The Castoriadis Reader

𝔅

BLACKWELL READERS

In a number of disciplines, across a number of decades, and in a number of languages, writers and texts have emerged which require the attention of students and scholars around the world. United only by a concern with radical ideas, *Blackwell Readers* collect and introduce the works of pre-eminent theorists. Often translating works for the first time (Levinas, Irigaray, Lyotard, Blanchot, Kristeva) or presenting material previously inaccessible (C. L. R. James, Fanon, Elias) each volume in the series introduces and represents work which is now fundamental to study in the humanities and social sciences. (See also *Blackwell Critical Readers.*)

Already published
The Lyotard Reader
Edited by Andrew Benjamin

The Irigaray Reader
Edited by Margaret Whitford

The Kristeva Reader
Edited by Toril Moi

The Levinas Reader
Edited by Sean Hand

The CLR James Reader
Edited by Anna Grimshaw

The Wittgenstein Reader
Edited by Sir Anthony Kenny

The Blanchot Reader
Edited by Michael Holland

The Guattari Reader
Edited by Gary Genesko

The Cavell Reader
Edited by Stephen Mulhall

The Castoriadis Reader
Edited by David Ames Curtis

The Lukács Reader
Edited by Arpad Kadarkay

Forthcoming
The Benjamin Reader
Edited by Drew Milne

The Fanon Reader
Edited by Homi Bhabha

The Castoriadis Reader

Cornelius Castoriadis

Translated and Edited by
David Ames Curtis

Copyright © Blackwell Publishers Ltd 1997

First published 1997

2 4 6 8 10 9 7 5 3 1

Blackwell Publishers Ltd
108 Cowley Road
Oxford OX4 1JF
UK

Blackwell Publishers Inc.
350 Main Street
Malden, MA 02148
USA

British Library Cataloguing in Publication Data

A CIP catalogue record for this book is available from the British Library.

Library of Congress Cataloging-in-Publication Data

Castoriadis, Cornelius.
  [Selections. English. 1997]
  The Castoriadis reader / Cornelius Castoriadis. Translated and
edited by David Ames Curtis.
    p. cm. — (Blackwell readers)
  Includes bibliographical references and index.
  ISBN 1-55786-703-8 (alk. paper). — ISBN 1-55786-704-6 (pbk.
alk. paper)
  1. Social sciences. 2. Political science. 3. Communism.
4. Socialism. I. Title. II. Series.
H61.C33213 1997
300-dc20   96-12037
                                            CIP

Printed in Great Britain by Hartnolls Ltd, Bodmin, Cornwall

This book is printed on acid-free paper

Contents

Foreword

Cornelius Castoriadis was born in 1922 in what was then known as Constantinople and would soon become Istanbul. In the troubled times surrounding the birth of the modern Turkish State, Castoriadis's father, a Voltairean Francophile of Greek extraction, removed the family to Athens. There the young Castoriadis grew up during the turbulent years leading up to the Metaxas dictatorship, the Second World War, the Nazi occupation, Greece's liberation, and the Greek Communists' December 1944 coup d'état attempt. In December 1945, under threat of death from both Fascists and Stalinists, Castoriadis, who had joined the Greek Communist Youth only to enter soon thereafter into opposition and then join the Trotskyists, departed from Piraeus for Paris. In Paris he founded with Claude Lefort the now legendary revolutionary journal *Socialisme ou Barbarie* (1949–65), to which Jean-François Lyotard also once belonged. The group by the same name is now generally credited with inspiring the May 1968 student–worker rebellion; French student leader Daniel Cohn-Bendit, for example, who appears in the *Reader* as Castoriadis's cospeaker at a 1980 ecology conference, proudly proclaimed in 1968 that he had largely 'plagiarized' Castoriadis's and *S. ou B.*'s views. Today Castoriadis – renowned 'Sovietologist', retired OECD economist, practising psychoanalyst, and innovative philosopher – is considered one of Europe's foremost social thinkers. He still lives in Paris, where he continues to develop his political 'project of autonomy' and his philosophical ideas on the 'imaginary institution of society'.

I shall not offer the reader of this Foreword an in-depth analysis of Castoriadis's views or a detailed biography of this author. The *Castoriadis Reader* has itself been designed to acquaint readers new and old with both him and his work. Rather, I shall briefly explain here my choices for this *Reader* as a way of introducing its contents and highlighting its potential significance.

A Reader, as I conceive it, should serve a variety of purposes. With the author's assistance, I have endeavoured to respond to these multiple requirements and I hope to have fulfilled them as editor of this *Reader*.

A first purpose is to provide a general overview of the author's work instead of concentrating on just one or a few topics or periods. The texts presented here start, after the introductory interview in Chapter 1, with the 1949 'Presentation' of the first issue of *Socialisme ou Barbarie* and end with some of Castoriadis's most recent writings. The *Reader*'s fifteen chapters also encompass most of the major themes of his life's work, including: workers' management and people's potential for creative and autonomous self-activity; the early, radical, and ever relentless critique of the erstwhile 'Union of Soviet Socialist Republics' ('four words, four lies', Milan Kundera once quoted Castoriadis as quipping); the 'positive content of socialism' and the economics of a self-managed society; the critique of the conservative and capitalist elements found in Marxism and the development of the idea of the 'imaginary institution of society'; ecology and the present dangers of an out-of-control, autonomized 'technoscience'; the 'crisis of Western societies' and the current waning of contestation on the levels of both philosophical thought and political action; the inspiration the author has drawn from ancient Greece in general and the Greek *polis*'s simultaneous creation of philosophy and politics in particular; the elucidation of an alternative logic to the traditional 'ensemblistic-identitary' one that has ruled Western 'inherited thought' for the past twenty-five centuries; the role of cultural creation in the process of democratic social transformation; and the contribution a properly understood and practised psychoanalysis can make to both philosophy and the project of autonomy.

A Reader must also offer, in some way, a series of 'greatest hits' if readers are to familiarize themselves with the author's major works. In Castoriadis's case, not all the classic texts could be presented in their entirety in a one-volume Reader. We therefore had to make choices among them and provide only excerpts from some we did eventually choose. A reader already familiar with Castoriadis's work will note, and perhaps lament, the absence of such key writings as 'Socialism or Barbarism' (1949) and 'Modern Capitalism and Revolution' (1960–1), which could not be included; but in these two cases other classic texts – the Presentation to *Socialisme ou Barbarie*, 'From the Critique of Bureaucracy to the Idea of the Proletariat's Autonomy' (1955), and 'Recommencing the Revolution' (1964) – serve to summarize many of the absent articles' main points. Also, the reader may be heartened to learn that other classics – such as the second part of 'On the Content of Socialism' (1957), *The Imaginary Institution of Society* (1964–5; 1975), and 'The Greek *Polis* and the Creation of Democracy' (1983) – have at least been presented in the form of excerpts. First-time readers will thus be able to familiarize themselves with the author's main ideas by reading some of his most important and best-known writings.

A Reader can also present hard-to-find texts for the benefit of both the first-time reader and 'old timers', those who have followed Castoriadis's contributions to the revolutionizing of thought and society over the past five decades. We have thus also selected a number of lesser-known pieces that were previously published in English only in small academic, political, literary, or arts journals. These texts include 'The Social Regime in Russia' (1978), 'From Ecology to Autonomy' (1980), 'The Logic of Magmas and the Question of Autonomy' (1983), 'Culture in a Democratic Society' (1994), and 'Psychoanalysis and Philosophy' (1996).

Many people, however, pick up a Reader in order to familiarize themselves quickly with the basics of an author's thought. Several chapters of this *Reader* offer programmatic accounts of Castoriadis's main topics of discussion: 'Recommencing the Revolution', 'The Social Regime in Russia', and 'The Logic of Magmas and the Question of Autonomy' respond to this desire for succinct thematic statements by presenting his views in the compact and ordered form of numbered theses. These three summary texts, along with many of the others, also refer the reader to additional writings by the author where his arguments were developed for the first time or in greater detail.

This last point suggests one further purpose a Reader can and, indeed, should serve: to provide a historical overview of the evolution of the author's views. Theses presented in summary, or even canonical, form, and without additional reference to where these ideas were first developed and were subsequently refined, revised, or altered in response to criticism, would provide the reader with a skewed and contextless idea of the author's intellectual and political life. Therefore, with the exceptions of the introductory first chapter and the final one (which features responses to critics), the texts have been organized in chronological order. This chronological ordering, along with the addition of a myriad of abbreviated references in most texts, goes far toward eliminating for readers this potential danger. A guide to the abbreviations used appears directly after this Foreword and the Acknowledgements page.

But even when a Reader answers to these varied purposes and avoids the above-mentioned danger, the reader might not yet get a clear sense of what the author really has wanted to say. Indeed, when one reads a Reader of some no longer living author one may still, even with the sense of closure afforded by that author's death, lack a sense of the whole, an understanding of what the author lived for and was willing to die for. As the present Reader is a collection of texts by a writer who is still very much alive, still very active, and still developing and deepening his thought, we are fortunate to have 'Done and To Be Done' (1989), a recent example of Castoriadis debating with his critics, extending his thinking, returning to previously covered ground in order to work it over once again. This final chapter contains the author's forceful and thoughtful replies to thirty discussions of his life's work which were written by an international collection of scholars.[1] Here we witness Castoriadis at his polemical and critical best, responding to objections, clarifying his positions, exposing misinformed or misguided assumptions held by critics, and developing his ideas and projects even further in a variety of directions while making frequent reference to his own past writings, including many of the texts presented here unabridged or in excerpts. No doubt 'Done and To Be Done' will whet the appetite of many a reader who will then desire to read other writings by the author. I believe the present volume provides readers with the necessary background for such further explorations and the necessary basis to make something meaningful of them.

I do not wish to prescribe in advance for readers the ways in which they are to evaluate and judge the innovative ideas contained in this last chapter, or the *Reader* as a whole; I hope – indeed, I am sure – that some readers will invent fresh responses and insights of their own, ones that no one has thought of before. Let me, in anticipation of the reader's own work, focus merely on one recent notion from 'Done and To Be Done' which I consider particularly fecund. I wish to highlight this notion also because Castoriadis makes specific reference there to 'On the Content of Socialism, II', a text I was determined to include in this selection from his fifty years of political, social, and philosophical writings.

As Castoriadis's English-language translator/editor, I am often asked by the more politically minded of his readers whether he still holds to the vision of a self-managed society as outlined in this 1957 article. In contrast, others interested less in his radical political positions than in the more recent developments in his social, psychoanalytical, or philosophical thought might simply view this forty-year-old text as outdated and perhaps not worth the bother of including in the present *Reader*. There are, however, as I have argued elsewhere,[2] a continuity and coherency to his life's work that authorize and, indeed, enable one to present his writings as a still relevant and evolving whole.

In 'Done and To Be Done' Castoriadis states his conviction that the spirit and principles of *CS II* remain valid, except for its (relatively) exclusive workerism and the obsolete notion of the 'dictatorship of the proletariat'. For him, socialism – or what he now calls the 'autonomous society' – must involve the socialization and democratization of the management of the economy (as opposed to its mere 'nationalization', with exclusive control over 'production' and 'planning' delegated to a separate stratum of bureaucratic managers), but also the socialization and democratization of society itself.[3] In contrast to all major schools of Western political thought with the sole exception of anarchism – from the libertarian 'minimal State' to Communism's extreme inflation of the State's role (on the factual, if not ideological, level) – Castoriadis argued in *CS II*, and still argues today, for the elimination of any stratum of rulers separated from the real life of society, any party or other instituted group that would claim responsibility, in society's absence, for society's overall orientation as well as for its specific doings and expressions. As he has stated many times, such a project is in head-on contradiction with totalitarian pretensions to eliminate the private and civil spheres of action or to absorb these spheres entirely into the State, or with other attempts to limit or circumscribe, from the outside or through extrasocial representations of society, people's freedom to contribute to the making and remaking of society – just as the direct democratic inspirations of this project stand in stark contrast to modern liberal-oligarchical compromises and to the not-even-half measures most post-totalitarian 'political philosophers' today are falling back on.

In 'Done and To Be Done' Castoriadis returns to the question of the State, civil society, and private conduct or initiative, but he does so in a new way that, inspired by his thinking on the *polis* in ancient Greece as well as by his elucidation of the simultaneously individual and social project of autonomy in Modern Times, leaves far behind the traditional conceptions and usages of these terms. In contrast to what he labels the 'private/private' (domestic) sphere – or *oikos* – as well as to the (explicitly political) 'public/public' sphere – or *ekklēsia* – Castoriadis designates and describes a third sphere of social action: the 'public/private' sphere – or *agora* – which is only implicitly political, but which also goes beyond the private concerns of individual and family.[4]

As an analytical concept, he explains, this 'public/private' sphere may be applied to any society. It is a *free agora* open to all, one in which everybody would have an equal effective possibility of participation, whose instauration[5] Castoriadis would be aiming at achieving.[6] This would be an *agora* that has emerged from the *oikos,* as occurred for the first time in ancient Greece – Hannah Arendt, too, identifies Greece as the birthplace of a 'public space' – but which would not be so identified with the public/public sphere, or so far removed from it, that it would have ceased to be an independent and genuinely private/public entity. Castoriadis is thus developing a conceptualization of social and political organization that clarifies, but also challenges, the binary civil society/State distinction now being much heralded again by formerly radical critical thinkers from both the West and the ex-dissident East who have decided to make their peace with a State whose existence they no longer challenge politically or even on the level of thought.

Today, we should recognize, the *agora* as commercial market is becoming little more than a privately owned and operated shopping mall,[7] or perhaps a home shopping network for the world's plugged-in agoraphobes. And, as financial market, it is being transformed more and more into a 'planetary casino', Castoriadis has remarked, where the amounts placed into worldwide electronic speculation every few days equal the US GNP. The classical sovereign nation-State is thus itself becoming irrelevant and impotent as the world rapidly coalesces into supranational, superregional trading blocs whose main purpose and passion are neither to foster direct democratic input nor to address the festering and even worsening problems of environmental degradation. Nor do either the traditional nation-States or these new superregional groupings appear particularly adept at facing up to the rise of religious fanaticisms and various deadly forms of separatist nationalism, communitarianism, and ethnic mania, their responses being mostly half-hearted, reactive, belated, and often counterproductive in the long run for lack of any meaningful and mobilizatory project of their own.

This 'public/private' sphere, or *agora*, is at present, in the absence of active contestation of the established disorder, rapidly atrophying through its thoroughgoing privatization (while the 'private/private' sphere is rapidly being oversocialized for commercial, financial, and advertising/media purposes). We should not, for all that, cease to fix as our implicitly political objective the emergence of this sphere. We should continue to work for this *agora*'s development – first of all by the exemplary means of making it exist through our actions – even though we recognize that the prospects for implicitly politial ('civil') action are at this time little more encouraging than the prospects for vigorously explicit political action and the establishment of a true *ekklēsia* (that is, democratic decision-making in properly political matters, as defined by general public assembly and by intermediate organs of all those involved at the various levels of social activity).[8]

Nevertheless, in aiming at the creation of the conditions under which this public/private sphere might emerge,[9] independently from and in solidarity with the two other spheres Castoriadis is describing, a problem immediately arises. 'The first condition for the existence of an autonomous society – of a democratic society – is that the public/public sphere become *effectively* public, become an *ekklēsia* and not an object of private appropriation by particular groups,' Castoriadis argues in 'Done and To Be Done'. In the contrary case, one would end up with neither the private/public sphere nor the private/private sphere being free and independent; both would be mere objects of publicity, of mystification, of manipulation and brute force, and/or the expression of a generalized conformism toward fashion and authority, as is presently the case to a very high degree. But if such is the 'first condition', and if this condition is to such an extent absent in the present state of society (which does not mean that we should cease to favour its implementation or that we should believe people collectively incapable of launching an effort, even today, toward its realization), why then aim at the creation of any other conditions for the eventual emergence of the public/private sphere as part of a future autonomous society?

An initial response may be found in another statement Castoriadis makes in this same text concerning these three spheres: 'The freedom of the private sphere, like the freedom of the *agora*, is a *sine qua non* condition for the freedom of the *ekklēsia* and for the becoming public of the public/public sphere.' But how can we harmonize this affirmation about '*sine qua non*' conditions for the emergence of the *ekklēsia* with the even more weighty, prior affirmation concerning the *ekklēsia* itself as the 'first condition' for a society in which each of these three spheres would be free and each would exist in social solidarity with the others? Why make any other efforts when the primary goal would appear to be the realization of this 'first condition', a free *ekklēsia*? (In classical Marxist terms, the establishment of a 'dictatorship of the proletariat' becomes the be-all and end-all of all revolutionary political activity.)

To wait for the first condition to be duly and completely fulfilled before doing anything else would be equivalent to renouncing all present efforts toward encouraging reflection and self-responsibility; all liberatory educational endeavours, whether formal or informal; any attempts by people, inspired by psychoanalytic practice or just mutual discussion and reflected experience, to engage in criticism/self-criticism and to confront lucidly their present problems or oppression as they come to define them. It would amount, in short, to an abandonment of all not explicitly political forms of *praxis*, in the sense Castoriadis intends the latter term: activities that aim at the autonomy of the other and of oneself (see 'Marxism and Revolutionary Theory' and 'Done and To Be Done'). Despite the fact that such renunciation seems in our day to be the prevailing 'norm', we ought to refuse to give in on this point.

Furthermore, to concentrate exclusively and unilaterally on this first condition relating to the *ekklēsia* in such a way as to prevent oneself from undertaking any action or reflection whatsoever in the other two spheres would be equivalent to ignoring the solidarity and the mutual implications among these three spheres of social life, their circle of continued creation. This is equally the reason we ought not to aim merely at reinforcing a 'civil society', or building a 'civic forum', alongside a State apparatus that is left standing – even a 'democratized' and now 'lustrated' one, as in the case of the Czech Republic.[10] In taking as our goal an autonomous society – whose 'first condition' remains the instauration of a genuinely public *ekklēsia* – the emancipation of the *agora* and the development of the capacity for critical reflection and deliberate action in the private/private sphere become indispensable co-aims. Indeed, 'to guarantee the greatest freedom possible' among these three spheres, all the while expressing and emphasizing their mutual solidarity and reciprocal responsibility, becomes the key imperative for such a society, Castoriadis says in 'Done and To Be Done'.

Still, we are immediately confronted with innumerable questions. We ought, for our part, to reject all forms of nationalism as an inappropriate *biological* figure for an autonomous *social* collectivity that should come to know itself as such and in its various social articulations; that is, we ought to reject nationalism as the allegedly natural (or even 'naturalized') self-substitute for the properly social sphere. But how can we aim at an international or transnational (or, better: forthrightly non-national) *agora* in the *absence* of an international *dēmos* and in the face of today's widespread and growing nationalist and religious motivations and sentiments of internal exclusiveness and external exclusion? The whole question of revolutionary social organization,[11] as well as that of the struggle against all forms of mystification – both of which are addressed in the 1974 introductory interview – arises anew; and this in a persistent and radical way. Faced with such questions, those who wish to engage in finding responses can take their shared activity of posing these questions and of seeking answers to them as a common field for creative reflection and action. In this work, originality, relevancy, exemplariness,[12] and a desire to share and scrutinize personal and collective experiences without essentializing these experiences or placing them somehow beyond the reach of criticism can become watchwords. It is my hope that this *Reader* will aid those still attracted by such aspirations to give them concrete expression.

Notes

1 I am guest editing a special issue of *Thesis Eleven*, which will present additional critical appreciations of Castoriadis's work, along with new texts by Castoriadis himself, on the occasion of his seventy-fifth birthday in 1997.

2 See my Foreword to the first volume of Castoriadis's *Political and Social Writings* and, especially, my Foreword to his recent book, *World in Fragments*.

3 To speak of the 'socialization . . . of society' might appear redundant to some – and impossible to others. But Castoriadis has been highlighting the phenomenon of the *privatization* of society since the 1960s (see *MCR*) while also endeavouring to show that there is no incoherency or impossibility in the goal of encouraging 'instituting society' to have a conscious, concerted, and continuing effect upon 'instituted society' (see *MRT* [1964–5]). Note, too, that I did *not* say 'socialization and democratization of the State'. A few years ago, at a Paris lecture given by Richard Rorty for which Castoriadis served as respondent, Chantal Mouffe called for a 'debureaucratization of the State'; Castoriadis aptly quipped that this would be like calling for a 'demilitarization of the army'.

4 Not that the latter should be considered sacrosanct, or even a 'haven'. Castoriadis develops further his ideas on the three spheres of social and political life in a recent text, 'Democracy as Procedure and Democracy as Regime', forthcoming in *Constellations*, the successor review to *Praxis International*.

5 As I noted in the Glossary to the first volume of Castoriadis's *Political and Social Writings* and in *World in Fragments*'s 'A Note on the Translation', I have revived the original meaning in English of 'instauration', which is *to establish something anew or for the first time*. I have not developed another glossary or translator's note for the *Reader*; instead, I have, more frequently than in my other volumes of translations of Castoriadis's writings, indicated in brackets the original French word or phrases whenever some ambiguity might be alleviated or a meaning might be clarified.

6 In some cities in ancient Greece, Aristotle notes in the *Politics*, the *agora* – not as marketplace but as site of discussion, reflection, and deliberation – was reserved for only a portion of the *polis*'s citizens, others being excluded therefrom.

7 Characteristic in this regard is the US Supreme Court ruling that refused to guarantee the exercise of First Amendment rights in privately owned shopping malls across the country. So much for the alleged compatibility or mutual implications between democracy and capitalism – whose mutual incompatibility we already recognized clearly in the capitalist workplace.

8 As I noted in the Foreword to *Cleisthenes the Athenian* (Atlantic Highlands, New Jersey: Humanities, 1996), my translation of Pierre Lévêque and Pierre Vidal-Naquet's classic 1963 essay on the reforms that led to the birth of democracy in Athens (Castoriadis appears there as a participant in a subsequent discussion that was printed as a supplement), a curious new phenomenon is the call by the 1992 presidential candidates William Jefferson Clinton and H. Ross Perot for a revival of the town meeting format, whether televised or 'electronic' – and this, in the absence of any widespread demand on the part of the populace for the use of such organs of public policy formation or ratification! In view of the lack of serious thought given to the formulation of these proposals and in the light of the character of the politicians advancing the idea, we should certainly avoid concluding that elite leadership groups or individuals have suddenly become gripped with a passion for direct democratic participation. Rather, as I argued in that Foreword, extending Castoriadis's ideas on the 'bureaucratic-capitalist project' (with its simultaneous need to exclude people from participation and to encourage such participation), we should see these proposals for what they really are: rather desperate and ill-thought-out attempts to come to terms with the ongoing depoliticization and privatization of society, where people's absence of involvement, itself mandated by the present system, inevitably leads to dysfunctions in the operation of that system which the system is obliged to address. Were we to borrow medical or psychoanalytical language to describe it, we would call this social and political phenomenon – like that of 'quality circles' – a significant symptom of something that clearly goes far beyond its explicit content and certainly bears further examination.

9 Its emergence, of course, could in no way be merely an illustration of any particular person's ideas. There is not, and I trust there never will be, any 'Castoriadianism'.

10 'Civic Forum' was the name of Vaclav Havel's opposition group which led to the overthrow of the Communist regime in Czechoslovakia. A forum is not an *agora*.

11 Recently I read that Jacques Derrida, in his book on the 'spectres of Marx' after the fall of Communism, calls for the creation of a 'new International' – one that would not be burdened, however, with any 'institutions', these presumably being intrinsically *bad* and, apparently, perfectly avoidable for an earnest cynic like Derrida. Inspired in great part by Castoriadis's work, Vassilis Lambropoulos in the third and final chapter of his book *The Rise of Eurocentrism: Anatomy of Interpretation* (Princeton: Princeton University Press, 1993) has developed many of the elements for a coherent and consequential critique of Derrida's deconstructionist errings.

12 There is a constant – and ineliminable – *tension* between excellence and commonality in a democratic society, fraught with risks but also pregnant with inspirations and hopes.

Acknowledgements

As Castoriadis has always emphasized, the work represented by his *Socialisme ou Barbarie* writings is collective in nature. Each text was discussed, dissected, and debated by the *S. ou B.* group before its publication. On the author's behalf, those who participated in these exchanges and proposed improvements are thanked here once again for their inestimable contributions.

The contributions to the making of this *Reader* are also of a collective nature. Thanks to the efforts of London and Philadelphia Solidarity, and then *Telos* at a certain stage in its existence, the Australian social theory journal *Thesis Eleven*, and other reviews and publishers, Castoriadis's writings have been available in English translation continuously for more than a third of a century. I dedicate this *Reader* to Maurice Brinton, some of whose fine London Solidarity translations appear here in slightly edited form, as an 'emerged part' of this collective experience and endeavour – of which I am but the latest participant.

The editor and publishers gratefully acknowledge the following for permission to reproduce copyright material:

Christian Bourgois Éditeur, Éditions 10/18, Éditions du Seuil, MIT Press, Oxford University Press, Inc., Polity Press, University of Minnesota Press, and Cornelius Castoriadis.

Chapter 10 – Excerpted from *Philosophy, Politics, Autonomy: Essays in Political Philosophy by Cornelius Castoriadis.* ©1991 Oxford University Press, Inc. Reprinted by permission.
Chapter 15 ©1989 Librairie Droz.

The publishers apologize for any errors or omissions in the above list and would be grateful to be notified of any corrections that should be incorporated in the next edition or reprint of this book.

The translations were made possible, in part, with a grant from the French Ministry of Culture.

Abbreviations

The dates provided below are always the dates of *first publication*, whether in French, English, or another language, *except* in the case of lectures or previously unpublished manuscripts, where the original date is given. Unless otherwise noted in the volume or text sections, all English-language translations published in book form are by David Ames Curtis, all French translations by Cornelius Castoriadis. The original-language version is always listed first, the translation thereafter. (Both in this section and in the body of the *Reader*, E = English-language version; F = French-language version.)

The reader is invited to consult the publication notes to individual articles for previous appearances of texts listed as 'now in' volumes written by Castoriadis. However, I have always noted the original appearance of texts published in *Socialisme ou Barbarie* (*S. ou B.*), the revolutionary journal Castoriadis edited and contributed to, from its inception in 1949 until its last issue in 1965.

Since this list of abbreviations of volumes and other texts written by Cornelius Castoriadis is based upon the texts he cites in the *Castoriadis Reader*, it may be considered a handy 'abbreviated' bibliography of what, in addition to the chapters published in the *Castoriadis Reader*, the author considers to be his key writings. More complete bibliographies may be found in the appendices to volumes 1 and 3 of Castoriadis's *Political and Social Writings* and in *World in Fragments*. Supplements may be obtained through the Translator/Editor (hereafter: T/E): David Ames Curtis, c/o Agora International, 27 rue Froidevaux, 75014 Paris, France or by E-mail <CURTIS@MSH-PARIS.FR>. A web page is under construction.

Abbreviations for Volumes Written by Cornelius Castoriadis

CL   *Les Carrefours du labyrinthe*. Paris: Seuil, 1978. *Crossroads in the Labyrinth*. Trans. Martin H. Ryle and Kate Soper. Brighton: Harvester, and Cambridge, Mass.: MIT, 1984.

CL 5	*Les Carrefours du labyrinthe V* (provisional title). Paris: Seuil (forthcoming).
CMR 1	*Capitalisme moderne et révolution, 1: L'Impérialisme et la guerre.* Paris: 10/18, 1979.
CMR 2	*Capitalisme moderne et révolution, 2: Le Mouvement révolutionnnaire sous le capitalisme moderne.* Paris: 10/18, 1979.
CR	*The Castoriadis Reader.* Oxford, England and Cambridge, Mass.: Blackwell, 1997.
CS	*Le Contenu du socialisme.* Paris: 10/18, 1979.
DG	*Devant la guerre.* Vol. 1: *Les Réalités.* Paris: Fayard, 1980. 2nd rev. edn 1981.
DH	*Domaines de l'homme. Les Carrefours du labyrinthe II.* Paris: Seuil, 1986.
EMO 1	*L'Expérience du mouvement ouvrier, 1: Comment Luter.* Paris: 10/18, 1974.
EMO 2	*L'Expérience du mouvement ouvrier, 2: Prolétariat et organisation.* Paris: 10/18, 1974.
IIS	*L'Institution imaginaire de la société.* Paris: Seuil, 1975. *The Imaginary Institution of Society.* Trans. Kathleen Blamey. Oxford, England: Polity and Cambridge, Mass.: MIT, 1987. *IIS* consists of *MRT I–V* and *SII.* Excerpts from both parts appear in *CR.*
MI	*La Montée de l'insignifiance. Les Carrefours du labyrinthe IV.* Paris: Seuil, 1996.
MM	*Le Monde morcelé. Les Carrefours du labyrinthe III.* Paris: Seuil, 1996.
PPA	*Philosophy, Politics, Autonomy.* Ed. David Ames Curtis. New York and Oxford, England: Oxford University Press, 1991.
PSW 1	*Political and Social Writings.* Vol. 1: *1946–1955: From the Critique of Bureaucracy to the Positive Content of Socialism.* Minneapolis: University of Minnesota Press, 1988.
PSW 2	*Political and Social Writings.* Vol. 2: *1955–1960: From the Workers' Struggle Against Bureaucracy to Revolution in the Age of Modern Capitalism.* Minneapolis: University of Minnesota Press, 1988.
PSW 3	*Political and Social Writings.* Vol. 3: *1961–1979: Recommencing the Revolution: From Socialism to the Autonomous Society.* Minneapolis: University of Minnesota Press, 1993.
SB 1	*La Société bureaucratique, 1: Les Rapports de production en Russie.* Paris: 10/18, 1973.
SB 2	*La Société bureaucratique, 2: La Révolution contre la*

	bureaucratie. Paris: 10/18, 1973.
SB★	*La Société bureaucratique (nouvelle édition)*. Paris: Christian Bourgois, 1990.
SF	*La Société française*. Paris: 10/18, 1979.
WIF	*World in Fragments*. Stanford: Stanford University Press, 1997.

Abbreviations for Texts Written by Cornelius Castoriadis

AR [1968]	'La Révolution anticipée': *La Brèche* (Paris: Fayard, 1968). 2nd edn. Brussels: Complexe, 1988. Now in *SF*. 'The Anticipated Revolution', trans. Basil Druitt. *PSW 3*.
ASE [1956]	'Les Grèves de l'automation en Angleterre', *S. ou B.*, 21 (March 1957). Reprinted in *EMO 1*. 'Automation Strikes in England'. *PSW 2*.
BPT [1957]	'Bilan, perspectives, tâches', *S. ou B.*, 21 (March 1957). Reprinted in *EMO 1*.
CCS [1986]	'The Crisis of Culture and the State' (1986 lecture). Now in *PPA*.
CFP [1948]	'La Concentration des forces productives' (March 1948 manuscript). *SB 1*. Reprinted in *SB*★.
CMS [1965]	*The Crisis of Modern Society* (1965 lecture). Now in *PSW 3*. 'La Crise de la société moderne'. *CMR 2*.
CP [1960]	'Conceptions et programme de *Socialisme ou Barbarie*'. Now in *SB 2* and *SB*★.
CS I [1955]	'Sur le Contenu du socialisme', *S. ou B.*, 17 (July 1955). Reprinted in *CS*. 'On the Content of Socialism, I'. *PSW 1*. Excerpts in *CR*.
CS II [1957]	'Sur le Contenu du socialisme', *S. ou B.*, 22 (July 1957). Reprinted in *CS*. 'On the Content of Socialism, II'. Based on the translation of Maurice Brinton. Now in *PSW 2*. Excerpts in *CR*.
CS III [1958]	'Sur le Contenu du socialisme', *S. ou B.*, 23 (January 1958). Reprinted in *EMO 2*. 'On the Content of Socialism, III'. *PSW 2*.
CWS [1982]	'La Crise des sociétés occidentales'. Abridged version now in *MI*. 'The Crisis of Western Societies'. Abridged version now in *CR*.
DC I [1953]	'Sur la dynamique du capitalisme', *S. ou B.*, 12 (August 1953).
DC II [1954]	'Sur la dynamique du capitalisme', *S. ou B.*, 13 (January 1954).

DE? [1987]   'Voie sans issue?' Now in *MM*. 'Dead End?' *PPA*.

DI [1978]   'La Découverte de l'imagination'. Now in *DH*. 'The Discovery of the Imagination'. Now in *WIF*.

DRR [1958]   'Sur la dégénérescence de la révolution russe'. Now in *SB 2* and *SB**.

DT [1981]   'Destinies of Totalitarianism' (1981 lecture). *Salmagundi*, 60 (Spring–Summer 1983), pp. 107–22. 'Destinées du totalitarisme', *DH*.

DW [1991]   'Le Délabrement de l'Occident' (1991 interview). Now in *MI*. 'The Dilapidation of the West. An Interview with Cornelius Castoriadis', *Thesis Eleven*, 41 (1995).

EP? [1988]   'The "End of Philosophy"?' (1988 lecture). Now in *PPA*. 'La "Fin de la philosophie"?' *MM*.

EPBC [1949]   'L'Exploitation de la paysannerie sous le capitalisme bureaucratique', *S. ou B.*, 4 (October 1949). Reprinted in *SB 1* and *SB**. 'The Exploitation of the Peasantry under Bureaucratic Capitalism'. *PSW 1*.

ETS [1968]   'Épilégomènes à une théorie de l'âme que l'on a pu présenter comme science'. Now in *CL* (F). 'Epilegomena to a Theory of the Soul Which Has Been Presented as a Science'. *CL* (E).

FISSI [1985]   'Institution première de la société et institutions secondes' (1985 lecture). *Y a-t-il une théorie de l'institution?* Paris: Centre d'Étude et de la famille Association, 1986. 'The First Institution of Society and Second-Order Institutions', *Free Associations*, 12 (1988).

GDA [1956]   'Les Grèves des dockers anglais', *S. ou B.*, 18 (January 1956). Reprinted in *EMO 1*.

GI [1973]   'Introduction générale'. *SB 1*. Reprinted in *SB**. 'General Introduction'. *PSW 1*.

GPCD [1983]   'The Greek *Polis* and the Creation of Democracy'. Now in *PPA*. Excerpts in *CR*. 'La *Polis* grecque et la création de la démocratie'. Now in *DH*.

HS [1976]   'The Hungarian Source'. Now in *PSW 3*. 'La Source hongroise', trans. Maurice Luciani. *CS*.

HWI [1974]   'La Hiérarchie des salaires et des revenus'. Now in *EMO 2*. 'Hierarchy of Wages and Incomes'. Now in *PSW 3*.

HWM [1974]   'Introduction: La Question de l'histoire du mouvement ouvrier'. *EMO 1*. 'The Question of the History of the Workers' Movement'. Now in *PSW 3*.

ICSHD [1981]   'The Imaginary: Creation in the Social-Historical Domain' (1981 lecture). Now in *WIF*. 'L'Imaginaire: la création dans le domaine social-historique'. *DH*.

ISR [1982]	'L'Institution de la société et religion'. Now in *DH*. 'Institution of Society and Religion'. Now in *WIF*.
ISRH [1988]	'Individu, société, rationalité, histoire'. Now in *MM*. 'Individual, Society, Rationality, History'. Now in *PPA*.
KDBI [1956]	'Khrouchtchev et la décomposition de l'idéologie bureaucratique', *S. ou B.*, 19 (July 1956). Reprinted in *SB 2* and *SB**. 'Khrushchev and the Decomposition of Bureaucratic Ideology'. *PSW 2*.
LIR [1991]	'Logique, imagination, réflexion'. Now in *CL 5*. 'Logic, Imagination, Reflection'. Now in *WIF*.
LMQA [1983]	'La Logique des magmas et la question de l'autonomie'. Now in *DH*. 'The Logic of Magmas and the Question of Autonomy'. Now in *CR*.
MCR I [1960]	'Le Mouvement révolutionnaire sous le capitalisme moderne', *S. ou B.*, 31 (December 1960). Reprinted in *CMR 2*. 'Modern Capitalism and Revolution', Part 1. Based on the translation of Maurice Brinton. Now in *PSW 2*.
MCR II [1961]	'Le Mouvement révolutionnaire sous le capitalisme moderne', *S. ou B.*, 32 (April 1961). Reprinted in *CMR 2*. 'Modern Capitalism and Revolution', Part 2. Based on the translation of Maurice Brinton. Now in *PSW 2*.
MCR III [1961]	'Le Mouvement révolutionnaire sous le capitalisme moderne', *S. ou B.*, 33 (December 1961). Reprinted in *CMR 2*. 'Modern Capitalism and Revolution', Part 3. Based on the translation of Maurice Brinton. Now in *PSW 2*.
MP [1986]	'Merleau-Ponty et le poids de l'héritage ontologique'. *CL 5*. 'Merleau-Ponty and the Weight of the Ontological Tradition'. Now in *WIF*.
MRT I [1964]	'Marxisme et théorie révolutionnaire', *S. ou B.*, 36 (April 1964). Reprinted in *IIS* (F). 'Marxism and Revolutionary Theory'. Now in the first part of *IIS* (E). Excerpts in *CR*.
MRT II [1964]	'Marxisme et théorie révolutionnaire', *S. ou B.*, 37 (July 1964). Reprinted in *IIS* (F). 'Marxism and Revolutionary Theory'. Now in the first part of *IIS* (E).
MRT III [1964]	'Marxisme et théorie révolutionnaire', *S. ou B.*, 38 (October 1964). Reprinted in *IIS* (F). 'Marxism and Revolutionary Theory'. Now in the first part of *IIS* (E). Excerpts in *CR*.
MRT IV [1965]	'Marxisme et théorie révolutionnaire', *S. ou B.*, 39 (March 1965). Reprinted in *IIS* (F). 'Marxism and Revolutionary Theory'. Now in the first part of *IIS* (E). Excerpts in *CR*.

MRT V [1965]   'Marxisme et théorie révolutionnaire', *S. ou B.*, 40 (June 1965). Reprinted in *IIS* (F). 'Marxism and Revolutionary Theory'. Now in the first part of *IIS* (E).

MSPI [1973]   'Science moderne et interrogation philosophique'. Now in *CL* (F). 'Modern Science and Philosophical Interrogation'. In *CL* (E).

OIHS [1986]   'Portée ontologique de l'histoire de la science'. *DH*. 'The Ontological Import of the History of Science'. *WIF*.

ORAD [1946]   'Sur le régime et contre la défense de l'URSS'. Now in *SB 1* and *SB**. 'On the Regime and Against the Defense of the USSR'. *PSW 1*.

PA [1986]   'Phusis, création, autonomie' (1986 lecture). *CL 5*. 'Phusis and Autonomy'. Now in *WIF*.

PL [1951]   'La Direction prolétarienne', *S. ou B.*, 10 (July 1952). Reprinted in *EMO 1*. 'Proletarian Leadership'. *PSW 1*.

PO I [1959]   'Prolétariat et organisation', *S. ou B.*, 27 (April 1959). Reprinted in *EMO 2*. 'Proletariat and Organization, I'. Based on the translation of Maurice Brinton. *PSW 2*.

PO II [1959]   'Prolétariat et organisation', *S. ou B.*, 28 (July 1959). Reprinted in *EMO 2*.

PoPA [1988]   'Pouvoir, politique, autonomie'. Now in *MM*. 'Power, Politics, Autonomy', trans. by Cornelius Castoriadis. Now in *PPA*.

PPE [1977]   'Psychanalyse, projet et élucidation'. Now in *CL* (F). 'Psychoanalysis: Project and Elucidation'. *CL* (E).

PRAB [1956]   'La Révolution prolétarienne contre la bureaucratie', *S. ou B.*, 20 (December 1956). Reprinted in *SB 2* and *SB**. 'The Proletarian Revolution Against the Bureaucracy'. *PSW 2*.

PsyPo [1987]   'Psychoanalysis and Politics' (1987 lecture). Now in *WIF*. 'Psychanalyse et politique'. Now in *MM*.

PUSSR [1947]   'Le Problème de l'URSS et la possibilité d'une troisième solution historique'. Now in *SB 1* and *SB**. 'The Problem of the USSR and the Possibility of a Third Historical Solution'. *PSW 1*.

QURSS [1947]   'Sur la question de l'URSS et du stalinisme mondiale'. Now in *SB 1* and *SB**.

RA [1989]   'The Retreat from Autonomy: Postmodernism as Generalized Conformism' (1989 lecture). Now in *WIF*. 'L'Époque du conformisme généralisé'. *MM*.

RBI [1964]   'Le Rôle de l'idéologie bolchevique dans la naissance de la bureaucratie', *S. ou B.*, 35 (January 1964). Reprinted in *EMO 2*. 'The Role of Bolshevik Ideology in the Birth of the Bureaucracy'. Based on the translation of Maurice Brinton. Now in *PSW 3*.

ReRa [1987]   'Réflexions sur le racisme'. Now in *MM*. 'Reflections on Racism'. Now in *WIF*.

RPR [1949]   'Les Rapports de production en Russie', *S. ou B.*, 2 (May 1949). Reprinted in *SB 1* and *SB**. 'The Relations of Production in Russia'. *PSW 1*.

RR [1964]   'Recommencer la révolution', *S. ou B.*, 35 (January 1964). Reprinted in *EMO 2*. 'Recommencing the Revolution'. Based on the translation of Maurice Brinton. Now in *PSW 3*.

RRD [1974]   'Reflections on "Rationality" and "Development"' (1974 lecture). Now in *PPA*. 'Réflexions sur le "développement" et la "rationalité"', trans. Mme de Venoge. Now in *DH*.

SAS [1979]   'Introduction: Socialisme et société autonome'. *CS*. 'Socialism and Autonomous Society'. Now in *PSW 3*.

SB [1949]   'Socialisme ou Barbarie', *S. ou B.*, 1 (March 1949). Reprinted in *SB 1* and *SB**. 'Socialism or Barbarism'. Now in *PSW 1*.

SH [1991]   'The Social-Historical: Mode of Being, Problems of Knowledge'. *PPA*.

SII [1975]   'L'Imaginaire social et l'institution'. Published as the second part of *IIS* (F). 'The Social Imaginary and the Institution'. Published as the second part of *IIS* (E). Excerpts in *CR*.

SMH [1974]   'Autogestion et hiérarchie'. Now in *CS*. 'Self-Management and Hierarchy'. *PSW 3*.

SP [1967]   'La Suspension de la publication de *Socialisme ou Barbarie*'. Now in *EMO 2*. 'The Suspension of Publication of *Socialisme ou Barbarie*'. *PSW 3*.

SRR [1978]   'Le Régime social de la Russie'. Now in *DH*. 'The Social Regime in Russia'. Now in *CR*.

SST [1986]   'L'État du sujet aujourd'hui'. Now in *MM*. 'The State of the Subject Today'. Now in *WIF*.

STCC [1979]   'Transformation sociale et création culturelle'. Now in *CS*. 'Social Transformation and Cultural Creation'. *PSW 3*.

SU [1971]   'Le dicible et l'indicible'. Now in *CL* (F). 'The Sayable and the Unsayable'. *CL* (E).

SY [1963]   'La Jeunesse étudiante', *S. ou B.*, 34 (March 1963). Reprinted in *CMR 2*. 'Student Youth'. *PSW 3*.

T [1973]   'Technique'. Now in *CL* (F). 'Technique'. *CL* (E).

VEJP [1975]   'Valeur, égalité, justice, politique: de Marx à Aristote et d'Aristote à nous'. Now in *CL* (F). 'Value, Equality, Justice, Politics: From Marx to Aristotle and from Aristotle to Ourselves'. Now in *CL* (E).

VPB [1957]   'La voie polonaise de la bureaucratisation', *S. ou B.*, 21 (March 1957). Reprinted in *SB 2* and *SB**.

WSAAI [1956]   'Les Grèves sauvages de l'industrie automobile américaine', *S. ou B.*, 18 (January 1956). Reprinted in *EMO 1*. 'Wildcat Strikes in the American Automobile Industry'. *PSW 2*.

1

'The Only Way to Find Out If You Can Swim Is to Get into the Water': An Introductory Interview (1974)*

History of Socialisme ou Barbarie

Socialisme ou Barbarie grew out of a tendency established during the summer of 1946 inside the Parti Communiste Internationaliste (PCI), the French Trotskyist Party. For my part, I had been developing a critique of the Trotskyist conception of Stalinism since late 1944/early 1945 on the basis of my experience of the December 1944/January 1945 Stalinist coup d'état in Greece. For Trotsky and the Trotskyists, the Stalinist parties in the capitalist countries had lined up definitively on the side of the bourgeois order (at least since the period of the Popular Fronts and the Spanish Civil War). These parties no longer represented, for Trotsky and the Trotskyists, anything but a repeat of reformism, and with regard to them one simply resumed the basics of the Leninist analysis and critique of classical reformism. From this perspective, if the Stalinists were ever to participate in a government, they could do so only in the manner and with the objectives of the reformist parties: that is, in order to save the bourgeois regime during a difficult phase of its existence.

Now, it was obvious in Greece in 1944 that it was not a matter of that, but really and fully an attempt by the CP to seize power and to instaurate its own dictatorship (a dictatorship it was already exercising, during the last phase of the Occupation, over almost the entire country). The insurrection at Athens in December 1944 failed, but we know what happened during the same period in Yugoslavia and then, as the months passed, in the other countries of Eastern Europe.

* 'Le Projet révolutionnaire aujourd'hui. Entretien avec C. Castoriadis (26 janvier 1974)' appeared as the last issue of *APL Basse Normandie (Analyse et popularisation des luttes)*. Bart Grahl and David Pugh's translation, 'An Interview with C. Castoriadis', was published in *Telos*, 23 (Spring 1975), pp. 131–55. It was preceded by Dick Howard's 'Introduction to Castoriadis', pp. 117–31. [Translator/Editor (hereafter: T/E): I have used Castoriadis's corrected copy of the original *APL* interview and I have on occasion consulted the *Telos* text for the preparation of the present translation.]

This experience already demonstrated the absurdity of the Trotskyist 'tactic', which consisted in supporting the CP and 'pushing' it to take power ('For a PC–PS–CGT Government' was the Trotskyist slogan [in France] and, unless I am mistaken, it remains so). This tactic was based on two ideas, each as illusory as the other:

- That the CP in power would be as fragile as Kerensky, for example, had been;

- That the contradiction between the motivations the masses had in joining or supporting the CP (the masses were supposed to want a revolutionary change of regime) and the real policy of the CP (which supposedly wanted to preserve the bourgeois order) would erupt when the CP came to power.

Now, when the CP is installed in power it is anything but fragile (were it in power, moreover, we would not be here discussing it, since the first act of the CP when in power is always to exterminate any revolutionaries it can lay its hands on). And the 'contradiction' between the CP's policy and the masses' desire for a social transformation does not erupt for the very good reason that the CP effectively *transforms* the regime, expropriating the traditional bourgeoisie, 'planning' the economy, etc., and that some time is needed before the masses can see clearly that they have done nothing but change exploiters.

But all this also led to a reopening of the 'Russian question' and to a rejection of the Trotskyist conception, according to which the Russian bureaucracy was only a parasitic and transitory stratum that maintained itself in power solely as a function of the unstable balance on the world scale between international capitalism, on the one side, and the Revolution on the other. Whence Trotsky's prognostic that the war would provoke the collapse of the Russian bureaucracy and could end only in either international revolution or a victory on the part of capitalism (which implied, in his view, a restoration of capitalism in Russia itself). This prognostic, totally disproved by the outcome of the war, was not merely journalistic: in it are effectively condensed all the tenets and consequences of Trotsky's conceptions both about the question of bureaucracy and about the contemporary era.

The fact that the bureaucracy exited from the war not weakened but considerably strengthened, that it extended its power over all of Eastern Europe, and that regimes in all respects identical to the Russian regime were in the process of being established under the aegis of the CP unavoidably led one to see the bureaucracy not as a 'parasitic stratum' but very much as a dominant and exploitative class – confirmation of which, moreover, was allowed by a new analysis of the Russian regime on the economic and sociological level.

When I came to France (at the end of 1945), the PCI was preparing the

Second Congress of the 'Fourth International', and the main topic was the question of the USSR and Stalinism. I participated in the preparatory discussions, developing there the ideas summarized above. It was during one of these discussions that I met Claude Lefort, who for his part was experiencing a growing sense of unease in relation to the official PCI line. We quickly noted the proximity of our views, and we set up with a few comrades a tendency inside the PCI starting in August 1946. In 1947, when the PCI reached its maximum postwar-era influence (some 700 militants in France), our tendency numbered a few dozen comrades. But after 1947 the PCI entered into one of its periodic phases of decomposition. On the one hand, its right wing left to join the Rassemblement Démocratique of David Rousset and Jean-Paul Sartre; on the other hand, the militants who remained had clearly become less and less capable of putting the party's ideology into question and of evolving (when they succeeded in comprehending the absurdity of this ideology, they simply dropped all political activity). At the same time, both events – the 1947 strikes in France, changes in the countries of Eastern Europe, the beginnings of the Cold War – and the development of our theoretical work led us to see the enormous distance that separated the Trotskyist discourses from what was relevant in the class struggle, contemporary world history, and revolutionary theory itself. Starting from the moment one conducted a thorough analysis and critique of the experience of the Russian Revolution, a fundamental reconsideration of the question, 'What is socialism?', became necessary, and this reconsideration could only start with the idea of the autonomous action of the proletariat as the central theoretical and practical idea of revolution and culminate in the definition of socialism as workers' management of production and as collective management of all social activities by all those who participate in them. All this was separated by an immense gulf from the Trotskyist conception of 'nationalization' and 'planning' as central objectives of the revolution, and of the complete power of the Party as the instrument for their realization.

As early as the summer of 1948, we had decided to leave the PCI and we were discussing the date and the modalities of this exit when, as if by accident, one of those events that seal a situation supervened, the break between Tito and the Cominform. To a man, the Trotskyists started shouting 'Long live Tito, long live the Yugoslavian Revolution' and writing to the Yugoslavian CP to propose a 'Front Unique' (*sic*). It must be recalled that on the eve of this break they were still writing that Yugoslavia (like the rest of Russia's satellite countries) had remained an 'essentially capitalist' country – this because the CP had not nationalized everything the first day and because it had kept in place a few puppet ministers who did not formally belong to the CP (generally they were CPers working under deep cover [*sous-marins*]) and who represented political formations that had been fabricated by the Stalinists and were completely controlled by them (as the 'People's Progressive Democratic Left Radicals' will perhaps one day be in France). The absurdity of these reasonings is such that one knows not by what end to begin to grasp them. What importance could there be in the fact that a few percentage points of production had not yet been 'nationalized' when the basic levers of the economy already had been, and when, moreover, this percentage was steadily decreasing month after month? And how can one discuss with people who thought that, if everything were nationalized, one would thereby have achieved the essence of socialism? They could see the countries of the East only in terms of the following dilemma: Is it socialism (which they identified with nationalization, etc.) or is it capitalism (which they identified with traditional private property ownership)? But the question could not be posed in those terms. One had to see that the structural assimilation of these countries to the Russian regime was proceeding ever further each day, that the CPs solidly implanted in power were installing their men everywhere, creating a new managerial apparatus for production and society, around which a new dominant and exploitative stratum was rapidly crystallizing, and that this process not only was not incompatible with 'nationalization' and 'planning' but found therein its perfectly adequate form. And what could it mean to form a 'Front Unique' between a Stalinist party in power, having at its disposal an army and the budget of a State, and a few dozen Trotskyists in Paris? That was the comical side. But for us the whole thing was the final straw as far as Trotskyism was concerned. Leaving the PCI, we set ourselves up as an independent group and published the first issue of *Socialisme ou Barbarie* in 1949.

I do not want to do the history of the S. ou B. group from start to finish. If one wanted to do it correctly, it would be necessary to study it as a 'case history', both in detail and by examining in a deep way all the aspects, which traditional conceptions evacuate, of the life of a small revolutionary organization over eighteen years, its real [*effective*] and not only its 'ideological' daily life, the persons who made it up, etc. This would take too long to do, and there are more urgent tasks. I shall endeavour only to describe certain aspects of the group's history – recalling that I was deeply and constantly involved in the group, that I am not neutral and that, no doubt, I never will be.

One can begin to 'periodize' the history of the group by defining a first phase that extended from 1949 until 1953. Let us recall here the social, political, and international context. In 1949 the Cold War was starting to develop. In June 1950 the Korean War broke out. People were frozen in place, they were living the situation as if the Third World War were imminent.

After the great strikes of 1947 very few struggles took place in France. The miners' strike of 1948, the last great conflict of the immediate postwar era, was totally controlled, in totalitarian fashion, by the Stalinists. During this period the immediate public of the group and the review was made up of what was left of the old-style ultraleft groups: Bordigists, Council Communists, a few anarchists, and some offspring of the 1920s German 'Leftists'. These groups, moreover, were breaking up or disappearing at a rather rapid pace (a majority of the largest group among them, the Bordigist group, joined S. ou B. in 1950). As for the life of the group, it is marked by two long discussions that took place over the 'organizational question', the second of which culminated in a scission (which was of short duration) with Claude Lefort and a few other comrades. Starting in 1950, the group suffered increasing isolation. Toward the end of 1952 it found itself reduced to a dozen comrades, and issues of the review came out infrequently and were small in size.

Then, through the strange power of history, the scene changed. Blow after blow, the Korean War ended, Stalin died, the workers of East Berlin revolted, the entire public sector in France went on strike. The life of the group was reanimated, some new people joined, the content of the review was enriched, and the frequency of its appearances increased. Daniel Mothé, who came to the group in 1952, did some systematic work at Renault; with some workers from the factory, he published and distributed a few hundred copies of *Tribune Ouvrière* on the inside. Henri Simon, for his part, played an important role in a movement of employees at a large insurance company; they set up a 'council' of their own and broke with the unions. Other working-class contacts were established here and there, a few correspondents from the provinces began to appear. The Twentieth Congress of the Russian CP, Poznan, then of course the Hungarian Revolution and the Polish movement considerably stimulated the life of the group through the massive confirmation these events gave to our orientation, and they tangibly increased (everything being relative) both the circulation of the review and participation in the public meetings we were holding in Paris. Since that time, at least 700 copies of each issue of the review were sold (up to 1,000 for some issues) and nearly a hundred people from outside the group attended our public meetings. You have lived in the period after May 1968, during which there has been a certain massification of the leftist public; it must be recalled that during our crossing of the desert we held public meetings at the Mutualité building with twenty people from outside the group.

The Algerian War began in November 1954; the Mollet government (early 1956) initiated a partial mobilization in order to send troops to Algeria. The soldiers who had been called up began to demonstrate, stopping trains that were to transport them, the economic mess grew worse, and movements frequently sprang up and lodged new demands. In autumn

1957 agitation in the factories was widespread, the situation was clearly unstable and open. This is when we published the text *Comment lutter* (now in *EMO 1*), a text that benefited enormously from the discussions that took place around the initial draft I had written; there was participation both by comrades within the group and by comrades from various companies who did not belong to the group but who came to the meetings to discuss it. But no large-scale movement developed during the winter of 1957–8, and then, suddenly, it was 13 May [1958] and de Gaulle had arrived in power.

On the eve of 13 May the group comprised approximately thirty members (those who regularly paid dues and participated regularly in meetings and in tasks decided upon in common). The events led several dozen sympathizers to approach us, to organize and to act with us. That posed once again for the group the 'organizational question', and this time in practical terms. Indeed, it had become clear that the mode of functioning we had when we were thirty, such that all those who wanted to could express themselves during the group's weekly meetings, could not remain the same if we were growing to a hundred; a general meeting of 100 persons almost inevitably becomes a general assembly where a few star performers speak and the others listen. Moreover, such a meeting cannot decide anything regarding practical tasks of the kind undertaken by the group. One therefore had to 'divide'. But if one divides, one must also reunite. How, and under what forms?

The conflict over the organizational question, which had been brewing for ever but had not reappeared in an explicit way since the discussions of 1950–1, re-emerged at this time. Ultimately, the discussion lasted a rather short time and ended in September 1958 in another scission: some of the comrades, with Claude Lefort and Henri Simon as spokesmen, left S. ou B. and formed a group, Informations et Liaisons Ouvrières (ILO; later Informations et Correspondance Ouvrières [ICO]). Their positions were formulated in Lefort's text 'Organisation et parti', which was published in no. 26 of *S. ou B.* (and reprinted now in *Élements d' une critique de la bureaucratie* (Geneva: Droz, 1971; 2nd edn, Paris: Gallimard, 1979, pp. 98–113). As for the majority, it regrouped around the text 'Prolétariat et organisation', published in *S. ou B.*, 28 and 29 (reprinted in *EMO 2* [T/E: *PO I* (1959) appears in *PSW 2*]).

In this text I tried to go beyond an 'external' critique of the traditional type of organization and of its activity. It was not only that Bolshevism had erected itself into a 'position of leadership [*direction*]' and that the party was subject to an authoritarian bureaucratic regime. In doing that, it was adopting the capitalist model of organization in the most general sense and was introducing this model into the workers' movement (as social democracy, with different variations, had done). The organization was divided into directors and executants; and it was posing, overall, as a director opposite this executant of the revolution that was the proletariat. The *type of labour* militants performed was that of executants. And, as the ultimate – but also the most important – aspect, the conception of revolutionary theory underlying the organizational model and the type of activity it implied, as well as the content of this theory, had remained essentially capitalist, and this from as early as Marx himself.

Symmetrical with this analysis and this critique was an effort to define the new revolutionary organization in another way. One had to repudiate the capitalist model in all domains and in all its implications; that could be done, to begin with, only by drawing one's inspiration from the creations of the working class over the preceding 150 years. It went without saying, but it was stated in any event, that the revolutionary organization could not be a 'director' of the working class but, rather, an instrument – one of the instruments – of the revolutionary struggle; and that it could be inspired only by the organizational forms the proletariat had created and by the 'spirit' of those creations. The revolutionary organization therefore had to regulate its structure and its internal operation on the basis of the principles that underlie the organization of soviets, or workers' councils (sovereign general assemblies, held as frequently as possible; committees of elected delegates, revocable at any moment, in all cases where decision by general assembly is not possible). But, beyond the changes in the type of organization, it was the traditional conception as a whole that was profoundly at issue.

Politics

Let us begin with a point that played a great role in the 1958 scission, even if it was not made explicit as such. In my view, Lefort's and Simon's conceptions ended up, without saying so, in a refusal or rejection of the political dimension of the organization. If by 'politics' one means what the French Communist Party or the Trotskyists mean by politics, we would obviously all be in agreement. But, obviously, it was not a matter of that.

The question of politics is the overall question of society; and one of the organization's tasks is to keep this question constantly open before the proletariat. I do not see how one can think and situate oneself as a revolutionary while evading it. We declared ourselves partisans of workers' management (or self-management, as one says today). What does this mean, what does it imply? Suppose the workers gain power in each factory, taken separately. The fact remains that all factories are directly and closely interdependent; that the integration of their activities must still be accomplished one way or another; and that, if it is not done in a revolutionary way, it will be done anyway, inevitably, and then in a bureaucratic way – that is to say, by specialists of the universal who will say, to begin with: 'You go manage your little corner, that's fine; as for us, we are going to take care of the general

coordination of activities.' Obviously, if that were to occur, local 'management' would very quickly be emptied of all meaning, since the question of
the integration of the various 'social units' at all levels (firms, localities,
types of activity, etc.) cannot miraculously be resolved all by itself, and it
does not constitute some sort of secondary and external aspect whose repercussions on each unit might remain strictly circumscribed and of limited
importance. It is absurd to think of socialist factories or simply self-
managed ones within the context of a bureaucratic 'coordination' of the
economy and of society.

On the other hand, as people are always in one way or another conscious
of this question, all their particular attempts are hampered and inhibited by
the fact that they doubt their own capacities or are unsure of the objective
possibility of confronting this overall question of society, of social organization as such. Independent of every other consideration, labouring people
clearly cannot reach the point of 'taking power' in the factory if they are not
already envisaging in a certain fashion – be it obscure, half-conscious,
ambiguous – the question of power on the scale of society as a whole. I am
not only taking the standpoint of the 'relation of forces' here; I do not mean
– a truism, again illustrated by the Lip case [T/E: a factory takeover] – that
the power of the workers in the factory can be liquidated, by hook or by
crook, by the bourgeoisie if this workers' power remains 'power in the
factory'. I mean that, beyond a certain point, people engaged in struggle
necessarily pose themselves the question, 'What comes afterward, on the
society-wide scale?' If this question is not made as explicit as possible, this
factor can only put a radical brake on the movement at one moment or
another. It is a task of the revolutionary organization to help labouring
people to elucidate this question, to render it explicit, and to demonstrate
that there is no *fatality* to the dilemma: collapse of the movement or else
central 'power' separated from the masses, therefore bureaucracy, therefore
a return after a short while to a variant of the previous state of things. It is a
task of the organization to show that an overall socialist organization of
society, beyond the factory as such, is possible.

But there is an even more important aspect to this question: in impugn-
ing, implicitly or explicitly, the political dimension of the organization's
existence and activity – starting from the principle that the organization
should express only what is preoccupying the workers *hic et nunc* and that
the workers do not *now* situate themselves on this terrain – one does nothing
more than repeat the premises of the Leninist position in *What Is to Be
Done?*, even if in other connections it is severely criticized. For, one is also
denying that there is a path or an internal relation between the 'immediate'
situation and struggles of the working class and the overall question of
society. Now, this path, this relation, they exist and they are of capital
importance. They reside in the following, that this or that struggle in this or

that factory, this or that activity of this or that occupational sector, this or that theme of 'everyday' concerns can contain and generally do potentially contain much more than at first glance appears there: they contain, in germinal form, an implicit – though, through its implications and its consequences, an overall – contestation of the established order in general. It is thus first a matter of sifting out this signification, of rendering explicit what, in all these 'particular' struggles, activities, etc., this contestation of the established system contains in potentiality, even though it almost always remains obscure for the participants themselves. This signification, these germs, are repressed by the entire contemporary social structure, by the reigning ideology, by the tireless effort of the traditional organizations to suppress it, and, of course, by individuals' psychical internalization of this structure: the self-repression of the new significations they create without completely knowing it.

It is, for example, a bit of a joke to say that the organization ought to spread the word about exemplary struggles by describing and summarizing them and then dodge the questions, 'How and why are these struggles exemplary, and who decides this?' Now, some struggles are exemplary only in terms of their potential signification, which goes beyond their immediate and manifest tenor, not only in as much as what is produced therein also holds in other cases 'numerically', but also in as much as its implications go far beyond what seems to be at issue as they unfold. An elected and revocable strike committee is not exemplary only in as much as all strike committees ought to be elected and revocable; it is also so in as much as, through its constitution and through the relations the strikers entertain with it, the mass of strikers *shatters* the principles of a political philosophy that have been around for twenty-five centuries and creates another one. But of course it is we who are saying this, and we can say it only on the basis of our overall conception. Now, not only ought we openly to take responsibility for this conception, but also it seems to me dishonest and manipulative not to be explicit about it.

If this conception is true, one can see that it unsettles straight away the traditional distinction between the 'immediate' and the 'political'. But it also opens up a path that allows one to go beyond the traditional views on revolutionary theory and the ways in which this theory is to be elaborated. The need for such an elaboration is obvious; it is also clear that the revolutionary organization cannot and should not be a think tank [*CNRS*] or an official Academy of the revolution. Theoretical activity is governed by a prior decision concerning the question, 'What really matters?' To this question we can respond only by granting a central place to what is germinating within the population and to what preoccupies it (while remaining, once again, repressed). Overcoming the traditional conception of theory, both as content and as mode of activity, requires, on the one hand, a change in the axes of one's concerns, a change in what are considered the central themes of theoretical activity, but this also necessarily goes together with a change in the method and the type of elaboration. If it is not to remain the isolated occupation of a separate category of specialists, with all that that fatally implies, revolutionary theory can be elaborated only in a setting [*milieu*] where those who can be called the spokespersons of the population and those who tend to give to what the latter have to say a general expression begin to mingle together and cooperate. And it is clear that an analogous circuit of cooperation and exchange must be instaurated between the organization as such and its surroundings [*milieu ambiant*], and ultimately the social setting in general.

In early 1959 we began to publish a mimeographed monthly, *Pouvoir Ouvrier*. Half of it was devoted to a column entitled 'Giving Labouring People a Voice'. Under this heading we published everything that was sent to the newspaper. But to let the workers really have a voice is an enormous task. It does not suffice to 'let' them have it, for they still have to *take* it. For people to talk, it does not serve much purpose to gather people together and tell them, 'You are free to speak and to say what comes into your mind; there is no taboo here, no authority, nothing that from the outset is considered trivial or unimportant.' Still less does it suffice to call a column 'Giving Labouring People a Voice' for labouring people to write in to it. People do not express themselves; the entire effort of instituted society has always aimed at persuading them that what they have to say does not really matter and that what really matters is what is said by Giscard, Marchais, or Mendès France, the economic and political specialists (generally, pseudospecialists of pseudosciences). This effort has reached its target, and people say, 'What concerns me does not really matter much, it is just some stupid personal stuff; I can't speak about the great affairs of society, because I don't know anything.' We have to destroy the effects of this effort, turn the tables, spread the obvious idea that all the speeches daily filling the newspapers, the radio, and television are of nearly no consequence and that people's preoccupations are the *only* things that really matter from the social point of view.

On the experience of ILO and ICO

After the split, Lefort and Simon founded a group and published a mimeographed newspaper, *ILO*. Some time afterward, Lefort separated from the others and Simon continued, the name of the group and the newspaper becoming *ICO*. Among the founders of ILO, there was a more than restrictive, and in my view profoundly contradictory, conception of revolutionary activity: the sole real task the group was to undertake was to gather and circulate information. The basis for this attitude was a certain interpretation of the idea of the proletariat's autonomy, which they thought implied a refusal to intervene and to contribute anything 'foreign' to the proletariat's own experience. For me this position remains prisoner to the problematic whose other outcome is bureaucracy: We have our ideas and we shall impose them on people – or (as simple negation of the preceding statement, but still situated on the *same* terrain): We have our own ideas, but we shall not state them, because to state them would be to impose them on people (and to adulterate their 'autonomous' evolution). In fact, the autonomous evolution of people does not mean anything. People's evolution is not 'autonomous' in the absolute; it occurs in the midst of a struggle and of a social dialectic in which capitalists, Stalinists, and so on are constantly present. The sole result we would bring about, then, would be that the only voice absent from the concert would be that of the revolutionaries. It is one thing to condemn the conception of the party as 'director', it is another to reject one's own responsibilities and say, 'Our sole point of view consists in putting our newspaper at the disposal of those who want to speak.'

No need to recall that I am giving here my view of things. In any case, the texts are there; those who want to can read them. I think that my criticisms of the time have been confirmed by the events that followed. I would like to illustrate what followed by looking more particularly at a problem that is important and still relevant.

One of the implications of the positions of the founders of ILO was that there was no question of saying in a clear-cut and firm way that there are some people who are members of the organization and some who are not – already because one does not say *on what basis* one would say so. Certainly, the quarrel over the question of membership in the organization has somewhat sinister historical reverberations: the scission between Bolsheviks and Mensheviks at the Second Congress of the RSDLP [Russian Social Democratic Labour Party] centred around Article 1 of the statutes: Who is a member? The Bolsheviks wanted a very clear cut-off, accepting as members only those who worked under the *leadership* of one of the organization's authorities; the Mensheviks wanted to consider as members those who were in agreement with the Party's programme and paid dues while doing any kind of work for the Party. The terms in which the question was posed at the time, the way in which the discussion unfolded, are obviously outdated today; the question itself remains and it cannot be avoided. Suppose one wanted to suppress it. A group is founded on the basis of an affinity of ideas, it goes about its little business, the participants, ten or fifteen of them, have known one another for a long time, they meet together and each has come to like the way the others smell, they are isolated but have a few outside contacts. No problem. One fine day – after May '68, let us say – a hundred guys, it matters little who they are, show up at their meeting and ask, 'Is it open? Can we come in?' They are told: 'Yes, of course.' Then, the person who was supposed to read the agenda for the meeting says, 'We had decided to discuss today subjects A, B, and C.' Cries from the hall: 'What is this shit? What is this fucking bureaucracy? Agendas are an invention of the bureaucracy.' 'But we have to decide on the table of contents for the next issue of our rag.' 'Why do you need to list the contents? We need an anti-rag, with an anti-list', or, 'The question of the contents is all settled, we're going to publish the Common Programme of the Left, which has to be circulated.' All that remains for the ten or fifteen initial participants is to leave quietly, accused by the others – and rightly so – of deceiving the world by saying that their group was 'open', and to meet elsewhere, in a 'closed' room.

One cannot eliminate the problems at issue here with the aid of some minor, negative recipes. If revolutionaries want to work together, this means that, so long as a degree of agreement remains among them, they assume together, collectively, a certain number of tasks. They alone can decide what these tasks are, how they are to be carried out, and by whom. Certainly, it is of the essence to break down the absolute opposition between militants from the organization and a formless morass of sympathizers who are good for indoctrinating, for shaking down, for buying the group's rag, or for supplying their addresses for correspondence. One must break with this conception of the environment [*milieu*] of the organization and the 'sympathizer', break it down through action, organizing frequent meetings where everyone is on the same footing, inventing activities that really can be shared. But one cannot avoid the fact that it is they who have committed themselves to assuming responsibility, in an ongoing way, for the tasks the collective, the militants, have set for themselves, and that it is they who assume responsibility as well for the decisions made as to their own orientation and activities.

To pretend to suppress the scission between militants, members of the organization, and the others by refusing to say who is and who is not a member of the group is to evade, in thought alone, the real difficulties that arise from the fact that there are people for whom work in a collectivity founded upon a revolutionary project is very important (this is a task that, for them, comes to an end only with their death) but that there are also other people who, at a given stage of their existence, are interested in it, really want to participate in it in a partial way, but do not make of this activity an axis of their life (which does not lessen their value in our eyes). The coexistence of these two categories of individuals is a fact to which one must face up. One does not face up to it by stating that the first type of individuals does not exist because they ought not to exist. That ends only in hypocrisy and manipulations of another kind: these individuals, those who are militants, whatever name they are masquerading under, are still there; they do things, be it silently, due to the fact they have some power, but this power is hidden [*occulte*] because formally they are no greater than anyone else. They have a *de facto* power, masked by the elimination of the question of power as an explicit question. This situation is sinister not only because it occults their power but because, what is infinitely more serious, it occults *the question of power*.

To finish with the 1958 scission, let me make one last point: it seems to me that, for Claude Lefort, this split was overdetermined – here I am interpreting, it was not written down at the time – by a conception already forming within him, one he did not express, more or less, until later on. I shall summarize it roughly as follows: One cannot aim at a radical revolution; certainly, there are struggles that shake up the established order, movements that prefigure another form of society; one is on their side and one tries to act in the same direction, but the idea that there might be a radical transformation of society, an overcoming of social alienation, is a philosophical absurdity. I did not follow the evolution of ILO/ICO closely, but I think that the break that occurred later on between Lefort and Simon was conditioned by this conception.

The interpretation of Gaullism

Between 1958 and 1961 the S. ou B. group grew numerically in a rather satisfactory way. Two or three cells were operating in Paris and several more were created in the provinces, with students and a few workers. At the end of 1960 we numbered nearly a hundred, which was not bad for the time. People attended public meetings, and the group exerted some influence over certain non-negligible strata of students in Paris and over some Renault workers, thanks to Mothé's efforts there. The way the group was evolving at the time was related to the struggle against the Algerian War and the ignominious stance the traditional organizations adopted all the way until the war ended.

There were in the group no divergences over the interpretation of Gaullism, which had settled into power. No one saw Gaullism as a form of fascism. Gaullism was immediately interpreted as the passage to modern capitalism, within the specific context of the history of the French bourgeoisie and French society, as the attempt to liquidate a whole set of 'backward' characteristics inherited from the previous regime, from the colonial empire, of course, but also from the economic and financial chaos and even from the political chaos of the bourgeois republic.

The text I wrote at the time provided this interpretation but insisted, as well, on the inability of the French bourgeoisie, with or without de Gaulle, to endow itself with a 'normal' and 'regular' form of political functioning. Today – in January 1974 – it can be said, in relation to this political problem, that it, too, in a sense has been 'resolved', because Pompidou is there. But it can also be said that it has not been resolved – precisely because Pompidou is there.

On the other hand, de Gaulle seized power in the population's absence. Even more than that, in November 1958 de Gaulle and his constitution were granted approval in a plebiscite. One cannot pass over the significance of this fact.

A new scission

The question was posed, then, of how to interpret the population's attitude toward politics. This interpretation had to include the overall evolution of all modern capitalist countries, since one noticed this same attitude occurring everywhere. Other threads, notably our critique of the traditional conception of socialism, were also leading us to think that a radical revision was becoming necessary.

I tried to tie together these different threads in *MCR* (1960–1). A first version was circulated within the group as early as 1959 and it immediately divided the group in two, for it served to crystallize opposition within the group from everybody who rejected the idea of undertaking a radical criticism. There were already some texts (such as *DC*, 1953–4) that implied a rejection of the classical positions on pauperization, economic crises, the growth of the reserve industrial army, in short, everything that passes for, and actually is, Marx's economic theory – as well as the classical conception of imperialism, just as there were some texts (*CS I–III*, 1955–8) that rejected another central idea of Marxism, viz., that the revolution could be conceived simply as receiving existing capitalist technique and placing it in the service of socialism. Also being challenged (see above) was the traditional conception of the role and content of theory, which conception partakes of the speculative attitude elaborated in the West over the past twenty-five centuries. All these things flowed together, converged into consequences, and there ultimately was, as comrade Mao would say, a transformation of quantity into quality. No longer was it this or that particular position, but Marxism as a whole, that was being put back in question. And naturally this immediately provoked Maille, Lyotard, Souyri into recoiling in horror, and into crying 'C. is abandoning Marxism', 'C. is becoming an existentialist.'

The ensuing brawl lasted three years. For a long time, those who had, characteristically, called themselves the *antitendency* opposed us only with self-contradictory polemical arguments ('There is no rise in the workers' standard of living', 'There is one, but it has no significance, or not the one you say', etc.). It was only during the three months preceding the scission that they finally produced three texts that attempted to defend an incoherent variant of neo-paleo-Marxism. For my part, I regret that their authors never published them.

Obviously, this brawl very quickly interfered with all the group's activities, blocking them in a rather serious way. At the same time, a sort of polarization occurred in relation to the tasks of the group: the 'antitendency' had more or less taken charge of *Pouvoir Ouvrier*, and the comrades who were in agreement with the line expressed in *MCR* had charge of the review. They tried to make of *P.O.* a sort of agitational newspaper centred around the traditional themes – an attempt we denounced, saying that they were just following a correct Trotskyism. They criticized the unions while saying that one must go further, do this or that on the occasion of some strike or other; they couldn't refrain from writing an editorial each time the Government had done or said something – which in our view was aberrant, since this amounted to placing oneself on the same terrain as the enemy. With scornful jokes, platitudes, and permanent obstruction they opposed our proposals aimed at a radical transformation in the axes of our propaganda and of our work so that we could address in depth the youth and student problems (all this was recorded in texts dating from 1960, several years before Berkeley), or the problems of woman and the family, pedagogy and the critique of the alleged education one receives today, the critique of the very existence of education, or the importance of struggles other than those of the industrial proletariat and wage-based strikes.

The chasm, both theoretical and practical, between the two sides grew ever deeper. The scission occurred in July 1963. In an amicable manner, the 'antitendency' kept *P.O.* and the rest of us *S. ou B.*

The suspension of publication of S. ou B. *and of the group's activities*

After the scission we published another six issues of the review (nos. 35–40), the last dated June 1965, and the group continued to function until spring 1966. During this final period the review's outside audience was perhaps at its greatest (around 1,000 copies sold per issue, public gatherings of up to 200 people). Nevertheless, there was almost no feedback. The readers of the review never or almost never wrote in, people came to meetings and went home (despite our attempts to break down the professorial structure of the traditional meeting); the ideas were being put into circulation, no doubt, but the public was behaving as a passive consumer of ideas. On the other hand, an increasingly insistent problem arose concerning recruitment into the group. Some very young, highly aware, very astute guys arrived, but they did not succeed in functioning in a collective way with the older comrades (or the reverse, which boils down to the same thing). My interpretation is that these young guys – who had obviously come, like everyone else, as a result of their own personal motivations – were constantly expressing these motivations via their behaviour within the group. And given the situation, the group did not provide the terrain on which these initial motivations might have been transformed into something else; in a sense, the group was becoming a substitute for the family, which led to feelings of ambivalence as strong as those in a real family. This, in turn, led to reactions on the part of the 'elders', and the functioning of the group, undermined by the resulting frictions, became less and less collective and less and less coherent.

Finally, the very character the review was tending to take on posed a grave problem. My last texts were challenging the Marxist conception as a whole and were attempting to return to the foundations of the conception of society and history. For this reason the review began to take a more and more 'abstract' or 'philosophical' turn. This remained solitary work, not only with respect to the writing, but because the group did not feel the need to discuss it. Other texts appeared in the review (those by Mothé or Châtel, for example), but the unity of the whole remained obscure. The review had become the group's main activity – and at the same time it no longer represented a truly collective effort. In the face of everything, it no longer made much sense to maintain the review and the group under these conditions. It was in the light of these observations that I proposed the suspension of publication of the review (see *GI* [1973] and *SP* [1967]). A comrade said to me at the time, 'But if it dies [*Si le grain ne meurt*] . . .' Its seed did indeed bring forth fruit later on . . .[1]

Why didn't we try to reconstitute the group later on? Because there is, for the moment, an enormous difficulty in maintaining revolutionary activity as soon as one no longer leans upon a theoretical or allegedly theoretical *corpus* saying, 'Keep quiet, the answer is in Marx or in Mao', and as soon as one tries to face up in an honest way to real problems.

The experience of all the post-May '68 groups shows that one cannot avoid the questions, 'Who are we? How do we function? Who is we and who is not we? Is there a "we"?' – and, especially, 'What is "we"?' This question is very important, for this 'we' can be mystificatory and alienating. Moreover, most of the time in an organization one does not say 'we', one says 'the Party', 'the group', etc. But in any case, this 'party', this 'group' – or this 'we' – had been defined, at least ideally, by implicit or explicit reference to a finite and definite theory. Now, what I am saying is that this conception of theory is a mystificatory phantasm. People ought to join together because they share a project – the revolutionary project. It will be said that in this way the difficulty has simply been displaced. I would say more than that: It is considerably aggravated, for a project includes a dimension that involves a perpetual, never fully achieved, and open-ended elucidation and implies a completely different subjective *attitude* toward theorization. In short, it is to reject categorically the idea that there might be a complete (or indefinitely perfectible) theory and that theory is sovereign, but it is not to allow oneself, for all that, to say just anything at all. (This 'anything at all' is today the almost universal practice of those who believe they have broken down the traditional barriers but who are all the more, in another way, merely the prisoners thereof. The 'reigning discourse' of a certain 'radical [*contestataire*]' circle today, this disgusting mish-mash that is Freudo-Nietzscheo-Marxism, is, strictly speaking, a *just anything*.) Now, such an attitude is difficult to uphold – I am not saying that it is impossible. But unless a sufficient number of persons who share it join together, I do not see how one could build up something that would have some possibility of surviving and of developing.

The Break with Marxism

QUESTIONER: What, according to you, makes it necessary to break with Marxism? In what way is this break tied to your analysis of the situation of the workers' movement?

C.C.: This question can be discussed on two planes: the theoretical tenor of Marxism and the way in which it poses the problem of theory, and the historical fate of Marxism.

On the theoretical plane, there is a Marxist metaphysics, a theory of history, and an economic theory, all three of them closely intertwined. All three are untenable. As Marxists consider the economic theory to be the cornerstone of the edifice, let us begin with the last of the three.

What is economic theory in Marx, what can it say, up to what point can it go, has it any limits? It is well known that, contrary to the spirit of certain expressions of the young Marx, in his systematic elaboration of theory the mature Marx aims at constituting a sovereign theory that has no limit, that defines the laws of the capitalist economy and shows that the functioning of the latter unavoidably leads to its collapse and to a new society. Now, such a theory is in principle impossible.

In short, all that is said in *Capital*, the theoretical elaboration carried out therein, is possible only by means of the elimination of two decisive factors in the functioning and evolution of the capitalist economy: the evolution of technique and the class struggle. And this is not by chance. It is an internal necessity of this type of theorization, for in the domain of the economy these two factors are expressive, *par excellence*, of the creativity of history, which ensures that there can be no question of establishing 'laws' of economic evolution other than in an always partial and passing sense.

The elimination of class struggle is absolutely flagrant. Marx posits that labour power is a commodity and treats it as such in his theory (starting from the idea that it *is* such in the reality of capitalism). Now, one knows that in the Marxist system a commodity has a definite exchange value and, if it is a 'means of production', also a definite use value. But labour power has neither a definite use value nor a definite exchange value. It has no definite use value: the capitalist who buys a ton of coal knows, in terms of the current state of technique, how many calories he can extract from it, but when he buys an hour of labour, he does not know what amount of output he will be able to extract from it. Now, Marx constantly works from the postulate that, just as the capitalist will extract from the ton of coal the maximum calories the techniques of the time will allow him to extract from it (and coal is indeed passive), so can he extract from the worker the maximum output allowed by the state of technique (type and speed of machinery, etc.), since the worker can only be passive. But that is false. Practically never does Marx speak of the bitter struggle over output that unfolds daily within industry; he speaks of the workers' resistance to output only incidentally, in two places in the first volume of *Capital*, and both times he presents it as inevitably doomed to defeat – which means that the worker is a pure passive object of capital in production, that there is no *struggle* between classes in production but, rather, complete and uncontested – since incontestable – domination of one class over another.

The history of modern industry, however, is not only the history of great pitched union battles; it is also and especially the history that unfolds eight hours a day, sixty minutes an hour, sixty seconds a minute in production and apropos of production; during each of these seconds each gesture of the worker has two sides to it, one that conforms to the imposed production norms, the other combating those norms. Effective output is the result of the struggle that unfolds upon this terrain. Labour power, therefore, has no definite use value that one might grasp independent of this struggle and its effects.

Now, it is easy to see that at the same time this struggle codetermines to a decisive degree labour power's exchange value. That is so not only because it codetermines labour productivity (and thereby the unit value of commodities that enter into the working class's level of consumption) but especially because it alone sets effective wage levels. Wages are not '*X* dollars an hour'. That is meaningless, since the capitalist does not in fact buy 'an hour'; he acts as if he is buying 'an hour', but in reality he is buying the effective output – the effective output which is, as a matter of fact, indeterminate – that he will try to determine by introducing new machines, by hiring time-study men, etc., and that the workers, for their part, will try to determine otherwise, by fooling the time-study men, by cutting corners, by organizing among themselves, etc. In reality, wages are a rate of exchange: so many dollars against the output achieved during an hour – and the second term is indeterminate. So many dollars for workers completely subject to the time-study men and so many dollars for workers who successfully resist them are not at all the same things.

And how does Marx think the determination of labour power's exchange value? Since labour power *is* a commodity, it is worth, like every other commodity, the 'labour' it contains, that is to say, the labour incorporated into the 'costs of production and reproduction of labour power', which is materially represented as the quantity of commodities a worker (or a working-class family) consumes in order to live and to reproduce a new generation of workers. If we call this quantity the working class's 'standard of living', the exchange value of labour power will be a mere function of two and only two factors: this 'standard of living' and the unit value of each of the commodities that make it up (in fact, the simple multiplicative product of the one balanced by the other). Now, this unit value of each commodity is only the inverse, roughly speaking, of labour productivity: the higher the latter is raised, the less labour time is incorporated into – and the lower the unit value of – each commodity produced. Therefore, *if* the working class's standard of living remains constant, the rise in labour productivity, tirelessly pursued and achieved by capitalism, signifies *ipso facto* a reduction in the value of the commodities that make up the working-class standard of living, *therefore* a reduction of the 'paid part' of the working day, therefore an increase in the rate of exploitation, assuming that the working day itself remains constant.

But can we postulate that the working class's standard of living remains constant? Marx does not have much to say on this topic; he posits that each time it is 'determined by historical and moral factors' and goes on to postulate in an implicit way that one must assume it is constant. But that is logically arbitrary and really false. For ease of presentation and as a first approximation, one can offer the hypothesis that the working-class standard of living remains constant if one is talking about the situation of the economy over a very short period. One absolutely cannot do so over a period of one or two centuries – and it is upon the latter that the Marxian theory of the capitalist economy bears. Now, it is obvious that there has been a considerable modification (a rise) in the real standard of living of the working class over the past 150 years. This rise has been the result of working-class struggles, both, as has already been said, informal, implicit struggles at the point of production and large or small overt struggles over wage demands. Marx abstracts from this struggle, and, as everything that follows in *Capital* necessarily rests upon this 'analysis' of the determination of the exchange value of labour power as a commodity, the whole edifice is built upon sand, the whole theory is conditioned by this 'forgetting' of class struggle. One must also reread the end of 'Wages, Price, and Profit' to convince oneself that, even when Marx grants that working-class struggle has had some influence over wage levels, for him this influence remains conjunctural and 'cyclical' and unable to alter the basic long-term distribution of the product as regulated by the law of value.

There is even more. Starting at a certain moment, the capitalists themselves came to understand that the steady rise of the working class's standard of living was inherently necessary to the operation of the system. For, without a continual enlargement of the market in consumer goods there can be no capitalist expansion – in any case, not of the type of expansion we know. Obviously, in certain situations (Nazi Germany, the USSR over a long period, times of war, etc.) the system orients production especially toward the manufacture of armaments or toward accelerated accumulation, and the real standard of living of the working class finds itself blocked or even declines. But the 'normal' long-term evolution of the system is impossible without a continual expansion of the market in consumer goods; and this market, for the most part, is made up of solvent demand, therefore the incomes, of workers and wage earners in general. For this reason, if today one wants, for ease of presentation and as a first approximation, to offer a hypothesis, one is obliged to hypothesize that there is a stability to the *pace of increase* of workers' real income during the short-term period one is studying.

One can certainly imagine on paper a hypertheory that would attempt to quantify the intensity of the class struggle and its relation with wage levels and to insert it into a 'more general' schema (some academic economists have indeed made such attempts, where, as if by chance, it is the rate of unionization that is taken as the variable representative of 'wage pressures'). I shall not discuss this attempt, as I consider such an outlook fundamentally absurd.

All this goes to show that the idea of a 'law of the increase in the rate of exploitation' is a myth. Also mythical, more generally, is any idea of a 'law' that would determine the evolution of the distribution of the social product between capitalists and labouring people without regard to class struggle.

The alleged law of the rise in the organic composition of capital likewise rests on a fallacy. Because in terms of *volume*, and even more rigorously in *physical* terms, one notices an increase in the mass of constant capital (of the *quantity* of machines, raw materials, etc.) in relation to 'variable capital' (that is to say, in fact, in relation to the number of workers or of hours worked), one draws the conclusion that constant capital, in terms of *value*, increases in relation to variable capital, also in *value* terms. This is what in logic is called a *non sequitur*. The evolution of the physical mass of constant capital still says nothing about the evolution of the mass of its *value*, for the latter equals physical mass multiplied by unit value, and this last element *decreases* with the rise of labour productivity (which there is no reason to assume increases less rapidly in the sector producing the means of production than in the economy as a whole). It is not because the quantity of machines, raw materials, etc. increases relative to the number of workers that the value of constant capital increases relative to that of variable capital. At the same time, Marx assumed that the value of variable capital decreases with time, with a constant number of workers, as a function of the increase in the rate of exploitation; and we have seen that the latter does not exist. One can therefore say nothing *a priori* about the evolution of organic composition.

As for the 'falling rate of profit', it is the very example of a nonproblem. Perhaps one day it will be necessary to write a psychoanalytic essay on the motives behind the fascination the idea of a long-term fall in the rate of profit exerted over Marx and the Marxists, and before them over classical political economy.

Marx's formula for profit is $sv/c + v$ (ratio of total surplus value to the sum of constant capital and variable capital). Sv is a function of the number of workers employed, since surplus value is extracted only from living labour. The 'law of the rise in organic composition of capital' says that c increases more rapidly than v. Therefore, sv depends only on v, and, the latter increasing less quickly than c, the numerator of the fraction should decrease over time, relative to the denominator. In this argument all the links are false. We have already seen that it is not necessarily true (and it is not true in reality) that organic composition rises. On the other hand, Marx states that the rate of exploitation (the ratio sv/v) increases over time; how do we know that this increase is not sufficient to compensate for an eventual increase in organic composition, or even for overcompensating it, in which case we would have for the rate of profit not a tendency to fall but a tendency to rise? Well, the formula itself is meaningless in relation to this 'problem': $sv/c + v$ is not a rate of profit on capital but a rate of profit on gross sales (capital is represented therein only by c, which is the portion productively consumed over a period, generally a small part of the capital engaged in production).

On the other hand, we may ask: In what way does all this have any interest or relevance? Let us grant that the rate of profit tends to decrease – what then? If it were a matter of the rate of profit *on capital*, we would be able to conclude, everything else being equal (an in no way trivial postulate), that the pace of capitalist accumulation tends to slacken – so what? (Let us note that, in reality, it is rather the opposite that, until now, has been observed.) For two centuries capitalist production has increased, let us say, at 4 per cent per annum on the average; in what way does it comfort us or affect our political outlook to think that *circa* 2175 its pace of annual growth will be only 2 per cent? And we are not even talking about the rate of profit on capital but about the rate of profit on gross sales, which does not have, as such, any direct relation to the pace of accumulation.

Finally, if one assumes that such a 'tendency to fall' does exist, why would it cease to exist in socialist society? The reasons that, according to Marx, the rate of profit tends to fall in capitalist society are of a technical character that have nothing to do with the social structure of capitalism; they boil down to this, that there are always more machines, raw materials, etc., for a given number of workers. Since we are not saying that in socialist society one will try to achieve reverse technical development (and in any case Marx and the Marxists would never say so), this factor will still be there; it will even worsen, since the other factor that can counterbalance it under a capitalist regime – the increase in the rate of exploitation – ought no longer to exist in socialist society. Well, is it that in socialist society there will be a fall in the rate of surplus production (since we can no longer speak of profit)? and what will be the consequences of that?

Now we come to what I have called Marx's elimination of the technological factor. Certainly, Marx saw with profundity the constantly repeated upheaval technical evolution introduces into capitalist society and into the capitalist economy, and he provided exemplary and incomparable sociohistorical analyses of this upheaval. But when he comes to construct his economic system, it is as though he had forgotten all that. The implicit postulate, without which everything said in *Capital* would have no meaning, is that there is technical progress (without which there would be no rise in labour productivity) but that this technical progress is represented by a continuous variable. There is a growing $f(t)$, a growing and continuous function of time, that determines output per hour of labour. That is all! If one wants to go further and take into account all that Marx saw when he spoke historically and concretely of technical progress, there is no longer anything that can be called the value of capital and that can be treated in economic theory as Marx treats it, namely, something *measurable* that corresponds to the piling up of buildings, machines, mines, etc.

Marx's conception presupposes, in effect, that one could *measure* the value of capital, represent it by a *number* of this heteroclite *assemblage* of objects, add together apples and oranges, and this is the purpose of the theory of labour value. Each machine, for example, has a value in as much as it incorporates past labour, which can be counted (in hours, etc.). If there is no technical progress at all, which means that one produces and reproduces the same type of machine by the same methods, there is no problem: the (direct or indirect) labour actually spent in manufacturing the machine, its 'historical' cost, unambiguously measures the latter's value. If there is technical progress, that means *ipso facto* that manufacturing methods have changed; the machines formerly produced, and still in operation today, have a different (generally higher) 'historical' cost than the cost of machines produced today by more efficient methods. It would nevertheless be bizarre to say that they have, for all that, 'more value' (disregarding depreciation, etc.). Logic (and the real practice of the capitalist economy) leads one to say that the value of this type of machine (as, moreover, that of every product) will have to be determined not by its effective 'historical' cost but by its present necessary cost (in other words, its cost were it to be reproduced).

If technical progress is continuous in the mathematical sense, that is to say, is made in infinitesimal increments, one can show, by means as well of other fairly restrictive conditions, that one can preserve a calculus of the 'value' of the machine according to its costs of production.

But if technical progress is made, as it is in the case of reality, by leaps and bounds, this possibility no longer exists. One will no longer have an infinitesimal 'obsolescence' (technical ageing) of each machine, which makes its value tend imperceptibly toward zero, but entirely new machines, others which, even if outmoded, continue to operate well but are no longer reproduced (and consequently one can no longer calculate in a meaningful way the cost of reproducing them), and others, finally, that suddenly lurch from being into nonbeing since, although still very good yesterday, they suffer from the effects of the invention of another machine that renders them positively and totally unprofitable, or because the final product they once served to produce is suddenly replaced by another whose manufacture is completely different. Under these conditions one can no longer establish a measurement of capital that would have some meaning over time; one can no longer say what c represents in the formulae and the alleged laws of development of capitalism, except in an absolutely 'instantaneous' sense.

Q: Doesn't this call all economic discourse into question?

C.C.: Of course.

Q: This would leave the science of economics only with a descriptive task?

C.C.: There is certainly more than that. Even in sociology, one can do much more than provide descriptions. In economics there are connections, repetitions, 'local' and partial regularities, general tendencies; there is an intelligibility of phenomena – provided, of course, one never forgets that, in order to understand anything about it, economics must be plunged back into the social-historical. But what does not exist is a political economy established on the model of a physicomathematical science. And it really is this model that Marx had in mind when he wrote *Capital*. Now, such a model presupposes invariants and conservations. The 'laws' of physics are invariant relations in which appear some parameters that remain constant ('universal constants'); there is a relation, always the same, that connects the pressure, volume, and temperature of a gas, and a constant of perfect gases. And through all the changes in a physical system there is always 'something' that *is conserved*: mass–energy, electrical charge, etc. But what 'is conserved' in an economy? And where can one find therein invariant functional relations? Each time one tries to establish such relations (academic economics has been exerting itself in vain on this issue for decades), one sooner or later notices that their form changes, that their parameters change, that their very type of dependency, in relation to 'initial conditions' or to the 'exogenous' ones under which it was posited that they were valid, changes. To reiterate, the economy is full of 'locally regular' linkages that are not unintelligible, but there can be no question of integrating them into an exhaustive and permanent system of invariant relations, still less of formalizing them.

Q: You have just shown how Marxist economic theory is untenable. In what way is Marx's theory of history untenable?

C.C.: Already, what has just been said about the economy shows that one cannot consider capitalist society as obeying the theoretical schema of historical materialism (such as it is formulated, for example, in the Preface to *A Contribution to the Critique of Political Economy*). Still less can one understand the history of humanity previous to the bourgeois era on the basis of this schema. How, for example, can one understand 'archaic' societies in this fashion? These societies very often exhibit, on the basis of the same state of the forces of production and the same type of relations of production, an incredible variety of social organizational forms and forms of social life. Faced with that, one of the Marxist responses is to say, 'We could care less about this variety, which is only apparent; forms of organization and forms of life are but a sauce on top, the substance is in all these cases the same; some may be totemized, and others not, some may live in a matriarchal system and others in a patriarchal system, but the essential point is that they all live by hunting or gathering.'

But this boils down to eliminating history and society, to deciding in advance that the sole reality is that of the 'forces of production' and all the rest mere epiphenomenon, whose mere existence and the variations therein then become, moreover, totally unintelligible: Why the devil aren't these savages content to go hunting and instead go off representing *different* things to themselves, since all they all do is hunt? This attitude also boils down to judging the whole of the history of humanity according to the crudest and coarsest mentality a capitalist boss ever could have: What is so-and-so? Well, he earns so much a month. What is this tribe?

It's just some hunters at such-and-such a stage of technical development. The entire history of humanity is thus seen as a series of less and less imperfect attempts to attain that final perfection, the capitalist factory. And to the extent that they have not reached that point, these poor savages are wasting their time inventing 'absurdities' (as Engels wrote, black on white). Finally, all this refers us back to Marxism's 'rationalist-materialist' philosophy, which is only a variant of a twenty-five-centuries-old metaphysics that is almost completely meaningless.

We must also speak, however, about the historical destiny of Marxism. It is strange to see people who proclaim themselves to be Marxists or want to 'defend Marx' and who remain stubbornly ignorant of this question. Would I be able to discuss Christianity while saying, 'I couldn't care less about the Inquisition; the Pope is an accident; the Catholic Church's participation in the Spanish Civil War on the side of Franco, well that's just a matter of empirical priests. All that is secondary in relation to the essence of Christianity, which manifests itself in such-and-such verses from the Gospels'? Christianity is a social and historical reality that has been instituted for going on two thousand years; this reality, which is certainly infinitely complex and ambiguous, nevertheless has a signification that I can at no moment ignore: Christianity has been and remains the religion of power that teaches people to render unto Caesar the things which be Caesar's, etc.

I cannot do otherwise when Marxism is at issue. Here, certainly, two thousand years have not elapsed, only a hundred and twenty, but the last sixty of them have been, historically, quite ponderous. The *reality* of Marxism is first of all, to an overwhelming degree which takes precedence over all the rest, that it is the avowed ideology of totalitarian regimes of exploitation and oppression which exercise their power over a billion men and women. And it is also that it is the ideology of other countries' bureaucratic parties whose aim, we know, is to install regimes identical to the previous ones and whose daily practice is a series of infamies. That has not lasted two thousand years but it weighs two billion tons.

If someone says, 'Brezhnev is not Marxist but a mystifier who uses Marx; the true thought of Marx has nothing to do with all that' – then it is no longer Marxism we are dealing with but the 'true thought of Marx'. But the 'true thought of Marx' – an expression that, moreover, remains mysterious – has the same status as the true thought of Freud, the true thought of Hegel, the true thought of Kant, and so on. It is a great work. It is ambiguous. It is also contradictory: there are different strata. Immense labour is required to begin to make something out of it – that is to say, chiefly to discover in it some questions to be explored. What the faithful still believe is that there is a full and plain truth and that it is physically deposited in Marx's writings. That said, we may add that of course Marx is very important. We could not hold this conversation for a second if we had not passed by way of his thought and if we were not living in a world that has been influenced by it.

Q: Is the proletariat still, as Marx said, the bearer of the revolutionary project?

C.C.: What we call the revolutionary project has been engendered in and through the struggles of workers, and this began before Marx (between 1790 and 1840 in England and in France). All the relevant ideas were formed and formulated during this period: the fact of exploitation and its conditions, the project of a radical transformation of society, that of a government by the producers and for the producers, the abolition of the wages system . . .

The history of the proletariat is a fundamental fact and an inexhaustible source. No other exploited class is known that has thus constituted itself as an active pole of society, that has engendered a project for such a radical sort of transformation, that has acted with such audacity, such heroism, that has achieved the following extraordinary thing: to have, as an exploited class, codetermined to a decisive degree the evolution of the social system. Everything that has happened in the Western world for the past 150 years is, in enormous part, the result of working-class struggles. These struggles have forced increases in wages, reductions in work time, the introduction of political rights, the 'true' bourgeois republic; and it is they, too, that have induced a certain type of technological evolution.

But at present, we have to acknowledge that in modern capitalist societies the proletariat is constantly decreasing as a percentage of the population and has by now become a minority in the most 'developed' countries. In the United States, manual workers represent barely a quarter of the labouring population; and the tendency is the same in the other countries of modern capitalism. Above all, for the past twenty-five years it has no longer, as it did in the past, posited itself as a class aiming at the radical transformation of society.

We therefore can no longer maintain the proletariat in the role Marx assigned to it, based on the idea that the process of capitalist accumulation was going to transform everyone (apart from a handful of capitalists and perhaps a few foremen) into industrial proletarians. That is not what happened. To say that everyone, or almost everyone, has become a wage earner does not mean that everyone has become proletarian with the content one used to give to this term. To be a wage earner is virtually the general condition in modern capitalist society; it is no longer the situation of a 'class'. Quite evidently, there are from several standpoints sizeable differentiations among wage earners. But they do not furnish us with a division into classes. For example, the strictly 'economic' criterion, one's income (or wage) level, cannot really be used. If one used it in a consistent way and on a world scale, one would have to say that the lowest-paid wage earner in a developed capitalist country is still an exploiter of the two-thirds of humanity living in the nondeveloped countries. The other dividing line among wage earners, that of directors and executants, is tending to become less and less relevant, for the categories of pure directors and pure executants are, numerically speaking, becoming less and less sizeable; the bureaucratic pyramid is bulging, so to speak, in the middle, since there is a proliferation of production tasks whose agents cannot be said to have been reduced to the role of simple executants.

The sole criterion of differentiation within the mass of wage earners that remains relevant for us is their attitude toward the established system. That boils down to saying that one must abandon 'objective criteria', of whatever kind they may be. With the exception of the tiny minority at the summit, the whole of the population is just as open – or closed – to a revolutionary outlook. It is possible that, conjuncturally speaking, this or that strata or category plays a larger role; but one can no longer maintain the idea that the proletariat is 'the' depositary of the revolutionary project. This idea has become a sort of incantation that permits, on the one hand, the CP to pose as *the* party that speaks 'in the name' of labouring people, and, on the other, the left and extreme-left groupuscules to mystify themselves by repeating, 'We are ten, but we are the potential party of the proletariat', or 'We *are de jure* this proletariat that still does not know itself.' It is clear, too, that one cannot both proclaim oneself a Marxist and try to find a substitute for the proletariat in the person of Third World peasants.

The political privilege of the proletariat in Marxism was homologous with the theoretical and philosophical privilege granted to the sphere of production. We have seen that the latter cannot be maintained. And symmetrically, one cannot neglect the historical importance of the evolution in the struggles of young people, nor of all that happens within the female part of the population (after all, the condition for production is the reproduction of the species . . .). This refers us back to the disruption of the relations between the sexes, of the traditional family structure, and to the crisis in all authoritarian structures. For us, these manifestations ought to be as important as any others.

A last point on the relation between this idea of the proletariat and Marxist theory. A kind of discourse still frequently encountered today comes in the form of the following circular argument: The proletariat has a privileged historical role, as demonstrated in Marx's work (which is true); Marx's work has a (truth) status that sets it apart, because it is the conscious expression of the movement of the proletariat (as a historically privileged class). This is not stated under that explicit form, but ten minutes of Socratic dialogue is all that is needed to bring these statements out from almost all Marxists. Thus, too: The proof of the truth of the Scriptures is Revelation; and the proof that there has been Revelation is that the Scriptures say so. This is a self-confirming system. In fact, it is true that Marx's work, in its spirit and in its very intention, stands and falls along with the following assertion: The proletariat is, and manifests itself as, the revolutionary class that is on the point of changing the world. If such is not the case – as it is not – Marx's work becomes again what in reality it always was, a (difficult, obscure, and deeply ambiguous) attempt to think society and history from the perspective of their revolutionary transformation – and we have to resume everything starting from our own situation, which certainly includes both Marx himself and the history of the proletariat as components.

The Revolutionary Project Today

Q: What you said shortly before about youths, women, etc. was like a beginning of a development of the formula, 'the revolutionary problematic today has to be extended to all spheres of social activity, and in the first place to everyday life'.

C.C.: Yes, certainly. The everyday is also the everyday life of the worker, for example. It is therefore eight hours, or more, of daily work in the factory, with labour conditions as we know them, the implicit, informal, incessant struggle at the point of production; the struggle against the time-study men contains, germinally, the workers' tendency to determine by themselves their pace of work, which is of capital significance. But the everyday is also the home in the evening, the neighbourhood, the whole of people's lives in all their ignored, neglected aspects which have been considered to be secondary by those who are obsessed solely by strikes, 'political' events, or 'international' crises.

Q: Do we end up then with Marcuse's problematic in relation to the youth struggle?

C.C.: It is difficult to discern what Marcuse is thinking in this regard. Sometimes he expresses himself as if he were thinking that there can no longer be a question of a revolution, but just revolutionary struggles doomed to remain minoritarian, as if he were saying, 'Long live the students, long live the prisoners in revolt, but we know that the world cannot change essentially. So much the better if people fight somewhere or other; this proves that human beings do not allow themselves to be enslaved and brutalized completely.' For my part, I categorically reject this attitude and the philosophy that corresponds to it.

Sometimes one has the impression that he is denying the revolutionary role of the proletariat, or more exactly that he is denying all possibility of a revolutionary attitude on the part of workers and reserves these possibilities for other categories (youth, etc.). This is Marx in reverse: there is a negative privilege on the part of the proletariat, and always a positive privilege on the part of a determinate someone. As for me, I say that it is from this universe of thought that we must exit.

Q: What can one say of revolutionary activity today?

C.C.: First, one must break with the imperialist conception that revolutionary activity is the doing of revolutionary militants alone. One cannot speak of *a* revolutionary activity, of *one type* of revolutionary activity. In contemporary society there is necessarily a plurality of potentially and effectively revolutionary activities. The activity of militants who organize themselves in a revolutionary organization is only one of the vectors of a multiform combat that unfolds in several spheres, potentially in all (and if such were not the case, the activity of revolutionaries would be intrinsically absurd). As such, the activity of revolutionary militants has no privilege; it is one component of a historical movement that outstrips it – that must outstrip it – to an infinite degree.

Q: But can one still speak of *a* revolutionary project?

C.C.: That is another thing, and perhaps we must specify what we mean here by *project*. We are not speaking about a 'programme', a set of concrete measures the masses in power, in France or in Venezuela, would do well to undertake. The revolutionary project is the historical aim of a society that would have gone beyond alienation; by alienation I mean a social-historical fact (instituted heteronomy), not a metaphysical given. In other words it is the aim of an autonomous society, one which is not *enslaved* to its past or to its own creations. I explicitly say 'enslaved'. One is certainly always 'determined' by one's past, and by one's own acts; but all that depends on what one means by 'determined' and up to what point this determination goes. Determination is not the same for a psychotic and for a 'normal' or neurotic person; neither is it the same for 'traditional' (archaic or Asiatic) societies, for the Greek cities, for the United States or France at the end of the eighteenth century.

What is an autonomous society? I had at first given to the concept of autonomy, as extended to society, the meaning of 'collective management'. I have now been led to give it a more radical content, which is no longer simply collective management ('self-management') but the *permanent and explicit self-institution of society*; that is to say, a state in which the collectivity knows that its institutions are its own creation and has become capable of regarding them as such, of taking them up again and transforming them. If one accepts this idea, it defines a unity of the revolutionary project.

Q: It seems that you have defined overall reflection [*la réflexion globale*] as both indispensable and impossible. One can also ask if your analysis does not assign to struggles a regulative effect. It seems that the self-institution of which you are speaking is an overall project, a sort of *petitio principii* according to which this globality is viable and that the outcome of struggles is a sort of rationality.

C.C.: I am not saying that everyday struggles, as such, become global. Nevertheless, when we analyse a given struggle – workers against time-study men, students over the curriculum – we notice that it contests, at a precise moment and on a precise point, *the* capitalist system which, whatever its contradictions and its faults, really does have a 'globality' to it that is expressed, here as oppressive education, there as rules relating to time-and-motion studies.

When someone refuses to remain a passive object of the educational system or of the factory's management or of her husband after having been that of her father, there really is, whether one knows it or not, a 'positive underside' to this refusal, *another* principle that contradicts head-on the fundamental principle of capitalism. My interpretation of these struggles leads me to see in them a unity, or at least a homology, to their signification. If I am mistaken, one could no longer speak indeed of a revolutionary project during the present period, and one would have to return to positions like those just imputed to Marcuse. But if I am not mistaken, these homologous significations necessarily refer us back, due to the very fact that their homology is being affirmed across different sectors and activities of society, to the question of social globality and to its reality.

Obviously, when one speaks of the globality of society one is speaking of a problem that only the whole of society as acting society is in a position to address. And this is what creates the impression of an enormous gap. I believe that the imaginative and creative capacities of society will allow it to resolve problems that today may appear to us insoluble, and others whose formulation we cannot even suspect at this time. If such a capacity does not exist, it really serves no purpose to worry over this or that aspect of the organization of the first phase of a socialist society or to talk about it. Such a discourse has meaning only if it aims at shedding the greatest possible light on the largest possible number of questions, at sweeping clear the terrain, at showing that certain difficulties are imaginary, that for such-and-such other ones this or that type of solution is already conceivable, etc. But all this still presupposes that one takes *people's determinative activity* to be capable of facing head-on the questions that will be raised – and presupposes that one takes such activity alone to be capable of doing so.

Let us take an example. For a very long time now I have perceived schooling not as an institution that must be reformed and improved upon but as a prison that must be destroyed. As the 'positive underside' of this negation, one can conceive of life in society taking on the task of reabsorbing the function of educating the younger generations. (I am thoroughly hostile to the mythology of the 'noble savage' which arose again a few years ago. This does not stop me from noting that, from this standpoint, archaic societies give us a glimpse of the real possibility of an 'education' – that is to say, an absorption of culture by the individual, as that individual grows up – that does not imply the institution of a separate sector of activity whose specialized purpose is to achieve this end.) But it is not a question of proposing a new utopia, for this utopia will always be hollow at its central point: the reabsorption of the educative function by social life has meaning only if people as a whole are capable of living their own children, and the children of others, therefore *children*, in another way than they now do. That implies thoroughgoing transformations in the organization and the nature of labour itself, as well as of people's habitat, their psychical apparatus, etc. – excuse me if I don't go on. That is to say, this refers back immediately to the globality of society – and to the activity and the very being of the collectivity as being capable of taking charge thereof.

Will society itself be capable of secreting from within a coherent response to these questions? We cannot demonstrate in advance through theoretical reflection that it will be so capable, still less that this response would have the meaning we are trying to sketch out in advance. Clearly, such a 'demonstration' would be a contradiction in terms.

What we do know, however, is that *all societies in history have been capable of giving coherent responses to the problem of their globality as such and to the (each time specific) particularities of this globality.* This coherency, let it be said in passing, leaves – or ought to leave – bewildered and speechless all sociologists, psychoanalysts, economists, etc. (I say 'ought to', because in fact they are hardly ever concerned with it at all), for it goes infinitely beyond all conceivable analytical abilities. Individuals' psychical apparatuses, the economic regime, social organization, the way in which objects are manufactured, the spirit animating one's mother tongue, etc. – all this *holds together*; it is impossible for one to exist without the others and for the society to exist without any one of them. It is society that posits them, it is society that institutes itself as overall society.

An immense enigma – and a blinding fact – is that there is no failed society, there never has been one. There are biological monsters, there are psychical failures; there are no failed societies. The Chinese, the Athenians, the French, innumerable collectivities down through history have always been capable of instituting, without their knowing it, a coherent social life. To say that postrevolutionary society would be the only one not so capable can only be based on the idea that there is a radical absurdity or an impossibility in this aim of an autonomous society. Now, until this idea is 'demonstrated' (and I say that such a 'demonstration' is in principle impossible), I shall continue to affirm that it expresses only a practico-politico-philosophical decision on the part of the person who states it.

Q: What can be done at present? And what are the tasks of revolutionaries more particularly as intellectuals?

C.C.: The first task is to try to organize as revolutionary militants. As long as a revolutionary remains isolated, the question you have posed remains without great mystery and without great interest. Isolated individuals have to try to do what they can where they find themselves, but no general answer is possible.

The question that really matters is the following: How is one to go beyond the problems faced by a collective of revolutionaries, the ones that stand in opposition to its survival and development? As for the rest, we can do nothing: the workers will struggle or they won't, the women's movement will spread or it won't, the high-school kids will persevere or they will return to the fold. But what one should feel responsible for is *that in France there are at least hundreds of people who are thinking nearly along the lines outlined by the framework of our discussion here, by the problematic that matters to us* (little matter if their responses may vary) – a framework and problematic that others reject. Nevertheless, each among them feels or knows that the plagues ravaging small revolutionary organizations have not disappeared, and they are no closer today than yesterday to believing that they could provide an answer to the problems that would arise again, were a [revolutionary] organization to be re-established at this time.

The only way to find out if you can swim is to get into the water. Of course, you might drown, but you can also choose to start at a place where you have a footing. One must first try to find out whether an embryo of an organization heading in the direction I alluded to right now is possible (whether people who would participate in it exist), then try to define a certain number of points of agreement necessary and sufficient for a collective activity to commence. Starting from a common frame of reference of problems and ideas, one can begin to apply the principle that the organization self-determines itself constantly, with all that this implies. The people involved must be disposed toward assuming responsibility for a permanent collective activity that is long term in nature and at least somewhat general in import. They also must be ready to examine the relations they develop with one another, and more generally the internal problems of organization, in tandem with those that are posed in connection with the outside world. In other words, the people involved must have understood and accepted that a group is composed of flesh-and-blood individuals and not pure political consciousnesses.

Beautiful solutions to these problems can be given on paper, but they will serve no practical purpose, for what determines people's effective behaviour in the organization is, much more than their 'ideas', their life, their personality, their preoccupations, their experience, the relations they maintain with others in the organization, etc. All this is all the more influential as the field of activity of the revolutionary organization offers none of the 'objective' constraints other types of collective activity present. In the case of productive labour, for example, whether or not it is alienated, there exists an 'objective' constraint that tends to minimize the effects of the factors mentioned above. The same does not hold in the case of a collective that, in a sense, is floating somewhat in midair and that has to draw from within itself the essential elements of what it thinks, what it wants to do, how it wants and is to do it.

Now, if by your question you mean, 'Suppose this organization exists, what ought its tasks to be?', I would respond that it is for the group to define them and that they depend in good part on conjunctural factors. For my part, I think that immense tasks are to be accomplished on the level of elucidating the problematic of revolution, of denouncing falsehoods and mystifications, of spreading just and justifiable ideas, as well as relevant, significant, and precise information; it can also promulgate a new attitude toward ideas and theory, for the type of relation people at present entertain with ideas and theory, an essentially religious type, must be shattered, and it must be shown at the same time that one cannot for all that authorize oneself to say just anything whatsoever.

It seems to me obviously just as essential for the organization to participate in struggles, where they unfold, and to become an instrument of them, provided that this participation is not fabricated out of thin air or parachuted in. To establish a new relation between revolutionaries, in the sense we give to this word, and the social setting in which these revolutionaries find themselves begins with the conviction that the organization has as much to learn from people in the street as the latter have to learn from it. But again, that does not mean anything unless it is made concrete, and here again an enormous field of invention opens for the activity of revolutionaries.

Note

1   *Telos* translator's note: *Si le grain ne meurt* . . . is the title of an autobiographical work by André Gide and is taken from John 12: 24: 'but if it die, it bringeth forth much fruit'.

2

Presentation of *Socialisme ou Barbarie.*
An Organ of Critique and Revolutionary
Orientation (1949)*

The group whose organ this Review is was set up inside the French section of the 'Fourth International' in 1946. As it developed politically and ideologically, it became increasingly distanced from the latter, and this led it to break decisively not only with the present positions of Trotsky's epigones but with what has constituted the genuine essence of Trotskyism since 1923, that is to say, its reformist attitude toward the Stalinist bureaucracy (in the profound sense of the term 'reformist'), an attitude which has strangely been combined with an attempt to maintain intact, within a reality that has constantly been evolving, the basic tenets of Bolshevik policy during its heroic period.

It is not by accident that our group was formed inside the Trotskyist organization. Indeed, even a passing awareness of the counterrevolutionary character of Stalinism leads, most often, to Trotskyism. But it is not an accident that we have separated ourselves from it, for the question of the nature of Stalinism is precisely the point on which the superficiality of the Trotskyist conceptions becomes most apparent.

Indeed, our positions were formed on the basis of a problem that all revolutionary militants feel is the fundamental problem of our time: the nature of the 'working-class' bureaucracy and especially of the Stalinist bureaucracy. We began, as all workers who have simply gone beyond Stalinism do, by asking ourselves: What is Russia today, what are the 'Communist' parties? What do the politics and ideology of Stalinism signify? What are the social bases? And, finally, what are the economic roots? This bureaucracy, which for twenty-five years has dominated Russian society, which since the end of the war has annexed the eastern half of Europe, and which is now in the process of conquering China at the same time as it is maintaining exclusive influence over key sections of the proletariat in the bourgeois countries – is it a mere temporary excrescence grafted onto the workers' movement, a simple historical accident, or does it correspond to

* 'Présentation', *S. ou B.*, 1 (March 1949). Reprinted in *SB 1*, pp. 131–7, and in *SB**, pp. 106–10.

deep-seated characteristics in the evolution of contemporary social and economic life? If it is the latter that is the true response to this question, if to speak of a 'historical accident' apropos of a phenomenon so vast and so enduring is quite simply ridiculous, the question then arises: How is it that this evolution of economic and social life, which according to Marxism ought to lead to the victory of the revolution, has led to the victory, even fleeting, of the bureaucracy? And what, from this perspective, becomes of the proletarian revolution?

It was, therefore, the most practical and immediate necessities of class struggle that led us to pose seriously the problem of bureaucracy and that in turn obliged us to pose anew the problem of the evolution of the modern economy, of the signification of a century of proletarian struggles, and, in the end, of the revolutionary outlook itself. A theoretical elaboration taking practical preoccupations as its point of departure once again became the prerequisite for any coherent, organized activity.

In introducing ourselves today, via this Review, to the avant-garde of manual and intellectual workers, we know ourselves to be the only ones who are responding in a systematic way to the fundamental problems of the contemporary revolutionary movement: we think we are the only ones who are resuming and continuing the Marxist analysis of the modern economy, who are posing on a scientific basis the problem of the historical development of the workers' movement and of its signification, who are providing a definition of Stalinism and, in general, of the 'working-class' bureaucracy, who are furnishing a characterization of the Third World War, who are finally once again laying down what is involved in the revolutionary outlook while also taking account of the original elements being created by our age. In questions of such breadth, there can be no question of either pride or modesty. Marxists have always deemed that, in representing the historical interests of the proletariat – the sole positive class in present-day society – they were able to have a view on reality that is infinitely superior to that of everyone else, whether in comparison to the capitalists or to all intermediate varieties of bastards. We think that we represent the living continuation of Marxism within society today. In this sense, we are in no way afraid of being confused with publishers of 'Marxist' reviews, 'clarifiers', 'men of good will', quibblers and gossipers of all sorts. If we pose problems, it is that we think we can resolve them.

The famous saying, 'Without revolutionary theory, no revolutionary action', really has to be comprehended in its full breadth and in its true meaning. The proletarian movement distinguishes itself from all previous political movements, however important the latter might have been, by this, that it is the first to be conscious of its objectives and of its means. In this sense, not only is theoretical elaboration for it inseparable from this activity, but this theoretical elaboration neither precedes nor follows revolutionary activity: it is simultaneous with the latter and each conditions the other. Separated from practice, from its preoccupations and from its control, attempts at theoretical elaboration cannot but be vain, sterile, and increasingly meaningless. Conversely, practical activity that does not base itself on constant research can lead only to a cretinized form of empiricism. 'Revolutionary' bonesetters are no less dangerous than other sorts of medical hacks.

But what is this revolutionary theory on which action must constantly base itself? Is it a dogma, plucked fully armed from the head of Marx or some other modern prophet, whose original splendour the rest of us would be charged only with maintaining in mint condition? To ask the question is to answer it. To say 'Without revolutionary theory, no revolutionary action' while understanding by 'theory' mere knowledge of Marxism and at the very most a scholastic exegesis of the classic texts is a pathetic joke expressing nothing but impotence. Revolutionary theory can be of value only if it is constantly being developed, only if it is enriched by all the conquests of scientific thought and of human thought in general, by the experience of the revolutionary movement more particularly, only if it undergoes, each time it proves necessary, all the modifications and internal revolutions reality imposes upon it. The classic saying therefore has meaning only if it is understood to be saying, 'Without *development* of revolutionary theory, no development of revolutionary action.'

By stating things in this way, we have already said that, while we consider ourselves to be Marxists, we in no way think that being Marxist signifies doing in relation to Marx what Catholic theologians do in relation to the Holy Scriptures. Being Marxist signifies for us situating oneself on the terrain of a tradition, posing problems starting at the point Marx and his continuators posed them, maintaining and defending traditional Marxist positions so long as a new examination has not persuaded us that these positions must be abandoned, amending them or replacing them by others that better correspond to subsequent experience and to the needs of the revolutionary movement.

All this does not signify merely that the development and propagation of revolutionary theory are already extremely important practical activities – which is correct, but insufficient. It signifies, above all, that without a renewal of the fundamental conceptions there will be no practical renewal. The reconstitution of the revolutionary movement will necessarily have to pass through a period during which the new conceptions will need to become the possession of the majority of the [working] class. This will take place through two processes that are independent of each other only in appearance: on the one hand, the mass will have to raise itself up, under pressure of objective conditions and of the necessities of its struggle, to a clear awareness, even if this awareness is rough and simple; on the other, the seeds of revolutionary organization, such as our own group, will have to, starting upon a firm theoretical basis, spread this new conception of the problems at hand and give it ever more concrete form. The meeting point of these two processes, the moment when the majority of the class raises itself up to a clear understanding of the historical situation and when the general theoretical conception of the movement can be expressed fully in directives for practical action, is the moment of Revolution.

It is obvious that the present-day situation is still far removed from that point. Both in France and in other countries, the majority of the proletariat is alienated and mystified by its bureaucracy. It is mystified ideologically when it adopts, either as its own interest or as a 'lesser evil', the bureaucracy's policy, whether this bureaucracy be 'reformist' or Stalinist; its very action is alienated, since the struggles it undertakes to defend its immediate interests are most often, and as soon as they take on a certain breadth, appropriated by the Stalinist bureaucracy as an instrument of its own national and international policy. Finally, the elements of the avant-garde that are now attaining awareness of this mystification and this alienation draw from it, for the moment and for lack of a general outlook, only a negative conclusion directed against the bureaucratic organizations; while this conclusion is well founded, it is evidently still inadequate. Under these conditions it is obvious that a correct general conception cannot in the present period be expressed at every moment by slogans for immediate action leading to revolution. To say that we support unconditionally every proletarian struggle, that we are on the side of the workers at each moment they struggle to defend their interests, even if we are in disagreement over the definition of the objectives and of the means of struggle, is an elementary truth that goes without saying. But to want, apropos of every partial struggle, to give oneself over to superficial and sterile agitation for the General Strike or for the Revolution, despite all reality and all evidence, is a task we want nothing to do with.

As appropriate as they are, these remarks nevertheless neither exhaust nor resolve the problem of the necessary connection between a general conception of the problems of the revolution on the one hand and present-day struggle on the other. These struggles are not only an extremely important material for analysis and verification; furthermore, and above all, they are the setting in which a real proletarian avant-garde, however numerically restricted it may be, can form and educate itself. On the other hand, a general conception has some value only to the extent that it proves capable of affecting a portion of the avant-garde of the working class and to the extent that it offers the framework, even if only a general one, for practical solutions, in other words, useful criteria for action. It is in terms of all these factors that we can define the immediate objective of this Review as being the popularization, to the greatest extent possible, of our theoretical and political conceptions, the discussion and clarification of the practical problems the struggle between classes constantly poses, even under the crippled forms this struggle presently takes.

We therefore constantly seek all occasions to deal with the practical questions of the day, even when these questions affect only one sector of the class; we shall avoid dealing with theoretical questions for their own sake. Our goal will be to provide working tools to the advanced workers in an age when the complexity of the problems, the confusion that reigns everywhere, and the constant effort of the capitalists and especially the Stalinists to mystify everyone apropos of everything necessitate an unprecedented effort in this direction. In treating these problems we shall always try not only to present them in the clearest language possible but especially to show their practical importance and the concrete conclusions that follow therefrom.

This Review is in no way an organ for the confrontation of opinions between people who 'pose problems' but, rather, the instrument for the expression of an overall conception which we believe to be systematic and coherent. The main lines of this conception are expressed in the article 'Socialisme ou Barbarie', contained in this first issue.[1] Nevertheless, neither on the organizational level nor on the theoretical level are we partisans of monolithism. We think that the development of revolutionary theory can occur only through the confrontation of divergent opinions and positions. We think, too, that this discussion must be carried out before the whole of the class; we think, quite specifically, that the conception according to which one party alone possesses the truth and the whole truth, and brings it to the class while hiding from the class its internal disagreements is, on the ideological plane, one of the roots as well as one of the most important expressions of bureaucratism in the workers' movement. This is why the divergencies that might appear on particular points among the comrades of our group will be able to be expressed in the Review, and the Review will note which articles express the position of their author and not of the group as such. Discussion will therefore be free within the framework of our general conceptions, our constant concern being to avoid having this discussion become an interminable dialogue between a few individuals.

We are certain that the workers and the intellectuals who, in France, have already become aware of the importance of the problems we are posing, who understand how urgent it is to give them an adequate response, one in conformity with the interests of the masses, will support us in the long and difficult effort the preparation and dissemination of our Review will represent.

Note

1. T/E: See *SB* (1949).

3

On the Content of Socialism (1955–1957): Excerpts

From the Critique of Bureaucracy to the Idea of the Proletariat's Autonomy (1955)*

The ideas set forth in this discussion will perhaps be understood more readily if we retrace the route that has led us to them. Indeed, we started off from positions in which a militant worker or a Marxist inevitably places himself at a certain stage in his development – positions therefore that everyone we are addressing has shared at one time or another. And if the conceptions set forth here have any value at all, their development cannot be the result of chance or personal traits but ought to embody an objective logic at work. Providing a description of this development, therefore, can only increase the reader's understanding of the end result and make it easier for him to check it against his experience.[1]

Like a host of other militants in the vanguard, we began with the discovery that the traditional large 'working-class' organizations no longer have a revolutionary Marxist politics nor do they represent any longer the interests of the proletariat. The Marxist arrives at this conclusion by comparing the activity of these 'socialist' (reformist) or 'communist' (Stalinist) organizations with his own theory. He sees the so-called Socialist parties participating in bourgeois governments, actively repressing strikes or movements of colonial peoples, and championing the defence of the capitalist fatherland while neglecting even to make reference to a socialist system of rule [régime]. He sees the Stalinist 'Communist' parties sometimes carrying out this same opportunistic policy of collaboration with the bourgeoisie and sometimes an 'extremist' policy, a violent adventurism unrelated to a consistent revolutionary strategy. The class-conscious worker makes the same discoveries on the level of his working-class experience. He sees the socialists squandering their energies trying to moderate his class's economic demands, to make any

* 'Sur le contenu du socialisme', S. ou B., 17 (July 1955). Reprinted as CS I in CS, pp. 67–102. Preceding the article was the following note: 'This article opens up a discussion on programmatic problems, which will be continued in forthcoming issues of Socialisme ou Barbarie.' [T/E: The present abridged version of CS I reprints the introductory section (PSW 1, pp. 290–7).]

effective action aimed at satisfying these demands impossible, and to substitute for the strike interminable discussions with the boss or the State. He
sees the Stalinists at certain times strictly forbidding strikes (as was the case
from 1945 to 1947) and even trying to curtail them through violence[2] or
frustrating them underhandedly[3] and at other times trying to horsewhip
workers into a strike they do not want because they perceive that it is alien
to their interests (as in 1951–2, with the 'anti-American' strikes). Outside
the factory, he also sees the Socialists and the Communists participate in
capitalist governments without it changing his lot one bit, and he sees them
join forces, in 1936 as well as in 1945, when his class is ready to act and the
regime has its back against the wall, in order to stop the movement and save
this regime, proclaiming that one must 'know to end a strike' and that one
must 'produce first and make economic demands later'.

Once they have established this radical opposition between the attitude of
the traditional organizations and a revolutionary Marxist politics expressing
the immediate and historical interests of the proletariat, both the Marxist
and the class-conscious worker might then think that these organizations
'err' [*se trompent*] or that they 'are betraying us'. But to the extent that they
reflect on the situation, and discover for themselves that reformists and
Stalinists behave the same way day after day, that they have always and
everywhere behaved in this way, in the past, today, here and everywhere else,
they begin to see that to speak of 'betrayal' or 'mistakes' does not make any
sense. It could be a question of 'mistakes' only if these parties pursued the
goals of the proletarian revolution with inadequate means, but these means,
applied in a coherent and systematic fashion for several dozen years, show
simply that the goals of these organizations are not our goals, that they
express interests other than those of the proletariat. Once this is understood,
saying that they 'are betraying us' makes no sense. If, in order to sell his junk,
a merchant tells me a load of crap and tries to persuade me that it is in my
interest to buy it, I can say that he is trying to deceive me [*il me trompe*] but
not that he is betraying me. Likewise, the Socialist or Stalinist party, in trying
to persuade the proletariat that it represents its interests, is trying to deceive
it but is not betraying it; they betrayed it once and for all a long time ago,
and since then they are not traitors to the working class but consistent and
faithful servants of other interests. What we need to do is determine whose
interests they serve.

Indeed, this policy does not merely appear consistent in its means or in
its results. It is embodied in the leadership stratum of these organizations or
trade unions. The militant quickly learns the hard way that this stratum is
irremovable, that it survives all defeats, and that it perpetuates itself through
co-option. Whether the internal organization of these groups is 'democratic'
(as is the case with the reformists) or dictatorial (as is the case with the
Stalinists), the mass of militants have absolutely no influence over its

orientation, which is determined without further appeal by a bureaucracy whose stability is never put into question; for even when the leadership core should happen to be replaced, it is replaced for the benefit of another, no less bureaucratic group.

At this point, the Marxist and the class-conscious worker are almost bound to collide with Trotskyism.[4] Indeed, Trotskyism has offered a permanent, step-by-step critique of reformist and Stalinist politics for the past quarter-century, showing that the defeats of the workers' movement – Germany, 1923; China, 1925–7; England, 1926; Germany, 1933; Austria, 1934; France, 1936; Spain, 1936–8; France and Italy, 1945–7; etc. – are due to the policies of the traditional organizations, and that these policies have constantly been in breach of Marxism. At the same time, Trotskyism[5] offers an explanation of the policies of these parties, starting from a sociological analysis of their makeup. For reformism, it takes up again the interpretation provided by Lenin: The reformism of the socialists expresses the interests of a labour aristocracy (since imperialist surplus profits allow the latter to be 'corrupted' by higher wages) and of a trade-union and political bureaucracy. As for Stalinism, its policy serves the Russian bureaucracy, this parasitic and privileged stratum that has usurped power in the first workers' State, thanks to the backward character of the country and the setback suffered by the world revolution after 1923.

We began our critical work, even back when we were within the Trotskyist movement, with this problem of Stalinist bureaucracy. Why we began with that problem in particular needs no long involved explanations. Whereas the problem of reformism seemed to be settled by history, at least on the theoretical level, as it became more and more an overt defender of the capitalist system,[6] on the most crucial problem of all, that of Stalinism – which is *the* contemporary problem *par excellence* and which in practice weighs on us more heavily than the first – the history of our times has disproved again and again both the Trotskyist viewpoint and the forecasts that have been derived from it. For Trotsky, Stalinist policy is to be explained by the interests of the Russian bureaucracy, a product of the degeneration of the October Revolution. This bureaucracy has no 'reality of its own', historically speaking; it is only an 'accident', the product of the constantly upset balance between the two fundamental forces of modern society, capitalism and the proletariat. Even in Russia it is based upon the 'conquests of October', which had provided socialist bases for the country's economy (nationalization, planning, monopoly over foreign trade, etc.), and upon the perpetuation of capitalism in the rest of the world; for the restoration of private property in Russia would signify the overthrow of the bureaucracy and help bring about the return of the capitalists, whereas the spread of the revolution worldwide would destroy Russia's isolation – the economic and political result of which was the bureaucracy – and would give rise to a new revolutionary explosion of the Russian proletariat, who would chase off these usurpers. Hence the necessarily empirical character of Stalinist politics, which is obliged to waver between two adversaries and makes its objective the utopian maintenance of the status quo; it even is obliged thereby to sabotage every proletarian movement any time the latter endangers the capitalist system and to over-compensate as well for the results of these acts of sabotage with extreme violence every time reactionaries, encouraged by the demoralization of the proletariat, try to set up a dictatorship and prepare a capitalist crusade against 'the remnants of the October conquests'. Thus, Stalinist parties are condemned to fluctuate between 'extremist' adventurism and opportunism.

But neither can these parties nor the Russian bureaucracy remain hanging indefinitely in midair like this. In the absence of a revolution, Trotsky said, the Stalinist parties would become more and more like the reformist parties and more and more attached to the bourgeois order, while the Russian bureaucracy would be overthrown with or without foreign intervention so as to bring about a restoration of capitalism.

Trotsky had tied this prognostication to the outcome of the Second World War. As is well known, this war disproved it in the most glaring terms. The Trotskyist leadership made itself look ridiculous by stating that it was just a matter of time. But it had become apparent to us, even before the war ended, that it was not and could not have been a question of some kind of time lag but, rather, of the *direction* of history, and that Trotsky's entire edifice was, down to its very foundations, mythological.

The Russian bureaucracy underwent the critical test of the war and showed it had as much cohesiveness as any other dominant class. If the Russian regime admitted of some contradictions, it also exhibited a degree of stability no less than that of the American or German regime. The Stalinist parties did not go over to the side of the bourgeois order. They have continued to follow Russian policy faithfully (apart, of course, from indi-vidual defections, as take place in all parties): they are partisans of national defence in countries allied to the USSR, adversaries of this kind of defence in countries that are enemies of the USSR (we include here the French CP's series of turnabouts in 1939, 1941, and 1947). Finally, the most important and extraordinary thing was that the Stalinist bureaucracy extended its power into other countries; whether it imposed its power on behalf of the Russian army, as in most of the satellite countries of Central Europe and the Balkans, or had complete domination over a confused mass movement, as in Yugoslavia (or later on in China and in Vietnam), it instaurated in these countries regimes that were in every respect similar to the Russian regime (taking into account, of course, local conditions). It was obviously ridicu-lous to describe these regimes as degenerated workers' States.[7]

From then on, therefore, we were obliged to look into what gave such stability and opportunities for expansion to the Stalinist bureaucracy, both in Russia and elsewhere. To do this, we had to resume the analysis of Russia's economic and social system of rule. Once rid of the Trotskyist outlook, it was easy to see, using the basic categories of Marxism, that Russian society is divided into classes, among which the two fundamental ones are the bureaucracy and the proletariat. The bureaucracy there plays the role of the dominant, exploiting class in the full sense of the term. It is not merely that it is a privileged class and that its unproductive consumption absorbs a part of the social product comparable to (and probably greater than) that absorbed by the unproductive consumption of the bourgeoisie in private capitalist countries. It also has sovereign control over how the total social product will be used. It does this first of all by determining how the total social product will be distributed among wages and surplus value (at the same time that it tries to dictate to the workers the lowest wages possible and to extract from them the greatest amount of labour possible), next by determining how this surplus value will be distributed between its own unproductive consumption and new investments, and finally by determining how these investments will be distributed among the various sectors of production.

But the bureaucracy can control how the social product will be utilized only because it controls production. Because it *manages* production at the factory level, it can always make the workers produce more for the same wage; because it manages production on the societal level, it can decide to manufacture cannons and silk rather than housing and cotton. We discover, therefore, that the essence, the foundation, of its bureaucratic domination over Russian society comes from the fact that it has dominance within the relations of production; at the same time, we discover that this same function has always been the basis for the domination of one class over society. In other words, at every instant the effective essence of class relations in production is the antagonistic division of those who participate in the production process into two fixed and stable categories, directors and executants. Everything else is concerned with the sociological and juridical mechanisms that guarantee the stability of the managerial stratum; that is how it is with feudal ownership of the land, capitalist private property, or this strange form of private, nonpersonal property ownership that characterizes present-day capitalism; that is how it is in Russia with the 'Communist Party', the totalitarian dictatorship by the organ that expresses the bureaucracy's general interests and that ensures that the members of the ruling class are recruited through co-option on the scale of society as a whole.[8]

It follows that planning and the nationalization of the means of production in no way resolve the problem of the class character of the economy, nor do they signify the abolition of exploitation; of course, they entail the abolition of the former dominant classes, but they do not answer the fundamental problem of who will now direct production and how. If a new stratum of individuals takes over this function of direction, 'all the old rubbish' Marx spoke about will quickly reappear, for this stratum will use its managerial position to create privileges for itself, it will reinforce its monopoly over managerial functions, in this way tending to make its domination more complete and more difficult to put into question; it will tend to assure the transmission of these privileges to its successors, etc.

For Trotsky, the bureaucracy is not a ruling class since bureaucratic privileges cannot be transmitted by inheritance. But in dealing with this argument, we need only recall (1) that hereditary transmission is in no way an element necessary to establish the category of 'ruling class', and (2) that, moreover, it is obvious how, in Russia, membership of the bureaucracy (not, of course, some particular bureaucratic post) can be passed down; a measure such as the abolition of free secondary education (laid down in 1936) suffices to set up an inexorable sociological mechanism assuring that only the children of bureaucrats will be able to enter into the career of being a bureaucrat. That, in addition, the bureaucracy might want to try (using educational grants or aptitude tests 'based upon merit alone') to bring in talented people from the proletariat or the peasantry not only does not contradict but even confirms its character as an exploiting class: similar mechanisms have always existed in capitalist countries, and their social function is to reinvigorate the ruling stratum with new blood, to mitigate in part the irrationalities resulting from the hereditary character of managerial functions, and to emasculate the exploited classes by corrupting their most gifted members.

It is easy to see that it is not a question here of a problem particular to Russia or to the 1920s. For the same problem is posed in every modern society, even apart from the proletarian revolution; it is just another expression of the process of concentration of the forces of production. What, indeed, creates the *objective* possibility for a bureaucratic degeneration of the revolution? It is the inexorable movement of the modern economy, under the pressure of technique, toward the more and more intense concentration of capital and power, the incompatibility of the actual degree of development of the forces of production with private property and the market as the way in which business enterprises are integrated. This movement is expressed in a host of structural transformations in Western capitalist countries, though we cannot dwell upon that right now. We need only recall that they are socially incarnated in a new bureaucracy, an economic bureaucracy as well as a workplace bureaucracy. Now, by making a *tabula rasa* of private property, of the market, etc., revolution *can* – if it stops at that point – make the route to total bureaucratic concentration easier. We see, therefore, that, far from being deprived of its own reality, bureaucracy personifies the final stage of capitalist development.

Since then it has become obvious that the programme of the socialist revolution and the proletariat's objective could no longer be merely the suppression of private property, the nationalization of the means of production and planning, but, rather, *workers' management* of the economy and of power. Returning to the degeneration of the Russian Revolution, we established that on the economic level the Bolshevik Party had as its programme not *workers' management* but *workers' control*. This was because the Party, which did not think the revolution could immediately be a socialist revolution, did not even pose for itself the task of expropriating the capitalists, and therefore thought that this latter class would remain as managers in the workplace. Under such conditions, the function of workers' control would be to prevent the capitalists from organizing to sabotage production, to gain control over their profits and over the disposition of the product, and to set up a 'school' of management for the workers. But this sociological monstrosity of a country where the proletariat exercises its dictatorship through the instrument of the soviets and of the Bolshevik Party, and where the capitalists keep their property and continue to direct their enterprises, could not last; where the capitalists had not fled they were expelled by the workers, who then took over the management of these enterprises.

This first experience of workers' management lasted only a short time; we cannot go into an analysis here of this period of the Russian Revolution (which is quite obscure and about which few sources exist),[9] or of the factors that determined the rapid changeover of power in the factories into the hands of a new managerial stratum. Among these factors are the backward state of the country, the proletariat's numerical and cultural weakness, the dilapidated condition of the productive apparatus, the long civil war with its unprecedented violence, and the international isolation of the revolution. There is one factor whose effect during this period we wish to emphasize: in its actions, the Bolshevik Party's policy was systematically opposed to workers' management and tended from the start to set up its own apparatus for directing production, responsible solely to the central power, i.e., in the last analysis, to the Party. This was done in the name of efficiency and the overriding necessities brought on by the civil war. Whether this policy was the most effective one even in the short term is open to question; in any case, in the long run it laid the foundations for bureaucracy.

If the management [*direction*] of the economy thus eluded the proletariat, Lenin thought the essential thing was for the power of the soviets to preserve for the workers at least the leadership [*direction*] of the State. On the other hand, he thought that by participating in the management of the economy through workers' control, trade unions, and so on, the working class would gradually 'learn' to manage. Nevertheless, a series of events that cannot be retraced here, but that were inevitable, quickly made the Bolshevik Party's domination over the soviets irreversible. From this point onward, the proletarian character of the whole system hinged on the proletarian character of the Bolshevik Party. We could easily show that under such conditions the Party, a highly centralized minority with monopoly control over the exercise of power, would no longer be able to preserve even its proletarian character (in the strong sense of this term), and that it was bound to separate itself from the class from which it had arisen. But there is no need to go as far as that. In 1923 'the Party numbered 50,000 workers and 300,000 functionaries in its total of 350,000 members. It no longer was a workers' party but a party of workers-turned-functionaries.'[10] Bringing together the 'elite' of the proletariat, the Party had been led to install this elite in the command posts of the economy and the State; hence this elite had to be accountable only to the Party, i.e. to itself. The working class's 'apprenticeship' in management merely signified that a certain number of workers, who were learning managerial techniques, left the rank and file and passed over to the side of the new bureaucracy. As people's social existence determines their consciousness, the Party members were going to act from then on, not according to the Bolshevik programme, but in terms of their concrete situation as privileged managers of the economy and the State. The trick has been played, the revolution has died, and if there is something to be surprised about, it is, rather, how long it took for the bureaucracy to consolidate its power.[11]

The conclusions that follow from this brief analysis are clear: The programme of the socialist revolution can be nothing other than *workers' management*. Workers' management of power, i.e. the power of the masses' autonomous organizations (soviets or councils); workers' management of the economy, i.e. the producers' direction of production, also organized in soviet-style organs. The proletariat's objective cannot be nationalization and planning without anything more, because that would signify that the domination of society would be handed over to a new stratum of rulers and exploiters; it cannot be achieved by handing over power to a party, however revolutionary and however proletarian this party might be at the outset, because this party will inevitably tend to exercise this power on its own behalf and will be used as the nucleus for the crystallization of a new ruling stratum. Indeed, in our time the problem of the division of society into classes appears more and more in its most direct and naked form, and stripped of all juridical cover, as the problem of the division of society into directors and executants. The proletarian revolution carries out its historical programme only in so far as it tends from the very beginning to abolish this division by reabsorbing every particular managerial stratum and by *collectivizing*, or more exactly by *completely socializing*, the functions of direction. The problem of the proletariat's historical capacity to achieve a classless society is not the problem of its capacity physically to overthrow the exploiters who are in power (of this there is no doubt); it is, rather, the problem of how positively to organize a collective, socialized management of production and power. From then on it becomes obvious that the realization of socialism on the proletariat's behalf by any party or bureaucracy whatsoever is an absurdity, a contradiction in terms, a square circle, an underwater bird; socialism is nothing but the masses' conscious and perpetual self-managerial activity. It becomes equally obvious that socialism cannot be 'objectively' inscribed, not even halfway, in any law or constitution, in the nationalization of the means of production, or in planning, nor even in a 'law' instaurating workers' management: if the working class cannot manage, no law can give it the power to do so, and if it does manage, such a 'law' would merely ratify this existing state of affairs.

Thus, beginning with a critique of the bureaucracy, we have succeeded in formulating a positive conception of the content of socialism; briefly speaking, 'socialism in all its aspects does not signify anything other than workers' management of society', and 'the working class can free itself only by achieving power for itself'. The proletariat can carry out the socialist revolution only if it acts autonomously, i.e. if it finds in itself both the will and the consciousness for the necessary transformation of society. Socialism can be neither the fated result of historical development, a violation of history by a party of supermen, nor still the application of a programme derived from a theory that is true in itself. Rather, it is the unleashing of the free creative activity of the oppressed masses. Such an unleashing of free creative activity is made *possible* by historical development, and the action of a party based on *this* theory can *facilitate* it to a tremendous degree.

Henceforth it is indispensable to develop on every level the consequences of this idea. [. . .]

Notes

1 In so far as this introduction gives a brief summary of the analysis of various problems already treated in this Review, we have taken the liberty of referring the reader to the corresponding articles published in *S. ou B.*

2 The April 1947 strike at Renault, the first great postwar working-class explosion in France, was able to take place only after the workers fought physically with Stalinist union officials.

3 See in *S. ou B.*, 13 (January 1954), pp. 34–46, the detailed description of the way in which the Stalinists were able to 'scuttle' the August 1953 strike at Renault without overtly opposing it.

4 Or with other, essentially similar currents (Bordigism, for example).

5 Among its serious representatives, which virtually amounts to just Trotsky himself. Present-day Trotskyists, knocked about by reality as no ideological current has ever been knocked about before, have reached such a degree of political and ideological decomposition that nothing precise can be said about them at all.

6 In the last analysis, our ultimate conception of working-class bureaucracy leads to a revision of the traditional Leninist conception of reformism. But we cannot dwell here on this question.

7 See the 'Lettre ouverte aux militants du P.C.I. et de la "IVᵉ Internationale"' in *S. ou B.*, 1 (March 1949), pp. 90–101. [T/E: This article, 'Open Letter to P.C.I. and "Fourth

International" Militants', is reprinted in *SB 1*, pp. 185–204 (and now reprinted again in *SB**, pp. 145–58).]
  8 See *RPR*.
  9 1979 Note: See now *RBI* and the Brinton text cited therein [T/E: Maurice Brinton, *Bolsheviks & Workers' Control* (London: Solidarity, 1970; Detroit: Black & Red, 1975)].
10 Victor Serge, *Russia Twenty Years After*, trans. Max Shachtman (New York: Hillman-Curl, 1937), p. 150.
11 See *SB*.

On the Content of Socialism, II (1957)*

[Introduction]

The development of modern society and what has happened to the working-class movement over the last hundred years (and in particular since 1917) have compelled us to make a radical revision of the ideas on which that movement has been based.

Forty years have elapsed since the proletarian revolution seized power in Russia. From that revolution it is not socialism that ultimately emerged but a new and monstrous form of exploiting society and totalitarian oppression that differed from the worst forms of capitalism only in that the bureaucracy replaced the private owners of capital and 'the plan' took the place of the 'free market'. Ten years ago only a few people like us defended these ideas. Since then the Hungarian workers have brought them to the world's attention.

Among the raw materials for such a revision are the vast experience of the Russian Revolution and of its degeneration, the Hungarian workers' councils, their actions, and their programme. But these are far from being the only elements useful for making such a revision. A look at modern capitalism and at the type of conflict it breeds shows that throughout the world working

---

* Originally published as 'Sur le contenu du socialisme', *S. ou B.*, 22 (July 1957). Reprinted as *CS II* in *CS*, pp. 103–221. The text was preceded by the following note:
  The first part of this text was published in *Socialisme ou Barbarie*, no. 17, pp. 1–22. The following pages represent a new draft of the entire text and a reading of the previously published part is not presupposed. This text opens a discussion on programmatic questions. The positions expressed here do not necessarily express the point of view of the entire Socialisme ou Barbarie group.
  [T/E: This text was originally translated by Maurice Brinton under the title *Workers' Councils and the Economics of a Self-Managed Society* (London: Solidarity, 1972), with 'Our Preface'. It was reprinted by Philadelphia Solidarity in 1974 (with forewords by Philadelphia Solidarity and the League for Economic Democracy) and 1984 as a Wooden Shoe Pamphlet (with a statement about the group, Philadelphia Solidarity, entitled 'About Ourselves', and a new introduction by Peter Dorman, 'Workers Councils . . . 25 Years Later'). In editing Brinton's translation, I have retained the headings he has added to the text, placing them in square brackets. *CS II* appeared in full in *PSW 2*, pp. 90–154. To save space, the present abridged version omits some of the more technical sections.]

people are faced with the same fundamental problems, often posed in surprisingly similar terms. These problems call everywhere for the same response. This answer is socialism, a social system that is the very opposite of the bureaucratic capitalism now installed in Russia, China, and elsewhere.

The experience of bureaucratic capitalism allows us clearly to perceive what socialism *is not* and *cannot be*. A close look both at past proletarian uprisings and at the everyday life and struggles of the proletariat enables us to say what socialism could and should be. Basing ourselves on a century of experience we can and must now define the positive content of socialism in a much fuller and more accurate way than was possible for previous revolutionaries. In today's vast ideological morass, people who call themselves socialists may be heard to say that they 'are no longer quite sure what the word means'. We hope to show that the very opposite is the case. Today, for the first time, one can begin to spell out in concrete and specific terms what socialism really could be like.

The task we are about to undertake not only leads us to challenge many widely held ideas about socialism, many of which go back to Lenin and some to Marx. It also leads us to question widely held ideas about capitalism, about the way it works and about the real nature of its crises, many of which have reached us (with or without distortion) from Marx himself. The two analyses are complementary and in fact the one necessitates the other.

The revision we propose did not of course start today. Various strands of the revolutionary movement – and a number of individual revolutionaries – have contributed to it over time. From the very first issue of *Socialisme ou Barbarie* we endeavoured to resume this effort in a systematic fashion. There we claimed that the fundamental division in contemporary societies was the division into directors and executants. We attempted to show how the working class's own development would lead it to a socialist consciousness. We stated that socialism could only be the product of the autonomous action of the working class. We stressed that a socialist society implied the abolition of any separate stratum of directors and that it therefore implied the power of mass organs and workers' management of production.

But in a sense, we ourselves have failed to develop the content of our own ideas to the full. It would hardly be worth mentioning this fact were it not that it expressed, at its own level, the influence of factors that have dominated the evolution of Marxism itself for a century, namely, the enormous dead weight of the ideology of exploiting society, the paralysing legacy of traditional concepts, and the difficulty of freeing oneself from inherited modes of thought.

In one sense our revision consists of making more explicit and precise what was the genuine, initial intention of Marxism and what has always been the deepest content of working-class struggles – whether at their dramatic and culminating moments or in the anonymity of working-class life in the factory. In another sense our revision consists of a freeing of revolutionary thought from the accumulated dross of a century. We want to break the distorting prisms through which so many revolutionaries have become accustomed to looking at the life and action of the proletariat.

Socialism aims at giving a meaning to people's life and work; at enabling their freedom, their creativity, and the most positive aspects of their personality to flourish; at creating organic links between the individual and those around him, and between the group and society; at reconciling people with themselves and with nature. It thereby rejoins the most basic goals of the working class in its daily struggles against capitalist alienation. These are not aspirations about some hazy and distant future but, rather, the content of tendencies existing and manifesting themselves today, both in revolutionary struggles and in everyday life. To understand this is to understand that, *for the worker, the ultimate problem of history is an everyday problem*. To grasp this is also to perceive that socialism is not 'nationalization' or 'planning' or even an 'increase in the standard of living'. It is to understand that the real crisis of capitalism is not due to 'the anarchy of the market' or to 'overproduction' or to 'the falling rate of profit'. Indeed, it is to see the tasks of revolutionary theory and the function of the revolutionary organization in an entirely new way.

Pushed to their ultimate consequences, grasped in their full strength, these ideas transform our vision of society and the world. They modify our conception of theory as well as of revolutionary practice.

The first part of this text is devoted to the positive definition of socialism. The following part[1] concerns the analysis of capitalism and the crisis it is undergoing. This order, which might not appear very logical, may be justified by the fact that the Polish and Hungarian revolutions have made the question of the positive definition of the socialist organization of society an immediate practical question.

This order of presentation also stems from another consideration. The very content of our ideas leads us to maintain that, ultimately, one cannot understand anything about the profound meaning of capitalism and the crisis it is undergoing unless one begins with the most total idea of socialism. For all that we have to say can be reduced, in the last analysis, to this: Socialism is autonomy, people's conscious direction of their own lives. Capitalism – whether private or bureaucratic – is the ultimate negation of this autonomy, and its crisis stems from the fact that the system necessarily creates this drive toward autonomy, while simultaneously being compelled to suppress it.

The Root of the Crisis of Capitalism

The capitalist organization of social life (we are speaking about private capitalism in the West and bureaucratic capitalism in the East) creates a perpetually renewed crisis in every sphere of human activity. This crisis appears most intensely in the realm of production – 'production' meaning here the shop floor, not 'the economy' or 'the market'. In its essence, however, the situation is the same in all other fields, whether one is dealing with the family, education, international relations, politics, or culture. Everywhere, the capitalist structure of society consists of organizing people's lives *from the outside*, in the absence of those directly concerned and against their aspirations and interests. This is but another way of saying that capitalism divides society into a narrow stratum of directors (whose function is to decide and organize everything) and the vast majority of the population, who are reduced to carrying out (executing) the decisions made by these directors. As a result of this very fact, most people experience their own lives as something alien to them.

This pattern of organization is profoundly irrational and full of contradictions. Under it, repeated crises of one kind or another are absolutely inevitable. It is nonsensical to seek to organize people, either in production or in politics, as if they were mere objects, systematically ignoring what they themselves wish or how they themselves think things should be done. In real life, capitalism is obliged to base itself on people's capacity for self-organization, on the individual and collective creativity of the producers. Without making use of these abilities the system could not survive for a day. But the whole 'official' organization of modern society both ignores and seeks to suppress these abilities to the utmost. The result is not only an enormous waste due to untapped capacity. The system does more: it *necessarily* engenders opposition, a struggle against it by those upon whom it seeks to impose itself. Long before one can speak of revolution or political consciousness, people refuse in their everyday working lives to be treated like objects. The capitalist organization of society is thereby compelled not only to structure itself in the absence of those most directly concerned but also to take shape against them. The net result is not only waste but perpetual conflict.

If a thousand individuals have among them a given capacity for self-organization, capitalism consists in more or less arbitrarily choosing fifty of these individuals, vesting them with managerial authority, and deciding that the others should just be cogs. Metaphorically speaking, this is already a 95 per cent loss of social initiative and drive. But there is more to it. As the 950 ignored individuals are *not* cogs, and as capitalism is obliged up to a point to base itself on their human capacities and in fact to develop them, these individuals will react and struggle against what the system imposes upon them. The creative faculties they are not allowed to exercise *on behalf* of a social order that rejects them (and which they reject) are now utilized *against* that social order. A permanent struggle develops at the very heart of social life. It soon becomes the source of further waste. The narrow stratum of directors has henceforth to divide its time between organizing the work of those 'below' and seeking to counteract, neutralize, deflect, or manipulate their resistance. The function of the managerial apparatus ceases to be merely organizational and soon assumes all sorts of *coercive* aspects. Those in authority in a large modern factory in fact spend less of their time organizing production than coping, directly or indirectly, with the resistance of the exploited – whether it be a question of supervision, of quality control, of determining piece rates, of 'human relations', of discussions with shop stewards or union representatives. On top of all this there is of course the permanent preoccupation of those in power with making sure that everything is measurable, quantifiable, verifiable and supervisable so as to deal in advance with any inventive counterreaction the workers might launch against new methods of exploitation. The same applies, with all due corrections, to the total overall organization of social life and to all the essential activities of any modern State.

The irrationality and contradictions of capitalism do not show up only in the way social life is organized. They appear even more clearly when one looks at the real *content* of the life this system proposes. More than any other social order, capitalism has put work at the centre of human activity – and more than any other social order capitalism makes of work something that is *absurd* (absurd not from the viewpoint of the philosopher or of the moralist, but from the point of view of those who have to perform it). What is challenged today is not only the 'human organization' of work but its nature, its contents, its methods, the very instruments and purpose of capitalist production. The two aspects are of course inseparable, but it is the second that needs to be stressed.

As a result of the nature of work in a capitalist enterprise, and however it may be organized, the activity of the worker, instead of being the organic expression of his human faculties, turns into an alien and hostile process that dominates the subject of this process. In theory the proletarian is tied to this activity only by a thin (but unbreakable) thread: the need to earn a living. But this ensures that one's work, even the day that is about to begin, dawns as something hostile. Work under capitalism therefore implies a permanent mutilation, a perpetual waste of creative capacity, and a constant struggle between the worker and his own activity, between what he would like to do and what he has to do.

From this angle, too, capitalism can survive only to the extent that reality does not yield to its methods and conform to its spirit. The system functions only to the extent that the 'official' organization of production and of society is constantly resisted, thwarted, corrected, and completed by the effective self-organization of people. Work processes can be effective under capitalism only to the extent that the real attitudes of workers toward their work differ from what is prescribed. Working people succeed in learning the general principles pertaining to their work – to which, according to the spirit of the system, they should have no access and concerning which the system seeks to keep them in the dark. They then apply these principles to the specific conditions in which they find themselves, whereas in theory this practical application can be spelled out only by the managerial apparatus.

Exploiting societies persist because those whom they exploit help them to survive. Slave-owning and feudal societies perpetuated themselves because ancient slaves and medieval serfs worked according to the norms set by the masters and lords of those societies. The proletariat enables capitalism to continue by acting *against* the system. Here we find the origin of the historical crisis of capitalism. And it is in this respect that capitalism is a society pregnant with revolutionary prospects. Slavery or serf society functioned in so far as the exploited did not struggle against the system. But capitalism can function only in so far as those whom it exploits actively oppose everything the system seeks to impose upon them. The final outcome of this struggle is socialism, namely, the elimination of all externally imposed norms, methods, and patterns of organization and the total liberation of the creative and self-organizing capacities of the masses.

The Principles of a Socialist Society

[. . .]

[Institutions that people can understand and control]

The guiding principle of our effort to elaborate the content of socialism is as follows: Workers' management will be possible only if people's attitudes to social organization alter radically. This in turn will take place only if the institutions embodying this organization become a *meaningful* part of their real daily lives. Just as work will have a meaning only when people *understand* and *dominate* it, so will the institutions of socialist society have to become *understandable* and *controllable*. (Bakunin once described the problem of socialism as being one of 'integrating individuals into structures that they can understand and control'.)

Modern society is a dark and hidden jungle, a confusion of apparatuses, structures, and institutions whose workings no one, or almost no one, understands and no one really dominates or takes any interest in. Socialist society will be possible only if it brings about a radical change in this state of affairs and massively simplifies social organization. Socialism implies that the *organization* of a society will have become transparent to its members.

To say that the workings and institutions of socialist society must be easy to understand implies that people must have a maximum of information. This 'maximum of information' is something quite different from an enormous mass of data. The problem is not to equip everybody with a portable version of the Bibliothèque Nationale or the Library of Congress. On the contrary, the *maximum of information* depends first and foremost on a *reduction of data to their essentials* so that they can readily be handled by everyone. This will be possible because socialism will result in an immediate and enormous simplification of problems and the disappearance, pure and simple, of most current rules and regulations, which will have become quite meaningless. It will be facilitated by a systematic effort to gather and disseminate information [*connaissance*] about social reality, and to *present* facts both adequately and simply. Further on, when discussing the functioning of socialist economy, we will give examples of the enormous possibilities that already exist in this field.

Under socialism, people will dominate the workings and institutions of society, instead of being dominated by them. Socialism will therefore have to realize democracy for the first time in human history. Etymologically, the word 'democracy' means *domination* by the masses. We are not concerned here with the formal aspects of the word 'domination'. Real domination must not be confused with voting. A vote, even a free vote, may be only – and often is only – a parody of democracy. Democracy is not the right to vote on secondary issues. It is not the right to appoint rulers who will then decide, without control from below, on all the essential questions. Nor does democracy lie in calling upon people to voice their opinions upon incomprehensible questions or upon questions that have no meaning for them. Real domination lies in being able to decide for oneself on all essential questions *in full knowledge of the relevant facts*.

'In full knowledge of the relevant facts': in these few words lies the whole problem of democracy.[2] It is meaningless to ask people to voice their opinions if they are not aware of the relevant facts. This has long been stressed by the reactionary or fascist critics of bourgeois 'democracy', and even by the most cynical Stalinist.[3] It is obvious that bourgeois democracy is a farce, if only because literally *nobody* in capitalist society can express an opinion in knowledge of the relevant facts, least of all the mass of the people from whom political and economic realities and the real meaning of the questions asked are systematically hidden. But the answer is not to vest power in the hands of a few incompetent and uncontrollable bureaucrats. The answer is to transform social reality in such a way that essential data

and fundamental problems are understood by everyone, enabling everyone
to express opinions in full knowledge of the relevant facts.

[Direct democracy and centralization]

To decide means to decide for oneself. To decide who is to decide, already
is not quite deciding for oneself. The only total form of democracy is therefore *direct democracy*. And the factory council exercises authority and
replaces the factory's general assembly only when the latter is not in session.[4]

To achieve the widest, the most meaningful direct democracy will require
that all the economic, political, and other structures of society be based on
local groups that are concrete collectivities, organic social units. Direct
democracy certainly requires the physical presence of citizens in a given
place when decisions have to be made. But this is not enough. It also requires
that these citizens form an organic community, that they live if possible in
the same milieu, that they be familiar through their daily experience with the
subject to be discussed and with the problems to be tackled. It is only in such
units that the political participation of individuals can become total, that
people can know and feel that their involvement will have an effect, and that
the real life of the community is, in large part, determined by its own
members and not by unknown or external authorities who decide for them.
There must therefore be the maximum amount of autonomy and self-
administration for the local units.

Modern social life has already created these collectivities and continues to
create them. They are based on medium-sized or large enterprises and are
to be found in industry, transportation, commerce, banking, insurance,
public administration, where people by the hundreds, thousands, or tens of
thousands spend the main part of their life harnessed to a common task,
where they encounter society in its most concrete form. A place of work is
not only a unit of production: it has become the primary unit of social life
for the vast majority of people.[5] Instead of basing itself on geographical units,
which economic developments have rendered completely artificial, the
political structure of socialism will be based largely on collectivities involved
in common work. Such collectivities will be the fertile soil on which direct
democracy can flourish, as the ancient city or the nineteenth-century democratic communities of free farmers in the United States were in their times,
and for similar reasons.

Direct democracy gives an idea of the amount of *decentralization* that
socialist society will be able to achieve. But this democratic society will have
to find a means of democratically *integrating* these basic units into the social
fabric as a whole as well as of achieving the necessary degree of *centralization*, without which the life of a modern nation would collapse.

It is not centralization as such that has brought about political alienation in modern societies or that has led to the expropriation of the power of the many for the benefit of the few. It comes, rather, from the constitution of separate, uncontrollable bodies, exclusively and specifically concerned with the function of centralization. As long as centralization is conceived of as the independent function of an independent apparatus, bureaucracy and bureaucratic rule will indeed be inseparable from centralization. But in a socialist society there will be no conflict between centralization and the autonomy of grass-roots organs, in so far as both functions will be exercised by the same institutions. There will be no separate apparatus whose function it will be to reunite what it has itself fragmented; this absurd task (need we recall it) is precisely the 'function' of a modern bureaucracy.

Bureaucratic centralization is a feature of all modern exploiting societies. The intimate links between centralization and totalitarian bureaucratic rule in such class societies provoke a healthy and understandable aversion to centralization among many people. But this response is often confused, and at times it reinforces the very things it seeks to correct. 'Centralization, there's the root of all evil' proclaim many honest militants as they break with Stalinism or Leninism in France as well as in Poland or Hungary. But this formulation, at best ambiguous, becomes positively harmful when it leads – as it often does – either to formal demands for the 'fragmentation of power' or to demands for a limitless extension of the power of grass-roots or factory organs, neglecting what is happening at the centre.

When Polish militants, for instance, imagine they have found the way to abolish bureaucracy when they advocate a social life organized and directed by 'several centres' (the State administration, a parliamentary assembly, the trade unions, workers' councils, and political parties), they are arguing beside the point. They fail to see that this 'polycentrism' is equivalent to the absence of any real and identifiable centre, controlled from below. And as modern society has to make certain central decisions, the 'constitution' they propose will exist only on paper. It will serve only to hide the re-emergence of a real, but this time masked (and therefore uncontrollable), 'centre' from amid the ranks of the State and political bureaucracy.

The reason is obvious: if one fragments any institution accomplishing a significant or vital function, one only creates ten times over an enhanced need for some other institution to reassemble the fragments. Similarly, if, in principle or in fact, one advocates extending the power of local councils merely to the level of the individual enterprise, one is thereby handing them over to domination by a central bureaucracy that alone would 'know' or 'understand' how to make the economy function as a whole (and modern economies, whether one likes it or not, *do* function as a whole). To refuse to face up to the question of central power is tantamount to leaving the solution of these problems to some bureaucracy or other.

Socialist society therefore will have to provide a socialist solution to the problem of centralization. This answer can only be the assumption of power by a federation of workers' councils and the institution of a central assembly of councils and of a council government. We will see further on that such an assembly and such a government do not signify a *delegation* of popular power but are, on the contrary, an *expression* of that power. At this stage we want to discuss only the principles that will govern the relationship of such bodies to the local councils and other grass-roots groups. These principles are important, for they will affect the functioning of all institutions in a socialist society.

[The flow of information and decisions]

In a society where the people have been robbed of political power, and where this power is in the hands of a centralizing authority, the essential relationship between this authority and its subordinate organs (and, ultimately, the people) can be summed up as follows: Channels of communication from the base to the summit transmit only *information*, whereas channels from the summit to the base transmit *decisions* (plus, perhaps, that minimum of information deemed necessary for the understanding and execution of the decisions made at the summit). The whole setup expresses not only a monopoly of power by the summit – a monopoly of decision-making authority – but also a monopoly of the *conditions* necessary for the exercise of power. The summit alone has the 'sum total' of information needed to evaluate and decide. In modern society it can only be by accident that any individual or body gains access to information other than that relating to his immediate milieu. The system seeks to avoid, or at any rate it does not encourage, such 'accidents'.

When we say that in a socialist society the central bodies will not constitute a delegation of power but will be the expression of the power of the people, we are implying a radical change in this way of doing things. Two-way communications will be instaurated between the 'base' and the 'summit'. One of the essential tasks of central bodies, including the council government, will be to collect, transmit, and disseminate information conveyed to them by local groups. In all essential fields decisions will be made at the grass-roots and will be sent back up to the 'summit', whose responsibility it will be to ensure their execution or to carry them out itself. A two-way flow of information and decisions thus will be instaurated and this will not only apply to relations between the government and the councils but will be a model for relations between all institutions and those who participate in them.

We must stress once again that we are not trying to draw up perfect blueprints. It is obvious, for instance, that to collect and disseminate information is not a socially neutral function. Not all information can be disseminated – that would be the surest way of smothering what is relevant and rendering it incomprehensible and therefore uncontrollable. The role of the government is therefore *political*, even in this respect. This is why we call it 'government' and not the 'central press service'. But more important is its explicit function of informing people, which shall be its responsibility. The explicit function of government today is to *hide* from the people what's going on.

Socialism is the Transformation of Work

Socialism can be instaurated only by the autonomous action of the working class; it *is* nothing other than this autonomous action. Socialist society is nothing other than the self-organization of this autonomy. Socialism both presupposes this autonomy and helps to develop it.

But if this autonomy is people's conscious domination over what they do and what they produce, clearly it cannot merely be a *political* autonomy. Political autonomy is but a derivative aspect of the inherent content and the basic problem of socialism: the instauration of people's domination over their primary activity, the work process. We deliberately say 'instauration' and not 'restoration', for never in history has this kind of domination existed. All comparisons with historical antecedents (for instance, with the situation of the artisan or of the free peasant), however fruitful they may be in some respects, have only a limited scope and risk leading one into a backward-looking type of utopian thinking.

A purely political autonomy would be meaningless. One cannot imagine a society where people would be slaves in production every day of the week and then enjoy Sundays of political freedom. (Yet this is what Lenin's definition of socialism as 'soviets plus electrification' boiled down to.) The idea that socialist production or a socialist economy could be run, at any political level, by 'technicians' supervised by councils, or by soviets or by any other body 'incarnating the political power of the working class' is pure nonsense. *Real* power in any such society would rapidly fall into the hands of those who managed production. The councils or soviets sooner or later would wither away amid the general indifference of the population. People would stop devoting time, interest, or activity to institutions that no longer really determined the pattern of their lives.

Autonomy is therefore meaningless unless it implies *workers' management*, that is, unless it involves organized workers determining the production process themselves at the level of the shop, the plant, entire industries, and the economy as a whole. But workers' management is not just a new administrative technique. It cannot remain external to the structure of work itself.

It does not mean keeping work as it is and just replacing the bureaucratic apparatus that currently manages production with a workers' council – however democratic or revocable such a council might be. It means that for the mass of workers new relations will have to be instaurated with their work and about their work. The very *content* of work will immediately have to be altered.

Today the purpose, means, methods, and rhythms of work are determined from the outside by a bureaucratic managerial apparatus. This apparatus can manage only through resort to abstract, universal rules determined 'once and for all'. Inevitably, though, they are revised periodically with each new 'crisis' in the organization of the production process. These rules cover such matters as production norms, technical specifications, rates of pay, bonuses, and the organization of production areas. Once the bureaucratic managerial apparatus has been eliminated, this way of regulating production will be unable to continue, in either its form or its substance.

In accordance with the deepest aspirations of the working class, production 'norms' (in their present meaning) will be abolished, and complete equality in wages will be instituted. Taken together, these measures mean the abolition of economic coercion and constraint in production – except in the most general form of 'those who do not work do not eat' – as a form of discipline externally imposed by a specific coercive apparatus. *Labour discipline* will be the discipline imposed by each group of workers upon its own members, by each shop on the groups that make it up, by each factory assembly upon its shops and departments. The integration of particular individual activities into a whole will be accomplished basically by the cooperation of various groups of workers or shops. It will be the object of the workers' permanent and ongoing coordinating activity. The essential *universality* of modern production will be freed from the concrete experience of particular jobs and will be formulated by meetings of workers.

Workers' management is therefore not the 'supervision' of a bureaucratic managerial apparatus by representatives of the workers. Nor is it the replacement of this apparatus by another, similar one made up of individuals of working-class origin. It is the *abolition* of *any* separate managerial apparatus and the restitution of the functions of such an apparatus to the community of workers. The factory council is not a new managerial apparatus. It is but one of the places in which coordination takes place, a 'local meeting area [*permanence*]' from which contacts between the factory and the outside world are regulated.

If this is achieved it will imply that the nature and content of work are already beginning to be transformed. Today work consists essentially in obeying instructions initiated elsewhere, the direction of this activity having been removed from the executant's control. Workers' management will mean the reunification of the *functions* of direction and execution.

But even this is insufficient – or, rather, it does and will immediately lead beyond mere reunification. By restituting to the workers the functions of direction, they necessarily will be led to tackle what is today at the core of alienation, namely, the *technological structure* of work, its objects, its tools and methods, which ensure that work dominates the workers instead of being dominated by them. This problem will not be solved by the workers overnight, but its solution will be the task of that historical period we call socialism. Socialism is first and foremost the solution to *this problem*.

Between capitalism and communism there are not thirty-six different types of 'transitional society', as some have sought to make us believe. There is but one: socialist society. And the main characteristic of this society is not 'the development of the productive forces' or 'the increasing satisfaction of consumer needs' or 'an increase in political freedom'. The hallmark of socialism is the *transformation it will bring about in the nature and content of work,* through the *conscious and deliberate transformation of an inherited technology.* For the first time in history, technology will be subordinated to human needs (not only to the people's needs as consumers but also to their needs as *producers*).

The socialist revolution will allow this process to begin. Its realization will mark the entry of humanity into the communist era. All other things – politics, consumption, etc. – are consequences, conditions, implications, and presuppositions that certainly must be looked at in their organic unity, but which can only acquire such a unity or meaning through their relation to this central problem: the transformation of work itself. Human freedom will remain an illusion and a mystification if it doesn't mean freedom in people's fundamental activity: their productive activity. And this freedom will not be a gift bestowed by nature. It will not arise automatically, by increments or out of other developments. People will have to create it consciously. In the last analysis, this is the content of socialism.

Important practical consequences pertaining to the *immediate* tasks of a socialist revolution follow from these considerations. Changing the nature of work will be tackled from both ends. On the one hand, the development of people's human capacities and faculties will have to become the revolution's highest priority. This will imply the systematic dismantling, stone by stone, of the entire edifice of the division of labour. On the other hand, people will have to give a whole new orientation to technical developments and to how such developments should be applied in the production process. These are but two aspects of the same thing: man's relationship to technique.

Let us start by looking at the second, more tangible point: technical development as such. As a first approximation, one could say that capitalist technology (the current application of technique to production) is rotten to the core, not only because it does not help people dominate their work, but also because its aim is exactly the opposite. Socialists often say that what is basically wrong with capitalist technology is that it seeks to develop production for purposes of profit, or that it develops production for production's sake, independently of human needs (people being conceived of, in these arguments, only as potential consumers of products). The same socialists then tell us that the purpose of socialism is to adapt production to the real consumer needs of society, in relation both to the volume and to the nature of the goods produced.

Of course, all this is true. But the fundamental problem lies elsewhere. Capitalism does not utilize a socially neutral technology for capitalist ends. Capitalism has created capitalist technology, which is by no means neutral. The real intention of capitalist technology is not to develop production for production's sake: it is to subordinate and dominate the producers. Capitalist technology is characterized essentially by its drive to eliminate the human element in productive labour and, in the long run, to eliminate man altogether from the production process. That here, as everywhere else, capitalism fails to fulfil its deepest tendency – and that it would fall to pieces if it achieved its purpose – does not affect the argument. On the contrary, it only highlights another aspect of the crisis of this contradictory system.

Capitalism cannot count on the voluntary cooperation of the producers. On the contrary, it constantly runs up against their hostility (or at best indifference) to the production process. This is why it is *essential* for the machine to impose *its* rhythm on the work process. Where this is not possible capitalism seeks at least to measure the work performed. In every productive process, work *must* therefore be definable, quantifiable, supervisable from the outside – otherwise this process has no meaning for capitalism. As long as capitalism cannot dispense with the producers altogether, it *has to* make them as interchangeable as possible and reduce their work to its simplest expression, that of unskilled labour. There is no conspiracy or conscious plot behind all this. There is only a process of 'natural selection', affecting technical inventions as they are applied to industry. Some are preferred to others and are, on the whole, more widely utilized. These are the ones that fit in with capitalism's basic need to deal with labour power as a measurable, supervisable, and interchangeable commodity.

There is no capitalist chemistry or capitalist physics as such. There is not even a specifically capitalist 'technique', in the general sense of the word. There certainly is, however, a capitalist *technology*, if by this one means that, of the 'spectrum' of techniques available at a given point in time (as determined by the development of science), a given group (or 'band') of processes actually will be selected. From the moment the development of science permits a choice of several possible procedures, a society will regularly choose those methods that have a meaning for it, that are 'rational' within the framework of its own class rationality. But the 'rationality' of an

exploiting society is not the rationality of socialism. The conscious transformation of technology will therefore be a central task of a society of free
workers. Correspondingly, the analysis of alienation and crisis in capitalist
society ought to begin with this central core of all social relationships, which
are found in the concrete relationships of production, people's relationships
in work, as seen in its three indissociable aspects: the relationship of the
workers with the means and objects of production, the relationships of
the workers among themselves, and the relationship of the workers with the
managerial apparatus of the production process. [. . .]

Workers' Management: The Factory

[Functions]

It is well known that workers can organize their own work at the level of a
workshop or of part of a factory. Bourgeois industrial sociologists not only
recognize this fact but point out that 'primary groups' of workers often get
on with their job better if management leaves them alone and doesn't
constantly try to 'direct' them.[6]

How can the work of these various 'primary groups' – or of various shops
and sections – be coordinated? Bourgeois theoreticians stress that the
present managerial apparatus, whose formal job it is to ensure such coordination, is not really up to the task: It has no real grip on the workers and
is itself torn by internal conflicts. But, having 'demolished' the present setup
by their criticisms, these modern industrial sociologists have nothing to put
in its place. And, as beyond the 'primary' organization of production there
has to be a 'secondary' organization, they finally fall back on the existing
bureaucratic apparatus, exhorting it 'to understand', 'to improve itself', 'to
trust people more', etc.[7] The same can be said, at another level, of 'democratically reformed' or 'de-Stalinized' Russian leaders.[8]

What no one seems prepared to recognize (or even to admit) is the
capacity of working people to manage their own affairs outside a very narrow
radius. The bureaucratic mind cannot see in the mass of workers employed
in a factory or an office an active subject, capable of managing and organizing. In the eyes of those in authority, both East and West, as soon as one
gets beyond a group of ten, fifteen, or twenty individuals the crowd begins
– the mob, the thousand-headed Hydra that cannot act collectively, or that
could only act collectively in the display of collective delirium or hysteria.
They believe that only a managerial apparatus specifically designed for this
purpose, and endowed of course with coercive functions, can master and
'organize' this mass.

The inconsistencies and shortcomings of the present managerial apparatus are such that even today individual workers or 'primary groups' are
obliged to take on quite a number of coordinating tasks.[9] Moreover, historical experience shows that the working class is quite capable of managing
whole enterprises. In Spain, in 1936 and 1937, workers ran the factories. In
Budapest, in 1956, according to the accounts of Hungarian refugees, big
bakeries employing hundreds of workers carried on during and immediately
after the insurrection. They worked better than ever before, under workers'
self-management. Many such examples could be cited.

The most useful way of discussing this problem is not to weigh up, in the
abstract, the 'self-managerial capacities' of the working class. It is to examine
the specific functions of the present managerial apparatus and to see which
of them retain meaning in a socialist enterprise and how they can be carried
out there.

Present managerial functions are of four main types and we will discuss
them in turn.

1 [Coercive functions]   These functions, and the jobs that go with them
(supervisors, foremen, part of the 'personnel' department), will be done
away with, purely and simply. Each group of workers is quite capable of
disciplining itself. It is also capable of granting authority to people drawn
from its own ranks should it feel this necessary to carry out a particular job.

2 [Administrative functions]   These relate to jobs that, in themselves, are in
no way managerial in character but, rather, involve the execution of tasks
necessary to the functioning of the company without being directly
connected with the manufacturing process. Most of these jobs are now
carried out in 'offices [*bureaux*]'. Among them are accountancy and the
'commercial' and 'general' services of the company. The development of
modern production has divided up, compartmentalized, and socialized this
work, just as it has done to production itself. Nine-tenths of people working
in offices attached to factories carry out compartmentalized tasks of execution. Throughout their life they will do little else. Important changes will
have to be brought about here.

The capitalist structure of the factory generally results in considerable
overstaffing of these areas,[10] and a socialist reorganization probably will
result in a substantial saving of labour in these fields. Some of these departments will not only diminish in size but will witness a radical transformation
of their functions. In the last few years 'commercial services' have everywhere grown enormously. In a planned socialist economy they will be
concerned mainly with the bookkeeping aspects of obtaining supplies and
making deliveries. They will be in contact with similar departments in supply
factories and with stores that sell to consumers. Once the necessary trans-

formations have been brought about, offices will be considered 'workshops' like all others, organizing their own work and keeping in contact with other shops for purposes of coordination. They will enjoy no particular rights by virtue of the nature of their work. They have, in fact, no such rights today, and it is as a result of other factors (the division between manual and 'intellectual' labour, the more pronounced hierarchy found in offices) that individuals heading these departments can sometimes rise to the summit of the genuine 'management' of the company.

3 [Technical functions]   These are at present carried out by people ranging from consultant engineers to draftsmen. Here too, modern industry has created a 'collective' apparatus in which work is divided up and socialized, and nine-tenths of which is made up of executants working in compartmentalized jobs. But while pointing this out in relation to what goes on *within* these particular departments, we must recognize too that these departments carry out managerial functions in relation to the rest of the factory – areas directly related to production. Once production targets have been set, it is this collective technical apparatus that selects – or is charged with selecting – the appropriate ways and means, looks into the necessary changes in tooling, determines the sequence and the details of various operations, etc. In theory the production areas merely carry out the instructions issued from the technical departments. Supposedly, a complete separation exists between those who draw up the plans and those who are charged with carrying them out under the concrete conditions of mass production.

Up to a point, all this is based on something real. Today, both specialization and technical and scientific competence are the privilege of a minority. But it does not follow at all that the best way to use this expertise is to leave it to the 'experts' to decide everything about the production process. Competence is, by definition, restricted in its scope. Outside his particular sector, or outside the particular processes he is familiar with, the technician is no better equipped to make a responsible decision than anyone else. Even within his own field, his viewpoint is inevitably limited. He will often know little about other sectors and may tend to minimize their importance although these sectors have a definite bearing on his own. Moreover – and this is more important – the technician is separated from the real process of production.

This separation is a source of waste and conflict in capitalist factories. It will be abolished only when 'technical' and 'productive' staff begin to cooperate thoroughly. This cooperation will be based on joint decisions made by technicians and by those who will be working on a given task. Together they will decide on the methods and means to be used.

Will such cooperation work smoothly? There is no intrinsic reason why insurmountable obstacles should arise. The workers will have no interest in challenging an answer that the technician, in his capacity as a technician, may give to purely technical problems. And if there are disagreements, these will rapidly be resolved in practice. The field of production allows for almost immediate verification of what this or that person proposes. That for this or that part or tool a certain type of metallic compound would be preferable (given a certain state of knowledge and certain conditions of production) cannot and will not be a matter of controversy.

But the answers provided by technique establish only a general framework. They suggest only some of the elements that will, in practice, influence the concrete production process. Within this given framework there will be a multitude of ways to organize this process. The choice will have to take into account, on the one hand, certain general considerations of 'economy' (economy of labour, of energy, of raw materials, of plant) and, on the other – and this is much more important – considerations relating to the fate of man in production. And on these questions, by definition, the only people who can decide are those directly involved. In this area the specific competence of the technician, as a technician, is nil.

In other words, what we are challenging deep down is the whole concept of a technique capable of organizing people from the outside. Such an idea is as absurd as the idea of a psychoanalytic session in which the patient would not appear, thus making psychoanalysis into just a 'technique' in the hands of the analyst. Such techniques are all just techniques of oppression and coercion offering 'personal incentives', which, ultimately, always remain ineffective.

Accordingly, the actual organization of the production process can be vested only in those who perform it. The producers will obviously take into account various technical points suggested by competent technicians. In fact, there will obviously be a permanent process of give and take, if only because the producers themselves will see new ways of organizing the manufacturing process, thereby posing new technical problems concerning which the technicians will in turn have to put forward their comments and evaluations before a joint decision can be made 'in full knowledge of the relevant facts'. But the decision, in this case as in others, will be in the hands of the producers (including the technicians) of a given shop (if it only affects a shop) – or of the factory as a whole (if it affects the whole factory).

The roots of possible conflict between workers and technicians therefore are not at all of a technical nature. If such a conflict emerged it would be a *social* and *political* conflict, arising from a possible tendency of the technicians to assume a dominating role, thereby constituting anew a bureaucratic managerial apparatus.

What would be the strength and probable evolution of such a tendency? We cannot discuss this problem in any depth. We can only re-emphasize that technicians do not constitute a majority – or even an essential part – of the upper strata of modern economic or political management. Incidentally, to become aware of this obvious fact helps one see through the mystificatory character of all those arguments that seek to prove that ordinary people cannot manage production because they lack the 'necessary technical capacity'. The vast majority of technicians occupy only subordinate positions. They carry out only compartmentalized work, on instructions from above. Those technicians who have 'reached the top' are not there as *technicians*, but as 'managers' or 'organizers'.

Modern capitalism is *bureaucratic* capitalism. It is not – and never will be – a *technocratic* capitalism. The concept of a technocracy is an empty generalization of superficial sociologists, or a daydream of technicians confronted with their own impotence and with the absurdity of the present system. Technicians do not constitute a separate class. From the formal point of view they are just a category of salaried worker. The evolution of modern capitalism, by increasing their numbers and by transforming them into people who carry out compartmentalized and interchangeable labour, tends to drive them closer to the working class. Counteracting these tendencies, it is true, is their position in the wage and status hierarchies – and also the scanty chances for 'moving up' still open to them. But these channels are gradually being closed as the number of technicians increases and as bureaucratization spreads within its own ranks. In parallel with all this, a kind of revolt is developing among these compartmentalized and bureaucratized [*fonctionnarisé*] technicians as they confront the irrationalities of the system of bureaucratic capitalism and increasingly experience difficulties in giving free rein to their capacities for creative or meaningful work.

Some technicians already at the top, or on their way there, will side squarely with exploiting society. They will be opposed, however, by a growing minority of disaffected colleagues, ready to work with others in overthrowing the system. In the middle, of course, there will be the great majority of technicians, today apathetically accepting their status as slightly privileged employees. Their present conservatism suggests that they would not risk a conflict with real power, whatever its nature. The evolution of events can only radicalize them.

It is therefore extremely likely that workers' power in the factory, after having swept aside a small number of technical bureaucrats, will find support among a substantial number of other technicians. It should succeed, without major conflict, in integrating the remainder into the cooperative network of the factory.

4 [Truly managerial functions] The people 'consulted' by a company chairman or managing director before he makes an important decision usually number less than a dozen, even in the largest of firms. This very narrow stratum of management has two main tasks. On the one hand, it has to make decisions concerning investment, stocks, output, etc., in relation to market fluctuations and long-term prospects. On the other hand, it has to 'coordinate' the various differences between various segments of the bureaucratic apparatus.

Some of these functions will disappear altogether in a planned economy, in particular those related to the fluctuations of the market (scale of production, levels of investment, etc.). Others would be considerably reduced: coordinating the different shops of a factory would be much easier if the producers organized their own work and if different groups, shops, or departments could contact one another directly. Still other functions might be enhanced, such as genuine discussions of what might be possible in the future, or of how to do things, or about the present or future role of the enterprise in the overall development of the economy.

[Institutions]

Under socialism, 'managerial' tasks at *factory* level could be carried out by two bodies:

1   *The factory council*, composed of delegates from the various shops and offices, all of them elected and instantly revocable. In an enterprise of, say, 5,000 to 10,000 workers, such a council might number 30–50 people. The delegates will remain at their jobs. They will meet in full session as often as experience proves it necessary (probably on one or two half-days a week). They will report back each time to their workmates in shop or office – and anyway will already have discussed the agenda with them. Rotating groups of delegates will ensure continuity. One of the main tasks of a factory council will be to ensure liaison and to act as a continuous regulating *locus* between the factory and the 'outside world'.

2   *The general assembly* of all those who work in the plant, whether manual workers, office workers, or technicians. This will be the highest decision-making body for all problems concerning the factory as a whole. Differences or conflicts between various sectors of the factory will be thrashed out at this level.

This general assembly will embody the restoration of direct democracy to what should, in modern society, be its basic unit: the place of work. The assembly will have to ratify all but routine decisions of the factory council. It will be empowered to question, challenge, amend, reject, or endorse any decision made by the council. The general assembly itself will decide on all sorts of questions to be submitted to the council. The assembly will meet regularly, say, one or two days each month. There will, in addition, exist procedures for calling such general assemblies, if this is desired by a given number of workers, shops, or delegates.

[The Content of Workers' Management at Factory Level]

What will be the *effective content* of workers' management at the factory level, the permanent tasks it will have to accomplish? It will help us to discuss this problem if we differentiate schematically between the static and the dynamic aspects of workers' management.

[Immediate content]

Looked at in a static way, the overall plan might allocate to a given enterprise a target to be achieved within a given period of time (we will examine further on how such targets are to be determined). The general means to be allocated to the enterprise (to achieve its target) also will be broadly outlined by the plan. For example, the plan will decide that the annual production of a given automobile factory should be so many cars and that for this purpose such and such a quantity of raw materials, power, machinery, etc., should be made available. At the same time, it will set how many work hours (in other words, the number of workers, since the length of the working day is fixed) will be allocated to achieve this goal.

Seen from this angle, workers' management implies that the workers' collective itself will bear the final responsibility for deciding *how* a proposed target could best be achieved, given the general means available. The task corresponds to the 'positive' functions of the present narrowly based managerial apparatus, which itself will have been superseded. The workers themselves will determine the organization of their work in each shop or department. They will ensure coordination between shops. This will take place through direct contacts whenever it is a question of routine problems or of shops engaged in closely related aspects of the production process. If more important matters arose, they would be discussed and solved by meetings of delegates (or by joint gatherings of workers) of two or more shops or sections. The overall coordination of the work would be undertaken by the factory council and by the general assembly of the factory. Relations with the rest of the economy, as already stated, would be in the hands of the factory council.

Under such conditions, *autonomy* in the production process means the ability to decide how to achieve designated targets with the aid of means that have been defined in general terms. A certain 'give and take' will undoubtedly occur between the 'targets set' and 'means to be used'. The plan must in general prescribe these 'targets' and 'means', for they are the product of other factories. But only the workers of the particular factory can carry out this process of concrete elaboration. By themselves, 'targets set' and 'means of production available for achieving them' do not automatically or exhaustively define all the possible methods that could be used, all the more so since the plan's definition of the means remains highly general and it cannot specify even all the important 'details'. Spelling out these methods in detail and deciding exactly how an objective will be achieved with the means provided will be the first area in which workers will exercise their autonomy. It is an important field but a *limited* one, and it is essential to be fully aware of its limitations. These limitations stem from (and define) the inevitable framework within which this new type of production will have to *begin*. It will be the task of socialist production constantly to expand this framework and constantly to push back these limitations on autonomy.

Autonomy, envisaged in this static way, is limited first of all in relation to the fixing of *targets*. True, the workers of a given enterprise will *participate* in determining the targets of their factory in so far as they participate in the elaboration of the overall plan. But they are not in total or sole control of these targets or objectives. In a modern economy, where the production of each enterprise both conditions and is conditioned by that of all the others, the determination of coherent targets cannot be vested in individual enterprises acting in isolation. It must be undertaken by and for all enterprises together, with general viewpoints prevailing over particular ones.

Autonomy is also limited in relation to available material *means*. The workers of a given enterprise cannot in full autonomy determine the means of production they would prefer to use, for these are but the products of other enterprises or factories. Total autonomy for every factory, in relation to means, would imply that each factory could determine the output of all the others. These various autonomies would immediately cancel one another out. This limitation is, however, less rigid than the first (the limitation in relation to targets). Alterations of its own equipment, as proposed by the user factory, could easily be accommodated by the producer factory without the latter saddling itself with a heavy extra load. On a small scale, this happens even today in integrated engineering factories (car factories, for instance), where a substantial part of the tooling utilized in one shop may be made in another shop of the same factory. Close cooperation between plants making machine tools and plants using them could quickly lead to considerable changes in the means of production currently used.[11]

[Subsequent possibilities]

Let us now take a look at workers' management at the factory level in its dynamic aspect, i.e. the function of workers' management in *developing and transforming* socialist production. More precisely, let us look at how the development and transformation of socialist production will become the *primary objective* of workers' management. Everything we have suggested so far will now have to be re-examined. In this way we shall see how the limits to autonomy will gradually be pushed back.

The change will be most obvious in relation to the *means* of production. As we have said, socialist society will attack the problem of how consciously to transform the technology it has inherited from capitalism. Under capitalism, production equipment – and, more generally, the means of production – are planned and manufactured *independently* of the user and of his preferences (manufacturers, of course, pretend to take the user's viewpoint into account, but this has little to do with the real user: the worker on the shop floor). But equipment is made to be used productively. The viewpoint of the 'productive consumers' (i.e. those who will *use* the equipment to *produce* the goods) is of primary importance. As the views of those who *make* the equipment are also important, the problem of the structure of the means of production will only be solved by the vital cooperation of these two categories of workers. In an integrated factory this involves permanent contacts between the corresponding shops. At the level of the economy as a whole, it will have to take place through the instauration of normal, permanent contacts between factories and between sectors of production. (This problem is *distinct* from that of overall planning. General planning is concerned with determining a quantitative framework – so much steel and so many hours of labour at one end, so many consumer goods at the other. It does not have to intervene in the form or the type of intermediate products.)

Cooperation will necessarily take two forms. The choice and popularization of the best methods, and the standardization and rationalization of their use, will be achieved through the *horizontal* cooperation of councils, organized according to branch or sector of industry (for instance, textiles, the chemical industry, engineering, electrical supply, etc.). On the other hand, the integration of the viewpoints of those who make and of those who utilize equipment (or, more generally, of those who make and those who utilize intermediate products) will require the *vertical* cooperation of councils representing the successive stages of a productive process (the steel industry and the machine-tool and engineering industries, for instance). In both cases, cooperation will have to be organized on a permanent basis through committees of factory council representatives (or wider conferences of producers) organized both horizontally and vertically.

Considering the problem from this dynamic angle – which ultimately is the only important one – we see at once that the terrain for exercising autonomy has expanded considerably. Already at the level of individual factories (but more significantly at the level of cooperation between factories), the producers are beginning to influence the structure of the means of production. They are, thereby, reaching a position where they are beginning to dominate the work process: they are not only determining its methods but are now also modifying its technological structure.

This fact now begins to alter what we have just said about *targets*. Three-quarters of gross modern production consists of intermediate products, of 'means of production' in the broadest sense. When producers and users of intermediate products decide together about the means of production, they are participating in a very direct and immediate way in decisions about the objectives of production. The remaining limitation, and it is an important one, flows from the fact that these means of production (whatever their exact nature) are destined, in the last analysis, to produce consumer goods. And the overall volume of these can be determined, in general terms, only by the plan.

But here, too, looking at things dynamically radically alters one's vision. Modern consumption is characterized by the constant appearance of new products. Factories producing consumer goods will conceive of, receive suggestions about, study, and finally produce such products.

This raises the broader problem of contact between producers and consumers. Capitalist society rests on a complete separation of these two aspects of human activity and on the exploitation of the consumer *qua* consumer. There are not just monetary exploitation (through overcharging) and limitations on one's income. Capitalism claims that it can satisfy people's needs better than any other system in history. But in fact capitalism, if it does not determine these needs themselves, decides upon the method of satisfying them. Consumer preference is only one of numerous variables that can be manipulated by modern sales techniques.

The division between producers and consumers appears most glaringly in relation to the *quality* of goods. This problem is insoluble in any exploiting society, as Daniel Mothé's dialogue between the human-worker and the robot-worker shows: 'Do you think this part's important? – What's it to you? You can always jam it in somehow.'[12] Those who look only at the surface of things see only a commodity as a commodity. They don't see in it a crystallized moment of the class struggle. They see faults or defects, instead of seeing in them the resultant of the worker's constant struggle with himself. Faults or defects embody the worker's struggles against exploitation. They also embody squabbles between different sections of the bureaucracy managing the plant.

The elimination of exploitation will of itself bring about a change in all this. At work, people will begin to assert their claims as future consumers of what they are producing. In its early phases, however, socialist society will undoubtedly have to instaurate regular forms of contact (other than 'the market') between producers and consumers.

We have assumed, as a starting point for all this, the division of labour inherited from present-day capitalism. But we have also pointed out that, from the very beginning, socialist society cannot survive unless it demolishes this division. This is an enormous subject with which we cannot even begin to deal in this text. Nevertheless, the first benchmarks of a solution can be seen even today. Modern production has destroyed many traditional professional qualifications. It has created universal automatic or semiautomatic machines. It has thereby itself demolished, on its own, the traditional framework for the industrial division of labour. It has given birth to a universal worker who is capable, after a relatively short apprenticeship, of using most existing machines. Once one gets beyond its class aspects, the 'posting' of workers to particular jobs in a big modern factory corresponds less and less to a genuine division of *labour* and more and more to a simple division of tasks. Workers are not allocated to given areas of the production process and then riveted to them because their 'occupational skills' invariably correspond to the 'skills required' by management. They are placed here rather than there because putting a particular worker in a particular place at a particular time happens to suit the personnel officer – or the foreman – or, more prosaically, just because a particular vacancy happened to exist.

Under socialism, factories would have no reason to accept the artificially rigid division of labour now prevailing. There will be every reason to encourage a rotation of workers *between shops and departments* – and between production and office areas. Such a rotation will greatly help workers to manage production in full knowledge of the relevant facts as more and more workers develop firsthand familiarity with what goes on where they work. The same applies to rotation of workers *between various enterprises*, and in particular between 'producing' and 'utilizing' units.

The residues of capitalism's division of labour will gradually have to be eliminated. This overlaps with the general problem of education not only of generations to come but of those adults who were brought up under the previous system. We cannot go into this problem here.

Simplification and Rationalization of General Economic Problems

[Simplification and rationalization of data]

The functioning of the socialist economy implies that the producers themselves will consciously manage all economic activity. This management will be exercised at all levels, and in particular at the overall or central level. It is completely illusory to believe that either a central bureaucracy left to itself or even a bureaucracy 'controlled' by the workers could guide the economy toward socialism. Such a bureaucracy could only lead society toward new forms of exploitation. It is also wrong to think that 'automatic' objective mechanisms could be established that, like the automatic pilot of a modern jet aircraft, could at each moment direct the economy in the desired direction. It is just as impossible for an 'enlightened' bureaucracy, the mechanisms of a 'true market' (supposedly restored to its pristine and original, precapitalist, purity), or the regulatory control afforded by some electronic supercomputer to achieve such an ideal end. Any plan presupposes a fundamental decision on the rate of growth of the economy, and this in turn depends essentially on decisions concerning the distribution of the social product between investment and consumption. [. . .]

Now, there is no 'objective' rational basis for determining how to distribute the social product. A decision to invest zero per cent of the social product is neither more nor less objectively rational than a decision to invest 90 per cent of it. The only rationality in the matter is the choice people make about their own fate, in full knowledge of the relevant facts. The fixing of plan targets by those who will have to fulfil them is, in the last analysis, the only guarantee of their willing and spontaneous participation and hence of an effective mobilization of individuals around both the management and the expansion of the economy.

But this does not mean that the plan and the management of the economy are 'just political matters'. Socialist planning will base itself on certain rational technical factors. It is in fact the only type of planning that could integrate such factors into a conscious management of the economy. These factors consist of a number of extremely useful and effective 'labour-saving' and 'thought-saving' devices that can be used to simplify the representation of the economy and its laws, thereby allowing the problems of central economic management to be made accessible to all. Workers' management of production (this time at the level of the economy as a whole and not just at the level of a particular factory) will be possible only if management tasks have been enormously simplified, so that the producers and their collective organs are in a position to judge the key issues in an informed way. What is needed, in other words, is for the vast chaos of today's economic facts and relations to be boiled down to certain propositions that adequately sum up the real problems and choices. These propositions should be few in number. They should be easy to grasp. They should summarize reality without distortion or mystification. If they can do this, they will form an adequate basis for meaningful judgements.

A condensation of this type is *possible*, first, because there is at least a rational outline to the economy; second, because there already exist today certain techniques allowing one to grasp the complexities of economic reality; and finally, because it is now possible to mechanize and to automate all that does not pertain to human decisions in the strict sense.

A discussion of the relevant devices, techniques, and possibilities is therefore indispensable, starting right now. They enable us to carry out a vast clearing of the ground. Without them workers' management would collapse under the weight of the very subject matter it ought to be getting a handle on. The content of such a discussion is in no sense a 'purely technical' one, and at each stage we will be guided by the general principles already outlined here.

[The 'Plan Factory']

A production plan, whether it deals with one factory or the economy as a whole, is a type of reasoning (made up of a great number of secondary arguments). It can be boiled down to two premises and one conclusion. The two premises are the material means initially at one's disposal (equipment, stocks, labour, etc.) and the target one is aiming at (production of so many specified objects and services, within a given period of time). We will refer to these premises as the *'initial conditions'* and the *'ultimate target'*. The 'conclusion' is the path to be followed from initial conditions to ultimate target. In practice this means a certain number of intermediate products to be made within a given period. We will call these conclusions the *'intermediate targets'*.

When passing from simple initial conditions to a simple ultimate target, the intermediate targets can be determined right away. As the initial conditions or the ultimate targets (or both) become more complex, or are more spread out in time, the establishment of intermediate targets becomes more difficult. In the case of the economy as a whole (where there are thousands of different products, many of which can be made by several different processes, and where the manufacture of any given category of products directly or indirectly involves most of the others), one might imagine that the level of complexity makes rational planning (in the sense of an *a priori* determination of the intermediate targets, given the initial conditions and ultimate target) impossible. The apologists for 'free enterprise' have been proclaiming this doctrine for ages. But it is false.[13] The problem can be solved and available mathematical techniques in fact allow it to be solved remarkably simply. Once the initial conditions (the economic situation at the start of the planning process) are known and the ultimate target or targets have been consciously set, all planning work (the determination of the intermediate targets) can be reduced to a purely technical task of execution, capable of being mechanized and automated to a very high degree.

The basis of the new methods is the concept of the total interdependence of all sectors of the economy (the fact that everything that one sector utilizes in production is itself the product of one or more other sectors; and the converse fact that every product of a given sector will ultimately be utilized or consumed by one or more other sectors). The idea, which goes back to Quesnay and which formed the basis of Marx's theory of accumulation, has been vastly developed in the past twenty years by a group of American economists around W. Leontief that has succeeded in giving it a statistical formulation that can be applied to a real economy in a state of constant expansion.[14] This interdependence is such that at any given moment (for a given level of technique and a given structure of available equipment) the production of each sector is related, in a relatively stable manner, to the products of other sectors that the first sector utilizes (or 'consumes productively').

It is easy to grasp that a given quantity of coal is needed to produce a ton of steel of a given type. Moreover, one will need so much scrap metal or iron ore, so many hours of labour, such and such an expenditure on upkeep and repairs. The ratio 'coal used/steel produced', expressed in terms of value, is known as the *current technical coefficient* determining the productive consumption of coal per unit of steel turned out. If one wants to increase steel production beyond a certain point, it will not help simply to go on delivering more coal or more scrap metal to the existing steel mills. New mills will have to be built. Or one will have to increase the productive capacity of existing mills. To increase steel output by a given amount one will have to produce a given amount of specified equipment. The ratio 'given amount of specified equipment/steel-producing capacity per given period', again expressed in terms of value, is known as the *technical coefficient of capital*. It determines the quantity of *capital* utilized per unit of steel produced in a given period.

One could stop at this point if one were dealing with only a single enterprise. Every firm bases itself on calculations of this sort (in fact, on much more detailed ones) whenever, in making decisions about how much to produce or how much to increase production, it buys raw materials, orders machinery, or recruits labour. But when one looks at the economy as a whole, things change. The interdependence of the various sectors has definite consequences. The *increase* of production in a given sector has repercussions (of varying intensity) on all other sectors and finally on the initial sector itself. For example, an increase in the production of steel immediately requires an increase in the production of coal. But this requires both an increase in certain types of mining equipment and the recruitment of more labour into mining. The increased demand for mining equipment in turn requires *more* steel, and more labour in the steel mills. This in turn leads to a demand for still more coal, etc., etc. For their part, newly hired workers get increased wages and therefore they buy more consumer goods of various kinds. The production of these new goods will require such and such an amount of raw materials, new equipment, etc. (and, again, more coal and steel). The question of how much the demand for nylon stockings would rise in West Virginia or the Basses-Pyrénées if a new blast furnace were to be built in Pennsylvania or the Lorraine is not a joke but one of the central problems to which planners should – and can – respond.

The use of Leontief's matrices, combined with other modern methods such as Koopmans's 'activity analysis'[15] (of which 'operational research' is a specific instance) would, in the case of a socialist economy, allow theoretically exact answers to be given to questions of this type. A matrix is a table on which the technical coefficients (both 'current technical coefficients' and 'technical coefficients of capital') expressing the dependence of each sector upon each of the others are laid out systematically. Every ultimate target that might be chosen is presented as a list of material means to be utilized (and therefore manufactured) in specific amounts, within the period in question. As soon as the ultimate target is chosen, the solution of a system of simultaneous equations enables one to define immediately all the intermediate targets and therefore the tasks to be fulfilled by each sector of the economy.

Solving these problems will be the task of a highly mechanized and automated specific *enterprise*, whose main work will consist of a veritable 'mass production' of various *plans* (*targets*) and of their various *components* (*implications*). This enterprise is the *plan factory*. Its central workshop will, to start with, probably consist of a computer whose 'memory' will store the technical coefficients and the initial productive capacity of each sector. If 'fed' a number of hypothetical targets, the computer will 'produce' the production implication of each target for each sector (including the amount of work to be provided, in each instance, by the 'manpower' sector).

(The division of the economy into some 100 sectors, which roughly corresponds to *present* [1957] computer capacity, is about 'halfway' between its division [by Marx] into two sectors [consumer goods and means of production] and the few thousand sectors that would be required to ensure a perfectly exact representation. Present computer capabilities would probably be sufficient in practice, and could be made more precise, even now, by tackling the problem in several stages.)

Around this central workshop there would be others whose tasks would be to study the distribution and variations of regional production and investment and possible technical optima (given the general interdependence of the various sectors). They would also determine the unit values (equivalences) of different categories of products. [. . .]

Let us not be misunderstood; the role of the 'plan factory' will not be to decide on the plan. The *targets* of the plan will be determined by society as a whole [. . .]. *Before* any proposals are voted upon, however, the plan factory will work out and present to society as a whole the *implications* and the consequences of the plan (or plans) suggested. *After* a plan has been adopted, the task of the plan factory will be to constantly *bring up to date* the facts on which the current plan is based, *and* to draw conclusions from these modifications, informing both the central assembly of councils and the relevant sectors of any alterations in the intermediate targets (and therefore in the production tasks) that might be worth considering.

In none of these instances would those actually working in the plan factory decide anything – except, as in every other factory, the organization of their own work.

The market for consumer goods

[. . .] It is obvious that [the answer to the question: What and how much is to be produced?] cannot be based on direct democracy. The plan cannot propose, as an ultimate target, a complete list of consumer goods or suggest in what proportions they should be produced. Such a proposal would not be democratic, for two reasons. First, it could never be based on 'full knowledge of the relevant facts', namely, on a full knowledge of everybody's preferences. Second, it would be tantamount to a pointless tyranny of the majority over the minority. If 40 per cent of the population wish to consume a certain article, there is no reason why they should be deprived of it under the pretext that the other 60 per cent prefer something else. No preference or taste is more logical than any other. Moreover, there is no reason at all to cut short the problem in this way, since consumer wishes are seldom incompatible with one another. Majority votes in this matter would amount to rationing, an irrational and absurd way of settling this kind of problem anywhere but on the raft of Medusa or in a besieged fortress.

Planning decisions therefore will relate not to particular items but to the general standard of living (the overall volume of consumption), expressed in terms of the disposable income of each person in a socialist society. They will not delve into the detailed composition of this consumption. [. . .]

Socialist society will have to regulate the pattern of its consumption according to the principle of *consumer sovereignty*, which implies the existence of a real market for consumer goods. The 'general decision' embodied in the plan will define: (1) what proportion of its overall product society wishes to devote to the satisfaction of individual consumer needs, (2) what proportion it would like to allocate to collective needs ('public consumption'), and (3) what proportion it wants to apply to the development of the productive forces (i.e. investment). But the *structure* of consumption will have to be determined by the demand of consumers themselves. [. . .]

Money, prices, wages, and value

Many absurdities have been spoken about money and its immediate abolition in a socialist society. It should be clear, however, that the role of money is radically transformed from the moment it can no longer be used as a means of *accumulation* (the means of production being owned in common) or as a means of *exerting social pressure* (wages being equal).

People will receive a *token* [*revenu*] in return for what they put into society. These 'tokens' will take the form of units [*signes*], allowing people to organize what they take out of society, spreading it out (1) in time and (2) between different objects and services, exactly as they wish. As we are seeking here to come to grips with realities and are not fighting against words, we see no objection to calling these tokens 'wages' and these units 'money' [. . .].

Under socialism, labour value will be the only rational basis for any kind of social accountancy and the only yardstick having any real meaning for people. As such, it will necessarily serve as the foundation for calculating profitability in the sphere of socialist production. The main objective of making such calculations will be to reduce both the direct and indirect costs of human labour power. Setting the prices of consumer goods on the basis of their labour value would mean that for each person the cost of consumer objects will clearly appear as the equivalent of the labour he himself would have had to expend to produce them (assuming he had both access to the average prevailing equipment and an average social capacity).

It would both simplify and clarify things if the monetary unit was considered the 'net product of an hour of labour' and if this were made the unit of value. It would also be helpful if the hourly wage, equal for all, were a given fraction of this unit, expressing the ratio *private consumption/total net production*. If these steps were taken and thoroughly explained, they would enable the fundamental planning decision (namely, the distribution of the social product between consumption and investment) to be immediately obvious to everyone, and repeatedly drawn to people's attention, every time anyone bought anything. Equally obvious would be the social cost of every object acquired.

Absolute wage equality

Whenever they succeed in expressing themselves independently of the trade-union bureaucracy, working-class aspirations and demands are directed increasingly against hierarchy and wage differentials.[16] Basing itself on this fact, socialist society will introduce absolute equality in the area of wages.

There is no justification, other than naked exploitation, for wage differentials,[17] whether these reflect differing professional qualifications or differences in productivity. If an individual himself advanced the costs of his professional training and if society considered him 'an enterprise', the recovery of those costs, spread over a working lifetime, would at most 'justify', at the extremes of the wage spectrum, a differential of 2:1 (between sweeper and neurosurgeon). Under socialism, training costs will be advanced by society (they often are, even today), and the question of their 'recovery' will not arise. As for productivity, it depends (already today) much less on bonuses and incentives and much more on the coercions exercised, on the one hand, by machines and supervisors and, on the other, by the discipline of production, imposed by primary working groups in the workshop. Socialist society could not increase productivity by economic constraints without resorting again to all the capitalist paraphernalia of norms, supervision, etc. Labour discipline will flow (as it already does, in part, today) from the self-organization of primary groups in each workshop, from the mutual cooperation and supervision among the factories' different shops, from gatherings of producers in different factories or different sectors of the economy. As a general rule, the primary group in a workshop ensures the discipline of any particular individual. Anyone who proves incorrigible can be made to leave that particular shop. It would then be up to this recalcitrant individual to seek entry into another primary group of workers and to gain their acceptance or else to remain jobless.

Wage equality will give a real meaning to the market in consumer goods, every individual being assured for the first time of an equal vote. It will abolish countless conflicts, both in everyday life and in production, and will enable an extraordinary cohesion to develop among working people. It will destroy at its very roots the whole mercantile monstrosity of capitalism (both private and bureaucratic), the commercialization of individuals, that whole universe where one does not earn what one is worth but where one is worth what one earns. A few years of wage equality and little will be left of the present-day mentality of individuals.

The fundamental decision

The fundamental decision, in a socialist economy, is the one whereby society as a whole determines what it wants (i.e. the ultimate targets of its plan).

This decision concerns two basic propositions. Given the 'initial conditions' of the economy, how much time does society want to devote to production? And how much of the total product does it want to see devoted respectively to private consumption, public consumption, and investment?

In both private and bureaucratic capitalist societies, the amount of time one has to work is determined by the ruling class by means of direct physical constraints (as was the case until quite recently in Russian factories) or economic ones. No one is consulted about the matter. Socialist society, taken as a whole, will not escape the impact of certain economic constraints (in the sense that any decision to modify labour time will – other things being equal – have a bearing on production). But it will differ from all previous societies in that for the first time in history people will be able to decide about work in full knowledge of the relevant facts, with the basic elements of the problem clearly presented to them.

Socialist society will also be the first society capable of deciding rationally how society's product should be divided between consumption and investment. (We leave aside for now the problem of public consumption.) Under private capitalism, this distribution takes place in an absolutely blind fashion and one would seek in vain any 'rationality' underlying what determines investment. (In his major work, which is devoted to this theme – and after a moderate use of differential equations – Keynes comes up with the conclusion that the main determinants of investment are the 'animal spirits' of entrepreneurs. *The General Theory of Employment, Interest and Money* [1936], pp. 161–2.) The idea that the volume of investment is determined primarily by the rate of interest (and that the latter results from the interplay of the 'real forces of productivity and thrift') was long ago demolished by academic economists themselves. (See, for example, Joan Robinson's *The Rate of Interest and Other Essays* [1952; reprinted, London: Hyperion, 1981].) In bureaucratic capitalist societies, the volume of investment is also decided quite arbitrarily, and the central bureaucracy in these societies has never been able to justify its choices except through monotonous recitations of litanies about the 'priority of heavy industry'. (One would seek in vain through the voluminous writings of Mr Charles Bettelheim for any attempt to justify the rate of accumulation 'chosen' by the Russian bureaucracy. The 'socialism' of such 'theoreticians' not only implies that Stalin [or Khrushchev] alone can know. It also implies that such knowledge, by its very nature, cannot be communicated to the rest of humanity. In another country, and in other times, this was known as the *Führerprinzip*.) Even if there were a rational, 'objective' basis for making a central decision on this matter, the decision arrived at would be *ipso facto* irrational if it was reached in the absence of those primarily concerned, namely, the members of society. Any decision made in this way would reproduce the basic contradiction of all exploiting regimes. It would treat people in the plan as just one variable of predictable behaviour among others and as theoretical 'objects'. It would soon lead to treating them as objects in real life, too. Such a policy would contain the seeds of its own failure: instead of encouraging the participation of the producers in carrying out the plan, it would irrevocably alienate them from a plan that was not of their choosing. There is no 'objective' rationality allowing one to decide, by means of mathematical formulae, about the future of society, work, consumption, and accumulation. The only rationality in these realms is the living reason of mankind, the decisions of ordinary people concerning their own fate.

But these decisions will not come from a toss of the dice. They will be based upon a complete clarification of the problem and they will be made in full knowledge of the relevant facts. This will be possible because there exists, for any given level of technique, a definite relation between a given amount of investment and the resulting increase in production. This relation is nothing other than the application to the economy as a whole of the 'technical coefficients of capital' we spoke of earlier. A given investment in steelworks will result in such and such an increase in what steelworks turn out – and a given *overall* investment in production will result in such and such a net increase in the overall social product. Therefore, a certain *rate* of accumulation will allow a certain *rate* of increase of the social product (and therefore of the standard of living or of the amount of leisure). Finally, a particular *fraction* of the product devoted to accumulation will also result in a particular *rate* of increase of living standards.

The overall problem can therefore be posed in the following terms. A large immediate increase in consumption is possible – but it would imply a significant cutback on further increases in the years to come. On the other hand, people might prefer to choose a more limited immediate increase in living standards, which would allow the social product (and hence living standards) to increase at the rate of x per cent per annum in the years to come. And so on. 'The antinomy between the present and the future', to which the apologists of private capitalism and of the bureaucracy are constantly referring, would still be with us. But it would be *laid out clearly*. And society itself would settle the matter, fully aware of the setting and of the implications of its decision. [. . .]

In conclusion, and to sum up, one could say that any overall plan submitted to the people for discussion would have to specify:

1 the productive implications for each sector of industry, and as far as possible the tasks to be completed by each enterprise;
2 the amount of work involved for everybody;
3 the level of consumption during the initial period;
4 the amount of resources to be devoted to public consumption and to investment; and
5 the rate of increase of future consumption.

To simplify things, we have at times presented the decisions about ultimate and intermediate targets (i.e. the implications of the plan concerning specific areas of production) as two separate and consecutive acts. In practice there would be a continuous give and take between these two phases, and a plurality of proposals. The producers will be in no position to decide on ultimate targets unless they know what the implications of particular targets are for themselves, not only as consumers but as *producers*, working in a specific factory. Moreover, there is no such thing as a decision made in full knowledge of the relevant facts if that decision is not founded on a *spectrum* of choices, each with its particular implications.

The fundamental process of decision therefore will take the following form. Starting from below, there would be discussions in the general assemblies. Initial proposals would emanate from the workers' councils of various enterprises and would deal with their own productive possibilities in the period to come. The plan factory would then regroup these various proposals, pointing out which ones were mutually incompatible or entailed undesirable effects on other sectors. It would elaborate a series of achievable targets, grouping them as far as possible in terms of their concrete implications. (Proposal A implies that factory X will increase production by r per cent next year with the help of additional equipment Y. Proposal B, on the other hand, implies . . .) There would then be a full discussion of the various overall proposals, throughout the general assemblies and by all the workers' councils, possibly with counterproposals and a repetition of the procedure described. A final discussion would then lead to a simple majority vote in the general assemblies of each enterprise.

The Management of the Economy

We have spelled out the implications of workers' management at the level of a particular factory. These consist in the abolition of any separate managerial apparatus and in the performance of managerial jobs by the workers themselves, organized in workers' councils and in general assemblies of one or more shops or offices, or of a whole enterprise.

Workers' management of the economy *as a whole* also implies that the management of the economy is not vested in the hands of a specific managerial stratum, but belongs instead to organized collectivities of producers.

What we have outlined in the previous sections shows that democratic management is perfectly feasible. Its basic assumption is the clarification of data and people's utilization of what modern techniques have now made possible. It implies the conscious use of a series of devices and mechanisms (such as a genuine consumer 'market', wage equality, the connections established between price and value – and, of course, the plan factory) combined with real knowledge concerning economic reality. Together, these will help clear the ground. The major part of planning is made up simply of tasks of execution and could safely be left to highly mechanized or automated offices, which would have no political or decisional role whatsoever and would confine themselves to placing before society a variety of feasible plans and their full respective implications for everyone, both from the standpoint of production and from that of consumption.

This general clearing of the ground having been achieved, and coherent possibilities having been presented to the people, the final choice will lie in their hands. Everyone will participate in deciding the ultimate targets 'in full knowledge of the relevant facts', i.e. knowing the implications of his choice for himself (both as producer and as consumer). The elements of the plan will begin as proposals emanating from various enterprises. They will be elaborated by the plan factory as a series of possible compatible plans. Finally, this spectrum of plans will be brought back before the general assemblies of each enterprise where they will be discussed and voted on.

Once adopted, a given plan provides the framework of economic activities for a given period of time. It establishes a starting point for economic life. But in a socialist society, the plan will not *dominate* economic life. It is only a starting point, to be constantly re-examined and modified as necessary. Neither the economic life of society – nor its life overall – can be based on a dead technical rationality, given once and for all. Society cannot alienate itself from its own decisions. It is not only that real life will almost of necessity diverge, in many aspects, from the 'most perfect' plan in the world. It is also that the workers' self-managerial activity will constantly tend to alter, both directly and indirectly, the basic data and targets of the plan. New products, new means of production, new methods, new problems, new difficulties, and new solutions will constantly be emerging. Working times will be reduced. Prices will fall, entailing consumer reactions and displacements of demand. Some of these modifications will affect only a single factory, others several factories, and yet others, no doubt, the economy as a whole. (From this angle – and if they weren't false in the first place – Russian figures that show that year after year the targets of the plan have been fulfilled to 101 per cent would provide the severest possible indictment of the Russian economy and of Russian society. They would signify, in effect, that during a given five-year period *nothing* happened in the country, that not a single new idea arose in anyone's mind – or else that Stalin, in his wisdom, had foreseen all such ideas and incorporated them in advance in the plan, allowing – in his kindness – inventors to savour the pleasures of illusory discovery.) The 'plan factory' therefore will not operate just once every five years; it will have to tackle some problem or another daily.

All this deals mainly with the *form* of workers' management of the economy and with the mechanisms and institutions that will ensure that it functions in a democratic manner. These forms will allow society to give to the management of the economy the *content* it chooses. In a narrower sense, they will enable society to orient economic development freely.

The content of the management of the economy

Everything we have said indicates that the direction chosen will be radically different from that proposed by the best-intentioned ideologists or philanthropists of modern society. All such ideologists (whether 'Marxist' or bourgeois) accept as self-evident that the ideal economy is one that allows the most rapid possible expansion of the productive forces and, as a corollary, the greatest possible reduction of the working day. This idea, considered in absolute terms, is absolutely absurd. It epitomizes the whole mentality, psychology, logic, and metaphysics of capitalism, its reality as well as its schizophrenia. 'Work is hell. It must be reduced.' Mr Harold Wilson and Mr Nikita Khrushchev have nothing to offer people besides cars and butter. The population must therefore be made to feel that it can be happy only if the roads are choked with cars or if it can 'catch up with American butter production within the next three years'. And when people acquire the said cars and the said butter, all that will be left for them to do will be to commit suicide, which is just what they do in the 'ideal' country called Sweden. This 'acquisitive' mentality that capitalism engenders, which engenders capitalism, without which capitalism could not operate, and which capitalism pushes to the point of paroxysm might just conceivably have been a useful aberration during a certain phase of human development. But this way of thinking will die along with capitalism. Socialist society will not be this absurd race after percentage increments in production. This will *not* be its basic concern.

In its initial phase, to be sure, socialist society will concern itself with satisfying consumer needs and with a more balanced allocation of people's time between production and other activities. But the development of people and of social communities will be socialism's central preoccupation. A very significant part of social investment will therefore be geared toward transforming machinery, toward a universal education, and toward abolishing divisions between town and country. The growth of freedom *within* work, the development of the creative faculties of the producers, the creation of integrated and complete human communities will be the paths along which socialist humanity will seek the meaning of its existence. These will, *in addition*, enable socialism to secure the material basis it requires.

The Management of Society

We have already discussed the type of change that will be brought about by the 'vertical' and 'horizontal' cooperation of workers' councils, a cooperation secured through industrial councils composed of delegates from various places of work. A similar regional cooperation will have to be instaurated through councils representing all the units of a region. Cooperation, finally, will be necessary on a national level for all the activities of society, whether or not they are economic.

A central organ that will be the expression of the workers themselves will be needed in order to ensure the general tasks of economic coordination, in as much as they were not dealt with by the plan itself – or more precisely, in as much as the plan will have to be frequently or constantly amended (the very decision to suggest that it should be amended would have to be initiated by someone). Such a body will also coordinate activities in other areas of social life that have little or nothing to do with general economic planning. This central body will be the direct emanation of the workers' councils and the local general assemblies themselves. It will consist of a central assembly of delegates. The assembly itself will elect, from within its own ranks, a central council, called 'the government'.

This network of general assemblies and councils is all that is left of the *State* or of *power* in a socialist society. It is the *whole* State and the *only* embodiment of power. There are no other institutions that could manage, direct, or make binding decisions about people's lives.

To convince people that there would be no other 'State' lurking in the background we must show:

1　　that such a pattern of organization can embrace the entire population of the nation, not just in industry; and
2　　that institutions of the type described can organize, direct, and coordinate all those social activities that the population felt needed to be organized, directed, and coordinated (in particular noneconomic activities), in other words, that they could fulfil *all* the functions needed of a socialist 'State' (which should not be confused with those of a modern State).

We will then have to discuss what the significations of the 'State', 'parties' and 'politics' would be in such a society.

The councils: exclusive and exhaustive form of organization for the whole population

Setting up workers' councils will create no particular problems in relation to *industry* (taking the term in its widest sense to include manufacture, transport, communications, building, mining, energy production, public services and public works, etc.). The revolutionary transformation of society will in fact be based on the establishment of such councils and would be impossible without it.

In the postrevolutionary period, however, when the new social relations become the norm, a problem will arise from the need to regroup people working in smaller enterprises. This regrouping will be necessary if only to ensure them their full democratic and representational rights. Initially, it will be based on some compromise between considerations of geographical proximity and considerations of industrial integration. This particular problem is not very important, for even if there are *many* such small enterprises, the number of those working in them represents only a *small* proportion of the total industrial workforce.

Paradoxical as it may seem, the self-organization of the population into councils could proceed as naturally in *agriculture* as in industry. It is traditional on the Left to see the peasantry as a source of constant problems for a working-class power because of its dispersion, its attachment to private property, and its political and ideological backwardness. These factors certainly exist, but it is doubtful that the peasantry would actively oppose a working-class power that has formulated an intelligent (i.e. socialist) farming policy. The 'peasant nightmare' currently obsessing so many revolutionaries results from the telescoping of two quite different problems: on the one hand, the relations of the peasantry with a socialist economy, in the context of a modern society; and on the other, the relations between the peasantry and the State in the Russia of 1921 (or of 1932) or in the satellite countries between 1945 and today.

The situation that led Russia to the New Economic Policy of 1921 is of no exemplary value to an even moderately industrialized country. There is no chance of its repeating itself in a modern setting. In 1921 it was a question of an agricultural system that did not depend on the rest of the national economy for its essential means of production; seven years of war and civil war had compelled it to fall back upon itself entirely. The Party was asking this system of agriculture to supply its produce to the towns without offering it anything in exchange. In 1932 in Russia (and after 1945 in the satellite countries), what happened was an absolutely healthy resistance of the peasantry to the monstrous exploitation imposed on it by a bureaucratic State through forced collectivization.

In a country such as France – classically considered 'backward' as far as the numerical importance of its peasantry is concerned – the workers' power will not have to fear a 'wheat strike'. It will not have to organize punitive expeditions into the countryside. Precisely because the peasant is concerned with his own interests, he will have no cause to quarrel with a State that supplies him with gas, electricity, fertilizers, insecticides, and spare parts.

Peasants would actively oppose such an administration only if pushed to the
limit, either by exploitation or by an absurd policy of forced collectivization.
The socialist organization of the economy would mean an *immediate*
improvement in the economic status of most peasants, if only through the
abolition of that specific kind of exploitation they are subjected to through
middlemen. As for forced collectivization, it is the very antithesis of socialist
policy in the realm of agriculture. The collectivization of agriculture could
come about only as the result of an organic development within the peasantry itself, helped along by technical developments. Under no
circumstances could it be imposed through direct or indirect (economic)
coercion.

A socialist society will start by recognizing the rights of the peasants to the
widest autonomy in the management of their own affairs. It will invite them
to organize themselves into rural communes, based on geographical or
cultural units and comprising approximately equal populations. Each such
commune will have, both in relation to the rest of society and in relation to
its own organizational structure, the status of an enterprise. Its sovereign
organ therefore will be the general assembly of peasants and its representational unit, the peasant council. Rural communes and their councils will be
in charge of local self-administration. They alone will decide when and how
they want to form producers' cooperatives and under what conditions. In
relation to the overall plan, it will be the rural communes and their councils
that will be responsible to the government, and not individual peasants.
Communes will undertake to deliver a certain percentage of their produce
(or a given amount of a specific product) in exchange for given amounts of
money or means of production. The rural communes themselves will decide
how these obligations and payments ought to be allocated among their own
members. [. . .]

What about groups of workers involved in *services* of various kinds (from
commercial, banking, and insurance company staff to workers in entertain-
ment to all the ex-State administrators)?[18] There is no reason why the pattern
of their self-organization should not resemble that pertaining to industry as
a whole. And what about the thousand-and-one petty trades existing in
towns (shopkeepers, 'personal services', artisans, some of the 'liberal profes-
sions', etc.)? Here the pattern of organization could resemble what we have
outlined for an 'atomized' occupation such as agriculture. A working-class
power will never seek to socialize these occupations by force. It will only
require that these categories group themselves into associations or cooperatives, which will at one and the same time constitute their representative
political organs and their responsible units in relation to the management of
the economy as a whole. There will be no question, for instance, of socialized industry individually supplying each particular shop or artisan. Instead,
it will supply the cooperatives that these shopkeepers or artisans will be

members of, and will entrust to these collectives the job of organizing within their own ranks. At the political level, people in these occupations will seek representation through councils or they won't be represented at all, for there won't be any elections of either the Western or Russian types.

These solutions present serious shortcomings when compared with industrially based workers' councils – or even when compared with rural communes. Workers' councils or rural communes are not based primarily on an *occupation* (when they are still so based, this would reflect their weakness rather than their strength). They are based on a *working* unity and on a shared *life*. In other words, workers' councils and rural communes represent organic social units. A cooperative of artisans or of petty traders, geographically scattered and living and working separately from one another, will only be based on a rather narrow community of interests. This fragmentation is a legacy of capitalism that socialist society ought to eliminate as soon as possible. These occupations are overcrowded today. Under socialism, some of the members of these strata will be absorbed into other occupations. Society will grant funds to the remainder to enable them to organize into larger, self-managed units.

When discussing people in these various occupations we must repeat what we said about farmers, namely, that we have no experience of what their attitudes might be toward a *socialist power*. To start with, and up to a point, they will doubtless remain 'attached to property'. But up to what point? All that we know is how they reacted when Stalinism sought forcibly to drive them into a *concentration camp* instead of into a socialist society. A society that will grant them a great deal of autonomy in their own affairs, that will peacefully and rationally seek to integrate them into the overall pattern of social life, that will furnish them with a living example of democratic self-management, and that will give them positive help if they want to proceed toward socialization will certainly enjoy a different prestige in their eyes (and will have a different kind of influence on their development) than did an exploiting and totalitarian bureaucracy that, by every one of its acts, reinforced their 'attachment to property' and drove them centuries backward.

The councils: universal form of organization for social activities

The basic units of social organization, as we have envisaged them so far, will not merely manage *production*. They will, at the same time and primarily, be organs for popular self-management *in all its aspects*. On the one hand, they will be organs of local self-administration and, on the other, they will be the *only* bases of the central power, which will exist only as a federation or regrouping of all the councils.

To say that a workers' council will be an organ of popular self-administration (and not just an organ of workers' management of production) is to recognize that a factory or office is not just a productive unit, but is also a social cell, and that it will become the primary *locus* of individual 'socialization'. Although this varies from country to country and from workplace to workplace, myriad activities other than just earning a living take place around it (canteens, cooperatives, vacation retreats, sports clubs, libraries, rest homes, collective outings, dances) – activities that allow the most important human ties (both private and 'public') to become established. To the extent that the average person is today active in 'public' affairs, it is more likely to be through some trade-union or political activity related to work than in a capacity as an abstract 'citizen', putting a ballot into a box once every few years. Under socialism, the transformation of the relations of production and of the very nature of work will enormously reinforce, for each worker, the positive significance of the working collective to which he belongs.

Workers' councils and rural communes will absorb all of today's 'municipal' functions. They also will take over many others, which the monstrous centralization of the modern capitalist State has removed from the hands of local groups with the sole aim of consolidating the control of the ruling class and of its central bureaucracy over the whole population. Local councils, for instance, will take over such city and county services and departments as the direct application of 'policing' powers (by detachments of armed workers assigned in rotation), the administration of local justice, and the local control of primary education.

The two forms of regroupment – productive and geographical – seldom coincide today. Peoples' homes are at variable distances from where they work. Where the scatter is small, as in a number of industrial towns or industrial suburbs (or in many rural communes), the management of production and local self-administration will be undertaken by the same general assemblies and by the same councils. Where home and workplace do not overlap, geographically based *local* councils (soviets) will have to be instituted, directly representing both the inhabitants of a given area and the enterprises in the area. Initially, such geographically based local councils will be necessary in many places. One might envisage them as 'collateral' institutions in charge of local affairs. They will collaborate at the local and national levels with the councils of producers, which alone represent the seat of power.

(Although the Russian word 'soviet' means 'council', one should not confuse the workers' councils we have been describing in this text with even the earliest Russian soviets. The workers' councils are based on one's place of work. They can play both a political role and a role in the industrial management of production. In its essence, a workers' council is a universal organ. The 1905 Petrograd Soviet (Council) of Workers' Deputies, although the product of a general strike and although exclusively proletarian in composition, remained a purely political organ. The soviets of 1917 were as a rule geographically based. They too were purely political institutions, in which all social layers opposed to the old regime formed a united front [see Trotsky's *1905* and his *History of the Russian Revolution*]. Their role corresponded to the 'backwardness' of the Russian economy and of Russian society at the time as well as to the 'bourgeois-democratic' aspects of the 1917 revolution. In this sense, they belonged to the past. The normal form of working-class representation in the present age undoubtedly is the workers' council.)

The problems created by the gaps between these two types of councils could soon be overcome if one were to organize changes in workers' living places. This is but a small aspect of an important problem that will hang over the general orientation of socialist society for decades to come. Underlying these questions are all the economic, social, and human problems of urban planning in the deepest sense of the term and, ultimately, the very problem of the division between town and country. It is not for us here to venture into these fields. All we can say is that, from the very start, a socialist society will have to tackle these problems as *total* problems, for they have an effect on every aspect of peoples' lives and on society's own economic, political, and cultural purpose.

What we have said about local self-administration also applies to *regional* self-administration. Regional federations of workers' councils or rural communes will be in charge of coordinating these bodies at a regional level and of organizing activities best tackled at such a level.

The industrial organization of the 'State'

We have seen that a large number of functions of the modern State (and not merely 'territorial' functions) will be taken over by local or regional organs of popular self-administration. But what about the truly 'central' functions, those whose content affects indivisibly the totality of the population?

In class societies, and in particular under classical nineteenth-century 'liberal' capitalism, the ultimate function of the State was to guarantee the maintenance of existing social relations through the exercise of a legal monopoly on violence. In this sense Lenin was right, against the reformists of his day, to adopt Engels's description of the State as nothing more than 'special bodies of armed men, and prisons'.[19] In the course of a socialist revolution, there was no doubt as to the fate of this State: its apparatus was to be smashed, the 'special detachments of armed men' dissolved and replaced by the arming of the people, and the permanent bureaucracy abolished and replaced by elected and revocable officials.

Under today's crisis-ridden capitalism, increasing economic concentration and the increasing concentration of all aspects of social life (with the corresponding need for the ruling class to submit everything to its control

and supervision) have led since Lenin's time to an enormous growth of the
State apparatus, its functions, and its bureaucracy. The State is no longer
just a coercive apparatus that has elevated itself 'above' society. It is the hub
of a whole series of mechanisms whereby society functions *from day to day*.
At the limit, the present-day State underlies *all* social activity, as in the fully
developed bureaucratic-capitalist regimes of Russia and the satellite countries. Even in the West, the State goes beyond the mere exercise of 'power'
in the narrow sense and takes on an ever-increasing role in the *management*
and *control* not only of the economy but of a host of social activities. Parallel
with all this, the State takes on a large number of functions that in themselves could perfectly well be carried out by other bodies, but which either
have become useful instruments of control or imply the mobilization of
considerable resources that the State alone possesses.

In many people's minds the myth of the 'State' as the 'incarnation of the
Absolute Idea' (which Engels mocked a century ago) has been replaced by
another myth, the myth of the State as the inevitable incarnation of centralization and of the 'technical rationalization' required by modern social life.
This has had two main effects. It has led some people to consider outmoded,
utopian, or inapplicable the conclusions Marx, Engels, and Lenin have
drawn from their theoretical analysis of the State and from the experience
of the revolutionary events of 1848, 1871, or 1905. It has led others to
swallow the reality of the modern Russian State, which simultaneously epitomizes (not in what it hides – police terror and the concentration camps –
but in what it officially proclaims, in its Constitution) the complete and total
negation of previous Marxist conceptions of what the socialist 'State' might
be like *and* exhibits a monstrous increase in those very features of capitalist
society that were criticized by Marx or Lenin (the total separation of rulers
and ruled, permanent officialdom, greater privileges for the few than were
ever allowed to the elite in any bourgeois State, etc.).

But this very evolution of the modern State contains the seed of a solution. The modern State has become a gigantic enterprise – by far the most
important enterprise in modern society. It can exercise its *managerial* functions only to the extent that it has created a whole network of organs of
execution, within which work has become collective, subject to a division
of labour, and specialized. What has happened here is the same as what has
happened to the management of production in particular enterprises. But it
has happened on a much vaster scale. In their overwhelming majority,
today's governmental departments carry out only specific and limited tasks.
They are 'enterprises', specializing in certain types of work. Some are
socially necessary. Others are purely parasitic or are necessary only in order
to maintain the class structure of society. The 'powers that be' have no more
intrinsic connection with the work of 'their' departments than they have, say,

with the production of automobiles. The notion of 'power' or 'administrative rights' that remains appended to what are in fact a series of 'public services' is a juridical legacy, without real content. Its only purpose is to shield from criticism the arbitrary and irresponsible behaviour of those at the top of various bureaucratic pyramids.[20]

Given these conditions, the solution does not lie in the 'election and revocability of all civil servants'. This is neither necessary (these officials exercise no real power) nor possible (they are specialized workers, whom one could no more 'elect' than one would elect electricians or doctors). The solution will lie in the *industrial organization*, pure and simple, of most of today's governmental departments. In many cases this would only be giving formal recognition to an existing state of affairs. Concretely, such industrial organization would mean:

1   The explicit transformation of these 'administrative' departments into *enterprises* having the same status as any other enterprise. In many of these new enterprises the mechanization and automation of work could be systematically developed to a considerable degree.

2   The *management* of these enterprises will be through workers' councils, representing those who work there. These office workers, like all others, will determine autonomously the organization of their own work. (The formation of workers' councils of State employees was one of the demands of the Hungarian workers' councils.)

3   The function of these enterprises will be *confined* to the execution of the tasks assigned to them by the representative institutions of society.

We have seen that the 'plan factory' will be organized in this way. The same will apply to whatever remains or could be used of any current structures relating to *the economy* (foreign trade, agriculture, finance, industry, etc.). Current State functions that are already *industrialized* (public works, public transport, communications, public health, and social security) will be similarly organized. And the same goes for *education*.

The central power: the assembly and the governmental council

What remains of the functions of a modern State will be discussed under three headings:

1   the material basis of authority and coercion, 'the specialized bands of armed men and prisons' (in other words, the army and the law);

2   foreign and domestic 'politics', in the narrow sense (in other words, the problems that might arise for a working-class power if it was confronted with internal opposition or with the persistence of hostile exploiting regimes in other countries);

3   real politics: the overall vision, coordination, and general purpose and direction of social life.

Concerning *the army*, it is obvious that 'the specialized bands of armed men' will be dissolved and then replaced by the armed populace. Workers in factories, offices, and rural communes will constitute the units of a nonpermanent, territorially based militia, each council being in charge of policing its own area. Regional regroupings will enable local units to become integrated and will allow the rational use of heavier armaments. The extent to which 'strategic' types of weapons (which can be used only on a centralized basis) will remain necessary cannot be decided *a priori*. If it proved necessary, each council would probably contribute a contingent to the formation of certain central units, which would be under the control of the central assembly of councils.

Neither the means nor the overall conception of war can be copied from those of an imperialist country. What we have said about capitalist technology is valid for military technique: there is no neutral military technique, there is no 'A-bomb for socialism'. Philippe Guillaume has clearly shown (in 'La Guerre et notre époque', *Socialisme ou Barbarie*, 3 and 5–6 [July 1949 and March 1950]) that a proletarian revolution of necessity will have to draw up its own strategy and methods suitable to its social and human objectives. The need for so-called strategic weapons does not go without saying for a revolutionary power.

As for the *administration of justice*, it will be in the hands of rank-and-file bodies. Each council will act as a 'lower court' in relation to 'offences' committed in its jurisdiction. Individual rights will be guaranteed by procedural rules established by the central assembly, and could also include the right of appeal to the regional councils or to the central assembly itself. There would be no question of a 'penal code' or of prisons, the very notion of 'punishment' being absurd from a socialist point of view. Judgements could aim only at re-educating the social delinquent and at reintegrating him into his social surroundings. Deprivation of freedom has a meaning only if it is judged that a particular individual constitutes a permanent threat to others (and in that case what is needed is not a penitentiary but 'pedagogical' and 'medical' – 'psychiatric' – institutions).

Political problems – in the narrow as well as in the broader sense – concern the whole population, and therefore only the population as a whole is in a position to solve them. But people can solve them only if they are organized to this end. (At the present time, everything is devised so as to prevent people from dealing with such problems. People are conned into believing that the sole possessors of solutions to political problems are the politicians, those specialists of the universal, whose most universal attribute is precisely their ignorance of any particular reality.)

This organization will be made up first of all of the workers' councils and the general assemblies of each particular enterprise, the vital collective setting within which there can be a confrontation of views and an elaboration of informed political opinions. They will be the ultimate sovereign authorities for all political decisions. But there will also be a central institution, directly emanating from these grass-roots organizations, namely, the central assembly of councils. The existence of such a body is necessary, not only because some problems require an immediate decision (even if such a decision may subsequently be reversed by the population), but more particularly because preliminary checking, clarification, and elaboration of the facts are almost always necessary before any meaningful decision can be made. To ask the people as a whole to voice their opinions without such preparation would often be a mystification and a negation of democracy (because it would eliminate the possibility of people deciding in full knowledge of the relevant facts). There must be a framework for discussing problems and for submitting them to popular decision – or even for suggesting that they should be discussed. These are not just 'technical' functions. They are *deeply political*, and the body that would initiate them would be a *central power* – although very different in its structure and role from any contemporary central body – that socialist society could not do without.

The real problem is not whether such a body should exist. It is how to organize it in such a manner that it no longer incarnates the alienation of political power in society and the vesting of authority in the hands of specialized institutions, separate from the population as a whole. The problem is to make any central body into the expression and instrument of the central power. We think this is perfectly possible under modern conditions.

The central assembly of councils will be composed of delegates elected directly by the general assemblies of the grass-roots organs (or by larger geographical or federated groups of these organs, enterprises, rural communes, etc.). These people will be revocable at all times by the bodies that elected them. *They will remain at work*, as will delegates to the local workers' councils. Delegates to the central assembly will meet in plenary session as often as necessary. In meeting twice a week, or during one week each month, they will almost certainly get through more work than any present legislature (which gets through hardly any). At frequent intervals (perhaps once a month) they will have to give an account of their mandate to those who had elected them. (In a country like France, such an assembly could consist of 1,000 or 2,000 delegates [one delegate per 20,000 or 10,000 workers]. A compromise would have to be reached between two requirements: as a *working* body, the central assembly of councils should not be too large, but on the other hand it must afford the most direct and most broadly based representation of the people, areas, and organs of which it is the outcome.)

Those elected to the central assembly will elect from within their own ranks – or will appoint to act in rotation – a central governmental council, composed perhaps of a few dozen members. The tasks of this body will be restricted to preparing the work of the central assembly of councils, acting in its stead when it is not in session, and convening the assembly for emergency sessions if necessary.

If this governmental council exceeded its jurisdiction and made a decision that could or should have been submitted to the central assembly, or if it made any unacceptable decisions, these could immediately be rescinded by the next meeting of the central assembly, which could also take any other necessary measures, up to and including the 'dissolution' of its own council. Likewise, if the central assembly made any decision that exceeded its jurisdiction, or that went against the will of the local workers' councils or the local general assemblies, it will be up to those bodies to take any steps necessary, beginning with the revocation of their delegates to the central assembly. Neither the central council nor the central assembly could persevere in unacceptable practices (they have no power of their own, they are revocable, and in the last analysis, the population is armed). But if the central assembly allowed its council to exceed its rights – or if members of local assemblies allowed their delegates to the central assembly to exceed their authority – nothing could be done. The population *can* exercise political power only if it *wants* to. The organization proposed merely ensures that the population *could* exercise such power, if it wanted to.

But this very will to take affairs into one's own hands is not some occult force, appearing and disappearing in some mysterious way. Political alienation in capitalist society does not stem just from the fact that existing institutions, by their very structure, make it 'technically' impossible for the political will of the people to express or exercise itself. Contemporary political alienation stems from the destruction of this will *at its roots*, the thwarting of its very growth, and, finally, the suppression of all interest in public affairs. There is nothing more sinister than the utterances of sundry liberals, bemoaning the 'political apathy of the people', an apathy that the political and social system they subscribe to would recreate daily, if it did not already exist. This suppression of political will in modern societies stems as much from the *content* of modern 'politics' as from the *means* available for political expression. It is based on the *unbridgeable gulf* that today separates 'politics' from people's real lives. The content of modern politics is the 'better' organization of exploiting society. The better to exploit society itself. Its methods of expression are necessarily mystifying: they resort either to direct lies or to meaningless abstractions. The world in which all this takes place is a world of 'specialists', underhand deals, and a spurious 'technicism'.

All this will be radically changed in a socialist society. Exploitation having been eliminated, the content of politics will be the better organization of our common life. An immediate result will be a different attitude on the part of ordinary people toward public affairs. Political problems will be everyone's problems, whether they relate to where one works or deal with national issues. People will begin to feel that their concerns have a real impact, and perceptible results should soon be obvious to everyone. The method of expression of the new politics will be geared toward making real problems accessible to everyone. The gulf separating 'political affairs' from people's everyday lives will be completely eliminated.

All this warrants some comment. Modern sociologists often claim that the content of modern politics and its modes of expression are inevitable. They believe that the separation of politics from life is due to irreversible technical changes that make any real democracy impossible.[21] It is alleged that the content of politics – namely, the direction and management of society – has become highly complex, embracing an extraordinary mass of data and problems, each of which can be mastered only through advanced specialization. All this allegedly being so, it is proclaimed as self-evident that these problems could never be put to the public in any intelligible way – or only by simplifying them to a degree that would distort them altogether. Why be surprised then that ordinary people take no more interest in politics than they do in differential calculus?

If these 'arguments' – presented as the very latest in political sociology but in fact as old as the world (Plato discusses them at length, and his *Protagoras* is in part devoted to them) – prove anything, it is not that democracy is a utopian illusion but that the *very management of society*, by whatever means, has become impossible. The politician, according to these premises, would have to be the Incarnation of Absolute and Total Knowledge. No technical specialization, however advanced, entitles its possessor to master areas other than his own. An assembly of technicians, each the highest authority in his particular field, would have no competence (as an assembly of technicians) to solve anything. Only one individual could comment on any specific point, and no one would be in a position to comment on any general problem.

Indeed, modern society is not managed by technicians as such (and never could be). Those who manage it do not incarnate Absolute Knowledge – but, rather, generalized incompetence. In fact, modern society is hardly managed at all – it merely drifts. Just like the top management of the bureaucratic apparatus at the head of some big factory, a modern political 'leadership' only renders verdicts – and thoroughly arbitrary ones at that. It decides between the opinions of the various technical departments that are designed to 'assist' it, but over which it has very little control. In this, our rulers feel the repercussions in their own social system and experience the same political alienation they impose on the rest of society. The chaos of their own social organization and the narrow development of each branch for its own exclusive ends render impossible a rational exercise of their own power – even in their own terms.[22]

We discuss this sophism because it puts us on the road to an important truth. In the case of politics as in the case of production, people tend to blame modern technique and modern 'technicization' in general instead of seeing that the problems stem from a *specifically capitalist technology*. In politics as in production, capitalism does not only mean the use of technically 'neutral' means for capitalist ends. It also means the creation and development of *specific* techniques, aimed at ensuring the exploitation of the producers – or the oppression, mystification, and political alienation and manipulation of citizens in general. At the level of production, socialism will mean the conscious transformation of technology. Technique will be put in the service of the people. On the political level, socialism will imply a similar transformation: *technique will be put in the service of democracy*.

Political technique is based essentially on the techniques of information and of communication. We are here using the term 'technique' in the widest sense (the *material means* of information and communication comprise only a part of the corresponding techniques). To place the *technique of information* at the service of democracy does not only mean to put material means of expression in the hands of the people (essential as this may be). Nor does it mean the dissemination of *all* information, or of *any* information whatsoever. It means first and foremost to put at the disposal of mankind the elements necessary to enable people to decide in full knowledge of the relevant facts. This means that each person will receive a faithful translation of essential data relating to the problems that will have to be decided upon. This information will be expressed in the form of a finite number of succinctly stated and meaningful details. With respect to the plan factory, we have given a specific example of how information could be used so as vastly to increase people's areas of freedom. In this case, genuine information would not end up burying everyone under whole libraries of textbooks on economics, technology, and statistics: the information that would result from this would be strictly nil. The information provided by the plan factory would be *compact, significant, sufficient*, and *true*. Everyone will know what he will have to contribute and the level of consumption he will enjoy if this or that variant of the plan is adopted. This is how technique (in this instance, economic analysis, statistics, and computers) can be put in the service of democracy in a key area. There is no 'cybernetic politics' that could tell us how to make a decision; only people can determine the elements required to make decisions.

The same applies to the *technique of communication*. It is claimed that the very size of modern societies precludes the exercise of any genuine democracy. Distances and numbers allegedly render direct democracy impossible. The only feasible democracy, it is claimed, is representative democracy, which 'inevitably' contains a kernel of political alienation, namely, the separation of representatives from those they represent.

In fact, there are several ways of envisaging and achieving representative democracy. A legislature is one form. Councils are another, and it is difficult to see how political alienation could arise in a council system operating according to its own rules. If modern techniques of communication were put in the service of democracy, the areas where representative democracy would remain necessary would narrow considerably. Material distances are smaller in the modern world than they were in Attica in the fifth century BCE. At that time, the voice range of the orator – and hence the number of people he could reach – was limited by the functional capacity of his vocal cords. Today it is unlimited.[23] In the realm of communicating ideas, distances have not only narrowed – they have disappeared. If society felt it were necessary, tomorrow it could establish a general assembly of the whole population in any modern country. Closed-circuit radio and television hookups could easily link a vast number of general assemblies, in various factories, offices, or rural communes. Similar, but more limited, hookups could be established in a vast number of cases. In any case, the sessions of the central assembly or of its council could easily be televised. This, combined with the revocability of all delegates, would readily ensure that any central institution remained under the permanent control of the population. It would profoundly alter the very notion of 'representation'. (It would certainly be amusing to televise today's parliamentary sessions; this would be an excellent way of lowering sales of TV sets.)

It might be claimed that the problem of numbers remains and that people would never be able to express themselves in a reasonable amount of time. This is not a valid argument. There would rarely be an assembly of over twenty people where everyone would want to speak, for the very good reason that when there is something to be decided upon there is not an infinite number of options or an infinite number of arguments. In unhampered rank-and-file workers' gatherings (convened, for instance, to decide on a strike) there have never been 'too many' speeches. The two or three fundamental opinions having been voiced, and various arguments having been exchanged, a decision is soon reached.

The length of speeches, moreover, often varies inversely with the weight of their content. Russian leaders sometimes talk on for four hours at Party Congresses without saying anything. The speech of the Ephor that persuaded the Spartans to launch the Peloponnesian War occupies twenty-one lines of Thucydides (1.86). For an account of the laconicism of revolutionary assemblies, see Trotsky's accounts of the Petrograd soviet of 1905[24] – or accounts of the meetings of factory representatives in Budapest in 1956 (*S. ou B.*, 21 [March 1957], pp. 91–2).

People bemoan the fact that the size of the modern 'city' compared with those of yesterday (tens of millions rather than tens of thousands) renders direct democracy impossible. They are doubly blind. They do not see, first, that modern society has recreated the very milieu (the workplace) where such democracy could be reinstaurated. Nor do they see that modern society has created and will continue to create for an indefinite period of time the technical means for a genuine democracy on a massive scale. They envisage the only solution to the problems of the supersonic age in the horse-and-buggy terms of parliamentary political machinery. And they then conclude that democracy has become 'impossible'. They claim to have made a 'new' analysis – and they have ignored what is *really* new in our epoch: the material possibilities of at last freely transforming the world through technique, and through the proletariat, which is its living vehicle.

The 'State', 'parties', and 'politics'

What will the 'State', 'politics', and 'parties' consist of in such a society? We have seen that the remnants of a 'State' will still exist in those instances where there will not immediately be a pure and simple 'administration of things', where there will still be the possibility of coercion and constraints against individuals or groups, where the majority will still prevail over the minority, and where, therefore, limitations on individual freedom persist. There will no longer be a 'State' to the extent that the bodies exercising power will be none other than the productive units or local organizations of the whole population, that the institutions organizing social life will be but one aspect of that life itself, and that what remained of central bodies will be under the direct and permanent control of the grass-roots organizations. This will be the starting point. Social development cannot but bring about a rapid reduction ('withering away') of the 'statist' features of social organization: the reasons for exercising constraints gradually will disappear, and the field of individual freedom will enlarge. (Needless to say, we are not talking here about formal 'democratic freedoms', which a socialist society will immediately and vastly expand, but about substantive freedoms: not only the right to live but the right to do what one wants with one's life.)

Freed from all the rubbish and mystifications currently surrounding it, politics in such a society will be nothing but the collective search for, debate about, and adoption of solutions to the general problems concerning the future of society – whether these be economic or educational, whether they deal with the rest of the world or with domestic relations between various social strata or classes. All these decisions concern the *whole* of the population and they will be theirs to make.

It is probable, even certain, that there will be different views about such problems. Each approach will seek to be as coherent and systematic as possible. People will subscribe to particular viewpoints, though they will be dispersed geographically or occupationally. These people will come together to defend their views – in other words, they will form political groups. On the national level, the councils will have to decide whether they consider the general orientation of this or that party compatible with the makeup of the new society, and therefore whether such parties will be allowed to function on a legal basis.

There would be no point in pretending that there would not be a contradiction between the existence of such groups and the role of the councils. The two could not develop simultaneously. If the councils fulfil their function, they will provide the principal and vital setting not only for political *confrontations* but also for the *formation* of political opinions. Political groups, on the other hand, are exclusive environments for the schooling of their members, as well as being exclusive poles for their loyalty. The parallel existence of both councils and political groups will imply that a part of real political life will be taking place outside the councils. People will then tend to act in the councils according to decisions already made elsewhere. Should this tendency predominate, it would bring about the rapid atrophy and finally the disappearance of the councils. Conversely, real socialist development would be characterized by the progressive atrophy of established political groups.

This contradiction could not be abolished by a stroke of the pen or by any 'statutory' decree. The persistence of political groups would reflect the continuation of characteristics inherited from capitalist society, in particular the persistence of divergent interests (and their corresponding ideologies) even after these capitalistic traits have disappeared. People will not form parties for or against quantum theory, or over simple differences of opinion about some particular point. The flowering or final atrophy of political groups will depend on the ability of workers' power to unite society.

The basis of parties is not a difference of opinion as such but, rather, differences on fundamentals and the more or less systematic unity of each 'set of views'. In other words, parties express a set orientation corresponding to a more or less clear ideology, in its turn flowing from the existence of social positions leading to conflicting aspirations. As long as such positions exist and lead to a political 'projection' of expectations, one cannot abolish political groups – but as they begin to disappear it is unlikely that groups will be formed about 'divergences' of opinion in general.

If political organizations expressing the survival of different interests and ideologies persist, a working-class socialist party, a partisan defender of proletarian socialist organization will exist also. It will be open to all those who favour total power for the councils and will differ from all others, both in its programme *and in its practice*, precisely on this point: its fundamental activity will be directed toward the concentration of power in the councils and to their becoming the *only* centres of political life. This implies that it will struggle against power being held by any particular party, whichever one it may be.

It is obvious that the democratic power structure of a socialist society excludes the possibility of a Party 'holding power'. The very words would be meaningless within the framework we have described. In so far as major trends of opinion might arise or diverge on important issues, the holders of majority viewpoints might be elected as delegates to the councils, assemblies, communes, etc., more often than others. (This does not necessarily follow, however, for delegates will be elected mainly on the basis of overall confidence, and not always according to their opinion on this or that issue.) Parties will not be organizations seeking power, and the central assembly of councils will not be a 'workers' parliament'; people will not be elected to it as members of a party. The same goes for any government chosen by this assembly.[25]

The role of a working-class socialist party will be quite important initially. It will have to defend these conceptions systematically and coherently. It will have to conduct an extensive struggle to unmask and denounce bureaucratic tendencies, not in general, but where they concretely show themselves; also, and perhaps above all, initially it will be the only group capable of showing the ways and means whereby technique and technicians could be organized and directed so as to allow working-class democracy both to stabilize itself and to blossom forth. The work of the party could, for instance, hasten considerably the setting-up of the democratic planning mechanisms we analysed earlier. The party is in fact the *only* form in which a coalescence of workers and intellectuals can now take place in our society of exploitation. And this fusion could also allow the working-class power to make rapid use of techniques that would advance its goals. But if, some years after the revolution, the party continued to grow, it would be the surest sign that it was dead – as a working-class socialist party. [. . .]

The programme we have outlined is a *programme for the present, capable of being realized in any reasonably industrial country*. It describes the steps – or the spirit guiding the steps – that the councils will have to take and the general orientation they will have to adopt, starting from the very first weeks of their power, whether this power has spread to several countries or is confined to one. Perhaps, if we were talking about Albania, there would be little we could do. But if tomorrow in France, or even in Poland (as yesterday in Hungary), workers' councils emerged without having to face a foreign military invasion, they could only:

- federate into a central assembly and declare themselves the only power in the land;

- proceed to arm the proletariat and order the dissolution of the police and of the standing army;

- proclaim the expropriation of the capitalists, the dismissal of all managers, and the takeover of the management of all factories by the workers, themselves organized into workers' councils;

- proclaim the abolition of work norms and instaurate full equality of wages and salaries;

- encourage other categories of wage earners to form councils and to take into their own hands the management of their respective enterprises;

- ask workers in governmental departments, in particular, to form councils and proclaim the transformation of these administrative bodies into enterprises managed by those who work in them;

- encourage the peasants and other self-employed sections of the population to group themselves into councils and to send their representatives to a central assembly;

- proceed to organize a 'plan factory' and promptly submit a provisional economic plan for discussion by the local councils;

- call on the workers of other countries and explain to them the content and meaning of these measures.

All this would be immediately necessary. And it would contain all that is essential to the process of building socialism.

Notes

1 This following part will be published in the next issue of *S. ou B.* [T/E: see *CS III*].
2 The expression is to be found in part 3 of Engels's *Anti-Dühring*. [T/E: The French phrase is 'en connaissance de cause'. Castoriadis refers to a passage in section 2 of this third part, pp. 309–10, of the edition we are using (trans. Emile Burns, ed. C. P. Dutt [New York: International Publishers, 1939]). This edition translates the phrase in question merely as 'with complete understanding'.]
3 A few years ago a certain 'philosopher' could seriously ask how one could even discuss Stalin's decisions, since one did not know the real facts upon which he alone could base them. (J.-P. Sartre, 'Les Communistes et la paix', in *Les Temps Modernes*, 81, 84–5, and 101 [July and October–November 1952, April 1954]; trans. Martha H. Fletcher, *The Communists and the Peace* [New York: George Braziller, 1968].)
4 Lenin took the opportunity, in *State and Revolution*, to defend the idea of direct democracy against the reformists of his day who contemptuously called it 'primitive democracy'.
5 On this feature of working life, see Paul Romano, 'L'Ouvrier américain', in *S. ou B.*, 5–6 (March 1950), pp. 129–32 [T/E: 'Life in the Factory', in *The American Worker* (1947; reprinted, Detroit: Bewick Editions, 1972), pp. 37–39], and R. Berthier, 'Une Expérience d'organisation ouvrière', in *S. ou B.*, 20 (December 1956), pp. 29–31.
6 Daniel Mothé's text, 'L'Usine et la gestion ouvrière', also in this issue [*S. ou B.*, 22 (July 1957), pp. 75ff] already is one *de facto* response – coming from the factory itself – to the concrete problem of shop-floor workers' management and that of how to organize work. In referring to this text, we are considering here only the problems of the factory *as a whole*.
7 In J. A. C. Brown's *The Social Psychology of Industry* (London: Penguin, 1954), there is a

striking contrast between the devastating analysis the author makes of present capitalist production and the only 'conclusions' he can draw, which are pious exhortations to management that it should 'do better', 'democratize itself', etc. Let it not be said, however, that an 'industrial sociologist' takes no position, that he merely describes facts and does not suggest norms. Advising the managerial apparatus to 'do better' is itself a taking of a position, one that has been shown here to be completely utopian.

8 See the Twentieth Congress texts analysed by Claude Lefort in 'Le Totalitarisme sans Staline', *S. ou B.*, 19 (July 1956), in particular pp. 59–62 [now in *Éléments d'une critique de la bureaucratie*, 2nd edn (Paris: Gallimard), pp. 219–23; T/E: these sections were omitted from the translation, 'Totalitarianism Without Stalin', *The Political Forms of Modern Society. Bureaucracy, Democracy, Totalitarianism*, John B. Thompson, ed. (Oxford, England: Polity, 1986)].

9 See Mothé, 'L'Usine et la gestion ouvrière'.

10 On the extreme overstaffing of 'nonproductive' departments in today's factories, see G. Vivier, 'La Vie en usine', *S. ou B.*, 12 (August 1953), pp. 39–41. Vivier estimates that in the business he describes, '*without a rational reorganization of these departments, 30% of the employees are already redundant*' (emphasis in the original).

11 See Mothé, 'L'Usine et la gestion ouvrière'.

12 Ibid.

13 Bureaucratic 'planning' as carried out in Russia and the Eastern European countries proves nothing, one way or the other. It is just as irrational and just as anarchic and wasteful as the capitalist 'market' – though in different ways. The waste is both 'external' (the wrong decisions being made) and 'internal' (brought about by the resistance of the workers) to the production process. For further details, see *PRAB* (1956).

14 The field is in constant expansion. The starting points remain, however, Leontief's *The Structure of American Economy, 1919–1939: An Empirical Application of Equilibrium Analysis* (1951; reprinted, Armonk, NY: Sharpe, 1976), and the essays by Leontief et al., *Studies in the Structure of the American Economy: Theoretical and Empirical Explorations in Input–Output Analysis* (1953; reprinted, Armonk, NY: Sharpe, 1976).

15 Tjalling Koopmans, *Activity Analysis of Production and Allocation* (1951; reprinted, New Haven, Conn.: Yale University Press, 1972).

16 The 1955 Nantes strikes took place around an antihierarchical demand for a uniform increase for everyone. The Hungarian workers' councils demanded the abolition of norms and severe limitations on hierarchy. What inadvertently is said in official Russian proclamations indicates that a permanent struggle against hierarchy is taking place in the factories of that country. See *PRAB*.

17 For a detailed discussion of the problem of hierarchy, see *RPR*, section 5, and *DC I*, in *S. ou B.*, 13 (January 1954), pp. 67–9.

18 On the structure of a large insurance company undergoing rapid 'industrialization', both technically as well as socially and politically, see the articles by Henri Collet ('La Grève aux A.G.-Vie', in *S. ou B.*, 7 [August 1951], pp. 103–10) and R. Berthier ('Une Expérience d'organisation ouvrière: Le Conseil du personnel des A.G.-Vie', in *S. ou B.*, 20 [December 1957], pp. 1–64). On the same process taking place within the United States, where 'tertiary' sectors are being merged, see C. Wright Mills, *White Collar* (New York: Oxford University Press, 1951), esp. pp. 192–8. In order to take stock of the significance of the changes that are expected to occur in these areas, we must remember that the industrialization of office and 'service' work (and, ultimately, the industrialization of 'intellectual' work) is still in its infancy. Cf. N. Wiener, *Cybernetics* (New York: Wiley, 1948), pp. 37–8. In an entirely different sector, that of theatre and film, it is interesting to compare the ideas expounded in this article with the multiple (economic, political, work management) role the Revolutionary Workers' Committee of this sector played during the Hungarian

Revolution. See 'Les Artistes du théâtre et du cinéma pendant la révolution hongroise', in *S. ou B.*, 20 (December 1957), pp. 96–104.

19 See section 2 of chapter 1 of *State and Revolution*.

20 See chapter 4 ('Technique and the State') of Jacques Ellul's *The Technological Society*, trans. J. Wilkinson, intro. Robert K. Merton (New York: Knopf, 1964). In spite of his fundamentally incorrect outlook, Ellul has the merit of analysing some of these key aspects of the reality of the modern State, aspects that are blithely ignored by most sociologists and political writers – whether 'Marxist' or not.

21 This is Ellul's point of view, as expressed in *The Technological Society*. Ellul concludes that 'it is futile to try to put a halt to this process or to grasp hold of it and guide it'. For him, technique is only the self-developing process of enslavement taking place independently of any social context. [T/E: I have translated Castoriadis's quotation of Ellul.]

22 See C. Wright Mills (*White Collar*, pp. 347–8, and *The Power Elite* [New York: Oxford University Press, 1956], pp. 134ff, 145ff, etc.) for an illustration of the total lack of *any* relationship between 'technical' capacities of any kind, on the one hand, and current industrial management or political leadership groups, on the other.

23 'Plato defined the limits of the size of the city as the number of people who could hear the voice of a single orator: today those limits do not define a city but a civilization. Wherever neotechnic instruments exist and a common language is used there are now the elements of almost as close a political unity as that which once was possible in the tiniest cities of Attica. The possibilities for good and evil here are immense' (Lewis Mumford, *Technics and Civilization* [New York: Harcourt, Brace, 1934], p. 241).

24 *1905*, trans. Anya Bostock (New York: Vintage, 1971), p. 109.

25 The events in Poland have furnished yet another confirmation of the idea that the Party cannot be a governmental organ (see *PRAB*, in *PSW 2*, pp. 84–5, and *VPB* [1957; now in *SB 2*, pp. 327–9 and 348–52; reprinted in *SB**, pp. 403–4 and 441–13]).

4

Recommencing the Revolution (1964)[*]

I. The End of Classical Marxism

1   Three massive facts today confront revolutionaries who still wish to claim they are acting in such a way that they understand what they are doing, that is, in full knowledge of the relevant facts:

- The way capitalism functions has been fundamentally altered in relation to the reality of the pre-1939 era. It has altered even more in relation to the analysis of it Marxism had provided.

- As an organized class movement explicitly and permanently contesting capitalist domination, the workers' movement has disappeared.

- Colonial or semicolonial domination by advanced countries over backward countries has been abolished without this abolition being accompanied anywhere by a revolutionary mutation [*transcroissance*] within the movement of the masses, nor have the foundations of capitalism in the ruling countries been shaken by this process.

2   For those who refuse to mystify themselves, it is clear that, in practice, the establishment of these facts means the ruination of classical Marxism as a *system* of thought and action as it was formulated, developed, and maintained between 1847 and 1939. For, these findings signify that Marx's analysis of capitalism in his masterwork (the analysis of the economy), Lenin's analysis of imperialism, and Marx–Trotsky's conception of the permanent revolution as applied to backward countries have been refuted or outstripped, and that virtually all traditional forms of organization and action in the workers' movement (save for those of revolutionary

* 'Recommencer la révolution' was circulated within the group in March 1963 and then published in *S. ou B.*, 35 (January 1964). Reprinted in *EMO 2*, pp. 307–65. [T/E: Translation by Maurice Brinton, as *Redefining Revolution*, Solidarity Pamphlet, 44 (no date), 24 pp., with a 'Solidarity Introduction'. The present version has been edited with a view toward standardizing terminology and providing a text more faithful to the original (Brinton's fine original translation was in some respects an adaptation). As with other Solidarity translations used, footnotes added by the original translator have been eliminated unless otherwise indicated. *RR* previously appeared in *PSW 3*, pp. 27–55; we have not included here the Postface (*PSW 3*, pp. 80–8).]

periods) are irreversibly bankrupt. They signify the ruination of classical Marxism as a *concrete system of thought* having some grasp on reality. Apart from a few abstract ideas, nothing that is essential in *Capital* is to be found in the reality of today. Conversely, what is essential in reality today (the changes in and the crisis of the nature of work, the scission and opposition between the formal organization and the real organization of production and between the formal and the real functioning of institutions, the phenomenon of bureaucratization, the consumer society, working-class apathy, the nature of Eastern-bloc countries, the changes in backward countries and their relations with the advanced countries, the crisis of all aspects of life and the increasing importance of phenomena previously considered peripheral, people's attempts to find a way out of this crisis) can be understood only in the light of different analyses. The best in Marx's work can serve as a source of inspiration for these analyses, but set in front of these analyses is instead a vulgar and bastardized Marxism, the only kind practised today by his self-proclaimed 'defenders' of every ilk, which acts as a screen blocking one's view. The findings also signify the ruination of classical Marxism (and of Leninism–Trotskyism–Bordigism, etc.) as a *programme of action* in which what was to be done by revolutionaries at any given moment was coherently linked (at least on the level of intentions) with the real actions of the working class and with an overall theoretical viewpoint. When, for instance, a Marxist organization supported or led a working-class strike for higher wages, it did so (a) with a strong likelihood of receiving a real hearing from the workers, (b) as the only instituted organization fighting on their side, and (c) in the belief that each working-class victory on the wages front was a blow delivered to the objective structure of the capitalist edifice. None of the measures advocated in the classical Marxist programmes can today fulfil these three requirements.

3   Certainly, society today still remains profoundly divided. It functions against the immense majority of working people. In their everyday lives these people express their opposition to this society with half of each one of their gestures. The present crisis of humanity will be able to be resolved only through a socialist revolution. But these ideas run the risk of remaining empty abstractions, pretexts for sermons or for a blind and spasmodic activism, if we do not strive to understand how society's divisions are concretely being realized at the present hour, how this society functions, what forms of reaction and struggle labouring people adopt against the ruling strata and their system, what new kinds of revolutionary activity related to people's concrete existence and struggle in society and to a coherent and lucid view of the world are possible under these conditions. For all of this, what is needed is nothing less than a radical theoretical and practical renewal. It is this effort at renewal and the specific *new* ideas through which this effort has taken on concrete form at each stage that have

characterized the Socialisme ou Barbarie group from the outset, not simple-minded rigid adherence to the idea of class struggle, of the proletariat as revolutionary force, or of revolution. Such blind adherence would have sterilized us, as it did the Trotskyists, Bordigists, and nearly all communists and 'left' socialists. From the first issue of our review we have affirmed, in conclusion of our critique of conservatism in the realm of theory, that 'without *development* of revolutionary theory, no development of revolutionary action'.[1] Ten years later, after having shown that the basic postulates as well as the logical structure of Marx's economic theory reflect 'essentially bourgeois ideas' and having affirmed that a total reconstruction of revolutionary theory was needed, we concluded, 'Whatever the contents of the organization's revolutionary theory or programme, and however deep their connections with the experience and needs of the proletariat, there always will be the possibility, the *certainty* even, that at some point this theory and programme will be outstripped by history, and there will always be the risk that those who have defended them up to that point will tend to make them into absolutes and to try to subordinate and adapt the creations of living history to fit them.'[2]

4   This theoretical reconstruction, which remains a permanent task, has nothing to do with a vague and irresponsible revisionism. We have never abandoned traditional positions because they were traditional, simply saying: They are out of date, times have changed. On the contrary, we have shown, on each occasion, why they were wrong or why they have been outstripped, and we have defined that with which they should be replaced (save in the cases where it was then and remains today impossible for a group of revolutionaries to define, in the absence of mass activity, new forms to replace those that history itself has refuted). But this has not prevented, even within the Socialisme ou Barbarie group, our reconstruction effort from encountering, at each of its crucial stages, bitter opposition from conservative elements representing the type of militant who retains nostalgia for the golden age of the workers' movement (a golden age that, like all golden ages, is, moreover, perfectly imaginary) and who moves forward in history only by proceeding backwards, constantly wishing to return to the era in which, as he believes, theory and programme were indisputable, established once and for all, and constantly corroborated by the activity of the masses.[3]

5   It is not possible to discuss this conservatism in depth, for its main characteristic is its failure to confront the problems that count today, usually denying that they exist. It is a negative and sterile current. This sterility obviously is not a personality or character trait. It is an objective phenomenon, the sure consequence of the terrain on which conservatives place themselves and the inevitable result of the very conception they have of revolutionary theory.

A contemporary physicist who would set himself the task of defending

Newtonian physics against all comers would condemn himself to total sterility and would throw a neurotic fit every time he heard someone speak about such monstrosities as antimatter, particles that also are waves, the expansion of the universe, or the collapse of causality, locality, and identity as absolute categories. The plight of the person who would today simply defend Marxism or a handful of ideas he has borrowed from it is just as desperate. For, taken in this form, the question of Marxism has been settled in the real world and is beyond discussion: leaving aside for the moment the theoretical reconstruction we have been carrying out, Marxism quite simply no longer exists historically as a living theory. Marxism was not, could not, and did not seek to be a theory like the others, whose truth was consigned to books; it was not another Platonism, another Spinozism, another Hegelianism. According to its own programme and its most deep-seated content, Marxism could live only as a constantly renewed theoretical search that sheds light on a world in constant change and as a practice that constantly transforms the world while also being transformed by it (the indissoluble unity of the two corresponding to the Marxian concept of praxis).

Where is that kind of Marxism today? Where, since 1923 (the year Lukács's *History and Class Consciousness* appeared), has a single study that has advanced Marxism been published? Where, since 1940 (the year of Trotsky's death), has a single text been written that defends the traditional ideas on a level high enough to allow one to discuss them without being ashamed of doing so? Where, since the Spanish Civil War, has there been a Marxist group that has actually acted on its principles and connected these with mass activity? Quite simply: nowhere!

It is not one of the least of the tragicomic paradoxes to which the self-proclaimed defenders of Marxism today have been condemned that they are carrying out this rape and killing of Marxism even as they undertake to defend it, and because of this very attempt. For they can defend Marxism only by remaining silent about what has happened to it over the past forty years. As if actual history did not count! As if the presence or absence in real history of a theory and a political programme had no effect on the truth or the signification of such a theory or programme, which somehow would reside 'elsewhere'. As if it were not one of the indestructible principles taught to us by Marx that an ideology is not to be judged by the words it employs but by what it becomes in social reality. They can defend Marxism only by transforming it into its contrary, into an eternal doctrine that could never be upset by any fact (forgetting in the process that if that were so, Marxism would no longer be able in its turn to 'upset the facts', i.e. it would then possess no historical effectiveness). Like a despairing lover whose mistress has died prematurely, they can now express their love only by raping the corpse.

6   Less and less does this conservative attitude take the overt form of a defence of Marxist orthodoxy as such. Obviously, it is difficult to uphold without fear of ridicule the idea that one should remain true to the truths revealed once and for all by Marx and Lenin. Rather, it now takes the following form: faced with the crisis and the disappearance of the workers' movement, one reasons as if this state of affairs affected only certain specifically designated organizations (the Communist Party, the SFIO [Socialist Party], the [Communist-affiliated] CGT labour federation, etc.); confronted by the transformations capitalism is undergoing, one reasons as if these transformations represented merely an accumulation of similar characteristics that was in no way altering its essence.

One thus forgets, and makes others forget, that the crisis of the workers' movement is not simply the degeneration of social-democratic or Bolshevik organizations but a crisis embracing practically all the traditional expressions of working-class activity; that it is not some scaly excrescence covering over the intact revolutionary body of the proletariat or a penalty of condemnation imposed from without, but an expression of problems lying at the very heart of the workers' situation, upon which, moreover, this crisis acts in its turn.[4] One forgets, and makes others forget, that the quantitative accumulation of such 'similar traits' of capitalist society is accompanied by qualitative changes, that 'proletarianization' in contemporary society in no way has the simple meaning attributed to it in classical Marxism and that bureaucratization is not a simple and superficial corollary to the process of capital concentration, but entails profound modifications in the structure and functioning of society.[5] Thus, what one does is simply to offer a few 'additional' interpretations – as if a conception of history and the world that would unite theory and practice, which is what classical Marxism wanted to be, could be subjected to some 'additions', like a pile of potato sacks whose nature would not be altered by the addition of a few more sacks to the pile.

In doing so, one reduces the unknown to the known, which is tantamount to eliminating what is new, and ends up reducing history to one huge tautology. In the best of cases one 'makes repairs at least cost', a practice that in the long run is an infallible way of going broke ideologically, just as it is a sure way of going broke financially in the business world. This attitude, while psychologically understandable, is henceforth impossible. Beyond a certain point it becomes clearly apparent that it can no longer be taken seriously, for a thousand reasons, the first of which is that it is intrinsically contradictory (ideas cannot remain intact while reality is changing, nor can a new reality be understood without a revolution in ideas) and the last of which is that it is theological (and, like every theology, it basically expresses fear and a fundamental feeling of insecurity toward the unknown, neither of which do we have any reason to share).

7   Indeed, the time has arrived to attain a clear awareness that con-

temporary reality can no longer be grasped simply at the cost of a low-budget revision of classical Marxism, or even through any kind of revision at all. In order to be understood, contemporary reality requires a new whole in which breaks with the classical ideas are just as important as (and much more significant than) the ties of kinship. This fact was able to be hidden even from our own eyes by the gradual character of our theoretical elaboration and, undoubtedly, also by a desire to maintain the greatest possible degree of historical continuity. Nevertheless, it becomes strikingly apparent when we look back over the path travelled and as we gauge the distance separating the ideas that appear essential to us today from those of classical Marxism. A few examples will suffice to demonstrate this point.[6]

(a)   For classical Marxism, the division of society was between capitalists who owned the means of production and propertyless proletarians. Today it should be seen as a division between directors and executants.

(b)   Society was seen as dominated by the abstract power of impersonal capital. Today, we see it as dominated by a hierarchical bureaucratic structure.

(c)   For Marx, the central category for understanding capitalist social relations was that of *reification*. Reification was the result of the transformation of all human relations into *market* relations.[7] For us, the central structuring moment of contemporary society is not the market but its bureaucratic-hierarchical 'organization'. The basic category to be used in grasping social relations is that of the *scission* between the processes of direction and execution of collective activities.

(d)   In Marx, the category of reification found its natural continuation in the analysis of labour power as a commodity, in the literal and full sense of this term. As a commodity, labour power had an exchange value defined by 'objective' factors (costs of production and reproduction of labour power) and a use value the purchaser was able to extract at will. The worker was seen as a passive object of the capitalist economy and of capitalist production. For us, this abstraction is halfway a mystification. Labour power can never become purely and simply a commodity (despite capitalism's best efforts). Labour power has no exchange value determined by 'objective' factors, for wage levels are determined essentially by formal and informal working-class struggles. Labour power has no predefined use value, for productivity levels are the stake in an incessant struggle at the point of production and the worker is an active as much as a passive subject in this struggle.

(e)   For Marx, the inherent 'contradiction' of capitalism was that the development of the forces of production was becoming, beyond a certain point, incompatible with capitalist forms of property ownership and of private appropriation of the social product, and would have to 'break them asunder'. For us, the inherent contradiction of capitalism is to be found in the type of scission between direction and execution that capitalism brings about, and in its consequent need simultaneously to seek the exclusion and to solicit the participation of individuals in their activities.

(f)   For the classical revolutionary way of thinking, the proletariat suffers its history until the day it explodes its situation. For us, the proletariat makes its history, under given conditions, and its struggles are constantly transforming capitalist society at the same time that these struggles transform the proletariat itself.

(g)   For the classical revolutionary way of thinking, capitalist culture produces mystifications pure and simple, which are then denounced as such, or it produces scientific truths and valid works, in which case one denounces the fact that they have been appropriated exclusively by the privileged strata of society. For us, this culture, in all its manifestations, both participates in the general crisis of society *and* helps to prepare the way for a new form of human life.

(h)   For Marx, production will always remain the 'realm of necessity'. Whence comes the Marxist movement's implicit idea that socialism is essentially a matter of rearranging the economic and social consequences of a technical infrastructure that is at the same time both neutral and inevitable. For us, production must become the realm of creativity for the associated producers. And the conscious transformation of technology, aimed at putting it at the service of *homo faber*, must be a central task of postrevolutionary society.

(i)   Already for Marx, and much more so for the Marxist movement, the development of the forces of production was at the centre of everything, and its incompatibility with capitalist forms brought history's condemnation down upon these forms. Whence the quite natural identification of socialism with nationalization and economic planning. For us, the essence of socialism is people's domination over all aspects of their lives and in the first place over their work. Whence the idea that socialism is inconceivable outside of the management of production by the associated producers and without the power of workers' councils.

(j)   For Marx, 'bourgeois right' and therefore wage inequality would still have to prevail during a period of transition. For us, a revolutionary society could not survive and develop if it did not immediately instaurate absolute wage equality.

(k)   Finally, and to stick to fundamentals, the traditional movement has always been dominated by the twin concepts of economic determinism and the leading role of the Party. For us, at the centre of everything is the autonomy of labouring people, the masses' capacity for self-direction, without which every idea of socialism immediately turns into a mystification. This entails a new conception of the revolutionary process, as well as of revolutionary organization and politics.

It is not difficult to see that these ideas – whether they are true or false matters little for the moment – represent neither 'additions' nor partial revisions but, rather, constitute the elements for an all-around theoretical reconstruction.

8   One must also grasp that this reconstruction affects not only the content of the ideas, but also the very type of theoretical conception we are attempting to make. Just as it is vain to search today for a type of organization that would be able to be, in the new period to come, a 'substitute' for trade unions, resuming somehow its previously positive role but without the negative traits now associated with unions – in short, to seek to invent a type of organization that would be a union without being one, while all the time

remaining one – so it is illusory to believe that it will be possible for 'another Marxism' to exist henceforth that would not be Marxism. The ruination of Marxism is not only the ruination of a certain number of specific ideas (though we should point out, if need be, that through this process of ruination a number of fundamental discoveries and a way of envisaging history and society remain that no one can any longer ignore). It is also the ruination of a certain type of connection among ideas, as well as between ideas and reality or action. In brief, it is the ruination of the conception of a closed theory (and, even more, of a closed theoretico-practical system) that thought it could enclose the truth, the whole truth, and nothing but the truth of the historical period presently occurring within a certain number of allegedly scientific schemata.

With this ruination, a phase in the history of the workers' movement – and, we should add, in the history of humanity – is drawing to a close. We can call it the theological phase, with the understanding that there can be and there is a theology of 'science' that is not better – but, rather, worse – than the other type of theology (in as much as it gives those who share in this belief the false conviction that their faith is 'rational'). It is the phase of faith, be it faith in a Supreme Being, be it in an 'exceptional' man or a group of 'exceptional' men, be it in an impersonal truth established once and for all and written up as a doctrine. It is the phase during which man became alienated in his own creations, whether imaginary or real, theoretical or practical. Never again will there be a complete theory that would need merely to be 'updated'. Incidentally, in real life there never was any theory of this sort, for all great theoretical discoveries have veered off into the imaginary as soon as one tried to convert them into systems, Marxism no less than the others.

What there has been, and what there will continue to be, is a living theoretical process, from whose womb emerge moments of truth destined to be outstripped (were it only through their integration into another whole within which they no longer have the same meaning). This does not entail some sort of scepticism: at each instant and for each stage in our experience *there are* truths and errors, and there is always the need to carry out a provisional totalization, ever changing and ever open, of what is true. The idea of a complete and definitive theory, however, is today only a bureaucrat's phantasm helping him to manipulate the oppressed; for the oppressed, it can only be the equivalent, in modern-day terms, of an essentially irrational faith.

At each stage in our development, we ought therefore to assert positively those elements about which we are certain, but we also must recognize – and not just by paying lip service – that at the frontiers of our reflection and our practice we encounter problems whose solution we do not know in advance, and perhaps we will not know for a good while; we may not even know whether the solution will oblige us to abandon positions we would have died defending the day before. Whether we like it or not, whether we know it or not, each of us is obliged in our personal lives to display this lucidity and this courage in the face of the unknownness of the perpetually renewed creation into which we are advancing. Revolutionary politics cannot be the last refuge for neurotic rigidity and the neurotic need for security.

9   More than ever before, the problem of the fate of human society is now posed in global terms. The fate of the two-thirds of humanity that live in nonindustrialized countries; the relations these countries maintain with the industrialized countries; more profound still, the structure and the dynamic of a world society that is gradually emerging – these questions are not only starting to take on central importance, they are being raised, in one form or another, day after day. For us, however, we who live in a modern capitalist society, the primary task is to analyse this society, the fate of the workers' movement born therein, the orientation revolutionaries should adopt for themselves. This task is *objectively* the primary one, since it is in fact the forms of life of modern capitalism that dominate the world and shape the evolution of other countries. This task is also the primary one *for us*, for we are nothing if we cannot define ourselves, both theoretically and practically, in relation to our own society. It is to this definition that the present text is devoted.[8]

II. Modern Bureaucratic Capitalism

10   In no way can it be said that capitalism, whether in its 'private' or in its totally bureaucratic form, is unable to continue to develop the forces of production. Nor is there any insurmountable economic contradiction to be found in its mode of operation. More generally speaking, there is no contradiction between the development of the forces of production and capitalist economic forms or capitalist production relations. To state that a socialist regime would be able to develop the forces of production infinitely faster is not to point out a contradiction. And to state that there is a contradiction between capitalist forms and the development of human beings is a sophism, for to speak of the development of human beings has meaning only to the exact extent that they are considered as something other than 'productive forces'. Capitalism is engaged in a movement of expanding the forces of production, and itself constantly creates the conditions for this expansion.

Classical economic crises of overproduction correspond to a historically obsolete phase characterized by the capitalist class's lack of organization. Such crises are completely unknown in totally bureaucratic capitalism (as exists in Eastern-bloc countries). And they only have a minor equivalent in the economic fluctuations of modern industrial countries, where state control over the economy can and actually does maintain such fluctuations within narrow limits.

11   There is neither a growing 'reserve army of the unemployed' nor a relative or absolute 'pauperization' of the working class that would prevent the system from selling off its products or would render its long-term operation impossible. 'Full employment' (in the capitalist sense and within capitalist limits) and the rise in mass consumption (a type of consumption that is capitalist in its form and in its content) are both the prerequisite for and the result of the expansion of production, which capitalism in actual fact achieves. Within its current limits, the continuous rise in workers' real wages not only does not undermine the foundations of capitalism as a system but is the condition for its survival. The same will go, to an increasing degree, for the shortening of the working week.

12   None of this prevents the capitalist economy from being full of irrationalities and antinomies in all its manifestations. Still less does it prevent capitalism from being immensely wasteful as compared with the possibilities of a socialist form of production. These irrationalities, however, do not come to our attention because of some analysis of the kind found in *Capital*. They are the irrationalities found in the bureaucratic management of the economy, which exists in its pure and unadulterated form in the Eastern-bloc countries. In the Western countries they are mixed with residues from the private-anarchic phase of capitalism.

These irrationalities express the incapacity of a separate ruling stratum to manage rationally any field of activity in an alienated society, not the autonomous functioning of 'economic laws' independent of the action of individuals, groups, and classes. This is the reason they are irrationalities, and never absolute impossibilities, except at the moment when the dominated classes refuse to make the system work any longer.

13   Under capitalism, changes in labour and in the way it is organized are dominated by two profoundly related tendencies: bureaucratization on the one hand, mechanization-automation on the other. Taken together, these tendencies constitute the directors' basic response to the executants' struggle against their exploitation and their alienation. But this fact does not lead to a simple, straightforward, and uniform evolution of labour, of its structure, of the skills it requires, of its relationship to the object of labour and to work machinery; nor does it entail a simple evolution of relations among labouring people themselves. If the reduction of all tasks to compartmentalized tasks has long been and remains the central phenomenon of capitalist production, this process of reducing labour to compartmentalized tasks is beginning to attain its limits in the sectors most characteristic of modern production, where it is becoming impossible to divide up tasks any further without making work itself impossible. Similarly, the reduction of tasks to simple jobs requiring no special qualifications (the destruction

of skilled jobs) encounters its limits in modern production too, and even tends to be reversed by the growing need for greater skills that most modern industries require. Mechanization and automation are leading to a compartmentalization of tasks, but tasks that have been sufficiently compartmentalized and simplified are taken over at the next stage by 'totally' automated units, which entail a restructuring of manpower that involves a division between a group of 'passive', isolated, and unskilled attendants, on the one hand, and highly skilled and specialized technicians working in teams, on the other.

Side by side with all this, and still the largest segment of the workforce in numerical terms, traditionally structured production sectors continue to exist. In these sectors are found all the historically sedimented strata of previous eras in the evolution of work, along with completely new sectors (notably office work) where traditional concepts and distinctions lose in this regard almost all their meaning. We therefore must consider as hasty and unverified extrapolations both the traditional idea (from Marx's *Capital*) that capitalism entails the pure and simple destruction of skills and the creation of an undifferentiated mass of automaton-workers, slaves to their machines, as well as the more recent idea (of Romano and Ria Stone [Grace (Lee) Boggs] in *The American Worker*)[9] of the growing importance of a category of universal workers working on universal machines. Both these tendencies exist as partial tendencies, together with a third tendency toward the proliferation of new categories both skilled and specialized at the same time, but it is neither possible nor necessary to decide in some arbitrary fashion that a single one of these categories represents the future.

14   It follows that neither the problem of uniting labouring people in the struggle against the present system nor that of workers' management of the business enterprise after the revolution has a guaranteed solution that relies on some automatic process incorporated into the evolution of technique itself. These problems remain, rather, political problems in the highest meaning of the term: their solution depends on a thoroughgoing raising of people's consciousnesses concerning the totality of society's problems.

Under capitalism there will always be a problem of uniting the struggles of different categories of labourers who are not and never will be in immediately identical situations. And during the revolution, and even afterward, workers' management will not consist in the labouring people taking charge of a production process that has become materialized in the form of mechanization and whose objective logic is watertight and beyond argument. Nor will it consist in the deployment of the aptitudes, somehow fully formed, of a collectivity of virtually universal producers, ready-made by capitalism. Workers' management will have to face up to an extraordinarily complex internal differentiation among the various strata of the labouring population; it will have to resolve the problem of how to integrate individuals, various categories of labourers, and different types of activity, for this will be its fundamental problem. Not in any foreseeable future will capitalism produce, through its own workings, a class of labourers that would already be, in itself, a concrete universal. Unless we stick to a sociological concept, actual labouring class unity can be realized only through the struggle by labouring people and against capitalism. (Let it be said, parenthetically, that to speak today of the proletariat as a class is merely to indulge in descriptive sociology, pure and simple; what unites labouring people as identical members of a group is simply the set of passively shared traits capitalism imposes upon them, and not their attempt to assert themselves as a class that unites itself and opposes itself to the rest of society through their activity, even if fragmentary in character, or through their organization, even if that of a minority.)

The two problems mentioned above [uniting workers in struggle and workers' management] can be resolved only by the association of all the nonexploiting categories of workers at the workplace, manual workers as well as intellectual workers or office workers and technicians. Any attempt at achieving workers' management that would eliminate a category of workers essential to the modern production process would lead to the collapse of this production process – which could be built back up again only through renewed bureaucratization and the use of coercion.

15   The changes in the structuring of society that have taken place over the past century were not those foreseen by classical Marxism. This has had important consequences. Certainly there has been a 'proletarianization' of society in the sense that the old 'petit bourgeois' classes have practically disappeared, and in the sense that the overwhelming majority of the population has been transformed into a population of wage and salary earners and has been integrated into the capitalist division of labour found in the business enterprise. But this 'proletarianization' differs essentially from the classical image, where society was supposed to have evolved in two opposite directions, toward an enormous pole of industrial workers and toward an infinitesimal one of capitalists. On the contrary, as it has become bureaucratized, and in accordance with the underlying logic of bureaucratization, society has been transformed into a pyramid, or, rather, a complex set of pyramids.

The transformation of virtually the whole population into a population of wage and salary earners does not signify that there no longer exists anyone but pure and simple executants on the bottom rungs of the ladder. The population absorbed by the bureaucratic-capitalist structure has come to inhabit all tiers of the bureaucratic pyramid. It will continue to do so. And in this pyramid one can detect no tendency toward a reduction of the intermediate layers. Quite the contrary. Although it is difficult to delimit clearly this concept and although it is impossible to make it coincide with the extant statistical categories of analysis, we can with certainty state that in no modern industrial country does the number of 'simple executants' (manual workers in industry and their counterparts in other branches: typists, sales personnel, etc.) exceed 50 per cent of the labouring population. Moreover, the previously nonproletarianized population has not been absorbed into the industrial sectors of the economy. Except for countries that have not 'completed' their industrialization process (Italy, for example), the percentage of the population in industry stopped growing after reaching a ceiling of between 30 and (rarely) 50 per cent of the active population. The rest are employed in the 'service' sectors of the economy (the proportion of the population employed in agriculture is declining rapidly all over and is already negligible in England and the United States).

Even if the increase in the percentages employed in the service sectors were to stop (due to the mechanization and automation now encroaching upon these sectors in their turn), it would be very difficult to *reverse* this tendency, given the increasingly rapid productivity increases occurring in the industrial sector and the consequent rapid decrease in demand for industrial manpower. The combined result of these two factors is that the industrial proletariat in the classical and strict sense (i.e. defined in terms of manual workers or as hourly paid workers, categories that are roughly overlapping) is in the process of declining in relative and sometimes even absolute size. Thus, in the United States, the percentage of the industrial proletariat ('production and allied workers' and 'unskilled workers other than those in agriculture and mining', statistics that *include the unemployed*, as listed according to their last job) has fallen from 28 per cent in 1947 to 24 per cent in 1961, this decline moreover having accelerated appreciably since 1955.[10]

16   In no way do these observations signify that the industrial proletariat has lost its importance, or that it does not have a central role to play in the unfolding of a revolutionary process, as has been confirmed both by the Hungarian Revolution (though in that case not under conditions of modern capitalism) and by the Belgian General Strike. However, our observations clearly show that the revolutionary movement could no longer claim to represent the interests of the immense majority of the population against a small minority if it did not address itself to all categories of the wage-earning and labouring population, excluding the small minority of capitalists and ruling bureaucrats, and if it did not seek to associate the strata of simple executants with intermediate strata of the pyramid, which numerically speaking are nearly as important.

17   Apart from the transformations in the nature of the capitalist State and of capitalist policy that we have analysed elsewhere,[11] we must understand what the new form of capitalist totalitarianism exactly signifies and what its methods of domination are in present-day society. In present-day

totalitarianism the State, as the central expression of domination of society by a minority, or its appendages and ultimately the ruling strata seize hold of all spheres of social activity and try to model them explicitly after their interests and their outlook. This in no way implies, however, a continuous use of violence or direct coercion, or the suppression of freedoms and formal rights. Violence of course remains the ultimate guarantor of the system, but the system need not have recourse to it every day. It need not resort to violence precisely to the extent that the extension of its grip into almost all fields of activity assures it a more 'economical' exercise of its authority, to the extent that its control over the economy and the continuous expansion of the latter allow it most of the time to appease economic demands without major conflict, and to the extent, finally, that rises in the material standard of living and the degeneration of the traditional organizations and ideas of the workers' movement serve as the constant condition for individual privatization, which, though contradictory and transitory, nonetheless signifies that the domination of the system is not explicitly contested by anyone in society.

We must reject the traditional idea that bourgeois democracy is a worm-eaten edifice doomed to give way to fascism in the absence of revolution. First, this 'democracy', even as bourgeois democracy, has already effectively disappeared, *not* through the reign of the Gestapo, but through the bureaucratization of all political and state institutions and the concomitant rise of apathy among the population. Second, this new pseudodemocracy (pseudo to the second degree) *is* precisely the adequate form of domination for modern capitalism, which could not do without parties (including socialist and communist ones) and unions, nowadays essential cogs of the system, whatever point of view you might adopt. This has been confirmed by what has happened over the last five years in France, where, despite the decomposition of the state apparatus and the Algerian crisis, there was never a serious chance of a fascist takeover and establishment of a dictatorship. It also has been confirmed by Khrushchevism in Russia, which expresses precisely the bureaucracy's attempt to move on to new methods of domination, the old ones (totalitarian in the traditional sense) having become incompatible with modern society (it is another thing that there are chances that everything might break apart *during* the passage to these new methods of domination). With the monopoly over violence as its last resort, capitalist domination presently rests on the bureaucratic manipulation of people in their work life, in their consumer life, and everywhere else in their lives.

18   Thus, modern capitalism is essentially a bureaucratized society with a pyramidal, hierarchical structure. In it are not opposed, as in two clearly separate tiers, a small class of exploiters and a large class of producers. The division of society is much more complex and stratified, and no simple criterion is available to sum it up.

The traditional concept of class corresponded to the relation of individuals and social groups to the ownership of the means of production. We have gone beyond this concept under that form, and rightly so, when we insisted upon looking at how individuals and groups are situated in the real relations of production, and when we introduced the concepts of directors and executants. These concepts remain valid for shedding light on the situation of contemporary capitalism, but they cannot be applied in a mechanical fashion. In their pure state, they can be concretely applied only at the very top and the very bottom of the pyramid, thus leaving aside all the intermediate strata, namely, almost half the population, the half whose tasks involve both execution (with regard to their superiors) and direction (toward those 'below'). Certainly, within these intermediate strata one can encounter again some practically 'pure' cases. Thus a part of the hierarchical network basically fulfils the functions of coercion and authority, while another part basically fulfils technical functions and includes those who could be called 'executants with status' (for example, well-paid technicians or scientists who carry out only the studies or research they are asked to perform). But the collectivization of production has made it such that these pure cases, increasingly rare nowadays, leave out the great majority of the intermediate strata. While a business enterprise's service personnel may have considerably expanded, it is clear that not only the typists but a good number of employees placed higher up in these departments play no role of their own in the system of coercion and constraints that their departments help to impose within the company. Conversely, when a research department or a department that performs 'studies' for the company is developed, a chain of command is set up there, too, for a good number of people in such departments will have as their function the management of the other people's work.

More generally, it is impossible for the bureaucracy – and here is one more expression of the contradiction it experiences – to separate entirely the two work requirements, of 'knowledge' or 'technical expertise', on the one hand, and of 'managerial ability' on the other. True, the logic of the system would want only those capable of 'handling the men' to participate in the managerial chain of command, but the logic of reality requires that those who do a job know something about it – and the system can never become entirely unstuck from reality. This is why the intermediate strata are populated with people who combine a professional qualification with the exercise of managerial functions. For some of these people, the problem of how to manage in a way other than through manipulation and coercion crops up daily. Ambiguity vanishes when one reaches the layer of those who really are directors. These are the people for whose interests everything ultimately functions. They make the important decisions. They reactivate and stimulate the workings of the system, which would otherwise tend to become bogged down in its own inertia. They take the initiative for plugging the leaks [*brèches*] during moments of crisis.

This definition is not of the same nature as the simple criteria previously adopted to characterize classes. The question today, however, is not to get wrapped up in how to define the concept of class: it is to understand and to show that bureaucratization does not diminish society's divisions but on the contrary aggravates them (by complicating them), that the system functions in the interests of a small minority at the top, that hierarchization does not suppress and never will suppress people's struggle against the ruling minority and its rules, that labouring people (whether they be workers, clerical staff, or engineers) will not be able to free themselves from oppression, from alienation, and from exploitation unless they overthrow this system by eliminating hierarchy and by instaurating their collective and egalitarian management of production. The revolution will come into being the day the immense majority of the labouring people who populate the bureaucratic pyramid attack this pyramid and the small minority who rule it. And it will not occur a day sooner. In the meantime, the only differentiation of genuinely practical importance is the one that exists at almost all levels of the pyramid (save at the very top, obviously) between those who *accept* the system and those who, in the everyday reality of production, *combat* it.

19   We already have defined elsewhere the profound contradiction of this society.[12] Briefly speaking, it resides in the fact that capitalism (and this reaches its point of paroxysm under bureaucratic capitalism) is obliged to try to realize simultaneously the exclusion and the participation of people in their activities, that people are forced to make the system run half the time *against* its rules and therefore in struggle against it. This fundamental contradiction is constantly appearing at the junction of the process of direction with the process of execution, this being, as a matter of fact, the *social* moment of production *par excellence*. And it is to be found again, in an indefinite number of refracted forms, within the process of direction itself, where it renders the bureaucracy's functioning irrational from the root up. If this contradiction can be analysed in a particularly clear-cut fashion in the *labour* process, that central manifestation of human activity found in modern Western societies, it is to be found again under other forms, transposed to a greater or lesser degree, in all spheres of social activity, whether one is dealing with political life, sexual and family life (where people are more or less obliged to conform to norms they no longer internalize), or cultural life.

20   The crisis of capitalist production, which is only the flipside of this contradiction, has already been analysed in *S. ou B.*,[13] along with the crises of political and other kinds of organizations and institutions. These analyses must be complemented by an analysis of the crisis in values and in social life as such, and ultimately by an analysis of the crisis in the very personality of modern man, a result of the contradictory situations with which he must

constantly grapple in his work and in his private life. This personality crisis also results from the collapse of values in the most profound sense of the term, namely, the fact that without values no culture is able to structure personalities adequate to it (i.e. to make the culture function, if only as the exploited).

Yet, our analysis of the crisis of production did not show that in this system of production there was only alienation. On the contrary, it has made clear that production occurred only to the extent that the producers have constantly struggled against this alienation. Likewise, our analysis of the crisis of capitalist culture in the broadest sense, and of the corresponding human personality, will take as its starting point the quite obvious fact that society is not and cannot be simply a 'society without culture'. Alongside the debris of the old culture are to be found positive (but ever ambiguous) elements created through the evolution of history. Above all, we find the permanent effort of people to live their lives, to give their lives a meaning in an era where nothing is certain any longer and where, in any case, nothing from without is accepted at face value. In the course of this effort there tends to be realized for the first time in the history of humanity people's aspiration for autonomy. For that very reason, this effort is just as important for the preparation of the socialist revolution as are the analogous manifestations in the domain of production.

21   The fundamental contradiction of capitalism and the multiple processes of conflict and irrationality in which its ramifications are brought out express themselves, and will express themselves so long as this society exists, through 'crises' of one kind or another, breakdowns in the regular functioning of the system. These crises can open the way to revolutionary periods if the labouring masses are combative enough to put the capitalist system into question and conscious enough to be able to knock it down and to organize on its ruins a new society. The very functioning of capitalism therefore guarantees that there always will be 'revolutionary opportunities'. It does not, however, guarantee their outcome, which can depend upon nothing other than the masses' level of consciousness and their degree of autonomy. There is no 'objective' dynamic guaranteeing socialism, and to say that one can exist is a contradiction in terms. All objective dynamics that can be detected in contemporary society are thoroughly ambiguous, as we have shown elsewhere.[14]

The only dynamic to which one can, and should, give the meaning of a dialectical progression toward revolution is the *historical* dialectic of the struggle of social groups, first of the proletariat in the strict sense of the term, and today more generally labouring people earning wages or salaries. The signification of this dialectic is that, through their struggle, those who are exploited transform reality as well as themselves, so that when the struggle resumes it can occur only at a higher level. This alone is the revolutionary perspective, and the search for another type of revolutionary perspective, even by those who condemn a mechanistic approach, proves that the true signification of their condemnation of such an approach has not really been understood. The ripening [*maturation*] of the conditions for socialism can never be an objective ripening (because no fact has signification outside human activity of one sort or another, and the will to read the certainty of the revolution in simple facts is no less absurd than the will to read it in the stars). Nor can it be a subjective ripening in a psychological sense (labouring people today do not have history and its lessons explicitly present in their minds, far from it; the main lesson of history is, as Hegel said, that there are no lessons of history, since history is always new). It is a historical process of maturation, that is, the accumulation of objective conditions for an adequate consciousness. This accumulation is itself the product of class action and the action of social groups. It cannot acquire its meaning, however, except through its resumption in a new consciousness and in new activity, which is not governed by 'laws' and which, while being probable, is never *fated*.

22   The present era remains within this perspective. The victory of reformism as well as of bureaucratism signifies that if labouring people are to undertake large-scale struggles, they will be able to do so only by combating reformism and bureaucracy. The bureaucratization of society poses in an explicit way the social problem as one of the *management* of society: management by whom, to what ends, by what means? The rise in standards of consumption will tend to lessen the effectiveness of consumption as a substitute in people's lives, as motive and as justification for what is already called in the United States the 'rat race'.[15] In as much as 'economic' problems in the narrow sense are diminishing in importance, the interests and preoccupations of labouring people will be able to turn toward the real problems of life in modern society: toward working conditions and the organization of the workplace, toward the very *meaning* of work under present conditions, toward the other aspects of social organization and of people's lives.

To these points[16] we must add another that is just as important. The crisis of culture and of traditional values increasingly raises for individuals the problem of how to orient their concrete life both in the workplace and in all its other manifestations (relationships between man and woman, between adults and children, with other social groups, with their neighbourhood and immediate surroundings, even with 'disinterested' activities), of its modes of being [*modalités*], but also, in the end, of its very *meaning*. Less and less can individuals resolve these problems simply by conforming to traditional and inherited ideas and roles – and even when they do conform they no longer internalize them, that is, they no longer accept them as valid and unchallengeable – because these ideas and these roles, which are incompatible with present-day social reality as well as with the needs of individuals, are collapsing from within. The ruling bureaucracy tries to replace them by means of manipulation, mystification, and propaganda – but these synthetic products cannot, any more than any other ones, resist next year's fashions, they can serve only as the basis for fleeting, external types of conformism. To an increasing degree, individuals are obliged to invent new responses to their problems. In doing so, not only do they manifest their tendency toward autonomy, but at the same time they tend to embody this autonomy, in their behaviour and in their relationships with others. More and more, one's actions are set on the idea that a relationship between human beings can be founded only on the recognition by each of the freedom and responsibility of the other in the conduct of his life. If one takes seriously the character of the revolution as total, if one understands that workers' management does not signify only a certain type of machinery but also a certain type of people, then it must also be recognized that this tendency is just as important, as an index of the revolution, as the workers' tendency to combat the bureaucratic management of the business enterprise – even if we do not yet see the collective manifestations of this former tendency, or how it could lead to organized activities.

III. The End of the Traditional Workers' Movement: A Balance Sheet

23   Today one cannot act or think as a revolutionary without becoming deeply and totally conscious of this fact: the result of the transformations of capitalism and of the degeneration of the organized workers' movement has been that its traditional organizational forms, its traditional forms of action, its traditional preoccupations, ideas, and very vocabulary no longer have any value, or even have only a negative value. As [Daniel] Mothé has written, when discussing the effective reality of this movement for workers, 'even the Roman Empire, when it disappeared, left behind it ruins; the workers' movement is leaving behind only refuse'.[17]

To become aware of this fact means to be done once and for all with the idea that, consciously or unconsciously, still dominates many people's attitudes, namely, that today's parties and trade unions – and all that goes with them (ideas, demands, etc.) – represent merely a screen interposed between a proletariat, ever and inalterably revolutionary in itself, and its class objectives, or a casting mould that distorts the form of workers' activities but does not modify their substance. The degeneration of the workers' movement has not only entailed the appearance of a bureaucratic stratum at the summit of these organizations, it has affected *all* its manifestations. This process of degeneration is due neither to chance nor simply to the 'outside' influence of capitalism, but expresses just as much the proletariat's reality during an entire historic phase, for the proletariat is not and cannot be unfamiliar with what happens to it, let alone what it does.[18]

To speak of the demise of the traditional workers' movement means to understand that a historical period is coming to a close, dragging with it into the nothingness of the past the near-totality of forms and contents it had produced to embody labouring people's struggle for liberation. Just as there will be a renewal of struggles against capitalist society only to the extent that labouring people will make a *tabula rasa* of the residues of their own past activity and hinder the rebirth of these struggles, so there can be a renewal of the activity of revolutionaries only to the extent that the corpses have been properly and definitively buried.

24   The workers' traditional forms of organization were the trade union and the party. What is a union today? It is a cog in capitalist society, indispensable for its 'smooth' functioning both at the level of production and at the level of distribution of the social product. (That it plays an ambiguous role in this regard does not suffice to distinguish it in any essential way from other institutions in established society; that the character of trade unions does not forbid revolutionary militants from belonging to them is also another matter.) This is what they are *necessarily*, and to seek to restore trade unions to their original purity is to live in a dream world under the pretext of being realistic.

What is a political party today (a 'working-class' one, I mean)? A managerial organ of capitalist society, a means for enrolling the masses into this society; when it is 'in power', it differs in no way from bourgeois parties except that it helps accelerate the evolution of capitalism toward its bureaucratic form and that it sometimes gives capitalism a more overtly totalitarian twist; in any case such 'working-class' parties organize repression of the exploited and of the colonial masses as well as, if not better than, their rivals. This is what they are necessarily, and there is no way these parties can be reformed. An abyss separates what we mean by revolutionary organization from the traditional party.

In the case of both the labour union and the 'working-class' political party, our critique[19] merely renders explicit the critique to which history itself has subjected these two institutions. And like history itself, it has offered not just a critique of events but also a critique of contents and forms of people's action over an entire period. It is not just *these* parties and *these* unions that are dead as institutions for working-class struggle, but The Party and The Union. Not only is it utopian to wish to reform them, to straighten them out, or to constitute new ones that would miraculously escape the fate of the old ones; it is false to want to find for them in the new period exact equivalents, replacements under 'new' forms that would still have the same old functions.

25   Traditional 'minimum' demands were first of all economic demands. Such economic demands not only coincided with workers' interests but were supposed to undermine the capitalist system. We have already shown[20] that steady wage increases are the condition for the expansion of the capitalist system and ultimately for its 'health', even if capitalists do not always understand this. (It is another thing if the capitalists' resistance to such increases can, under certain completely exceptional circumstances, become the point of departure for conflicts that go beyond the level of economic issues.)

Then there were political demands. In the great tradition of the real workers' movement (and in Marx, Lenin, and Trotsky, if not for the ultraleft sects), these consisted in demanding and defending 'democratic rights' and the extension of such rights, in making use of parliamentary institutions, and in demanding the right to manage municipal affairs. The justifications for these demands were (a) that these rights were necessary to the development of the workers' movement; (b) that the bourgeoisie could not grant them or tolerate in the long run their exercise, since it was 'choking on its own legality'. Now, we have seen the system accommodate itself very well to its pseudodemocracy. 'Rights' do not mean very much for the workers' movement since they have been cancelled out by the bureaucratization of 'working-class' organizations themselves. We must add that these 'rights' have been achieved in almost all cases in modern Western societies, and that challenges to these rights by the ruling strata, when they do take place, stir up large-scale reactions on the part of the populace only quite seldom. As for the so-called transitional demands put forth by Trotsky, we have shown well enough their false and illusory character, so we need not return to that issue here.

Finally, it must be stated and repeated that the central points of traditional 'maximum' demands (which remain alive in the minds of the overwhelming majority of people) were nationalization and economic planning. We have shown that these were organically the programme of the bureaucracy (the expression 'workers' management' is mentioned only once in passing in the *Theses, Resolutions, and Manifestos of the First Four Congresses of the Third International*, without being elaborated at all or even defined, never to appear again).

26   The traditional forms of action (we are not talking here about armed insurrection, which does not take place every day or even every year) basically were the strike and the mass demonstration.

What is the strike today – not the idea of the strike, but striking in its effective social reality? Basically there are mass strikes, controlled and marshalled by trade unions into confrontations whose unfolding is set like a theatre piece (whatever the sacrifices such strikes may demand of the mass of workers). Or else there are 'symbolic' strikes lasting fifteen minutes, an hour, etc.; these too are controlled and marshalled from above. The only cases in which strikes go beyond the institutionalized procedure that is now part of union–management negotiations are the wildcat strikes in England and the United States, precisely because they put this procedure into question, either in its form or in its content. There are also, we should add, a few cases of strikes limited to one company or to one department of a company; for this very reason, the grass-roots are able to play a more active role in them.

As for mass demonstrations, it is better not even to mention them.

What must be understood in these two cases is that, in their reality, these forms of action are necessarily and indissociably linked both to the organizations that control them and to the objectives these organizations pursue. It is true, for example, that the idea of the big strike still remains valid 'in itself', and that one can imagine a process in which 'real' strike committees would be elected (and not appointed from above), would put forward the 'real' demands of the workers, would remain under their control, etc. In relation to the real world today, however, such speculations are empty and gratuitous. To achieve this on a larger scale than that of a single enterprise or shop within one enterprise would require both a deep break between workers and the union bureaucracy and the masses' capacity to set up autonomous organs and to formulate demands that would cut through the present context of reformism. In short, it would signify that society was entering into a revolutionary period. The enormous difficulties that the Belgian strikes of 1960–1 encountered, as well as their ultimate failure, dramatically highlight the problem.

27   This same irreversible historical wear and tear has had its effect on the traditional vocabulary of the workers' movement as well as on what can be called its *idées-forces*. If we take into account the real way words are used in society, their signification for people and not their dictionary definitions, a communist is today a member of the Communist Party, that is all; socialism is the type of regime that exists in the USSR and other similar countries; the proletariat is a term used by no one outside a few extreme left-wing sects, and so on. Words have their historical destiny, and whatever difficulties this creates for us (difficulties that are resolved only in appearance when we write 'communist' in quotation marks), we should understand that we cannot play in relation to this language the role of a revolutionary counterpart of the Académie Française, more conservative than the real one, as we would be rejecting the living meaning of words in their everyday social usage while maintaining, for example, that 'sensible' means 'pertaining to the mode of knowing' rather than 'reasonable'[21] or that a communist is someone in favour of a society in which everyone gives according to his ability and receives according to his needs, and not a supporter of Maurice Thorez.[22]

As for the *idées-forces* of the workers' movement, no one outside a few sects knows any longer, even vaguely, what 'social revolution', for example, means. At most one thinks of a civil war. The 'abolition of the wages system', once the top priority in labour-union programmes, no longer signifies anything to anyone. The last manifestations of actual internationalism date from the Spanish Civil War (not that opportunities have been lacking since then). The very idea of working-class unity or, more generally, unity of the entire population of labouring people (in as much as they basically share the same interests, which indeed are radically opposed to those of the ruling strata) hardly manifests itself at all in reality (apart from solidarity strikes and the 'blacking' of strike-bound companies that take place in England). As background to all this there is the collapse of traditional theoretical conceptions and ideology, to which we will not here return.

28   At the same time that we are witnessing the irreversible bankruptcy of the forms that are characteristic of the traditional movement, we have witnessed, we are witnessing, and we will continue to witness the birth, rebirth, or resumption of new forms that, to the best of our ability to judge at the present time, are pointing to the direction the revolutionary process will take in the future. These new forms should guide us in our present thinking and action. The Hungarian Workers' Councils, their demands concerning the management of production, the abolition of [externally prescribed work] norms, and so on; the shop stewards' movement in England and wildcat strikes in the United States; demands concerning working conditions in the most general sense and those directed against hierarchy, which various categories of workers in several countries are putting forward, almost always *against* the unions: these are the new forms that ought to be the certain and positive points of departure in our effort to reconstruct a revolutionary movement. We have made an extensive analysis of these movements in *S. ou B.*, and this analysis remains valid (even if it must be re-examined and developed further). These insights, however, will not allow our reflections and our action to become truly fruitful unless we come to understand fully how they represent a *rupture*, certainly not with the high points of past revolutions, but with the everyday historical reality of the traditional movement today, and unless we take them not as amendments or additions to past forms, but as new bases upon which we must continue to reflect and to act, together with what our analysis and our renewed critique of established society teach us.

29   Present conditions allow us, therefore, to deepen and to enlarge both the idea of socialism and its bases in social reality. This claim seems to be in direct conflict with the total disappearance of the revolutionary socialist movement and of political activity on the part of labouring people. And this opposition is not merely apparent. It is real, and it constitutes the central problem of our age. The workers' movement has been integrated into official society; its institutions (parties, unions) have become those of

official society. Moreover, labouring people have in fact abandoned all political and sometimes even trade-union activity. This privatization of the working class and even of all other social strata is the combined result of two factors: on the one hand, the bureaucratization of parties and unions distances these organizations from the mass of labouring people; on the other, rising living standards and the massive proliferation of new types of consumer objects and new consumer life-styles provide them with the substitute for and the simulacrum of reasons for living. This phase is neither superficial nor accidental. It expresses one possible destiny of present-day society. If the term *barbarism* has a meaning today, it is neither fascism nor poverty nor a return to the Stone Age. It is precisely this 'air-conditioned nightmare', consumption for the sake of consumption in private life, organization for the sake of organization in collective life, as well as their corollaries: privatization, withdrawal, and apathy as regards matters shared in common, and dehumanization of social relationships. This process is well under way in industrialized countries, but it also engenders its own opposites. People have abandoned bureaucratized institutions, and ultimately they enter into opposition against them. The race after 'ever higher' levels of consumption and 'ever newer' consumer objects sooner or later condemns itself by its very absurdity. Those elements that may allow a raising of consciousness, socialist activity, and, in the last analysis, revolution have not disappeared, but on the contrary are proliferating in contemporary society. Each labouring person can observe the anarchy and incoherencies that characterize the ruling classes and their system in their management of the grand affairs of society. And in his daily existence – and in the first place, in his work – he lives the absurdity of a system that tries to reduce him to the status of an automaton but is obliged to call upon his inventiveness and his initiative to correct its own mistakes.

Here lies the fundamental contradiction we have analysed, the decrepitude and the crisis of all traditional forms of organization and life. Here too we find people's aspirations for autonomy, such as these are manifested in their concrete existence. Here, finally, we discover labouring people constantly struggling in an informal way against the bureaucratic management of production, the movements and just demands we mentioned in point 28. Thus the elements of a socialist solution continue being produced, even if they are hidden underground, deformed, or mutilated by the functioning of bureaucratic society.

Moreover, this society does not succeed in rationalizing its operation (not even from its own point of view). It is doomed to go on producing 'crises', which, as accidental as they may appear to be each time they occur, are nonetheless inevitable, and never fail to raise before humanity the totality of its problems. These two elements provide the necessary and sufficient basis upon which a revolutionary perspective and project can be founded. It is a vain mystification to seek another perspective, to try to deduce the revolution, to provide a 'proof' for it, or to describe the way in which the conjunction of these two elements (the conscious revolt of the masses and the temporary inability of the established system to go on functioning) will take place and lead to revolution. Besides, no description of this kind ever existed in classical Marxism, except for the passage at the end of the chapter entitled 'Historical Tendency of Capitalist Accumulation' in *Capital*. Moreover, this passage is theoretically false, for no revolution that has ever actually taken place in history took place in this way. Every revolution that has occurred began as an unforeseeable 'accident' of the system, setting off an explosion of mass activity. (Later on, the historians – whether Marxist or not – who have never been able to foresee anything, but are always very wise after the fact, furnish us with *a posteriori* explanations for such explosions, explanations that explain nothing at all.)

A long time ago we wrote that it is not a matter of deducing the revolution, but of making it. And the only factor making a connection between these two elements about which *we*, as revolutionaries, can speak is our own activity, the activity of a revolutionary organization. Of course, such activity does not constitute a 'guarantee' of any sort, but it is the only factor dependent on us that can increase the likelihood that the innumerable individual and collective revolts taking place throughout society will be able to respond to one another and unite among themselves, take on the same meaning, explicitly aim at the radical reconstruction of society, and finally transform what is, at the beginning, never anything other than 'just another crisis of the system' into a revolutionary crisis. In this sense the unification of the two elements of the revolutionary perspective can take place only through our activity and by means of the concrete content of our orientation.

IV. Elements for a New Orientation[23]

30   As an organized movement, the revolutionary movement must be rebuilt totally. This reconstruction will find a solid base in the development of working-class experience, but it presupposes a radical rupture with present-day organizations, their ideology, their mentality, their methods, and their actions. Everything that has existed and exists today in instituted form in the labour movement – parties, unions, etc. – is irremediably and irrevocably finished, rotten, integrated into exploiting society. There can be no miraculous solutions. Everything must be remade at the cost of long and patient labour. Everything must be started over again [*recommencer*], but starting from the immense experience of a century of working-class struggles and with labouring people, who find themselves closer than ever to genuine solutions.

31   Equivocations about the socialist programme created by degenerated 'working-class' organizations (whether Stalinist or reformist) must be destroyed down to their very roots. The idea that socialism coincides in any way with the nationalization of the means of production or with planning, that it basically aims at – or that people ought to aim at – increasing production and consumption are ideas that must be mercilessly denounced. Their basic identity with the underlying orientation of capitalism must be repeatedly shown.

Workers' management of production and society and the power of workers' councils as the necessary form of socialism should be demonstrated and illustrated, starting from recent historical experience. The basic content of socialism is the restitution of people's domination over their own lives; the transformation of work from an absurd form of breadwinning into the free deployment of the creative forces of individuals and groups; the constitution of integrated human communities; the unification of people's culture and lives. This content should not be embarrassingly hidden as some kind of speculation about an indeterminate future but, rather, put forward as the sole response to the problems that today torment and stifle people and society. The socialist programme ought to be presented for what it is: a programme for the humanization of work and of society. It ought to be shouted from the rooftops that socialism is not a backyard of leisure attached to the industrial prison, or transistors for the prisoners, but the destruction of the industrial prison itself.

32   Revolutionary criticism of society must switch its axis. In the first place, it should denounce in all its forms the inhuman and absurd character of work today. It should unveil the arbitrariness and monstrosity of hierarchy in production and in society, its lack of justification, the tremendous wastefulness and strife it generates, the incompetency of those who rule, the contradictions and irrationality of bureaucratic management of each enterprise, of the economy, of the State, and of society. It ought to show that, whatever the rise in the 'standard of living', the problem of people's needs is not resolved even in the richest of societies, that consumption in the capitalist mode is full of contradictions and ultimately absurd. Finally, it ought to broaden itself to encompass all aspects of life, to denounce the disintegration of communities, the dehumanization of relations between individuals, the content and methods of capitalist education, the monstrousness of modern cities, and the double oppression imposed upon women and youth.

33   The analysis of social reality today cannot and must not simply explain and denounce alienation. It must constantly show the *double reality* of every social activity under present-day conditions (which is but the expression of what we have defined above as the fundamental contradiction of the system), namely, that people's creativity and their struggle against

alienation, at times individual, at times collective, necessarily manifest themselves in every domain, especially during the contemporary era (were this not so, there would never be a question of socialism).

We have attacked the absurd idea that the factory is *nothing but* a hard-labour camp. And we have shown that alienation can never be total (for then production would simply grind to a halt). Rather, production is dominated just as much by the tendency of the producers, both individually and collectively, partially to take on the management of production. Similarly, we must denounce the absurd idea that people's lives under capitalism consist of *nothing but* passivity toward capitalist manipulation and mystification (if this were so, we would be living in a world of zombies for whom the question of socialism would never arise). On the contrary, we must highlight and recognize the positive value of people's efforts (which are at once the cause and the effect of the collapse of traditional values and forms of living) to orient for themselves their own lives and their own attitudes in a period where nothing is certain any longer.

These efforts open up – no more, no less – an absolutely new phase in the history of humanity, and, in so far as they embody the aspiration for autonomy, they are a condition for socialism as essential as, if not more essential than, the development of technology. And we must also show the positive content the exercise of this autonomy often takes on, for instance in the growing transformation of the relations between the sexes or between parents and children in the family. This transformation contains within itself the recognition that the other person is or ought in the last analysis to be the master of his life and responsible for it. It is equally important to show the similar contents that appear in the most radical currents in contemporary culture (tendencies in psychoanalysis, sociology, and ethnology, for example), to the extent that these currents both complete the demolition of what remains of oppressive ideologies and are bound to spread within society.

34   Traditional organizations were based upon the idea that economic demands constituted the central problem confronting workers and that capitalism was incapable of satisfying these demands. This idea should be categorically repudiated since it corresponds to nothing in present-day reality. The revolutionary organization and the trade-union activity of revolutionary militants cannot be founded upon a game of outbidding others over economic demands, which the unions have more or less successfully defended and which are achievable within the capitalist system without major difficulties. The basis for permanent trade-union reformism is to be found in the possibility of wage increases. This is also one of the conditions for their irreversible degeneration into bureaucratic organizations. Capitalism can survive only by granting wage increases. For this reason, bureaucratized, reformist trade unions are indispensable to it.

This does not mean that revolutionary militants ought necessarily to leave the unions or no longer interest themselves in economic demands. But neither of these two points retains the central importance they once were given.

35   The wage earner's humanity is less and less subject to attack by economic poverty that puts his physical existence into danger. It is more and more threatened by the nature and conditions of his work, by the oppression and alienation he suffers in the production process. Now, in this field there is not, and cannot be, lasting reform, but only a struggle with unstable results that are never fully established, for one cannot reduce alienation by 3 per cent per annum. Nor is the organization of the production process ever free from the upheavals of technical change. In this field, too, the trade unions cooperate with management down the line. A key task for the revolutionary movement is to help workers organize their struggle against living and working conditions in the capitalist enterprise.

36   Exploitation in contemporary society occurs more and more under the form of inequality within the hierarchy. Respect for the value of hierarchy, which is sustained by 'working-class' organizations, becomes the last ideological support for the whole system. The revolutionary movement ought to organize a systematic struggle against the ideology of hierarchy in all its forms, including the wage and salary hierarchy and the hierarchy among different jobs in each company.

This struggle can no longer continue, however, simply on the basis of an analysis of the respective situations of semiskilled machine operators and foremen within traditional industries. Such an analysis would have no grasp over the growing number of categories of labourers, to whom it would be false to present hierarchy as merely a veil of mystification covering over a reality in which all roles would be identical, save for those that involve the exercise of coercion. What we must show is that in the overwhelming majority of cases, differences in skills among labouring people result from the very functioning of a society that is unequal and hierarchized from the outset.

With each new generation, such a society constantly reproduces itself as a stratified society. We must show that it is not simply these differences in skill levels that determine where individuals are situated on the hierarchical pyramid; their situations are defined as much (and more and more so, as one moves up from one echelon to the next) by each individual's ability to remain afloat amid the struggle between bureaucratic cliques and clans – an ability of no social value. In any case, we must show that it is only the collectivity of labouring people that can and should manage work in a rational manner, as to its general objectives and to its conditions. To the extent that certain technical aspects of work require a differentiation in people's responsibilities, we must show that those given positions of responsibility should remain under the control of the collectivity. We must show that in no case can there be a justification for any kind of wage differentials whatsoever, wage equality being a central plank of any socialist programme. In this same context, it must be understood that labouring people's desire to improve their skills or to take on posts of responsibility does not always or necessarily express an aspiration to pass over to the other side of the class barrier. Indeed, to an increasing degree it expresses people's need to find some interest in their work. (It is another thing that this need cannot be satisfied within the present system just by getting a promotion, either. Nor is there any point in saying that such a solution remains purely personal and individualistic; it is no more so than that of individuals who raise their children the best they can, instead of just saying, 'The problem is insoluble anyhow under the present system.')

37   In all struggles, the way in which a result is obtained is as important as, even more important than, what is obtained. Even with regard to immediate effectiveness, actions organized and directed by labouring people themselves are superior to actions decided and directed bureaucratically. But above all, these alone create the conditions for pushing the movement forward, for they alone teach labouring people how to manage their own affairs. The supreme criterion guiding the activity of the revolutionary movement ought to be the idea that when it intervenes it aims not at replacing but at developing labouring people's initiative and autonomy.

38   Even when struggles in production reach a great intensity and attain a high level, the passage to the overall problem of society remains the hardest one for labouring people to make. In this field, therefore, the revolutionary movement has a key task to perform. This task must not be confused with sterile agitation about incidents in the 'political life' of capitalism. It lies instead in showing that the system always operates against labouring people, that they cannot resolve their problems without abolishing capitalism and the bureaucracy and totally reconstructing society; that there is a profound and intimate similarity between their fate as producers in the workplace and their fate as people in society, in the sense that neither one nor the other can be modified without the division between a class of directors and a class of executants being suppressed. Only through long and patient work in this direction can the problem of how to mobilize labouring people around general questions be posed again in correct terms.

39   Experience has proved that internationalism is not an automatic product of working-class life. Formerly it had been developed into a real political factor by the actions of working-class organizations, but it disappeared when the latter degenerated and lapsed into chauvinism.

The revolutionary movement will have to struggle to help the proletariat reclimb the long path down which it has been descending for the past quarter-century. It will have to breathe life back into the international solidarity of labour struggles and especially the solidarity of labouring people in imperialist countries with the struggles of colonized peoples.

40   The revolutionary movement must cease to appear as a political movement in the traditional sense of the term. Traditional politics is dead, and for good reasons. The population has abandoned it because it sees it for what it is in social reality: the activity of a stratum of professional mystifiers hovering around the state machinery and its appendages in order to penetrate into them or to take them over. The revolutionary movement ought to appear as a total movement concerned with everything that people do and are subject to in society, and above all with their real daily life.

41   The revolutionary movement ought therefore to cease being an organization of specialists. It ought to become the place – the only place in present-day society outside the workplace – where a growing number of individuals relearn how to live a truly collective life, manage their own affairs, and realize and develop themselves while working in mutual recognition for a common objective [*projet*].

42   The propaganda and recruitment efforts of the revolutionary movement must take into account the transformations in the structure of capitalist society described above, as well as the generalization of its state of crisis. The revolutionary movement cannot address itself to manual labourers to the exclusion of almost everyone else, or pretend that everyone has been or ultimately is going to be transformed into a simple executant at the base of the bureaucratic pyramid. What really is the case, and what can serve as an adequate basis for propaganda and recruitment efforts, is that the great majority of individuals, whatever their qualifications or level of pay, have been integrated into a bureaucratically organized production process. They feel the alienation in their work as well as the absurdity of the system, and they tend to revolt against it. Similarly, the crisis of culture and the decomposition of values in capitalist society are driving large sections of intellectuals and students (whose numerical weight, indeed, is growing) toward a radical critique of the system.

In order to achieve unity in the struggles against the system and to make the collective management of production by labouring people a realizable goal, the role of these 'new strata' will be fundamental. Indeed, it will be much more fundamental than was, for example, 'unity with the poor peasantry' in Lenin's time, for, as such, the peasantry represented only a negative force, capable merely of destroying the old system, whereas the 'new strata' have an essential, positive role to play in the socialist reconstruction of society.

The revolutionary movement alone can give a positive meaning and provide the positive outcome to the revolt of these strata against the system. And in return, the movement will be greatly enriched by them. Under the conditions of an exploitative society, the revolutionary movement alone can serve as the link between manual workers, 'tertiary' employees, and intellectuals. Without this link-up there can be no victory for the revolution.

43 The rupture between generations and the youth revolt in modern society are not comparable to the 'generational conflicts' of former times. Youth no longer oppose adults as part of a strategy to take their place in an accepted and established system. They reject this system. They no longer recognize its values. Contemporary society is losing its hold over the generations it produces. This rupture is especially brutal when it comes to politics.

On the one hand, the overwhelming majority of adult cadres and labour militants cannot regear themselves to the changing situation, no matter how hard they try or how sincere they may be. They mechanically repeat the lessons and phrases learned long ago, even though these ideas have become devoid of meaning. They remain attached to forms of action and organization that are in the process of collapsing. Conversely, traditional organizations are succeeding less and less in recruiting youth. In the eyes of young people, nothing separates these organizations from all the stupid, worm-eaten pomposity they meet when they come into the social world.

The revolutionary movement will be able to give a positive direction to the immense revolt of youth today. It will make of it the leaven for social transformation, if it can find the new and genuine language for which youth is searching and if it can show young people an effective form of action and struggle against a world they reject.

44 The crisis and wearing down of the capitalist system today extend to all sectors of life. Its leaders tire themselves out trying to plug the leaks [*brèches*] in the system, without ever succeeding in doing so. In this society, the richest and most powerful the earth has ever known, people's dissatisfaction and their impotence in the face of their own creations are greater than ever.

Today capitalism may succeed in privatizing the labouring population, in driving them away from dealing with their social problems and from acting collectively. But this phase cannot last forever, if only because established society will put a stop to it first. Sooner or later, due to one of those inevitable 'accidents' that take place under the present system, the masses will enter into action again to change the conditions of their existence. The fate of this action will depend on the degree of consciousness, of initiative, of will and of capacity for autonomy that labouring people will then exhibit.

But the development of this awareness and the consolidation of this autonomy depend to a decisive degree on the continuing work of a revolutionary organization. This organization must have a clear understanding of a century of working-class struggles. Above all, it must understand that both the end and the means of all revolutionary activity are the development of the conscious and autonomous action of labouring people. It must be capable of tracing out the perspective of a new human society for which it is worth living and dying. Finally, it must itself embody the example of a collective activity that people can both understand and dominate.

Notes

1 *S. ou B.*, 1 (March 1949), p. 4 (emphasis in the original) [T/E: see, now, the 'Presentation' above in *CR*].
2 *PO I*, in *PSW 2*, pp. 202–3, 213–14, and 220.
3 This opposition reached the point of paroxysm in *MCR* (1960–1), and in the ideas that, developed on the basis of that text, were formulated in the present article. The ultimate result was a scission within the group. The comrades who have separated themselves from us, among whom are P[ierre] Brune, J[ean]-F[rançois] Lyotard, and R. Maille, propose to continue publication of the monthly journal *Pouvoir Ouvrier* [T/E: *S. ou B.*'s popularized, mimeographed newsletter, *Workers' power*]. The customary and logical thing would have been to discuss publicly the reasons for this scission, and the opposing theses. Unfortunately, that is not possible for us to do. This opposition has remained without any definable content, positive or even negative; to this day we know nothing about what those who reject our ideas want to put in their place, and just as little about what precisely they are opposed to. We therefore can only explain ourselves concerning our own positions and, for the rest, we can merely note once again the ideological and political sterility of conservatism. [See *MCR*; T/E: see now the Postface to *RR*, chapter 7 in *PSW 3*.]
4 See *PO I*, in *PSW 2*, pp. 207–9.
5 See *MCR*, in *PSW 2*, pp. 272ff.
6 The ideas that follow have been developed in a number of texts published in *S. ou B.* See in particular the editorial, *SB* (1949); *RPR* (1949); 'Sur le programme socialiste', *S. ou B.*, 10 (July 1952) [T/E: reprinted in *CS*, pp. 47–65]; 'L'Expérience prolétarienne', *S. ou B.*, 11 (November 1952) [T/E: by Claude Lefort, reprinted in *Éléments d'une critique de la bureaucratie* (Geneva: Droz, 1971; 2nd edn, Paris: Gallimard, 1979), pp. 39–58 and 71–97, respectively]; 'La Bureaucratie syndicale et les ouvriers', *S. ou B.*, 13 (January 1954) [T/E: by Daniel Mothé]; *CS I–III* (1955–8) [T/E: excerpts from *CS I* and *CS II* appear above in *CR*]; 'La Révolution en Pologne et en Hongrie', *S. ou B.*, 20 (December 1956) [T/E: Castoriadis is referring to a special section of this issue of *S. ou B.*, which included 'Questions aux militants du P.C.F.' (reprinted in *SB 2*, pp. 231–65, and *SB**, pp. 353–70, as 'L'Insurrection hongroise: questions aux militants du P.C.F.'); Claude Lefort, 'L'Insurrection hongroise' (reprinted in the 1971 edition of *Éléments*, pp. 191–220); Philippe Guillaume, 'Comment ils se sont battus'; D. Mothé, 'Chez Renault on parle de la Hongrie'; and Pierre Chaulieu (Cornelius Castoriadis), *PRAB* (1956)]; 'L'Usine et la gestion ouvrière', *S. ou B.*, 22 (July 1957) [T/E: by Daniel Mothé]; *PO I* and *PO II* (1959); 'Les Ouvriers et la culture', *S. ou B.*, 30 (April 1960) [T/E: by Daniel Mothé]; and *MCR*.
7 It is in a spirit of profound fidelity to this, the most important aspect of Marx's doctrine, that Lukács devoted the main part of *History and Class Consciousness* to an analysis of reification.
8 Several of the ideas summarized below have been developed or demonstrated in *MCR*.
9 *S. ou B.*, 1–8. [T/E: *The American Worker*, which includes 'The American Worker' by Paul Romano and 'The Reconstruction of Society' by Ria Stone (Grace [Lee] Boggs), was originally published in English by Correspondence in 1947; a 1974 reprint is still available from Bewick in Detroit.]
10 Solidarity text footnote: By 1971 the proportion had declined to 21 per cent. (Figures calculated from *Manpower Report of the President* [Washington, DC: GPO, 1973],

pp. 188–9; and *Statistical Abstracts of the United States* [1963; T/E: this last date presumably should read 1973]).

11 See *CS II* in *PSW 2*, pp. 137–9 [T/E: see *CR*, pp. 91–93] and *MCR*, in *PSW 2*, pp. 267–71.

12 See *CS III*, in *PSW 2*, pp. 158ff, and *MCR*, in *PSW 2*, pp. 258ff.

13 See Paul Romano and Ria Stone, 'L'Ouvrier américain', *S. ou B.*, 1–8 [T/E: see note 9 above for the original English-language version]; D[aniel] Mothé, 'L'Usine et la gestion ouvrière', *S. ou B.*, 22 (July 1957); R[oger] Berthier, 'Une expérience d'organisation ouvrière', *S. ou B.*, 20 (December 1956), and *CS III*.

14 See *MCR*, in *PSW 2*, p. 299.

15 T/E: Castoriadis uses the French phrase 'la course de rats' in quotation marks followed by the English phrase 'rat race', in parentheses and italics.

16 Developed in *MCR*, in *PSW 2*, pp. 301–3.

17 'Les Ouvriers et la culture', *S. ou B.*, 30 (April 1960), p. 37.

18 See *PO I*, in *PSW 2*, pp. 207–9.

19 See *PO I*, in *PSW 2*, pp. 201–9.

20 See *MCR*, in *PSW 2*, pp. 249–50.

21 T/E: We have followed the Solidarity text here, beginning with the word 'sensible'. The accompanying footnote reads: 'This is an English adaptation of Cardan's [i.e. Castoriadis's] text. The original stated, ". . . qui refuserait le sens vivant des mots dans l'usage social et insisterait qu'étonner signifie 'faire trembler par une violente commotion' et non 'surprendre' . . ." (Solidarity footnote).' The reprinted French text, we might also note, replaced 'insisterait' with 'maintiendrait'.

22 T/E: Maurice Thorez (1900–64) was general secretary of the French Communist Party at the time.

23 T/E: This fourth and final section of *RR*, 'Elements for a New Orientation', is an almost verbatim restatement of the eighth and final section of *MCR*, 'For a Modern Revolutionary Movement', with a few slight, but quite significant, alterations. See note 23 to *RR* in *PSW 3*, p. 55, for the details of these changes. (In this *Reader* text and in others in this volume, some additional slight changes have been made in order to conform to specifically British parlance or to Blackwell Publishers' house style or in order simply to improve upon the previous translations.)

5

Marxism and Revolutionary Theory (1964–1965)[*]: Excerpts

Marxism: A Provisional Assessment

The Historical Situation of Marxism and the Notion of Orthodoxy

For anyone who is preoccupied with the question of society, the encounter with Marxism is immediate and inevitable. Even to speak of an encounter in this case is inappropriate, in as much as this word denotes a contingent and external event. Ceasing to be a particular theory or a political programme professed by a few, Marxism has so impregnated language, ideas, and reality that it has become part of the atmosphere we breathe when we come into the social world, part of the historical landscape that frames our comings and goings.

For this very reason, however, to speak of Marxism has become one of the most difficult tasks. To begin with, we ourselves are implicated in a thousand different ways in this matter. And Marxism, in 'realizing' itself, has become ungraspable. Of which Marxism, in fact, should we be speaking? That of Khrushchev, of Mao Tse-tung, of Togliatti or Thorez? Or that of Castro, of the Yugoslavs, of the Polish revisionists? Or, rather, of the Trotskyists (and here again this depends on geography: French and English Trotskyists, those from the United States and those from Latin America fight among themselves and denounce one another), Bordigists, or any given far-left group that accuses all the others of betraying the spirit of 'true' Marxism, which it alone would possess? There is not simply the abyss that separates official Marxisms and oppositional Marxisms. There is an

---

[*] 'Marxisme et théorie révolutionnaire' originally appeared in the final five issues of *Socialisme ou Barbarie*, 36–40 (April 1964–June 1965) and was reprinted as the first part of *IIS*. The present abridged translation, which includes the first section of chapter 1 and all of chapter 2 of *MRT*, first appeared in its entirety in the translation of *IIS* by Kathleen Blamey. [T/E: I have made some editorial changes in order to standardize terminology and style and to correct some translated passages.]

enormous range of variants, each presenting itself as excluding all the others.

No simple criterion allows us to reduce this complexity all at once. There is obviously no factual test that speaks for itself, since both the public official and the political prisoner find themselves in particular social situations which, as such, confer no privilege on their views and, on the contrary, render indispensable a double interpretation of what they say. The consecration of power must not carry greater weight for us than the halo of irreducible opposition, and it is Marxism itself that forbids us to forget the suspicion that is cast on established powers as well as on the oppositions that remain indefinitely in the margins of historical reality.

Nor could the solution be 'a return to Marx', pure and simple, whereby the historical evolution of ideas and practices over the past eighty years[1] would be considered no more than a layer of impurities concealing the resplendent body of a doctrine intact. Not only is it that the doctrine of Marx itself, as is well known and as I shall attempt once more to show, far from possesses the systematic simplicity and the consistency that some would like to attribute to it. Nor is it that such a 'return' necessarily involves an academic character – since, at best, it could do no more than restore the correct theoretical content belonging to a past doctrine, as could be done for Descartes or Thomas Aquinas, while at the same time leaving entirely in the shadows the problem that counts above all others, namely, the importance and the signification of Marxism for us and for contemporary history. The return to Marx is impossible because, under the pretext of being faithful to Marx and in order to realize this fidelity, it begins by violating some essential principles posited by Marx himself.

Marx was, in fact, the first to show that the signification of a theory cannot be understood in isolation from the historical and social practice to which it corresponds, which is an extension of it or which it serves to cover. Who today would dare to claim that the one and only meaning of Christianity is that which restores a purified reading of the Gospels, and that the social reality and the historical practice of the Churches and of Christianity over two millennia have nothing essential to teach us on this account? The 'faithfulness to Marx' that brackets the historical fate of Marxism is no less laughable. It is even more so, because for a Christian the revelation of Scripture has a transcendent ground and a timeless truth that no theory could possess in the eyes of a Marxist. To want to find the meaning of Marxism exclusively in what Marx wrote, ignoring what this doctrine has become in history, is to claim, in direct contradiction to the central ideas of this doctrine, that real history does not count, that the truth of a theory is always and exclusively 'beyond', and, finally, it is to replace revolution by revelation and the reflection on facts by the exegesis of texts.

This in itself would be serious enough. But there is more to it, for the necessity of confrontation with historical reality[2] is explicitly inscribed in

Marx's work and bound up with its most profound meaning. The Marxism of Marx did not aspire to be, and could not have been, a theory like any other, paying no attention to its rootedness and its historical resonance. The point was no longer 'to interpret but to change the world',[3] and the full meaning of the theory *is*, according to the theory itself, the one that appears in the practice it inspires. Those who say, believing they thus 'exonerate' Marxist theory: None of the historical practices that claim to belong to Marxism are 'truly' inspired by it – these very people, in saying this, 'condemn' Marxism to being a 'mere theory' and level an irrevocable judgement upon it. This could even be called, quite literally, a Last Judgement, for Marx assumed entirely as his own Hegel's great idea: *Weltgeschichte ist Weltgericht.*[4]

In fact, if the practice inspired by Marxism effectively was revolutionary during certain phases of modern history, it was also the opposite during other periods. And if these two phenomena require interpretation (I shall return to this), it is nevertheless the case that they indicate beyond any doubt the essential ambiguity of Marxism. It is also the case, and this is even more important, that in history and in politics the present carries infinitely greater weight than the past. Now, this 'present' is the fact that for over forty years Marxism has become an *ideology* in the very sense Marx gave to this term: a set of ideas that relate to a reality not in order to shed light on it and to change it, but in order to veil it and to justify it in the imaginary, which permits people to say one thing and do another, to appear as other than they are.

Marxism first became an ideology as the official dogma of the established powers in countries described by antiphrasis as 'socialist'. Invoked by governments that visibly do not embody the power of the proletariat and are no more 'controlled' by the latter than any bourgeois government; represented by brilliant leaders treated by their equally brilliant successors as no more than criminal madmen, without further ado; serving as a foundation for the policies of Tito as well as those of the Albanians, the policies of Khrushchev as well as those of Mao, Marxism has become the 'solemn complement of justification' discussed by Marx, which allows one to teach students the mandatory work, *The State and Revolution*, and at the same time to maintain the most oppressive and most rigid state apparatus ever known,[5] thereby helping the bureaucracy to conceal itself behind the 'collective ownership' of the means of production.

Marxism has also become an ideology as the doctrine of the multitude of sects that proliferated as a result of the degeneration of the official Marxist movement. The word 'sect' is not used here simply as an epithet; it has a precise sociological and historical meaning. A group with few members is not necessarily a sect; Marx and Engels did not form a sect even at the times they were most isolated. A sect is a group that sets up as an absolute a single side, aspect, or phase of the movement from which it stems, makes this aspect the truth of the doctrine and *the* truth as such, subordinates every-thing else to it, and, in order to maintain its 'faithfulness' to this aspect, severs itself radically from the world, so as to live henceforth in 'its' own separate world. The invocation of Marxism by these sects allows them to think of themselves and to present themselves as something other than what they really are, that is, as the future revolutionary party of the proletariat, in which they are unable to take root.

Finally, Marxism has become an ideology in an entirely different sense, as well: for the past several decades, it is no longer, even as a simple theory, a living theory, and it is useless to search in the literature of the last forty years for any fecund applications of the theory, and even less for any attempts to extend it or deepen it.

It may be that what we are saying will be received as a scandal by those who, making it their profession to 'defend Marx', bury his remains every day a little deeper under the thick layers of their lies or their stupidity. I could not care less about this. It is clear that by analysing the historical destiny of Marxism, we are not, in any ethical sense, 'imputing' the responsibility to Marx. It is Marxism itself in what is best in its spirit, in its merciless denun-ciation of empty phrases and of ideologies, in its continual demand for self-criticism, that forces us to concern ourselves with its real fate.

Moreover, the question goes far beyond Marxism. For, just as the de-generation of the Russian Revolution poses the problem: Is it the fate of *every* socialist revolution that is indicated by this degeneration?, so, too, we must ask: Is it the lot of *every* revolutionary theory that is indicated by the fate of Marxism? This is the question I shall deal with at length at the end of this text.[6]

It is therefore not possible to maintain or to rediscover any sort of 'ortho-doxy' – whether in the laughable and comically complementary form given to it at once by the Stalinist pontiffs and the sectarian hermits, that of a doctrine alleged to be intact and 'amended', 'improved', or 'brought up to date' by one or the other at their convenience on a particular point; or, in the dramatic and ultimatum-like form given to it by Trotsky in 1940,[7] stating more or less as follows: We know that Marxism is an imperfect theory, bound to a given historical epoch, and that its theoretical development must continue, but, since revolution is the order of the day, this task can and must wait. Acceptable on the very day of armed insurrection, when it is anyhow useless, this argument, after a quarter of a century, serves only to conceal the inertia and sterility that have indeed characterized the Trotskyist move-ment since the death of its founder.

Nor is it possible to attempt to maintain an orthodoxy as Lukács did in 1919 by limiting it to Marxist *method*, which is held to be separate from its content and, so to speak, indifferent to it.[8] Although it marks an advance with respect to the diverse varieties of 'orthodox' cretinism, this position is untenable for a reason that Lukács, who was nonetheless steeped in dialectic, overlooked: unless we are to take the term in its most superficial sense, method cannot be separated from content in this way, especially not when it is a question of historical and social theory. Method, in the philosophical sense, is simply the operating set of categories. A rigid distinction between method and content belongs only to the most naive forms of transcendental idealism or criticism, which, in its initial steps, separates and opposes an infinite or indefinite matter or content and the categories that the eternal flow of the material cannot affect, categories that are the form without which this matter could not be grasped. But this rigid distinction is already superseded in the more advanced, more dialectical phases of critical thinking. For the problem immediately appears: How are we to know which category corresponds to which material? If the material bears in itself the 'distinctive sign' allowing it to be subsumed under a given category, it is therefore not merely shapeless matter; and if it is truly without form, then the application of this or that category becomes indifferent, and the distinction between true and false collapses. It is precisely this antinomy that has led, upon a number of occasions in the history of philosophy, from critical thinking to thinking of a dialectical type.[9]

Such is the way the question is posed on the level of logic. And, on the historical-genetic level, that is to say, when the process of the development of knowledge is considered from the point of view of its unfolding as *history*, it is most often the 'unfolding of the material' that leads to a revision or a shattering of the categories. The properly philosophical revolution produced in modern physics as a result of relativity and quantum theory is only one striking example among others.[10]

However, the impossibility of establishing a rigid distinction between method and content, between category and material, appears even more clearly when we consider, not knowledge of nature but knowledge of history. For, in this case there is not simply the fact that the further exploration of the material already given or the appearance of new material can lead to a modification of the categories, that is, of method. There is especially, and more profoundly, another fact, one brought to light, precisely, by Marx and by Lukács himself:[11] the categories we use to think of history are, for an essential part, real products of historical development. These categories can clearly and effectively become forms of *knowledge* of history only when they are embodied or realized in forms of *effective social life*.

To cite only the simplest example: if in Antiquity, the dominant categories under which social and historical relations are grasped are essentially *political* categories (power in the city, relations between cities, the relation between force and right, etc.), and if the economic receives only marginal attention, this is neither because intelligence or reflection was less 'advanced', nor because the economic material was absent or neglected. The reason is that, in the reality of the ancient world, the economy was not yet constituted as a separate, 'autonomous' moment (as Marx would say), 'for itself', of human activity. A genuine analysis of the economy itself and of its importance for society could occur only starting in the seventeenth, and in particular, in the eighteenth century, that is, with the birth of capitalism, which in fact set up the economy as dominant moment of social life. And the central importance accorded by Marx and the Marxists to the economic likewise expresses this historical reality.

It is therefore clear that there can be no 'method' in history which would remain unaffected by real historical development. And this for reasons more profound than the notions of the 'progress of knowledge', 'new discoveries', and so on, reasons that concern directly the very *structure* of historical knowledge, and first and foremost the structure of its object, that is, the mode of being of history. Since the object of historical knowledge is itself a signifying object, or an object constituted by significations, the development of the historical world is *ipso facto* the unfolding of a world of significations. There can thus be no break between matter and category, between fact and meaning. And since this world of significations is that in which the 'subject' of historical knowledge lives, it is also that through which this subject necessarily grasps, to begin with, the whole of the historical material.

Of course, these observations, too, are to be relativized. They cannot imply that at every instant every category and every method are put into question, superseded, or destroyed by the evolution of real history at the very moment one thinks. In other words, each time it is a concrete question whether historical change has reached the point where the old categories and the old method are to be reconsidered. But it then becomes apparent that this cannot be done independent of a discussion about content, and is even nothing other than a discussion about the content which, by starting with the old method, may eventually show the need to go beyond this method when it is placed in contact with the material.

To say that being Marxist is being faithful to Marx's method, which continues to be true, is to say that nothing in the content of the history of the past hundred years either authorizes us or compels us to put Marx's categories into question, that everything can be understood by means of his method. This is, therefore, to take a position with reference to content, to have a definite theory about it, and yet to refuse to state it.

In fact, it is precisely the elaboration of the content that forces us to reconsider the method and hence the Marxist system. If we have been led to pose, at first gradually and in the end bluntly, the question of Marxism, it is because we have been forced to recognize, not only and not so much that this or that particular theory of Marx, this or that specific idea of traditional Marxism was 'false', but that the history we are living can no longer be grasped with the help of Marxist categories as they stand, not even when they are 'amended', 'extended', etc. It appeared to us that this history can be neither understood nor changed with this method. The re-examination of Marxism that we have undertaken does not occur in a void, nor are we speaking by placing ourselves anywhere at all or nowhere at all. Starting from revolutionary Marxism, we have arrived at the point where we have to choose between remaining Marxist and remaining revolutionaries, between faithfulness to a doctrine that, for a long time now, has ceased to fuel either reflection or action and faithfulness to the project of a radical change of society, which demands that we first understand what we want to change and that we identify what in society truly challenges this society and is struggling against its present form. Method cannot be separated from content, and their unity, that is to say, theory, cannot in turn be separated from the requirements of a revolutionary action which, as the example both of great parties and of sects has shown, can no longer be clarified and guided by the traditional schemata. [. . .]

Notes

1 T/E: Dating back from 1964, the year this text was written, to the year following Marx's death in 1883.

2 By historical reality we, of course, do not mean particular events and facts separated from the rest, but the dominant tendencies in their evolution, after all the necessary interpretations.

3 Marx, 'Eleventh Thesis on Feuerbach', in Marx and Engels, *Selected Works* (New York: International Publishers, 1968), p. 30.

4 'Universal history is the Last Judgement.' Despite its theological overtones, this is Hegel's most radically atheistic idea: there is no transcendence, no recourse against what happens here, we *are* definitely what we become, what we will have become.

5 As one 'knows', the need to destroy, on the first day of the revolution, every state apparatus separate from the masses is the central thesis of *State and Revolution*.

6 T/E: See below, 'Theory and Revolutionary Project'.

7 See *In Defense of Marxism*, 2nd edn (New York: Pathfinder, 1973).

8 'What is Orthodox Marxism?' in *History and Class Consciousness*, trans. Rodney Livingstone (Cambridge, Mass.: MIT, 1971), pp. 1–26. C. Wright Mills also appears to adopt this viewpoint. See *The Marxists* (Harmondsworth: Penguin, 1962), pp. 98 and 129.

9 The classic example of this shift is obviously the passage from Kant to Hegel, by way of Fichte and Schelling. The problematic is the same, however, in the later works of Plato or in the neo-Kantians, from Rickert to Lask.

10 To be sure, the positions must not simply be reversed. Neither logically nor historically can physical categories be considered merely the result of the material (still less a 'reflection' of it). A revolution in the domain of categories can lead to the grasp of a material previously undefined (as with Galileo). Furthermore, an advance in experimentation can 'force' a new material to appear. Ultimately there is a twofold relation, but there is certainly no independence of the categories in relation to the content.

11 'The Changing Function of Historical Materialism', in *History and Class Consciousness*, pp. 223–55.

Theory and Revolutionary Project

Praxis and Project

Knowing and making/doing

If what we say is true, if not only the specific content of Marxism as a theory is unacceptable, but the very idea of a complete and definitive theory is a pipe dream and a mystification, can we then still speak of a socialist revolution and maintain the project of a radical transformation of society? Is not a revolution, like the one aimed at by Marxism and like the one we continue to aim at, a conscious enterprise? Does it not presuppose both a rational knowledge of present society and the possibility of rationally anticipating future society? To say that a socialist transformation is possible and desirable, is this not to say that our effective knowledge of present society ensures this possibility, that our expected knowledge of future society justifies this choice? In both cases, do we not raise the claim that our thought possesses present and future social organization as totalities in act and that it provides at the same time a criterion permitting us to judge them? On what can we base all this, if there is not and cannot be a theory, and even, behind it, a philosophy of history and of society?

These questions, these objections can be – and indeed are – formulated from two diametrically opposed points of view, which, nevertheless, ultimately share the same premises.

For the first, the critique of the alleged absolute certainties of Marxism is interesting, perhaps even true – yet unacceptable because it would destroy the revolutionary movement. Since this movement must be supported, the theory must be preserved whatever the cost, even if this means cutting back on claims and requirements, or, if need be, shutting one's eyes.

For the second group, since a total theory cannot exist, one is forced to give up the revolutionary project, unless it is posited, in utter contradiction with its content, as the blind will to transform at any price something one does not know into something one knows even less.

In both instances the implicit postulate is the same: Without a total theory there can be no conscious action. In both cases, the phantasy of Absolute Knowledge remains sovereign. And in both cases the same ironic reversal of values occurs. The person who considers himself a man of action grants, instead, the primacy of theory; he sets up as the supreme criterion the possibility of safeguarding revolutionary activity, while making this possibility dependent on maintaining, in appearance anyway, a definitive theory. The philosopher who wants to be radical remains a prisoner of what has been criticized. A conscious revolution, he says, would presuppose Absolute

Knowledge. Eternally absent, this knowledge nevertheless remains the measure of our acts and of our life.

This postulate, however, is worthless. We already have an inkling that by forcing us to choose between geometry and chaos, between Absolute Knowledge and blind reflex, between God and beast, these objections move within a world of pure fiction and allow to slip through unnoticed a trifle: all that is and ever will be given to us, human reality. Nothing we do, nothing we have anything to do with, ever affords complete transparency, any more than it displays utter molecular disorder. The historical and human world (that is to say, with the exception of an infinitely distant point, as mathematicians say, the world as such) is of a different order. It cannot even be called 'the mixed' for it is not made of a mixture. Total order and total disorder are not the components of the real but limiting concepts we abstract from it, or, rather, pure constructions which, taken in absolute terms, become illegitimate and incoherent. They belong to the mythical extension of the world created by philosophy over the past twenty-five centuries, and this is something we must rid ourselves of if we want to stop importing our own phantasies into what is to be thought.

The historical world is the world of human *making/doing* [*faire*]. This making/doing is always related to knowledge, but the relation itself has to be elucidated. For this elucidation, we shall look to two examples, two extremes – the limiting cases of 'reflex action' and 'technique'.

Consider a 'purely reflex' human activity, one that is absolutely non-conscious. By definition, this sort of activity would have no relation to any type of knowledge. But it is also clear that it would not belong to the domain of history.[1]

Consider, at the other extreme, a 'purely rational' activity. This would be based on an exhaustive, or practically exhaustive, knowledge of its domain. By practically exhaustive, we mean that any question relevant for practice and arising out of this domain would be decidable.[2] In terms of this knowledge and in conclusion to the reasoning it permits, action would be confined to positing in reality the means to reach the ends it aims at and to establishing the causes that would lead to the intended results. An approximation of this type of activity is realized in history; it is *technique*.[3] An approximation, because an exhaustive knowledge cannot exist (rather, only the fragments of such a knowledge) even within a well-defined domain and because the delimitation of domains in this way is never airtight.[4] Under this concept of 'rational activity' can be placed a host of cases which, without belonging to technique in the strict sense, come close to it and which we shall henceforth include under this term. The repetitive activity of an assembly-line worker; solving a second-degree algebraic equation for someone who knows the general formula; deriving new mathematical theorems by means of the 'mechanized' formalism of Hilbert; many simple games, and so forth, are examples of technical activity in the broad sense.

What is essential in human activities can be grasped neither as reflex nor as technique. No human making/doing is nonconscious, and yet none could continue one second longer if a prior exhaustive knowledge were required, if a total elucidation of its object and its mode of operation were necessary. This is obvious in the case of all the 'trivial' activities that make up daily life, both individual and collective. But this is also the case for more 'elevated' activities with the weightiest consequences, those directly involving other people's lives and those aimed at the most universal and lasting creations.

Raising a child (whether as parent or as teacher) can be done with greater or lesser consciousness and lucidity, but it is excluded by definition that this be done on the basis of a total elucidation of the child's being and of the pedagogical relationship. When a doctor, or better yet an analyst,[5] begins a treatment, do we think of asking him to put his patient into concepts first, to draw the diagrams of his conflictual structures and the *ne varietur* course of treatment? Here, as in the case of the pedagogue, we are dealing with something quite other than a provisional ignorance or a 'therapeutic' silence. The illness and the patient are not two separate things, one containing the other (any more than the future of the child is something contained in the child-thing), of which we could define the essence and the reciprocal relationship while awaiting a more thorough investigation. It is a mode of being of the patient, whose entire life, past as well as yet to come, is at issue and the signification of this life cannot be fixed and closed off at a given moment since it continues and thus modifies past significations. What is essential in this treatment, just as in education, corresponds to the very relationship that will be established between the patient and the doctor, or between the child and the adult, and to the evolution of this relationship, which depends on what each of them will *do*. One does not ask the teacher or the doctor for a complete theory of their activity, which, moreover, they would be incapable of supplying. But one should not, for all that, say that these are blind activities, that raising a child or treating a patient is a game of roulette. The requirements with which human making/doing confronts us are of another order.[6]

The same thing is true for the other manifestations of human making/doing, even those in which others are not explicitly implicated, in which the 'isolated' subject undertakes a task or an 'impersonal' work. When an artist begins a work, and even when an author begins a theoretical book, he both does and does not know what he is going to say – even less does he know what that which he will say *will mean*. And it is no different for the most 'rational' activity of all, theoretical activity. We were saying earlier that the use of Hilbert's formalism for the relatively mechanical derivation of new theorems is a technical activity. However, the attempt to constitute this formalism in itself is absolutely not a technique, but instead a genuine making/doing, a conscious activity which can rationally assure neither its foundations nor its results. The proof of this, I dare say, lies in its grandiose failure.[7] More generally, if the application of 'proven' results and methods within this or that branch of mathematics can be assimilated to a technique, once mathematical research approaches the foundations or the ultimate consequences of the discipline, it reveals its essence as a making/doing which rests on no ultimate certainty. The construction of mathematics is a project pursued by humanity for thousands of years; during the course of this elaboration, increased rigorousness within the discipline has led *ipso facto* to a growing uncertainty as to the foundations and as to the meaning of this activity.[8] With respect to physics, this is not even a making/doing, but a sort of Western, where one surprising event after another creates an accelerating pace, astounding even the actors themselves who first set off the series of actions.[9]

Theory as such is a making/doing, the always uncertain attempt to realize the project of elucidating the world.[10] And this is also true for that supreme or extreme form of theory – philosophy – the attempt to think the world without knowing, either before or after the fact, whether the world is effectively thinkable, or even just what thinking exactly means. It is for this reason, moreover, that one does not have to 'go beyond philosophy by realizing it'. Philosophy is 'surpassed' as soon as one has 'realized' what it is: it is philosophy – that is to say, both a lot and very little. One has 'surpassed' philosophy – namely, not forgotten it, still less despised it, but put it in its place – when it is understood that it is simply a project, one which is necessary yet uncertain as to its origin, its import, and its fate; not exactly an adventure, perhaps, but also not a chess game, and certainly not the realization of the total transparency of the world for the subject and of the subject for itself. And if philosophy were to set down for a politics that aspired to be both lucid and radical the prior condition of total rigorousness, demanding that this politics be founded wholly on reason, politics would be within its rights to answer: Have you then no mirrors at home? Or does your activity consist in setting up standards for others which you are incapable of applying to yourself?

Finally, if particular techniques are 'rational activities', technique itself (we are using the term here in its restricted, ordinary sense) is absolutely not. Various techniques belong to technique, but technique itself is not technical. In its historical reality, technique is a project whose meaning remains uncertain, whose future is obscure, and whose end [*finalité*] is indeterminate, since, to be sure, the idea of making ourselves 'the masters and possessors of nature' is strictly meaningless.

To demand that the revolutionary project be founded on a complete theory is therefore to assimilate politics to a technique and to posit its sphere of action – history – as the possible object of a finished and exhaustive knowledge. To invert this reasoning and conclude on the basis of the impossibility of this sort of knowledge that all lucid revolutionary politics is impossible amounts, finally, to a wholesale rejection of all human activity and history as unsatisfactory according to a fictitious standard. Politics, however, is neither the concretization of an Absolute Knowledge nor a technique; neither is it the blind will of no one knows what. It belongs to another domain, that of making/doing, and to the specific mode of making/doing that is *praxis*.

Praxis and project

We call praxis that making/doing in which the other or others are intended as autonomous beings and considered as the essential agents of the development of their own autonomy. True politics, true pedagogy, true medicine, to the extent that these have ever existed, belong to praxis.

In praxis there is something *to be made/to be done*, but what is *to be made/to be done* is something specific: it is precisely the development of the autonomy of the other or of others (this not being the case in relationships that are purely personal, as in friendship or love, where autonomy is recognized but its development is not posited as a separate object, for these relationships have no end outside the relationship itself).One could say that for praxis the autonomy of the other or of others is at once the end and the means; praxis is what intends the development of autonomy as its end and, for this end, uses autonomy as its means. This way of speaking is handy for it is easily comprehensible. But it is, strictly speaking, an abuse of language, and the terms 'end' and 'means' are absolutely incorrect in this context. Praxis cannot be circumscribed in a model of ends and means. The model of the end and of the means to attain this end belongs, precisely, in its proper usage, to technical activity, for the latter has to do with a real end, an end which is an end, a finished and definite end which can be posited as a necessary or probable result in view of which the choice of means amounts to a matter of more or less exact calculation. With respect to this end, the means have no internal relation, simply a relation of cause to effect.[11]

In praxis, however, the autonomy of others is not an end; it is, all word-play aside, a beginning, anything but an end. It is not finished; it cannot be defined in terms of a state or any particular characteristics. There is an internal relation between what is intended (the development of autonomy) and that through which it is intended (the exercise of this autonomy). These are two moments of a single process. Finally, although it evolves within a concrete context which conditions it and has to take into consideration the complex network of causal relations crisscrossing its terrain, praxis can never reduce the choice of its manner of operating to mere calculation, not that this would be too complicated, but because it would, by definition, allow the escape of the essential factor – autonomy.

To be sure, praxis is a conscious activity and can exist only as lucid activity, but it is something quite other than the application of prior knowledge (and cannot be justified by calling upon knowledge like this – which does not mean that it cannot justify itself). It is based on knowledge, but this knowledge is always fragmentary and provisional. It is fragmentary because there can be no exhaustive theory of man and of history; it is provisional because praxis itself constantly gives rise to new knowledge, for *it makes the world speak in a language that is at once singular and universal*. This is why the relations of praxis to theory, true theory correctly conceived, are infinitely tighter and more profound than those of any 'strictly rational' technique or practice; for the latter, theory is only a code of lifeless prescriptions which can never, in its manipulations, encounter meaning. The parallel development of psychoanalytic practice and theory by Freud, from 1886 until his death, probably provides the best illustration of this twofold relation. The theory cannot be given beforehand, because it constantly emerges out of the activity itself. The elucidation and transformation of reality progress together in praxis, each conditioning the other. And this twofold progression is the justification of praxis. However, in the logical structure of the ensemble they form, activity precedes elucidation; for praxis, the ultimate goal is not the elucidation but the transformation of the given.[12]

We have spoken of fragmentary and provisional knowledge, and this may give the impression that praxis (and all making/doing) is essentially negative, a privation or a deficiency in relation to another situation which would be full and would possess an exhaustive theory or Absolute Knowledge. This appearance, however, stems from our language, bound to a several-millennia-old manner of treating problems, which consists in judging or thinking the effective after the pattern of the fictive. If we were certain of being properly understood, if we did not have to take into consideration the tenacious prejudices and presuppositions holding sway even in the most critical of minds, we would simply say: Praxis is based on an effective knowledge (one which, of course, is limited, provisional – as is everything that is effective), and we would not feel the need to add: Being a lucid activity, it obviously cannot call upon the phantasy of an illusory Absolute Knowledge. What grounds praxis is not a temporary deficiency in our knowledge, which could gradually be reduced. Even less is it the transformation of the present horizon of our knowledge into an absolute boundary.[13] The 'relative' lucidity of praxis is not a stopgap solution, better than nothing – this is so not only because something 'better' exists nowhere, but also because this is but another side to its positive substance: the very object of praxis is the new, and this cannot be reduced to the simply materialized tracing of a preconstituted rational order; in other words, its object is the real itself and not a stable, limited, dead artifact.

This 'relative' lucidity also corresponds to another aspect of praxis which is just as essential: its subject, too, is constantly transformed on the basis of the experience in which it is engaged, which the subject *does* or *makes*, but which also *makes* the subject. 'Pedagogues are educated', 'the poem makes the poet'. And it goes without saying that a continuous modification results, both in form and in content, with respect to the *relation* between a subject and an object, which themselves cannot be defined once and for all.

What has, up to now, been called politics has almost always been a mixture in which the dominant component has been manipulation, treating people as things in terms of their properties and their supposed known reactions. What we call revolutionary politics is a praxis which takes as its object the organization and orientation of society with a view toward fostering the autonomy of all its members and which recognizes that this presupposes a radical transformation of society, which will be possible, in turn, only through people's autonomous activity.

It can readily be granted (after a brief inventory of a few phases of history) that a politics such as this has not existed until now. How and why might it exist now? On what could it be based?

The answer to this question leads us to the discussion of the very content of the *revolutionary project*, which is, precisely, the reorganization and re-orientation of society by means of people's autonomous action.

The project is the element of praxis (and of all activity). It is a determinate praxis, considered in its ties with the real, in the concrete definition of its objectives, in the specification of its mediations. It is the intention of transforming the real, guided by a representation of the meaning of this transformation, taking into consideration the real conditions and inspiring an activity.

We must not confuse project and plan. The plan corresponds to the *technical* moment of an activity, when conditions, objectives, and means can be and are 'exactly' determined, and when the mutual ordering of means and ends is based on a sufficient knowledge of the domain concerned. (It is apparent from this that the expression 'economic plan', despite its convenience in other respects, is, strictly speaking, an abuse of language.)

We must also distinguish between the project and the activity of an 'ethical subject' in traditional philosophy. The latter is guided – like the navigator by the North Star, following Kant's famous image – by the idea of morality, but at the same time remains at an infinite distance from this idea. There is thus a perpetual noncoincidence between the real activity of an ethical subject and the moral idea, even though they are related to each other. This relation however, is equivocal, for the idea is at once an end and a non-end.

An end because it expresses, without excess or deficit, what should be; a non-end because in principle there is no question that it be attained or realized. The project, however, regards its realization as an essential moment. If there is a gap between representation and realization, it is not one of principle, or, rather, it depends on categories other than the gap between 'idea' and 'reality': it refers to a new modification affecting representation as well as reality. The core of the project, in this respect, is a meaning and an orientation (a direction toward) which cannot simply be fixed in 'clear and distinct ideas' and which go beyond the representation of the project as it might be fixed at any given moment.

When it is a matter of politics, the representation of the intended transformation, the definition of objectives, can take – and must necessarily take, under certain conditions – the form of a *programme*. The programme is a provisional concretization of the objectives of the project on certain points judged to be essential in given circumstances, in so far as their realization would lead to or would facilitate the realization of the project as a whole by its own inner dynamics. The programme is but a fragmentary and provisional figure of the project. Programmes come and go, the project remains. Like anything else, the programme can easily deteriorate and degenerate. The programme may be taken as an absolute; it may foster the alienation of people and their activities. This in itself proves nothing against the necessity of a programme.

Our topic here, however, is not the philosophy of practice as such, nor is it the elucidation of the concept of project for itself. We want to show the possibility and render explicit the meaning of the revolutionary project as the project of transforming present society into a society organized and oriented toward fostering the autonomy of all, this transformation being accomplished by the autonomous action of human beings, such as they are produced by present society.[14]

This discussion, no more than any other, does not take place on a *tabula rasa*. What we say today is necessarily leaning on – and we might even say, if we were not careful: is sunk in – what has already been said for ages, by others and by ourselves. The conflicts that divide present society, the irrationality that predominates in it; the perpetual oscillation of individuals and the masses between struggle and apathy, the system's incapacity to deal with either one; the experience of past revolutions and, from our point of view, the ascending line that joins their apexes; the possibilities for the socialist organization of society and its modalities, to the extent that these can be defined as of now – all this is necessarily presupposed in what we are saying and it is not possible to go over it again here. For the moment, we should like simply to shed light on the main questions opened up by the critique of Marxism and the rejection of its analysis of capitalism, its theory of history and its general philosophy. If there is no economic analysis that can show, in the form of an objective mechanism, both the grounds of the crisis of present society and the necessary shape of future society, what can serve as the bases of the revolutionary project in the real situation and from where can we form any idea with regard to another society? Does not the critique of rationalism exclude the possibility of establishing a destructive and constructive 'revolutionary dynamics'? How can one posit a revolutionary project without wanting to grasp present society, and especially future society, as a totality and, moreover, as a rational totality, without succumbing to one of the pitfalls cited above? Once the guarantee of 'objective processes' has been eliminated, what remains? Why do we *want* revolution – and why would others want it? Why would they be capable of it? For, does not the project of a socialist revolution presuppose the idea of a 'total man' to come, of an Absolute Subject, a notion we have denounced? Just what does autonomy signify, and to what extent can it be realized? Does this not blow the role of consciousness out of all proportion? Does it not make alienation a bad dream from which we are about to awaken, and prior history an unfortunate accident? Is there any sense in postulating a radical reversal; are we not pursuing the illusion of an absolute novelty? Is there not behind all this another philosophy of history?

Roots of the Revolutionary Project

Social roots of the revolutionary project

There can be no complete theory of history, and the idea of the total rationality of history is absurd. However, neither can we say that history and society are *ir*rational in a positive sense. We have already tried to show that rational and nonrational are constantly intersecting in historical and social reality, and it is precisely this intersection that provides the condition for action.

Historical reality is not completely and exhaustively rational. If it were, *making/doing* would never be a problem, for everything would already have been *said*. Making/doing implies that reality is not rational through and through. It also implies that it is not simply chaos, that it contains grooves, lines of force, veins, which mark out the possible, the feasible, indicate the probable, and permit action to find points of support in the given.

The mere existence of instituted societies suffices to demonstrate this. However, along with the 'reasons' for its stability, existing society also reveals, upon analysis, its cracks and the force lines of its crisis.

The discussion of the relation between the revolutionary project and reality must be dislodged from the metaphysical terrain of the historical inevitability of socialism – or of the historical inevitability of nonsocialism. To begin with, it must include a discussion of the possibility of transforming society in a particular direction.

We shall only begin this discussion here, restricting ourselves to two examples.[15]

In that fundamental social activity – *labour* – and in the *relations of production* in which this labour is performed, capitalist organization presents itself, since its origins, as dominated by a central conflict. The workers only halfway accept – execute, as it were, with only one hand – the tasks they are assigned. The workers cannot effectively participate in production, and yet cannot help but participate in it. Management cannot do otherwise than exclude the workers from production and, at the same time, it cannot exclude them from it. The conflict resulting from this – which is at once 'external', between directors and executants, and 'internalized', within each executant and each director – could get bogged down and would become blurred if production were static and technique petrified, but economic expansion and technological upheaval keep it constantly alive.

The crisis of the capitalist enterprise presents a number of other aspects, and if one were to consider only the upper stages, one could perhaps speak simply of 'bureaucratic dysfunction'. But at the base, on the ground floor of the shops and offices, it is not a question of 'dysfunction', but of a conflict which is expressed in an incessant struggle, even if it is implicit and masked. Long before the revolutionaries, theoreticians and practitioners of capitalism discovered the existence and the gravity of this conflict and described it accurately, even if they stopped short, naturally, of the conclusions that could have been drawn from this analysis and if they remained bound to the idea of finding at any cost a 'solution' without upsetting the existing order.

This conflict, this struggle, display a logic and a dynamic, out of which three tendencies emerge:

- workers organize in informal groups and set up a fragmentary 'counter-management' of labour in opposition to the official management established by the employer;

- workers set forth demands concerning the conditions and the organization of labour;

- during the phases of social crisis, workers openly and directly demand the management of production and attempt to realize this (Russia 1917–18, Catalonia 1936–7, Hungary 1956).[16]

These tendencies express the same problem in different countries and in different phases. The analysis of the conditions of capitalist production shows that they are not accidental but consubstantial with the most profound characteristics of this kind of production. They cannot be amended or eliminated by partial reforms of the system, since they follow from the fundamental relation of capitalism, the division of the labour process into a moment of direction and a moment of execution, each embodied in a different social pole. The meaning they embody defines, beyond the framework of production, a type of antinomy, of struggle, *and* of overcoming of this antinomy that are essential to the understanding of a great number of other phenomena in contemporary society. In short, these phenomena are articulated together, they are articulated with the fundamental structure of capitalism, articulated with the rest of social relations. And they express not only a conflict but a tendency towards the solution of this conflict through the realization of workers' management of production, which implies the elimination of bureaucracy. We therefore find in social reality itself a conflictual structure and the seeds of a solution.[17]

It is, therefore, a description and a critical analysis of what *is* that unearths, in this case, one of the roots of the revolutionary project. This description and this analysis are not even, truly speaking, 'our own' in any specific sense. Our theorizing only sets in place *what society itself expresses confusedly about itself at every level.* It is the capitalist leaders or bureaucrats who are constantly complaining about people's opposition; it is their own sociologists who analyse this opposition, who exist in order to defuse it, and who most of the time confess that it is impossible. It is the workers who, once we begin to look closer, constantly combat the existing organization of production, *even if they do not know they are doing it.* And, if we feel satisfied with ourselves for having 'predicted' the content of the Hungarian Revolution far in advance,[18] we did not, for all that, invent it (any more than in the case of Yugoslavia, where the problem is posed even if it is to a large extent mystified). Society itself speaks of its own crisis in a language which scarcely requires any interpretation.[19] One section of society, that which is most vitally concerned by this crisis and which, moreover, includes the vast majority of people, behaves in actual fact in a way that, at one and the same time, *constitutes* the crisis and shows a possible way out of it. And under certain conditions, this section attacks the present organization, destroys it, and begins to replace it with another. In this other organization – in the management of production by the producers – it is impossible not to see the incarnation of autonomy in the fundamental domain of labour.

The questions that can legitimately be raised are therefore not: Where do you see the crisis? Where will you find a solution? The question is: Is this solution – workers' management – truly possible? Can it lastingly be realized? And supposing that, considered 'in itself', it appears possible, does not workers' management imply much more than workers' management?

However closely, however deeply one may try to look at it, the management of a firm by the collectivity of those who work there presents no insur-mountable problem. Quite the opposite, it reveals the possibility of doing away with an extraordinary number of problems which constantly hamper the functioning of firms today, resulting in immense wastage and wear on human and material resources.[20] At the same time, however, it becomes clear that the problem of management goes far beyond the firm and produc-tion and refers back to society as a whole, and that any solution to it implies a radical change in people's attitudes with respect to labour and the collec-tivity. We are therefore led to raise the questions of society as a totality and of people's responsibility – which we shall examine later.

The *economy* provides a second example which will allow us to clarify other aspects of the problem.

We have tried to show that there is not and that there cannot be a system-atic and complete theory of the capitalist economy.[21] The attempt to establish such a theory runs up against the determining influence exerted on the economy by a factor not reducible to the economic, namely, class struggle. It also collides with the impossibility, at another level, of estab-lishing a unit of measurement for economic phenomena, which nevertheless are presented as magnitudes. This does not prevent the possibility of a knowledge of the economy, or of finding out certain facts and of stating some tendencies (with regard to which, of course, precise discussion is open). For the industrialized countries, these facts and tendencies are, in our opinion:

1   The productivity of labour is increasing at an accelerating pace. In any event, no limit to this growth can be seen.

2   Despite the continuous rise in the standard of living, a problem of absorbing the fruits of this productivity is beginning to be posed in a virtual manner, in the form of the saturation of most traditional needs and in that of the latent underemployment of a growing portion of the workforce. Capitalism replies to these two phenomena by synthetically fabricating new needs, manipulating consumers, developing a mentality oriented towards 'status' and social rank tied to the level of consumption, and creating or maintaining outmoded or parasitic forms of employment. But it is by no means certain that these expedients will suffice for long. There are two apparent outcomes: turning the productive apparatus more and more towards the satisfaction of 'collective needs' (according to their capitalist definition and conception, to be sure), which seems hard to reconcile with the private economic mentality in the West and in the East (a policy such as this would imply a more rapid increase in 'taxes' than in wages), or, instead, introducing a more rapid reduction of labour time, which in the current social context would create enormous problems.[22] Either way, the basis for the system's functioning, economic motivation and constraint, would suffer what would probably be an irreparable blow.[23] What is more, if these

solutions are 'rational' from the point of view of the interests of capitalism as such, they are rarely so considered from the point of view of the specific interests of the dominant and influential capitalist and bureaucratic groups. To say that there is no absolute impossibility preventing capitalism from finding a way out of the situation that is being created today does not mean that it is a sure thing capitalism will get out of it. The stubborn and hitherto victorious resistance with which the dominant groups in the United States oppose the adoption of measures that would be beneficial to them – increases in public expenditure, the extension of 'aid' to underdeveloped countries, the reduction of labour time (which appear to them to be the height of extravagance, a squandering of funds, and sheer madness) – shows that an explosive crisis is as possible an evolution as is the pacific mutation of capitalism. This is all the more likely as this mutation would, at the present moment, put into question aspects of the social structure even more important than those concerned, in their time, by the New Deal, the introduction of economic controls, etc. Automation is progressing much more quickly than the decretinizing of American senators – although the latter might actually be speeded up by the very fact of a crisis. But whether it be through a crisis or through peaceful transformation, these problems will be resolved only by shaking the present social edifice to its very foundations.

3   There is a tremendous potential waste (or possibilities lost) in the use of productive resources (despite 'full employment'), stemming from a number of factors, all of which are related to the nature of the system: the lack of participation by the workers in production; bureaucratic dysfunction on the level of the firm as well as on that of the economy; competition and monopolistic competition (artificial product differentiation, lack of standardization of products and machinery, secrecy surrounding inventions and manufacturing processes, advertising, intentional restrictions in production); the irrational nature of the distribution of productive capacity among firms and branches, this distribution reflecting the past history of the economy as much as current needs; the protection of certain strata or sectors and the maintenance of the status quo; the irrational nature of the geographical and professional distribution of the workforce; the impossibility of any rational planning with respect to investments, resulting from ignorance of the present state of affairs as well as from avoidable uncertainties about the future (connected with the functioning of the 'market' or of the bureaucratic 'plan'); the radical impossibility of rational economic calculations (theoretically, if the price of one item of production contains an arbitrary element, all calculations throughout the system may thereby be jeopardized; now, prices have only a very distant relationship to costs, both in the West with its prevailing oligopolies and in the USSR where it is officially admitted that prices are essentially arbitrary); the use of a part of the product and of resources for ends that have a meaning only in relation to the system's class

structure (cost of the control bureaucracy in the firm and elsewhere, army, police, and so on). It is by definition impossible to quantify this wastage. Sociologists of labour have on occasion estimated at 50 per cent the loss in production due to the first factor we mentioned, undoubtedly the most important one, namely, workers' nonparticipation in production. If we were to advance an estimate, we would say that the current output of the United States must be of the order of a quarter to a fifth of that which could be attained by the elimination of the various above-mentioned factors [or that this output could be attained with a quarter of the labour currently expended].

4   Finally, an analysis of the possibilities that would result from making available to society, organized into councils of producers, economic knowledge and the existing techniques of information, communication, and computation – the 'cybernization' of the overall economy in the service of human beings' collective management – shows that, however far we can see, not only is there no technical or economic obstacle to the instauration and functioning of a socialist economy, but that this functioning would be, in its essential aspects, infinitely simpler and infinitely more rational – or infinitely less irrational – than the functioning of the current economy, whether private or 'planned'.[24]

There is, therefore, in modern society, an immense economic problem (which, ultimately, is the problem of 'suppression of the economy'), pregnant with an impending crisis. There are incalculable possibilities, currently being wasted, which, if put into effect, would allow a general well-being, a rapid reduction of labour time to perhaps half of what it is now, and the freeing of resources to satisfy needs that at the present moment are not even formulated. And there are positive solutions which, in a fragmentary, truncated, deformed manner are being proposed or introduced even now, and which, if they were applied radically and universally, would permit one to resolve this problem, realize these possibilities, and bring about an immense change in the life of humanity while rapidly eliminating 'economic need'.

It is clear that the application of this solution would require a radical transformation of the social structure – and a transformation of people's attitude toward society. We therefore find ourselves once again face to face with the problems of totalization and responsibility, which we shall attempt to analyse later.

Revolution and rationalization

The example of the economy allows us to see another essential aspect of the revolutionary problematic. A transformation in the direction indicated would signify an unprecedented *rationalization* of the economy. The metaphysical objection appears here, and appears here again as a sophism: Is a *complete* rationalization of the economy ever possible? The reply is: We do not care.

It is enough for us to know that a vast rationalization is possible and that it can only have a positive effect on people's lives. In the present economy we have a system that is only very partially rational but which contains possibilities for rationalization without assignable limit. These possibilities can begin to be realized only at the price of a radical transformation of the economic system and of the vaster system in which it is embedded. Conversely, it is only in relation to this rationalization that such a radical transformation is conceivable.

The rationalization in question concerns not only the use of the economic system (allocate the output to the ends that are expressly desired by the collectivity). It also concerns the system's functioning and, ultimately, the possibility of the very knowledge of the system. On this final point we can see the difference between the contemplative attitude and praxis. The contemplative attitude confines itself to observing that the economy (both past and present) contains profoundly irrational elements, which forbid a complete knowledge of it. It finds therein the particular expression of a general truth, the irreducible opacity of the given, which obviously is just as valid for the future. This attitude will assert, as a result (and it has every right to do so on these grounds), that a totally transparent economy is impossible. From this, it could easily – should it be the slightest bit lacking in rigour – rush to the conclusion that it is not worth the bother of trying to change anything, or that all the possible changes, however desirable they may be, will never change anything essential but will instead remain on the same line of being, since they can never accomplish the jump from the relative to the absolute.

The political attitude notes that the irrational character of the economy is not simply to be confused with the opacity of all being, that it is connected (not only from the human or social point of view but even from the purely analytical point of view) in great part to the entire present social structure which, to be sure, is by no means eternal or fatal. It asks to what degree this irrationality can be eliminated by a modification of this structure, and it concludes (in this it can, of course, be mistaken, but this is a *concrete* question) that it can be eliminated to a considerable extent, so considerable that it would bring about an essential modification, a qualitative change: the possibility for people consciously to direct the economy, to make decisions in full knowledge of the relevant facts – instead of submitting to the economy, as is now the case.[25] Will this economy be totally transparent, rational through and through? Praxis will reply that this question is meaningless for it, that what matters to it is not speculating on the impossibility of the absolute but transforming the real in order to eliminate as much as possible all that is adverse to human beings. It does not concern itself with the possibility of moving from the 'relative' to the 'absolute', it observes that radical innovations have already taken place in history. It is not interested in complete rationality as a finished state but, as concerns the economy, in rationalization as the continuous process of realizing the conditions for autonomy. Praxis knows that this process has already crossed different stages and that it will cross more. After all, the discovery of fire or of America, the invention of the wheel, of metalwork, of democracy, of philosophy, of the Soviets, and certain other events in the history of humanity indeed took place *at a particular moment* and have introduced a deep split between what went *before* and what came *after*.

Revolution and social totality

We have endeavoured to show, in relation to production and to labour, that the conflict displayed there contains at the same time the seeds of a possible solution in the form of the *workers' management* of production.

These seeds of a solution, both as a 'model' and through their implications, go far beyond the problem of production. This is self-evident *a priori*, since production is already much more than production. But it is helpful to show this concretely.

Workers' management goes beyond production when it is considered as a model: if workers' management is valid, it is because it suppresses a conflict by realizing a given mode of socialization, which would allow participation. Now, the same type of conflict exists in other social spheres as well (in a sense, with the necessary transpositions, in all of them); the mode of socialization represented by workers' management appears here, too, in principle as a possible solution.

Workers' management goes beyond production through its implications: it cannot simply remain workers' management of production in the narrow sense, at the cost of becoming a simulacrum. Its effective realization implies a practically total rearrangement of society, just as its consolidation, in the long run, implies another type of human personality. Another type of direction of the economy and of its organization, another type of power, another education, and so forth must, of necessity, accompany it.

In both cases we are led to pose the problem of the social totality. And we are also led to propose solutions which are presented as global solutions (a 'maximum programme'). Is this not to postulate that society forms potentially a rational whole, that nothing that may arise in another sector would render impossible what seems possible to us after an examination that is necessarily partial, that what is germinating here can blossom forth everywhere, and that we henceforth possess the key to this rational totality?

No. In posing the revolutionary project, in giving to it the concrete form of a 'maximum programme', not only are we not claiming to exhaust the problems, not only do we know that we cannot exhaust them; rather, we can and must indicate the problems that remain, tracing their outlines to the very limit of the unthinkable. We know and we must state that problems remain which we can do no more than formulate; others we cannot even suspect; and still others which will have to be posed in different terms, currently unimaginable to us. We know that questions that cause us anguish now, because they are insoluble, may very well disappear by themselves, and that, conversely, replies that today appear self-evident may upon application reveal practically infinite degrees of difficulty. We also know that all this could possibly (but not necessarily) obliterate the meaning of what we are saying now.

These considerations, however, cannot constitute the basis for objecting to revolutionary praxis any more than to any kind of praxis or making/doing in general – except for someone who wills nothingness or who claims to stand on the ground of Absolute Knowledge and to judge everything from there. To do something, to write a book, to make a child, a revolution, or just making or doing as such, is projecting oneself into a future situation which is opened up on all sides to the unknown, which, therefore, one cannot possess beforehand in thought, but which one must necessarily assume to be defined in its aspects relevant to present decisions. This making/doing is lucid when it does not alienate itself to an already established image of this future situation, but modifies this image as it goes along; when it does not confuse intention and reality, the desirable and the probable; when it does not lose itself in conjectures and speculations concerning aspects of the future irrelevant to what is to be done now or beyond our control. But lucidity in making/doing also does not give up this image, for, if it did, not only would it 'not know where it is going', it would not even know where it *wants* to go (it is for this reason that the motto of all reformism, 'The goal is nothing, the movement is everything', is absurd; every movement is a movement *toward*; it is something else if, since there are no preassigned goals in history, all the definitions of the goal prove to be provisional).

If the necessity and the impossibility of taking into consideration the totality of society could be opposed to revolutionary politics, they could and should be opposed to *every* sort of politics. For a reference to the whole of society is necessarily implied whenever there is a politics. The most narrowly reformist action must, if it is to be coherent and lucid (but what is essential to reformism in this respect is precisely the lack of coherency and lucidity), take into consideration the social whole. If it does not do so, it will see its reforms swept aside by the reaction of this totality which it has neglected, or a result completely different from the one it had intended. The same thing can be said with respect to purely conservative action. Completing an existing arrangement, filling in the breaches in the system's defences, how can these actions fail to raise the question of whether the remedy is not worse than the illness and, in order to decide this, to look as far as possible into the ramifications of its effects, how can these actions dispense with the effort of aiming at the social totality, not only with respect to their intended end, the preservation of the overall system [*régime global*], but also with respect to the possible consequences and coherency of the network of means employed? At the very most, this aim (and the knowledge it implies) can remain implicit. Revolutionary action differs in this regard only in that it attempts to make its own presuppositions explicit, so far as is possible.

The situation is the same outside politics. Under the pretext that there is no satisfactory theory of the organism as a totality, or any well-defined concept of health, would we dream of forbidding doctors from practising medicine? And during this practice, could any doctor worthy of the name abstain from taking this totality into account, as far as possible? And let no one say: Society is not sick. Besides the fact that this is not certain, sickness or health is not what is at issue here. It is a question of practice, which can have as its field the sickness or the health of an individual, the functioning of a group or a society, but which constantly encounters the totality both as a certitude and as a problem – for its 'object' is given only as a totality and it is also as a totality that it slips away.

The speculative philosopher can protest against the 'lack of rigour' implied by these considerations touching on a totality that can never be grasped. But these very protests point to the greatest lack of rigour, for without this 'lack of rigour' the speculative philosopher could not survive a single instant. If he survives, it is only because he allows his right hand to be unaware of what the left hand is doing. It is because he divides his life into a theoretical activity, including absolute criteria for defining rigour – which, moreover, are never satisfied – and a simple living to which these criteria by no means apply, and for good reason, since they are inapplicable. The speculative philosopher is thus caught within an insoluble antinomy. But in fact he generates this antinomy himself. The problems resulting for praxis from the attempt to take into account the totality are real ones in so far as they are concrete problems: but they are purely illusory when they are considered as absolute impossibilities. They arise only when one tries to gauge real activities after the mythical standards of a certain philosophical ideology, of a 'philosophy' which is simply the ideology of a certain philosophy.

The mode in which praxis *faces* the totality and the mode in which speculative philosophy *claims* to *give* itself the totality are radically different.

If there is an activity that addresses itself to a 'subject' or to a lasting collectivity of subjects, this activity can exist only by being grounded in two ideas: the idea that it encounters, in its 'object', a unity that is not posited by the activity itself as a theoretical or a practical category but which exists first of all *for itself* (whether clearly or dimly, implicitly or explicitly); and the idea that what is specific to this unity-for-itself lies in the capacity to supersede every prior determination, to produce the new, new forms and new contents (new in the mode of organization and in what is organized, the distinction between these being, of course, relative and 'optical'). As concerns praxis, one can sum up the situation by saying that it encounters the totality as an *open-ended unity in the process of making itself* [*se faisant elle-même*].

When the traditional speculative theory encounters the totality, it has to postulate that it already possesses the latter. Otherwise, it has to admit that it cannot fulfil the role it has assigned to itself. If 'truth is not in the things but in the relations', and if, as is self-evident, relation has no boundaries, then, necessarily, 'Truth is the Whole.' And if the theory is to be true, it must possess everything, or else deny its own claims and accept what, for it, is the supreme downfall, relativism and scepticism. Possessing the whole in this way must be *actual* in the philosophical as well as in the everyday sense: explicitly realized and present at every instant.

For praxis, too, relation has no boundaries. But from this does not follow any need to fix and to possess the totality of the system of relations. The requirement of taking the totality into consideration is always present for praxis, but praxis is not thereby obliged to come to the end of this process, to complete it at any time. And this is so because this totality is not, for it, a passive object of contemplation, whose existence would hang in midair until such time as it would be wholly actualized by theory. This totality can, and does, constantly take itself into consideration.

For speculative theory, the object does not exist if it is not complete and the theory itself does not exist if it cannot complete its object. Praxis, on the other hand, can exist only if its object, by its very nature, surpasses all completion; praxis is a perpetually transformed relation to the object. Praxis begins with the explicit acknowledgement of the open character of its object and exists only to the extent that it acknowledges this. Its 'partial grasp' of the object is not a shortcoming it regrets but something positively asserted and intended as such. For speculative theory, only that which, in one way or another, it has managed to pack away and lock up in the strongboxes of its 'proofs' is valid. Its dream – its phantasy – is the accumulation of a treasure of unusable truths. In as much as theory goes beyond this phantasy, it becomes a true theory, the praxis of truth. For praxis, what is already constituted as such is already dead once it has been constituted, what has been acquired must, without exception, be reinserted within living actuality in order to maintain its existence. However, it is not up to praxis to assure this existence wholly by itself. Its object is not something inert, whose entire fate is to be assumed by praxis. The object itself is active, it possesses tendencies, it is productive and it organizes itself – for, if it is not capacity for production and capacity for self-organization it is nothing. Speculative theory collapses, for it assigns to itself the impossible task of taking the entire world on its shoulders. But praxis does not have to carry its object in its arms;

while acting on its object, and in the same stroke, it recognizes in act that the object does effectively exist for itself. There is no sense in showing an interest in a child or in a sick person, in a group or in a society, if one does not see in them first and foremost *life*, the capacity of being grounded on itself, self-production and self-organization.

Revolutionary politics consists in recognizing and making explicit the problems of society considered as a totality. But, precisely because society is a totality, it acknowledges that society is something other than inertia in relation to its own problems. It observes that every society, in one way or another, has been able to deal with its own weight and its own complexity. And, on this level as well, it broaches the problem actively: Cannot this problem, which it does not invent, a problem which, in any event, is constantly implied in social and political life, be faced by humanity under different conditions? If it is a matter of managing social life, is there not at the present time an immense gap between needs and reality, between what is possible and what is there? Would not this society be in an infinitely better position to face up to itself if it did not condemn to inertia and to opposition nine-tenths of its own substance?

Revolutionary praxis is, therefore, not required to produce the complete and detailed scheme of the society it intends to establish. Nor does it have to 'demonstrate' and provide an absolute guarantee that this society could solve all the problems that might ever arise for it. It is enough that it show that there is nothing incoherent in what it proposes and that, as far as can be seen, its realization would greatly increase society's capacity to face up to its own problems.

The subjective roots of the revolutionary project

We sometimes hear it said that the idea of another society is presented as a project but in fact is simply a projection of unacknowledged desires, a garment woven of motivations that remain hidden to those who wear them. In some people it serves only as a vehicle for a desire for power; in others it simply marks the refusal of the reality principle, the phantasy of a world without conflict where everyone would be reconciled with everyone else and each person with himself, an infantile daydream which would attempt to do away with the tragic side of human existence, a fleeing that allows one to live at once in two different worlds, an imaginary compensation.

When the discussion takes this turn, it must first be recalled that we are all in the same boat. No one can be sure that what he says is unrelated to unconscious desires or unavowed motivations. When one hears 'psychoanalysts' of a particular tendency classify all revolutionaires in broad terms as 'neurotics', one can only congratulate oneself on not sharing their bargain-basement 'health', and it would be only too easy to take apart the unconscious mechanism behind their conformism. More generally, those who believe they discover at the roots of the revolutionary project this or that unconscious desire ought at the same time to ask themselves what is the motive conveyed by their own critique and to what extent this critique is not a rationalization.

For us, however, this reversal is of slight interest. The question does indeed exist and even if no one were to raise it, whoever speaks of revolution should ask it to himself. Leave it up to the others to decide the amount of lucidity involved in their own positions; revolutionaries cannot impose limits on their desire for lucidity. Nor can they reject the problem by saying, What counts is not unconscious motivations but the signification and the objective value of ideas and acts; Robespierre's or Baudelaire's neurosis or madness was more fecund for humanity than the 'health' of a certain shop-keeper of the period. For, revolution as we conceive of it refuses as a matter of fact to accept once and for all this split between motivation and result; it would be impossible in reality and incoherent in its meaning if it were borne by unconscious intentions unrelated to its articulated content. It would, then, simply reproduce once again previous history, and it would continue to be dominated by obscure motivations which, in the long run, would impose their own finality and their own logic.

The true dimension of this problem is the collective dimension. It is on the scale of the masses, who alone can realize a new society, that we must examine the birth of new motivations and new attitudes capable of bringing the revolutionary project to its outcome. This examination will be easier, however, if we first attempt to render explicit what the desire and the motivations of a revolutionary might be.

What we can say about this is, by definition, highly subjective. It is also, by definition, open to all possible interpretations. If it can help someone see more clearly into another human being (even if only into the illusions and the errors of this human being) and through this into one's own self, it will not have been useless to state it.

I desire and I feel the need to live in a society *other* than the one surrounding me. Like the great majority of people, I can live in this one and accommodate myself to it – at any rate, I do live in it. However critically I may try to look at myself, neither my capacity for adaptation nor my assimilation of reality seems to me to be inferior to the sociological average. I am not asking for immortality, ubiquity, or omniscience. I am not asking society to 'give me happiness'; I know that this is not a ration that can be handed out by the town hall or my neighbourhood workers' council and that, if this thing exists, I have to make it for myself, tailored to my own needs, as has happened to me already and as will no doubt happen to me again. In life, however, as it comes to me and to others, I run up against a lot of unacceptable things; I say that they are not inevitable and that they stem from the organization of society. I desire, and I ask, first of all that my work be meaningful, that I may approve what it is used for and the way in which it is done, that it allow me genuinely to expend myself, to make use of my faculties and at the same time to enrich and develop myself. And I say that this is possible, with a different organization of society, possible for me and for everyone. I say that it would already be a basic change in this direction if I were allowed to decide, together with everyone else, what I had to do and, with my fellow workers, how to do it.

I should like, together with everyone else, to know what is going on in society, to control the extent and the quality of the information I receive. I ask to be able to participate directly in all the social decisions that may affect my existence, or the general course of the world in which I live. I do not accept the fact that my lot is decided, day after day, by people whose projects are hostile to me or simply unknown to me, and for whom we, that is, I and everyone else, are only numbers in a general plan or pawns on a chessboard, and that, ultimately, my life and my death are in the hands of people whom I know to be, necessarily, blind.

I know perfectly well that realizing another social organization, and the life it would imply, would by no means be simple, that difficult problems would arise at every step. But I prefer contending with real problems rather than with the consequences of de Gaulle's delirium, Johnson's schemes, or Khrushchev's intrigues. Even if I and the others should fail along this path, I prefer failure in a meaningful attempt to a state that falls short of both failure and nonfailure, and which is merely *ridiculous*.

I wish to be able to meet the other person as a being like myself and yet absolutely different, not like a number or a bird perched on another level (higher or lower, it matters little) of the hierarchy of incomes and powers. I wish to see the other, and for the other to see me, as another human being. I want our relationships to be something other than a field for the expression of aggressiveness, our competition to remain within the limits of play, our conflicts – to the extent that they cannot be resolved or overcome – to concern real problems and real stakes, carrying with them the least amount of unconsciousness possible, and that they be as lightly loaded as possible with the imaginary. I want the other to be free, for my freedom *begins* where the other's freedom begins, and, all alone, I can at best be merely 'virtuous in misfortune'. I do not count on people changing into angels, or on their souls becoming as pure as mountain lakes – which, moreover, I have always found deeply boring. But I know how much present culture aggravates and exasperates their difficulty to be and to be with others, and I see that it multiplies to infinity the obstacles placed in the way of their freedom.

I know, of course, that this desire cannot be realized today; nor, even were the revolution to take place tomorrow, could it be fully realized in my lifetime. I know that one day people will live, for whom the problems that cause us the most anguish today will no longer even exist. This is my fate, which I have to assume and which I do assume. But this cannot reduce me to despair or to catatonic ruminations. Possessing this desire, which indeed is mine, I can only work to realize it. And already in the choice of my main interest in life, in the work I devote to it, which for me is meaningful (even when I encounter, and accept, partial failure, delays, detours, and tasks that have no sense in themselves), in the participation in a group of revolutionaries which is attempting to go beyond the reified and alienated relations of present society – I am in a position partially to realize this desire. If I had been born in a communist society, would happiness have been easier to attain? – I really do not know, and at any rate I can do nothing about it. I am not, under this pretext, going to spend my free time watching television or reading detective novels.

Does my attitude amount to denying the reality principle? But what is the content of this principle? Is it that work is necessary – or that it is necessary that work be meaningless, exploited, that it contradict the objectives for which it is allegedly done? Is this principle valid, *in this form*, for someone of independent means? Was it valid, *in this form*, for the natives of the Trobriand islands or Samoa? Is it still valid today for fishermen in a poor Mediterranean village? Up to what point does the reality principle reveal nature, and at what point does it begin to reveal society? Why not serfdom, slave galleys, concentration camps? Where does a philosophy get the right to tell me, 'Here, on exactly this inch of existing institutions, I am going to show you the borderline between the phenomenon and the essence, between passing historical forms and the eternal being of society'? I accept the reality principle, for I accept the necessity of work (as long, in any case, as it is real, for this is becoming less obvious every day) and the necessity of a social organization of work. But I do not accept the appeal to a false psychoanalysis and to a false metaphysics, which introduces into this precise discussion of historical possibilities some gratuitous assertions about alleged impossibilities, about which this philosophy *knows nothing at all*.

Might my desire be infantile? But the infantile situation is that life is given to you and that the Law is given to you. In the infantile situation, life is given to you for nothing; and the Law is given to you without anything else, without anything more, without any possible discussion. What I want is just the opposite: I want to make my life and to give life if possible, and in any event to give something for my life. I want the Law not to be simply given, but for me to give it to myself at the same time. The person who remains constantly in the infantile situation is the conformist or the apolitical person, for he accepts the Law without any discussion and does not want to participate in shaping it. Someone who lives in society without any will concerning the Law, without any political will, has merely replaced the private father with the anonymous social father. The infantile situation is, first, receiving without giving, and then doing or being in order to receive. What I want is a just exchange to begin with, passing beyond exchange afterward. The infantile situation is the relation of duality, the phantasy of fusion – and in this sense it is the present society that constantly infantilizes everyone, by the imaginary fusion with unreal entities: leaders, nations, cosmonauts, or idols. What I want is for society to cease to be a family, moreover a false one to the point of being grotesque; I want it to acquire its peculiar dimension as a society, a network of relationships among autonomous adults.

Is my desire a desire for power? But what I want is the abolition of power in the current sense; I want the power of each and every one. For current power, other people are things, and all that I want goes against this. The person for whom others are things is himself a thing, and I do not want to be a thing either for myself or for others. I do not want others to be things, I would have no use for this. If I may exist for others, be recognized by them, I do not want this to be in terms of the possession of something external to me – power; nor do I want to exist for them only in an imaginary realm. The recognition of others has value to me only in as much as I recognize them as well. Am I in danger of forgetting all this if ever events were to carry me close to 'power'? This seems more than improbable to me. If this were to happen, a battle would perhaps be lost but not the war, and am I to rule my entire life on the assumption that I might one day slip back into childhood?

Might I be pursuing the chimera of wanting to eliminate the tragic side of human existence? It seems to me, instead, that I want to eliminate the melo-dramatic aspect, the false tragedy – the one where catastrophe arrives without necessity, where everything could have been otherwise if only the characters had known this or had done that. That people should die of hunger in India, while in America and in Europe governments penalize farmers who 'over'-produce – this is a macabre farce, this is Grand Guignol in which the corpses and the suffering are real, but this is not tragedy, there is nothing ineluctable here. And if one day humanity perishes by hydrogen bombs, I refuse to call this a tragedy. I call it stupidity. I would like an end to Guignol and to the transformation of people into puppets by other puppets who 'govern' them. When a neurotic repeats for the fourteenth time the same behaviour pattern of failure, reproducing for himself and for those nearby the same type of misfortune, helping this person get out of such a situation is to rid his life of grotesque farce, not tragedy; it is to allow the person finally to see the real problems of life and the tragic element they may contain – which the neurosis served in part to express but especially to *mask*.

When one of Buddha's disciples came to tell him, after a long voyage in the West, that miraculous things, instruments, medications, methods of thinking, and institutions had transformed people's lives since the time the

Master had retreated into the mountains, Buddha stopped him after a few words. Have they wiped out sadness, sickness, old age, and death? he asked. No, replied the disciple. Then, they might as well have kept still, thought the Master. And he plunged back into his contemplation, without bothering to show his disciple that he was no longer listening.

The logic of the revolutionary project

The socialist revolution aims at transforming society through people's autonomous action and at instaurating a society organized to promote the autonomy of all its members. This is a *project*. It is not a theorem, the conclusion of a demonstration indicating what must unavoidably occur. The very idea of such a demonstration is absurd. But neither is it a utopia, an act of faith, an arbitrary wager.

The revolutionary project finds its roots and its points of support in effective historical reality, in the *crisis* of established society, and in its *contestation* by the great majority of the people who live in it. This is not the crisis that Marxism believed it saw, the 'contradiction between the development of the productive forces and the continuation of the capitalist relations of production'. It consists in the fact that the social organization can attain the ends it sets for itself only be setting forth means that contradict these ends, by creating demands it cannot satisfy, by positing criteria it is incapable of applying, norms it is obliged to transgress. It requires that people, as producers or as citizens, remain passive and restrict themselves to executing the task it has imposed on them. When it notices that this passivity is like a cancer within it, it encourages initiative and participation, only to discover that it cannot bear them, for they question the very essence of the existing order. Society must live with a double reality, distinguishing between an official version and the real one that are irreducibly opposed to each other. It does not suffer simply from an opposition between classes which would remain separate, outside one another; it is conflictual in itself, the *yes* and the *no* existing together as active intentions within the very core of its being, in the values it proclaims and denies, in its mode of organizing and of disorganizing, in the extreme socialization and the extreme atomization of the society it creates. In the same way, the *contestation* of which we were speaking is not merely the struggle of labouring people against exploitation, nor is it their political mobilization against the regime. Manifest in the great open conflicts that mark the history of capitalism, it is constantly present, in an implicit and latent manner, in their work, in their daily life, in their mode of existence.

People sometimes say to us: You are inventing a crisis in society, you are labelling 'crisis' something that has always been there. You want, at all costs, to find a radical novelty in the nature or the intensity of current social conflicts, for this alone would permit you to claim that a radically new state is in the making. What you call contestation of the essence of social relations is something that has always existed as a result of the different and opposing interests of groups and classes. All societies, at any rate all historical societies, have been divided and this has only led them to produce other societies, divided as well.

We are in fact saying that a precise analysis shows that the deep-lying elements of the crisis of contemporary society are specific and *qualitatively unique*. There are, doubtless, naive pseudo-Marxists who, even today, are only able to appeal to class struggle and fill their mouths with it, forgetting that class struggle has been going on for thousands of years and that it can by no means supply, in itself, a point of support for the socialist project. But there are also pseudo-objective – and just as naive – sociologists who, having learned to be suspicious of ethnocentric and 'epoch-centric' projections and to reject our tendency to privilege our own epoch as something absolutely distinct, cannot go further; they flatten historical reality and bury under a paper mountain of methodology the central problem of historical reflection, namely, the specificity of each society as a specificity of meaning and of the dynamics proper to this meaning, the undeniable fact – even if it remains mysterious – without which there would be no history, that certain societies introduce dimensions that did not exist before, the qualitatively new in another sense than merely descriptive. It is of no interest to discuss these pseudophilosophical arguments. Anyone who cannot see that between the Greek world and the Egyptian–Assyrian–Babylonian world, or even between the medieval world and the world of the Renaissance, there is – despite the obvious continuities and cause and effect relations – *another* difference, another type, degree, and sense of difference than that between two trees or even two human individuals living in the same period – this person is missing an essential sense for the comprehension of things historical, and would be better off working in entomology or in botany.

Analysis shows a difference such as this between contemporary society and those preceding it, taken *overall*. This is precisely the result, first of all, of a rigorous sociological description that respects its object and makes it truly speak out, instead of squashing it under a cheap metaphysics which asserts that everything always amounts to the same thing. Consider the problem of labour: it is one thing when the slave or the serf rises up in opposition to his exploitation, that is to say, refuses to make an additional effort or demands a greater share of the product, combats the orders of the master or the lord on the level, so to speak, of 'quantity'. It is something else again, something radically different, when the worker is forced to combat the orders of management *in order to* be able to apply them, when not simply the quantity of labour or of the product but its content as well and the mode of doing it become the object of an incessant struggle – in short, when the labour process no longer gives rise to a conflict external to labour itself but has to be based on an *internal* contradiction, the simultaneous requirement of being excluded from *and* of participating in the organization and the direction of labour.

Consider, likewise, the problem of the family and of the structure of the personality. To be sure, the family organization has always contained a repressive principle; individuals have always been obliged to internalize a conflict between their drives and the demands of a given social organization; every culture, whether archaic or historical, has always presented in its 'basic personality' a particular 'neurotic' tint. But what is radically different is that there is no longer any principle discernible at the base of the present organisation or rather disorganization of the family, or any integrated structure in the personality of contemporary human beings. It is, of course, stupid to think that the Florentines, the Romans, the Spartans, the Mundugumors, or the Kwakiutl were 'healthy' and that our contemporaries are 'neurotic'. But it is hardly more intelligent to forget that the personality type of the Spartan or of the Mundugumor, regardless of their 'neurotic' components, was *functionally adequate* to their society, that the individual felt adapted to it and could make it function in accordance with his own requirements and shape a new generation which would do likewise; whereas the 'neurosis' or 'neuroses' of people today appear, from a sociological point of view, as essentially phenomena of maladjustment, which not only are experienced subjectively as misfortune but, moreover, hamper the social functioning of individuals, preventing them from responding adequately to the demands of life as it is, and being reproduced as an amplified maladjustment in the second generation. *The Spartan's 'neurosis' was what allowed him to be integrated into his society – the 'neurosis' of modern man is what prevents him from being integrated.* It is superficial to recall, for example, that homosexuality has existed in all human societies while forgetting that each time it has been something socially defined – a marginal deviance that is tolerated, or despised, or sanctioned; a custom that is accorded a value, institutionalized, possessing a positive social function; a widespread vice – and that today it is – well, just what in fact is it? Or to say that different societies have been able to adjust to an immense variety of different roles for women, only to forget and to make others forget that current society is the first in which there is *no* definite role for women – and, as a direct and immediate result, none for men either.

Consider, finally, the question of society's values. Whether explicit or implicit, there has been a system of values in every society – or even two systems, which were in conflict but which were present. No material coercion has ever been lastingly – that is to say, socially – efficacious, without this 'complement of justification'; no psychical repression has every played a *social* role without this extension into broad daylight; an *exclusively* unconscious Superego is not conceivable.[26] The existence of society has always presupposed the existence of rules of conduct, and the sanctions for these rules were neither simply unconscious nor merely material-juridical; they always also included informal social sanctions and metasocial 'sanctions' (metaphysical, religious sanctions and so forth – in short, *imaginary* sanctions, but this in no way diminishes their importance). In the extremely rare cases in which these rules were openly transgressed, this was the act of a small minority (by part of the aristocracy in eighteenth-century France, for instance). Currently, rules and their sanctions are almost exclusively the province of the legal code, and unconscious formations no longer correspond to the rules, in the sociological sense, either because, as certain psychoanalysts have said, the Superego is being considerably weakened[27] or because the specifically social component (and hence function) of the Superego is crumbling away amid the pulverization and mixing together of situations and 'personality types' which intersect in modern society. Beyond legal sanctions, most of the time these rules have no extension of their justification in people's consciousness. But what matters most is not the weakening of sanctions surrounding rules and prohibitions: it is the almost complete disappearance of positive rules and values. The life of a society cannot be based solely on a network of prohibitions, of negative orders. Individuals have always received from the society in which they lived positive injunctions, orientations, the representation of value-charged ends – at once formulated universally and 'embodied' in what was, for each epoch, its 'collective Ego Ideal'. In comparison, there exists in contemporary society no more than residues of prior phases which are becoming more moth-eaten every day, reduced to abstractions bearing no relation to life ('morality' or a 'humanitarian' attitude), or else we find flattened pseudovalues, whose realization is at the same time their self-condemnation (consumption as an end in itself, or fashion and the 'new').

People say to us: Even admitting that there is a crisis of contemporary society, you cannot legitimately posit the project of a new society, for where could you draw the content for it, if not from your own head, your ideas, your desires – in short, from your subjective arbitrariness?

We answer: Yes, if by that you mean that we cannot 'demonstrate' the necessity or the excellence of socialism, as one can 'demonstrate' Pythagoras' theorem, or that we cannot show you socialism in the process of growing within established society, as one can show a foal growing in the womb of the mare, you are doubtless correct, but at the same time you pretend to be unaware that one is never dealing with this kind of self-evidence in any real activity, whether individual or collective, and that you yourself thrust aside such requirements whenever you undertake anything. But if you mean that the revolutionary project merely conveys the subjective arbitrariness of a few individuals, this is because you have first chosen to forget, in defiance of the principles you defend elsewhere, the history of the past fifty years and the fact that the problem of a different organization of society has constantly been posed, not by reformers or by ideologues, but by massive collective movements, which have changed the face of the world, even if they have failed with regard to their original intentions. Next, this is because you do not see that the crisis of which we are speaking is not simply a 'crisis in itself', this conflictual society is not a beam rotting with the ages, a machine that rusts or wears out. The crisis is due to the fact that it is at the same time contestation, it is the result of contestation and it constantly feeds this contestation. Labour conflict, the destructuring of the personality, the collapse of standards and values are not and cannot be lived by people as mere facts or as external calamities; they also give rise to responses and to intentions, and the latter, while they complete the shaping of the crisis as a genuine crisis, also go beyond mere crisis. To be sure, it is erroneous and mythologizing to want to find, in the 'negative' element of capitalism, a 'positive' element which would be symmetrically constituted in it, inch by inch – whether this be conceived in the objectivist style of some of Marx's formulations (when, for example, the 'negative' element of alienation is seen as depositing itself and becoming sedimented in the material infrastructure of technology and accumulated capital which contain – with their inevitable human corollary, the proletariat – the necessary and sufficient conditions for socialism) or in the subjectivist style of some Marxists (who see socialist society already constituted, so to speak, in the working-class community of the factory and in the new type of human relations displayed there). The development of the productive forces as well as the evolution of human attitudes in capitalist society display significations which are not simple, not simply contradictory in the sense of a naive dialectic which would proceed by the juxtaposition of contraries – significations which, for lack of another term, can be called ambiguous. However, the ambiguous, in the sense we intend it here, is not the indeterminate or the indefinite, it is not just anything whatsoever. The ambiguous is ambiguous only through the conjoining of several significations capable of being specified, none of which, for the moment, predominates. In the crisis and in the contestation of the forms of social life by our contemporaries there are some facts that are heavy with meaning – the wear and tear on authority, the gradual exhaustion of economic motivation, the loosening of the hold of the instituted imaginary, the nonacceptance of rules that are simply inherited or passed down – and these facts can only be organized around one or the other of two central significations: either the progressive decomposition of the content of histor-ical life, the gradual emergence of a new society which, ultimately, would be one where people were external to one another and to themselves, an over-populated desert, a lonely crowd, not even an air-conditioned nightmare but a generalized anaesthesia; or, if we look instead to what appears in people's *work* as a tendency toward cooperation, the collective self-management of activities and responsibility, we can interpret the whole of these phenomena as the emergence in society of the *possibility* of and the *demand* for autonomy.

People may still say to us: Yours is only one reading, and you agree that it is not the only one possible. In the name of what do you read the facts this way, in the name of what do you claim that the future you envisage is possible and coherent, in the name of what, in particular, are you making this choice?

Our reading is not arbitrary. In a certain fashion it is only the interpretation of the discourse that contemporary society holds with respect to itself, the sole perspective in which the crisis of business and of politics, the appearance of psychoanalysis as well as of psychosociology, and so on all become comprehensible. And we have tried to show that, as far as we can see, the idea of a socialist society presents no impossibility or incoherency. But our reading is also, indeed, the result of a choice: an interpretation of this type and on this scale is possible, ultimately, only in relation to a project. We are affirming something which is not 'naturally' or geometrically imposed on us, we prefer one future to another – and even to any other.

Is this choice arbitrary? If you like, in the sense that every choice is. But of all historical choices, it seems to us the least arbitrary of any that have ever existed.

Why should we prefer a socialist future to any other? We are deciphering, or believe we can decipher, a signification in actual [*effective*] history – the possibility of and the demand for autonomy. But this signification takes on its full weight only in relation to other considerations. This simple 'factual' datum is not enough; it could not as such impose itself upon us. We do not approve of what contemporary history offers us simply because it 'is' or because it 'tends to be'. Should we arrive at the conclusion that the most probable, even certain, tendency of contemporary history is the universal instauration of concentration camps, we would not deduce from this that we have to support them.[28] If we assert the tendency of contemporary society towards autonomy, if we want to work for its realization, this is because we are asserting autonomy as a mode of being of humans, because we are ascribing value to it, because we recognize it as our essential aspiration and as an aspiration that surpasses the peculiarities of our personal constitution, the only one that can be defended publicly with lucidity and coherency.

This, therefore, involves a twofold relation. The reasons we are aiming at autonomy are and are not of this epoch. They are not, because we would assert the value of autonomy regardless of the circumstances, and more profoundly, because we think that the aim of autonomy ineluctably tends to emerge wherever we find humans and history, that, like consciousness, the aim of autonomy is human destiny and that, present from the start, it constitutes history rather than being constituted by it.

These reasons, however, are also bound to our epoch, in so many ways that it would be pointless to state them. Not only because the links by which we and others arrive at this aim and at the ways of concretizing it are related to our epoch. But also because the content we may give to it, the way in which we think it can be embodied, can be possible only today and presuppose all previous history, in more ways than we may suspect. In particular, the explicit social dimension we are able to give to this aim today, the possibility of another form of society, the passage from an ethic to a politics of autonomy (which, without *suppressing* ethics, preserves it by outstripping it) are clearly tied to the concrete phase of history we are living.

Finally, one can ask: And why, then, do you think that this possibility is appearing just now? We say: If your 'why' is a concrete one, we have already replied to your question. The why is to be found in all the particular historical links which have led humanity where it is now, which have made capitalist society and its current phase this singularly unique epoch we were trying to define above. But if your why is a metaphysical why, if it amounts to asking: What is the precise place of the current phase in a total dialectic of universal history, why should the possibility of socialism emerge at this precise moment in the plan of Creation, what is the relation that has been worked out between this originary constituent of history – autonomy – and the successive figures it assumes in time? – if this is what is meant, then we refuse to answer. Even if the question had any sense it would be a purely speculative one, and we consider it absurd to suspend all doing and not-doing waiting for someone rigorously to work out this total dialectic, or to discover at the back of an old cupboard the plan of Creation. We are not going to fall back into a stupor simply because we do not possess Absolute Knowledge. However, we deny the legitimacy of the question, we deny that there is any sense in thinking in terms of total dialectic, of a plan of Creation, of an exhaustive elucidation of the relation between what is founded *with* time and what is founded *in* time. History has given birth to a project, and this project we take as our own because in it we recognize our deepest aspirations, and we think that it is possible to realize it. We find ourselves here, at this precise place in time and space, among these people, within this horizon. Knowing that this horizon is not the only possible one does not prevent it from being ours and giving a shape to the landscape of our existence. All the rest, total history, from everywhere and from nowhere, is the work of a horizonless thought, which is only another name for nonthought.

Autonomy and Alienation

The sense of autonomy – the individual

If autonomy is at the centre of the objectives and at the crossroads of the paths of the revolutionary project, this term must be specified and elucidated. We shall attempt to elucidate it first on the level where it is easiest to grasp, in relation to the individual, and then we shall move to the level which is of particular interest to us here, the collective level. We shall try to understand what an autonomous individual is – and what an autonomous or unalienated society is.

Freud proposed, as a maxim of psychoanalysis: 'Where Id was, Ego shall come to be' (*Wo Es war, soll Ich werden*).[29] *Ego* is here, as a first approximation, consciousness in general. The *Id*, which properly speaking is the origin and the place of drives ('instincts'), must be taken in this context as representing the Unconscious in the broadest sense. *Ego*, consciousness and will, must take the place of the dark forces which, 'in me', dominate, act for me – 'act me' as G. Groddeck said.[30] These forces are not simply – are not so much, but we shall return to this later – pure drives, libido or death instinct. What is at issue is instead their interminable, phantasmatic and fantastic alchemy, and along with this, and in particular, the unconscious forces of rearing and repression, the Superego and the unconscious Self. It is necessary, straight away, to interpret this sentence. Ego must take the place of Id – this can mean neither the suppression of drives nor the elimination or the absorption of the Unconscious. It is a matter of taking their place as an *agency [instance] of decision*. Autonomy would then be consciousness's domination over the Unconscious. Without prejudice to the new depth dimension revealed by Freud,[31] this is the programme proposed by philosophical reflection on the individual for the past twenty-five centuries, at once the assumption and the outcome of ethics as it has been viewed by Plato and the Stoics, Spinoza or Kant. (It is of immense importance in itself, but not for this discussion, that Freud proposes an efficacious way to attain what, for philosophers, had remained an 'ideal' accessible through abstract knowledge.)[32] If to autonomy – that is, to self-legislation or self-regulation – one opposes heteronomy – that is, legislation or regulation by another – then autonomy is my law, opposed to the regulation by the Unconscious, which is another law, the law of another, other than myself.

In what sense can we say that the regulation by the Unconscious is the law of another? Of what other? Of a literal other, not of another, unknown 'Self', but of another *in* me. As Jacques Lacan says, 'The Unconscious is the discourse of the Other'; it is to a great extent the depository of intentions, desires, cathexes, demands, expectations – significations to which the individual has been exposed from the moment of conception and even before, as these stem from those who engendered and raised him.[33] Autonomy then becomes: My discourse must take the place of the discourse of the Other, of a foreign discourse that is in me, dominating me: speaking through myself. This elucidation immediately indicates the *social* dimension of the problem (little matter that the Other in question at the start is the 'narrow' parental other; through a series of obvious articulations, the parental couple finally refers to society as a whole and to its history).

What, however, is this discourse of the Other – no longer as to its origin but as to its quality? And up to what point can it be eliminated?

The essential characteristic of the discourse of the Other, from the point of view that interests us here, is its relation to the *imaginary*. It has to do with the fact that, dominated by this discourse, the subject takes himself to be something he is not (or is not necessarily) and that for him, others and the entire world undergo a corresponding disguised misrepresentation [*travestissement*]. The subject does not express himself but is expressed by someone, and therefore exists as a part of another's world (certainly disguised in turn). The subject is dominated by an imaginary, lived as even more real than the real, yet not known as such, precisely *because* it is not known as such.[34] What is essential to heteronomy – or to alienation in the general sense of the term – on the level of the individual, is domination by an autonomized imaginary which has assumed for itself the function of defining for the subject both reality and desire. The 'repression of drives' as such, the conflict between the 'pleasure principle' and the 'reality principle' do not constitute individual alienation, which is finally the almost unlimited reign of a principle of *de*-reality. The important conflict in this respect is not that between drives and reality (if this conflict sufficed as a pathogenic cause, there would never have been a single, even approximately normal resolution of the Oedipus complex from the beginning of time, and never would a man and a woman have walked upon the earth). The important conflict is that between drives and reality, on the one hand, and their imaginary elaboration within the subject, on the other.[35]

The *Id* in Freud's adage therefore is to be understood as signifying essentially this function of the Unconscious which cathects imaginary reality, autonomizes it, and confers on it the power of decision – the content of this imaginary being related to the discourse of the Other ('repetition', but also amplified transformation of this discourse).

It is thus where this function of the Unconscious was, and along with it the discourse of the Other which fuels it, that Ego is to come to be. This means that my discourse is to take the place of the discourse of the Other. But what is my discourse? What is a discourse that is mine?

A discourse that is mine is a discourse that has negated the discourse of the Other, that has negated it not necessarily in its content but in as much as it is the discourse of the Other. In other words, a discourse that, by making clear both the origin and the sense of this discourse, has negated it or affirmed it in full knowledge of the relevant facts, by relating its sense to that which is constituted as the subject's own truth – as my own truth.

If in this interpretation Freud's adage were taken in an absolute sense, it would be proposing an inaccessible objective. Never will my discourse be wholly mine in the sense defined above. Obviously, I could never begin everything all over again, even if only to ratify what already happened. This is also because – and we shall return to this later – the notion of the subject's own truth is itself much more a problem than a solution.

This is just as true of the relation to the imaginary function of the Unconscious. How can we conceive of a subject that would have entirely 'absorbed' the imaginative function, how could we dry up this spring in the depths of ourselves from which flow both alienating phantasies and free creations truer than truth, unreal deliria and surreal poems, this eternally new beginning and ground of all things, without which nothing would have a ground, how can we eliminate what is at the base of, or in any case what is inextricably bound up with, what makes us human beings – our symbolic function, which presupposes our capacity to see and to think in a thing something which it is not?

In as much as we do not want to make Freud's maxim a mere regulative idea defined in reference to an impossible state – and thus a new mystification – another sense is to be given to it. It must be understood as referring not to an attained state but to an active situation; not to an ideal person who has become a pure Ego once and for all, who would proffer a discourse all its own, who would never produce phantasies, but to a real person who would be unceasingly involved in the movement of taking up again what had been acquired, the discourse of the Other, who is capable of uncovering his phantasies as phantasies and who, finally, never allows them to dominate – unless he is so willing. This is not a mere 'tending toward', it is really a situation, definable in terms of characteristics that trace a radical separation between it and the state of heteronomy. These characteristics do not consist in an 'awareness' achieved once and for all, but in *another relation* between the Conscious and the Unconscious, between lucidity and the function of the imaginary, in *another attitude* of the subject with respect to himself, in a profound modification of the activity–passivity mix, of the sign under which this takes place, of the respective place of the two elements that compose it. How little it is a question in all this of a power grab by consciousness in the narrow sense is shown in the fact that Freud's proposition can be completed by its inverse: 'Where Ego is, Id must spring forth' (*Wo Ich bin, soll Es auftauchen*). Desire, drives – whether it be Eros or Thanatos – this is me, too, and these have to be brought not only to consciousness but to expression and to existence.[36] An autonomous subject is one who knows himself to be well founded in concluding: This is indeed true, and: This is indeed my desire.

Autonomy is therefore not an elucidation without remainder, nor is it the total elimination of the discourse of the Other unrecognized as such. It is the establishment of another relation between the discourse of the Other and the subject's discourse. The total elimination of the discourse of the Other unrecognized as such is an unhistorical state. The weight of the discourse of the Other unrecognized as such can be seen even in those who have made the most radical attempts to pursue the interrogation and the critique of tacit presuppositions to the end – whether this be Plato, Descartes, Kant, Marx, or Freud himself. However, there are indeed those who – like Plato and Freud – never *gave up* this pursuit, and there are those who stopped and who, as a result, at times became alienated to their own discourse, which became other. There is the permanent and permanently actualizable possibility of regarding, objectifying, setting at a distance, detaching, and finally transforming the discourse of the Other into the discourse of the subject.

But just what is this subject? This third term of Freud's sentence, which is to come about where Id was, is certainly not the point-like ego of the 'I think'. It is not the subject as pure activity, possessing no constraints, no inertia, this will o' the wisp of subjectivist philosophers, this flame unencumbered by any physical support, ties, or nourishment. This activity of the subject who is 'working on itself' encounters as its object the wealth of contents (the discourse of the Other) with which it has never finished. And, without this object, it simply *is* not at all. The subject is also activity, but this activity is acting on something, otherwise it is nothing. It is therefore co-determined by what it gives itself as an object. But this aspect of mutual inherence between subject and object – intentionality, the fact that the subject exists only to the extent that it posits an object – is only an initial, relatively superficial determination, it is what carries the subject into the world, it is what continually puts the subject in the street. There is another determination, one that does not concern the orientation of the intentional fibres of the subject, but their very material, which carries the world into the subject and introduces the street into what the subject may take to be its own den. The active subject, which is *subject* of . . ., which evokes before itself, posits, objectifies, looks at, and sets at a distance, what is it – is it a pure gaze, the naked capacity for evoking something, setting it at a distance, a spark outside of time, nondimensionality? No, it is gaze *and* support for the gaze, thought *and* the support for thought, it is activity *and* acting body – the material body and the metaphorical body. A gaze in which there is not already something that has itself been looked at can see nothing; a thought in which there is not something that has been thought can think nothing.[37] What we have been calling *support* here is not simply the biological support; it is the fact that *some content, no matter which, is always already present* and that it is not a residue, scoria, encumbrance, or indifferent material, but the *efficient condition for the subject's activity.* This support, this content belongs neither simply to the subject nor simply to the other (or to the world). It is the produced and productive union of the self and the other (or the world). In the subject *as subject* there is the nonsubject, and all the traps it falls into have been dug out by subjectivist philosophy itself for having forgotten this fundamental truth. In the subject there is, to be sure, as one of its moments 'that which can never become an object', inalienable freedom, the ever-present possibility of redirecting the gaze, of abstracting from any particular content, of bracketing everything, including oneself, except in as much as the self is this capacity that springs forth [*resurgit*] as presence and absolute proximity at the very moment it places itself at a distance from itself. However, this moment is abstract, empty; it never has and never will produce anything other than the silent and useless self-evidence of the *cogito sum*, the immediate certainty of existing as thinking, which cannot even legit-imately express itself through language. For, once even unpronounced speech makes a first breach, the world and others infiltrate from every direc-tion, consciousness is inundated by the torrent of significations, which come, so to speak, not from the outside but from the inside. It is only through the world that one can think the world. Once thought is the thought of some-thing, the content re-emerges [*resurgit*], not only in what is to be thought but in that by means of which it is thought (*darin, wodurch es gedacht wird*). Without this content, in the place of the subject one would find no more than its ghost. And in this content, there is always to be found, directly or indirectly, the other and others. The other is just as fully present in the form as in the fact of discourse, as the demand for confrontation and for truth (which obviously does not mean that truth is confused with the agreement of opinions). Finally, and it is only apparently far removed from our discus-sion to recall that the support for this union of the subject and the nonsubject in the subject, the point of articulation between the self and the other, is the body, that 'material' structure heavy with virtual meaning. The body, which is not alienation – this would be meaningless – but participation in the world and in sense, attachment and mobility, preconstitution of a universe of significations before any reflective thought.

It is because it 'forgets' this concrete structure of the subject that tradi-tional philosophy, the narcissism of consciousness fascinated by its own naked forms, reduces to the level of the conditions of servitude both the other and corporeality. And it is because it wants to found itself upon the pure freedom of a fictive subject that it condemns itself to rediscover the alienation of the effective subject as an insoluble problem. In the same way, wanting to found itself on exhaustive rationality, it must constantly run up against the impossible reality of an irreducibly irrational element. This is how it finally ends up being an irrational and alienated undertaking; all the more irrational as it seeks, digs out, and purifies indefinitely the conditions for its rationality; all the more alienated as it unceasingly affirms its naked freedom, whereas this freedom is at once incontestable and vain.

The subject in question is, therefore, not the abstract moment of philosophical subjectivity; it is the effective subject traversed through and through by the world and by others. The Ego of autonomy is not Absolute Self, the monad cleaning and polishing its external–internal surface in order to eliminate the impurities resulting from contact with others. It is the active and lucid agency that constantly reorganizes its contents, through the help of these same contents, that produces by means of a material and in relation to needs and ideas, all of which are themselves mixtures of what it has already found there before it and what it has itself produced.

In this relation too, it cannot be a matter of eliminating entirely the discourse of the other – not only because this is an interminable task, but because the other is each time present in the activity that 'eliminates' him.[38] And this is why there can never exist any 'proper truth' of the subject in any absolute sense. The subject's own truth is always participation in a truth that surpasses him, a truth rooted in him and that finally roots him in society and in history, even as the subject realizes his autonomy.

The social dimension of autonomy

We have spoken at length about the meaning of autonomy for the individual. This was because, first of all, it was necessary to distinguish clearly and forcefully between this concept and the old philosophical idea of abstract freedom, echoes of which can be found even in Marxism.

Next, this was because only this conception of autonomy and of the structure of the subject makes praxis, as we have defined it, possible and comprehensible.[39] In any other conception this 'action of one freedom upon another freedom' remains a contradiction in terms, a perpetual impossibility, a mirage – or a miracle. Or else it is confused with the conditions and the factors of heteronomy, since all that comes from the other concerns the 'contents of consciousness', 'psychology', and is therefore of the order of a cause. Subjectivist idealism and psychologistic positivism ultimately meet in this view. In reality, however, it is because the autonomy of the other is not absolute fulguration and sheer spontaneity that I can aim at its development. It is because autonomy is not the pure and simple elimination of the discourse of the other but the elaboration of this discourse, wherein the other is not an indifferent material but counts for the content of what it says, that an intersubjective action is possible and that it is not condemned to remain vain or to violate by its very existence what it posits as its principle. It is for this reason that there can be a politics of freedom and that we are not reduced to choosing between silence and manipulation, consoling ourselves with 'After all, the other will do whatever he wants with it.' It is for this reason that I am finally responsible for what I say (and for what I leave unsaid).[40]

The final reason for beginning with the autonomy of the individual is because autonomy, as we have defined it, leads directly to the political and social problem. The conception we have discussed shows both that one cannot want autonomy without wanting it for everyone and that its realization cannot be conceived in its full scope except as a collective enterprise. If by this term we no longer mean the inalienable freedom of an abstract subject or the domination of a pure consciousness over an undifferentiated material, essentially 'the same' for all and for ever, a primary obstacle that freedom would have to overcome ('passions', 'inertia', etc.); if the problem of autonomy is that the subject meets in itself a meaning that is not its own and that it must transform this meaning in using it; if autonomy is the relation in which others are always present as the otherness *and* as the selfness of the subject, then autonomy can be conceived, even in philosophical terms, only as a social problem and as a social relation.

However, the term 'social' contains more than we have explicated and immediately reveals a new dimension of the problem. Until now we have referred directly to intersubjectivity, even if we have taken it in an unlimited sense – the relation of person to person, even if it is endlessly articulated. But this relation is located in a larger ensemble, which is *the social*, properly speaking.

In other words: the fact that the problem of autonomy immediately refers to, is even identified with, the problem of the relation of one subject to another – or to others; the fact that the other or others do not appear there as external obstacles or as a malediction to be suffered – 'Hell is other people',[41] 'living with others is like being under an evil spell' – but instead as constitutive of the subject, of the problem of the subject and of its possible solution; these facts recall what, after all, was certain from the start for anyone who is not mystified by the ideology of a certain philosophy, namely, that human existence is multiple [*à plusieurs*] and that whatever is said neglecting this presupposition is sheer nonsense (even when one strives painfully to bring 'the other' back, for 'the other', avenging himself for having been excluded at the outset from 'pure' subjectivity, refuses to allow anything of the kind). This multiple existence, however, which appears in this way as an extended intersubjectivity, does not remain – and, indeed, is not from the start – mere intersubjectivity. It is social and historical existence and, to us, this is the essential dimension of the problem. In a way, the intersubjective is the material out of which the social is made but this material exists only as a part and a moment of the social, which it composes but which it also presupposes.

The *social-historical*[42] is neither the indefinite addition of intersubjective networks (although it is this *too*), nor, of course, is it their simple 'product'. The social-historical is the anonymous collective, the impersonal-human element that fills every given social formation but which also encompasses it, setting each society in the midst of others, inscribing them all within a continuity in which those who are no longer, those who are elsewhere, and even those yet to be born are in a certain sense present. It is, on the one hand, given structures, 'materialized' institutions and works, whether these be material or not; and, on the other hand, *that which* structures, institutes, materializes. In short, it is the union *and* the tension of instituting society and of instituted society, of history made and of history in the making [*se faisant*].

Instituted heteronomy: alienation as a social phenomenon

Beyond the individual Unconscious and the intersubjective relation that is played out there, the conditions for alienation are to be found in the social world. Beyond the 'discourse of the other' lies that which gives it its unshiftable weight, limiting and rendering almost futile all individual autonomy.[43] This is manifested as a mass of conditions of privation and oppression, as a solidified global, material and institutional structure of the economy, of power and of ideology, as induction, mystification, manipulation, and violence. No individual autonomy can overcome the consequences of this state of affairs, can cancel the effects on our life of the oppressive structure of the society in which we live.[44]

This is because alienation, social heteronomy, does not appear simply as the 'discourse of the other' – although the latter plays an essential role here as a determining factor and as a content of the Unconscious and of the consciousness of the mass of individuals. The other, however, disappears into collective anonymity, in the impersonal nature of the 'economic mechanisms of the market' or in the 'rationality of the Plan', of the law of a few presented as the law as such. And, along with this, what henceforth represents the other is no longer a discourse: it is a machine gun, military call-up papers, a pay packet and high-priced essential goods, a court decision and a prison. The 'other' is now 'embodied' elsewhere than in the individual Unconscious – even if its presence by proxy [45] in the Unconscious of all those concerned (the one holding the machine gun, the one for whom it is held, and the one at whom it is pointing) is the necessary condition for this embodiment. The opposite is also true; the fact that a few people possess the machine guns is without doubt the condition for maintaining alienation, but on this level the question of the primacy of one condition or the other is meaningless, and what matters to us here is the properly social dimension.[46]

Alienation therefore appears as *instituted*, in any case as heavily conditioned by institutions (the word being taken here in its broadest sense, including in particular the structure of the real relations of production). And its relation to institutions appears twofold.

In the first place, institutions can be, and effectively are, alienating in their specific content. They are alienating to the extent that they express and sanction a class structure, more generally an antagonistic division of society and, concurrent with this, the power of one determinate social category over the whole. They are alienating in a specific way, as well, for each of the classes or strata of a given society. In this way, the capitalist economy – production, distribution, market, etc. – is alienating in as much as it goes along with the division of society into proletariat and capitalists. The same thing holds in a specific manner for each of the two opposing classes, for the proletariat, to be sure, but also for the capitalists. In the past we corrected the simplistic Marxist view of capitalists as the mere toys of economic mechanisms,[47] but one must obviously be careful not to fall into the opposite error and dream of capitalists who are free in relation to 'their' institutions.

However, beyond this aspect and in a more general manner – for, this holds also for societies which do not display an antagonistic division, as is the case in many archaic societies – there is an alienation of society, *irrespective of class*, with regard to its institutions. By this we do not mean the specific aspects that affect all classes 'equally' – the fact that even if the law serves the bourgeoisie it binds it as well. We are instead thinking of the fact, of greater importance in its own right, that once an institution is established it seems to become autonomized, the fact that it possesses its own inertia and its own logic, that, in its continuance and in its effects, it outstrips its function, its 'ends', and its *'raisons d'être'*. The apparent plain truths are turned upside-down: what could have been seen 'at the start' as an ensemble of institutions in the service of society becomes a society in the service of institutions.

'Communism' in its mythical sense

Surpassing alienation in these two forms was, we know, one of the central ideas of Marxism. The proletarian revolution was, after a transitional period, to lead to the 'higher phase of communism' and this passage was to mark 'the end of the prehistory of humanity and the entry into its true history', 'the leap from the realm of necessity to the realm of freedom'. These ideas, however, remained imprecise,[48] and we shall not attempt here to present them systematically, or to discuss them in detail. It is enough to recall that they involved, more or less explicitly, not only the abolition of classes but the elimination of the division of labour ('there will be no more painters, there will be men who paint'), a transformation of social institutions which is hard to distinguish, ultimately, from the idea of the total suppression of all institutions ('the withering away of the State', the elimination of all economic constraints) and, on the philosophical plane, the emergence of a 'total man' and of a humanity that henceforth 'would dominate its history'.

These ideas, despite their vague, remote, almost gratuitous character, not only express a real problem, they unavoidably spring up along the path of revolutionary political reflection. In Marxism it is indisputable that they lock tight its philosophy of history, which without them would be indefinable. What we might regret is not that Marx and Engels spoke of them but that they did not say enough about them – not in order to give 'recipes for the socialist kitchens of the future', not in order to devote themselves to a definition and utopian description of future society, but in order to attempt to discern the meaning of future society in relation to present problems, and in particular in relation to the problem of alienation. Praxis cannot do away with the need to elucidate the future it wants to bring about. No more than psychoanalysis can rid itself of the problem of the *end* of the analysis can revolutionary politics sidestep the question of its outcome and of the meaning of this outcome.

Exegesis and polemics concerning a problem that until now has remained vague matter little to us. There are numerous elements of undeniable truth in Marx's intuitions concerning the overcoming of alienation: first of all, to be sure, the necessity of abolishing classes but also the idea of the transformation of institutions to such an extent that a vast distance would indeed separate them from what institutions have represented until now in history. And all this both presupposes and leads to an upheaval in the mode of existence of human beings – individually and collectively, the limits of which are difficult to glimpse. These elements, however, have undergone – at times in Marx and Engels themselves and, at any rate, in Marxists – a shift toward an ill-defined mythology that is ultimately mystifying and that feeds an equally mythological polemics or antimythology in the adversaries of revolution. A demarcation of these two mythologies, which share a common base moreover, is necessary for its own sake and will also allow us to make some progress in the positive comprehension of the problem.

If by communism ('higher phase') is meant a society in which all resistance, all thickness, all opaqueness would be absent; a society that would be purely transparent to itself; in which everyone's desires would spontaneously harmonize with everybody else's or, in order to harmonize, would require merely an airborne dialogue which would never by weighted down by the gum of symbolism; a society that would discover, formulate, and realize its collective will without having to pass through institutions, or in which institutions would never pose a problem – if this is what is meant, then we must clearly state that this is an incoherent reverie, an unreal and unrealizable state, the representation of which should be eliminated. This is a mythical formation equivalent and analogous to that of Absolute Knowledge or of an individual whose 'consciousness' has absorbed his entire being.

No society will ever be totally transparent, first because the individuals who make it up will never be transparent to themselves, since there can be no question of eliminating the *Unconscious*. Then, because the social implies not only individual consciousnesses, nor even simply their mutual inter-subjective inherencies, the relationships between persons, both conscious and unconscious, which could never be given in their entirety as a content to all, unless we were to introduce the double myth of an Absolute Knowledge possessed equally by all: the social implies something that can never be given as such. The social-historical dimension, as dimension of the collective and the anonymous, instaurates for each and every one of us a simultaneous relation of interiority and of exteriority, of participation and of exclusion, which can in no way be abolished or even 'dominated', in any even slightly definite sense of this term. The social is what is everyone and what is no one, what is never absent and almost never present as such, a nonbeing that is more real than any being, that in which we are wholly immersed yet which we can never apprehend 'in person'. The social is an indefinite dimension, even if it is enclosed at each instant – a definite struc-ture and at the same time one that changes, an objectifiable articulation of categories of individuals and that which, beyond all articulations, sustains their unity. It is what is given as the structure – indissociable form and content – of human ensembles, yet which goes beyond any given structure, an ungraspable productive element, an unformed forming element, some-thing that is always more and always other. It is something that can present itself only in and through the *institution* but which is always infinitely more than the institution, since it is, paradoxically, at once what fills in the insti-tution, what allows itself to be formed by it, what continually overdetermines its functioning, and what in the final analysis founds it: creates it, maintains it in existence, alters it, destroys it. There is the social as instituted, but this always presupposes the social as instituting. 'In ordinary times' the social is manifested in the institution, but this manifestation is at once true and, in a sense, fallacious – as in those moments in which the social as instituting bursts on to the stage and rolls up its sleeves to get to work, the moments of revolution. But this work aims at an immediate result, which is to provide itself once again with an institution in order to exist in a visible manner – and once this institution is set in place the social as instituting slips away, places itself at a distance, is already somewhere else.[49]

Our relation to the social – and to the historical which is its unfolding in time – cannot be called a relation of dependence, for this would be mean-ingless. It is, rather, a relation of *inherence*, which as such is neither freedom nor alienation but the sole ground upon which freedom and alienation can exist, and which only the delirium of an absolute narcissism could wish to abolish, to deplore, or to see as a 'negative condition'. If one wants at all costs to find an analogue or a metaphor for this relation it will be found in our relationship to nature. This belonging to society and to history, infinitely obvious and infinitely obscure, this consubstantiality, partial identity, participation in something that surpasses us on every side, is not an alienation – no more than our spatial character, our corporeality, as 'natural' aspects of our existence, which 'subject' this existence to the laws of physics, chemistry, or biology. These are forms of alienation only in the phantasies of an ideology which refuses what is in the name of a desire aimed at a mirage – the total possession or the Absolute Subject, which in fact has not yet learned to live or even to see, and so can see in being no more than intolerable privation and deficiency, to which it opposes (fictive) Being.

This ideology, which cannot accept inherence, finitude, limitation, and lack, cultivates scorn for this all too green reality that it is unable to reach in two ways: by constructing a 'full' fiction and by an indifference with respect to what is and to what one can do with it. This is manifest on the theoretical plane in the exorbitant requirement of recovering in its entirety the 'meaning' of history, past and to come. On the practical plane we see this in the no less exorbitant idea of man 'dominating his history' – being the master and possessor of history, as he is about to (or so it seems) become the master and possessor of nature. These ideas, to the extent that they are found in Marxism, express Marxism's dependency on traditional ideology; the symmetrical protests of those who, annoyed at the observation that history cannot be an object of possession or transformable into an Absolute Subject, conclude that alienation is perennial, likewise betray their dependence on traditional ideology *and* on Marxism. However, to term 'alienation' the inherence of individuals or of any given society in the social and in the historical that surpass them in every dimension, this is meaningful only from the perspective of 'man's Misery without God'.

Revolutionary praxis, because it is revolutionary and because it must dare beyond the possible, is 'realistic' in the truest sense and begins by accepting being in its profound determinations. For it, a subject that would loosen all its inherent ties to history – even if this be by recovering 'the full meaning of history' – and that would take a tangential line with respect to society – even if this be by exhaustively 'dominating' its relation to society – is not an autonomous subject, it is a psychotic subject. And *mutatis mutandis*, the same thing holds for every determinate society, which, even if it be communist, can emerge, exist, and define itself only against the backdrop of the social-historical, which itself is beyond every particular society and history and nourishes them all. Revolutionary praxis knows not only that there is no question of recovering a unique 'meaning' of past history but that there is no question of 'dominating', in the accepted sense of this term, history to come, unless one is aiming to destroy history's creativity – fortunately, a hopeless endeavour. Let us recall, as a mere image, what we said about the sense of autonomy for the individual: one can no more eliminate or absorb the Unconscious than one can eliminate or absorb the unlimited and unfathomable ground upon which every given society reposes.

Nor can there be any question of a society without institutions, whatever the degree of individual development, technical progress, or economic abundance. None of these factors will ever do away with the innumerable problems people's collective existence constantly raises. There is no way to do away with the necessity for arrangements and procedures that will permit discussion and choice – unless one postulates a biological mutation in humanity, which would realize the immediate presence of each in all and of all in each (but science fiction writers have already seen that a state of universal telepathy would only lead to an immense, generalized confusion, producing only noise and not information). Nor can there be any question of a society that would completely coincide with its institutions, that would be covered exactly, without excess or deficit, by the institutional fabric and which, behind this fabric, would have no flesh on it, a society that would be a network of infinitely flat institutions. There will always be a distance between society as instituting and what is, at each moment, instituted – and this distance is not something negative or deficient; it is one of the expressions of the creativity of history, what prevents it from fixing itself once and for all in the 'finally found form' of social relations and of human activities, what makes a society always contain *more* than what it presents. To wish to abolish this distance, in one way or another, is not to leap from prehistory to history or from necessity to freedom, it is to wish to leap into the Immediate Absolute, that is to say, into nothingness. Just as an individual cannot grasp or provide himself with anything at all – neither the world nor himself – outside the symbolic dimension, no society can provide itself with anything outside this second-order symbolism represented by institutions. And, just as I cannot label *alienation* my relation to language as such – in which I can both say everything and yet not just anything at all, opposite which I am at once determinate and free, and in relation to which a stumbling is possible but not inevitable – so is there no reason to label *alienation* society's relation to the institution. Alienation appears *in* this relation, but it *is* not this relation – just as error or delusion is possible only *in* language but *is* not language.

Notes

1 We are speaking here, to be sure, of activities that go beyond the body of a subject and substantially modify the external world. The 'biological' functions of the human organism

are obviously another matter, including an infinite number of 'reflex' or nonconscious activities. It will be granted that discussion of them cannot shed light on the problem of the relations of knowing and doing in history.

2	It is enough that it be decidable in terms of probabilities; what we are saying does not presuppose a complete, deterministic knowledge of the area considered.

3	Technique, that is, to the extent that is is applied to *objects*. Technique in the more general sense as this is commonly used today – 'military technique', 'political technique', etc., and, more generally, the activities Max Weber included under the term *Zweckrational* – does not enter into our definition in as much as it deals with people, for reasons that will be explained in the text.

4	It is not a matter of exhaustive knowledge in the absolute. The engineer who builds a bridge or a dam does not need to know the nuclear structure of matter; it is enough for him to know statics, the theory of elasticity, the resistance of the materials, and so on. It is not knowledge of matter as such that concerns him but knowledge of the factors that can have a practical importance. This sort of knowledge does exist in the vast majority of cases; but the surprises (and catastrophes) that occur from time to time also show the limits thereof. Precise answers to a host of questions are possible, but not to *all* questions. To be sure, we are leaving aside here the other – essential – limit of the rationality of technique, namely, the fact that technique can never account for the ends it serves.

5	Better yet, because in large part today's medicine is practised in a trivial and fragmentary manner, the doctor trying to act almost as a 'technician'.

6	1975 Note: I have attempted to clarify this idea in relation to psychoanalysis, defined as a pratico-poetic activity, in *ETS* (1968).

7	This attempt failed once it was demonstrated that it is impossible to demonstrate the noncontradiction of systems thus constituted and that undecidable propositions can appear therein (Gödel, 1931).

8	This uncertainty was far less for the Greeks, since the 'rational' foundation of mathematical rigour was, for them, of a nature which is clearly 'irrational' for us (the divine essence of number or the natural character of space as receptacle of the cosmos). The uncertainty is much greater for the Moderns, where the attempt to establish this rigour ends up completely shattering the idea that there can be a rational foundation to mathematics. It is not futile in this regard to remind those who maintain a nostalgia for absolute certainties of the tragic fate of the efforts of Hilbert, who proclaimed that his programme was to 'eliminate from the world once and for all the questions of foundation' (*die Grundlagenfrage ein für allemal aus der Welt zu schaffen*'), thereby setting off an investigation which would show, and even demonstrate, that the question of foundations will always exist in this world *as an insoluble question*. Once more, hubris provoked nemesis.

9	1975 Note: For a justification of these ideas, see 'Le Monde morcelé' (*Textures*, 4–5 [1972], pp. 3–40) [T/E: an expanded version of this text appeared in *CL* as *MSPI* (1973)].

10	The moment of elucidation is always necessarily contained in making/doing. It does not result from this, however, that making/doing and theory are symmetrical at every level, each encompassing the other. Making/doing constitutes the human universe to which theory belongs as a segment. Humanity is engaged in a multiform conscious activity, it *defines itself as* making/doing (which contains elucidation in the context of and in relation to making/doing as a necessary but not sovereign moment). Theory as such is a specific making/doing, it emerges once the moment of elucidation becomes a project for itself. In this sense one can say that there is actually a 'primacy of practical reason'. One can conceive of, and indeed there existed for millennia, a humanity without theory; but there cannot exist a humanity without making/doing.

11	'Are my profession and my children ends or means or both? They are nothing of the sort, certainly not means for my life, which loses itself in them instead of using them; and they are much more than ends, since an end is *what* one wants, and since I want my profession and my children without measuring in advance where this will lead me, which will be far beyond what I can know of them. Not that I dedicate myself to something I do not know – I see them with the kind of precision that belongs to existing things. I recognize them among all others without completely knowing of what they are made. Our concrete decisions do not aim at closed meanings.' This text by Maurice Merleau-Ponty (*The Adventures of the Dialectic*, trans. Joseph Bien [Evanston, Ill.: Northwestern University Press, 1973], p. 127) implicitly contains the closest definition, to my knowledge, given until now of praxis.

12 In an experimental science or an observational science, it may seem that 'activity' precedes elucidation as well; but it precedes the latter only in time, not in logical order. One undertakes an experiment in order to elucidate, and not the other way around. And the activity of the experimenter is transformative only in a superficial or formal sense: it is not aimed at transforming its object as such and, if it does modify the object, this is only to make another, more 'deeply hidden' level appear as 'identical' or as 'constant'. [1975 addition: 'Invariants' are the obsession of science.]

13 Assuming that one day physics might attain an 'exhaustive knowledge' of its object (an assumption which, anyhow, is absurd), this would in no way affect what we are saying about historical praxis.

14 This means: a revolution of the labouring masses that eliminates the domination of any particular stratum over the whole of society and instaurates the power of councils of labouring people over all aspects of social life. On the *programme* that makes the objectives of this revolution concrete in current historical circumstances, see *CS II*.

15 Once again, our discussion here certainly takes up only a very small part of this question and we must refer here to various texts published previously in *Socialisme ou Barbarie* on these matters.

16 When we speak of logic and dynamics, this obviously concerns *historical* logic and dynamics. On the analysis of informal struggle in production, see D[aniel] Mothé, 'L'Usine et la gestion ouvrière', *S. ou B.*, 22 (July 1957), reprinted in *Journal d'un ouvrier* (Paris: Minuit, 1959), and my text *CS III* (1958). On 'workers' management' demands, see *WSAAI* (1956), *GDA* (1956), and *ASE* (1956). On the Hungarian workers' councils and their demands, see all of the texts on the Hungarian Revolution published in issue no. 20 of *S. ou B.* and Pannonicus, 'Les Conseils ouvriers de la révolution hongroise', *S. ou B.*, 21 (March 1957). Let us recall, moreover, that a permanent dialectic appears in this struggle; just as the means used by management against the workers can be taken by the latter and turned against management itself, so management is able to co-opt the positions conquered by the workers and, ultimately, even to make use of their informal organization. Each of these types of co-option, however, gives rise in the end to a response on another level.

17 Finicky sociologists can be found who will protest: How can one include under the same signification data coming from fields as diverse as investigations in industrial sociology, strikes at Standard in England and at General Motors in the United States, and the Hungarian Revolution? This breaks all methodological rules. The same hypersensitive critics fall into trances, however, when they see Freud compare 'the return of the repressed' in a patient during the course of an analysis and in the entire Jewish people ten centuries after the alleged murder of Moses.

18 By affirming, since 1948, that the experience of bureaucratization henceforth made the workers' management of production the central demand of all revolution (*SB* [1949]).

19 We have, for our part, recapped the analyses of industrial sociology and, assisted by concrete information contributed by workers who constantly live this conflict, attempted to elucidate its signification and bring out the conclusions that may be drawn therefrom.

For this, we have recently been reproached, by reformed Marxists like Lucien Sebag, for 'partiality' (*Marxisme et structuralisme* [Paris: Payot, 1964], p. 130): we are supposed to have committed the sin of 'admitting that the *truth of the business enterprise* is concretely given to certain of its members, namely the workers'. In other words: ascertaining that a war exists; that both adversaries agree on its existence, on the way it unfolds, on its modalities and even on its causes, this point of view is deemed to be partial (in both senses of the term). One can then only wonder what, for Lucien Sebag, would not be partial: Might this be the point of view of university professors or 'researchers' who themselves would, perhaps, belong to no social subgroup? Or does he mean that one can never say anything about society, but then why does he bother to write? On this level, a revolutionary theorist has no need to postulate that the 'truth of the business enterprise' is given to certain of its members; once it is analysed, the discourse of capitalists says nothing else; from top to bottom, society expresses its crisis. The problem begins when one wants to know what one is to *do* with this crisis (and this overdetermines, ultimately, theoretical analyses); then, indeed, one can only place oneself in the perspective of a particular group (since society is divided), but then the question is no longer 'the truth of the business enterprise' (or of society) as it is but the 'truth' of what is to be done by this group *against* another. At this moment one effectively does take sides, but this is the case for everyone, including the philosopher who, by holding forth on the impossibility of taking sides, actually does take sides in favour of what is and so in favour of a few people. Moreover, Sebag mixes up two different considerations in his critique: the difficulty of which we have just spoken and which is held to result from the fact that the 'Marxist sociologist' attempts to express a 'global signification of the factory' whose depositary is the proletariat, which in turn is only one part of the factory; and the difficulty relating to the 'disparity of attitudes and stands on the part of the workers', which the Marxist sociologist would resolve by giving preference to 'certain types of conduct', 'based on a more general schema relating to capitalist society as a whole'. The second difficulty exists, to be sure, but it is by no means a curse specific to Marxist sociology; it exists for all scientific thought, for all thought as such, as well as for the most ordinary, everyday discourse. Whether I speak about sociology, economics, meteorology, or the behaviour of my butcher, I am constantly forced to distinguish what appears to me to be significant from the rest, to give preference to certain aspects and to pass over others. I do this in accordance with certain criteria, rules, and conceptions which can always be argued about and which are periodically revised – but I could cease to do so only if I were to cease to think. The fact that preference is given to *these particular* types of behaviour can be concretely criticized, but not the fact of according preference as such. It is distressing to note once again here that the alleged advances over Marxism are in most cases clear regressions based not on new knowledge but on the forgetfulness of what had previously been learned – poorly learned, it would seem.

20 For the justification of what is stated here, we must refer the reader to Mothé's 'L'Usine et la gestion ouvrière', cited above, as well as to S. Chatel's article, 'Hiérarchie et gestion collective', *S. ou B.*, 37 and 38 (July and October 1964).

21 See *MCR I* (1960), now in *PSW 2*, pp. 242–58.

22 Up to a certain point, a very considerable increase in 'aid' to underdeveloped countries could also help to alleviate this problem.

23 What is actually at issue in all this is the fact that we are living the *beginning of the end of the economic* as such. Herbert Marcuse in *Eros and Civilization* (London: Routledge & Kegan Paul, 1956) and Paul Goodman in *Growing Up Absurd* (New York: Random House, 1960) were the first, to my knowledge, to examine the implications of this potential upheaval – to which we shall return later.

24 For the possibility of an organization and management of the economy in this direction, see *CS I*, in *PSW 1*, pp. 303–5, and *CS II*, in abridged form in *CR*, pp. 74–85, and reprinted

in full in *PSW 2*, pp. 117–31. The extent to which these problems are at the heart of the current economic situation is shown by the fact that the idea of the 'automatization' of a great part of the management of the overall economy, formulated in *S. ou B.*, 1955–7, has since 1960 inspired one of the 'reforming' tendencies of Russian economists, concerning the 'automatization' of planning (Kantorovich, Novozhilov, etc.). However, the achievement of this solution is scarcely compatible with the continuing power of the bureaucracy.

25 The demand for a more comprehensible economy *precedes* logically and even politically that of an economy in the service of human beings; no one can say in the service of whom the economy is functioning, if this functioning is incomprehensible.

26 1975 Note: This question is discussed at length in chapter 6 of *IIS*.

27 See, for example, Allen Wheelis, *The Quest for Identity* (London: Victor Gollancz, 1956), in particular pp. 97–138. This is also the sense of David Riesman's analyses in *The Lonely Crowd* (New Haven, Conn.: Yale University Press, 1950).

28 1975 Note: As 'Marxists' should have done – and actually did – in this case.

29 The passage in which this sentence occurs, at the end of the third (31st in the consecutive numbering adopted by Freud) of the 'lectures' of the *New Introductory Lectures on Psychoanalysis*, reads as follows: '[The] intention [of the therapeutic efforts of psychoanalysis] is, indeed, to strengthen the ego, to make it more independent of the superego, to widen its field of perception and enlarge its organization, so that it can appropriate fresh portions of the id. Where id was, there ego shall be. It is a work of culture – not unlike the draining of the Zuider Zee' (*Standard Edition*, vol. 22, p. 80). Jacques Lacan renders the *Wo Es war, soll Ich werden* by 'Là où fut ça, il me faut advenir' (Where that was, I must come to be) ('L'Instance de la lettre dans l'inconscient' (1957), in *Écrits* [Paris: Seuil, 1966, p. 524]) and he adds, concerning 'the end which Freud's discovery proposes to man': 'This is one [an end] of reintegration and harmony, I could even say of reconciliation [*Versöhnung*]' (*Écrits. A Selection* [London: Tavistock, 1977], p. 171).

30 In *The Book of the It* (1923) by G. Groddeck, trans. V. M. E. Collins (London: Vision Press, 1950; New York: Vintage, 1961).

31 It would be fairer to say: concerning the clarification and the exploration of the depth dimension of the psyche, which neither Heraclitus nor Plato was unaware of, as even the most superficial reading of the *Symposium* reveals for all to see.

32 '. . . the nucleus of our being, but it is not so much that Freud commands us to seek it as so many others before him have with the empty adage "know thyself" – as to reconsider the ways that lead to it, and which he shows us' (Jacques Lacan, *Écrits. A Selection*, pp. 173–4).

33 See Jacques Lacan, 'Remarques sur le rapport de D. Lagache', in *Psychanalyse*, 6 (1961), p. 116. 'A pole of attributes – this is the subject before its birth (and perhaps one day it will suffocate under their mass). Attributes, that is to say, signifiers tied more or less closely together in a discourse . . .' (*Écrits*, p. 652F).

34 This is obviously the essential difference in relation to other forms of the imaginary (such as, for example, art or the 'rational' use of the imaginary in mathematics) which do not become autonomized as such. We shall return to this at length later. [1975 addition: The term 'imaginary' here and in the two pages that follow is still used in an ambiguous sense, bearing its common usage.]

35 [1975 Note: This is also indicated by Freud's abandonment of the hypothesis of 'infantile seduction' as well as, more especially, by the gradual – although never definitive – questioning, throughout the account of the analysis of *The Wolf Man*, of the 'reality' of the primitive scene.] This is not a matter of 'reality' or of the 'demands of life in society' as such, but of what becomes of these demands in the discourse of the Other (which, moreover, is by no means a neutral vehicle) and in the imaginary elaboration of the latter by the subject. This obviously does not deny the capital importance, for the *content* of the

discourse of the Other and for the specific tenor which its imaginary elaboration will take on, of the concrete character of the society considered, or the importance of the excessive and irrational nature of the social formulation of these 'requirements' with respect to the frequency and the seriousness of pathogenic situations: on this matter, Freud was extremely clear (cf., in particular, *Civilization and its Discontents*). But at this level we encounter once again the fact that these 'requirements' of society cannot be reduced to the demands of 'reality', to those of 'life in society' in general, or even, finally, to those of a 'society divided into classes' but instead go beyond what these demands would rationally imply. Here we find the point of connection between the individual imaginary and the social imaginary – a topic to which we shall return later.

36 'An ethic announces itself . . . through the advent not of fear but of desire' (Jacques Lacan, *Écrits*, p. 684F).

37 This is not a description of the empirical–psychological conditions for the functioning of the subject but an articulation of the logical (transcendental) structure of subjectivity: there is no thinking subject except as the disposition of contents, every particular content can be bracketed but not just any content as such. The same thing is true concerning the problem of the genesis of the subject, considered in its logical aspect: at any given instant the subject is a producer produced and 'at the origin' the subject constitutes itself as that which is simultaneously given as Self and as Other. [1975 addition: The subject in question here is the one that is established with the break-up of the psychical monad. See chapter 6 of *IIS*.]

38 1975 Note: This ultimately leads to denying that the traditional distinction between 'activity' and 'passivity' possesses any originary signification. I return to this in the second half of *IIS*.

39 As that making/doing which is aimed at the other or at others as autonomous beings. See 'Praxis and Project' above.

40 Political praxis has a second foundation, which will be distinguished later: the possibility of institutions that favour autonomy.

41 The author of this statement [Jean-Paul Sartre] was no doubt certain that he carried no trace at all of another within himself (otherwise, he might just as well have said that Hell was himself). He has, moreover, recently confirmed this interpretation by stating that he had no Superego. How could we object to this, as we have always thought that he spoke of matters on this Earth as if he were a being arriving here from another planet?

42 By this expression we are intending the unity of the twofold multiplicity of dimensions, in 'simultaneity' (synchrony) and in 'succession' (diachrony), which are traditionally denoted by the terms 'society' and 'history'. We shall at times speak of the social or of the historical, without specifying them further, depending on the aspect we wish to underscore. [1975 addition: We shall return to this matter at length in the second part of *IIS*.]

43 In a society of alienation, even for those rare individuals for whom autonomy has a meaning, it can only be truncated, for it runs up, in material conditions and in other individuals, against continually renewed obstacles as soon as it is to be embodied in an activity, to unfold and exist in a social dimension; autonomy can be manifested in the effective life of these individuals only in ever uneven openings [*interstices*], hewn out by chance and through a certain skill.

44 It is hardly necessary to recall that the idea of autonomy and that of responsibility of each individual for his life can easily become mystifications if they are severed from the social context and posited as self-sufficient responses.

45 This delegation poses multiple complex problems which it is impossible to discuss here. There is, obviously, at once homology and an essential difference between the 'family' relation and class relations, or power relations, in society. Freud's basic contribution (*Totem and Taboo* or *Group Psychology and the Analysis of the Ego*), that of Wilhelm Reich (*The Function of the Orgasm*), and the numerous contributions of American anthropologists

(in particular, Kardiner and Margaret Mead) far from exhaust the question, in as much as they relegate the properly institutional dimension to a secondary level.

46 If factory workers wanted to question the existing order, they would run up against the police and, if the movement were to spread, the army. Through historical experience we know that neither the police nor the army are impermeable in the face of widespread movements; can they hold fast against the main part of the population? Rosa Luxemburg said: 'If the entire population *knew*, the capitalist regime would not last 24 hours.' Never mind the 'intellectual' overtones of the statement: let us ascribe to *knowing* its full depth and let us connect it to *willing*. Is it not true beyond a shadow of a doubt? Yes and no. The *yes* is obvious. The *no* follows from the other fact, which is equally obvious, that the social regime as a matter of fact *prevents* the population from knowing and willing. Unless one is to postulate a miraculous coincidence of positive spontaneities from one end of the country to the other, every seed, every embryo of this knowing and this willing which can be manifested in a given place in society is constantly hampered, combated and, finally, crushed by the existing institutions. It is for this reason that the purely 'psychological' view of alienation, the one which seeks the conditions for alienation solely in the structure of individuals, in their 'masochism', etc., and which would finally say: If people are exploited, it is because they want to be, is itself unilateral and, ultimately, false. People are this *and* something else, but in their individual life the combat is grotesquely uneven, for the other factor (the tendency towards autonomy) has to confront the entire weight of instituted society. If it is essential to recall that heteronomy must in each case also find its conditions in each exploited individual, it has to find them to the same extent in social structures, which make the individuals' 'chances' (in Max Weber's sense) of knowing and willing practically nonexistent. Knowing and willing are not purely a matter of knowing and willing, we are not dealing with subjects who would be pure will to autonomy and entirely responsible, for if this were the case there would be no problem in any domain whatsoever. It is not simply that the social structure is 'designed for' instilling passivity, respect for authority, etc. even before an individual's birth; it is that institutions are there, in the long struggle of each person's life, to place blocks and obstacles in the way at every instant, to push the waters in a certain direction, and finally to rage against whatever might be manifested as autonomy. This is why the person who says he wants autonomy while refusing the revolution in institutions knows neither what he is saying nor what he wants. The individual imaginary, as we shall see later, finds a correspondence in a social imaginary embodied in institutions, but this embodiment exists as such and it is also as such that it must be attacked.

47 See *MCR*, now in *PSW 2*, pp. 267ff.

48 It is, moreover, very hard to evaluate the role these ideas have effectively played in the case of workers or even of militants. It is certain that both have always been much more preoccupied with the problems posed by their condition and their struggle than with the need to define a 'final' objective; but it is equally certain that something like the image of a promised land, or of a radical redemption, has always been present in them, carrying the ambiguous signification of an eschatological Millennium, of a Kingdom of God without God, *and* of the desire for a society in which man would no longer be the main enemy of man.

49 1975 Note: These are the features of the social that are at the root of inherited thought's inability to reflect upon the social for its own sake – without reducing it to what it is not. We shall return at length to this in the second part of *IIS*.

6

The Social Imaginary and the Institution (1975)*: Excerpt

The Social-Historical

Our aim in this chapter is to elucidate the question of society and that of history, questions that can be understood only when they are taken as one and the same: the question of the social-historical. Inherited ways of thinking can make only fragmentary contributions to this elucidation. Perhaps this contribution is mostly negative, marking out the limits of a mode of thought and displaying its impossibilities.

This assertion may seem surprising, considering the quantity and the quality of what, at least since Plato and especially over the past few centuries, has been provided by reflection in this domain. However, the essential part of this reflection – except for germinal asides, lightning strokes quickly dying out, moments of the intractable presence of the aporia – has been spent not in opening and broadening the question but in covering it over as soon as it was discovered, in reducing it as soon as it emerged. The same mechanism and the same motivations are to be found in this covering over and this reduction as in the covering over and the reduction of the question of the imagination and the imaginary – and for the same profound reasons.

On the one hand, inherited reflection has never succeeded in separating out the true object of this question and in considering it for its own sake. This object has almost always been split into a society, referred to something other than itself and, generally, to a norm, end, or *telos* grounded in something else, and a history, considered as something that happens to this society, as a disturbance in relation to a given norm, or as an organic or dialectical development towards this norm, end, or *telos*. In this way, the object in question, the being proper to the social-historical, is constantly shifted towards something other than itself and absorbed by this something else. The most profound views, those that are truest with respect to the social-historical, those that have taught us the most and without which we

* 'Le Social-historique' was originally published as chapter 4 in *SII* (1975), the second part of *IIS*. The present version contains excerpts from the first three sections of Kathleen Blamey's translation of this chapter. [T/E: Again, I have edited this translation for purposes of standardization and clarity.]

would still be babbling incoherently, these are still implicitly governed by an elsewhere – and this, too, appertains to the essence and the history of thought; it is in the direction of this elsewhere that these views attempt to orient what they do say about the social-historical. What rules *a tergo* inherited reflection upon society and history, that in spite of which it discovers what it does manage to discover, is, for example, the place of society and of history in the divine economy of creation or in the infinite life of reason; or the possibility they have of encouraging or hampering the individual's fulfilment as an ethical subject; or their standing as the final avatar of natural beings; or the relation of social matter and its corruption or historical instability (its being indefinite-indeterminate, *apeiron*, determined by its privation of determinability; its character of always becoming, *aei gignomenon*) to the form and the norm of the determinate and stable political city, implying the subordination of the study of the former to the requirements of the latter, hence to the right form of the right city, even if one must then deny its very possibility.[1]

Thus, too, representation, imagination, and imaginary have never been seen for themselves but always in relation to something else – to sensation, intellection, perception, or reality – submitted to the normativity incorporated in the inherited ontology, brought within the viewpoint of the true and the false, instrumentalized within a function, means judged according to their possible contribution to the accomplishment of the end that is truth or access to true being, the being of being (*ontos on*).

In this way, finally, there has not been the slightest concern with knowing what *making/doing* means, what the being of making/doing is and what it is that making/doing makes be, so obsessed have people been with these questions alone: What is it to do good or to do well, to do evil or to do badly? Making/doing has not been thought because no one has attempted to think of anything other than two particular moments of making/doing, the ethical moment and the technical moment. And even these moments have not been truly thought, since that of which they are the moments was never thought and since their very substance had been eliminated from the outset when doing as making-be was ignored, and when it was subordinated to its partial determinations, which are the products of making/doing but were presented as absolutes, reigning from an elsewhere, good and evil (of which the efficient and the inefficient are derivatives).

Moreover, reflection on history and society has always been situated on the terrain and within the boundaries of the inherited logic-ontology – and how could it have been otherwise? Society and history cannot be the objects of reflection if they are not. But what are they, how are they, in what sense are they? The classical rule enjoins: Do not multiply beings unnecessarily. At a deeper level lies another rule: Do not multiply the meanings of being; being must have a single meaning.[2] This meaning, determined from start to finish as determinacy – *peras* in the Greeks, *Bestimmtheit* in Hegel – already in itself excluded the possibility of recognizing a type of being that essentially escapes determinacy, like the social-historical or the imaginary. Consequently, whether or not it recognized this, whether or not it intended this, and even in the instances when it may have explicitly intended the opposite, inherited thought has necessarily been led to reduce the social-historical to the primitive types of being it knew or thought it knew – having constructed them and hence determined them – from elsewhere, making the social-historical a variant, a combination, or a synthesis of the corresponding beings: thing, subject, idea or concept. Consequently, too, society and history found themselves subordinated to already guaranteed logical operations and functions that apparently could be thought by means of categories established in fact to grasp a few entities, themselves particular but posited by philosophy as universal.

These are but two aspects of the same movement, two indissociable effects of imposing the inherited logic-ontology on the social-historical. If the social-historical is thinkable by means of the categories that are valid for other beings, then it cannot help but be essentially homogeneous with them; its mode of being poses no particular question, and it allows itself to be re-absorbed within total being. Reciprocally, if to be means to be determined, then society and history *are* only to the extent that their place within the total order of being (as the result of causes, as means to an end, or as a moment in a process), their internal order, and the necessary relation between the two, are determined; these orders, relations, and necessities take the form of categories, that is to say, of determinations of all that can be in as much as it can be (thought). The best that can be obtained this way is the Hegelian–Marxist view of society and of history: the sum and sequence of actions (whether conscious or not) of a multiplicity of subjects, determined by necessary relations, and by means of which a system of ideas is embodied in an ensemble of things (or reflects it). Whatever in effective history appears as irreducibly in excess or in deficit in relation to this schema becomes scoria, illusion, contingency, chance – in short, unintelligible; this is not scandalous in itself, but it should be so for a philosophy for which the unintelligible is only another name for the impossible.

However, if we decide to consider the social-historical for its own sake; if we understand that it is to be questioned and reflected upon starting from itself; if we refuse to eliminate the questions it poses by subjecting it in advance to determinations that we know or believe we know from elsewhere – then we observe that it shatters the inherited logic and ontology. For, we see that it does not fall under traditional categories – except in a nominal and empty manner; that, instead, it makes us recognize the narrow limits of their validity; and that it permits us to glimpse a new and different logic and, above all, to alter radically the meaning of being.

Possible Types of Traditional Responses

The question, What is the social-historical?, joins together the two questions that tradition and convention generally separate, that of society and that of history.[3] A brief study of the *status* of traditional responses will be facilitated by formulating the core of these two questions in a more specific way.

What is society? In particular, what are the unity and identity (*ecceity*) of a society, or what holds a society together?

What is history? In particular, how and why is there temporal alteration in a society; in what way is this an alteration; is there emergence of the new in history, and what does this emergence signify?

The meaning and the unity of these questions can be further clarified if we ask ourselves: In what way and why are there many societies and not just one; in what way and why are there differences between societies? If we were to reply that the differences between societies, and their histories, are merely apparent, the question would still remain, just as before: Why, then, do we find this appearance, why does the identical appear as different?[4]

The countless replies given since reflection originated on these two questions can be grouped under two basic types and their various mixtures.

The first type of reply is the physicalist type, which reduces, directly or indirectly, immediately or in the final analysis, society and history to nature. This nature is, first of all, human biological nature; it matters little whether this is seen to be reducible, in turn, to a simple physical mechanism, or whether it is held to go beyond the latter, for example a generic being (*Gattungswesen*) for the young Marx, a Hegelian concept[5] representing a later stage in the logico-ontological elaboration of the *phusis* of the Aristotelian living being, the aspect/species (*eidos*) that reproduces itself without ever changing. Functionalism is the purest and most typical exemplar of this point of view: it takes human needs as fixed and explains social organization as the ensemble of functions intended to satisfy these needs. This explanation, as we saw above, explains nothing at all. A host of activities in every society fill no specific function in the functionalist sense. And, what is more, the very question that matters, that concerning differences between societies, is eliminated or covered over by platitudes. The alleged explanation is left hanging in midair for lack of a stable point to which it could relate the functions that social organization is supposed to serve. This stable point can be supplied only by postulating an identity of human needs in all societies and in all historical periods, an identity contradicted by the most superficial look at history. One is then forced to resort to the fiction of an inalterable core of abstract needs that would receive from place to place different specifications or varying modes of satisfaction and to platitudes or tautologies in order to account for this difference and variability. The essential fact is thereby covered over: human needs, to the extent that they are social and not simply biological, are inseparable from their objects, and both these needs and their objects are each time instituted by the society considered. The same is true with respect to the impostures propagated nowadays, ever since 'desire' has become the fashion; society is, in fact, reduced to desire and to its repression, without any effort to explain the difference between the objects and the forms of desire, without expressing any surprise at the strange division into desire and the desire for the repression of desire which is, according to them, supposed to characterize most societies, the possibility of this division, and the reasons for its appearance.

The second type is the logicist type, which takes on different forms depending on the acceptation of the *log-* root in this term. When the logic in question ultimately amounts (irrespective of its surface complications) to arranging a finite number of black and white pebbles in a predetermined number of boxes following a few simple rules (for example, no more than *n* pebbles of the same colour in the same line or column), we have the most impoverished form of logicism – structuralism. The same logical operation, repeated a certain number of times, is thereby held to account for the totality of human history and for the different forms of society; the latter would then be no more than different possible combinations of a finite number of the same discrete elements. This elementary combinatorics – which mobilizes the same intellectual faculties as those used in constructing magic squares or solving crossword puzzles – must, each time, unquestionably take for granted both the finite set [*ensemble*] of elements on which the operations are performed and the oppositions or differences it postulates between them. However, even in phonology – of which structuralism is but an abusive extrapolation – one cannot take as a basis the *natural* givenness of a finite set of discrete elements – here, the phonemes or distinctive features that can be uttered and perceived by man; as Plato already knew,[6] sounds that are uttered and perceived are indeterminate, *apeiron*; and *peras*, determination, the simultaneous positing of phonemes and of their relevant differences is an institution of language [*langue*] in general, and of each specific tongue [*langue*]. This institution and its differences – the difference between French phonology and English phonology, for example – phonology accepts as a fact and is not obliged to question. As a positive and limited form of knowledge it can leave the question of the origin of its object dormant. How could one proceed in the same way when the question of society and of history is, essentially, a question of the nature and the origin of differences? Structuralism's naivety in this respect is disarming. It has nothing to say about the sets of elements it manipulates, about the reasons for their being-thus, or about their modifications in time. Masculine and feminine, north and south, high and low, dry and wet, seem self-evident to structuralism; simply found there by humans, stones of meaning scattered on the Earth since the origins, in a being-thus which is at once completely natural and totally significant, among which each society selects a few (following the results of a game of chance),[7] provided that it can choose elements only by pairs of opposites and that the choice of certain pairs leads to or excludes the choice of others. As if social organization could be reduced to a finite sequence of yes/no, and as if, wherever a yes/no is involved, the terms it bears upon were themselves given from somewhere else and from all time – whereas they are, as terms and as these particular terms, the creation of the society concerned.

Or else, at the extreme opposite end and in its richest form, the logic employed claims to stir all the figures of the material and spiritual universe. Accepting no limit, it wants to and has to bring everything into play, into relation with everything else, into complete determinacy and exhaustive reciprocal determination. It must then generate them, some on the basis of others, and all on the basis of the same first or last element, as its necessary figures or moments, necessarily unfolding in a necessary order, of which the logic itself must necessarily be a part as a reflecting on, reflecting back, repetition, or apex. No matter whether this element is termed reason, as in Hegelianism, matter or nature, as in the canonical version of Marxism (matter or nature that, in principle, is reducible to rational determinations). We have already indicated [in *MRT*] a few of the countless and interminable aporias to which this conception leads.

Thus, the question of the unity and identity of society and of any particular society is brought back to the assertion of a given unity and identity of an ensemble of living organisms; or of a hyperorganism containing its own needs and functions; or of a natural-logical group of elements; or of a system of rational determinations. Of society as such in all this, there remains nothing; nothing that might be the proper being of society, nothing that manifests a mode of being any different from what we already know from elsewhere. Nor does there remain much of history, of the temporal alteration produced in and through society. Faced with the question of history, physicalism naturally becomes causalism, that is, the elimination of the question. For the question of history is the question of the emergence of radical alterity or of the absolutely new (even the assertion of the contrary would attest to this, for neither amoebae nor galaxies talk in order to say that everything is eternally the same). And causality is always the negation of alterity, the positing of a double identity: an identity in the repetition of the same causes producing the same effects; an ultimate identity of the cause and the effect since each necessarily belongs to the other, or both to the same.[8] It is therefore not by chance that the pre-eminent element in and through which the social-historical unfolds, namely, significations, is neglected or else transformed into a mere epiphenomenon, a redundant accompaniment to what is really supposed to be happening. How, indeed, could one signification be the cause of another signification, and how could they be the effects of nonsignifications?

Precisely the same elimination of the question of history is brought about by the form that logicism takes, becoming, in the face of history, rationalistic finalism. For, if logicism sees in significations the element of history, it is incapable of considering these significations other than as rational (this, of course, does not imply that it must posit them as conscious for the agents of history). But rational significations can and must be deduced or produced on the basis of other rational significations. Their unfolding is then no more than a spreading out, and the new is, each time, constructed through *identitary* operations[9] (even if they are termed dialectical) by means of what was already there; the totality of the process is only the displaying of the necessarily realized virtualities inherent in a primordial principle, present from all time and for all time. Historical time thus becomes a simple abstract medium of successive coexistence or a mere receptacle for the dialectical sequences. True time, the time of radical alterity, an alterity that can be neither deduced nor produced, has to be abolished, and no reason other than contingent reason can explain why the totality of past and future history is not, in principle, deducible. The end of history annoys Hegel's commentators because it seems absurd to them to situate it in 1830; this displays insufficient knowledge of the necessities of the philosopher's thought, for which this end had already occurred before the beginning of history. For history cannot be Reason if it does not have a *raison d'être* that is its end (*telos*), that is just as necessarily fixed for it (from all time) as the paths of its progress. This is simply another way of saying that time is abolished, as it is in every true teleology, since, for every complete and necessary teleology, everything is controlled from the end, and the end is already posited and determined at the start of the process, positing and determining the means that will make it appear as accomplished. Time is then only a pseudonym for the order of positing and of reciprocal generation of the terms of the process, or, as effective time, mere external condition that has nothing to do with the process itself. I have already indicated, in *MRT* and in other texts,[10] that canonical Marxism represents an attempt to glue back together the causalist and the finalist view.

Let us note that, beyond the contingent incapacity of the exponents of structuralism to confront the problem of history (apart from denying, more or less explicitly, that such a problem exists), nothing would prevent one from positing the fiction of a structure of history in its temporal unfolding; or, rather, that the postulate of a structure such as this would be required by a structuralist conception that desired to be self-consistent. Actually, structuralism cannot be taken seriously as a general conception so long as it does not venture to affirm that the different social structures it claims to describe are themselves simply elements of a hyper- or metastructure that would constitute total history. And since this would amount to bringing history to a close, as far as ideas are concerned – speaking of structures means nothing unless all the elements and their relations can be determined once and for all – and to placing oneself in the spot of Absolute Knowledge,[11] structuralism cannot be taken seriously in this case either.

It is not these conceptions, as such, that truly matter, or their critique, and even less the critique of their authors. With important authors, conceptions are never pure; the application of such conceptions in contact with the material these authors are attempting to think reveals something other than what they explicitly think, and the results are infinitely richer than their programmatic theses. A great author, by definition, thinks beyond his means. He is great to the extent that he thinks something other than what has already been thought, and his means are the result of what has already been thought, which continually encroaches on what he does think, if only because he cannot wipe away all that he has received and place himself before a *tabula rasa*, even when he is under the illusion that he can. The contradictions that are always present in a great author bear witness to this fact; I am speaking of true, raw, irreducible contradictions, which it is just as stupid to think cancel by themselves the author's contribution as it is useless to try to dissolve or to recover at successive and ever deeper levels of interpretation.

The most pregnant, the richest form that these contradictions may take is the one which results from the impossibility simply to think together and with the same means what the author discovers – which is, in the important cases, another region of what is, another mode and another sense of: being – and what was already known. Nothing guarantees in advance the coherency or, more precisely, the identity (immediate or mediated) of the mode of being belonging to the objects of a new region, hence of the logic and the ontology a new region requires, and of the logic and the ontology already developed somewhere else; even less is it guaranteed that this coherency will be of the same order and type as that existing within already known regions. In particular, the regions at issue here – the radical imaginary and the social-historical – imply a profound questioning of the received significations of being as determinacy and of logic as determination. To the extent that the resulting conflict is perceived by the author, it tends to be resolved by subordinating the new object to the significations and determinations already acquired, leading to the concealment of what has been discovered, the occultation of what has been revealed, its marginalization, the impossibility of thematizing it, its denaturing through its resorption into a system to which it remains alien, its retention under the form of an intractable aporia.

Thus, Aristotle discovers the imagination – *phantasia* – philosophically, but what he says about it thematically, when he treats it *ex professo* (fixing the imagination in its alleged place, between sensation, of which it would be a reproduction, and intellection, thereby governing for twenty-five centuries what everyone thinks about it), is of little consequence next to what he truly has to say about it, which he says elsewhere, and which he has no way of reconciling with what he thinks about *phusis*, the soul, thinking, and being. Thus, too, Kant, repeating the same move three times (in the two editions of the *Critique of Pure Reason* and in the *Critique of Judgment*), discovers and conceals the role of what he calls the transcendental imagination. Thus Hegel, and Marx incomparably more, who can say what they have to say that is fundamental about society and history only by transgressing what they believe they know about what being and thinking mean, and who finally reduce it, by forcing it to enter into a system that cannot contain it. Thus, finally, Freud, who unveils the Unconscious, affirms its mode of being to be incompatible with diurnal logic-ontology, and yet never manages to think it, up to the end, except by calling upon all the machinery of the psychical apparatus, agencies, places, forces, causes, and ends in order to manage to conceal its indetermination as radical imagination.

The reproduction of these situations with features that are essentially analogous, considering the depth and the audacity of minds such as these, shows that fundamental factors are involved here. The inherited logic-ontology is solidly anchored in the very institution of social-historical life; it is rooted in the unavoidable necessities of this institution, and it is, in a sense, the elaboration and branching out [*arborescence*] of these necessities. Its core is the *identitary* or *ensemblist* logic, and it is this logic that rules sovereignly and ineluctably over the two institutions without which no social life can exist: the institution of *legein*, the ineffaceable component of language and of social representing, and the institution of *teukhein*, the ineffaceable component of social making/doing.[12] The fact that social life has been able to exist shows that this identitary or ensemblist logic has a grip on what there is – not only on the natural world in which society emerges, but on society itself, which cannot represent things and represent itself, speak and speak (of) itself, make things and make itself without at the same time applying this identitary or ensemblist logic, which can establish institutions and institute itself only by instituting *legein* and *teukhein*, as well.

This logic – and the ontology that is homologous to it – far from exhausting what there is and its mode of being, touches only the first stratum; but at the same time, its internal exigency is to cover over or to exhaust every possible stratum. The problematic sketched out above is simply the concrete realization, in the areas of the imaginary and of the social-historical, of this antinomy. Physicalism and logicism, causalism and finalism are only ways of extending the exigencies and the basic schemata of identitary logic to society and to history. For, identitary logic is the logic of determination, which particularizes itself, depending on the case, as a cause and effect relation, as means and end, or as the logic of implication.

This logic can operate only by positing these relations as relations among the elements of a set (in the sense that these terms have in contemporary mathematics, but which is already at work from the start of the institution of *legein* and *teukhein*). This is what is essential and not the fact that it defines the mode of being of these elements as that of physical entities or logical terms. For it, just as for the ontology that follows from it, to be means to be determined. It is only starting from this position that oppositions develop concerning what truly is, that is to say, what is truly, solidly, and fully *determined*. From this point of view, not only is the opposition between materialism and spiritualism secondary; but secondary, too, is the opposition between Hegel and Gorgias, for example, between Absolute Knowledge and Absolute Nonknowledge. Both do, in fact, share a common conception of: being. The first posits being as infinite self-determination; the nerve centre of the second's arguments (like all sceptical and nihilist arguments ever uttered), when he wants to demonstrate that nothing is, and that if something is, it is not knowable, amounts to this: Nothing is really determinable, the requirement of determination will forever remain empty and unsatisfied, for every determination is contradictory (hence indetermination) – which is meaningful only on the basis of the tacit criterion: If something did exist, it would be determined.

Any discussion of the inherited concepts of society and history is, therefore, inseparable from bringing to light their logical and ontological foundations, just as their critique can only be the critique of these foundations and the elucidation of the social-historical as a domain irreducible to inherited logic and ontology. The typology of the answers to the question of society and history sketched out above is important in as much as these types of answers are the only ones possible on the basis of this logic-ontology. They concretize the ways in which inherited thought can conceive of coexistence and succession, the being, the being-thus, and the *raison d'être* (the why) of coexistence and succession.

Society and the Schemata of Coexistence

Society presents itself immediately as the coexistence of a host of terms or entities of different orders. What is available to inherited thinking in order to think coexistence and the mode of being-together of a diversity of terms?

Either this coexistence, this being-together of a manifold, is considered to be a real system, whatever its complexity. In which case there must be the possibility of effectively decomposing (whether in reality or ideally and abstractly) the system into well-defined subsystems, into parts, and, finally, into elements taken provisionally or definitively as ultimate. These elements, clearly distinct and well defined, must be amenable to univocal definition. They must be connected together by relations of causal determination, linear or cyclical (reciprocal), categorical or probabilist – relations which themselves are amenable to univocal definition; and relations of the same type must hold between parts, subsystems, and so on, of the overall system. It results from this, too, that there must be a possibility of recomposing (whether in reality or ideally and abstractly), without excess or deficit, the system starting from these elements and relations, which alone are considered to possess ultimate reality. Or, the being-together of the manifold [*diversité*] can be that of a logical system (in the broad sense, including mathematics). In this case as well, ultimate elements must be posited that are clearly distinct and well defined, amenable to univocal definition, and, with them, univocal relations among these elements.

In both cases ensemblistic-identitary logic is applied. In both cases society is thought as an ensemble of distinct and well-defined elements, relating to one another by means of well-determined relations. To the extent that – and we shall return to this at length – society is something quite other than a set or a hierarchy of sets, there is no way that anything essential about it can be thought along this line. But also the question arises immediately: What are the elements and the relations with respect to which society, considered as coexistence-composition, would be the (real or ideal-abstract) system, and which ones are they? The difficulty or the refusal to recognize the mode of being proper to the social-historical necessarily signifies that, whatever the concomitant reservations, qualifications, restrictions, or modalizations may be, these elements and relations will, in the final analysis, be those whose being and mode of being have already been recognized elsewhere, and hence both will ultimately be determined in other ways and from elsewhere. Such are the relations of causation, finality, or logical implication. Such, also, are the elements to which inherited thought, for deep-seated reasons, was led at a very early stage to ascribe an ultimate substantiality and consistency: individuals, things, ideas or concepts.

Thus, for example, every society immediately presents itself as a collection of individuals. This immediate appearance is rapidly challenged by serious thinkers. But is it really challenged? For centuries one hears it affirmed that man does not exist as man outside the city: 'Robinsonades' and social contracts are condemned and the irreducibility of the social to the individual is proclaimed. But when we take a closer look, we see not only that nothing is said concerning what it is that would remain irreducible but that, in fact, this irreducible something is in reality reduced: society repeatedly reappears as determined by the individual considered its efficient or the final cause, the social as constructible or composable from the individual. This was already the situation in Aristotle, for whom 'the city is first according to nature' in relation to the individual man, but for whom, as well, the being of the city is determined by its end, and this end is the well-being of the individual man.[13] But this is also the situation in Marx: 'the real basis' of society that 'conditions' all the rest is 'the set of the relations of production', which are 'determined, necessary, independent of the will' of men. But *what* are these relations of production? They are 'relations between persons mediated by things'. And by what are they 'determined'? By the 'state of the productive forces' – that is to say, by another aspect of the relation of persons to things, an aspect that is mediated, at the same time as it is determined, by concepts, those that are embodied in the technical know-how of each period.[14] Despite inassimilable and explosive formulations, the same is true with respect to Freud, to the extent that he does consider the social dimension: it is the *psyche*, with its corporeal anchor, its confrontation with a natural *anankē*, its internal conflicts and its phylogenetic history, that must account for the whole of the human world.[15]

But how could we think of society as the coexistence or the composition of elements that are held to pre-exist it or that are supposed to be determined – really, logically, or teleologically – from elsewhere, when these so-called elements are in general and are what they are only in and through society? One could not compose a society – if this expression had any meaning – except with individuals, who themselves would already have to be social, who would already contain the social within themselves. Nor would it be possible to use here the schema that seems to apply, more or less, in other domains, namely, the idea that on the level of a totality properties emerge that do not exist or that are meaningless on the level of the components – what physicists call cooperative or collective phenomena,[16] corresponding to the well-known theme of the transformation of quantity into quality. There is no sense in considering language, production, social rules to be additional properties that would emerge if a sufficient number of individuals were juxtaposed; these individuals would not be just different, but inexistent and inconceivable, outside or prior to these collective properties – without their being, for all that, reducible to the latter.

Society is not a thing, not a subject, and not an idea – nor is it a collection or system of subjects, things, and ideas. This observation seems quite banal to those who are quick to forget to ask themselves how and why one can then speak of a society and of this particular one. For, in conventional language and in the logic it contains, '*a*' and '*this*' apply only to what we are able to name, and we are able to name only things, subjects, concepts, and their collections or unions, relations, attributes, states, and so on. However, the unity of a society, like its *ecceity* – the fact that it is this particular society and not some other one – cannot be analysed into relations between subjects mediated by things, since every relation between subjects is a social one between social subjects, every relation to things is a social relation to social objects, and since subjects, things, and relations are what they are and such as they are here only because they are instituted in the way they are by the society concerned (or by society in general). The fact that some men can kill and die for gold, while others do not, has nothing to do with the chemical element *Au*, or with the DNA properties of each group; and what is one to say when people kill or die for Christ and for Allah?

These difficulties are resolved merely in words when a collective consciousness or a collective unconscious is invoked, illegitimate metaphors, terms for which the only possible signified is the very problem discussed here. And they are also resolved merely in words when one simply affirms the existence of a social totality, of society as a whole, different from its parts, superseding them and determining them. For, if no more than this is said, one cannot help but slip back toward the only schema available to inherited thought for thinking a whole that is not a system *partes extra partes*: the schema of the organism – a schema that, despite the rhetorical precautions that are taken, in fact returns more often than one believes, and still today, in discussions about society. But, to speak of an organism, whether literally or figuratively, or of a hyperorganism, is to speak of a system of inter-dependent functions determined by an end; and this end is the conservation and the reproduction of the same, the affirmation of permanence across time and accidents, of essence, *eidos* (aspect/species).[17] What would the same be that is conserved and reproduced here? And what would be the stable and determined functions enslaved to this goal of conservation–reproduction?

It is only in appearance and in the most superficial fashion that the various sectors or domains in which social activities unfold – economics, law, politics, religion, etc. – could be identified or made to correspond with such functions. It is useful, beyond any critique of functionalism, or organicism, or of other similar conceptions, to take a closer look at the question posed by the relation between these sectors or domains and the organization or the overall life of society. For, here again, we have a type of coexistence between a whole and its parts, even a type of existence of these parts, that cannot be apprehended within the framework of inherited thought. There is obviously no question of constituting society starting with an economy, a law, a religion that would be its components, each possessing an independent existence, whose union would bring about the appearance of a society (with or without additional new properties). The economy, for example, is conceivable and can exist only as social economy, the economy of a society and of this particular society. The problem, however, extends much further than these self-evident facts (the implications of which, going far beyond the question of society, have yet to be drawn). No available schema permits us truly to grasp the relations between the economy, law, politics, and religion, on the one hand, and society on the other; nor does it permit us to grasp the relations among these sectors themselves. For – and this precedes any discussion of content, any critique, for example, of the causal determination of the alleged superstructure by the alleged infrastructure – every known schema of relation presupposes that the schema of separation is applicable in the field considered and permits the constitution of the entities (whether real or abstract) that are placed into relation. This is not the case here, for the domains of social activity are not genuinely separable – I mean, not even ideally – they are so only in a nominal and empty sense. And this refers us back to a much deeper level of the question: nothing in inherited thought allows us to say what these are or in what manner they exist as particular entities. They are certainly not abstract aspects, correlative to the place chosen to observe the object or to the categories used to grasp it. And this is so, first, because these places and categories exist only starting from and in relation to a particular – though in no way privileged – social-historical institution that has brought them into existence in and through a particular social reality. If the theorist distinguishes between a religious aspect and a legal aspect in the activities of a given traditional or archaic society which itself does not distinguish between them, this is not due to the progress of knowledge or to the purification and the refinement of reason but to the fact that the society in which the theorist lives has, for a long period of time, instituted in its own reality legal categories and religious categories as relatively distinct. He then extrapolates these categories and the distinction between them into the past, without questioning, in general, the legitimacy of this extrapolation, and tacitly postulating that the distinctions established in his own society correspond to the essence of every society and express its true articulation.

But neither can we consider these sectors of social life as coordinated partial systems – like the circulatory, respiratory, digestive, and nervous systems of an organism – since we can, and often do, encounter the predominance or relative autonomization of one or another of these sectors in a given social organization.

What, then, are these sectors? We see already that, if we are to begin to think seriously about this question, we have to take full consideration of this massive, irreducible fact which remains, in reality, inassimilable for traditional thought: there is no articulation of social life that is given once and for all, neither on the surface nor at a greater depth, neither really nor abstractly. This articulation, whether with respect to the parts it posits or to the relations it establishes among these parts and between the parts and the whole, is each time the creation of the society in question. And this creation is an ontological genesis, the positing of an *eidos*, for what is thus posited, established, instituted each time, although it is always borne by the concrete materiality of acts and things, goes beyond this concrete materiality and any particular *this*, and is a *type* permitting the indefinite reproduction of its instances, which are in general and are what they are only as instances of this type. A specific tool (*teukhos*) – knife, adze, hammer, wheel, boat – is such a type, a created *eidos*. So, too, is a word (*lexis*), as are marriage, purchase and sale, enterprise, temple, school, book, inheritance, election, painting. At another, and yet not entirely separate level, the self-articulation of each society and the sectors or domains in and through which it exists equally are created *eidē*. Society institutes itself as a mode and a type of coexistence: as a mode and type of coexistence in general, with no ana-logue or precedent in another region of being, and as *this* particular mode and type of coexistence, the specific creation of the society considered. (In the same way, as we shall see, it institutes itself as a mode and type of suc-cession, that is, as a social-historical temporality.) Thus, the articulation of society into technique, economy, law, politics, religion, art, etc., which seems self-evident to us, is only one mode of the institution of the social, particular to a series of societies to which our own belongs. We know per-fectly well, for example, that only of late do the economy and law appear as explicitly posited moments of social organization; that religion and art con-sidered as separate domains are, on the scale of history, quite recent creations; that the type (and not just the content) of the relation between productive labour and other social activities displays, throughout history and across different societies, vast modifications. The organization of society redeploys itself each time in a different way, not only in as much as it posits different moments, sectors, or domains in and through which it exists, but also in as much as it brings into being a type of relation among these moments that can be new and even that is always new in a nontrivial sense.[18] Neither the former nor the latter can be inferred inductively from the forms of social life observed until now, deduced *a priori* by theoretical reflection, or thought within a logical framework that is given once and for all.

Reflecting on society refers us thus to two limits of inherited thought, limits that, in truth, are but the single limit characteristic of identitary logic-ontology. There is no way, within this limit, to think the self-deployment of an entity as the positing of new terms of an articulation and of new relations among these terms, hence as the positing of a new organization, of a new form, of another *eidos*. For, there is no way within the logic-ontology of the same, of repetition, of the forever intemporal (*aei*) to think a creation, a genesis that is not a mere becoming, generation and corruption, engendering of the same by the same as a different exemplar of the same type, but is instead the emergence of alterity, ontological genesis, which makes beings be as *eidos*, and as the *ousia* of *eidos*, another manner and another type of being and of being-a-being [*être-étant*]. And it may be that this self-evidence is in effect blinding; it may be that it is, at most, recognizable but not think-able. This question, however, will not be able to be resolved until it has been recognized, perceived, experienced, until it is no longer denied or covered over by the veil of tautology.

There is no way, within this same limit, to think society as coexistence or as the unity of a manifold. For, reflection on society places us before a requirement, one we can never satisfy by means of inherited logic: the requirement that we consider terms that are not discrete, separate, individualizable entities (entities that can be posited in this way only temporarily, as markers), in other words, terms that are not elements of a set, and that are not reducible to such elements; relations among these terms which themselves are neither separable nor definable in any univocal way; finally, the pair, terms/relation, as it presents itself each time at a given level, as impossible to grasp at this level independently of the others. What is in question here is not a greater logical complexity, which could be handled by increasing the traditional logical operations, but an unprecedented logical-ontological situation.

This situation is unprecedented from an ontological point of view: *what* the social is, and the way in which it is, has no analogue anywhere else. It therefore forces us to reconsider the sense of: being, or else to shed light on another, previously unseen, side of this sense. By this very fact, we once again see that what has been termed 'ontological difference', the distinction between the question of being and the question of beings, is impossible to maintain or, to say the same thing another way, simply exposes the limit of inherited thought. Briefly speaking, traditional ontology has been no more than the surreptitious positing of the mode of being of these particular categories of beings on which its gaze has remained riveted as the meaning of: being. It is from these categories, as well as from – practically the same thing – the necessities of language as *legein* (as ensemblistic-identitary instrument) that traditional ontology has drawn the meaning of: being as being determined. This has not always prevented it from envisaging other types of being, but it has always led it to characterize them as being-less (*hetton on*, in opposition to being-more, *mallon on*), by which it has always meant to say this and only this: less determined or less determinable.

This situation is also unprecedented from the logical point of view – an aspect that is indissociable from the preceding one, since, despite the apparently strange – but in truth natural – alliance between Heidegger and the positivists on this point, there is no thought of being that is not also a *logos* of being, an ordered and self-ordered, hence logical *logos*, just as there is no logic without a positing of being (even if only as being in and through language). We cannot think the social, as coexistence, by means of inherited logic, and this means: we cannot think it as the unity of a plurality in the usual sense of these terms; we cannot think it as a determinable set of clearly distinct and well-defined elements. We have to think it as a *magma*, and even as a *magma of magmas* – by which I mean not chaos but the mode of organization belonging to a nonensemblizable diversity, as exemplified by the social, the imaginary, or the Unconscious.[19] In order to speak of it, which we can do only in the existing social language, we unavoidably call upon the terms of ensemblistic *legein*, such as one and many, part and whole, composition and inclusion. These terms, however, function here only as markers, not as genuine categories. For, there are no transregional categories: the rule of connection dictated by a category is empty if that which is to be connected in this way is not taken into account. This is merely another way of saying that being is always only the being of the beings [*l'être des étants*], and that each region of beings unveils another side of the sense of: being.

History and the Schemata of Succession

History presents itself immediately as succession. What is available to inherited thought to think of a succession? The schemata of causality, of finality, or of logical consequence. These schemata presuppose that what is to be grasped or thought by their means can, essentially, be reduced to an ensemble. One must be able to separate elements or discrete entities, clearly distinct and well defined, in order to be able to say that *a* is the cause of *b*, that *x* is the means of *y*, or that *q* is a logical consequence of *p*.

Inherited thought is therefore unable to grasp a succession in the social, except on the condition that it has made the latter an ensemble or is in the process of doing so; we have just seen, and we shall see again at length, that this is impossible. It amounts to the same thing to say that it can think *succession* only from the point of view of *identity*. Causality, finality, and implication are merely amplified and unfolded forms of an enriched identity; they aim at positing differences as merely apparent and at finding, at another level, the same to which these differences belong. It is of no importance in the present context whether the same is understood as an entity or as a law. To be sure, the question of knowing how and why the same is given as or appears in and through difference remains the central aporia of inherited thought in all its forms, in the most ancient ontology or in the most modern positive science. This aporia follows from the fact that it has been decided that the same is and, what is more, that, in an ultimate sense, the same alone is. It is easy to see that this proposition goes hand in hand with another, namely, that *what is* is fully determined from and in all time, an 'in all time' that can be rigorously thought only as an intemporal *aei*, which may or may not be minted in an omnitemporal always.

It is self-evident and well known that logical implication is an elaborated identity, that the conclusion is simply a disimplication of what is already in the premises (analyticity). But the same thing is true with respect to the frameworks of causality and finality. Cause and effect belong to the same; if we can separate and determine a set of causes, it goes with the set of its effects, neither of these two sets can exist without the other, and they therefore both partake of the same, are the parts of a single set.[20] Likewise as concerns means and ends. Likewise, finally, if we consider not entities but laws, whether causal or final: a law is only in and through the same; it is the essential and internal identity to which the external difference of phenomena refers, without which this difference could not exist. Or: this differing exteriority of phenomena as such must ideally be brought back to the identical interiority of a law.

Causes go with effects, means go with ends. This *going with* is explicitly present at least since the Aristotelean definition of the syllogism: 'a discourse in which, some things being posited, another thing . . . necessarily goes with them (*ex anankēs sumbainei*), by reason of the being of the former'. *Sumbainein*, to walk together, to go with, *comitari* (*cum-eo*); *sumbēbēkos*, translated by *accidens* in Latin, in reality means what *goes with*, which one can and should translate by *comitant*. *Sumbainein*, *sumbēbēkos* most often designate for Aristotle what is found to go with, what has externally coincided with – the accident; but they also designate, in the opposite sense, what essentially and necessarily goes with something else.[21] In his definition of the syllogism, Aristotle obviously can leave no room for ambiguity: conclusion and premises *ex anankēs sumbainei*, necessarily go with each other, ineluctably walk together.

However, that which necessarily goes with something else, what is it if not a part of that other thing, or else, together with it, a part of the same other thing? How and why do the legs and the body of an animal go together if not because they belong to one and the same animal?

If what follows necessarily goes with that which it follows, succession is at best only a subjective arrangement for inspecting the total thing, the effective counterpart of which in the thing is, and is only, an order of coexistence. In truth, the conclusion is given together with the premises; the Philosophy of Mind together with the Science of Logic; and the expansion of the universe together with the initial hyperdense state and the laws governing physical being. If succession is determined, or necessary, it is given as soon as are given its law and its first term; it is itself but an order of being-together. Time is then simply a relation of order that nothing permits us to distinguish intrinsically from other relations of order, for example from a spatial arrangement or from the relation of 'greater or lesser'. And, to the extent that the terms are necessarily *taken up* in this order, they are no more than 'parts' of the One-Whole and *co*exist as parts of One-Same. In the intemporal always, there can be, at most, an order of coexistences but not an order of successions; and in the omnitemporal always of determination, the order of succession is simply a variant of the order of coexistence, for succession can and must be reduced to a particular type of coexistence.[22]

However, just as society cannot be thought within any of the traditional schemata of coexistence, so history cannot be thought within any of the traditional schemata of succession. For, what is given in and through history is not the determined sequence of the determinate but the emergence of radical alterity, immanent creation, nontrivial novelty. This is manifested by the existence of history *in toto*, as well as by the appearance of new societies (of new *types* of society) and the incessant self-transformation of each society. And it is only on the basis of this radical alterity or creation that we can truly think temporality and time, the excellent and eminent effective actuality [*effectivité*] of which we find in history. For, either time is nothing, a strange psychological illusion masking the essential intemporality of a relation of order, or else time is the very manifestation of the fact that something other than what is is making itself be, and is making itself be as new or as other and not simply as a consequence or as a different exemplar of the same.

It may be helpful to stop here and consider a confusion that seems to have been spreading for some time. The emergence of the new appears with a special intensity at times of upheaval, of catastrophic or great events that mark and punctuate the existence of societies often termed 'historical' in a restricted sense of the term. Authors sometimes express themselves as though historicity belongs only to this category of societies, to which could be opposed 'cold' societies – where change would be marginal or simply nonexistent, the essence of their life unfolding as stability and repetition – as well as societies 'without history', in particular so-called archaic societies, where not only do repetition and absence of change seem self-evident but another mode of relating to their own past and future seems to prevail that distinguishes them radically from so-called 'historical' societies. These distinctions are not false and do, indeed, point to something important. They would become fallacious if we were to forget that to which they refer: different *modes* of historicity and not the presence of history here as opposed to the absence of history there. Different modes of the effective institution of social-historical time by different societies, in other words, different modalities according to which different societies represent and make their incessant self-alteration – even if, in the extreme case, they deny it or, rather, attempt to deny it. To be sure, this makes a difference not only with respect to the pace or the rhythm of this self-alteration but also with respect to its content. It does not, for all that, prevent it from being.

Thus, the extraordinary stability of living conditions, of rules, and of representations that characterizes the existence of European peasants over a period of centuries (and, in a sense, all peasants from the neolithic age to the twentieth century) cannot but strike us when it is opposed to the stage of the theatre of 'history', as it is commonly called, constantly shaken by the sound and fury of wars, discoveries, the movement of representations and ideas, changes of government and regimes. And yet, large segments of European peasantry passed, in the space of a few decades, from a universe of papism and witchcraft to the Reformation. The question posed by this passage – and by every passage – is obviously not eliminated, or even reduced by a hair's breadth, by the illusion of the alleged – and unrealizable – division *ad infinitum* of the gap that separates the before and the after (a division that merely multiplies the problem *ad infinitum*). To underscore just one aspect of the problem: the Reformation implies an upheaval in the psychical organization of the individuals concerned, who are obliged to pass from a state in which everything is tied to the representation of the Absolute, the Law, the Master in and through the visible organization of the Church and its flesh and blood officials, to a state in which there is, for the individual, no conceivable intermediary between himself and transcendence other than the Text, which he interprets at his own risk and peril. We must, neverthe-less, insert this upheaval within the apparently stable and repetitive self-reproduction of the preceding stage: Catholic fathers and mothers, in a cold society, produced sons and daughters ready to become Protestants. The fact that this took place in the space of one generation or of ten changes absolutely nothing here. It is obviously the illusion of the historian – our illusion, necessary to all of us – to measure eternity on the basis of his own life expectancy and to consider that whatever does not change for three centuries is 'stable'. But change the scale of time, and the stars in the heavens will step to a dizzy dance.

The same is true for archaic societies, even if it is infinitely more difficult, for obvious reasons, to illustrate by its apparent consequences the implacable and incessant self-alteration that unfolds in their depths.[23] The 'static', 'repetitive', 'ahistorical', or 'atemporal' character of this class of societies is simply their way of instituting their own particular historical temporality.

It is impossible, however, to manage without a discussion of the question of time in general. For, on the one hand, this is where all the threads that inherited thought uses to weave its denial of history and of creation stem from and the place to which they return – the denial of genuine time as that in which and through which there is alterity, in the name of being inter-preted as determined and determined in the always: *aei*. On the other hand, it is possible, on the question of time, to attempt an initial elucidation of the infinitely complex relations entertained among: (1) society's reception of a 'natural datum' and what could be termed, to borrow an expression from Freud, the *Anlehnung*, the leaning of the social-historical institution on the natural stratum; (2) this institution itself as the simultaneous and indis-sociable institution of identitary relations and of nonidentitary significations; and, finally, (3) the philosophical problematic that emerges, at a particular moment, in society, and the philosophical negation/ affirmation of the social-historical world of significations. [. . .]

Notes

1 Thus, for example, what Marx has to say that is true, profound, important, and new about society and history, he says *despite* this 'elsewhere' which governs his entire thought: that history *must* (*muß, soll,* and *wird*) lead to a classless society. The result is that what is essential in his discovery cannot fit within his own system. See *HWM* (1974).

2 The difficulty or the impossibility of satisfying this requirement was recognized, we know, at least as early as Plato's *Sophist*. Aristotle's effort in the *Metaphysics* was aimed essentially at surmounting the multiple meanings of being, what he called *pollachos legomenon*. Intending this meaning as *one* will also govern all of later philosophy, and this will almost always lead to expressing the differences in the meanings of: being in terms of gradations in the quality of being or in the 'ontological intensity' accorded to corresponding types of entities.

3 We know that, as early as the *Republic*, Plato examines the alteration in the order of the city as a historical process, and that, at the other end, Marx's entire effort concerns the determination of the relation between the organization and the functioning of social systems and their dynamics, or their history. It will be evident later that what I mean by the unity and indivisibility of the social-historical is situated on another level. The examples of Husserl and Heidegger still show to what extent the separation is ingrained and deeply rooted in inherited thought. For both of them, although in different ways, an (impoverished) question of history appears as a philosophical question – but never a philosophical question of society.

4 If a justification of these formulations is sought, one may refer to what was stated above concerning the historical emergence of capitalist society and its unity, or the establishment of an asymmetrical division of society into classes (see *MRT* [1964–5], in *IIS*, pp. 45–54E, and *SII*, in *IIS*, pp. 150–6E).

5 Hegel, *Wissenschaft der Logik*, ed. Georg Lasson (Leipzig: Felix Meiner, 1923), vol. 2, pp. 426–9.

6 *Philebus* 17b–18d.

7 Claude Lévi-Strauss, *Race and History. The Race Question in Modern Science* (Paris: UNESCO, 1968).

8 'The same and identically disposed always makes be, by its nature, the same' (Aristotle *On Generation and Corruption* 336a27–8). The same, under the same conditions, engenders the same: the set formed by the cause, the conditions, and the effect contains these as its parts. Cf. *Metaphysics* 1026a16–17: 'Now, all causes must be eternal . . .'

9 The meaning of this term will be discussed at length in chapter 5 of *IIS*.

10 See, in addition to *MRT, HWM*.

11 This is what Claude Lévi-Strauss now does explicitly: 'only structural interpretation can account both for itself and for the other kinds' (*The Naked Man, Introduction to a Science of Mythology* [New York: Harper & Row, 1981], p. 628).

12 Chapter 5 of *IIS* is devoted to clarifying these two terms. *Legein* is the identitary dimension of social representing/saying: *legein* (whence *logos*, logic) signifies distinguishing–choosing–positing–assembling–counting–saying. In language, *legein* is represented by the component *code*; the signifying component of language will here be termed *tongue*. *Teukhein* is the identitary (or functional, or instrumental) dimension of social making/doing; *teukhein* (whence *technē*) signifies assembling–adjusting–fabricating– constructing.

13 See *HWM*, in *PSW 3*, pp. 166–8.

14 'Machines . . . locomotives, railways, . . . etc. . . . *are organs of the human brain, created by human hand*; the power of knowledge, objectified', Marx wrote in the *Grundrisse: Foundations of the Critique of Political Economy*, trans. Martin Nicolaus (New York: Vintage, 1973), p. 706.

15 We shall return to this at length. See chapter 6 of *IIS*.

16 See D. Park, *Contemporary Physics* (New York: Harcourt Brace, 1964), pp. 131–49.

17 The fact that this permanence is no longer viewed within the framework of the fixed and unchanging Aristotelean *phusis*, but as limited and relativized through evolution, changes nothing at bottom. The living being is nothing if not a stable *eidos*, and this stability is essentially determined as the capacity for *self*-preservation and *self*-reproduction, in the repetition of the same.

18 Thus the bourgeoisie establishes a new *mode of being* of production and a new type of relation between production and the rest of social life, which is *its* creation – and which Marx retrospectively projects on to all of history. See *HWM*, in *PSW 3*, pp. 171–81.

19 See chapter 7 of *IIS*, pp. 341Eff.

20 Set theory, like all mathematics, formally presupposes a logic, the so-called formal or symbolic logic, and is based upon it; but formal or symbolic logic presupposes that the object it speaks about to begin with, the propositions it treats as unanalysable and indifferent with respect to their content, are themselves a set, an ensemble, on which it defines a determinate relation, implication. The situation remains basically the same when, in an alleged second stage, quantifiers are introduced. There is, thus, a logico-mathematical circle, evident also in the fact that one cannot do formal logic without numbering – and which is eliminated only in words when it is asserted that the numbers involved here are 'other' than the numbers of arithmetic. Logic and mathematics are indissociable, posited together, two aspects of the same – of the ensemblistic-identitarian.

21 This has been a torture for commentators, forced to speak of 'essential accidents'; in fact, there are, for Aristotle, essential comitants and accidental comitants.

22 It is obviously not by chance that a genuine particularizing of time in relation to space begins to appear in physics only when the schema of complete determination has to be abandoned, namely, in thermodynamics, where the vector of time is identified with increasing probability and an irreversibility of time is introduced and interpreted as an extreme impossibility (whereas mechanical phenomena as such are reversible). We shall return to the question of the irreversibility of time from the social-historical point of view. It is enough to note here that the probabilist definition of physical time is also, in the final analysis, an ensemblistic-identitary definition (such is the logico-ontological foundation of any theory of probability) and that thermodynamic 'time' is a 'time' of equalization and of de-differentiation (growth of entropy).

23 The recent development of work in ethnohistory tends to show how erroneous and ideologically determined was the denial of the historicity of so-called 'archaic' societies. See also Claude Lefort, 'Sociétés "sans histoire" et historicité', in *Cahiers Internationaux de Sociologie*, 12 (1952), pp. 91–114.

7

The Social Regime in Russia (1978)*

Prefatory Note (1985)

This text summarizes the results of more than thirty years (1944–77) of reflection and work on the 'Russian question', its interminable theoretical implications, its incalculable real repercussions. Shortly after it was drafted, the Russian invasion of Afghanistan induced me to prolong and perfect these analyses, which is what I did in the article 'Devant la guerre' (*Libre*, 8 [May 1980]), then in the book by the same name, the first volume of which was published in May 1981 (Fayard) and whose second volume I hope to publish soon.[1]

The publication of *Devant la guerre* had varying results that, objectively speaking, were bizarre. Among them, one was for me entirely foreseeable: the 'pacifists' of various stripes began accusing me of being a supporter of Western rearmament and of intentionally inflating the quantities of Russian arms (in this they are, as is their wont, more royalist than the king, since in arms reduction talks the Russians have in fact never contested the figures that establish the nuclear 'parity' they had already attained between 1970 and 1975). Another result was less foreseeable: people began to speak of (and to write about) my 'theory about Russian stratocracy' as if I had never written *anything else* about Russia than *Devant la guerre* – or else, in the best of hypotheses, as if the new analyses of this book signified the abandonment of my previous analyses or rendered them null and void. This was a curious method of reading. *Devant la guerre* was explicitly based upon my earlier writings concerning total and totalitarian bureaucratic capitalism, which I cited on several occasions in the book and whose results I used therein. Without these still valid results, the analysis of Russian society as a

---

* Introductory report to the fourth and last day of the historical seminar held in Venice as part of the biennial devoted to dissidence in Eastern-bloc countries (15–18 November 1977). Time limitations obliged me to present in this report, under the form of theses, some of the ideas I have been working out since 1946 on the 'Russian question' and its implications. The development of these ideas and the arguments for them may be found in the references included in the text.

The text was published in *Esprit*, July–August 1978, then, in the form of a brochure, by Les Cahiers du vent du ch'min (Saint-Denis, 1982). 'Le Régime social de la Russie' was reprinted in *DH*, pp. 175–200, preceded by a November 1985 'Avertissement' (Prefatory Note). An earlier translation of the main text appeared in *Telos*, 38 (Winter 1978–9), pp. 32–47. [T/E: I have on occasion consulted this translation.]

stratocracy loses both its social and its historical bases. The problem I posed to myself – as the reader of *DT* (1981) will easily be convinced – was how to account for the evolution of the regime, its own dynamic, starting from the moment the failure of the bureaucracy's attempt at self-reform (Khrushchev, 1964) left free rein to the process of necrosis going on within the Party and its ideology. One cannot respond to this problem – or to the fact that, in a thousand ways, the evolution of Russia is highly singular – by chanting 'totalitarianism, totalitarianism' or 'ideocracy, ideocracy' morning, noon, and night. Ideocracy in 1921 and in 1985? Totalitarianism in Stalin's Russia and in the Hungary of Kádár? The ongoing incapacity to think that which is *historical* is expressed in the impotence to do anything other than keep on varnishing over, with one and the same abstraction, realities that have been changing continually for going on seventy years now and that concern societies as improbably different, at the outset, as Ethiopia and East Germany, Czechoslovakia and Vietnam, Cuba, China, and Russia itself. And given that this abstraction is becoming, if one may say so, each day more abstract, the result is that one loses sight of what constitutes the genuine unity of Russia's history since 1917 – or the genuine kinship among Communist regimes, whatever the region onto which they have been grafted.

November 1985

1   One need only glance at the most elementary and well-known facts to see that it is immediately self-evident that Russian society is a divided society, subject to the domination of a particular social group, where exploitation and oppression reign. To present the Russian regime as 'socialist' or as a 'workers' State', as do the 'Left' and the 'Right' in near-universal complicity, or simply to discuss its nature in reference to socialism in order to find out on what points and to what degree it deviates therefrom, represents one of the most dreadful attempts at mystification known to history. The persistent success of this enterprise evidently poses a question of the first magnitude concerning the function and the importance of ideology in the contemporary world.

I

2   Russian society, like the societies of the countries of Eastern Europe, China, etc., is an asymmetrically and antagonistically divided society – to use the traditional terminology, it is a 'class society'. It is subject to the domination of a particular social group, the bureaucracy, whose active core is the political bureaucracy of the CPSU. This domination takes concrete form as economic exploitation, political oppression, mental enslavement of

the population by and for the bureaucracy. No more than any other dominant stratum in any other society does the bureaucracy, for all that, exercise
absolute mastery over its society. It must face up to the conflict by which it
is opposed to the population, a conflict whose manifestations the regime
stifles without being able to eliminate them. It is subject to antinomies and
to irrationalities that are consubstantial with the existence of a modern
bureaucratic regime. Lastly, the bureaucracy itself is dominated by its own
system, by the institution of the society correlative with itself, and by the social
imaginary significations this institution bears and conveys. Russian society,
too, is an alienated or heteronomous society, 'all classes thrown together'.

3   The relations of production in Russia are antagonistic; they divide
directors from executants and oppose one group to the other. These
relations imply exploitation of the producers (workers, peasants, 'service'
labourers) and their enslavement to a labour and production process that
escapes entirely from their control. In no way do the 'nationalization' of the
means of production (state control) and bureaucratic 'planning' entail
the abolition of exploitation or have nothing to do with socialism. The
suppression of 'private ownership' leaves entirely open the question: Who
now *effectively* has the means of production and production itself at its
disposal? In Russia (as in the countries of Eastern Europe, China, etc.), it is
the bureaucracy (that of the factories and other state enterprises, of the
economy, of the State itself, and especially of the CPSU) that disposes
(*verfügt*) collectively of the means of production, of the time of the labouring
population, and of the results of production. Under cover of the juridical
form of 'nationalized' (i.e. state-controlled) property, it has *jus fruendi,
utendi, and abutendi*. State control and bureaucratic 'planning' are the
adequate and necessary means for this disposition. 'Statically' speaking, at
every instant the bureaucracy has at its disposal the means of production
and production itself. It does with them 'what it wants', physically and
economically, as much as and more than a capitalist 'does what he wants'
with his capital. But above all, it has them at its disposal 'dynamically'. It
decides on the means by which a surplus is extracted and how this surplus
is to be allotted (its distribution between bureaucratic consumption and
accumulation, as well as the orientation of this accumulation). Russian
'capital' today is nothing else, in its 'essence', than the accumulated surplus
of the exploitation of the Russian people over the past sixty years and, in its
form, nothing else than the sedimented result of the decisions made by the
bureaucracy and of the functioning of its system during this same period
(*ORAD* [1946], *PUSSR* [1947], *QURSS* [1947], *SB* [1949], *RPR* [1949],
EPBC [1949], *BPT* [1957], *DRR* [1958], *CP* [1960]).

4   The nature of these relations of production, and of the social regime,
is inscribed in the actual material condition of the means of production and
is borne by the latter. *Qua* instruments of labour – via the form and the

content they imprint upon the labour process – these means aim to ensure the enslavement of the producers to the labour process, both through the kind of labour they impose and through the type of labour organization they entail. *Qua* instruments of production – via the nature of the products they are destined to manufacture – they embody the orientation the bureaucracy imprints upon social life, its specific goals, the values and significations to which the bureaucracy itself is enslaved. The production of armaments, of consumer goods intended for the bureaucracy, the type and nature of objects produced for popular consumption, and especially the production of machines meant to reproduce the same type of production and the same labour and production relations amply illustrate how the nature of the social regime corresponds to the productive 'means' it develops. The total identity of these 'means' with those invented and implemented by Western-style capitalism testifies to the profound kinship between the two regimes. It also creates identical problems on the political level. Far from being able merely to inherit the 'development of the productive forces' and an allegedly neutral technology to be placed in the service of socialism, just as much as in the Western countries a social revolution in Russia will have to grapple with the material–technical basis of production and to focus on its transformation (*CS II* [1957]).

    5   For the past sixty years the situation and the effective fate in production of the Russian labourer have been essentially identical to what they had always been under capitalism. The conjuring away of this fact by almost all 'Marxist' currents, including 'oppositional' ones (such as Trotskyism), is highly revelatory. The enslavement of labourers in the labour process is not a major or secondary 'defect' in the system, nor is it simply an inhuman trait to be deplored. In it the essence of the Russian regime as a regime of alienation is exposed on the most concrete as well as on the most philosophical level. Limiting oneself strictly to the labour process and to the production process, one can see that the Russian working class is subject to the 'wage' relation as much as any other working class. The workers dispose neither of the means nor of the product of their labour, nor of their own activity as labouring people. They 'sell' their time, their vital forces, their life to the bureaucracy, which disposes of it according to its own interests. The constant effort of the bureaucracy is to increase labour output to the greatest extent possible while curbing levels of remuneration and it does this through the same methods as those utilized in the West. The ever more extended division of tasks, the definition of tasks so as to aim at rendering labour ever more subject to control and ever more impersonal and the labourer ever more interchangeable, the measurement and control of the labourer's gestures, piece wages and output-based wages, the 'quantification' of all aspects of work and of the very personality of the labourer are sustained, there as well as here, by a technology that, far from expressing a neutral

'rationality', is destined to subject the labourer to a pace of production independent of the labourer, to break up the 'informal' groups set up among labouring people, to expropriate from living labour all autonomy, and to transfer the moment of the management of activity, however insignificant this activity might be, to mechanical units, on the one hand, and to the bureaucratic Apparatus that manages factories and other enterprises, on the other (*CS III* [1958]).

6   This analysis (which would in fact be the true Marxian analysis) is nevertheless incomplete and insufficient, because abstract. In considering production in itself, in separating it from the whole of life and social organization, it would end up identifying completely the situation of the Russian worker with that of the Western worker. Yet the fate of the worker, and of the population in general, outside production, is not an added characteristic but, rather, an essential component of the worker's situation. Deprived of political, civic, and trade-union rights, forcibly enrolled in 'unions' that are mere appendages of the State, the Party, and the KGB, subject to permanent police control, to spying inside as well as outside the workplace, constantly harassed by the omnipresent voice of official mendacious propaganda, the Russian working class is subject to an oppressive effort of totalitarian control and mental and physical expropriation that, quite clearly, surpasses the Fascist and Nazi models and has experienced some additional improvements only in Maoist China. This situation has no analogy in the 'classical' capitalist countries, where very early on the working class was able to wrest some civic, political, and trade-union rights and contest explicitly and overtly the existing social order – doing so at the same time as it was constantly exerting decisive pressure upon the evolution of the system, this pressure ultimately being the principal factor in imposing limitations on the irrationality of that system (*DC I* [1953], *PO I* [1959], *MCR* [1960–1], *GI* [1973], *RRD* [1974]). The difference is of capital importance, including from the narrow and abstract point of view of production and the economy. Under the classical capitalist regime the working class explicitly negotiates the level of nominal wages and other, still more important elements of the 'labour contract' (the daily, weekly, yearly, and 'lifetime' duration of labour, labour conditions, etc.). The 'labour contract' is certainly a juridical form – but it is not an *empty* form, because the working class can struggle, and does struggle, explicitly to change it. Without a class of 'free' labourers, in both senses of this term, there might have been a 'slave capitalism' or a 'serf capitalism' – not capitalism such as it has effectively existed. Through these struggles and this freedom, which it is stupid to label 'formal', the working class has been able, for the past 175 years, to reduce the time spent working, prevent an increase in the rate of exploitation, limit unemployment, etc. Now, it is precisely the suppression of all freedom in Russia and the impossibility of all overt struggle there that turns the 'labour contract' into an

empty form, so that one cannot speak in this case of 'wage earning', except in a formal sense. The consequence of this is not just that exploitation is much heavier there than elsewhere. The suppression of all possibility for the working class, and for the population in general, to exert pressure openly upon events gives free rein to the deployment of bureaucratic irrationality and ends in the monstrous waste of human labour and of productive resources in general that is characteristic of the Russian economy (not to mention the Gulag, which poses problems that go far beyond the above considerations).

7   It is all the more striking, then, to see that totalitarian oppression is still incapable of stifling the workers' (and peasants') ongoing and implicit struggle inside production against the system. Under the Russian regime, as well as in the West, the point of departure and the primary object of this struggle are the level of effective rates of remuneration/output (ratio between wages received and labour effectively furnished). But in both cases this struggle, far from being simply 'economic', is expressive of the resistance of labouring people to the oppression and alienation to which the established relations of production tend to subject them. In Russia this struggle is expressed in a particularly acute manner by the permanent crisis of quantitative and qualitative production, absenteeism, chronic overshooting of the firm's planned 'wage targets', etc. (*RPR, EPBC, PRAB* [1956], *CS II–III, MCR*).

8   The ultimate condition for this struggle is bureaucratic capitalism's fundamental contradiction. In production, as in all spheres of social life, the regime aims at excluding individuals and groups from the direction of their activities and at transferring it to a bureaucratic Apparatus. External to these activities, and encountering the opposition of the executants, this Apparatus becomes incapable half the time of managing them or of controlling them, and even of knowing what is really going on. It is thus obliged to appeal constantly to these same executants, whom it had wanted to exclude, in order to obtain their participation; it must at all times call upon the initiative of those whom it had wanted to transform into robots. This contradiction could congeal into a simple opposition between two groups, were they situated within a static society. The continual upheaval of the means and methods of production, which the regime itself is obliged to introduce, transforms it into a conflict that never abates (*PRAB, CS II–III, MCR, RR* [1964]).

9   This fundamental contradiction, and the very nature of the bureaucratic Apparatus, ensure that bureaucratic 'planning' will in its essence be chaotic and irrational, even from the standpoint of the goals it sets for itself. Examining the capitalist society of his time, Marx contrasted the despotism present in the workplace to the anarchy present in society. But bureaucratic capitalism, in the East as in the West, is both despotism *and* anarchy, both

in the workplace *and* in society. The immense wastage and the absurdities of bureaucratic 'planning', amply well known for a long time, are in no way an accidental or reformable trait; they result from the most important characteristics of bureaucratic organization. The very existence of the bureaucratic Apparatus raises social opacity to a hitherto unknown level, rendering the information needed for planning – of the economy, or even of production in a large firm – constantly lacking. The mass of executants hide the truth from the Apparatus. The vital condition for the existence of every sector of the bureaucracy is the falsification of the facts for the rest of the bureaucracy. The Apparatus tries to resolve the problem through the multiplication of control mechanisms and bureaucratic agencies, which does nothing more than multiply the factors that had given birth to them in the first place. Half blind, the Apparatus is also half-brained. The 'expertise', 'knowledge', and 'competency' of the bureaucracy are just so many ideological illusions. In a *modern* bureaucratic-hierarchical system (as opposed to a traditional one) there neither does nor can exist any 'rational' device or procedure for the nomination and promotion of bureaucrats. Consequently, a great deal of the activity of these persons is aimed at trying by all available means to resolve their private problem. The struggle among cliques and clans thus becomes an essential sociological factor that dominates the life of the Apparatus and radically undermines its functioning, most often transforming the objective options at issue in that struggle. Creating a radical split in society through its very existence, fragmenting the latter more and more the better to control it, introducing of necessity within itself this same fragmentation, this same division of labour and of tasks that it also imposes everywhere else, the Apparatus claims to be the site of synthesis in society, the site for the recomposition of social life – but it is so only fictively. The particular bureaucratic agencies regularly become bogged down in their own inertia. The Summit of the Apparatus brutally intervenes each time *in extremis*, settling in an arbitrary manner those problems that can no longer be postponed (*PRAB, MCR, HS* [1976]).

10   No more than it has reduced the power of the bureaucracy, the industrialization of Russia – and the extension of the bureaucratic regime over the lives of 1.3 billion individuals – has hardly attenuated at all the conflicts and the antinomies that tear at Russian society. Certainly, the level of police terror, along with its methods, has changed since Stalin's death, and at the same time the bureaucracy has tried to enter onto the path of a 'consumer society'. But both the content as well as the failure of Khrushchevism go to show the limits of attempts at self-reform on the part of the bureaucracy, and also the contradictions these efforts encounter. Thus, a certain degree of 'democratization' appears as a prerequisite for overcoming the most irrational traits of the system. But attempts, even timid ones, in this direction risk ending in explosions (the events of 1956 in

Eastern Europe) or else open the door to a utilization of these conceded 'rights' that rapidly would become intolerable for the bureaucracy (the case of dissidence on the part of intellectuals over the past fifteen years). The fact is that all possibility of putting the Party's power into question would constitute suicide for the bureaucracy, and every 'democratization' of the Party, even of limited import, would constitute suicide for the instance that embodies, personifies, and exercises power, namely, the Summit of the Apparatus.

Similarly, the need to reform the management of the economy at all levels, in order to limit the absurdities from which it suffers, collides with the need, in order to do this, to reduce the role and the discretionary powers of the bureaucracy – that is, to proceed to the self-mutilation of the dominant stratum. Such would be the case if one tried to inject 'market mechanisms' into the present system, but also if one wanted to proceed to a 'cybernetization' of the economy, which – unrealizable in any case in the Russian situation – would require the elimination of a great portion of the existing 'productive' and overall economic bureaucracy and would lead only to the proliferation of new bureaucratic agencies. Thus, the bureaucracy's economic 'reforms' are expressed essentially by recurrent oscillations between attempts at greater and lesser centralization (*PRAB*, *VPB* [1957]). Certainly, a more 'supple' bureaucratic regime is not inconceivable, either *de facto* or *de jure* (cf. Yugoslavia). It is the concrete conditions of Russia that render this eventuality extremely improbable: the risk of collapse of the Russian Empire (cf. both the events of 1956 and the invasion of Czechoslovakia in 1968) and the virtually explosive situation existing inside the country itself.

11   Indeed, the fundamental problems posed within the empire of the Czars, which provoked its downfall, not only have not been resolved but find themselves considerably aggravated.

First, there is the agrarian problem. The peasants were, until very recently, in a state of legal serfdom, bound by law to the soil (they had no domestic passports), and undoubtedly they in fact still are so. Russia, already Europe's granary before the time of Herodotus, hardly succeeds in feeding its own people now, whereas the Western countries subsidize farmers not to produce. And the 'organization' of agriculture has to be brought up for discussion again and again, though without any tangible results.

Next, there is the problem of industrial development. The system still does not succeed in satisfying the population's solvent demand for current-use objects. The manufacture of products of acceptable and reliable quality still constitutes an insoluble problem. Military balance with the United States is maintained only be devoting an exorbitant share of productive resources (probably three to four times greater than in the United States) to weapons production, and at the price of considerable underdevelopment in all civilian sectors. After sixty years of 'socialism' and overexploitation of the population, the per capita national product is of the same order of magnitude as that of Spain, if not of Greece. This 'socialist' regime has still not been able to resolve the problem people resolved as early as the neolithic era: ensuring that one can survive from one harvest to the next. Nor has it resolved another problem, which has been resolved elsewhere since the time of the Phoenicians: supplying those ready to pay the price with the merchandise they are demanding.

Then there is the national question. Great Russian chauvinism and anti-Semitism, as strong as ever, must still face the hatred of nationalities that have been forcibly locked up in the modernized prison of peoples. Russia remains the sole major, 'developed' country in which entire nations are kept in a state of servitude.

There is also the political question. Independent of the fact that the people are radically excluded from all control over and knowledge of public affairs, the bureaucracy has not been able and is not able to find any regular mode of operation for resolving the problem of its own management, except via struggles among cliques and clans and via court intrigues. As changes at the Summit must be spaced as far apart as possible, so as to avoid a fatal collapse of the entire edifice, the inevitable consequence is gerontocracy. Claiming to regulate all aspects of social life and to resolve all problems in the place of those directly interested, the State, and the Party which is its soul, do no more than multiply these problems through their very existence and through their mode of operation. Their swelling growth, itself monstrous, testifies to how extremely acute is the antagonistic split within society.

The persistence and aggravation of these problems are accompanied by a veritable involution of culture. The people that produced Dostoyevsky, Mussorgsky, Mayakovsky must now suffer the cretinism, uninspired conventionality [*pompiérisme*], and bewildering sterility of the 'official' state culture. At the same time, state ideology is decomposing. The invocation of 'Marxism–Leninism' has become a mere ritual (*KDBI* [1956]). The bureaucracy condemns Russian culture to sterility, because it is itself condemned to silence.

The bureaucracy cannot speak or allow anyone to speak of its original sin, of its bloody birth in and through Stalin's terror – whom it neither condemns nor rehabilitates fully. This bureaucracy cannot erase, without further ado, thirty or forty years of Russian history, in as much as the latter continues on without any essential alterations. It is equally impossible for the bureaucracy to allow anyone to present a truthful image, even an artistic one, of its present state, accept any discussion about the state of Russian society, or tolerate any investigations or initiatives that might escape its control.

The result of all this is a wearing away, if not a total disappearance, of its hold over the younger generations, but also over a growing proportion of the general population. In fact, the sole cement holding bureaucratic society together, besides repression, is now cynicism. Russian society is the first *cynical* society in History. One knows in history of no example of a society that could survive for very long in a state of pure and simple cynicism. Nor is it by chance that Great Russian chauvinism and nationalism are becoming more and more pronounced. Held in check by bureaucratic terror, these conflicts explode only that much more violently when the occasion presents itself (see the examples described by Solzhenitsyn and Plyushch). Among industrialized countries Russia remains the prime candidate for a social revolution.

12   The Russian regime is an integral part of the contemporary world system of domination. With the United States and China, it constitutes one of the three pillars of that system. It is, in solidarity with the others, both manager and guarantee [*le gérant et le garant*] of the maintenance of the social and political status quo on a planetary scale. This solidarity and complicity, which are constantly at work behind the scenes, strikingly manifested themselves for example when the Big Three intervened in concert to help the government of Ceylon crush the 1971 uprising. Likewise, it is more than possible that the United States and Russia would intervene in concert to stifle a revolution in Europe or elsewhere as soon as they became convinced that they could not take control of it or make use of it. In parallel, we may note that the imperialist antagonism of the Big Three remains acute and continues to have the prospect of a world war as its horizon. Contrary to the claims of the official propaganda, such a war has in no way been rendered impossible by the balance of nuclear terror.

II

13   Let us agree to call *social regime* a given type of institution of society to the extent that it goes beyond one particular society. The notion and the term 'mode of production' has some validity if it is a question of characterizing production as such, not a society or a class of societies. Such could be the case only if production and 'mode of production' determined necessarily and sufficiently the whole of social organization and life – which is not even false, but meaningless. The very relationship between production (and the relations of production) and the overall organization of society is each time specific to the *social regime* in question, to the given institution of society, and partakes of this institution (*MRT, HWM* [1974], *SII* [1975]). The social regime of Russia (and of the countries of Eastern Europe, China, etc.) is *total bureaucratic capitalism*; the social regimes of the industrialized countries of the 'West' are *fragmented bureaucratic capitalism* (*SB, RPR, HS*).

14   The emergence of modern bureaucracy and of bureaucratic capitalism, whether total or fragmented, raises an immense number of problems, only a few of which can be lightly touched upon here. Reflection upon these problems explodes the inherited conceptions about society and history. The historical advent of the bureaucracy and the functioning of bureaucratic society remain ungraspable within the framework of the great traditional theories (*SB, RR, RBI, MRT, GI, SII*). The world today lives upon representations of society and of history that, already formed in 1848, have nothing to do with the world today. This is immediately evident with respect to 'liberal' and 'neoliberal' economic and sociological conceptions [in the Continental sense of a capitalist 'free-market' ideology]. What, for them, can the bureaucratic regime be – seeing that it constantly transgresses 'economic rationality' – if not a bad accident that is contrary to human nature? What is to be made of the transformation of citizens into cogs of the state machine if it is not an inexplicable resurgence, in the midst of 'democracy' and the 'spread of knowledge', of the transhistorical form of tyranny?

The situation is different in part with Marx's conception, but only on the condition that one breaks its systematic-dogmatic framework, understands its limits, and relates it to changes in historical reality. *Capital* is to be read in the light of Russia, not Russia in the light of *Capital*. In remaining enslaved not even to Marx's thought but to those aspects of this thought that they have transformed into a mechanistic schema, contemporary 'Marxists' have rendered themselves incapable of saying anything relevant at all about the modern world. In particular, the bureaucracy and the bureaucratic regime remain for them thoroughly impossible as objects of thought.

15   Thus, for almost all Marxist currents and authors (leaving aside, obviously, orthodox Communists), everything seems to have been said already when the Russian regime is pronounced to be the product of the October Revolution's degeneration, itself caused by the 'backwardness' of the country and the 'isolation' of the new power. That the Russian regime should have originated in a revolution that demanded socialism and in which workers and peasants played a decisive and in large part autonomous role is one thing. That one might, when invoking this origin, evacuate the question of the present nature of the regime, the question of the end product of this 'degeneration', is something else completely. The historical combination of circumstances through which a regime is instaurated has its importance, but in no way does it suffice as a characterization thereof. A capitalism established through the peaceful merger of the bourgeoisie with the old aristocracy or even the mere transformation of the latter into a capitalist class (Japan) does not essentially differ in this regard from a capitalism that would be instaurated in the aftermath of the aristocracy's violent elimination by the bourgeoisie. The very term *degeneration* does not correspond to what is at issue here. The 'dual power' of the Provisional Government and the Soviets

between February and October 1917 was succeeded by the 'dual power' of the Bolshevik Party and the organs of the labouring people (basically, factory committees), the latter being gradually repressed and then definitively eliminated in 1921 (*RPR, DRR, CP, RBI*). The explanation of the advent of the bureaucratic regime in terms of the degeneration of a revolution collapses when one examines the accession to power of the bureaucracy in China and elsewhere. The interpretation of degeneration itself as an effect of 'backwardness' and 'isolation' – which is ridiculously superficial and whose function is to mask the *political* problematic of a socialist revolution and the bureaucratic-totalitarian character of the Bolshevik Party from the outset – has become totally anachronistic, since the industrialization of Russia and the extension of the bureaucratic Empire have in no way undermined the bureaucracy's domination. If, these alleged causes having disappeared, the effect persists, and if the same effect is produced where the causes do not exist, one is obliged to recognize that this effect is rooted in reality in another way than under the circumstances surrounding its initial appearance. Continuing to appeal to Marx – who wrote 'to the hand mill corresponds feudal society, to the steam mill capitalist society' – these conceptions implicitly affirm that to the assembly line corresponds, here, capitalism, there, 'socialism' or the 'workers' State'. Incapable of reflecting upon this new social-historical entity that is the modern bureaucracy, in these conceptions one can speak of Russia, China, etc., only with reference to a socialist society, these regimes representing deformations thereof. They thus preserve of Marx in fact only his metaphysical/deterministic schema of history: there should exist a predetermined stage of history, socialism, that necessarily succeeds capitalism. Consequently, what is not 'capitalism' (conceived, furthermore, in the most superficial way on the basis of 'private property', 'commodities', etc.) could only be socialism – if need be, a socialism that is deformed, degenerated, very degenerated, etc. But socialism is not a necessary stage of history. It is the historical project of a new institution of society, whose content is direct self-government, the direction and collective management by human beings of all aspects of their social life, and the explicit self-institution of society. In reducing socialism to a purely 'economic' affair and economic reality to the juridical forms of ownership; in presenting as socialist state control and bureaucratic 'planning', the social function of these conceptions is to mask the bureaucracy's domination, to occult its roots and its conditions, so as to justify the bureaucracy already in place or to camouflage the aims of 'revolutionary' bureaucrats who are candidates for power.

16   Modern bureaucracy is, up to a certain point, thinkable within the Marxian frame of reference. But also, beyond this point it blows apart this frame of reference. At a certain level of abstraction (as Max Weber had seen, and as Marx had not seen), it constitutes the immanent culmination of the

'ideal' evolution of capitalism. From the narrow productive-economic standpoint, technological evolution, the concomitant organization of production, and the process of capital concentration entail the elimination of the 'independent' individual capitalist and the emergence of a bureaucratic stratum that 'organizes' the labour of thousands of labouring people in giant firms, takes on the effective management of the company and of complexes of companies, and takes charge of the incessant modifications in the instruments and methods of production (whereby it differs radically from every 'traditional' bureaucracy that manages a *static* system). When it reaches its full development, this stratum appropriates for itself a portion of the surplus product (under the form of 'salaries', etc.) and decides how to allocate the other part of this surplus by mechanisms for which 'the private ownership of capital' is neither a necessary nor a sufficient condition. The capitalist 'owner' or 'owners', if they remain, can play a role in the modern business enterprise only by means of the place they occupy within the bureaucratic pyramid. If, as Marx thought, the concentration of capital 'does not stop before all social capital is concentrated in the hands of a single capitalist or group of capitalists', this single capitalist or group of capitalists would never be able to dominate in person hundreds of millions of labouring people; such a situation is inconceivable without the emergence and the proliferation of a stratum that effectively controls, manages, directs production and in fact has the latter at its disposal, and this capitalist himself would be dependent upon it. In the effective history of the classical capitalist countries, concentration does not attain (and could not attain) its 'ideal limit' in this way (as a function of economic evolution alone). But the tendencies just described are amply achieved therein, sufficiently so as to allow one to define the social regime of Western countries as *fragmented bureaucratic capitalism*. Modern bureaucracy may therefore be interpreted, within Marx's frame of reference, as the organic product of the evolution of capitalist production and of capital concentration, as the 'personification of capital' at a certain stage in its history, as one of the poles in the capitalist relation of production, the directors/executants division, and the active agent of the achievement, the expansion, and the ever greater penetration of this relation into production activities (and into all other activities). The separation of management and immediate production, the transfer of management from the activity of labour to an instance of authority external to labour and to the labourer; pseudo-'rationalization'; 'calculation' and 'planning' extended to greater and greater segments of production and of the economy, etc. – it is out of the question that all these functions could be accomplished by 'persons' and simply by means of the 'ownership of capital'. It is equally out of the question that they would be accomplished by the 'market', unless one thinks the latter according to the mythology of political economy (which Marx, in fact, shared). These functions can be accomplished only by the bureaucracy and by means of the creation of the bureaucratic Apparatus (*SB, PO I* [1959], *MCR*). And domination by the bureaucracy appears as the adequate form, *par excellence*, of domination by the 'spirit' of capitalism (here again, Max Weber had seen things much more clearly than Marx) – or, by the magma of social imaginary significations the institution of capitalism realizes.

17   Marx's blindness before the implications of his own correct view of capital concentration is not an accident (and the reasons for this blindness are the same as those that explain the poverty of most other theoretical approaches to modern bureaucracy). At its limit, concentration implies not only the elimination of 'individual capitalists' but also the abolition of 'capital' as such and of the 'economy' as a sector effectively separate from the rest of social life. Concentration and monopolization entail an increasing reduction of the 'market', an essential alteration in the character of what remains of it, its replacement by a condominium of oligopolies and monopolies, and ultimately by an 'integrated' ('planned') organization of production and of the economy. At the limit point of total concentration (and in fact, long before this limit is attained), there no longer is any genuine 'market', no 'production price', no 'law of value', and ultimately no more 'capital' in the sense Marx gave to this term (which contains, as an ineliminable moment, the idea of a sum of 'values' engaged in the process of self-aggrandizement). At best, the 'law of value' is transformed in this case into a rule (norm, prescription) of 'rational' subjective behaviour on the part of the sole capitalist or the bureaucracy, but nothing guarantees that it would be followed, and everything ensures that it could not be (*CFP* [1948], *DC I*). Under total bureaucratic capitalism, one can no longer speak of 'economic laws', trivialities excepted (physical and technical constraints are not 'economic laws'). This is also why conceptions that see in Russia a kind of 'state capitalism', and that claim that the 'economic laws of capitalism' continue to prevail, with a simple substitution of the State for the 'capitalist class', are devoid of content.

18   Nevertheless, to remain with this conception of the bureaucracy would be to neglect essential dimensions of its reality – those, as a matter of fact, that put the Marxian conception into question and ultimately render it untenable. Even in 'classical' capitalist countries, the emergence and growth of the bureaucracy are in no way reducible to the concentration of 'capital' and to the concomitant bureaucratization of production and of the business enterprise. In fact, from the outset the Western-style industrial organization borrows its model from the age-old bureaucratic-hierarchical organization of States and armies, which it transforms for its own purposes – not only by adapting it to the necessities of production but especially, in contrast to the traditional 'static' bureaucracy, by making it the instrument and the bearer of 'change'. Later on, the 'industrial' bureaucratic model is in turn

taken up again by the State, the army, and political parties. The bureaucratization of 'classical' capitalist societies finds a powerful source in the considerable expansion of the State's role and functions, which are as much general as properly economic, independent of all formal state nationalization of production (cf. the United States). This expansion entails a proliferation of the bureaucratic stratum and a broadening of its powers, as well as the multiplication of noncommercial institutional mechanisms for the integration and management of social activities. Finally, it finds an important source in the evolution of the workers' movement. The constitution of a trade-union and 'working-class' political bureaucracy expresses the adoption of the capitalist model by working-class organizations and its acceptance by their members (*PO I*); or it expresses the continued domination of the imaginary significations of capitalism and of the corresponding institutional devices (the division between directors and executants, hierarchy, specialization, etc.) over the working class outside production and in the very instruments this class has created in order to struggle against capitalism.

19   Already, therefore, the evolution of a 'classical' capitalist society toward fragmented bureaucratic capitalism is not interpretable solely in terms of production and the economy. Still more important, however, is the fact that the bureaucracy's emergence in Russia and its domination there results not from such an 'organic' evolution but from the rupture that was the Revolution of 1917 and from an essentially political process. The first modern bureaucracy to constitute itself as a dominant stratum – and which served, on a world scale, as catalyser and accelerator of the process of bureaucratization – is not the 'canonical' bureaucracy that traditional capitalism would have engendered, but is born, rather, in and through the destruction of traditional capitalism (*RBI, MRT*). Still more illuminating is the case of 'precapitalist' countries, China being the example *par excellence*. Here, the bureaucracy, coming to power through a political process and instaurating relations of domination for its own benefit, creates practically *ab ovo* 'capitalist relations of production' and the corresponding material infrastructure. It is not the Chinese bureaucracy that is the product of the industrialization of China but, rather, the industrialization of China that is the work of the Chinese bureaucracy. The effective and concrete mediation between the world system of domination and the bureaucratic transformation of China was not furnished by 'infrastructures', except negatively, in as much as the penetration and the impact of capitalism had dislocated traditional forms of organization in China; this had also occurred elsewhere, but without the result being the same. The 'material' bearers of the conditions for the bureaucratic transformation of China have been 'Marxist' catechisms and the Bolshevik militaro-political model, not machines or even rifles (Chiang Kai-shek had as many and more). The concrete mediation between

world capitalism and the bureaucratic transformation of China is to be found in the penetration, into China, of the social imaginary significations of capitalism and of the corresponding institutional and organizational types ('Marxist' ideology, political party, 'progress', 'production', etc.). And it is in this sense – and not because there would have been domination by 'capital' – that China, like Russia, and so on, ultimately belongs to the same social-historical universe as the 'Western-style' countries, that of bureaucratic capitalism.

20   Total bureaucratic capitalism is therefore neither a mere variant of traditional capitalism nor a moment in the 'organic' evolution of the latter. Belonging to the social-historical universe of capitalism, it also represents a rupture and a new historical creation. And the relation between what is altered and what is not altered when one passes from traditional capitalism to complete bureaucratic capitalism is itself new (*RBI, MRT, SII*). This break is obvious when one looks at the concrete social group that exercises, in both cases, domination. It is just as obvious when one looks at the specific institution of the social regime, notably the explicit and implicit, formal and informal mechanisms and devices by means of which the domination of a particular social group over the whole of society is achieved and assured. The core and germinal institution of capitalism – the *business enterprise* – remains the tie between these phases. But the 'private ownership' (or, better, the *disposition*) of 'capital', the 'market' as mechanism for economic integration, the formal distinction between 'State' and 'civil society', all essential for the existence of traditional capitalism, disappear under total bureaucratic capitalism, which is characterized by the universal extension of the modern bureaucratic-hierarchical Apparatus, the 'plan' as integrative mechanism, the erasure of the distinction between 'civil society' and the 'State'. The dominant stratum's relation to these mechanisms is obviously different in the two cases – since, in all social regimes, the relation of the dominant stratum to the instituted mechanisms corresponding to its domination is each time *sui generis*, its proper and specific part of the institution of *this* social regime. In good part, lack of understanding of the Russian regime also comes from the fact that one always wants to view the relationship between the bureaucracy and its instituted mechanisms on the basis of the model of the bourgeoisie's relationship to capital ownership and to the market (whether this be to affirm that the two relationships are identical or to conclude from their difference that there is in Russia no exploitation). But the relationship between slaveholders and the mechanisms of a slave-based regime, between lords and the mechanisms of the feudal regime, between the bourgeoisie and the mechanisms of the capitalist regime is each time different and partakes of the mode of institution of the corresponding social regimes (*MRT, HWM, SII*).

Likewise, it is just as false to think of the dominant social group as a simple 'personification' of instituted mechanisms and devices (as Marx did for capitalists and 'capital') as it is to see in these mechanisms a simple 'instrument' of this group (as most Marxists do for the State). This relation is not thinkable under the categories of 'instrumentality', 'personification', or 'expression'; it is a relation without analogy elsewhere, and it is to be thought for its own sake. And politically speaking, it is just as fallacious to speak of 'power' while evacuating the fact that it is always also power of a group over others as it is to speak of groups or classes while evacuating the instituted systems that correspond to them. In total bureaucratic capitalism, the intricate connections between the 'economic', the 'political', the 'ideological', and so on take on a new character in comparison with 'classical' capitalist societies; there is *another* institution of the spheres of social activity and of their articulation. It is absurd to reason in its regard as if the social categories posited and instituted as separate by other types of society, and *par excellence* by 'classical' capitalist society (economy, right, State, 'culture', etc.), have remained unaltered therein (*MRT, HWM, SII*).

21   The advent of total bureaucratic capitalism confirms what the study of precapitalist societies could already have shown: it is not in and through production that 'classes' in general are formed (*MRT, HWM*). The institution of a social regime of asymmetrical and antagonistic division is equivalent to the instauration of a relation of domination between a social group and the rest of society, to which corresponds a set of 'second-order' institutions (*SII*, in *IIS*, p. 371E; T/E: see now *FISSI* [1985]). Such are the institutions that embody and realize in the narrowly political and coercive sphere the power of the dominant group, and notably the State; those that allow for the creation of an economic *surplus* and its appropriation by the dominant group; and those, finally, that assure the domination of myths, religious beliefs, ideas – in short, the representations and social significations that correspond to the institution of society, their internalization by individuals, and the indefinite fabrication of individuals who conform to this institution. Thus, for example, antagonistic relations of production can exist neither logically nor really except as a moment and dimension of the relations of domination. They *are* intrinsically relations of domination in the specific sphere of production and labour: relations of domination external to the labour process itself in a slave-based or feudal regime penetrate deeper and deeper into this process under the capitalist regime (*RPR, MRT*). And they imply the constitution of a power over society and the appropriation of this power by a particular social group. The origin, and the basis for the unity, of this group is not necessarily to be found in the identical position, relative to production, of the individuals who make up the group but, rather, in their participation in the above-mentioned power over the rest of society – a power that, of course, must also be expressed as 'economic power', or the ability

to dispose of people's time and to allot a portion of this time to activities that serve the dominant group or whose results it appropriates for itself. It is possible that such a power might, historically, already be constituted within the society in question and that a social category set up on the basis of production/the economy (or even otherwise) might seize it, transforming it a little or a lot, in order to attain a position of full domination. Such was the case with the bourgeoisie – and wrongly extrapolated, by Marx, onto the whole of history. Even in this case, moreover, it would be false to see in power and in the State something that is added over and above a productive-economic structure while remaining external to it, or a simple instrument of a social stratum that is in the process of acceding to a dominant position. But it is also possible that it be by the direct instauration of a new relation of domination and of a new form of power that a social group (a victorious ethnic group, a political grouping) creates and imposes relations of production that correspond to this domination and allow for its social reproduction. Such has been, in all likelihood, the origin of slave-based societies and, certainly, the most frequent origin of feudal regimes; and such is the origin of the contemporary bureaucratic regimes in Russia, in China, or in Eastern Europe.

22   Under total bureaucratic capitalism, the abolition of the 'economy' as a separate and relatively autonomous sphere is part of an essential alteration between 'civil society' and the State. In truth, this distinction itself – which remains encumbered with large ideological elements that correspond to the classical bourgeoisie's view of society – has to be re-examined. The reality of the relations between 'civil society' and the State has never been such as they have been presented in theoretical constructs (including in Hegel and Marx). But in any case, bourgeois society lives and develops within the distinction between a private sphere, a 'civil' public sphere, and a state public sphere. This distinction is already upset by the evolution that leads to fragmented bureaucratic capitalism: the extension of state activities increasingly restrains the 'civil' public domain and the 'private' sphere itself tends to become, under multiple forms, 'public' (*MCR, RR*). With total bureaucratic capitalism, a qualitative leap takes place. The distinction between the 'civil' public sphere and the state public sphere is wiped out, the 'private' sphere is reduced to the minimum (at the limit, it is reduced to the biological functions of individuals). There is not, for all that, a domination of the State *as such* over society – or an 'absorption of civil society by the State'. The State is itself dominated by a separate 'political' organism – in the typical and prevailing case, the Party, which is the ultimate instance of decision-making and power, and, within the Party itself, the Summit of the Apparatus. The Party, as organization and unifying setting of the dominant group, can identify itself in words with society only so long as the terror it exercises over the latter, in reducing

society to silence, disproves this very identification. And it could not 'absorb' society without ceasing to be what it is and what its name clearly indicates: a *part* of society, a *particular* body within the latter. Also, the formal erasure of the distinction between civil society and the State signifies neither the 'absorption' of the former by the latter nor a 'unification' of society. The claim that it is unifying and homogenizing society (as formulated in the Party's ideology) bears some relation to reality from one angle alone: the undifferentiated submission of all to the unlimited power and arbitrariness of the Summit of the Apparatus. Beyond that, it can mask the persistence neither of a social (and not simply 'occupational') differentiation that is as strong as under traditional capitalism (city-dwellers/peasants, manual labourers/intellectual workers, men/women, etc.), nor of an asymmetrical and antagonistic division of society between directors and executants (which has become more and more complex through the mutual interpenetration of different bureaucratic-hierarchical pyramids), nor, finally, of cleavages and conflicts within the bureaucracy itself. Still more, this pretension gives rise to a new opposition between the formal existence of a State, which ought to cover the totality of the social sphere and coincide with the latter, and the reality of the social sphere, which constantly escapes the control of this State and differs from it both by excess (doing more and other than what it is supposed to do) and by default (not doing, by far, what it is supposed to do). On this opposition depends, when one considers the State itself, a new split between its appearance and its reality. 'Civil public' life has become an object of state control. But state-controlled life is no longer public at all; its unfolding has to be hidden, even in the tiniest details, and what elsewhere is 'public' without any difficulty here becomes a state secret (from the most banal economic statistics to telephone books and Moscow transport maps).

23   The Russian regime belongs to the social-historical universe of capitalism because the magma of social imaginary significations that animate its institution and are realized in and through this institution is the very same one that arises in history with and through capitalism. The core of this magma can be described as the unlimited expansion of 'rational' mastery. We are dealing here, of course, with a sort of mastery that in great part is illusory, and a pseudo-'rationality' of the Understanding and of abstraction (*CS I* [1955], *CS II, MCR, RBI, MRT, GI, RRD, SII*). It is this imaginary signification that constitutes the main junction point for the ideas that become effective forces and processes dominating the operation and evolution of capitalism: the unlimited expansion of the forces of production; the obsessive preoccupation with 'development', pseudorational 'technical progress', production, and 'the economy'; 'rationalization' and control of all activities; the ever heightened division of tasks; organization as end in itself, and so on. Its correlates are the institutional forms of the business enter-

prise, the bureaucratic-hierarchical Apparatus, the modern State and Party, and so on. Several of these elements – significations and institutional forms – were created in the course of historical periods that preceded capitalism. But it is the bourgeoisie, during its transformation into a capitalist bourgeoisie, that, in taking them over, altered their meaning and their function, reuniting them and subordinating them to the signification of the unlimited expansion of 'rational' mastery (which was explicitly formulated as early as Descartes, which is still central in Marx, and through which the latter's thought remains anchored in the capitalist universe). And this signification, mediated by Marxism's transformation into an ideology and by the political organization of the Party, rallies together, unifies, animates, and guides the bureaucracy as it comes to dominate society, in the specific institution of its regime and in the management of the latter.

24   The 'realization' of this social imaginary signification is profoundly antinomic. Here we have a decisive trait of modern societies, which serves to contrast them radically from traditional, 'archaic', or 'historical' societies, where one does not encounter an antinomy of this type (*MCR, MRT, SII*). Modern society aims only at 'rationality' and produces, on a massive scale, only 'irrationality' (from the point of view of this 'rationality' itself). Or else, it can be said: In no other known society does the system of representations society itself gives itself happen to be in flagrant and violent opposition to the reality of that society, as is the case under the regime of bureaucratic capitalism. It is perfectly logical that this antinomy should reach the point of delirious paroxysm under the extreme forms of 'Marxist' totalitarianism, under the reign of Stalin and of Mao.

25   In modern societies this system of representations tends more and more to be reduced to the level of ideology. Ideology is the 'rationalized-systematized' elaboration of the emergent, explicit part of the social imaginary significations that correspond to a given institution of society – or to the place and to the aims of a particular social stratum within this institution. It therefore can appear neither in 'mythical' societies nor in 'simply' religious societies. It experiences genuine development only starting with the institution of capitalism, which is easily comprehensible. There it takes on increasing importance due to the fact that the central imaginary signification of capitalism is alleged rationality and that its very content requires this 'rational' form of expression that is ideology. Ideology thus has to render everything explicit, transparent, explicable, and rationalizable – at the same time that its function is to occult everything. Subject to this intrinsic contradiction, and in head-on opposition to social reality, ideology is obliged to flatten everything and is itself obliged to flatten itself; it becomes empty form and is condemned to wear itself down from within at an ever accelerated pace. The present-day fate of 'Marxism–Leninism' in Russia and in China furnishes a striking and extreme illustration of this fact.

Note

1 T/E: A second, revised edition of the first volume of *Devant la guerre* was published by Fayard in 1981. The second volume never appeared. Around this time, however, *CWS* (1982), which appears below, served as a supplement, for Western societies, to the analyses of Russia conducted in *Devant la guerre*.

8

From Ecology to Autonomy (1980)*

I am happy to be here and to see you. And I am very surprised by the number of participants, very pleasantly surprised and happy. But at the same time, this increases my fear of disappointing you, in as much as when I spoke with Dany before coming here he told me that he did not know what he was going to say, that he would improvise. Well, he has a habit of doing that and as one knows, historically, he comes out quite well. [*Laughter.*] As for myself, I would have liked to have devoted more time than I was able to preparing what I wish to say to you.

But perhaps, in the last analysis, this would not have made a difference since the four or five things I have to say, you will see, end in the interrogatory mode and they would have ended that way in any case. And I believe that the point of an evening like this is precisely to get you to speak, either on the questions that for you are already open or – and this would be a considerable gain – on new questions that would arise in the course of the debate, perhaps with the help of those who have been charged with introducing it.

Today, everyone knows, everyone thinks they know – this was not the case a short time ago – that science and technique are in their very essence inserted, inscribed, rooted in a given institution of society. Likewise, everyone knows that the science and the technique of today have nothing transhistorical about them, have no value that lies beyond question; these belong, on the contrary, to the social-historical institution that is capitalism as it was born in the West a few centuries ago.

That is a general truth. People know that each society creates its technique and its type of knowledge, as well as its type of transmission of knowledge.

* *De l'Écologie à l'autonomie* (Paris: Seuil, 1981) presents the acts of a meeting on 'The Antinuclear Struggle, Ecology, and Politics' held on 27 February 1980 at Louvain-la-Neuve, Belgium. [T/E: The other principal speaker was Daniel Cohn-Bendit, the former May 1968 Paris student leader and current German Greens Party member. This was the first time Cohn-Bendit, who was deported from France at the height of the May 1968 protests, had met Castoriadis, whose ideas he proudly 'plagiarized' in *Obsolete Communism: The Left-Wing Alternative* (trans. Arnold Pomerans [New York: McGraw-Hill, 1968]). Exceeding the organizers' expected turnout, some eight hundred people, mostly ecological and antinuclear activists, were reported to have attended the conference. Alastair Davidson's translation of the bulk of Castoriadis's speech appeared as 'From Ecology to Autonomy' in *Thesis Eleven*, 3 (1981), pp. 8–22. The present abridged version, a new translation which on occasion consulted Davidson's, includes pp. 20–50 of the original French edition.]

People know, too, that capitalist society not only has gone very far toward the creation and the development of a type of technology that distinguishes it from all others but – and this also distinguishes it from all others – that it has placed these activities at the centre of its social life and granted them an importance they did not have previously or elsewhere.

Likewise, everyone knows today, or everyone thinks they know, that the alleged neutrality, the alleged instrumentality of technique and even of scientific knowledge are illusions. In truth, even this expression is inadequate, and it masks the essential aspect of the question. The presentation of science and of technique as neutral means or as instruments pure and simple is not a mere 'illusion': it is an integral part of the contemporary institution of society – that is, it partakes of the dominant social imaginary of our age.

This dominant social imaginary can be encapsulated in one sentence: The central aim of social life is the unlimited expansion of rational mastery. Of course, when one looks from close up – and it is not necessary to go very, very close to see it – this mastery is a pseudomastery, this rationality a pseudorationality. That does not stop it from being the core of the social imaginary significations now holding society together. And this is not only the case in the countries of so-called private or Western capitalism. It is equally the case in the allegedly socialist countries, in the countries of the East, where the same instruments, the same factories, the same organizational procedures and knowledge procedures are equally put in the service of this same social imaginary signification, namely, the unlimited expansion of an allegedly rational alleged mastery.

Here I shall open a parenthesis, for in no way can we discuss these matters in abstraction from the serious things now going on around the world. We see much more clearly today, with Afghanistan – more exactly, I shall say: People can see; as for myself, I claim to have seen it for going on thirty-five years – that the coexistence and the antagonism of these two subsystems, each of which claims to have a monopoly on the way in which 'rational mastery' over everything shall be attained, are now reaching the point where we run the risk of total rational mastery by the one true master, as Hegel would say, that is, by death.

You know that the domination of this imaginary begins first via the form of the unlimited expansion of the forces of production – of 'wealth', of 'capital'. This expansion rapidly becomes the extension and the development of the knowledge necessary for increased production, that is to say, of technology and science. Finally, the tendency toward 'rationally' reorganizing and reconstructing all spheres of social life – production, administration, education, culture, etc. – transforms the whole institution of society and penetrates ever further into all activities.

But you also know that, despite its pretensions, this institution of society is torn by a host of internal contradictions, that its history is shot through with large-scale social conflicts. In our view, these conflicts basically express the fact that contemporary society is divided asymmetrically and antagonistically between dominators and dominated, and that this division is expressed, notably, in the facts of exploitation and oppression. From this point of view we ought to say that, *de facto*, the immense majority of people who live in present-day society ought to be opposed to the established form of the institution of society. But it is equally difficult for us to believe that if such were the case, this society could last for long or even could have lasted until today. A very important question therefore arises. How does this society succeed in maintaining itself and holding itself together when it 'ought' to arouse the opposition of the great majority of its members?

There is a response to this question that we must eliminate once and for all from our minds, the one characteristic of the old mentality of the Left. This is the idea that the system is held together only through the repression and manipulation of people, in an external and superficial sense of the term *manipulation*.

This idea is totally false and, what is graver still, it is pernicious because it masks the depth of the social and political problem. If we truly want to struggle against the system and, also, if we want to see the problems which, for example, today confront a movement like the ecology movement, we have to comprehend an elementary truth that will seem very disagreeable to certain people: *The system holds together because it succeeds in creating people's adherence to the way things are [ce qui est]*. It succeeds in creating, somehow or other, for the majority of people and over the great majority of the moments of their life, their adherence to the effective, instituted, concrete way of life of this society. If we want to engage in an activity that is not vain and futile, it is from a recognition of this fundamental fact that we must begin our efforts.

This adherence is, of course, contradictory. It goes hand in hand with moments of revolt against the system. But it nevertheless is a form of adherence, and *it is not mere passivity*. Just look around you and you can easily see it. Moreover, if people didn't effectively adhere to the system, everything would collapse in the next six hours. To take just one example: that marvel of 'organization' and 'rationality' that is the capitalist factory – or, more generally, every capitalist business enterprise, in the West as in the East – would then produce nothing at all, it would quickly collapse under the weight of its absurd regulations and of the internal antinomies characteristic of its pseudorationality if the labouring population did not make it function half the time *against* the regulations – and quite beyond what could ever be explained by coercion or by the effect of 'material stimulants'.

This adherence depends on extremely complex processes, which there can be no question of analysing here. These processes constitute what I call the social fabrication of the individual and of individuals – of us all – in and through instituted capitalist society, such as it exists.

I shall simply mention two aspects of this fabrication process. One concerns the instillation in people, from their most tender infancy, of a relationship to authority, of a certain type of relationship to a certain type of authority. And the other, the instillation in people of a set of 'needs', to the 'satisfaction' of which they will then be harnessed their whole life long.

First, authority. When one looks at contemporary society and one compares it to previous societies, one notes one important difference: today, authority is presented as desacralized; no more are there kings by the grace of God.

DANIEL COHN-BENDIT: You are in Belgium.

CASTORIADIS: I am not forgetting that I am in Belgium. But I do not believe that the king of the Belgians is considered a king by the grace of God. I think that this must be a principle of Belgian constitutional law, that if there is a king of the Belgians, it is because the Belgian people have sovereignly decided to have a king – no? [*Laughter.*]

One would think, then, that authority today is desacralized. But in reality it is not. What, in former times, sacralized authority was religion: as Saint Paul said in Romans, 'There is no power but of God.' Today, something else has taken the place of religion and of God, something that is not for us 'sacred' but which has succeeded, somehow or other, in setting itself up as the practical equivalent of the sacred, a sort of substitute for religion, a flat and deflated religion. And this is the idea, the representation, the imaginary signification of *knowledge* and of *technique*.

I do not mean thereby, of course, that those who exercise power 'know'. But they pretend to know and it is in the name of this alleged knowledge – specialized, scientific, technical knowledge – that they justify their power in the eyes of the populace. And if they are able to do so, it is because the population believes this, it is because the populace has been trained to believe this.

Thus, in France one is saddled with a president of the Republic who claims to be an economic specialist. This 'specialist', when he was Minister of Finance, held forth in the Chamber of Deputies with a three-hour speech in which he laid out statistics rounded to four decimal places. This means he would have flunked first-year economics, since when it comes to prices and production a four-decimal statistic is strictly meaningless: at best, in these areas, one can speak about roughly 10 per cent. That did not stop President Giscard, who is not an economist, from unearthing a dinosaur of economic knowledge by the name of Raymond Barre [*laughter and applause*], whom he publicly baptized as 'the best economist in France'. The result is that the mess the French economy is in at present is much greater than it was three years ago and also than what it would have been had a cleaning lady been prime minister. [*Laughter.*]

There is a practical conclusion to be drawn from this. There is a field of struggle, especially for people like us here who are more or less involved in intellectual or scientific activities. It is a matter of showing, in the first place, that in the present age power is *not* knowledge, that not only does it not know everything but even that it knows many fewer things than people in general know, and that there are profound and organic reasons for this. And in the second place, it is a matter of showing that this 'knowledge' claimed by power, even when it does exist, is at bottom of a quite particular, partial, and biased character.

But there is also a *question* I do not want to pass over in silence – although it is only one of the questions we will have to dwell on this evening. It is that – forgetting completely now about Messrs Giscard, Barre, and their fellow plotters – there is a genuine problem of knowledge, and even of technique, that really does challenge us in as much as this knowledge and even this technique go beyond [*dépassent*] the present institution of society. Even if one grants – as I do – that the orientation, the ends, the mode of transmission, and internal organization of scientific knowledge are anchored in the present-day social system and, even more, that they are, in a sense, consubstantial with it; even then it must be granted that here there is a creation of something that certainly outstrips [*dépasse*] the contemporary era. This is also true, moreover, for previous eras of history. To take one easy example, Pythagoras's theorem was discovered and demonstrated on Samos or wherever twenty-five centuries ago. Clearly, it was discovered in a context that in no way was 'neutral', this context being formed as it was by a set of imaginary schemata indissociably and profoundly tied to the Greek conception of the world, to the Greek imaginary institution of the world, as is the case for all Greek geometry. That does not prevent, twenty-five centuries later, Pythagoras's theorem, or something that has the same name, not only from continuing to 'be true' (one can add as many quotation marks and question marks to this expression as one wishes), but also from appearing infinitely truer than Pythagoras himself could have thought it to be, since the present statement of Pythagoras's theorem, such as you will find it in a contemporary analytical geometry textbook, constitutes an immense generalization of its original formulation. It is still called Pythagoras's theorem, but now it states: In every pre-Hilbertian space, the square of the measure of the sum of two orthogonal vectors is equal to the sum of the squares of their measures. Or, to take another example, no society is possible without arithmetic – no matter how archaic, primitive, or savage this society might be. But where, then, does arithmetic stop? This, too, is part of the question of knowledge. It is too easy to evacuate this question by saying, as a recent small-minded Parisian clown [*microfarceur*] said, that totalitarianism is the scientists in power, which evidently serves only to condone and to reinforce the dominant ideological mystification. As if Stalin, who directed the operations of the Russian Army during the Second World War on an ordinary globe, as Khrushchev revealed, was a 'scientist in power'! But it is also too easy to evacuate the question, as is often done in our circles and by people close to us, by trying to jettison science and technique as such because they are said to be the pure products of the established system; one would thus end up eliminating any interrogations bearing on the world, on ourselves, on our knowledge.

I come now to the other dimension of the process whereby the individual is socially fabricated, that concerning 'needs'. Quite evidently, the human being has no 'natural needs', in any definition of the term *natural* – save, perhaps, in a philosophical definition in which 'nature' would be something completely different from what you usually think of under this term: a 'nature' according to Aristotle, or Spinoza, something like a norm that is both ideal and real. Beyond the fact that we are not here tonight to discuss these kinds of philosophical questions, this acceptation of the term *nature* does not interest us for a precise reason: it is unclear how one could agree *socially* on how to define what would correspond to a 'nature' of that kind.

There are no natural needs. Every society creates a set of needs for its members and teaches them that life is not worth living, and cannot even be lived physically, unless those created needs are 'satisfied' somehow or other. What is capitalism's specificity in this regard? In the first place, capitalism was able to arise, maintain itself, develop, and become stabilized (despite and along with the intense working-class struggles tearing through its history) only by putting 'economic' needs at the centre of everything. A Muslim, or a Hindu, will put aside some money his whole life long in order to make a pilgrimage to Mecca or to some temple; for him, that is a 'need'. It is not one for an individual fabricated by capitalist culture: this pilgrimage is a superstition or a whim. But for this same individual it is not a superstition or a whim, but an absolute 'need', to have a car or to change one's car every three years, or to have a colour television set as soon as one exists.

In the second place, therefore, capitalism succeeds in creating a humanity for which, more or less and somehow or other, these 'needs' are almost all that count in life. In the third place – and this is one of the points radically separating us from a view such as the one Marx could have of capitalist society – these needs that capitalism creates, somehow-or-other-and-most-of-the-time *it satisfies them*. As one says in English, 'It promises the goods and it delivers the goods'. The junk is there, the stores are overflowing with the stuff – and you have only to work in order to be able to buy some. You have only to be well-behaved and work, and you will earn more, you will clamber up, you will buy more, and there you are. And historical experience shows that, with a few exceptions, *it works*: production goes on, people work, things are bought, consumption continues, and it works all over again.

At this stage in the discussion, the question is not whether we are 'criticizing' this set of needs from a personal point of view, tastewise, from the human, philosophical, biological, medical, or what have you point of view. The question bears upon the facts, about which one should not nourish any illusions. Briefly speaking, this society works because people yearn to have a car and because they can, in general, have one, and because they can buy petrol for this car. This is why one of the things that might knock down the social system in the West is not 'pauperization', whether absolute or relative, but, rather, for example, the fact that governments might not be able to furnish drivers with petrol.

We really must realize what this means. When we speak of the energy problem, nuclear power, and so on, what in fact is involved is the entire political and social functioning of society, and the whole contemporary way of life. It is so both 'objectively' and from people's point of view, and *in this regard* our criticisms of the brutality of a consumer society count for little.

This situation may easily be illustrated by means of the future – and already past and present – political speeches of citizen [and Communist Party leader Georges] Marchais, who explains (1) if you no longer have any petrol to drive around with, it is the fault of the trusts, the multinationals, and of the government that is in bed with them; and (2) if the Communist Party comes to power, it will give you petrol because it will not be subject to the multinationals and because our great ally, friend of the French people, and great oil producer the Soviet Union will provide us with petrol (little matter if things are starting to go very badly over there, too, in this regard as well). That, clearly, is one possible scenario, just as there exists a possible scenario from an apparently opposite quarter, that is to say, from a neo-Fascist demagogue who might emerge from an energy crisis and the attendant fallout.

The energy crisis has meaning as a crisis, and is a crisis, only in relation to the present model of society. It is *this* society that has need, each year, of 10 per cent more oil or energy in order to be able to keep running. This means that the energy crisis is, in a sense, a crisis of this society. Thus, it contains in germ – and here is a question to which it is for you, much more than for me, to respond – a challenge on people's part to the whole system. But perhaps it contains, as well, in germinal form the possibility that people will follow the most aberrant, the most monstrous political currents. For, this society, such as it is, probably could not continue if the process of ever increased consumption did not keep droning on. It might be able to challenge itself by saying: What we are doing is completely mad, the way we live is absurd. But it could also cling to the present-day way of life, saying to itself: This or that party has the solution; or, We only have to kick out the Jews, the Arabs, or whoever, in order to solve our problems.

This is the question that is posed, and I pose it now to you: Where are people now at, concerning the crisis of their way of life? And what might a lucid political activity be that would accelerate the raising of people's consciousness concerning the absurdity of the system and would aid them in sorting things out among the various critiques of the system already now forming both on the Right and on the Left.

I now would like to broach, in immediate connection with the foregoing, the question of the ecology movement. It seems to me that one can observe, in the history of modern society, a sort of evolution in the field on which challenges, contestation, revolts, and revolutions take place. It also seems to me that one can shed some light on this evolution if one looks at the two dimensions of the institution of society I mentioned earlier: the instillation in individuals of a scheme of authority and the instillation in individuals of a scheme of needs. From the outset, the workers' movement challenged the entire organization of society, but it did so in a way that, retrospectively, cannot help but appear to us to be somewhat abstract. What the workers' movement attacked above all was the dimension of authority – that is to say, domination, which is its 'objective' side. Even on this point it left in the shadows – as was almost inevitable at the time – some completely decisive aspects of the problem of authority and domination, therefore also political problems concerning the reconstruction of an autonomous society. Some of these aspects were put into question later on, and especially, more recently, by the women's movement and the youth movement, both of which attacked the schemata, the figures, and the relations of authority as these existed in other spheres of social life.

What the ecology movement has put into question, on its side, is the other dimension: the scheme and structure of needs, the way of life, of society. And this constitutes a capital breakthrough [*dépassement*] in comparison with what can be seen as the unilateral character of previous movements. What is at issue in the ecology movement is the entire conception, the entire position of the relations between humanity and the world, and ultimately the central and eternal question: What is human life? What are we living for?

To this question there already exists, as we know, an answer: it is the capitalist response. Allow me here to open a parenthesis, proceeding rapidly in reverse. The most beautiful and concise formulation of the spirit of capitalism I know of is Descartes's well-known programmatic statement: We are to attain knowledge and truth in order to 'make ourselves masters and possessors of nature'. It is in this statement of the great rationalist philosopher that one sees most clearly the illusion, the madness, the absurdity of capitalism (as well as of a certain philosophy and a certain theology that precedes it). What does it mean to 'make ourselves the masters and possessors of nature'? Note, too, that both capitalism and the work of Marx and of Marxism are founded upon this meaningless idea.

Now, what becomes apparent, perhaps in fits and starts, through the ecology movement is that we certainly do not want to be masters and possessors of nature. First of all, because we have understood that this does not mean anything, it has no meaning – except to enslave society to an absurd project and to the structures of domination embodying that project. And next, because we want another relationship with nature and with the world – which means, too, another way of life and other needs.

The question, however, is this: What way of life, and what needs? What do we want? And who can answer to these questions, how, and on what basis? By *answer* I mean not in a state of absolute knowledge but, rather, in full knowledge of the relevant facts and lucidly.

In my view, the ecology movement has appeared as one of the movements that tend toward the autonomy of society. Each time I have spoken of it, either orally or in writing, I have included it in the series of those movements I just mentioned. In the ecology movement it is a matter, in the first place, of autonomy in relation to a technico-productive system that is alleged to be inevitable or optimal, the technico-productive system present in society today. But it is absolutely certain that, by the questions it raises, the ecology movement goes far beyond this question of the technico-productive system, since it engages potentially the entire political problem and the entire social problem. I shall explain myself here and end on this point.

That the ecology movement engages the entire political problem and the entire social problem can immediately be seen by starting with an apparently limited question. I hope you will excuse me if I tell you things you must already have heard dozens of times, and if I say them abruptly. The antinuclear struggle: Yes, very good, bravo. But does that mean at the same time an *antielectricity* struggle? If yes, then one must say so, right away, loud and clear. And one must also say: We are against electricity and we know all the implications of what we are saying: no sound system in a hall like this one – but that's already happened [*laughter*]; no telephones; no surgery rooms (after all, Illich says medicine only increases the mortality rate); no radio, pirated or otherwise; no tape recorders; no Keith Jarrett records like the one I just heard in your club, and so on. It must be realized that there is practically *no* object of modern-day life that in one way or another, directly or indirectly, does not imply electricity. This total rejection is perhaps acceptable – but one must know it and say it.

Or else, the only logical thing would be to propose other sources of energy, stating and showing that it is not necessary to deprive oneself of electricity if one rules out nuclear power plants, provided that the entire system of energy production be reformed in such a way that only renewable sources of energy would be allowed. As I am sure you know many more things than I do about renewable energy sources, I won't bother to extend my remarks on this question considered in its own right. But the question of renewable energy sources goes far beyond the question of renewable energy sources. First, it implies the *totality* of production. And then (or, rather, at the same time), it implies the totality of social organization. The only attempt I personally know of to take the question in its entirety into account is the *Alter* project Philippe Courrège is working on in France with a tiny group of volunteer workers. I say *seriously* because Courrège saw straight away that it is not only a question of ensuring the production of renewable sources of energy; he saw that this implies the totality of production and, consequently, he proceeded to construct a small complete 'system' (or, rather, a broad range of such systems, each depending upon the final objectives one sets for oneself), a closed matrix covering the totality of 'inputs' and 'outputs' of a small, fairly much autarkic region. But I also say *seriously* because Courrège also saw, and said, that what on the 'technical' or 'economic' level is, if not a simple solution, at least a feasible one raises immense political and social (he says 'societal') problems: the definition of the final objective of production, the community's acceptance of a steady state, the management of the whole, and so on. Here I can say I feel I am on familiar ground – not that I, of course, have the solution, but because these are the questions on which I have been reflecting and working for thirty years and they become both more precise and more clear when one gives concrete underpinning to the idea of self-governed social units living in large part upon locally renewable resources. But there remains the 'negative' aspect, so to speak, which the *Alter* project also shows: if one wants to touch upon the problem of energy, one has to touch upon everything. Now, all that is neither theory nor literary posturing. As is known, governments are saying even now that without nuclear power plants there will be no more electricity in a few years. Certainly, if nothing else happens – and as, since 1973, these governments have done nothing but blow hot air on the energy problem without doing anything real about it – we really will end with something happening like the breakdown of the power grid last year in France.

Now, on the other hand, projects that deal with renewable energy resources can in part be co-opted towards ends that could not even be labelled reformist – that is, toward the end of plugging up the holes in the existing system. And beyond this question of co-option, this leads to another question: Does an antinuclear, energy-oriented ecological 'reformism' have any meaning and can it be lucidly supported? I mean here by 'reformism' the support given to partial measures we consider viable and meaningful (that is to say, those not cancelled out by the very fact that they are inserted into an overall system that, itself, is not changed); for example, the laws against the pollution of waterways – laws that leave everything else in place: multinational companies, the State, the Communist Party, the king, etc. A certain traditional position responded in the negative to this question. It was said: We are fighting for the Revolution, and one of the by-products of the Revolution will be the nonpollution of rivers (as well as the emancipation of women, the reform of education, etc.). We know that this response is absurd and mystificatory, and fortunately women and students have stopped waiting for the Revolution to demand and obtain real changes in their condition. I think that the same thing holds for the ecology strug-gle: there is, for example and among a thousand other issues, a grave question of the pollution of waterways, and the struggle against this state of affairs makes complete sense, provided one knows what one is doing, pro-vided one is lucid. This means that one knows that at present one is struggling for this or that partial objective because it has a certain value, and that one knows, too, that the measure of which one is demanding the intro-duction or the implementation will, so long as the present system exists, necessarily have an ambiguous signification and can even be diverted from its initial objective. You know that Social Security was, in many countries, a conquest wrested by the working class in the midst of struggle. But you know, too, that there are Marxists who explain – and after all, it is not totally false from a certain point of view – that Social Security makes the capitalist system function because it serves the upkeep of the labour force. Well, so what? Should one demand the abolition of Social Security on the basis of that argument?

I shall close in broaching the problem that to me seems the most profound, the most *critical* – critical in the initial sense of the word *crisis*: the moment· and process of decision. To speak of an autonomous society, of the auton-omy of society, not only with regard to this or that particular dominant stratum but with regard to its own institution, needs, techniques, etc., pre-supposes both the capacity and the will of human beings to govern themselves [*s'auto-gouverner*], in the strongest sense of this term. For a very long time, in fact from the beginning of the period I was engaged in Socialisme ou Barbarie with my comrades, it was basically in these terms that for me the question of the possibility of a radical, revolutionary trans-formation of society was formulated: Do human beings have the capacity and especially the will to govern themselves? (I say especially *will* to gov-ern themselves, for in my view 'capacity' does not really pose a problem.) Do they truly want to be their own masters? For, after all, if they really wanted it, nothing could stop them: this has been known since Rosa Luxemburg, since La Boétie, even since the Greeks. But little by little another aspect of this question – the question of the possibility of a radical transformation of society – began to appear to me, and to preoccupy me more and more. It is that another society, an autonomous society, does not imply only self-management, self-government, self-institution. It implies another *culture*, in the most profound sense of this term. It implies another way of life, other needs, other orientations for human life. You will agree with me if I say that a socialism of traffic jams is an absurd contradiction in terms and that the socialist solution to this problem would not be to eliminate traffic jams by quadrupling the width of the Champs-Élysées. What are these cities, then? What do the people who fill them truly desire to do? How the devil does it happen that they 'prefer' to have their cars and spend hours each day in traffic jams, rather than something else?

To pose the problem of a new society is to pose the problem of an extraordinary cultural creation. And the question that is posed, and that I pose to *you*, is the following: Do we have, before us, some precursory and premonitory signs of this cultural creation? We who reject, at least in words, the capitalist way of life and what it involves – and it involves everything, absolutely everything that exists today – do we see coming to life around us another way of life that heralds, that prefigures something new, something that would give some *substantive* content to the idea of self-management, self-government, autonomy, self-institution? In other words, can the idea of self-government take on its full force, attain its full appeal, if it is not also borne by other desires, by other 'needs' that cannot be satisfied within the contemporary social system?

The rest of us, probably, we who are here, can no doubt think of such needs, we feel them, and perhaps for us they count for a lot. For example, I don't know, to be able to go when one wants to wander in the woods for two days. But the question does not lie there. At issue are not *our* wishes and needs, but those of the great mass of people. What is being asked is this: Is something of this sort, a rejection of the needs being nourished at present by the system and the appearance of other aims, beginning to dawn, to appear to be important to people living today?

And finally, what is being asked is this: Don't we effectively encounter on this point, on this line, the limit to political thought and action? Like all thought and all action, this kind, too, must have a limit – and must endeavour to recognize it. Is not this limit, on this point, the following: that neither we ourselves nor anyone else can decide on a way of life for others? We are saying, we can say, we have the right to say that we are against the contemporary way of life – which, once again, implies nearly everything that exists and not only the construction of such and such a nuclear power plant, which is only one of its implications to the nth degree. But to say that we are against such a way of life introduces, in a roundabout way, a tremendous problem, what can be called the problem of right in the most general sense, not simply formal rights, but right in terms of *content*. What is going to happen if others continue to want this other way of life? I intentionally take an extreme and absurd example, since it is close to the starting point of our meeting. Suppose there were people who not only want electricity but specifically want electricity of nuclear origin? You offer them all the electricity in the world, but they don't want it: they want it to be nuclear. All sorts of tastes exist in nature, after all. What would you say in such a case, what shall we say? We will say, I suppose, that there will be a majority decision (at least we hope it will be) that forbids people from satisfying their taste for nuclear-powered electricity. Again, this is an absurd example – and one easy to resolve. But you can easily imagine thousands of others that are neither absurd nor easy to resolve, for what is posed in this issue of one's way of life is ultimately the following question: How far can the 'right' (the legally and collectively assured effective possibility) of each individual, of each group, of each commune, of each nation to act as it wants, extend once we know – and we have always known it, but the ecology movement forcefully reminds us of it – that we are all embarked on the same planetary boat and that what each one of us does can have repercussions on everyone else? The question of self-government, of the autonomy of society, is *also* the question of the *self-limitation* of society. Self-limitation has two sides to it: limitation by the society of what it considers to be the unacceptable wishes, tendencies, acts, and so on of this or that portion of its members, but also self-limitation of society itself in its rules and regulations, the legislative authority it exercises over its members. The positive and substantive problem of right lies in the ability to conceive a society that is founded upon *substantive* universal rules (the prohibition of murder is not a 'formal' rule) and at the same time is compatible with the greatest possible diversity of cultural creation and therefore also of ways of life and systems of needs (I am not talking here about folklore for tourists). And this synthesis, this conciliation is not something we can just pull out of our heads. It will come out of society itself, or it will not come out at all.

To recognize this limit to political thought and to political action is to prohibit oneself from redoing the work of the political philosophers of the past, substituting oneself for society and deciding, as Plato and even Aristotle did, that some musical scale is good for the education of the young, whereas some other one is bad and ought therefore to be banned from the city. This in no way implies that we are to renounce our own thinking, our own action, our own point of view, or that we are to accept blindly and religiously all that society and history can produce. Again, it is ultimately an abstract philosophical point of view that led Marx to decide (for it was *he* who decided) that what history will decide or has already decided is good. (History almost decided for the Gulag.) We maintain our responsibility, our judgement, our thought, and our action, but we also recognize the limit thereto. And to recognize this limit is to give full content to what at bottom we are saying, namely, that first and foremost a revolutionary politics today entails recognition of people's autonomy, that is to say, the recognition of society itself as the ultimate source of institutional creation. [*Applause.*]

9

The Crisis of Western Societies (1982)*

Prefatory Paragraph (1995)

I have omitted from this chapter the first three pages of the 1982 French text, which dealt with the situations of Russia and the West in the early 1980s. Today, these pages would have no more than a historical interest, though in my view the substance of my remarks remains true. For forty years, a coalition of the richest countries on Earth trembled before the power of Russia, which had half the population and paltry productive resources in comparison with theirs and was hobbled by an ongoing and deep-seated internal crisis. Contrary to what we have been told, the matter was settled not by the 'victory of the West' but by an implosion of the bureaucratic regime that was the first to surrender to what has been called the 'process of competitive decadence' between the West and Russia. It is the Western side of this decadence that is examined in the pages that follow.

Just like the explanation of the relative strength of Russia, our understanding of the relative weakness of Western regimes refers us back to causes that are social and historical in nature. Behind the facts described are found factors that each person can observe for himself: the incoherency, the blindness, and the incompetency of the dominant strata in Western countries as well as of their political personnel. But these factors are, in turn, not the last word on the matter, either, for they still require analysis. How and why is it that the ruling strata of these countries, which dominated the planet for five centuries, are abruptly revealing themselves to be in a state of decrepitude that places them in a position of inferiority *vis-à-vis* the Russian stratocracy? How and why do the richest, most productive societies the Earth has ever borne find themselves mortally threatened by a regime that does not even succeed in nourishing and housing its own population decently? How and why has this fantastic wilful blindness of Western populations toward the monstrous virtual possibilities quite evidently contained in

* 'La Crise des sociétés occidentales' was originally published in *Politique Internationale*, 15 (Spring 1982), pp. 131–47. David J. Parent's translation, 'The Crisis of Western Societies', appeared in *Telos*, 53 (Fall 1982), pp. 17–28. [T/E: I have, on occasion, consulted the *Telos* translation while preparing this new translation of the version that now appears in *MI*, pp. 11–26, with a 1995 introduction.]

these facts ever come about and how and why does it continue to exist?

Behind these phenomena is hidden a process of decomposition of Western societies, all classes thrown together. Despite the various discourses produced over the past three-quarters of a century – decline of the West, civilizational crisis, a crisis of society – this decomposition remains to be understood and analysed. In the pages that follow I propose to furnish a few, fragmentary elements of this analysis.

The Decomposition of Leadership Mechanisms

The manifestations of this decomposition can easily be catalogued through listing the abiding failures of the policies being pursued (or, still more radically, in the absence of any policy at all) in key areas. If the Western societies continue to function, it is assuredly not the fault of their leaders but, rather, the result of the extraordinary resilience of capitalist and liberal institutions (characteristics totally unrecognized by the regime's critics and adversaries) and of the enormous reserves of all sorts (and not just wealth) previously accumulated.

I have already alluded [in the introduction not reprinted here] to the absence (and/or radical inadequacy) of Western policies with regard to the Third World and in matters of weaponry. I can do no more than mention briefly two other decisive areas where the same situation is manifest.

The first is the economy. Capitalism has been able to continue operating, as a social system, basically thanks to its 'economic' success: approximately full employment, expansion of production and consumption. This successful evolution has nothing 'fated' about it (any more, conversely, than does a 'collapse'). The enlargement of domestic markets – indispensable on a global scale, for the system taken as a whole – which is due to the long-term rise in real pay, was imposed upon capitalism via the struggles of labouring people. A century and a half was needed before this regime finally 'understood' that one of the conditions for its dynamic equilibrium was a rough equality between the pace of increase in consumption and the pace of the rise in productivity. Nevertheless, this single condition was not sufficient because of near-inevitable fluctuations in investment and the cycles of expansion/contraction these fluctuations engender. Finally, after the Second World War governments were forced to assume management of overall demand in order to maintain approximately full employment. This is how the long wave of expansion from 1945 to 1974 was able to develop with only minor fluctuations in the capitalist economy.

One does not have to be a rocket scientist [*grand clerc*] to foresee that a phase of uninterrupted full employment was going to create other problems for the capitalist economy.[1] Already manifest (and aggravated by other factors) in the Great Britain of the 1950s, these difficulties were generalized to embrace all industrialized capitalist countries during the second half of the 1960s, which led to an ongoing acceleration of price increases. The successive 'accidents' represented by the Vietnam War and its mode of (non)financing in the United States, the international monetary crisis of 1970, and finally the Yom Kippur War and the oil embargo led to an explosion of such problems.

For eight years now [since 1974], the Western governments have strikingly demonstrated their impotence in the face of this situation. The sole result of the policies being applied has been to shatter the expansion phase and provoke a grave and ongoing rise in unemployment, without for all that tangibly reducing price hikes. To this self-sustaining inflation has been added a self-sustaining stagnation, each reinforcing the other. The absolute mental pauperization of the ruling strata is expressed in the proclamations being made about the bankruptcy of Keynesianism (which amounts to saying that our failure to contain cancer proves Pasteur's bankruptcy), the fad of monetarism (a rehash of the old quantitative theory of money, a tautology whose transformation into an 'explanatory' theory has long been known to be fallacious), or new demonological inventions like 'supply-side economics'.

How long will the system be able to face up to the continuous rise in the number of unemployed and to the stagnation in the standard of living of those who work? The pockets of poverty and relative (and sometimes absolute) misery in the industrialized countries, whose importance has until now been attenuated by the general economic expansion and the accompanying expectations (Roosevelt's 'depressed third' had successively been transformed into a 'quarter' and then into a 'fifth'), are becoming permanent and growing pockets filled with people without resources or hope. Those elements that had, amid the dislocation of values and motivations, somehow or other succeeded in cementing society together (expectations of rises in living standards and non-null possibilities of 'advancement'/ ascending the skills and incomes ladder) are now in the process of disappearing. Finally, in growthless capitalist economies unemployment cannot but continue to rise a few percentage points for the active working population per annum (corresponding to the natural increase in population, and augmented by the effects of labour-saving investments).

[1995 addition: The capitalist economy's entry during the past two years into a phase of expansion does not basically modify the preceding analysis. This moderate expansion is taking place, moreover, on the basis of new evolutionary changes that are heavy with consequences. For going on fifteen years, the thoroughgoing mental regression of the ruling classes and of political personnel, which has led to the economy's out-and-out 'liberalization' (the heroic protagonists of which in France were the 'Socialists'), and the more and more effectively real globalization of production and trade have resulted in nation-States losing control over their economies. As was foreseen, these changes have been accompanied by an explosion of speculation which each day is transforming the capitalist economy more and more into a casino. Under these circumstances, even a return to Keynesian policies, which presuppose that the State has control over foreign trade and over monetary and credit policies, would hardly be meaningful. See, also, the Postscript to *DW* (1991).]

The second area (which I can do no more than mention here) is that of the complex of problems designated by the terms energy, nonrenewable resources, environment, and ecology. In part masked by the current phase of economic stagnation, these problems are worsening over time. Here again, policies are nonexistent, or disproportionate to the potential gravity of these questions.

Superficiality, incoherency, a sterility of ideas, and a versatility of attitudes are therefore, quite evidently, the characteristic traits of Western political leadership groups [*directions*]. But how is one to explain their generalization and their persistence?

Undoubtedly, the mechanisms of personnel recruitment and selection among politicians play an important part here. Even more than in the bureaucratic apparatuses that dominate other social activities, the dissociation between possibilities of promotion and one's ability to work efficiently is reaching a limit within political parties. 'Politics', in the prevailing sense of the term, has at all times been a bizarre profession. It has always demanded that one combine the faculties and specific abilities required, according to the type of regime under consideration, in order to 'attain power' and the faculties and capacities required in order to know how to utilize this power. In itself, the art of oratory, the recollection of people's faces, and the ability to make friends and gain partisan supporters and to divide and weaken opponents have nothing to do with legislative genius, administrative talent, leadership in war or in foreign policy, any more than, under an absolutist regime, the art of pleasing the monarch has any relation to the art of governing.

It is nevertheless clear that any regime whatsoever can survive only if, in one manner or another, its mechanisms and devices for the selection of political personnel succeed in combining, somehow or other, these two requirements. We do not have to examine here how Western parliamentary (or 'republican') regimes have in the past resolved the problem. The fact is that, if during a hundred or hundred and fifty years 'capable' or 'incapable' leaders have alternated in power, rare are the cases where governmental incapacity has constituted a decisive evolutionary factor.

The opposite is true today. One can find general sociological causes for this phenomenon: a vast movement of depoliticization and privatization, the disintegration of the control and correction devices that were operative under classical parliamentary regimes, a fragmentation of power among lobbies of all sorts. I shall return to this below. But two factors specific to the modern 'political' organization must be emphasized quite particularly here.

The first factor is connected with the bureaucratization of the political Apparatuses (i.e. parties). The absolute rule of the contemporary totalitarian bureaucratic party holds more or less for all parties: the capacity to rise within the Apparatus has, in principle, nothing to do with the capacity to manage the affairs this Apparatus is charged with overseeing.[2] The selection of the fittest is the selection of those fittest at getting themselves selected.

The second factor is specific to the liberal countries. The choice of the principal leaders in these countries, we know, boils down to designating the most 'sellable' personalities.[3] In the contemporary totalitarian bureaucratic Apparatus, the type of authority is neither rational nor traditional nor charismatic, to adopt Max Weber's distinctions. It is difficult, for example, to discern wherein lies Mr Brezhnev's charisma. This type of authority being new, we must find a name for it. Let us call it *inertial authority*. But in liberal (or soft) bureaucratic Apparatuses, such as Western political parties, we witness a return of a 'charismatic' type of authority: charisma is here, simply, the particular talent of a kind of actor who plays the role of 'chief', or 'statesman'. (This was obvious long before the election of Mr Reagan, who is, in this regard, only a symbol of this trend magnified to the point of becoming a platitude.) Of course, this trend has been provoked by the fantastic expansion of the power of the media and the servile attitudes they impose. As for the succeeding stages of the process, Kafka already described them wonderfully in 'Josephine the Singer'. Starting from the moment the tribe has agreed publicly that Mr X is a 'great leader', it feels vaguely compelled to continue playing its own role: that of applauding.

These accidental and inevitable leaders find themselves placed at the head of the vast bureaucratic Apparatus that is the modern State. This Apparatus is the bearer and organic producer of a proliferation of irrationality,[4] and among its agents the old *ethos* (that of the high-level official and the conscientious low-level civil servant) grows increasingly rare. And these leaders are faced with a society that is becoming less and less interested in 'politics' – that is to say, in its fate as society.

The Evanescence of Social and Political Conflict

For centuries one of the characteristics of Western countries was the very existence (practically unknown elsewhere in history) of a sociopolitical dynamic. This dynamic continually gave rise to currents and movements that aimed at taking charge of society, the proposed basic changes in its institutions and definite orientations for its social activities – both of them proceeding from, or connected with, systems of belief (or 'ideologies', etc.) and opposed, certainly, to contrary tendencies and currents.

Over the past thirty years, however, we have been witnessing the *de facto* disappearance of such movements. On the 'political' level in the strict sense, parties, completely transformed into bureaucratic machines, no longer obtain anything more than a purely electoral form of support from citizens they have become incapable of 'mobilizing' in any sense of the term. These same parties, dying of ideological starvation, either hark back to litanies no one believes in any longer (Socialists and Communists in Western Europe) or camouflage as 'new theories' and 'new policies' some superannuated superstitions (Thatcher, Reagan, etc.).

Unions today are no more than lobbies defending the sectoral or corporative interests of their members. Here we have something more than what I, following others, analysed as their bureaucratization. On the one hand, one can no longer speak of even a more or less 'unified' union bureaucracy pursuing its own objectives (little matter which ones); the sole goal of this bureaucracy is its self-preservation. On the other hand, it no longer suffices to state that these unions 'betray' the interests of their constituents or 'negotiate' them away while trying above all to avoid conflicts with capitalists and the managerial bureaucracy. When the occasion arises they really do enter into conflict, but they do so in order to defend corporative interests, defining the latter in such a way as to transform the various categories of labouring people into so many lobbies.

The great movements that shook Western societies for twenty years – youth, women, ethnic and cultural minorities, ecologists – have certainly had (and potentially retain) considerable importance from all standpoints, and it would be frivolous to maintain that their role has ended. But their present ebb leaves them in the state of groups that are not just minoritarian, but fragmented and sectoral, and incapable of articulating their goals and their means in universal terms that would be both objectively relevant and mobilizing.

These movements shook the Western world, they even changed it – but at the same time they rendered it even less viable. This is a striking but ultimately not a surprising phenomenon, for if these movements have been able to contest powerfully the established disorder, they have been neither able nor willing to assume a positive political project. The net result for now, following their ebb, has been the accentuated dislocation of existing social regimes without the appearance of new overall objectives or supports for such objectives. The extreme case is illustrated by the acts and the gestures of the movement of contestation occurring in Germany. Three hundred thousand demonstrators against the Pershing missiles, tens of thousands of demonstrators in Frankfurt against an airport extension, but not a single demonstrator against the instauration of military terror in Poland. People really do want to demonstrate against the biological dangers of war, or against the destruction of a forest, but they are totally uninterested in the political and human stakes connected with the current world situation.

Present-day 'political' society is more and more fragmented, more and more dominated by lobbies of all sorts, and this creates a general blockage of the system. Each of these lobbies is indeed capable of effectively hindering every policy that is contrary to its real or imaginary interests; none of them has any general policy; and, even if they had one, they would not have the ability to impose it.

Education, Culture, Values

The question is thus raised: To what extent do Western societies remain capable of fabricating the type of individual necessary for their continued functioning?

The first and the main workshop for the fabrication of conformal (true-to-form) individuals is the family. The crisis of the family today does not consist only, and not so much, in its statistical fragility. What is at issue is the crumbling and disintegration of the traditional roles – man, woman, parents, children – and the consequence thereof: the *formless disorientation* of new generations. What has been said above about the movements of the last twenty years also holds in this domain (although the process dates back, in the case of the family, much further, and already it is three-quarters of a century old in the most 'evolved' countries). The disintegration of traditional roles expresses individuals' push toward autonomy and contains the germs of emancipation. But the ambiguities of its effects have long been noted.[5] The more time passes, the more one is justified in asking oneself whether this process is expressed more by a blossoming forth of new ways of living than by sheer disorientation and anomie.

One can perfectly well conceive of a social system in which the role of the family would be granted less emphasis while other institutions of training and rearing would be granted greater emphasis. In fact, numerous archaic tribes, such as the Spartans, achieved such systems. Even in the West, starting in a certain era this role increasingly came to be fulfilled by the educational system on the one hand, the surrounding culture on the other – whether general or particular (local: village – or work-related: factory, etc.).

The Western educational system has entered, for going on twenty years now, a phase of accelerated disaggregation.[6] It is undergoing a crisis of contents: What is being transmitted, and what *ought to* be transmitted, and according to what criteria? In other words, there is a crisis of curricula and a crisis of that *in view of which* these curricula are defined. It is also experiencing a crisis of the educational relationship: the traditional type of undisputed authority has collapsed, and new types – the master–pal [*maître-copain*] type, for example – have succeeded neither in defining themselves, nor in affirming themselves, nor in extending themselves. But all these observations would still remain abstract if they were not related to the most flagrant and blinding manifestation of the crisis of the educational system, the one no one dares even mention. Neither pupils nor teachers [*maîtres*] are interested any longer in what happens in the school as such; education is no longer *cathected* as education by the participants. It has become a bread–winning chore for educators, a boring burden for pupils, for whom it has ceased to be the only extrafamilial opening and who are not of the age (nor in possession of the physical structure) required to see in it an instrumental investment (the profitability of which, moreover, is becoming more and more problematic). In general, it has become a question of obtaining a piece of paper (a diploma) that will allow one to exercise a profession (if one finds work).

It will be said that, at bottom, it never has been otherwise. Perhaps. The question does not lie there. Formerly – just a short while ago – all dimensions of the educational system (and the values to which they referred) were incontestable. They have ceased to be so.

Leaving a weakened family, frequenting – or not frequenting – a school lived as a chore, the young individual finds herself confronted by a society in which all 'values' and 'norms' are pretty much replaced by one's 'standard of living', one's general welfare, comfort, and consumerism. No religion, no 'political' ideas, no social solidarity with a local or work community or with 'schoolmates'. If she is not marginalized (drugs, delinquency, unstable 'personality'), there remains the royal road of privatization, which she may enrich by indulging in one or several personal crazes. We are living the society of *lobbies* and *hobbies*.

The classical educational system was nourished, 'from above', by the living culture of its time. This is still the case with today's educational system – to its detriment. Contemporary culture is becoming, more and more, a mixture of 'modernist' imposture and museum-ism.[7] Ages ago 'modernism' became old hat, began to be cultivated for its own sake, and now is often based on instances of mere plagiarism tolerated only because of the neo-illiteracy of the public (as is illustrated, for example, by the admiration the 'cultivated' Parisian public has in recent years shown for productions that repeat, in a diluted way, inventions from the 1920s). No longer is past culture alive within a living tradition, but instead it has become an object of knowledge for museum-goers or for tourists who seek out curiosities ruled by the latest fashions. On this level, and as banal as it may be, the label of 'Alexandrianism' is becoming applicable (and is even beginning to be insulting to Alexandria) – all the more so as, in the domain of reflection itself, history, commentary, and interpretation are progressively becoming substitutes for creative thought.

The Collapse of Society's Self-Representation

There can be no society that *is* not something for itself, that does not *represent* itself *as* being something – this being consequence, part, and dimension of the fact that it has to *posit itself as* 'something'.

This 'something' is neither a simple ordinary 'attribute' nor an 'assimilation' of itself to any natural or other kind of object. Society posits itself as being something, a singular and unique self, named (i.e. identifiable [*repérable*]) but otherwise 'indefinable' (in a physical or logical sense); in fact, it posits itself as a supranatural but sufficiently identified and detailed substance, re-presented by 'attributes' that are the currency of the imaginary significations that hold society – and *this* society – together. 'For itself', society is never a collection of perishable and substitutable individuals living on some territory or other, speaking this or that language, practising 'outwardly' some customs or other. On the contrary, these individuals 'belong' to this society *because* they participate in its social imaginary significations, its 'norms', 'values', 'myths', 'representations', 'projects', 'traditions', etc., and because they share (whether they know it or not) the will to be *of* this society and to make it be on a continuing basis.

All this evidently partakes of the institution of society in general – and of each society examined. Individuals are its sole 'real' or 'concrete' bearers, such as they have been fashioned, fabricated by its institutions – that is to say, by other individuals, who are themselves bearers of these institutions and of the correlative significations.

This boils down to saying that every individual has to be a bearer, 'sufficiently as to need/usage' [as Aristotle would say], of this *self-representation* of society. Here is a vital condition for the *psychical* existence of the singular individual. But, what is much more important in the present context, this is a vital condition for the existence of society itself. The individual's 'I am something' – Athenian citizen, Florentine merchant, or whatever – which covers over for this individual the psychical Abyss over which it lives, is identifiable and, above all, acquires meaning and content only by reference to the imaginary significations and the constitution of the (natural and social) world created by its society. The effort of the individual to be X or to remain X is, *ipso facto*, an effort to make be and to give life to the institution of its society. It is through individuals that society realizes itself and reflects itself through complementary parts that can be realized and be reflected (can reflect) only by realizing society and reflecting it (by reflecting). Now, the crisis of contemporary Western societies can be grasped most fully by reference to this dimension: the collapse of society's self-representation, the fact that these societies can no longer posit themselves *as* 'something' (other than in an external and descriptive way) – or that what they posit themselves as is crumbling apart, flattening out, and becoming empty and self-contradictory.

This is but another way of saying that there is a crisis of social imaginary significations, that these significations no longer provide individuals with the norms, values, bearings, and motivations that would permit them both to make society function and to maintain themselves, somehow or other, in a livable state of 'equilibrium' (the 'everyday unhappiness' Freud contrasted with 'neurotic misery').

In order to try to avoid all misunderstandings or sophisms (which in any case are inevitable), let me add that I am not saying that previous societies offered humans 'happiness' or 'truth' – nor am I saying that their illusions are more valid than the illusions, or absence of illusions, of contemporary society. I am speaking from a *factual* viewpoint: the conditions for an adequate socialization of human beings, the conditions for the fabrication of social individuals capable of making society function and of reproducing the society that made them be. It is from this standpoint that *valuing* (*Gelten*) social imaginary significations is a *sine qua non* condition for the existence of a society. Nor could it be said that the crisis of social imaginary significations in contemporary society implies, purely and simply, a dis-alienation, a disengagement, an opening of society onto the question of itself. For such an 'opening' to take place, this society would still need to be something other than a simple collection of externally uniformized and homogenized individuals. Society can open itself onto its own question only if, in and through this question, it still affirms itself as society; in other words, only if *sociality as such* (and, moreover, historicity as such) is positively affirmed and posited as what, in its *fact of being* (*Das-sein*), does not raise a question, even if it raises a question in its determinate being (*Was-sein*).

Now, what precisely is in crisis today is very much *society as such* for contemporary man.[8] We are paradoxically witnessing, at the same time as a (factual or external) hyper- or oversocialization of life and of human activities, a 'rejection' of social life, of others, of the necessity of the institution, etc. The war cry of early nineteenth-century Liberalism, 'The State is evil', has become today, 'Society is evil.' I am not speaking here of the confused pseudophilosophies of the age (which express, moreover, on this point, and without knowing it, a historical movement that far surpasses them), but, first of all, the increasingly typical 'subjective lived experience' of contemporary man. Here is the extreme outcome of what I have been analysing for twenty years as the privatization of modern societies, other aspects of which some recent analyses have illustrated under the heading of 'narcissism'. Let us leave aside this aspect, which may easily be open to dispute, and let us pose the question in brutal fashion: Does contemporary man *want* the society in which he lives? Does he *want* another one? Does he *want* society in general? The answer may be read in acts, and in the absence of acts. Contemporary man behaves as if existence in society were an odious chore, which only an unfortunate fate has prevented him from avoiding. (That this may be the most monstrously infantile of illusions obviously changes nothing as to the facts.) The typical contemporary man acts as if he were *submitting* to the society which, moreover (under the form of the State, or of others), he is ever ready to blame all evils on and to make – at the same time – demands for help from or to ask for 'solutions to his problems'. He no longer nourishes any project relating to his society – neither that of its transformation nor even that of its preservation/reproduction. He no longer accepts social relations; he feels caught in them and he reproduces them only in so far as he cannot do otherwise. The Athenians or the Romans *wanted themselves* (and quite explicitly) to be Athenians or Romans; the proletarians of yesteryear ceased to be mere matter for exploitation starting from the moment they *wanted themselves* to be something other than what the regime was forcing them to be – and this 'something else' was for them a collective project. Who could say, then, *what* contemporary man wants himself to be? Let us pass from individuals to the whole: present-day society does not want itself as society, it endures itself. And if it does not want itself, this is because it can neither sustain or forge for itself a representation of itself that it might affirm and give value to nor engender a project for social transformation to which it might adhere and for which it would want to struggle.

An analogous collapse affects the other dimension of society's self-representation: the dimension of historicity, society's definition of itself by reference to its own temporality, its relationship with its past and its future.

I shall limit myself here, as concerns the past, to underscoring the paradox in which contemporary society lives its relationship to 'tradition' and through which, in fact, it tends to abolish this tradition. Here we see the coexistence of a glut of information with a basic ignorance and sense of indifference. The collection of information and objects (never practised to such an extent before) goes hand in hand with the neutralization of the past: object of knowledge for some, a tourist's curio or a hobby for others, the past is a source and a root for no one. It is as if it were impossible to stand straight up in front of the past, as if one could not escape from the absurd dilemma of servile imitation vs denial for the sake of denial, except through indifference. Neither 'traditionalistic' nor creative and revolutionary (despite the tales being told on this score), the era lives its relationship to the past in a mode that itself certainly represents as such a historical novation: that of the most perfect exteriority.

For a long time, the era could think – and one could think – that this strange abolition of one's relationship to the past proceeded from a new and intense relationship society was instaurating with its future, its time-to-come [*à-venir*]. In singing the praises of the bourgeois era, Marx on the one hand, and the reality (a certain reality) of American society on the other, joined forces on this score. It was supposed that an intense preoccupation with the future, a concentration on transformational projects, and the changes modernity itself had wrought signified (and justified) a radical break with the past. 'History is bunk,' said Henry ford; the Model T, obviously, was not.

This was true, for a time (and it remains to be explored, which we cannot do here). It no longer is so. As concerns substantive culture, the era of great modern creativity reached its end around 1930.[9]

How, then, did this society see its future? Other societies before it had seen theirs as indefinite repetition or as expectation of the realization of a mythical Promise. Western society lived its future within the ideology of 'progress' – ever gradual (Liberalism) or leading, by a sudden leap, to a qualitative transformation (Marxism/Anarchism).

In fact, the two variants (mundane progressivism and 'revolutionary' progressivism) are inscribed within the same overall interpretation of History. For this interpretation, there was an 'inevitability of progress' (this was also Marx's explicit position and the one implicitly required for his work as a whole to have a meaning). There was also, at a deeper level, a need for History to 'make sense' (the role of the Judeo-Christian heritage has been decisive in this regard; but its position is also consubstantial with the dominant Greco-Western philosophical position, that of the centrality of *logos*, become Reason, and Divine Reason). Little matter that this 'meaning' should have been expressed in terms of 'progress' (and not as a 'test', for example), and ultimately coined in the hard cash of the accumulation of the forces of production and 'rising living standards'.[10]

This representation (criticized, as one knows, as early as the nineteenth century) was severely shaken by the First World War, by Fascism, Nazism, and the Second World War. The elimination of Nazism, the expansion phase in the capitalist economy, and decolonization gave it a new lease on life for an additional quarter-century. It also enjoyed another support, for it permitted Westerners to remain blind to the fact that the 'victory over Nazism' had been accompanied by the consolidation and considerable expansion of Communist totalitarianism. The inevitability of progress authorized one to treat Communism – or its most disagreeable traits – as a 'transitory' phenomenon and to await the inevitable 'liberalization' of the regime, which one was and remains ready to finance.

The final awakening was late, but it was brutal. The recently decolonized countries did not rush toward the delights of parliamentarianism. *Homo economicus* delayed making his appearance; and when he did appear, as in several Latin American countries, his appearance was made in order to condemn the great majority of his brothers to the most atrocious misery, under protection of military men and torturers educated *ad hoc* by 'the greatest democracy in the world'. The environmental crisis and the outlook of 'zero growth' came to undermine from without the representation of the future as indefinite exponential growth – before the oil shocks and an inflation rebellious to all remedies did so from within. Western man was long able to regard savages as ethnographic curiosities and previous phases of history as stages in the march toward today's happiness; he could ignore the fact that, without anything obliging them to do so, six hundred million Hindus continue to live under a rigid caste system [*régime*] (at the same time that they practise 'parliamentary politics' and construct a nuclear bomb). Nevertheless, the exploits of Idi Amin and Bokassa in Africa, the Islamic explosion in Iran, the tribulations of the Chinese regime, the Cambodian massacres, and the boat people of Vietnam finally shook his sense of certainty that he represents the realization of the innate goal [*finalité*] of humanity as a whole. If he had comprehended something of what is going on in Russia and in the countries Russia has enslaved, the Afghanistan invasion, and the instauration of a military dictatorship in 'socialist', 'People's' Poland, he would have had to account for the fact that the society in which he lives constitutes but a very improbable exception in the history of humanity as well as in its current geography.

This challenge to the apparent 'universalism' of Western culture could not help but have repercussions on the self-representation of this culture and the image it could make for itself of its future. The nature of these repercussions was not determined *a priori*. Western culture could have found in them the motivations that would have provided firmer support for the values to which it still claims adherence. But on the contrary, it seems to be losing, through this crisis, the self-confirmation it was seeking from without. Everything is happening as if, by a curious phenomenon of negative resonance, Western societies' discovery of their historical specificity were succeeding in undermining their adherence to what they were able and willing – and still more, their will to know what they want in the future – to be.

Notes

1 Michal Kalecki had foreseen it in a famous article published in 1943. For my part, I had analysed the problem, using the example of Great Britain, in *MCR III* (1961), in *PSW 2*, pp. 283–5; for the problem in general, and the inflation of the years 1960–70, see 'Author's Introduction to the 1974 English Edition' of *MCR*, in *PSW 2*, pp. 326–43.

2 *DG*, pp. 242–7 and the texts cited in ibid., p. 245.

3 *MCR*, in *PSW 2*, pp. 273–8.

4 See the texts cited in note 2.

5 *CMS* (1965).

6 *SY* (1963). [T/E: There may be a pun here in the contrast between the current 'disaggregation' of the educational system and the *concours d'agrégation*, France's traditional
   teacher's certificate examination.]

7 *STCC* (1979). [T/E: See also *CCS* (1986) and *RA* (1989).]

8 For Russian society, see the fourth chapter of *DG*, in particular pp. 251–64.

9 *STCC*. [T/E: See also *CCS* (1986).]

10 *RRD* (1974).

10

The Greek *Polis* and the Creation of Democracy (1983)*

How can we orient ourselves in history and politics? How can we judge and choose? It is from this political interest that I start – and in this spirit that I ask: In ancient Greek democracy is there anything of political relevance for us?

In a sense, Greece is obviously a presupposition of this discussion. The reasoned investigation of what is right and wrong, of the very principles that are the basis of our ever being able to say, beyond trivialities and traditional preconceptions, that something is right or wrong, arises for the first time in Greece. Our political questioning is, *ipso facto*, a continuation of the Greek position, although of course we have transcended it in many important respects and are still trying to transcend it.

Modern discussions of Greece have been plagued by two opposite and symmetrical – thus, in a sense, equivalent – preconceptions. The first, and most frequently encountered over the last four or five centuries, is Greece as eternal model, prototype, or paradigm.[1] (One contemporary outlook merely inverts this preconception: Greece as antimodel, as negative model.) The second and more recent preconception involves the complete 'sociologization' or 'ethnologization' of the examination of Greece. Thus, the differences between the Greeks, the Nambikwara, and the Bamileke are only descriptive. No doubt, this second attitude is formally correct. Not only, needless to say, is there not nor could there be any difference in 'human value', 'worthiness', or 'dignity' between different peoples and cultures, but

* The principal ideas found in this article were presented for the first time during a lecture given on 29 October 1979, to a seminar at the Max Planck Institute in Starnberg led by Jürgen Habermas; Johann Arnason, Ernst Tugendhat, and Albrecht Wellmer were among the main participants. Since then, these ideas have been at the centre of my work in my seminar at the École des Hautes Études en Sciences Sociales in Paris, beginning in 1980, and they have provided the substance for a course in August 1982 at the University of São Paulo, a seminar in April 1985 at the University of Rio Grande do Sul (Porto Alegre), and several other presentations. The text published here is that of a lecture read on 15 April 1982, in New York, during one of the Hannah Arendt Memorial Symposia in Political Philosophy organized by the New School for Social Research which dealt with 'The Origins of Our Institutions'. The original English version was published in the *Graduate Faculty Philosophy Journal* of the New School, 9:2 (Fall 1983), pp. 79–115, and reprinted in *PPA*, pp. 81–123. A French translation appeared in *DH*, pp. 261–306. [T/E: The present abridged reprint omits, for reasons of space, a middle section dealing with Kant's *Critique of Judgment*.]

neither could there be any objection to applying to the Greek world the methods – if there be any – applied to the Aranda or to the Babylonians.

The second approach, however, misses a minute and decisive point. The reasoned investigation of other cultures and the reflection upon them do not begin within the Aranda or the Babylonian cultures. Indeed, one could show that neither could have begun with them. Before Greece and outside the Greco-Western tradition, societies are instituted on a principle of strict closure: our view of the world is the only meaningful one, the 'others' are bizarre, inferior, perverse, evil, or unfaithful. As Hannah Arendt has said, impartiality enters this world with Homer.[2] This is not just 'affective' impartiality. It is the impartiality of knowledge and understanding. The keen interest in the other starts with the Greeks. This interest is but another side of the critical examination and interrogation of their own institutions. That is to say, it is a component of the democratic and philosophical movement created by the Greeks.

That the ethnologist, the historian, or the philosopher is in a position to reflect upon societies other than his own and, indeed, even upon his own society becomes a possibility and a reality only within this particular historical tradition – the Greco-Western tradition. Now, on one hand, this activity may have no theoretical privilege over any other – say, poison divination by the Azanda. Then, for example, the psychoanalyst is but a Western variety of shaman, as Lévi-Strauss has written, and Lévi-Strauss himself, along with the entire society of ethnologists, is but the local variety of sorcerer within this particular group of tribes exorcising, if you will, the alien tribes. The only difference is that, rather than fumigating them out of existence, they structuralize them out of existence. Or on the other hand, we may postulate or posit a qualitative difference between our theorizing about other societies and about 'savages' and attach to this difference a specific, limited but firm, positive valuation.[3] Then, a philosophical discussion starts. *Then*, and not before. To start a philosophical discussion is to imply that one has already affirmed that for oneself unrestricted thinking is the way of entering upon problems and tasks. Thus, since we know that this attitude is by no means universal but extremely exceptional in the history of human societies,[4] we have to ask how, under what conditions, in which ways, human society was capable, in one particular case, of breaking the closure by virtue of which it generally exists?

In this sense, though describing and analysing Greece is equivalent to describing and analysing any other randomly chosen culture, thinking and reflecting about Greece is not and cannot be. For in this latter case, we are reflecting and thinking about the social and historical conditions of thought itself – at least, thought as we know and practise it. One has to eliminate these twin attitudes: there was, once upon a time, a society which remains for us the inaccessible model: *or*, history is essentially flat, there are no significant differences between cultures other than descriptive ones. Greece is the social-historical *locus* where democracy and philosophy are created; thus, of course, it is our own origin. In so far as the meaning and the potency of this creation are not exhausted – and I firmly believe that they are not – Greece is for us a *germ*, neither a 'model', nor one specimen among others, but a germ.

History is creation: the creation of total forms of human life. Social-historical forms are not 'determined' by natural or historical 'laws'. Society is self-creation. 'That which' creates society and history is the instituting society, as opposed to the instituted society. The instituting society is the social imaginary in the radical sense.

The self-institution of society is the creation of a human world: of 'things', 'reality', language, norms, values, ways of life and death, objects for which we live and objects for which we die – and of course, first and foremost, the creation of the human individual in which the institution of society is massively embedded.

Within this wholesale creation of society, each particular, historically given institution represents a particular creation. Creation, as I use the term, means the positing of a new *eidos*, a new essence, a new form in the full and strong sense: new determinations, new norms, new laws. The Chinese, the classical Hebrew, the ancient Greek, or the modern capitalist institution of society each means the positing of different determinations and laws, not just 'juridical' laws but obligatory ways of perceiving and conceiving the social and 'physical' world and acting within it. Within, and by virtue of, this over-all institution of society emerge specific creations: science, for example, as we know and conceive it, is a particular creation of the Greco-Western world.

There follows a series of crucial questions, about which I can only sketch some reflections here.

First, how can we understand previous or 'foreign' institutions of society? (For that matter, how and in what sense can we say that we understand our own society?) We do not have, in the social-historical domain, 'explanation' in the same sense the physical sciences do. Any 'explanation' of this sort is either trivial or fragmentary and conditional. The innumerable regularities of social life – without which, of course, this life would not exist – are what they are because the institution of this particular society has posited this particular complex of rules, laws, meanings, values, tools, motivations, etc. And this institution is nothing but the socially sanctioned (sanctioned formally or informally) magma of social imaginary significations created by this particular society. Thus, to understand a society means, first and fore-most, to penetrate or reappropriate the social imaginary significations which hold this society together. Is this at all possible? We have to take into account two facts here.

The first, indisputable fact is that *almost all* of the people in a given society do not and cannot understand a 'foreign' society. (I am not speaking, of course, about trivial obstacles.) This points to what I have called the cognitive closure of the institution. The second (which can be and is disputed, but to which I nevertheless hold) is that under some very specific social, historical, and personal preconditions, some people can understand something about a foreign society. This points to some sort of 'potential universality' in whatever is human for humans. Contrary to inherited commonplaces, the root of this universality is not human 'rationality' (if 'rationality' were at stake here nobody would ever have understood anything about the Hebrew God, or, for that matter, about any religion whatsoever) but creative imagination as the core component of nontrivial thinking.[5] Whatever has been imagined strongly enough to shape behaviour, speech, or objects can, in principle, be reimagined (rerepresented, *wiedervorgestellt*) by somebody else.

Two significant polarities have to be stressed here.

In this social-historical understanding, there is a distinction between 'true' and 'false' – and not just in the trivial sense. One can talk sense about 'foreign' societies, and one can talk nonsense – of which there is no dearth of examples. The 'true' cannot be subjected in this case (as, more generally, it never can in matters of thought) to the banal 'verification' or 'falsification' procedures which are currently (platitudinously and wrongly) considered to demarcate 'science' from 'nonscience'. For instance, Burckhardt's realization of the importance of the agonistic element in the Greek world (which looms so large in Hannah Arendt's thinking about Greece) is *true* – but not in the same sense as $E = mc^2$ is true. What does 'true' mean in this former case? That the idea of the agonistic brings together an indefinite class of social and historical phenomena in Greece that would otherwise remain unconnected – not necessarily unconnected in their 'causal' or 'structural' relation but unconnected in their *meaning*; and that its claim to possess a 'real' or 'actual' referent (i.e. that is not just a delusion, or convenient fiction, or even an *Idealtypus*, an observer's limiting rational construction[6]) can be discussed in a fecund way, though this discussion may be and, in the decisive cases, *has to* be interminable. In brief, it *elucidates* and initiates a process of elucidation.

The situation is different, at first glance, when we are speaking about our own history or tradition, about societies which though 'other' are not 'foreign' since there is a strong genealogical connection between their imaginary significations and ours, since we still somehow 'share' the same world, since there is still some active, intrinsic relationship between their institutions and our own. It would seem that since we succeed this creation but fall within the same concatenation, since we find ourselves, so to speak, downstream, since we live, at least partly, within the mental framework and the universe of beings which they have posited, our understanding of our 'ancestral' societies would present no mystery. But of course, other problems arise. This 'common belonging' is by necessity partly illusory, but often tends to be taken as fully real. Projective 'value judgements' become important and interfere with understanding. The proper distance between ourselves and 'our own past' is very difficult to establish; the attitudes toward Greece cited earlier are examples. The illusion of the *Selbstverständlichkeit* can be catastrophic: thus, people today consider democracy or rational inquiry to go without saying, naively projecting onto the whole of history the exceptional situation of their own society, and are unable to understand what democracy or rational inquiry could mean for the society where they were created for the first time.

The second question is: If history is creation, how can we judge and choose? It is to be stressed that this question would not arise if history were simply and strictly a causal concatenation, or if it did contain its *phusis* and *telos*. It is precisely because history is creation that the question of judging and choosing emerges as a radical, nontrivial question.

The radicality of the question stems from the fact that, despite a widespread naive illusion, there is not and cannot be a rigorous and ultimate foundation of anything – not of knowledge itself, not even of mathematics. One should remember that this foundational illusion has never been shared by the great philosophers: not by Plato, not by Aristotle, not by Kant, not by Hegel. The first outstanding philosopher who was under the delusion of 'foundation' was Descartes, and this is one of the respects in which his influence has been catastrophic. Since Plato, it has been known that every demonstration presupposes something which is not demonstrable. Here I want to stress one other aspect of the question: the judgements and choices we make belong to the history of the society in which we live and depend upon it. I do not mean that they depend upon particular social-historical 'contents' (though this is also true). I mean that the sheer fact of judging and choosing in a nontrivial sense presupposes not only that we belong to that particular history, to that particular tradition where judging and choosing first become effectively possible, but that we have already, before any judgement and choice of 'contents', judged affirmatively and chosen this history and this tradition in this respect. For, this activity of judging and choosing, and the very idea of it, is a Greco-Western activity and idea – it has been created within this world and nowhere else. The idea would not and could not occur to a Hindu, to a classical Hebrew, to a true Christian or to a Muslim. Classical Hebrews have nothing to choose. They have been given the truth and the Law once and for all by God, and if they started judging and choosing about that they would no longer be Hebrew. Likewise, true Christians have nothing to judge or choose: they have to believe and to love.

For, it is written: *Judge not, that ye be not judged* (Matt. 7: 1). Conversely, Greco-Westerners ('Europeans') who produce rational arguments for rejecting the European tradition confirm *eo ipso* this tradition and that they belong to it.

But neither does this tradition offer us repose. For, while it has produced democracy and philosophy, both the American and the French Revolutions, the Paris Commune and the Hungarian Workers' Councils, the Parthenon and *Macbeth*, it has produced as well the massacre of the Melians by the Athenians, the Inquisition, Auschwitz, the Gulag, and the H-bomb. It created reason, freedom, and beauty – and it also created massive monstrosity. No animal species could ever create Auschwitz or the Gulag; to create that you must be a human being. These extreme possibilities of humanity in the field of the monstrous have been realized *par excellence* in our own tradition. The problem of judging and choosing thus also arises within this tradition, which we cannot validate for a moment *en bloc*. And of course, it does not arise as a simple intellectual possibility. The very history of the Greco-Western world can be viewed as the history of the struggle between autonomy and heteronomy. [. . .]

Judging and choosing, in a radical sense, were created in Greece, and this is one of the meanings of the Greek creation of politics and philosophy. By politics I do not mean court intrigues or fighting among social groups over interest or position (both of which existed elsewhere), but a collective activity whose object is the institution of society as such. In Greece we have the first instance of a community explicitly deliberating about its laws and changing those laws.[7] Elsewhere laws are inherited from the ancestors or given by gods or by the One True God; but they are not posited as created by men after a collective confrontation and discussion about right and wrong law. This position leads to other questions, which also originated in Greece: not only 'Is *this* law right or wrong' but 'What is it for a law to be right or wrong, that is, what is justice?' Just as in Greek political activity the existing institution of society is called into question and altered for the first time, similarly Greece is the first society where we find the explicit questioning of the instituted collective representation of the world – that is, where we find philosophy. Further, just as political activity in Greece leads to the question not merely of whether this particular law is right or wrong, just or unjust, but of what justice is in general, so philosophical interrogation leads rapidly to the question not only of whether this or that representation of the world is true, but of what truth is. Both questions are genuine questions – that is, they must remain open forever.

The creation of democracy and philosophy and the link between them has its essential precondition in the Greek vision of the world and human life, the nucleus of the Greek imaginary. This can perhaps best be clarified by the three questions in which Kant summarizes the interests of man. About the first two: What can I know? What ought I to do? an endless discussion begins in Greece, and there is no 'Greek answer' to them. But to the third question: What am I allowed to hope? there is a definite and clear Greek answer, and this is a massive and resounding *nothing*. And evidently it is the true answer. 'Hope' is not to be taken here in the everyday trivial sense – that the sun will again shine tomorrow, or that a child will be born alive. The hope to which Kant refers is the hope of the Christian or religious tradition, the hope corresponding to that central human wish and delusion that there be some essential correspondence, some consonance, some *adequatio* between our desires and decisions, on the one hand, and the world, the nature of being, on the other. Hope is the ontological, cosmological, and ethical assumption that the world is not just something out there, but *cosmos* in the archaic and proper sense, a total order which includes us, our wishes, and our strivings as its organic and central components. The philosophical translation of this assumption is that being is ultimately good. As is well known, the first one who dared to proclaim this philosophical monstrosity clearly was Plato – after the classical period had ended. This remained the fundamental tenet of theological philosophy in Kant, of course, but in Marx as well. The Greek view is expressed as early as the myth of Pandora. For Hesiod hope is forever imprisoned in Pandora's box. In preclassical and classical Greek religion, there is no hope for an afterlife: either there is no afterlife, or if there is one, it is worse than the worst life on earth – as Achilles reveals to Odysseus in the Land of the Dead. Having nothing to hope for from an afterlife or from a caring and benevolent God, man is liberated for action and thought in *this* world.

This is intimately linked with the fundamental Greek idea of *chaos*. For Hesiod, in the beginning there is chaos. In the proper, initial sense 'chaos' in Greek means void, nothingness. It is out of the total void that the world emerges.[8] But already in Hesiod, the world is also chaos in the sense that there is no complete order in it, that it is not subject to meaningful laws. First there is total disorder, and then order, *cosmos*, is created. But at the 'roots' of the world, beyond the familiar landscape, chaos always reigns supreme. The order of the world has no 'meaning' for man: it posits the blind necessity of genesis and birth, on one hand, of corruption and catastrophe – death of the forms – on the other. In Anaximander, the first philosopher for whom we possess reliable testimony, the 'element' of being is the *apeiron*, the indeterminate, indefinite – another way of thinking chaos. Form, the particularized and determinate existence of the various beings, is *adikia*, injustice – one may well call it *hubris*. That is why the particular beings have to render justice to one another and pay compensation for their injustice through their decay and disappearance.[9] There is a strong though implicit connection between the two pairs of opposite terms, *chaos/cosmos* and *hubris/dikē*. In a sense the latter is the transposition of the former into the human domain.

This vision conditions, so to speak, the creation of philosophy. Philosophy, as the Greeks created and practised it, is possible because the world is not fully ordered. If it were, there would not be any philosophy, but only one, final system of knowledge. And if the world were sheer chaos, there would be no possibility of thinking at all. But this vision of the world also conditions the creation of politics. If the human world were fully ordered, either externally or through its own 'spontaneous operation', if human laws were given by God or by nature or by the 'nature of society' or by the laws of history', then there would be no room for political thinking and no field for political action and no sense in asking what the proper law is or what justice is (cf. Hayek). But furthermore, if human beings could not create some order for themselves by positing laws, then again there would be no possibility of political, instituting action. If a full and certain knowledge (*epistēmē*) of the human domain were possible, politics would immediately come to an end, and democracy would be both impossible and absurd: democracy implies that all citizens have the possibility of attaining a correct *doxa* and that nobody posseses an *epistēmē* of things political.

I think it is important to stress these connections because a great many of the difficulties of modern political thinking are related to the persisting dominant influence of theological (that is, Platonic) philosophy. The operative postulate that there is a total and 'rational' (and therefore 'meaningful') order in the world, along with the necessary implication that there is an order of human affairs linked to the order of the world – what one could call unitary ontology – has plagued political philosophy from Plato through modern Liberalism and Marxism. The postulate conceals the fundamental fact that human history is creation – without which there would be no genuine question of judging and choosing, either 'objectively' or 'subjectively'. By the same token, it conceals or eliminates the question of responsibility. Unitary ontology, in whatever disguise, is essentially linked to heteronomy. The emergence of autonomy in Greece was conditioned by the nonunitary Greek view of the world that is expressed from the beginning in the Greek 'myths'.

A curious but inevitable consequence of the 'model/antimodel' mentality employed when examining Greece, and in particular Greek political institutions, is that these are taken, so to speak, 'statically', as if there were *one* 'constitution', with its various 'articles' fixed once for all, that could and must be 'judged' or 'evaluated' as such. This is an approach for people who seek recipes – whose number, indeed, does not seem to be on the decrease. But, of course, what is important in ancient Greek political life – the *germ* – is the *historical instituting process*: the activity and struggle around the change of the institutions, the explicit (even if partial) self-institution of the *polis* as a permanent process. This process goes on for almost four centuries. The annual election of the *thesmothetai* in Athens is established in 683/2 BCE, and it is probably around the same time that the citizens in Sparta (9,000 of them) are instated as *homoioi* ('similar', i.e. equals) and the rule of *nomos* (law) affirmed. The widening of democracy in Athens continues well into the fourth century. The *poleis* – at any rate Athens, about which our information is most complete – do not stop questioning their respective institutions; the *dēmos* goes on modifying the rules under which it lives. This is, of course, inseparable from the hectic pace of creation during this period in all fields beyond the strictly political one.

This movement is a movement of explicit self-institution. The cardinal meaning of explicit self-institution is autonomy: we posit our own laws. Of all the questions arising out of this movement, I will briefly survey three: 'Who' is the 'subject' of this autonomy? What are the limits of his action? What is the 'object' of autonomous self-institution?[10]

The community of citizens – the *dēmos* – proclaims that it is absolutely sovereign (*autonomos, autodikos, autotelēs*, self-legislating, self-judging, self-governing, in Thucydides' words). It also affirms the political equality (equal sharing of activity and power) of all free men. This is the self-position, self-definition, of the political body, which contains an element of arbitrariness – and always will. *Who* posits the *Grundnorm* – in Kelsen's terminology, the norm ruling the positing of norms – is a *fact*. For the Greeks, this 'who' is the body of adult, male, free citizens (which means, in principle, [those men born] of other citizens, though naturalization is known and practised). Of course, the exclusion of women, foreigners, and slaves from citizenship is a limitation we do not accept. This limitation was never lifted in practice in ancient Greece (at the level of ideas, things are less simple, but I will not discuss this aspect here). But indulging for a moment in the absurd 'comparative merits' game, let us remember that slavery was present in the United States until 1865 and in Brazil until the end of the nineteenth century. Further, in most 'democratic' countries, voting rights were granted to women only after the Second World War; no country today grants political rights to foreigners, and in most cases naturalization of resident foreigners is by no means automatic (a quarter of the resident population of very 'democratic' Switzerland are *metoikoi*).

Equality of the citizens is of course equality in respect of the law (*isonomia*), but it is essentially much more than that. It is not the granting of equal passive 'rights', but active general participation in public affairs. This participation is not left to chance, but actively promoted both through formal rules and through the general *ethos* of the *polis*. According to Athenian law, a citizen who will not take sides while the city is in civil strife becomes *atimos* – deprived of political rights.[11]

Participation materializes in the *ekklēsia*, the Assembly of the people, which is the acting sovereign body. All citizens have the right to speak (*isēgoria*), their votes carry the same weight (*isopsēphia*), and they are under a moral obligation to speak their minds (*parrhēsia*). Participation also materializes in the courts. There are no professional judges; virtually all courts are juries with their jurors chosen by lot.

The *ekklēsia*, assisted by the *boulē* (council), legislates and governs. This is *direct democracy*. Three of its aspects deserve further comment.

1   *The people versus 'representatives'*. Direct democracy has been rediscovered or reinvented in modern history every time a political collectivity has entered a process of radical self-constitution and self-activity: town meetings during the American Revolution, *sections* during the French Revolution, the Paris Commune, the workers' councils, or the soviets in their original form. Hannah Arendt has repeatedly stressed the importance of these forms. In all these cases, the sovereign body is the totality of those concerned; whenever delegation is inevitable, delegates are not just elected but subject to permanent recall. One should remember that for classical political philosophy, the notion of 'representation' is unknown. For Herodotus as well as for Aristotle, democracy is the power of the *dēmos*, unmitigated in matters of legislation, and the designation of magistrates (not 'representatives'!) by sortition [lot] or rotation. Scholars merely repeat today that Aristotle's preferred constitution, what he calls *politeia*, is a mixture of democracy and aristocracy, and forget to add that for Aristotle the 'aristocratic' element in this *politeia* is the *election* of the magistrates – for, Aristotle clearly and repeatedly defines election as an aristocratic principle. This is also clear for Montesquieu and Rousseau. It is Rousseau, not Marx or Lenin, who writes that Englishmen believe that they are free because they elect their Parliament, but in reality are free only one day every five years. When Rousseau says that democracy is a regime too perfect for men, suitable only for a people of gods, what he means by democracy is the identity of the *souverain* and the *prince* – that is, there are no *magistrates*. Serious modern liberals – in contradistinction to contemporary 'political philosophers' – knew all this perfectly well. Benjamin Constant did not glorify elections and 'representation' as such; he defended them as lesser evils on the grounds that democracy was impossible in modern nations because of their size *and* because people were not interested in public affairs. Whatever the value of these arguments, they are based upon the explicit recognition that representation is a principle alien to democracy. This hardly bears discussion. Once permanent 'representatives' are present, political authority, activity, and initiative are expropriated from the body of citizens and transferred to the restricted body of 'representatives', who also use it to consolidate their position and create the conditions whereby the next 'election' becomes biased in many ways.

2   *The people versus the 'experts'*. Linked to the principle of direct democracy is the Greek view of 'experts'. Not only legislative decisions but important political ones – on matters of *government* – are made by the *ekklēsia* after it has listened to various speakers, possibly including those who claim some specific knowledge about the affairs at hand. There are not and cannot be 'experts' on political affairs. Political expertise – or political 'wisdom' – belongs to the political community, for expertise, *technē*, in the strict sense is always related to a specific, 'technical' occupation and is, of course, recognized in its proper field. Thus, Plato says in the *Protagoras*, the Athenians will listen to technicians, when the building of proper walls or ships is discussed, but will listen to anybody when it comes to matters of politics. (The popular courts embody the same idea in the domain of justice.) War is, of course, a specific field entailing a proper *technē*, and thus the war chiefs, the *stratēgoi*, are elected – as are the technicians in other fields charged by the *polis* with a particular task. So Athens was, after all, a *politeia* in Aristotle's sense since some (and very important) magistrates were elected.

Now, the *election* of the experts entails another principle central to the Greek view, clearly formulated and accepted not only by Aristotle but, despite its massive democratic implications, even by that archenemy of democracy, Plato. The proper judge of the expert is not another expert, but the *user*: the warrior and not the blacksmith for the sword, the horseman and not the saddler for the saddle. And evidently, for all public (common) affairs, the user, and thus the best judge, is the *polis*. From the results – the Acropolis, or the tragedy prizes – the judgement of this user appears to have been quite sound.

One can hardly overemphasize the contrast between this view and the modern one. The dominant idea that experts can be judged only by other experts is one of the conditions for the expansion and the growing irresponsibility of the modern hierarchical-bureaucratic apparatus. The prevalent idea that there exist 'experts' in politics, that is, specialists of the universal and technicians of the totality, makes a mockery of the idea of democracy: the power of the politicians is justified by the 'expertise' they would alone possess, and the, inexpert by definition, populace is called upon periodically to pass judgement on these 'experts'. It also – given the emptiness of the notion of a specialization in the universal – contains the seeds of the growing divorce between the capacity to attain power and the capacity to govern – which plagues Western societies more and more.

3   *The community versus the 'State'*. The Greek polis is *not* a 'State' in the modern sense. The very term 'State' does not exist in ancient Greek (characteristically, modern Greeks had to invent a word, and they used the ancient *kratos*, which means 'sheer force'). *Politeia* (e.g., in the title of Plato's work) does not mean *der Staat* as in the standard German translation (the

Latin *respublica* is less opposed to the meaning of *politeia*). It means both the political institution/constitution and the way people go about common affairs. It is a scandal of modern philology that the title of Aristotle's treatise, *Athēnaiōn Politeia*, is everywhere translated as '*The Constitution of Athens*', both a straightforward linguistic error and the inexplicable sign of ignorance or incomprehension on the part of very erudite men. Aristotle wrote *The Constitution of the Athenians*. Thucydides is perfectly explicit about this: *Andres gar polis*, 'for the *polis* is the men'. For example, before the Battle of Salamis, when Themistocles has to resort to a last-ditch argument to impose his tactics, he threatens the other allied chiefs that the Athenians will take their families and their fleet and found anew their city in the West. This notwithstanding the fact that for the Athenians – even more than for the other Greeks – their land was sacred and they took pride in their claim to autochthony.

The idea of a 'State' as an institution distinct and separated from the body of citizens would not have been understandable to a Greek. Of course, the political community exists at a level which is not identical with the concrete, 'empirical' reality of so many thousands of people assembled in a given place at a given time. The political community of the Athenians, the *polis*, has an existence of its own: for example, treaties are honoured irrespective of their age, responsibility for past acts is accepted, etc. But the distinction is not between a 'State' and a 'population'; it is between the continuous corporate body of perennial and impersonal Athenians and the living and breathing ones.

No 'State' and no 'State apparatus'. There is, of course, in ancient Athens a technical-administrative mechanism, but it does not possess any political function. Characteristically, this administration, up to and including its higher echelons – police, keepers of the public archives, public finance – is composed of slaves (possibly Treasury Secretary Donald Regan and certainly Federal Reserve Chairman Paul Volcker would have been slaves in Athens). These slaves were supervised by citizen magistrates usually drawn by lot. 'Permanent bureaucracy', the task of *execution* in the strictest sense, is left to the slaves.

The designation of magistrates through lot or rotation in most cases ensures participation by a great number of citizens in official tasks – and knowledge of those tasks. That the *ekklēsia* decides all important governmental matters ensures the control of the political body over elected magistrates, as does the fact that they are subject to what amounts in practice to the possibility of recall at any time: conviction in a judicial procedure entails, *inter alia*, that they lose their office. Of course all magistrates are responsible for their performance in office as a matter of routine (*euthuna*); accounts are given, in the classical period, to the *boulē*.

In a sense, the unity and very existence of the political body are 'prepolitical', at least in so far as explicit political self-institution is concerned. The community 'receives itself', as it were, from its own past, with all that this past entails. (In part, this is what the moderns call the question of 'civil society' versus the 'State'.) Elements of this given may be politically irrelevant or nontransformable. But *de jure*, 'civil society' is itself an object of instituting political action. This is strikingly exemplified by some aspects of Cleisthenes' reform in Athens (506 BCE). The traditional division of the population among tribes is superseded by a redivision having two main objects. First, the number of tribes is changed. The traditional (Ionian) four *phulai* become ten, each subdivided into three *trittyes*, all sharing equally in all magistratures through rotation (which entails what is in fact the creation of a new, 'political' year and calendar). Second, each tribe is formed by a balanced composition of agricultural, maritime, and urban people. Thus, the tribes – which henceforth have their 'headquarters' in the city of Athens – become neutral as to territorial or professional particularities; they are clearly political units.

What we have here is the creation of a properly political social space, founded on social (economic) and geographical elements, but not *determined* by these. No phantasm of 'homogeneity' here: an articulation of the citizen body within a political perspective is created and superimposed on the 'prepolitical' articulations without crushing them. This articulation obeys strictly political imperatives: equality of power-sharing on the one hand, unity of the body politic (as against 'particular interests') on the other.

The same spirit is exemplified by a most striking Athenian disposition (Aristotle *Politics* 1330a20): when the *ekklēsia* deliberates on matters entailing the possibility of a conflict such as a war with a neighbouring *polis*, the inhabitants of the frontier zone are excluded from the vote. For, they could not vote without their particular interests overwhelming their motives, while the decision must be made on general grounds only.

This again shows a conception of politics diametrically opposed to the modern mentality of the defence and assertion of 'interests'. Interests have, as far as possible, to be kept at bay when political decisions are made. (Imagine the following disposition in the US Constitution: 'Whenever questions pertaining to agriculture are to be decided, senators and representatives from predominantly agricultural States cannot participate in the vote'.) At this point one may comment on the ambiguity of Hannah Arendt's position concerning what she calls 'the social'. She rightly saw that politics is destroyed when it becomes a mask for the defence and assertion of 'interests'. The political space is then hopelessly fragmented. But *if* society is, in reality, strongly divided along conflicting 'interests' – as it is today – insistence on the autonomy of politics becomes gratuitous. The answer, then, is not to ignore the 'social', but to change it so that the conflict of 'social' – that is, economic – interests ceases to be the dominant factor in shaping political attitudes. If this is not done, the present situation among Western societies results: the decomposition of the body politic and its fragmentation into lobbies. In this case, as the 'algebraic sum' of opposing interests is very often zero, the consequence is political impotence and aimless drift, such as is observed today.

The unity of the body politic has to be preserved even against extreme forms of *political* strife. This is, to my mind, the meaning of the Athenian law on ostracism (not the usual interpretation, which sees in it a safeguard against would-be tyrants). In Athens political division and antagonism should not be allowed to tear the community apart; one of the two opposing leaders must go into temporary exile.

General participation in politics entails the creation for the first time in history of a *public space*. The emphasis Hannah Arendt has put on this, her elucidation of its meaning, is one of her outstanding contributions to the understanding of Greek institutional creation. I will confine myself, therefore, to a few additional points.

The emergence of a public space means that a political domain is created which 'belongs to all' (*ta koina*).[12] The 'public' ceases to be a '*private*' affair – of the king, the priests, the bureaucracy, the politicians, and the experts. Decisions on common affairs have to be made by the community.

But the essence of the public space does not refer only to 'final decisions'; if it did, it would be more or less empty. It refers as well to the presuppositions of the decisions, to everything that leads to them. Whatever is of importance has to appear publicly. This is, for example, effectively realized in the *presentation* of the law: laws are engraved in marble and publicly exposed for everybody to see. But much more importantly, law materializes in the discourse of the people, freely talking to one another in the *agora* about politics and about everything they care about before deliberating in the *ekklēsia*. To understand the tremendous historical change involved, one has only to contrast this with the typical 'Asiatic' situation.

This is equivalent to the creation of the possibility – and actuality – of free speech, free thinking, free examination and questioning without restraint. It establishes *logos* as circulation of speech and thought within the community. It accompanies the two basic traits of the citizen already mentioned: *isgēoria*, the right for all equally to speak their minds, and *parrhēsia*, the commitment for all really to speak their minds concerning public affairs.

It is important to stress here the distinction between the 'formal' and the 'real'. The existence of a public space is not just a matter of legal provisions guaranteeing rights of free speech, etc. Such provisions are but conditions for a public space to exist. The important question is: What are the people actually doing with these rights? The decisive traits in this respect are courage, responsibility, and shame (*aidos, aischunē*). Lacking these, the 'public space' becomes just an open space for advertising, mystification, and pornography – as is, increasingly, the case today. Against such development, legal provisions are of no avail or produce evils worse than the ones they pretend to cure. Only the education (*paideia*) of the citizens as citizens can give valuable, substantive content to the 'public space'. This *paideia* is not primarily a matter of books and academic credits. First and foremost, it involves becoming conscious that the *polis* is also oneself and that its fate also depends upon one's mind, behaviour, and decisions; in other words, it is participation in political life.

Equally important, hand in hand with the creation of a public space goes the creation of a *public time*. By this I do not mean just 'social', 'calendar' time, a system of sociotemporal benchmarks which, of course, already exists everywhere. I mean the emergence of a dimension where the collectivity can inspect its own past as the result of its own actions, and where an indeterminate future opens up as domain for its activities. This is the meaning of the creation of historiography in Greece. It is a striking fact that historiography properly speaking has existed only during two periods of human history: in ancient Greece and in modern Europe – that is, in the cases of the two societies where questioning of the existing institutions has occurred. In other societies, there is only the undisputed reign of tradition, and/or simple 'recording of events' by the priests or the chroniclers of the kings. But Herodotus starts with the declaration that the traditions of the Greeks are not trustworthy. The disruption of tradition and critical inquiry into 'true causes' of course go together. Moreover, this knowledge of the past is open to all. Herodotus, for example, is reported to have read his *Histories* to the Greeks assembled for the Olympic games (*si non e vero, e ben trovato*). And the Funeral Speech of Pericles contains a survey of the history of the Athenians from the viewpoint of the spirit of the activities of the successive generations – a survey leading up to the present and clearly pointing toward new things to be done in the future.

What are the limits of political action – the limits of autonomy? If the law is God-given, or if there is a philosophical or scientific 'grounding' of substantive political truths (with Nature, Reason, or History as ultimate 'principle'), then there exists an extrasocial standard for society. There is a norm of the norm, a law of the law, a criterion on the basis of which the question of whether a particular law (or state of affairs) is just or unjust, proper or improper, can be discussed and decided. This criterion is given once and for all and, *ex hypothesi*, does not depend upon human action.

Once it is recognized that no such ground exists, either because there is a separation between religion and politics, as is, imperfectly, the case in modern societies, or because, as in Greece, religion is kept strictly at bay by political activities, and once it is also recognized that there is no 'science', no *epistēmē* or *technē*, of political matters, the question of what a just law is, what justice is – what 'the proper' institution of society is – opens up as a genuine, that is, interminable, question.

Autonomy is possible only if society recognizes itself as the source of its norms. Thus, society cannot evade the question: Why this norm rather than that? – in other words, it cannot evade the question of justice by answering, for example, that justice is the will of God, or the will of the Czar, or the reflection of the relations of production. Neither can it evade the question of *limits* to its actions. In a democracy people *can* do anything – and must know that they *ought not* to do just anything. Democracy is the regime of self-limitation; therefore it is also the regime of historical risk – another way of saying that it is the regime of freedom – and a tragic regime. The fate of Athenian democracy offers an illustration of this. The fall of Athens – its defeat in the Peloponnesian War – was the result of the *hubris* of the Athenians: *hubris* does not simply presuppose freedom, it presupposes the absence of fixed norms, the essential vagueness of the ultimate bearings of our actions. (Christian sin is, of course, a heteronomous concept.) Transgressing the law is not *hubris*, it is a definite and limited misdemeanour. *Hubris* exists where self-limitation is the only 'norm', where 'limits' are transgressed which were nowhere defined.

The question of the limits to the self-instituting activity of a community unfolds in two moments. Is there any intrinsic criterion of and for the law? Can there be an effective guarantee that this criterion, however defined, will not be transgressed?

With the move to fundamentals, the answer to both questions is a definite *no*. There is no norm of norms which would not itself be a historical creation. And there is no way of eliminating the risks of collective *hubris*. Nobody can protect humanity from folly or suicide.

Moderns have thought – have pretended – that they they have found the answer to these two questions by fusing them into one. This answer would be the 'Constitution' as a fundamental Charter embodying the norms of norms and defining particularly stringent provisions for its revision. It is hardly necessary to recall that this 'answer' does not hold water either logically or effectively, that modern history has for two centuries now in all conceivable ways made a mockery of this notion of a 'Constitution'; or that the oldest 'democracy' in the liberal West, Britain, has no 'Constitution' at all. It is sufficient to point to the shallowness and duplicity of modern thinking in this respect, as exemplified both in the field of international relations and in the arena of changes in political regimes. At the international level, despite the rhetoric of professors of 'International Public Law', there is in fact no law but the 'law of force', that is, there is a 'law' as long as matters are not really important – as long as you hardly need a law. The 'law of force' also rules concerning the establishment of a new 'legal order' within a country: 'A victorious revolution creates right' is the dictum which almost all teachers of international public law avow, and all countries follow in practice. (This 'revolution' need not be, and usually is not, a revolution properly speaking; most of the time, it is a successful *Putsch*.) And, in the European experience of the last sixty years, the legislation introduced by 'illegal' and even 'monstrous' regimes has always been maintained in its bulk after their overthrow.

The very simple point here is of course that in the face of a historical movement which marshals *force* – be it by actively mobilizing a large majority or a passionate and ruthless minority in the forefront of a passive or indifferent population, or be it even just brute force in the hands of a group of colonels – legal provisions are of no avail. If we can be reasonably certain that the re-establishment of slavery tomorrow in the United States or in a European country is extremely improbable, the 'reasonable' character of our forecast is based *not* on the existing laws or constitutions (for then we would be simply idiotic) but on a judgement concerning the active response of a huge majority of the people to such an attempt.

In Greek practice and thinking the distinction between 'constitution' and 'law' does not exist. The Athenian distinction between laws and decrees of the *ekklēsia* (*psēphismata*) did not have the same formal character and in fact disappeared during the fourth century. But the question of self-limitation was dealt with in a different (and, I think, more profound) way. I will consider only two institutions related to this problem.

The first is an apparently strange but fascinating procedure called *graphē paranomon* (accusation of unlawfulness).[13] The procedure can be briefly described as follows. You have made a proposal to the *ekklēsia*, and this proposal has been voted for. Then another citizen can bring you before a court, accusing you of inducing the people to vote for an unlawful law. You can be acquitted or convicted – and in the latter case the law is annulled. Thus, you have the right to propose anything you please, but you have to think carefully before proposing something on the basis of a momentary fit of popular mood and having it approved by a bare majority. For, the action would be judged by a popular court of considerable dimensions (501, sometimes 1,001 or even 1,501 citizens sitting as judges), drawn by lot. Thus, the *dēmos* was appealing against itself in front of itself: the appeal was from the whole body of citizens (or whichever part of it was present when the proposal in question was adopted) to a huge random sample of the same body sitting after passions had calmed, listening again to contradictory arguments and assessing the matter from a relative distance. Since the source of the law is the people, 'control of constitutionality' could not be entrusted to 'professionals' – in any case, the idea would have sounded ridiculous to a Greek – but only to the people themselves acting in a different guise. The people say what the law is; the people can err; the people can correct themselves. This is a magnificent example of an effective institution of self-limitation.

Tragedy is another institution of self-limitation. People usually speak of 'Greek tragedy', but there is no such thing. There is only *Athenian* tragedy. Only in the city where the democratic process, the process of self-institution, reached its climax, only there could tragedy (as opposed to simple 'theatre') be created.

Tragedy has, of course, many layers of signification, and there can be no question of reducing it to a narrow 'political' function. But there is certainly a cardinal political dimension to tragedy, not to be confused with the 'political positions' taken by the poets, not even with the much commented upon (rightly, if insufficiently) Aeschylean vindication of public justice against private vengeance in the *Oresteia*.

The political dimension of tragedy lies first and foremost in its ontological grounding. What tragedy, not 'discursively' but through *presentation*, gives to all to see, is that Being is Chaos. Chaos is exhibited here, first, as the absence of order *for* man, the lack of positive correspondence between human intentions and actions, on one hand, and their result or outcome, on the other. More than that, tragedy shows not only that we are not masters of the consequences of our actions but that we are not even masters of their *meaning*. Chaos is also presented as Chaos *in* man, that is, as his *hubris*. And the ultimately prevailing order is, as in Anaximander, order through catastrophe – a 'meaningless' order. From the universal experience of catastrophe stems the fundamental *Einstellung* of tragedy: universality and impartiality.

Hannah Arendt has rightly said that impartiality enters this world through the Greeks. This is already fully apparent in Homer. Not only can one not find in the Homeric poems any disparagement of the 'enemy', the Trojans, for example, but the truly central figure in the *Iliad* is Hector, not Achilles, and the most moving characters are Hector and Andromache. The same is true for Aeschylus' *Persians* – a play performed in 472 BCE, seven years after the battle at Plataea, with the war still going on. In this tragedy, there is not a single word of hatred or contempt for the Persians; the Persian queen, Atossa, is a majestic and venerable figure, and the defeat and ruin of the Persians is ascribed exclusively to the *hubris* of Xerxes. And in his *Trojan Women* (415 BCE), Euripides presents the Greeks as the cruellest and most monstrous beasts – as if he were saying to the Athenians: this is what you are. Indeed, the play was performed a year after the horrible massacre of the Melians by the Athenians (416 BCE).

But perhaps the most profound play, from the point of view of tragedy's political dimension, is *Antigone* (442 BCE). The play has been persistently interpreted as a tract against human and in favour of divine law, or at least as depicting an insurmountable conflict between these two principles (or between 'family' and State', as in Hegel). This is indeed the manifest content of the text, repeated again and again. Since the spectators cannot fail to 'identify' with the pure, heroic, helpless, and desperate Antigone against the hard-headed, authoritarian, arrogant, and suspicious Creon, they find the 'thesis' of the play clear. But the meaning of the play is multilayered and the standard interpretation misses what I think is most important. A full justification of the interpretation I propose would require a complete analysis of the play, which is out of the question here. I will only draw attention to a few points. The insistence on the obvious – and rather shallow – opposition between human and divine law forgets that for the Greeks to bury their dead is *also* a human law, as to defend one's country is *also* divine law (Creon mentions this explicitly). The chorus oscillates from beginning to end between the two positions, always putting them on the same plane. The famous hymn (332–75) to the glory of man, the builder of cities and creator of institutions, ends with praise for the one who is able to *weave together* (*pareirein*) 'the laws of the land and the justice of gods to which he has sworn' (cf. also 725: 'well said from both sides'). Antigone's upholding of 'divine law' is remarkably weakened by her argument that she did what she did because a brother is irreplaceable when one's parents are dead, and that with a husband or a son the situation would have been different. To be sure, neither the divine nor the human law regarding the burial of the dead recognizes such a distinction. Moreover, what speaks through Antigone, here and throughout the play, more than respect for the divine law, is her passionate love for her brother. We need not go to the extremes of interpretation and invoke incestuous attraction, but we certainly must remember that the play would not be the masterpiece it is if Antigone and Creon were bloodless representatives of principles and not moved by strong passions – love for her brother, in Antigone's case, love for the city *and* for his own power, in Creon's case. Against this passionate background, the characters' arguments appear additionally as rationalizations. Finally, to present Creon as unilaterally 'wrong' goes against the deepest spirit of tragedy, and certainly of Sophoclean tragedy.

What the final lines of the chorus (1348–55) glorify is not divine law, but *phronein*, an untranslatable word, unbearably flattened in its Latin rendering by *prudentia*. The chorus lauds *phronein*, advises against impiety, and reverts again to *phronein*, warning against 'big words' and the '*huperauchoi*', the excessively proud.[14] Now, the content of this *phronein* is clearly indicated in the play. The catastrophe is brought about because *both* Creon *and* Antigone insist on their own reasons, without listening to the reasons of the other. No need to repeat here Antigone's reasons; let us remember only that

Creon's reasons are irrefutable. No city can exist – and therefore no gods can be worshipped – without *nomoi*; no city can tolerate treason and bearing arms against one's own country in alliance with foreigners out of pure greed for power, as Polynices did. Creon's own son, Haemon, clearly says that he cannot prove his father wrong (685–6); he voices the play's main idea when he begs Creon not to *monos phronein*, 'not to be wise alone' (707–9).

Creon's is a political decision, taken on very solid grounds. But very solid political grounds can turn out to be very shaky, if they are only 'political'. To put it in another way, precisely because of the totalistic character of the domain of politics (in this case, inclusive of decisions about burial and about life and death), a correct political decision must take into account all factors, beyond the strictly 'political' ones. Even when we think, on the best of rational grounds, that we have made the right decision, this decision may turn out to be wrong, and catastrophically so. Nothing can guarantee *a priori* the correctness of action – not even reason. And above all, it is folly to insist on *monos phronein*, 'being wise alone'.

Antigone addresses itself to the problem of political action in terms which acquire their acute relevance in the democratic framework more than in any other. It exhibits the uncertainty pervading the field, it sketches the impurity of motives, it exposes the inconclusive character of the reasoning upon which we base our decisions. It shows that *hubris* has nothing to do with the transgression of definite norms, that it can take the form of the adamant will to apply the norms, disguise itself behind noble and worthy motivations, be they rational or pious. With its denunciation of the *monos phronein*, it formulates the fundamental maxim of democratic politics.[15]

What is the 'object' of autonomous self-institution? This question may be rejected at the outset if one thinks that autonomy – collective and individual freedom – is an end in itself, or that, once significant autonomy has been established in and through the political institution of society, the rest is no more a matter of politics but a field for the free activity of individuals, groups and 'civil society'.

I do not share these points of view. The idea of autonomy as an end in itself would lead to a purely formal, 'Kantian' conception. We will autonomy both for itself and in order to be able *to do*. But to do what? Further, political autonomy cannot be separated from 'the rest', from the 'substance' of life in society. Finally, a very important part of that life concerns common objectives and works, which have to be decided in common and therefore become objects of political discussion and activity.

Hannah Arendt did have a substantive conception of what democracy – the *polis* – was about. For her, the value of democracy derived from the fact that it is the political regime in which humans can reveal who they are through words and deeds. To be sure, this element was present and important in Greece – but not only in democracy. Hannah Arendt (after Jacob Burckhardt) rightly emphasized the agonistic character of Greek culture in general – not only in politics but in all spheres and, one should add, not only in democracy but in all cities, Greeks cared above all for *kleos* and *kudos* and the elusive immortality they represented.

However, the reduction of the meaning and purposes of politics and of democracy in Greece to this element is impossible, as the foregoing brief account, I hope, makes clear. Moreover, it is surely very difficult to defend or support democracy on this basis. First, though of course democracy more than any other regime allows people to 'manifest' themselves, this 'manifestation' cannot involve everybody – in fact not even anybody apart from a tiny number of people who are active and deploy initiative in the political field as narrowly defined. Second, and more importantly, Hannah Arendt's position defers the crucial question of the content, the substance, of this 'manifestation'. To take it to extremes, surely Hitler and Stalin and their infamous companions have revealed who they were through words and deeds. The difference between Themistocles and Pericles on the one hand, and Cleon and Alcibiades on the other, between the builders and the gravediggers of democracy, cannot be found in the sheer fact of 'manifestation', but in the content of this manifestation. Even more so, it is precisely because for Cleon and Alcibiades the only thing that mattered was 'manifestation' as such, sheer 'appearance in the public space', that they brought about catastrophe.

The substantive conception of democracy in Greece can be seen clearly in the entirety of the *works* of the *polis* in general. It has been explicitly formulated with unsurpassed depth and intensity in the most important political monument of political thought I have ever read, the Funeral Speech of Pericles (Thuc. 2.35–46). It will always remain puzzling to me that Hannah Arendt, who admired this text and supplied brilliant clues to its interpretation, did not see that it offers a *substantive* conception of democracy hardly compatible with her own.

In the Funeral Speech, Pericles describes the ways of the Athenians (2.37–41) and presents in a half-sentence (beginning of 2.40) a definition of what is, in fact, the 'object' of this life. The half-sentence in question is the famous *Philokaloumen gar met'euteleias kai philosophoumen aneu malakias*. In 'The Crisis of Culture' Hannah Arendt offers a rich and penetrating commentary on this phrase. But I fail to find in her text what is, to my mind, the most important point.

Pericles' sentence is impossible to translate into a modern language. The two verbs of the phrase can be rendered literally by 'we love beauty . . . and we love wisdom . . .', but the essential would be lost (as Hannah Arendt correctly saw). The verbs do not allow this separation of the 'we' and the 'object' – beauty or wisdom – external to this 'we'. The verbs are not 'transitive', and they are not even simply 'active': they are at the same time 'verbs of state'. Like the verb *to live*, they point to an 'activity' which is at the same time a way of being or, rather, *the* way be means of which the subject of the verb *is*. Pericles does not say we love beautiful things (and put them in museums), we love wisdom (and pay professors or buy books). He says we *are* in and by the love of beauty and wisdom and the activity this love brings forth, we live by and with and through them – but far from extravagance, and far from flabbiness.[16] This is why he feels able to call Athens *paideusis* – the education and educator – of Greece.

In the Funeral Speech, Pericles implicitly shows the futility of the false dilemmas that plague modern political philosophy and the modern mentality in general: the 'individual' versus 'society', or 'civil society' versus 'the State'. The object of the institution of the *polis* is for him the creation of a human being, the Athenian citizen, who exists and lives in and through the unity of these three: the love and 'practice' of beauty, the love and 'practice' of wisdom, the care and responsibility for the common good, the collectivity, the *polis* ('they died bravely in battle rightly pretending not to be deprived of such a *polis*, and it is understandable that everyone among those living is willing to suffer for her' 2.41). Among the three there can be no separation; beauty and wisdom such as the Athenians loved them and lived them could exist only in Athens. The Athenian citizen is not a 'private philosopher', or a 'private artist', he is a citizen for whom philosophy and art have become ways of life. This, I think, is the real, materialized, answer of ancient democracy to the question about the 'object' of the political institution.

When I say that the Greeks are for us a germ, I mean, first, that they never stopped thinking about this question: What is it that the institution of society ought to achieve? And second, I mean that in the paradigmatic case, Athens, they gave this answer: the creation of human beings living with beauty, living with wisdom, and loving the common good.

Paris and New York, March 1982–June 1983

Notes

1 Marx himself wrote in the *Introduction to the Critique of Political Economy* that Greek art presented an *inaccessible* model – not insuperable or insurmountable, but *inaccessible*.
2 'The Concept of History', in *Between Past and Future* (New York: Viking Press, 1968), p. 51.
3 Needless to add, this in itself does not allow any 'practical' or 'political' conclusions.
4 Linguists seem to recognize and register some 4,000 languages extant *today*. Though there is of course no one-to-one correspondence between language and total institution of society, this gives a very rough indication of the order of magnitude of different types of

society that have existed in the very recent past.

5 Relying on 'rationality' alone has led, e.g., to the nineteenth-century characterizations of primitive religion and myth as sheer nonsense (or 'junk', as Marx and Engels wrote) – or to contemporary Structuralism and other Procrustean beds.

6 1986 Note: A 'central limit' one would say in mathematics.

7 I cannot agree with Hannah Arendt's idea that in Greece legislative activity was a secondary aspect of politics. This would hold only in a limited sense of the term 'legislative'. Aristotle counts thirteen 'revolutions' in Athens, that is, changes in the fundamental ('constitutional') legislation.

8 1986 Note: As Olof Gigon has clearly established in *Der Ursprung der griechischen Philosophie von Hesiod bis Parmenides* (Basel, 1945).

9 The meaning of Anaximander's fragment (Diels B1) is clear, and 'classical' historians of philosophy have, for once, interpreted it correctly. Heidegger's 'interpretation' of it ('Der Spruch des Anaximander', in *Holzwege*) is, as usual, Heidegger dressed up as Anaximander.

10 Given the constraints of space, I will have to speak 'statically' myself, ignoring the movement and considering only some of its most significant 'results'. I beg the reader to bear in mind this inevitable limitation.

11 Aristotle *Constitution of the Athenians* Book 8, chapter 5.

12 Something similar can be found in some savage societies, but it is confined to the handling of 'current' affairs, since in these societies the 'traditional' law cannot be called into question.

13 M. I. Finley has recently stressed the importance and elucidated the spirit of this procedure: *Democracy, Ancient and Modern* (New Brunswick, NJ: Rutgers University Press, 1973). See also V. Ehrenberg, *The Greek State*, 2nd edn (London: Methuen, 1969), pp. 73, 79, 267 – where two other important procedures or provisions similar in spirit are also discussed: *apatē tou demou* (deceit of the demos) and the exception *ton nomon mē epitēdeion einai* (inappropriateness of a law).

14 I must leave open here the question raised by Hannah Arendt's (and Hölderlin's) interpretation of these last lines (*The Human Condition*, p. 25, n. 8), which does not, in any case, create difficulties for my comment. Curiously, Michael Denneny in his excellent paper ('The Privilege of Ourselves: Hannah Arendt on Judgment', in *Hannah Arendt: The Recovery of the Public World*, ed. M. A. Hill [New York: St Martin's Press, 1979], pp. 268–9 and 274) does not mention the translation offered in *The Human Condition* and supplies instead a different (oral) rendering by Hannah Arendt, which is totally unacceptable, both philologically and from the point of view of the play's whole meaning.

15 An additional support for my interpretation can be found at the end (1065–75) of Aeschylus' *Seven Against Thebes*. This is certainly an addition to the initial text, probably dating from 409–5 BCE (according to Mazon, in the Budé edition, p. 103). This addition has been inserted to prepare for the performance of *Antigone* immediately afterward. It makes the *Seven* end with the two halves of the chorus divided, the one chanting that they will support those who are united with their blood (*genea*), because what the *polis* holds to be right is different at different times, i.e. the *polis*'s laws change though blood right is perennial; and the other asserting their support for the *polis* and *dikaion*, i.e. right. [1986 addition: The first half chorus makes no mention of a 'divine law'; the second mentions, in contrast, the 'blessed', no doubt the patron heroes of the city, and Zeus himself. Once again, all this appertains to the *manifest* text.] A non-negligible testimony of how Athenians at the end of the fifth century viewed the matter and the meaning of *Antigone*.

16 I follow the usual translation of *euteleia*. Hannah Arendt's rendering of this word, ending with the interpretation 'we love beauty within the limits of political judgment', while not strictly impossible, is extremely improbable.

11

The Logic of Magmas and the Question of Autonomy (1983)*

In memory of Claude Chevalley

What I have to say may appear disordered and heterogeneous, and I beg your forgiveness. I hope that the discussion will allow one to see the strong connections that tie together the six points I have decided to treat: ensembles; magmas; the power of ensemblistic-identitary logic; ontological theses; questions about the living being [*le vivant*]; the question of social and individual autonomy.

Ensembles

In a letter from Cantor to Dedekind dated 28 July 1899 one comes across this striking and important sentence: 'Every multiplicity is either an inconsistent multiplicity or it is a set [*ensemble*]'.[1] To say of a multiplicity that it is inconsistent implies obviously that this multiplicity *is*, it *is* in a certain fashion that remains to be specified and that Cantor does not specify. Clearly, we are not dealing here with an empty set, which is a set in full right, with its place in set theory.

It is toward these inconsistent multiplicities – inconsistent from the standpoint of a logic that claims to be consistent or rigorous – that I turned, starting from the moment, in 1964–5, when the importance of what I have called the radical imaginary in the human world became apparent to me. The discovery that the human psychism cannot be 'explained' by biological factors or considered as a logical automaton of no matter what richness and

*   The main part of this text was first presented at a seminar led by Claude Chevalley, Norbert Borgel, and Denis Guedj at the University of Paris-VIII in May 1981, then at the Cerisy colloquium on 'Self-Organization' (10–17 June 1981). For the version published in the record of the proceedings of this colloquium (*L'Auto-organisation. De la physique au politique* [Paris: Seuil, 1983], pp. 421–3), I had to remove, for reasons of space and time, a few paragraphs that later were restored within brackets when the article, 'La Logique des magmas et la question de l'autonomie', was reprinted in *DH*, pp. 385–418. 'The Logic of Magmas and the Question of Autonomy' first appeared in *Philosophy and Social Criticism*, 20:1/2 (1994), pp. 123–54.

complexity and, also and especially, that society cannot be reduced to any rational-functional determinations whatsoever (for example, economic/productive, or 'sexual', in a narrow view of the 'sexual') indicated that one had to think something else and to think otherwise in order to be able to comprehend the nature and specific mode of being of these two domains, the psychical on the one hand, the social-historical on the other. Simply to posit a new type of being, unprecedented and previously unthought of, which would be that of the psyche and the social-historical, did not suffice. Only if one succeeded in saying something about the specificity of these two strata, the psychical and the social-historical, not only in phenomenological and descriptive terms but also in logical and ontological ones, could this position have acquired some content. Let us note in passing that their specificity is already indicated [*se marque*] in their unique mode of coexistence: the psychical sphere and the social sphere are radically irreducible each to the other and yet at the same time absolutely indissociable, the one being impossible without the other.

After various terminological peregrinations – cluster [*amas*], conglomerate, and others – for this mode of being, as well as the logico-ontological organization it bears, I have ended up with the term *magma*. I was later to discover that the editions of Nicolas Bourbaki's *Algèbre* from 1970 on utilized the term with an acceptation that bears no relation at all to the one I have tried to give it and that is, of course, strictly ensemblistic-identitary in character. As the term, by its connotations, admirably lends itself to what I want to express, and as, dare I say, its utilization by Bourbaki seems to me both rare and superfluous, I have decided to retain it.[2]

Before going any further, it seems to me useful to provide an intuitive benchmark [*repère*] with the help of two illustrations. Let each person think of the totality of representations she is capable of making: everything that can present itself, and be represented, as present perception of 'reality', as memory, as fantasy, as reverie, as dream. And let each try to reflect upon this question: could one, within this totality, truly go about the task of separation, of carving up, arranging, putting in order, counting up – or are these operations both impossible and absurd with regard to what we are dealing with here? Or: let each person think of the totality of significations that could be conveyed by statements in contemporary English. These statements are in themselves certainly finite in number: they correspond to combinations of elements of a finite set, themselves each time having a finite number of terms. Let us note in passing that it is wrong to say – as Chomsky does – that the 'creativity of native speakers' may be expressed in the fact that they can form an infinity of statements. In the first place, in this fact as such there is no 'creativity': it is a matter of a purely combinatory activity (which, precisely because the *semantic* dimension is absent, has been, for years, reproducible in a trivial way by a computer). Second, it is false to talk in this regard about an *infinite* number of statements. There could be an infinite number of statements only if statements of an arbitrarily great length could be made, which neither exists nor can exist in any natural language (or even in any system with a physical basis). The statements of a language (even if an upper bound for their permissible length cannot be fixed) are arrangements, with repetition, of a finite (and relative small) number of terms, terms themselves taken up in a finite (and relatively small) set. No matter how great their number might be, it is finite.[3] This aspect, however, is still of secondary importance in relation to what really matters here. For, what I have to say about magmas, the relevant opposition is not finite/infinite, but determinate/indeterminate. Now, all mathematical entities are perfectly determinate. Within the set of real numbers, for example, any number whatsoever – be it rational, algebraic, transcendental – is perfectly determinate; there exists not the least ambiguity concerning what it is, where it is, between what other numbers it is, etc. And the discrete/continuous (or digital/continuous) opposition, with which one has attempted to 'soften' traditional logic, is no more relevant here than the finite/infinite opposition. From *this* standpoint, there is no essential difference between topology and arithmetic. The two belong to ensemblistic-identitary logic. Both elaborate the world of the determinate and of determination, the world of categorical distinctions (even if they are 'probabilistic': a probability is determinate or is nothing), the world of separation (in the everyday sense of the term separation, of course, not in the topological sense).

Let us recall the definition of sets given by set theory's founder, Cantor: 'A set is a collection into a whole of definite and distinct objects of our intuition or of our thought. These objects are called the elements of the set.'[4] (Intuition here is *Anschauung*: not Bergsonian intuition but what one can 'see' or inspect.) This definition, which one would now label 'naive', is fantastically profound and illuminating, for it exhibits the indefinable within the definition of the definite, the ineliminable circularity within every attempt at foundation.

As one knows, the elaboration of set theory very quickly brought out antinomies and paradoxes (of which Russell's Paradox is only the most famous). To avoid them, there were attempts at formalizing the theory. This has led to various systems of axioms, which, at the price of an ever more unwieldy formalism, have suppressed the clear intuitive content of Cantor's definition, and this, in my opinion, without any genuine gain on the formal level.[5] This may be illustrated through two examples.

In a relatively recent monograph on the axiomatic theory of sets, the theory appears to make intensive and very heavy use of mathematics in its presently constituted state; enormous chunks of other branches of mathematics (themselves bringing into play, obviously, a host of presuppositions) are drawn upon. The existence of a vicious circle is manifest. The author is certainly perfectly conscious of this, and his response boils down to saying that the axiomatic theory of sets does not come 'at the beginning' of mathematics, though that would, 'perhaps', be true for the 'naive theory'.[6] Of this 'perhaps' one could easily make lots of fun. Let us retain simply the admission that one does not know with *certitude* what should come 'at the beginning' of mathematics – namely, on what basis and by what means one proves anything at all in mathematics.

For my part, I dare believe that the 'naive' theory of sets does indeed come 'at the beginning', that it is ineliminable, and that it must be posited *from the outset*, with its circularities and its axioms tying together between them indefinable terms that acquire the consistency they will have only later on, in their actual utilization. The axiomatic circle is only the formalized manifestation of the originary circle implied by all *creation*.

This point may be illustrated, if need be, by the pseudodefinition of the term 'set' which Bourbaki furnished at a moment when his courage weakened and when, thinking perhaps of his grandmother, he deigned to express himself in French, recalling that there can be no 'definition' of this term. 'A *set* consists of *elements* which are capable of possessing certain *properties* and of having certain *relations* between themselves or with elements of other sets.'[7] Are the four words which are underlined in the original – set, elements, properties, relations – underlined because they introduce terms specific to this theory, or because they are considered indefinable, or else again because they are considered to be still more indefinable than other terms in this statement? But are the terms 'consist', 'capable of possessing', 'having', or 'other' any less mysterious than 'set', 'property', etc.?

Of course, from the standpoint of mathematics the genuine 'definition' of sets is to be found in the groups of axioms furnished by the various formalizations of the theory. It is not my intention to discuss them here. Rather, I will try to sift out what I consider the basic traits or, still better, the 'categories' or logico-ontological operators that necessarily are put to work [*mis en œuvre*] by ensemblistic-identitary logic, whether the latter functions in the activity of a mathematician or in that of a savage who classifies birds, fish, and the clans of his society. The principal ones among these operators are: the principles of identity, noncontradiction, and the excluded third; the property ≡ class equivalence; the existence, strongly stated, of relations of equivalence; the existence, strongly stated, of well-ordered relations; determinacy. A brief commentary on these terms may be useful.

In place of the excluded third, one may speak of the excluded nth; there is no essential difference. The property ≡ class equivalence has been challenged, as we know, because, taken absolutely, it leads to Russell's Paradox. In fact, however, one could not function for a second either in mathematics or in everyday life without constantly positing that a property defines a class and that a class defines a property of its elements (to belong to this class).

To infer from such and such a property of an element that it belongs or does not belong to such and such a set, or the inverse, is the daily bread of every mathematical proof.

The existence, strongly stated, of relations of equivalence poses more complex questions. We know that, in formalized theories, the relation of equivalence is a concept defined at a rather advanced stage in their construction. In fact, however, from the very first step taken by mathematics (as well as with ordinary thought), the relation of equivalence is presupposed, as is, with the strongest content possible, that of absolute identicalness of self to self. Paradoxically, it is even posited as (implicit) counterfactual postulate. The x that appears at two different places in any proof *has to* be taken as *the same x* – though, 'materially', it is quite obviously *not the same*. There is no mathematics without *signs*, and to use signs one must be able to posit that two different 'realizations' of x are *absolutely* the same x. Certainly, from the standpoint of formalized mathematics it will be said that this absolute identicalness of self to self imposed upon what is 'materially' different is simply an equivalence *modulo* every relation that could be defined. Here we have the definition of identity in mathematics; it is the same as the one already given by Leibniz, when he said, *eadem sunt quae substitui possunt salva veritate*, 'they are identical, those things that can be substituted the ones for the others while saving *the* truth' – while saving *all* truths. But it is clear that one cannot substitute one thing for *another* while saving *all* truths; that would happen only if it were a matter of absolutely indiscernible things – in which case there could be no question of *substitution*. We remain then – beyond the identicalness of self to self – simply with equivalence *modulo* such and such a relation, relative equivalence, equivalence *as to* . . . .

The well-ordered relation, too, appears in formalized mathematics as a construction that comes at an advanced stage of development. In fact, it is utilized and is operant from the very first moment. No matter what formula, no matter what proof presupposes well-orderedness as well as applies it [*le mettent en œuvre*]. As one knows, there is no equivalence between the statements 'Whatever x is there exists y such that $R(x,y)$' and 'There exists y such that whatever x is $R(x,y)$', which differ from each other only in the order of the signs (terms). Certainly, here too – as also in the case, previously mentioned, of the relation of equivalence which is presupposed before it is 'constructed' – the formalist objection is well known. The formalist would reproach us – rightly, in a certain sense – for confusing the levels; she would assert that the well-orderedness that reigns over the signs of a formula or of a proof is not the well-orderedness that is defined within mathematics, just as the equivalence of different occurrences of a sign is not mathematical equivalence; in both cases it would be a matter of metamathematical notions. The objection is irrefutable – and lacking in all interest. Likewise, it is simply 'logical and empty', as Aristotle would say ('logical', here, meaning in Aristotle's vocabulary in fact eristical), to assert that in a stratified theory (such as Russell's theory of types) 'equivalence' does not have the same meaning at the first level, at the second level, at the nth level, etc. For, to say that equivalence does not have the same meaning across the various levels implies already that one is given, as inspectable from the outset and simultaneously (from the logical point of view), the (enumerable) totality of these levels *and* that there exists a category of equivalence outside any level (or valid across and for all levels) that is applied (and, in some cases, is not applied) to 'equivalences' encountered on particular levels. We are interested here in the logico-mathematical operators (categories) involved, from the first step, in the construction of mathematics itself. The formalization of set theory, and of ensemblistic-identitary logic, absolutely presupposes the application [*mise en œuvre*] of categories and operators of 'natural logic', that is to say, of the ensemblistic-identitary logic already immanent in language as one of its dimensions. The 'construction' of ensemblistic-identitary logic *presupposes* ensemblistic-identitary logic (and certainly also something else: the radical imaginary).

Lastly, by means of all these terms there operates a hypercategory, this originary schema of ensemblistic-identitary logic that is *determinacy*. In the entire history of philosophy (and of logic) determinacy has functioned as a supreme, but more or less implicit or hidden, requirement. It is relatively less hidden among the ancient Greeks: the *peras* ('limit', 'determination') that they opposed to the *apeiron* ('indeterminate') was, for them, the decisive characteristic of every thing that one can truly speak of, that is to say, that truly is. At the other end of the history of philosophy, in Hegel, the same schema operates just as powerfully, but in a much more implicit manner: it is *Bestimmtheit*, determinacy, that one encounters on every page of the *Science of Logic*, but that is nowhere thematized or made explicit. Here we are speaking about the dominant tendency, the main stream of philosophical thought. One will find, certainly, among the great philosophers, qualifications or restrictions added to this thesis. Already the Pythagorean Philolaos affirmed that all that is is made of *peras* and of *apeiron*, an idea that Plato takes up and enriches when he writes: 'All that can be said to be is made of one and many, and includes growing with it from the outset the *peras* and the *apeiron*.'[8] But the dominant current of philosophy's fixation on determinacy and the determinate is expressed by this, that while it recognizes a place for the indeterminate, for the *apeiron*, the latter is posited as hierarchically 'inferior': what truly is is what is determined, and what is not determined is not, or is less, or has an inferior quality of being.

In all this there is not only a 'logic'. There is an *ontological decision* – clearly affirmed, from philosophy's beginnings, by Parmenides – and a constitution/creation. By means of the categories or operators mentioned, a region of being is constituted – and, at the same time, it is decided either that it exhausts being (full-scale rationalism, absolute idealism, or mechanistic-materialistic reductionism are merely some of its forms) or that it represents the paradigm of truly being (*ontos on*, the rest being accident, illusion and error, or deficient imitation, or amorphous and essentially 'passive' 'matter'. Even for Kant it is the being ≡ being-determined equivalence that remains the ontological polar star.

> *Everything* is subject, in its possibility, to the principle of *complete determination*, according to which one of *all* the possible predicates of things, as compared to their opposites, must be applicable to it . . . The proposition, that *everything which exists is completely determined*, does not signify only that one of every pair of *given* contradictory predicates, but that one of all *possible* predicates must always belong to a thing.[9]

One will note the very profound and in no way accidental proximity of this idea to the mathematical concept of an ultrafilter.[10] One will also note that this properly metaphysical decision [being ≡ being-determined] remains central in contemporary science, despite the upheavals the latter has undergone during the past sixty years as a result of its very evolution.

Magmas

Magmas can be spoken of only in ordinary language. This implies that they can be spoken of only in using the ensemblistic-identitary logic of this language. This is what I am going to do in what follows. The situation is even going to be aggravated to the extent that, in trying to speak of them in a rigorous manner, we will have to appeal to terms and notions that either belong to logic and mathematics in their constituted states or refer to them. The situation is even more unwieldy than that encountered in the case of the 'foundation' of set theory [*la théorie des ensembles*] or mathematics, since here it is a question not only of a 'vicious circle' but of an undertaking that can be qualified as antinomic or inconsistent. We are going to use language and, to a certain extent, the resources of ensemblistic-identitary logic in order to define, illuminate, and even justify the positing of something that goes beyond ensemblistic-identitary logic and even transgresses it. We are going to try to describe magmas by using ensembles. And, ideally, starting from magmas, we should try to describe ensembles as 'immersed in' magmas. At the most, we can take a moral precaution by drawing the reader's attention to the fact that all the logical and mathematical terms being used in what follows are, ideally, placed within an arbitrarily large number of quotation marks.

To begin with, let me recall the 'definition' of the magma I gave in *The Imaginary Institution of Society* (p. 343):

A magma is that from which one can extract (or in which one can construct) an indefinite number of ensemblist organizations but which can never be reconstituted (ideally) by a (finite or infinte) ensemblist composition of these organizations.

Thus, if one once again takes the totality of significations contemporary English language conveys or can convey, one can extract therefrom an arbitrary number of ensemblistic orgzanizations. One would not be able, however, to refabricate this totality starting from any ensemblistic elements whatsoever.

I note in passing that Jean-Pierre Dupuy remarked to me that the 'definition' cited above is unsatisfactory, for it would cover just as well what, to avoid Russell's Paradox, has been called in mathematics a 'class'. The objection is formally correct. It does not trouble me much, for I have always thought, and still think, that the 'class', in this acceptation of the word, is a logical artifact constructed *ad hoc* to get around Russell's Paradox, and that it succeeds in doing so only by means of an infinite regress.

Rather than comment on this 'definition', however, we are going to try here to illuminate other aspects of the idea of magma by exploring the paths (and the impasses) of a more 'formal' language.

For this, one must introduce a primitive (undefinable and undecomposable) term/relation: the *marking* [*repérer*] term/relation, whose valence is both unary and binary. So, let us suppose that the reader unambiguously understands the expressions: 'to mark X'; 'X marks Y'; 'to mark X in Y' (to mark a dog; the collar marks the dog; to mark or locate the dog in the field).[11] In using this term/relation, I 'define' a magma by the following properties:

M1: If M is a magma, one can mark, in M, an indefinite number of ensembles.

M2: If M is a magma, one can mark, in M, magmas other than M.

M3: If M is a magma, M cannot be partitioned into magmas.

M4: If M is a magma, every decomposition of M into ensembles leaves a magma as residue.

M5: What is not a magma is an ensemble or is nothing.

The first property (*M1*) secures the indispensable bridge to the domains that are formalizable, as well as their applications, that is to say, 'exact' knowledge. It equally allows an illumination of the term/relation (or operation) of marking [*repérage*]. Indeed, to be able to speak of M, I have to be able, at the outset, to mark M vaguely 'as such' – *and* the marking *in* M of a 'series' of definite ensembles allows me to render the identification of M progressively less 'vague'.

The second property (*M2*) expresses an inexhaustibility, or an indefinite potentiality. What it expresses implicitly, however, and what especially matters here, is that it is not only and not so much a matter of quantitative inexhaustibility. It is not cardinality that is at stake here, the 'number of objects' that a magma can 'contain' (on this level one can go no further than existing mathematics), but the inexhaustibility of modes of being (and of types of organization) that can be discovered (and which obviously remain, each time, to be specified as far as possible).

The formulation of this second property (*M2*) gives rise to a question: 'When is a magma *other* than an (other) magma – or: How do you know it?' We can answer with another question: 'When is a sign of a mathematical theory *other* than an (other) sign, and how do you know it?' What is brought into play by property *M2* pertains to the same thing as that which is brought into play, *non-* or *pre-mathematically*, in every mathematical theory and, more simply, in every language act: to posit, originally and simultaneously, the sign and that of which it is sign in their identicalness to themselves and their difference relative to everything else.[12]

The third property (*M3*) is undoubtedly the most decisive. It expresses the impossibility of applying here the schema/operator of *separation* – and, above all, its irrelevance in this domain. In the magma of my representations, I cannot rigorously separate out those that 'refer to my family' from the others. (In other words, in the representations that at first sight 'do not refer to my family', there always originates at least one associative chain that, itself, leads to 'my family'. This amounts to saying that a representation is not a 'distinct and well-defined being', but is everything that it brings along with it.) In the significations conveyed by contemporary English, I cannot rigorously separate out those that (not in my representation, but in this tongue [*langue*] itself) refer in any way at all to mathematics from the others. A weaker formulation may be given: the 'intersections' of submagmas are almost never empty. (Let us note that in this respect the language we would have to use would have to be full of such expressions as 'almost everywhere', 'almost never', 'strongly', 'weakly', etc.)

The fourth property (*M4*) is especially useful via its 'complement': if X is exhaustively decomposable into ensembles, then X is an ensemble and not a magma. For example, a mathematical being as monstrous as $\mathscr{F}(\mathbb{R}^\mathbb{R}, \mathbb{R}^\mathbb{R})$, the ensemble of applications of $\mathbb{R}^\mathbb{R}$ in itself, is decomposable into ensembles to an exhaustive degree, and this in an infinity of ways.

The fifth property (*M5*) amounts to affirming that the idea of magma is absolutely universal – or, more pragmatically speaking, that we call magmatic every non-ensemblistic-identitary mode of being/mode of organization that we encounter or can think of. (This boils down to saying that everything that is/everything that is conceivable, and that wherein we ourselves are, is a supermagma.)

Let us now attempt to 'reascend above' magmas – or to 'descend below' magmas – in order to 'construct' them, at the same time as ensembles, starting from something else. This attempt fails, but I believe this failure is instructive.

We take again the term/relation/operation 'to mark' and, as before, the notion of ensemble. A *diversity* (*polueides* in Plato; *Mannigfaltigkeit* in Kant) may be defined as follows:

D1: If in D one can mark a family of nonempty ensembles, D is called a diversity.

D2: Let N be the union of ensembles marked in D. If D – N = ø, D is an ensemble. If D – N ≠ ø, D is a magma.

Let us add to *D1* and *D2*, the properties *M1* to *M4*. We need hardly recall the multiple abuses of language and of notation committed in the foregoing. (D – N has meaning only if N is a part of an *ensemble* D; X ≠ ø has meaning only if X is an ensemble, etc.) Let us note simply this: if D – N ≠ ø, D – N is a magma according to *D2* and *M4*; therefore (*M1*), there exist ensembles that can be marked in D – N. Therefore, N defined as the union of markable ensembles in D does not contain all these ensembles: contradiction.

This example 'proves' nothing, certainly. Beyond illustrating that it is impossible to 'reascend above' magmas, however, it perhaps also indicates something else. The fruitful path is perhaps not the 'constructive' or 'finitary' one, the one that proceeds through the positing of 'elements' and 'inclusions', but, rather, another. Magmas exceed ensembles not from the standpoint of the 'wealth of cardinality' (from this standpoint, nothing can exceed the Cantorian scale of transfinite numbers), but from the standpoint of the 'nature of their constitution'. The latter is reflected only very imperfectly, and in a very impoverished manner, in properties *M1* to *M4* and, I believe, in all other properties of the same type that one might invent. And this, once again, independent of the circles and *petitio principii* that necessarily make their appearance there.

This is why, while conserving properties *M1* to *M4* as 'descriptive' or 'intuitive', we will try another path.

Let us take mathematics in its constituted state, and another 'primitive' term: the classes of statements bearing on a domain D. One can say that a class of statements possesses an ensemblistic-identitary organization if all its statements are axioms, theorems, or undecidable propositions in Gödel's sense (which boils down to saying that all its statements are formally constructible and that they are 'locally decidable' almost everywhere). One can say that a class of statements C is referred to D if there exists a biuni-vocal (one-to-one) correspondence (bijection) between a (nonempty) part of the signs of C and a (nonempty) family of parts of D. Once can say, lastly, that a statement *s* in C is *significant* in the ensemblistic-identitary sense if the metastatement 'There exist objects of D that satisfy *s* or *non-s*; or, *s* (or *non-s*) belongs to a deductive chain wherein *s* is connected to an *s'* that satisfies the preceding condition' is true.

If the statements that are significant in the ensemblistic-identitary sense exhaust the class of significant statements referred to D, then D is an ensemble. If there exist significant statements referred to D and these statements are not significant in the ensemblistic-identitary sense, then D is a magma.

It will be noted that the distinction thus made seems to include (and actually does include) an 'empirical', 'historical', or 'contingent' dimension: one cannot say in advance whether a domain D that for a long time has appeared nonensemblizable will not, later on, be ensemblized (this is, as we know, what has progressively happened with some considerable domains). The question is then posed whether the distinction we are trying to establish is not simply historical or relative – relative to a stage in the process of formal-ization/ensemblization. In other words, do irreducible magmas exist?

The answer is 'Yes', and we can immediately show an example of such a magma: the activity of formalization itself is not formalizable. Every formal-ization presupposes an activity of formalization and the latter is not formalizable (save, perhaps, in trivial cases). Every formalization rests upon originary operations of the *institution* of signs, of a syntax and even of a semantics (without which such formalization is vain and void of interest). These operations are the presupposition for all formalization; every attempt at pseudoformalization would only push them back a notch. This is what Bourbaki is finally obliged to admit in his Preface: we are not claiming to teach mathematics to 'beings that would not know how to read, write, and count'.[13]

From this, interesting consequences follow. For example, if it is admitted (as seems to be evident) that every deterministic theory must correspond to a chain of statements that are significant in the ensemblistic-identitary sense, the result is that there exist domains to which significant statements can be referred, but which satisfy no deterministic theory. (Of course, the usual distinction between the deterministic and the probabilistic is of no interest here: probabilistic statements are deterministic statements, for they assign determinate probabilities to classes of determinate events. Probability theory fully pertains to ensemblistic-identitary logic.) In other words, every deter-ministic theory is formed by chains of statements that are significant in the ensemblistic-identitary sense and, consequently, no deterministic theory can have a validity other than 'local'. Quite obviously, this settles nothing about the question whether some particular domain – the domain of 'physics', for example – does or does not satisfy one or several deterministic theories.

[I do not wish to close this aspect of my examination without mentioning the happy theoretical accident I experienced in encountering one of the participants in the colloquium, Ms Mugur-Schächter, who was kind enough to offer me an offprint of a text she had published in *Einstein 1879–1955* (Colloque du Centenaire, Collège de France, 6–9 June 1979 [Paris: CNRS, 1980], pp. 249–64). Presented at a round-table discussion at this colloquium devoted to what is called the Einstein–Podolsky–Rosen Paradox [in brief, the EPR Paradox] – which ceased to be a 'paradox' after the experiments of Freedman and Clauser, Fry and Thompson, and finally Alain Aspect and his colleagues – this text contains a host of formulations that I find enchanting. I recall first the tragic irony contained in the definition and the history of this 'paradox': formulated in 1935 by Einstein and his two colleagues at the time to show, on the basis of a mental experiment, that the hypothesis of the completeness of quantum mechanics is incompatible with the idea of an 'objective reality', it led, via the formulation of 'Bell's inequalities' (1965), to the experiments mentioned above, which, it very well seems, can only be interpreted as requiring the abandonment of the idea of a 'reality with local determinism', or of the *separability* of 'elementary phenomena'. (See also my text, *MSPI* (1973), in *CL*, pp. 160–4E; for more recent bibliographical references, beyond those furnished by Ms Mugur-Schächter in her article cited above, see those in Bernard d'Espagnat, *À la Recherche du réel* [Paris: Gauthier-Villars, 1979], p. 175 [T/E: the English edition, *In Search of Reality*, does not include the bibliography] and *Reality and the Physicist: Knowledge, Duration, and the Quantum World*, trans. Dr J. C. Whitehouse and Bernard d'Espagnat [New York and Cambridge: Cambridge University Press, 1989], pp. 271–4; for previous discussions of the 'paradox', see Abraham Pais, *'Subtle is the Lord': Science and Life of Albert Einstein* [Oxford: Clarendon, 1982], pp. 455–9, with bibliography.) This nonseparability undoubtedly possesses a capital philosophical importance which, it seems to me, is far from having been worked out. What concerns me here, however, is the admirable description by Ms Mugur-Schächter of the manner in which the physicist extracts from (or imposes upon) what I will call *the magma of physical Being/being* [*être/étant physique*] an ensemblistic-identitary grid – which she designates respectively by 'semantic mud' and 'syntactical organization'. It is worth citing *in extenso*, however, the lines where, after a series of formulae, she looks back upon her own activity:

I stop an instant and look at what I have just written. What a mixture of 'necessities' and arbitrariness, signs and words that have the appearance of pointing toward a specified *designatum* and yet beneath which one finds only fuzzy, moving images hung on these words and these signs in an *unseparated* way [emphasis added – C.C.]. I write 'time value' in quotation marks, for example, because each time I reflect on the degree of unexploredness still found in the concepts of duration and time and their relation, I feel a reticence to write anything beyond an algorithm that sets a rule of the game. The setting of parameters for the fundamental property of duration with the aid of time variable t, as this setting of parameters is practised in existing theories – and even in Relativity – is still certainly very much of a simplification and often a falsification; it is rigidifying, mechanistic in a sort of way. Changes are not always displacements of internally stable entities. [Not to forget that *all* physics since Galileo is founded on the postulate that *everything* is reducible to displacements of *internally stable* 'elementary' entities. Here I am speaking of theoretical physics, not of cooking up some numerical predictions. – C.C.] To be able to take fully into account the whole diversity of types and intensities of changes, one would need a sort of vectorial magnitude, a field of processual time defined in each point of abstract space framed by the axis of duration and by the axes of the changes envisioned. But would such a time be transformable along Lorenzian lines? What role would the speed of a *light* 'signal' play in relation to the propagational speeds of 'influences' (?) in such a processual space? What does Relativity genuinely impose upon *any* process, and what does it leave out? When it is a matter of a process that is (relatively) very intense locally, 'catastrophic', as is probably the case with 'pair creation', what does time become? In the general relativity theory of gravitation, for example, a non-null gradient of the gravitational field [or more simply put, the mere *existence* of a gravitational field, without which real 'observers' are obviously impossible – C.C.] is tied to the non-definability of *one* unique time for observers of the same frame of reference, if these observers are spatially distant from each other. [In other terms: in General Relativity, for real distant observers *there is no* unique time, nor, contrary to special relativity, any possibility of univocal transformation between the times of different observers. – C.C.] As to the invariance of the *speed of light* itself (and not the speed of other sorts of 'influences') when one passes from one frame of reference to another, it is postulated only locally, for no univocal definition of distances and times exists in variable gravitational fields (Weinberg, *Gravitation and Cosmology* [New York: J. Wiley Sons, 1975]) (curvature of space-time). How can we know what sort of local 'curvature' of space-time produces (or does not produce) an – essentially variable

– process of pair creation? [Obviously, the 'local' is a *nonlocal stratum.*
– C.C.] Finally, Relativity introduces no quantification, its description
is continuous. When one writes speed=distance/time, time is a continuous parameter.

If we then ask ourselves how one finds the value of t, we notice that
it is of the form NT_H, where N is an integer and T_H a (*supposedly*
constant!) 'period of clock time', which brings us back to the discrete.
Macroscopically or in cosmology, that can be of negligible importance
both on the level of principle and on the numerical level. However,
when we consider microscopic processes which, like pair creation, are
essentially quantum and relatively brief, what is the degree of significance of a condition like

$$V = \frac{distance}{time} = \frac{distance}{NT_H} = const.?$$

What clock should be chosen, with that T_H, and how, moreover, can
one be assured that, when one writes $\Delta t = 10^{-x}$, one is doing anything
more than a meaningless calculation?

Faced with such questions, we comprehend better the positivist
displays of prudence and the norms that counsel us to remain within
the wholesome zone of the operationally defined and of the well
syntaxed, where thought circulates on well-laid-out and reinforced
pathways. Beyond, we sink into a genuine semantic mud. *Nevertheless,
it is only here, in this mud, and when we force our gaze to make out the
moving forms, that we can perceive the contrasts between what is not done
and what is partially done and thus initiate something anew.* [*Einstein
1879–1955*, pp. 256–7; emphasis added in the final sentence. – C.C.]

I do not wish to comment on this excerpt, which seems to speak
adequately well for itself. I note simply that what Ms Mugur-Schächter calls
the semantic mud could just as well be called the humus or the limon in
which significations are born; it is this limon – the radical imaginary – that
engenders the schemata that permit the physicist to proceed further precisely
in the ensemblization of physical Being/being – which, moreover, lends itself
indefinitely to this ensemblization, *and* not just anyhow, as the entire history
of physics shows. Furthermore, starting from these formulations the determinist's thesis (whose logicistic substance now appears in striking fashion)
can be illustrated once again: the 'mud' – the magma – is 'provisional', it is
illusion or residue, due to the state of our ignorance; *tomorrow,* it will be
completely dried up (a well-known sign in the window of a dishonest and
deterministic barber).[14]]

We must return to the question of signification. We have tried to specify what a significant statement in the ensemblistic-identitary sense might be. Can we go further?

We can interpret the term 'sense [*sens*]' in its *two* basic acceptations. These, I believe, exhaust the sense of 'sense' for ensemblistic-identitary logic (and, perhaps, for the 'logic of living beings' – of the living being *as such*).

> 1 '*Sinn*' in German does not have completely the same meaning [*sens*] as 'sense' in English. Here, sense has the acceptation of 'valued as' or 'standing for' [*valoir comme*] = 'exchange value' = equivalence = 'class'.
>
> 2 'What you are doing makes no sense', 'to treat pneumonia with hot and cold showers makes no sense'. Here, sense has the acceptation of 'valued for', 'serving for' [*valoir pour*] = 'use value' = adaptation, adequation, belonging = 'relation'.

Quite obviously, each of the two acceptations refers [*renvoie*] to the other, both horizontally and 'stepwise'.[15]

Thesis: Signification in the ensemblistic-identitary sense is reducible to combinations of these two acceptations of 'sense' – and, reciprocally: Every signification reducible to combinations of these two acceptations of 'sense' is ensemblistic-identitary. In other words: Significant statements in the ensemblistic-identitary sense always concern inclusions within classes, insertions within relations, and the combinatory that is constructible thereupon.

Another formulation of the thesis: Significations in the ensemblistic-identitary sense are constructible by classes, properties, and relations ('by figures and movements', Descartes would have said).

Corollary of the thesis: Significations exist that cannot be constructed by classes, properties, and relations.

The immediate example is, obviously, that of the significations that 'primitively' constitute a domain of classes, properties, and relations (such as the minimal domain of signs, syntax, and semantics necessary to begin doing mathematics). This is also undoubtedly the most constraining for formalists and positivists. But the essential domain (and the one of which the preceding example is, in fact, only a particular case) is that of social imaginary significations and of those significations that can be designated, by an abuse of language, as psychical significations.[16]

For, in fact, as one should have glimpsed already, we have given ourselves another 'primitive term': the significant statement. This amounts to saying: one has given oneself natural language, as well as a class of speakers of this language, for whom there exist criteria – perhaps changing and fuzzy, but sufficient as to need/usage – for discriminating between significant and nonsignificant statements. And, quite obviously, every attempt to 'begin' mathematics, in whatever fashion, is obliged to presuppose this natural language, and to 'give itself' natural language, as well as the capacity of its speakers to distinguish significant statements from nonsignificant statements.

Now, this 'natural language' – which obviously has nothing 'natural' about it – is each time socially instituted and exists only by means of its social institution. From this very fact, it bears – it conveys – significations that are not ensemblistic-identitary, viz.: social imaginary significations. But we know too – and we have discovered it anew – that it is impossible to speak, in any context [*cadre*] whatsoever, without utilizing ensemblistic-identitary operators (and, for example, the operators: class, relation, property). Whence: *the ensemblistic 'part' is 'everywhere dense' in natural language.*

Here is not the place to try to advance our elucidation of the mode of being and of the organization of social imaginary significations. I have limited myself to jotting down a few notes.

Undoubtedly, we must distinguish a first stratum, in an originary and founding sense, of the signifier. It may be called, in memory of Kant, *transcendental* and it presupposes *radical imagining*. Radical imagining is the *positing, ex nihilo*, of something that 'is' not and the connection (without previous determination, or 'arbitrarily' made) between this something that 'is' not and something that, in another sense [*par ailleurs*], 'is' or 'is not'. Every signitive relation[17] and every language obviously *presupposes* this positing and this connection. The latter thereby are founders of the ensemblistic-identitary domain, as well as of every other humanly conceivable domain. Thus, to write (or to read or to understand) '$0 \neq 1$' presupposes the positing of 'material-abstract' 'rounds' and 'bars' (always identical to themselves, whatever their concrete 'realization') as 'signs' (which, as such, 'are' not 'naturally'), but also the positing of 'notions', 'ideas', 'concepts', or, as you wish, *zero, one, different*, which, themselves too, as such 'are' not naturally, as well as the connection of each of them with the others. It is by means of this connection that '$0 \neq 1$' *signifies* – and for it to signify, one must have the capacity to see in '$0 \neq 1$' what 'is' not there, *zeros* and *ones* where 'there are only' rounds and bars.

At the other extreme, there are core or central social imaginary significations, which we do not have to worry about here. Suffice it to recall, once again, that these significations constantly involve ensemblistic-identitary operations but are not exhausted thereby. They always are 'instrumented' in classes, relations, and properties – but are not *constructible* therefrom.

On the contrary: it is by means of social imaginary significations that the *positing* of classes, properties, and relations operates in the world created by society. The imaginary institution of society boils down to the constitution of 'arbitrary' points of view, starting from which 'equivalences' and 'relations' are established. (For instance, specific words pronounced by a particular individual in a specific place and context [*contexte*] establish the equivalence between a scrap of bread and the body of a God – or bring some object into the circle of relations that are characteristic of the 'sacred'.) And, certainly, one of the fields to be explored here would be the way in which 'equivalence' and 'relation' are transformed when they function no longer in the ensemblistic-identitary domain but in the imaginary domain in the proper and strong sense of the term.

Power of Ensemblistic-Identitary Logic

Why the fantastic power of ensemblistic-identitary logic (what Hegel called the 'terrible power of the Understanding')?

First of all, without doubt this logic *leans on* on stratum of what is – in other words, it does indeed 'correspond' to a dimension of being. One can go even further: either there exists an ensemblizable part of being that is 'everywhere dense' or being is 'locally' (or 'piecewise'; or by strata) ensemblizable. I return briefly to this below.

This leaning of ensemblistic-identitary logic on what is appears to us in two forms – which, moreover, are indissociable. The first, ensemblistic-identitary logic, repeats, prolongs, elaborates the logic of the living being. Incontestably, for an enormous part of its operations – for *all* its operations? – the living being works by means of classes, properties, and relations. The living being constitutes a world – *itself* constitutes *its* world[18] – that is organized and whose organization is obviously correlative to (is only the other side of) the proper organization of the living being. Equivalence and relation are its everywhere present ingredients. The living being creates *for itself* its own universality and its own order. This universality and this order we ourselves inherit *qua* living beings. I return to this below.

But could the living being organize an *absolutely chaotic* world? For the living being to be able to organize, for itself, a world, starting from X, X would still have to be organiz*able*. This is the old problem of Kantian criticism, which one could never glide over.[19] All organizational forms immanent to the transcendental consciousness – or within the genome: the logical position of the problem remains strictly identical in the two cases – cannot provide anything if the 'material' they are to 'form' does not already include in itself the 'minimal form' of being form*able*. Let it be noted in passing that the idea of an *absolutely* disordered universe is for us unthinkable; and we can liken this to the impossibility of proving that an infinite series is random.[20]

We are therefore obliged to postulate that there is something in the world 'independent of the living being' that corresponds to the organization (by classes, properties, and relations) by means of which the living being constitutes *its* world – which amounts to saying that there exists *in itself* a stratum of total being [*étant total*] that 'possesses' an ensemblistic-identitary organization (in the minimal sense that it can *lend itself* to such an organization). But we are also obliged to state, further, that this organization goes far beyond the simple *ex post* (and apparently tautological) implications that may be drawn from the fact that the living being exists, that it really presents a universality *in itself*. Perhaps the existence of terrestrial living beings as we know them would not have been possible without the fall of apples. But there is not only the fall of apples: the rotation of galaxies or the expansion of star clusters is ruled by the same law. If the living being exists in parasitizing, or in ontological symbiosis with, a stratum of total being that is locally ensemblistic-identitary, this stratum extends even where the living being does not. And obviously that is what accounts both for the extraordinary success of modern Western science and for the 'unreasonable effectiveness of mathematics' (Wigner).

But the power of ensemblistic-identitary logic also sinks its roots into the institution of society. It expresses a functional-instrumental necessity for the social institution in all domains: any society whatsoever must have the determinate and the necessary in order for it to function – and even for it to be able to presentify, to itself, its properly imaginary significations. There is no society without myth, and there is no society without arithmetic. And still more important, there is no myth (or poems or music) without arithmetic – and certainly, too, there is no arithmetic without myth (be it the myth of the 'pure rationality' of arithmetic).

To this (transhistorical) necessity is added, for us, a particular historical development, one that may be thought to be surmountable: the specific turn that philosophy has taken since Parmenides, and especially since Plato, as ontology of determinacy or as exorbitant dilation of the ensemblistic-identitarian, covering almost the entire domain of thought, thus also constituting a 'rational political philosophy', to culminate ultimately – of course also with the help of other contributions – in the reign of pseudo-rationality that we know today in the modern world.

Ontological Theses

What is is not ensemble or system of ensembles. What is is not fully determined.

What is is Chaos, or Abyss, or Groundlessness. What is is Chaos with nonregular stratification.

What is bears with it [*comporte*] an ensemblistic-identitary dimension – or an ensemblistic-identitary part everywhere dense. Question: Does it bear this dimension with it or do we impose this dimension on it? The response (to be done with constructivism, reflections [*reflets*], and *tabulae rasae)* is as follows:

For the 'near-perfect' observer, the question of knowing, in an ultimate sense, what comes from the observer and what comes from the observed is undecidable. (Nothing absolutely chaotic is observable. No absolutely unorganized observer can exist. The observation is a not fully decomposable coproduct.)

The nondetermination of what is is not mere 'indetermination' in the privative and ultimately trivial sense. It is creation, namely, emergence of *other* determinations, new laws, new domains of lawfulness. 'Indetermination' (if it does not simply signify 'our state of ignorance' or a 'statistical situation') has a precise meaning: No state of being is such that it renders impossible the emergence of *other* determinations than those already existing.

If being is not creation, then there is no time ('time' would be, in that case, only the fourth dimension of a fully spatialized R^4 – an ontologically supernumerary fourth dimension).

Questions about the Living Being

That the living being is fundamentally characterized by the constitution of a world of its own, including its own organization, of a world *for itself* in which nothing can be given or appear except in so far as it is set apart (from an 'external' X) and transformed, that is to say, formed/informed by this organization of the living being itself, all this has seemed evident to me for a long time.[21] In this regard, [Francesco] Varela, with his idea of the living being's operational, informational, and cognitive closure, offers, I believe, clarifications of decisive importance.

I am less happy with his use of the term 'biological autonomy', which he uses to characterize this situation, for the term autonomy has been used for a long time – and anew by me since 1949 – to designate, in the human domain, a radically different state of affairs: briefly speaking, the state in which 'someone' – singluar subject or collectivity – is explicitly and, as far as possible, lucidly (not 'blindly') author of its own law. This implies (I shall return to this in the last section of this paper) that this 'someone' instaurates a new relation with 'its law', which signifies, among other things, that this singular or collective 'someone' can modify that law, knowing that it is doing so. To identify autonomy, as Varela's usage of the term entails, with cognitive closure leads to paradoxical results. A paranoiac – who immediately transforms every datum in order to adapt it to his perfectly sealed and watertight system of interpretation – would then be the paradigm for a (psychically) autonomous being. Likewise, a society whose system of the world is totally closed and rigid – whether it be a matter of an archaic society or the society of *1984* – would be 'autonomous'. To avoid this polysemic situation, which leaves us in sum with a strict equivoke (the same term to designate two contradictories), I would prefer the word self-constitution. (Self-organization', a term more and more in use, does not seem to me radical enough.) Neither do I think, let it be said in passing, that the 'second level' Paul Dumouchel has tried to distinguish – an 'autonomy of the social' that would be situated between what he calls 'autonomy in Varela's sense' and 'autonomy in Castoriadis's sense' – is truly an independent level.[22]

I come now to the questions I ask myself and which I would like to put in particular to [Henri] Atlan and to Varela. The living being can be considered as an *automaton*, in the true and etymological sense of the term. Automaton signifies not 'robot' but that which moves of itself (a meaning already to be found in Homer). This clarification is useful: indeed, Aristotle defined the animal [and natural being in general] as that which 'has within itself the principle of movement' (*arkhēn kinēseōs*). Now, Aristotle is obviously pre-Cartesian and pre-Galilean: movement, for him, is not simply local movement; local movement is only one of the species of movement; among the others, generation and corruption on the one hand, alteration on the other, are to be counted. In other words, in this place Aristotle speaks as if he considered the animal as having in itself the principle of its generation and corruption, as well as of its alteration; this is, in fact, very close to what we are saying.

Now, can one think the living being as a *fully* ensemblistic-identitary automaton? And can one think that an automaton that is fully ensemblistic-identitary, but also fully *automatic*, namely, one that has in itself the principles of its generation and corruption as well as of its alteration – or, in still other words, capable not only of self-preservation but also of self-reproduction and self-alteration – can one really think that such an automaton is 'producible' by strictly ensemblistic-identitary (in other words, 'deterministic') procedures? I do not know the answer to these two questions. Let me simply comment on a few aspects of them.

To say that the living being is 'autonomous' (in Varela's sense) or 'self-constituting', in the terminology I prefer, means that the living being posits its own 'significations', namely, that it itself primitively constitutes its domains of classes, properties, and relations. That seems to me evident. But to what extent can we say that the being of the living being is exhausted in and through this functioning by classes, properties, and relations? And to what extent does a primitive 'self-constitution' make sense in a strictly ensemblistic-identitary system? Various criteria could be examined. For example, one could say that the living being is only an ensemblistic-identitary automaton if the 'primitive significations' for a given living species (those that constitute its organization and its closure) can be constructed by classes, properties, and relations in another ensemblistic-identitary system. Thus, a dog would be such an automaton if one could construct the forms and the partitions that constitute the world of the dog by ensemblistic-identitary operations in a system that would be external to the dog and that would not itself be that of the living being. But is this satisfactory and sufficient? It does not seem so to me; it seems to me that, formally, one could perhaps perform this construction, but one would have neither the reason nor the *criterion* for doing so *if the dog did not already exist.* It seems to me that the effective, already realized being-thus of the dog is the *a-priori logic* of its ensemblistic-identitary 'recomposition'; that the latter is (perhaps!) always formally possible does not signify anything more, at the limit, than this: to every 'dog state' corresponds, biunivocally, a physically realizable state of a cloud of elementary particles. From the 'prebiological' point of view, however, this state has no privilege and no characteristic of its own; nothing allows us physically to distinguish it from the infinity of other possible states of the same cloud of particles (nothing that is not trivially descriptive). In brief: to fabricate a dog, one would have to have the idea of a dog. Ideas: *eidos*, 'form' in the full sense of the term (union of the organization and of the organized).

I think that the existence, the emergence of this *eidos* is an instance, a manifestation of being as creation. I think that the living being represents a self-creation (though certainly a 'blind' one). How could this view be refuted? It could be said: We will prove that the living being does not represent an example of self-creation when its existence – its necessity, its extreme probability? – will have become a theorem in a deterministic theory of a vaster domain. That would imply, first of all, that the following question has already been settled in the affirmative: 'Is the living being a fully ensemblistic-identitary automaton?' It would also imply that one accepts the idea that the self is rigorously deducible from the nonself and according to the laws of the nonself – an idea which, I am convinced, is devoid of meaning.

The Question of Social and Individual Autonomy

Autonomy is not closure but, rather, opening: ontological opening, the possibility of going beyond the informational, cognitive, and organizational closure characteristic of self-constituting, but *heteronomous* beings. It is ontological opening, since to go beyond this closure signifies altering the already existing cognitive and organizational 'system', *therefore* constituting one's world and one's self according to *other* laws, *therefore* creating a new ontological *eidos*, another self in another world.

This possibility appears, as far as I know, only with the human. It appears as the possibility of challenging – not by chance or blindly, but knowing that one is doing so – one's own laws, one's own institution when society is involved.

The human domain appears, at the start, as a highly heteronomous domain ('autonomous' in Varela's sense). Archaic societies, like traditional societies, are very highly closed societies informationally, cognitively, and organizationally. In fact, this is the state of almost all societies we know of, almost everywhere, almost always. And not only does nothing in this type of society prepare such a society to challenge established institutions and significations (which, in this case, represent the principles and bearers of closure), but everything is constituted therein so as to render impossible and unthinkable this sort of challenging (this is in fact a tautology).

This is why one can conceive only as a radical rupture, an ontological creation, the emergence of societies that put into question their own institutions and significations – their 'organization' in the most profound sense of the term. In these societies, ideas such as 'Our gods are perhaps false gods, our laws are perhaps unjust' not only cease to be unthinkable and unpronounceable but become the active ingredient [*ferment*] in a self-alteration of society. And, as always, this creation occurs 'circularly'; its 'elements', which presuppose one another and have no meaning except through one another, are posited straight off. Concretely speaking, the existence of societies that call themselves into question means that there are individuals capable of putting existing laws into question – and the appearance of such individuals is possible only if something has changed at the same time on the level of the overall institution of society. This rupture, you know my thesis, has taken place only twice in history: in ancient Greece and then, in a related and profoundly different [*autre*] manner, in western Europe.

[Should we say more about the relationship between the idea of magma as I have developed it at the beginning of the present text, the ontological theses formulated above, and the ontological rupture that the human creation of autonomy represents? If ensemblistic-identitary logic totally [*de part en part*] exhausts what is, there could never be any question of a 'rupture' of any kind, or of any autonomy. Everything would be deducible/producible from the 'already given', and even our contemplation of the effects of eternal causes (or of laws given once and for all) would be merely an inevitable effect, coupled here with the inexplicable illusion that we are able to tend towards the true and to try to avoid the false. Far from being able to change something therein, a subject totally caught in an ensemblistic-identitary universe could not even *know* that it was caught in such a universe. It could, in effect, *know* only in the ensemblistic-identitary mode, that is to say, it could only try eternally and always in vain to prove as theorems the axioms of its universe, for, of course, from the ensemblistic-identitary standpoint *meta*considerations have no meaning. It is into this absurd situation, let it be said in passing, that determinists of every ilk still place themselves today; they rigorously oblige themselves to produce, *starting from nothing*, the 'initial conditions' of the universe (its number of dimensions, the numerical value of universal constants, 'total quantity' of energy-matter, etc.) as *necessary*.[23]

At the same time, as I have recalled above, society (*every* society) has a functional-instrumental need whereby its social-historical being can exist only by *positing*, by *instituting* an ensemblistic-identitary dimension.[24] Likewise, all thought must constantly rest on the ensemblistic-identitarian. In our historical tradition – basically since Plato – these two facts ultimately have conspired together to lead to various so-called political philosophies, as well as to a diffuse political imaginary (expressed and 'rationalized' by 'ideologies'), placed under the sign of 'rationality' (or of its pure and simple negation, though this remains, by far, a marginal phenomenon). Favoured also by the retreat of religion and by a thousand other factors, this pseudo-rationality ultimately functions as the sole explicit and 'explicitable' imaginary signification today capable of cementing the institution, of legit-imating it, of holding society together. It is perhaps not God that has willed the existing social order, but it is the Reason of things, and you can do nothing about it.

To this extent, breaking the grip of the ensemblistic-identitary logic-ontology under its various disguises is at present a political task that is directly inscribed in our work toward achieving an autonomous society. What is, such as it is, permits us to act and to create; and yet it dictates nothing to us. We make our laws; this is also why we are *responsible* for them.]

We are the inheritors of this rupture. It is this that continues to live on and to act within the democratic and revolutionary movement that has animated the European world for centuries. And the historical ups and downs of this movement, known as they are, permit us today – also and especially via its failures – to give a new formulation to its objectives, viz., the instauration of an autonomous society.

Permit me here to make a detour by way of my personal history. In my work, the idea of autonomy appears very early on, in fact from the outset, and not as a 'philosophical' or 'epistemological' idea but as an essentially political one. Its origin is my constant preoccupation, along with the revo-lutionary question, the question of the self-transformation of society.

Greece, December 1944: my political ideas were then, at bottom, the same as they are today. The Communist Party, the Stalinist party, tried to seize power. The masses were with it. The masses were with it, therefore it was not a *Putsch*, it was a revolution. But it was not a revolution. The masses were led around by the nose and constantly watched over by the Stalinist party; there was no creation of *autonomous* mass organs – organs that do not receive their directives from the outside, that are not subjected to the domi-nation and control of a separate, outside authority, a party or a State. Question: When does a revolutionary period begin? Answer: When the population forms *its own autonomous* organs – when it enters into activity in order to give to itself its own organizational forms and its own norms.

And where does this Stalinist party come from? In a sense, 'from Russia'. In Russia, however, such a revolution had in fact occurred in 1917, and autonomous organizations such as I have described (soviets, factory committees) were created. Question: When does a revolution end, when does it 'degenerate', when does it cease to be a revolution? Answer: When the population's autonomous organs cease to exist and to act, either because they are actually eliminated or because they have been domesticated, enslaved, used by a new *separate* power as mere instruments or decorative elements. This is how it was in Russia; the soviets and the factory committees created by the population in 1917 were gradually domesticated by the Bolshevik Party and finally deprived of all power during the period from 1917 to 1921. The crushing of the Kronstadt Commune in March 1921 put the final touch on this process, which was thenceforth irreversible in the sense that, after that date, nothing less than a full revolution would have been needed to dislodge the Bolshevik Party from power. That settled at the same time the question of the nature of the Russian regime, at least negatively: one thing was certain, this regime was not 'socialist' nor was it preparing 'socialism'.[25]

If therefore a new society should emerge from the revolution, it can be constituted only on the power of the population's autonomous organizations, extended to all spheres of collective activity and existence: not only 'politics' in the narrow sense, but production and the economy, daily life, etc. Therefore, self-government and self-management [*autogestion*] (what at that time I called workers' management and collective management) resting on the self-organization of the collectivities concerned.[26]

But self-management and self-government of what? Would it be a matter of the self-managment of prisons by the prisoners, of assembly lines by compartmentalized [*parcellisés*] workers? [Would the object of self-organization be simply the decoration of the factories?] Self-organization, self-management, has no meaning except when it comes to grips with the instituted conditions of heteronomy. Marx saw in technique only something positive, and others have seen in it a 'neutral' means capable of being put into the service of any ends whatsoever. We know that there is nothing of the sort, that contemporary technique is an integral part of the heteronomous institution of society. The same goes for the educational system, and so on. If therefore self-management, self-government, is not to become a mystification, or merely a mask for something else, all the conditions of social life have to be put into question. This is not a matter of making a *tabula rasa*, still less of doing so from one day to the next; rather, it is a matter of comprehending the solidarity of all the elements of social life and drawing therefrom the following conclusion: Nothing can, in principle, be excluded from the instituting activity of an autonomous society.

We thus arrive at the idea that what defines an autonomous society is its activity of explicit and lucid self-institution – the fact that it gives itself its own law, knowing that it is doing so. This has nothing to do with the fiction of some sort of social 'transparency'.[27] Even less than an individual, a society will never be able to become 'transparent' to itself. It can, however, be free and reflective – and this freedom and this reflection can themselves be objects and objectives of its instituting activity.

Starting from this idea, a look back upon the overall conception of society and history became unavoidable. Indeed, this instituting activity which we would like to liberate in our society has always been self-institution; the laws have not been given by the gods, by God, or imposed by the 'state of the forces of production' (these 'productive forces' being, in themselves, only one of the faces of the institution of society), they have been created by the Assyrians, the Jews, the Greeks, etc. In this sense, society has always been 'autonomous in Varela's sense'. This self-institution, however, has always been occulted, covered over by the representation, itself highly instituted, of an extrasocial source of the institution (the gods, the ancestors – or 'Reason', 'Nature', etc.). And this representation aimed, and still aims, at quashing the process of calling the existing institution into question; it locks in, as a matter of fact, its *closure*. In this sense, these societies are heteronomous. For they are enslaved to their own creation, their law, which they posit as intangible, as it proceeds from a qualitatively other origin than living men and women. In this sense, too, the emergence of societies that put their own 'organization' into question, in the broadest and most profound sense of 'organization', represents an ontological creation: the advent of a 'form' (*eidos*) that explicitly alters itself *qua form*. This signifies that, in the case of these societies, representational-cognitive 'closure' has been 'in part', 'in some sort' *shattered*. In other words, man is the only animal capable of breaking the closure in and through which every other living being *is*.

Autonomy is therefore, for us, at the social level, explicit self-institution, knowing itself as such. And this idea animates the political project of the instauration of an autonomous society.

Starting from here there begins, certainly, a host of political as well as philosophical questions. I will evoke, very briefly, only a few of them that are connected with our discussion here.

Autonomy as objective: Yes, but is that enough? Autonomy is an objective that we want [*voulons*] for itself – but also for something else. Without that, we fall back into Kantian formalism, as well as into its impasses. We will [*voulons*] the autonomy of society – as well as of individuals – both for itself and in order to be abel to *make/do* [*faire*] things. To make/do *what*? This is perhaps the most weighty interrogation to which the contemporary situation gives rise: this *what* is related to *contents*, to substantive values – and this is what appears to be in crisis in the society in which we live. We are not seeing – or are seeing very little of – the emergence of new contents for people's lives, new orientations that would be synchronous with the tendency – which, itself, actually appears in many sectors of society – toward an autonomy, a liberation *vis-à-vis* simply inherited rules. Nevertheless, we may think that, without the emergence of such new contents, these tendencies will be able neither to expand nor to deepen and to become universalized.[28]

Let us go further. What are the 'functions' of the institution? The social institution is, first of all, its own end, which also means that one of its essential functions is self-preservation. The institution contains devices it has incorporated that tend to reproduce it through time and across generations; it even, generally speaking, imposes this reproductive process with an effectiveness that, when we really reflect upon it, appears quite miraculous. This the institution can do, however, only if it carries out another of its 'functions', namely, the socialization of the psyche, the fabrication of adapted and true-to-form [*appropriés et conformes*] social individuals. In the process of the psyche's socialization, the institution of society can, trivialities apart, do nearly anything, yet there is a minimum of things it cannot do that are imposed upon it by the nature of the psyche. Clearly, it has to furnish the psyche with 'objects' that divert the psyche from its own drives and desires; it also has to provide the psyche with points of identification. Above all, however, it has to provide the psyche with *meaning* [*sens*]. This implies, in particular, that the institution of society has always aimed at – and to a greater of lesser extent has succeeded in – covering over what I have called above Chaos, the Groundless, the Abyss; Abyss of the world, of the psyche itself for itself, of society itself for itself. This *meaning-giving*, which has been at the same time a covering over of the Abyss, has been the 'role' of the most central, core social imaginary significations: religious significations. Religion is at once presentation and occultation of the Abyss. The Abyss is announced, presentified in and through religion – and at the same time, it is essentially occulted. Thus, for example, Death in Christianity: obsessive presence, interminable lamentation – and, at the same time, absolute denial, since this Death is not truly a death, it is access to another life. The sacred is the instituted simulacrum of the Abyss: religion confers a figure or figuration upon the Abyss – and this figure is presented as both Ultimate Meaning and source of all meaning. To take the clearest example, the God of rational Christian theology is both ultimate meaning and source of all meaning. It is also, therefore, both source and guarantee of the being of society and of its institution. The result is – the result has always been, under different forms – the occultation of the *metacontingency* of meaning, namely, of the fact that meaning is a creation of society, that it is radically contingent for anyone who stands on the outside, and absolutely necessary for those who stand on the inside – therefore, neither necessary nor contingent. This boils down to saying that this occultation is occultation of society's self-institution and of this double piece of evidence, viz., that society cannot be without the institutions and significations it creates – and that the latter cannot have any 'absolute' foundation.[29]

However, if autonomous society is that society which self-institutes itself [*s'auto-institue*] explicitly and lucidly, the one that knows that it itself posits its institutions and its significations, this means that it knows as well that they have no source other than its own instituting and signification-giving activity, no extrasocial 'guarantee'. We thereby encounter once again the radical problem of democracy. Democracy, when it is true democracy, is the regime that explicitly renounces all ultimate 'guarantees' and knows no limitations other than its self-limitation. It certainly can transgress such self-limitation, as has so often been the case in history; it can thereby sink into oblivion [*s'abîmer*] or turn into its contrary. This amounts to saying that democracy is the only tragic political regime – it is the sole regime that *takes risks*, that faces openly the possibility of its self-destruction. Tyranny or totalitarianism 'risks' nothing, for they have already made real everything that can exist as risk in historical life. Democracy always lives [*est*] within the problem of its self-limitation, and nothing can 'resolve' this problem in advance. One cannot draw up a constitution that would prevent, for example, 67 per cent of the individuals from one day making the 'democratic' decision to deprive the other 33 per cent of their rights. Imprescriptible rights of individuals can be written into the constitution; one cannot inscribe within it a clause that absolutely forbids any revision of the constitution – and were one to do so, this provision would sooner or later prove impotent. The sole essential limitation democracy can know is self-limitation. And this form of limitation, in its turn, can only be the task of individuals educated in, through, and for democracy.[30]

Such an education, however, necessarily includes acceptance of the fact that institutions, such as they are, are neither 'necessary' nor 'contingent', which amounts to saying: acceptance of the fact that there is no meaning given as a gift or any guarantee of meaning, that there is no meaning other than that created in and through history. And this amounts to saying that democracy thrusts aside the sacred, or that – and this is the same thing – human beings finally accept what they have never, until now, truly wanted to accept (and which deep down within ourselves we never truly accept): that they are mortal, that nothing lies 'beyond'. It is only starting from this profound and impossible conviction of the mortality of each and every one of us, and of all that we do, that one can truly live as an autonomous being – and that an autonomous society becomes possible.

Notes

1 Georg Cantor, *Gesammelte Abhandlungen*, p. 444.

2 In the 1951 edition of the *Algèbre* (chapter 1), the term 'magma' does not appear. It is worked out in detail in the 1970 edition (chapters 2 and 3). [T/E: Magmas are discussed on the first page of chapter 1 in the 1974 English-language edition, *Elements of Mathematics. Algebra I* (Reading, Mass.: Addison-Wesley, 1974). Nicolas Bourbaki is the collective pseudonym for a group of French mathematicians.]

3 See *IIS*, p. 253E.

4 *Beiträge zur Begründung der transfiniten Mengenlehre. I. Math. Annalen*, 46 (1895), p. 481.

5 In fact, the genuine gain, on both the formal and substantive levels, produced by the work of formalization has been that it has led to different theorems of undecidability and incompleteness, which evidently signify the failure of the initial intention of formalization.

6 Jean-Louis Krivine, *Théorie axiomatique des ensembles* (Paris: PUF, 1969), p. 6.

7 Nicolas Bourbaki, *Elements of Mathematics. Theory of Sets* (Reading, Mass.: Addison-Wesley, 1968), p. 347.

8 Deils Frs. 1, 3, 4; *Philebus* 16c–d. [T/E: I have translated into English Castoriadis's own translation from the Greek.]

9 *Critique of Pure Reason* (Second Division, Book 2, chapter 3, section 2: 'Of the Transcendental Ideal'), trans. F. Max Müller (Garden City, New York: Anchor, 1966), pp. 386 and 387.

10 1986 Note: Let it be recalled that a *filter F* is a family of parts of a set *S* such that: (1) the empty set does not belong as a part of *F*; (2) every intersection of elements of *F* belongs to *F*; (3) every part of *S* containing an element of *F* belongs to *F*. An *ultrafilter U* is a filter such that, whatever may be part *A* of *S*, either *A* belongs to *U* or the complement of *A* belongs to *U*. I cannot pursue here the discussion of this analogy, as it would take us too far afield. No need to recall, either, that for Kant this definition of the 'thing that exists' leads to the 'Transcendental Ideal' as *omnitudo realitatis* and *ens realissimum* – namely, God – which, *from the standpoint of theoretical reason*, however, has to remain 'idea of such a being' and must not be transformed into 'hypostasis' (for, 'such an employment' would 'be overstepping the limits of its purpose and admissibility', ibid., pp. 392–3). And yet it must be noted: (a) that it is nevertheless, therefore, the idea of God as 'being completely determined' that gives meaning to 'being', and (b) that it is the continued validity of this metaphysical decision (being = being-determined) that indicates, in a Kantian perspective, the origin of the deficit of being of *our* objects and constitutes one of the sources of Kantian phenomenalism.

11 T/E: The verb *repérer* in French includes the actions of marking, indicating, identifying, spotting, and locating. For convenience's sake, I use the English verb 'to mark' in order, so to speak, to mark all these connotations.

12 See *IIS*, chapter 5, passim.

13 Bourbaki, *Elements of Mathematics. Theory of Sets*, p. 10.

14 T/E: The reference here is to the French joke about the barber who places a sign in his window announcing 'Free Shaves Tomorrow'. When a customer who has seen the sign comes in the next day for his free shave, he is told by the barber at the end of the shave that he must pay, for it is not until 'tomorrow' (that is, never) that free shaves will be given.

15 *IIS*, chapter 5, pp. 252–5E.

16 Ibid., chapters 6 and 7.

17 Ibid., pp. 244–52E.

18 See my text, *MSPI* (1973), now in *CL*, pp. 182–3E. [T/E: See also, now, *SST* (1986).]

19 See *IIS*, pp. 341–2E.

20 1986 Note: This question and those that follow are discussed again at length in *OIHS* (1986).

21 See again *MSPI*, as well as *IIS*, pp. 332–7E.

22 1986 Note: See *L'Auto-organisation*, p. 354.

23 See *MSPI*, in *CL*, pp. 163–4E.

24 See *IIS*, chapters 4 and 6, passim, and *ICSHD* (1981).

25 See *GI* (1973).

26 See *SB* (1949).

27 1986 Note: I have denounced the absurdity of such fictional 'transparency' since 1965, in *MRT IV*, now in *IIS*, pp. 110–14E [T/E: this section appears above in the present volume as '"Communism" in its Mythical Sense'].

28 1986 Note: I have discussed this question at length in *STCC* (1979). [T/E: See, now, an updated version of this text, *CCS* (1986).]

29 1986 Note: See *ISR* (1982).

30 1986 Note: See *GPCD* (1983).

12

Radical Imagination and the Social Instituting Imaginary (1994)*

I

I have chosen to speak about imagination and the social instituting imaginary not only because these are central themes in my work but also for two much less contingent reasons. First, because imagination – the radical imagination of the singular human being, that is, the psyche or soul – though discovered and discussed twenty-three centuries ago by Aristotle, never won its proper place, which is central in the philosophy of the subject. Second, because the social imaginary, the radical instituting imaginary, has been totally ignored throughout the whole history of philosophical, sociological, and political thought.

Given the limitations of space and time, I shall not enter into the history of the subject, which includes the vacillations of Aristotle in the treatise *De Anima*, the Stoics and Damascius, a long development in Britain going from Hobbes to Coleridge, the rediscovery of imagination by Kant in the first edition of the *Critique of Pure Reason* and the reduction of its role in the second edition, the rediscovery of the Kantian discovery and retreat by Heidegger in the 1928 *Kantbuch*, the subsequent total silence of Heidegger on the subject, the hesitations of Merleau-Ponty in *The Visible and the Invisible* as to what is 'reason' and what is 'imaginary',[1] not to mention Freud, who talks throughout his work about what is in fact imagination, and accomplishes the feat of never mentioning the term.

I shall limit myself to two remarks about the Aristotelean discovery and, later, to a brief discussion of some problems raised by Kant's treatment of the subject in the first edition of the first *Critique*.

It has not been noticed, as far as I am aware, that the Aristotelean *phantasia*, in the treatise *De Anima*, covers two completely different ideas. Most of the treatment corresponds to what I have called *second* (secondary) imagination, imitative, reproductive, or combinatory imagination – and

* Originally published in *Rethinking Imagination: Culture and Creativity*, Gillian Robinson and John Rundell, eds (London and New York: Routledge, 1994). Translation forthcoming in *CL 5*.

has provided the substance of what, for centuries and up to now, passes for imagination. But in the middle of Book Three, Aristotle introduces, without warning, a totally different *phantasia*, without which there can be no thought and which possibly precedes any thought. This I have called *prime* (primary) imagination; it corresponds, roughly, to my radical imagination.[2]

It is, at the same time, characteristic that Aristotle does not establish any relation whatsoever between *phantasia* and *poiēsis*, for him, is *technē*, and *technē* 'imitates' nature, even in the loftiest case, the case of *technē noiētikē*.

This ballet, this hide-and-seek game, should of course be explained, or, rather, understood. The main factor seems to me to be that philosophy from the start has been a search for the truth (*alētheia*) as opposed to mere opinion (*doxa*), and truth was immediately correlated with *logos*, *nous*, *ratio*, Reason, *Verstand* and *Vernunft*. *Doxa* was linked with sense impressions, or imagination, or both, and left at best to the 'sophists' and sceptics. Truth about the world and about being was to be found along the ways of *logos*, of Reason, without the question being raised: How can a world, and being, exist for a human subject in the first place? And how is it that these human subjects possess *logos*, language? (In Aristotle *logos* is an extremely polysemous term; but in his dictum, *anthrōpos esti zoon logon ekhon* – humans are living beings possessing *logos* – *logos*, I believe, refers centrally to language; the translation *animal rationale* is Seneca's in the first century CE.) Animals are certainly much more 'logical' or 'rational' than humans: they never do something wrongly or in vain. And human reason, as I shall try to sketch, entails radical imagination, but also would be nothing without language. It would, of course, be preposterous to argue that language is a 'product' of reason. But then where does language come from? It is significant that the dispute about the 'natural' or 'conventional/instituted' character of language was already very heated in Greece in the fifth century BCE, with Democritus supplying already unsurpassable arguments for the 'conventional/instituted' character of language; that Plato's *Cratylus* is inconclusive, though it obviously makes fun of the idea of a 'natural' character of words; and that Aristotle defines the word as *phōnē sēmantikē kata sunthēken*, a 'voice' (or 'sound') signifying according to a convention, but does not push his reflection further. The Greeks had discovered the *phusis/nomos* (nature/institution-convention) distinction and had already put it into practice by *changing* their institutions. But their most important philosophies stopped short of using it, obviously – at least in the case of Plato – out of fear of opening the way to 'arbitrariness' and freedom.

This also allows us to understand why the social origin – that is, creation – of language and of all institutions, though explicitly known and practically demonstrated at least in the democratic cities, remained without consequences for philosophy. When tradition and/or religion stopped supplying an indisputable source and formulation for the law and for the meaning of the world, philosophy rushed in to take its place. For this it had to find a *fundamentum inconcussum*, an unshakeable foundation, which was to be Reason. And according to the already emerging basic ontological categories, this Reason could be found in Things, in Ideas, or in Subjects – that is, Substantive Individuals – but certainly not in the anonymous social collective which could only be a collection of such individuals entering into commerce because of need, of fear, or of 'rational calculation'.

Also, almost from the beginning (and already in Parmenides) the philosophical tenet *ex nihilo nihil* – a constitutive axiom of ensemblistic-identitary logic[3] – imposed itself. But imagination, and social instituting imaginary, create – *ex nihilo*. Therefore, what they create must be a nonbeing, *Unsein* – at best, fictions and illusions. Of course, this is a nonsolution, since illusions *are* (e.g., they may have tremendous consequences). But this was covered up by the idea of 'degrees of being' – or of 'intensity of existence' – linked very rapidly with the criteria of *duration*, so that permanence, eternity, and, finally, atemporality became fundamental characteristics of 'true being' – of *immutability* – so that everything belonging to the Heraclitean flux became disqualified – and of *universality* – opposing what must be for everybody to what just happens to be for somebody. *Mutatis mutandis*, all this remains true today, despite talk about imagination and creativity, both of which are rapidly becoming advertising slogans.

II

Before going further, a preliminary explanation of the use of the terms imagination, imaginary, and radical may be helpful.

I talk about imagination because of the two connotations of the word: the connection with images in the most general sense, that is, *forms* (*Bilder-*, *Einbildung*, etc.); and the connection with the idea of invention or, better and properly speaking, with *creation*.

The term *radical* I use, first, to oppose what I am talking about to the 'secondary' imagination which is either reproductive or simply combinatory (and usually both), and, second, to emphasize the idea that this imagination is *before* the distinction between 'real' and 'fictitious'. To put it bluntly: it is because radical imagination exists that 'reality' exists *for us* – exists *tout court* – and exists *as* it exists.

Both considerations apply as well to the radical instituting social imaginary. It is radical because it creates *ex nihilo* (not *in nihilo* or *cum nihilo*). It does not create 'images' in the visual sense (though it does this as well: totem poles, emblems, flags, etc.). It creates, rather, forms which can be images in a general sense (linguists speak about the acoustic image of a word), but in the main are significations and institutions (each of those being impossible without the other).

So, to put it briefly, in both cases we talk about an a-causal *vis formandi*. A-causal does not mean 'unconditioned' or absolute, *ab-solutus*, separated, detached, without relations. All actual and factual relations are *not* casual. The seat of this *vis formandi* as radical imagination is the singular human being, more specifically its psyche. The seat of this *vis* as instituting social imaginary is the anonymous collective and, more generally, the social-historical field.

III

I turn now to the radical imagination of the singular human being. One may take two paths in order to elucidate this idea: the philosophical and the psychoanalytical.

On the philosophical path, we may well start with an *Auseinandersetzung* with Kant. In the *Critique of Pure Reason* (§24, B151) a proper definition is given: '*Einbildungskraft ist das Vermögen einen Gegenstand auch ohne dessen Gegenwart in der Anschauung vorzustellen*' – 'Imagination is the power (the capacity, the faculty) to represent in the intuition an object even without its presence.' One may note that Parmenides was already saying as much, if not more: 'Consider how the absent (things) are with certainty present to thought (*noo*).' And Socrates was going much further when he asserted that imagination is the power to represent that which *is not*. Kant goes on to add: 'As all our intuitions are sensuous, imagination therefore belongs to the sensibility.' Of course, just the reverse is true as I shall try to show presently.

We shall see that Kant certainly intends much more than what is entailed by the above definition: the conception of 'transcendental imagination', the paragraphs on the Schematism, and even the substance of the chapters on space and time go far beyond this definition. But the latter is useful in order to oppose to it what I consider to be the proper definition: *Einbildungskraft ist das Vermögen Vorstellungen hervorzubringen, ob diese einen äusseren Anlass haben oder nicht*. Imagination is the power (the capacity, the faculty) to make appear representations ('ideas' is the old English term, e.g. in Locke), whether with or without an external incitement. In other words: imagination is the power to make be that which '*realiter*' *is not* (I shall return later to the term '*realiter*'.

We take first the case of an external incitement (or excitation!). Fichte, who in the first version of the *Wissenschaftslehre* gives much greater weight to the imagination than Kant, speaks of *Anstoß* (shock). In this he is, I think, correct. But Kant speaks about the senses, opposing the 'receptivity of impressions' to the 'spontaneity of concepts'. Imagination obviously should go with spontaneity; but curiously, it is left out of this opposition. (And, if it is taken to belong to 'sensibility', as in the citation above, then it should be passive – an idea difficult to make sense of.) But what about this 'receptivity of the impressions'? What about *Sinnlichkeit* – sensibility or sensoriality?

In truth, there is no 'receptivity' or passivity of the 'impressions'. To begin with, there are no such things as 'impressions'. 'Impressions' are a philosophical or psychological artifact. There are, in *some* cases, *perceptions* – that is, representations of 'external' and more or less 'independent' objects. (*Some* cases only: there is an exorbitant privilege of perception in the whole of inherited philosophy, up to and including Husserl, Heidegger, and Merleau-Ponty.) These possess, certainly, a 'sensorial' component. But this component is *itself* a creation of the imagination. The 'senses' make emerge, out of an *X*, something which 'physically' or 'really' *is not* (if one equates 'reality' with the 'reality' of physics): colours, sounds, smells, etc. In 'physical' nature there are no colours, sounds, or smells: there are only electromagnetic waves, air waves, kinds of molecules, etc. The sensible *quale* (the famous 'secondary qualities') is a pure *creation* of the 'senses', that is, of imagination in its most elementary manifestation, giving a form and a specific form to something which, 'in itself', has no relation with *that* form.

These are, of course, Eddington's 'two tables'. *This* table – the one I touch, I see, I lean on, etc. – contains an indefinite plurality of 'elements' created by the singular imagination *and* the social imaginary. The other 'table' – in fact, no 'table' at all – is a scientific construct, *such as* science makes it *today*. (And this does not make it any less imaginary in the sense of the word I am intending.)

As the meaningfulness (at least, the philosophical meaningfulness) of this distinction has been recently disputed, especially from phenomenological quarters advocating the 'first-person stance',[4] a digression seems useful.

There is, of course, no real distinction between 'primary' and 'secondary' qualities – number, figure, size as opposed to colour, sound, taste, touch, smell, pain, or pleasure. They are all creations of the living body, that is, of the embodied psyche in humans, creations more or less permanent or transient, more or less generic or singular. These creations are often conditioned by an 'external' *X* – *not* 'caused' by it. Light waves are not coloured, and they do not cause the colour *qua* colour. They induce, *under certain conditions*, the subject to create an 'image' which, in many cases – and, so to speak, by definition in all the cases we can *speak about* – is generically *and* socially *shared*.

This does not mean (the 'idealistic' or 'Cartesian' fallacy) that these images are 'confused ideas' 'in the mind'. They are not 'confused' or 'more or less confused', nor are they 'in the mind'. They are just what they are: images, not in the sense of 'ikons' or 'imitations', but *Vorstellungen*, representations, or, better, *presentations*: presentations of something about which nothing can be said except by means of another presentation, about which the discourse will be eternally open, but which is certainly neither 'identical' nor even 'isomorphic' to them. (Analysis of, for example, the 'constancy of colour' on a surface shows this clearly.) They are original ways of 'reacting' (and this only in *some* cases: a composer getting a musical idea is not 'reacting' to anything, at any rate *not* at *this* level and certainly nothing 'external'). This 'reaction' is not an 'idea in the mind': it is a total state of the subject ('body' and 'soul').

But neither does this mean (the phenomenological fallacy) that the 'first-person' or 'intentional' stance presents to, or for, me 'the things as they are'. This is the curious realistic delusion of phenomenology, paradoxically co-existing with fatal solipsistic consequences: How do I know that something exists for the next person, or, indeed, that a next person exists at all if I am confined to my 'first-person stance'? From the strict phenomenological point of view I have *no access* to the experience of 'other persons'; they and their 'experiences' exist just as *phenomena for me*. The simple *naming* of the problem in Husserl's *Cartesian Meditations* (or in Merleau-Ponty's *Phenomenology of Perception*) is no solution.

The 'first-person stance' is bluntly contradictory, even if we leave aside the 'other person'. It tells me, for example, that to move an object, or to move myself, I need *force*. But if I am in a car and the driver brakes abruptly, I am projected through the windscreen without deploying any force. The 'privilege' or 'authenticity' of the 'first-person stance' looks philosophically very funny if this stance leads, as lead it must, to contradictions or incoherences in the very 'experience' it keeps celebrating. Husserl's 'The Earth, as Ur-arkhē, does not move' forces me, for instance, to dismiss as absurd or illusory phenomena of equally compelling immediacy (e.g., Foucault's pendulum, or the yearly parallax of the fixed stars).

Neither does the escape of the later Husserl towards the 'life-world' (*Lebenswelt*) redeem phenomenology. Certainly, the immediate 'first-person stance' presents things as they 'appear' in the life-world. But this only means that it presents them as they have been shaped by the generic biological (species) imagination *and* the social imaginary I am sharing with my fellow human *socii*. Now, philosophy starts when we begin trying to *break the closure* of this life-world in both its biological and social-historical dimensions. Of course, we can never break it to such a degree as to be able to fly outside any closure, to have a 'view from nowhere'. But break it we do, and there is no point in pretending that we do not know that there is no 'red' except for, in, and through a living body – or, for that matter, that there are no nymphs in the springs and gods in the rivers, which were a perfectly legitimate part of the life-world of the ancient Greeks.

Red, or the red object, is not a 'confused idea in my mind' and neither is it a reality 'down there' (Sartre). My, and our, creation of a world entails *also* the creation of an 'exterior' *where* object, colour, etc., present themselves as different and distant from me – me being always and irrevocably *here* – as it entails *also* the creation of a double temporal horizon ('backward' and 'forward') within which I am the permanently moving *now*.

To be sure, all this presupposes that I, somehow or other, 'know' first-hand what it is like to see red – but also, that I know first-hand what it is like to live in a society where the most important things are social imaginary significations – for example, nymphs. It is true that nobody and nothing can make us 'stop living "in" or "through" the experience, to treat it itself as an object, or, what is the same thing, as an experience which could as well have been someone else's'.[5] And, equally true, to continue quoting Taylor, I cannot 'experience my toothache as a mere idea in the mind, caused by decay in the tooth, sending signals up the nerves to the brain'. But neither am I obliged to stick with this 'experience' and ignore other ways of access to the phenomenal fact of toothache, such as they lead me, for example, to take an aspirin or rush to my dentist.

Behind the phenomenological, or 'first-person', stance stands the attempt to present 'my own' experience as the only authentic or, at any rate, privileged one – the only one giving access to '*die Sache selbst*'. But in fact this 'experience' is not just 'my own' but shares in a biological and social genericity, otherwise we could never even talk, however 'in-adequately', about it; it is not an 'experience', but an imaginary creation; it does not give access to the 'thing itself', but only *encounters* an *X*, and this only in some cases and only partly. It has no absolute philosophical privi-lege. It is only an eternally recurring starting and (provisionally) ending point. 'Home is where we start from', wrote, I think, T. S. Eliot. Our 'per-sonal' experience is our personal home – and this home would not be a home, but a solitary cave, if it was not in a village or a town. For, it is the collectivity that teaches us how to build homes and how to live in them. We cannot live without a home but neither can we remain hermetically enclosed in 'our' home.

And when one moves, as the last Husserl and the first Heidegger, from the egological, strictly phenomenological point of view (the *je meiniges, je eigenes* of *Sein und Zeit*) to the 'life-world', one has just exchanged the egocentric for an ethno- or sociocentric point of view: solipsism on a larger scale. For, to know, as we must, that our *Lebenswelt* is but one among an indefinite number of others is to recognize that there is a multiplicity of 'first-person' collective 'experiences' among which there is, at first glance, no privileged one; at second glance, the only 'privileged' one – philosophically and, I would add, politically – is the one which made itself capable of *recog-nizing* and *accepting* this very multiplicity of human worlds, thereby breaking as far as possible the closure of its own world.

IV

As already stated, we never deal with 'impressions'. We deal with perceptions, that is, a class of representations (*Vorstellungen*). And it is impossible to compose a perceptual representation (or any representation) by sheer juxtaposition of 'sense data'. A *Vorstellung*, however vague or bizarre, possesses a unity and a formidable organization; it is never a sheer amorphous multiplicity, a pure *Mannigfaltigkeit*. There is therefore a tremendous amount of 'logical' work contained in the representation, entailing some of Kant's categories, some of his (wrongly named and placed) *Reflexionsbegriffen* and some others, notably topological schemata (e.g., neighbourhood/separation or continuity/discreteness) which I cannot dwell upon here.

These last considerations are certainly true of any living being – any being-for-itself – but in this case the 'logical' functions are, in general, simpler and, at any rate, unadulterated by the other functions of imagination in humans. Categories are intrinsic, immanent to the perception. A dog chases *a* (= *one*) rabbit, and usually catches it. A catch surely devoid of transcendental validity since the unity of the rabbit caught has not been established through mediations of transcendental schemata from the dog's unity of transcendental apperception. Kant is bound to a Cartesian conception of '*animaux machines*'. True, the third *Critique* sketches another view, but only 'reflectively' and only as part of a heavy teleological metaphysics. Let us, incidentally, outline my status under the Kantian regime: from the determining point of view I am a (somatical and psychical) machine; from the reflective point of view I am a mechanistically un-understandable but teleologically understandable being; from the transcendental point of view I simply *am* not – *Ich gelte*; from the ethical point of view I *ought* to be what in fact (from the determining point of view) I could *never* be: an agent acting 'outside' any psychological motives. To say, in these circumstances, that I am made out of 'crooked wood' is certainly the understatement of the millennium.

To revert to our main argument: radical imagination (as source of the perceptual *quale* and of logical forms) is what makes it possible for any being-for-itself (including humans) to *create for* itself an own [or proper] world (*eine Eigenwelt*) 'within' which it also posits itself. The ultimately indescribable *X* 'out there' becomes something definite and specific *for* a particular being, through the functioning of its sensory and logical imagination, which 'filters', 'forms', and 'organizes' the external 'shocks'. It is clear that no being-for-itself could 'organize' something out of the world, if this world were not intrinsically organiz*able* – which means that it cannot be simply 'chaotic'. But this is another dimension of the question – the properly ontological dimension – which cannot be discussed here.

But we do not have to do only with representations provoked by external 'shocks'. In relative (and often, absolute) independence from these, we do have an 'inside'. Here we part company with animals, etc. – not because they do not have an 'inside' but because we cannot say anything meaningful about it ('how it feels to be a bat'). The 'inside' is a perpetual, truly Heraclitean, flux of representations *cum* affects *cum* intentions, in fact indissociable. (On this indissociation neither Kant, nor Fichte, nor for that matter most of the inherited philosophy, has much to say. At best all this would be relegated to 'empirical psychology', etc.) I shall not insist upon this aspect: the whole psychoanalytical path has it as its main concern. Suffice it to say that here representations (and affects, and intentions or desires) emerge in an 'absolutely spontaneous' way, and even more: we have affects and intentions (desires, drives) which are creations of this a-causal *vis formandi* in their sheer being, their mode of being and their being-thus (*Sosein*). And, for all we know, this stream of representations *cum* affects *cum* desires is absolutely singular for each singular human being. It may be said that our sensory imagination and its logical components are, for all of us, 'identical' (though essentially similar would be a better term). But, to the extent that its products are decisively co-created by the 'inside', even this sensory imagination is, in the end, singular (*de gustibus et coloribus . . .*).

If, in its first aspect ('perceptual', geared to the 'outside'), the radical imagination creates a 'generic' own [or proper] world for the singular human being, a world sufficiently shared with the other members of the human species, in its second, fully psychical, aspect it creates a singular proper world. The importance of this could not be exaggerated. It is this 'inside' which conditions and makes possible, first, a 'distanciation' relative to the world considered as simply 'given', and, second, an active and acting *Einstellung*, position and disposition, towards the world. Representation, affect, and intention are at the same time principles of the formation of the proper world – even *materialiter spectati* – and principles of distanciation from it and action upon it.

A few words on a subject alluded to above: Kant's 'transcendental imagination'. Without in the least minimizing the importance of Kant's discovery, one must point to its limits. First, Kant's imagination is subject, throughout, to the requirements of 'true knowledge'. Second – and for this very reason – it is eternally 'the same'. If Kant's transcendental imagination started to *imagine* anything, the world, as constructed by Kant, would instantly collapse. For this very reason Kant cannot or will not see the creative function of the imagination in the cognitive (scientific or philosophical) domain. This is why the existence of a *history* of science must remain in the Kantian framework an enigma or, at best, a sheer cumulation of *inductions*.

Two additional remarks are here in order. The strongest – and truest – point in Kant's conception of the imagination is, of course, the schematism mediating between the categories and the 'sensory data'. Introducing it, Kant says: 'There is an art hidden in the depths of the human soul . . .', which is the source of the transcendental schemata. But, one wonders, what business have 'the human soul' and its 'depths' here? The human soul belongs in the domain of 'empirical psychology', where causality reigns supreme, etc. It has nothing to do with the 'transcendental' dimension, which is supposed to ensure the possibility of *a priori* synthetic knowledge.

The imagination appears also in the *Critique of Judgment* but is only mentioned, not used. A creative power is recognized but is not called creative (*schaffen*, not *schöpfen*; the latter word appears only once and in an indifferent context). This is the power of the genius – but the genius works like nature (*als Natur*). We enjoy in the work of art 'the free play of imagination in conformity with the laws of understanding', but the worth of the work of art lies in that it presents in the intuition the Ideas of Reason. (I confess that I am unable to see the Ideas of Reason presented in *Antigone* or in *King Lear*.)

I have already mentioned the 'logical' organization contained even in the simplest representation, perceptual or not. That this is so should not surprise us. Everything that is must contain an ensemblistic-identitary ('logical', in the largest sense possible) dimension; otherwise it would be *absolutely* indeterminate, and (at least for us) nonexistent. *A posteriori*, this is confirmed by the grasp logical categories have on whatever there is (e.g., 'the unreasonable effectiveness of mathematics', to quote Wigner). This, of course, by no means entails that 'what there is' is exhaustively determined by or reducible to 'logic' (not even when we consider 'physical' reality).

This is the 'objective' (or 'in itself') side of the question. The 'for itself' side emerges with life. Living beings would not be there if they had not developed, as a constituent of the proper world they create, a (however rudimentary) logical apparatus fit to cope, somehow or other, with the intrinsic ensemblistic-identitary dimension of the world. There are Kantian categories obviously embedded in the behaviour of dogs, not imposed on this behaviour by the scientific observer.

For all we know, these categories are not 'conscious' in animals (though obviously self-awareness is there), and even less reflected upon. For this to happen, two further conditions are required, which obtain only in the human domain. The first pertains to the radical imagination of the human psyche and its 'pathological' development expressed in its defunctionalization. I have dealt with this aspect somewhat extensively in other texts,[6] so I shall be very brief. Defunctionalization makes possible, first, the detachment of the representation from the object of the biological 'need', therefore the cathexis of biologically irrelevant objects (Gods, King, Country, etc.); and, second, the (biologically equally irrelevant) possibility that the activities of the psyche become objects for themselves, and the labile *quid pro quo*, which is the prerequisite of symbolism.

The second, equally important, condition is the creation, by the radical social imaginary, of institutions and, of course, first and foremost, of language. Neither life as such nor the singular psyche as such can produce institutions and language. Understanding and reason are socially instituted, though, of course, this institution leans on intrinsic possibilities and drives of the human psyche.

A last point must be made in this respect. The (Kantian) distinction between categories, 'transcendental' schemata, and 'empirical' representations cannot, of course, be taken as a distinction *in re* (nor is it taken as such by Kant himself). But one can be more precise. Any representation (I am abstracting here from affects and intentions) contains *qualia* and an organization of these *qualia*; this organization, in turn, consists in generic figures and traits and in categorial schemata. In other words, genericity and categoriality are intrinsic and immanent to the representation. To become categories and schemata they have to be *named* and *reflected upon*. And this – that is, abstract thought as such – is a relatively recent historical creation, not a biological trait of the 'human species', though all members of this species can share in this creation once it is there. But abstract thought itself always has to lean on some figure or image, be it, minimally, the image of the words through which it is carried on.

V

I shall be much briefer on the psychoanalytical path, which I have dealt with at length elsewhere.[7]

This path was opened, as we know, through the immense discoveries of Freud. But as I noted in the beginning, Freud never thematizes imagination as such. One has to use unsystematized, though seminal, indications in his work to draw rigorous and radical consequences from these and also to go beyond them in order to reach the reality of radical imagination. Among these indications, the main ones are the 'magical omnipotence of thought' (better called the *effective* omnipotence of thought, since we are dealing here with unconscious thought, where, in the first approximation, thinking makes it so purely and simply), and the (practically equivalent) assertion that there is no distinction, in the Unconscious, between a strongly cathected representation and an actual 'perception', that is, that there are not in the Unconscious 'indices of reality'. Wherefrom we can draw almost immediately a cardinal principle: for humans, representational pleasure prevails as a rule over organ pleasure, from which it also results that both representation and pleasure are *de*functionalized in humans. Another equally decisive consequence follows: projective schemata and processes have precedence over introjective ones, which should come as no surprise for any nonempiricist philosopher, and in which we just rediscover the very essence of any being for itself: creation of a proper world precedes by necessity any 'lesson' events in this world could supply. One particular remark on this: there is, nevertheless, in humans, certainly the specific strength and importance of the *introjective* processes and schemata, which can be understood if we realize that the human psyche cannot live outside a world of meaning and, when its own, initial, monadic meaning is, in the course of socialization, disrupted, as it must be, the resulting catastrophe has to be repaired by the internalization of the meaning supplied by the cathected persons of its environment. This is what is sometimes mistaken as an intrinsic disposition (*Anlage*) of the psyche towards socialization, and which is nothing more than a leaning on of the socialization process, made possible by the vital need of the psyche for meaning and the fact that society itself is nothing but the institution of meanings (social imaginary significations). Socialization is the process whereby the psyche is forced to abandon (never fully) its pristine solipsistic meaning for the shared meanings provided by society. Introjection goes always much further than animal *mimesis*, because it is always reinterpretation of that which is introjected, and this reinterpretation can only take place on the basis of the existing proper schemata. 'Below' the Freudian Unconscious, we have to postulate a psychical monad, initially closed upon itself and, until the end, constantly endeavouring to enclose in itself whatever is 'presented' to it. *Ich bin die Brust* (I am the bosom), wrote Freud in one of his last Notes in 1938.

Here again a digression seems useful. Paradoxically, inevitably, and despite his intentions and his formation, Freud remains a dualist. Soul and body, psyche and soma, remain for him essentially distinct – despite his elaboration of hysterical symptoms, and so on (we could add today what we know about psychosomatic illnesses). There can be no question of eliminating or 'solving' the time-honoured enigmas of this relation; let us just remember the amazing antinomies with which the most elementary evidence confronts us. The psyche is strongly dependent on the soma: even short of piercing your head with a bullet, I can make you talk nonsense with the help of some additional glasses of bourbon. The soma is strongly dependent on the psyche: even without mentioning hysterical symptoms or psychosomatic illnesses, I decided to write this text, therefore I am banging on my typewriter. The soma is strongly independent from the psyche: I have no control over the innumerable organic processes going on all the time within my body, some of which prepare my death. The psyche is strongly independent from the soma: even under the most horrible tortures, there are people who will not hand their comrades over to the police. This strange relationship definitely requires from us new modes of thinking. These should certainly start from something different from a reduction of one of the two entities to the other, or an irreversible and irreparable separation of soul and body.

Here are some indications along this line. We should posit 'behind' or 'below' the Freudian Unconscious (or the Id) a Nonconscious which is the living body *qua* human animated body in continuity with the psyche. There is no frontier between this living, animated body and the originary psychical monad. The monad is neither repressed nor repressible: it is *unsayable*. Nor do we 'repress' the life of the body. We vaguely 'feel' it, without knowing why and how – the beats of the heart, the movements of the bowels, probably already, very long ago, our movements within the amniotic fluid. There is a presence of the living body to itself, inextricably mixed with what we normally consider as the 'movements of the soul' proper. And there is the obvious and understandable substantive homogeneity between the singular person's psyche and soma. Socrates's dead body is no longer Socrates. Kant's soul could not inhabit Ava Gardner's body, nor the reverse. Human physiology is already soul-like; autoimmune disorders, where the *body's* 'defence mechanisms' turn against the body they are supposed to protect, can hardly be understood as the result of an external 'influence' of the soul on the body. (This example shows, incidentally, the nonfunctional, non-'logical' character of the human imagination.) It is in this light that we should consider the idea of a sensory, and more generally bodily, imagination.

These are tentative, embryonic thoughts. But there is a solid conclusion we reach on the psychoanalytic path: that the imagination of the singular human being is defunctionalized. Hegel has said that man is a sick animal. In truth, man is a mad animal, totally unfit for life, a species that would have disappeared as soon as it emerged if it had not proven itself capable, at the collective level, of another creation: society in the strict sense, that is, institutions embodying social imaginary significations. This creation we cannot help but impute to the creative capacity of anonymous human collectives, that is, to the radical instituting imaginary.

VI

To elucidate the idea of the instituting social imaginary we can again follow the two paths: the philosophical and the psychoanalytical.

Along the philosophical path, the discussion need not be long. Philosophy itself, and thought in general, cannot exist without language or, at least, without strong links with language. But any individual or 'contractual' primordial production of language is logically (not only historically) an absurdity. Language can only be a spontaneous creation of a human collective. And the same is true of all primordial institutions, without which there is no social life, therefore also no human beings.

From the psychoanalytic point of view, we never encounter singular psychosomatic humans in the 'pure' state; we encounter only socialized individuals. The psychical nucleus manifests itself very rarely, and only indirectly. In itself it forms the perpetually unattainable limit of psychoanalytic work. Ego, Super-Ego, Ego-ideal are unthinkable except as the products (at most, the coproducts) of a socialization process. Socialized individuals are walking and talking fragments of a given society; and they are *total* fragments: that is, they embody, in part actually, in part potentially, the essential core of the institutions and the significations of their society. There is no opposition between individual and society: the individual is a social creation, both as such and in its each time given social-historical form. The true polarity is between society and the psyche (the psyche-soma, in the sense indicated above). These are both irreducible to each other and effectively inseparable. The society as such cannot produce souls, the idea is meaningless; and an assembly of nonsocialized souls would not produce a society, but a hyper-Boschian nightmare. An assembly of *individuals* can, of course, produce a society (e.g., the *Mayflower* pilgrims), because these individuals are already *socialized* (otherwise they would not exist, even biologically).

The question of society (and, indissolubly, of history) is, of course, an abyssal subject, and I shall not try to summarize inadequately here what I have written at length elsewhere.[8] I shall only outline a few points.

A.   Society is creation, and creation of itself: self-creation. It is the emergence of a new ontological form – *eidos* – and of a new mode and level of being. It is a quasi-totality held together by institutions (language, norms, family forms, tools and production modes, etc.) and by the significations these institutions embody (totem, taboos, gods, God, *polis*, commodities, wealth, fatherland, etc.). Both of these represent ontological creations. We do not encounter anywhere else institutions as a mode of relation holding together the components of a totality; and we can 'explain' – causally produce or rationally deduce – neither the form institution as such, nor the fact of the institution, nor the particular primary institutions of a given society. And we do not encounter anywhere else signification, that is, the mode of being of an effective and 'acting' ideality, the immanent unperceivable; nor can we 'explain' the emergence of primary significations (e.g., the Hebrew God, the Greek *polis*, etc.).

I talk about self-creation, *not* 'self-organization'. In the case of society we do not have an assembly of already existing elements, the combination of which could possibly produce new or additional qualities of the whole; the quasi- (or rather pseudo-) 'elements' of society are created by society itself. Athens cannot exist without Athenians (*not* humans in general!) – but Athenians are created only in and by

Athens. Thus society is always self-institution – but for almost the whole of human history this fact of the self-institution has been veiled by the very institutions of society itself.

B.   Society as such is self-creation; and each particular society is a specific creation, the emergence of another *eidos* within the generic *eidos* of society.

C.   Society is always historical in the broad, but proper sense of the word: it is always undergoing a process of self-alteration. This process can be, and almost always has been, so slow as to be imperceptible; in our small social-historical province it happens to have been, over the last 4,000 years, rather rapid and violent. The question: 'When does a self-altering society stop being "the same" and become another?' is a concrete historical question for which standard logic has no answer (are the Romes of the early Republic, of Marius and Sulla, of the Antonins, etc., 'the same'?).

D.   In so far as they are neither causally producible nor rationally deducible, the institutions and social imaginary significations of each society are free creations of the anonymous collective concerned. They are creations *ex nihilo* – but not *in nihilo* or *cum nihilo*. This means, in particular, that they are creations *under constraints*. To mention the most important among these constraints:

i.   There are 'external' constraints – especially those imposed by· the first natural stratum, including the biological constitution of the human being. These are essentially trivial (which does not mean unimportant): the society is, each time, conditioned by its 'natural' habitat – it is not 'caused' by it. In so far as the first natural stratum exhibits, to a decisive degree, an ensemblistic-identitary dimension – two stones and two stones make four stones, a bull and a cow will always produce calves and not chickens, etc. – the social institution has to recreate this dimension in its 'representation' of the world, and of itself, that is, in the creation of its *Eigenwelt*. This dimension is also, of course, present in language; it corresponds to language as *code*, that is, as a quasi-univocal instrument of making/doing, reckoning and elementary reasoning. The code aspect of language (the cat is on the mat) is opposed to but also inextricably entangled with its poietic aspect which conveys the imaginary significations proper (God is one person in three). To these 'external' constraints responds the *functionality* of institutions, especially relative to the production of material life and to sexual reproduction.

ii.   There are 'internal' constraints, relative to the 'raw material' out of which society creates itself, that is, the psyche. The psyche has to be socialized and for this it has to abandon more or less its own world, its objects of investment, what is for it meaning, and to cathect socially created and valued objects, orientations, actions, roles, etc.; it has to abandon its own time and insert itself into a public time and a public world ('natural' as well as 'human'). When we consider the unbelievable variety of types of society known, we are almost led to think that the social institution can make out of the psyche whatever it pleases – make it polygamous, polyandrous, monogamous, fetishistic, pagan, monotheistic, pacific, bellicose, etc. On close inspection we see that this is indeed true, provided one condition is fulfilled: that the institution supplies the psyche with *meaning* – meaning for its life and meaning for its death. This is accomplished by the social imaginary significations, almost always religious ones, which tie together the meaning of the individual's life and death, the meaning of the existence and of the ways of the particular society, and the meaning of the world as a whole.

iii.   There are 'historical' constraints. We cannot fathom the 'origin' of societies, but no societies we can speak of emerge *in vacuo*. There are always, even if in pieces, a past and a tradition. But the relation to this past is itself a part of the institution of society. Thus, primitive or traditional societies attempt to reproduce and repeat almost literally the past. In the other cases, the 'reception' of past and tradition is, partly at least, conscious – but this 'reception' is, in fact, re-creation (present-day parlance would call it 'reinterpretation'). Athenian tragedy 'receives' Greek mythology, and it re-creates it. The history of Christianity is but the history of continuous 'reinterpretations' of the same sacred texts, with amazingly differing outcomes. Classical Greeks have been the object of an incessant 'reinterpretation' by the Western Europeans since the thirteenth century. This re-creation is, of course, always done according to the imaginary significations of the *present* – but, of course also, what is 'reinterpreted' is a given, not an indeterminate, material. Still, it is instructive to compare what the Byzantines, the Arabs, and the Western Europeans have done with the same Greek heritage. The Byzantines just kept the manuscripts, adding some scholia here and there. The Arabs used only the scientific and philosophical texts, ignoring the rest (see the beautiful short story by Borges on Averroes and Aristotle's *Poetics*). The Western Europeans have been struggling with the remnants of this heritage for eight centuries now, and do not seem to be through with it.

iv.   Finally, there are 'intrinsic' constraints – the most interesting of all. I can deal with only two of them.

   a.   Institutions and social imaginary significations have to be *coherent*. Coherence has to be assessed immanently, that is, relative to the main characters and 'drives' of the given society, taking into account the conformal behaviour of the socialized individuals, etc. Pyramid building with starving peasants is coherent when referred to the whole organization and social imaginary significations of the Pharaonic or Mayan societies.

   Coherence does not preclude internal divisions, oppositions, and strife. Slave-owning or feudal societies are, of course, coherent. Things are different with capitalist society, especially latter-day capitalist society, but in this case this is a historical novation, and belongs to another discussion. Coherence is not, generally, endangered by 'contradictions' between the strictly imaginary and the ensemblistic-identitary dimensions of the institution for, as a rule, the former prevail over the latter. Arithmetic and commerce have not been hampered in Christian societies by the fundamental equation $1 = 3$ implicit in the dogma of the Holy Trinity.

   Here belongs also the imaginary reciprocal entailment of the 'parts' of the institution and of the social imaginary significations. This is the enigmatic unity and substantive kinship between artifacts, beliefs, political regimes, artistic works, and, of course, human types belonging to the same society and the same historical period. Needless to say, any idea of a 'causal' or 'logical' explanation of this unity is meaningless.

   b.   On the other hand, institutions and social imaginary significations have to be *complete*. This is clearly and absolutely so in *heteronomous* societies, where *closure of meaning* prevails. The term *closure* has to be taken here in its strict, mathematical sense. Mathematicians say that an algebraic field is *closed* if the roots of any polynomial of the field are elements of the field. Likewise, in any closed society, any 'question' which can be formulated at all in the language of this society must find its answer within the magma of the social imaginary significations of the society. This entails, in particular, that questions concerning the *validity* of the social institutions and significations cannot be posed. The exclusion of such questions is ensured by the position of a *transcendent*, extrasocial, source of the institutions and significations, that is, religion.

E.   Some additional comments on the term social imaginary *significations* may help to prevent misunderstandings. I have chosen the term *significations* because it seems to me the least inappropriate to convey what I have in mind. But it should absolutely not be taken in a 'mentalistic' sense. Social imaginary significations create a proper world for the society considered – in fact, they *are* this world; and they shape the psyche of individuals. They create thus a 'representation' of the world, including the society itself and its place in this world; but this is far from being an intellectual construct. It goes together with the creation of a *drive* for the society considered (so to speak, a global intention) and of a specific *Stimmung* or mood (so to speak, of an affect, or a cluster of affects, permeating the whole of the social life). For example, Christian *faith* is a specific and pure historical creation entailing particular 'aims' (to be loved by God, saved, etc.) and most particular and peculiar *affects*, which would have been totally un-understandable (and nonsensical – *moria*, very rightly, says Saint Paul) for any classical Greek or Roman (and, for that matter, any Chinese or Japanese). And this is understandable, if one realizes that society is a being for itself.

VII

How is it possible that *we* are capable of talking in this way (correctly or not, that is another matter) about societies in general, putting ourselves, as it were, at an equal distance from all of them (be it an illusion, this is also another matter)?

Almost all societies we know have instituted themselves in and through the closure of meaning. They are heteronomous; they cannot put into question their own institution and they produce conformal and heteronomous individuals for whom the putting into question of the existing law is not just forbidden but mentally inconceivable and psychically unbearable. These individuals are 'conscious', but not self-reflective subjectivities.

This state of affairs was broken for the first time in ancient Greece, and this breaking was repeated fifteen centuries later, with much greater difficulty but also on an incomparably large scale, in Western Europe. In both cases the institutions and the ultimate beliefs of the tribe have been explicitly called into question and, to a large extent, modified. Partially open societies have emerged, together with self-reflective individuals. The main carriers of this new historical creation were politics as collective emancipatory movement and philosophy as self-reflecting, uninhibitedly critical thought. Thus emerged what I call the project of collective and individual autonomy.

In both cases the project has not been brought to its completion. One might say that it *could* not be brought to a completion. To this I would answer that neither this statement nor its contradiction can be 'theoretically' demonstrated or established, it being understood that the project of autonomy does not aim at establishing Paradise on Earth or at bringing about the end of human history; nor does it purport to ensure universal happiness. The object of politics is not happiness but freedom; autonomy is freedom understood not in the inherited, metaphysical sense, but as effective, humanly feasible, lucid and reflective positing of the rules of individual and collective activity. This is why the social-historical struggles animated by this project have left so many important results, among which are whatever intellectual and political freedom we may be enjoying today. But the philosophically important point is that, even if it finally failed, as in Athens, or if it is in danger of waning, as in the present Western world, its effect has been the creation of a totally new, unheard of, ontological *eidos*: a type of being which, consciously and explicitly, alters the laws of its own existence as it is, however partially, materialized in a self-legislating society and in a new type of human being: reflective and deliberating subjectivity. And this is what allows us to take some distance from our own society, to talk about society and history in general, and to accept rational criticism of what we say in this or any other respect.

Notes

1   See *MP* (1986).
2   See *DI* (1978).
3   On ensemblistic-identitary logic, see chapter 4 of *IIS*.
4   See, e.g., Charles Taylor, *Sources of the Self* (Cambridge, England: Cambridge University Press, 1989), pp. 162ff. Richard Rorty has also, from another point of view, attacked this distinction.
5   Taylor on Descartes, *Sources of the Self*, p. 162.
6   See *SST* (1986) and *LIR* (1991).
7   See the texts cited in note 6, and chapter 6 of *IIS*.
8   See *CL*, *IIS*, *PPA*, and *WIF*.

13

Culture in a Democratic Society (1994)*

I

Nothing, in appearance, is more obvious than the question implied by the title of the present text. What, indeed, could be more immediately evident, for those who think that they live in a democratic society, than to inquire about the place of culture in their society – all the more so as we are witnessing today, apparently, both an unprecedented dissemination of what is called culture and an intensification of questions and criticisms that bear upon what is thus being disseminated as well as upon its ways of being disseminated?

There is a way of responding to this question that is, in truth, a way of avoiding it. That response has consisted, for going on two centuries now, in affirming the specificity of the place of culture in a democratic society (as opposed to what was the case in nondemocratic societies). It is claimed, in this nonresponse, that this specificity consists solely in the following: that here culture is for everyone and not for an elite (however that elite may be defined). This 'for everyone' may, in turn, be taken in a simply quantitative fashion: whatever the existing culture may be, it should be put at everyone's disposal, not only 'in principle' (which was not the case, for example, in Pharaonic Egypt), but sociologically, in the sense that the existing culture should become effectively accessible to all – as is facilitated today, supposedly, by universal, free, and mandatory education as well as by museums, public concerts, etc.

Yet this sociological 'for everyone' may also be taken in another, stronger sense. Taking the existing culture to be a product of a class society, made

---

*   The ideas developed in the present text were first presented in a number of talks, notably in Paris in 1991, in Ankara in 1992, in Alexandroupolis in 1993, in Madrid in 1994, and at New York University in 1995. The version given here corresponds to the lecture delivered in Madrid 3 March 1994, as part of a colloquium on contemporary French political thought organized by the Ortega y Gasset Foundation in collaboration with the Cultural Service of the French Embassy. 'La Culture dans une société démocratique' was originally published in *Esprit*, October 1994, pp. 40–50, with a title provided by this Paris review: 'En Mal de culture'. Reprinted with original title in *MI*, pp. 194–205. The present translation is forthcoming in *Drunken Boat*, 3 (1997). [T/E: Translating from the original French typescript, I have also made use of 'Fragmentation and Creativity in a Democratic Society', Castoriadis's hand-corrected transcription of his 1992 English-language Ankara talk.]

by and/or for the dominant strata of that society, one may demand a 'culture for the masses'. As we know, this demand sums up the theory and the practice of *Proletkult* in Russia during the first years after the Revolution of 1917 and, in mystification and horror, the Stalinist and Zhdanovist theory and practice of 'socialist realism' a few decades later.

I shall not discuss here this last conception of cultural dissemination, resuscitated today by various (feminist, Black, etc.) movements that condemn the totality of the Greco-European legacy as being a product of 'dead white males'. I ask only why one does not also condemn, on the basis of the same principle, the Chinese, Islamic, or Aztec cultural legacy, products of dead males, respectively yellow, white, and 'red'. At bottom, the question boils down to an old philosophical interrogation: Do the effective conditions for the genesis of a work (of an idea, of a reasoned argument, etc.) determine, without further ado, its *validity*? To answer in the affirmative is to fall into the old contradiction of self-referentiality, for this response implicitly boils down to passing judgement as to the validity of this very statement, a judgement that claims to be independent of the effective conditions for its genesis – unless one arbitrarily places oneself in the position of prophet or messiah. This is what was done, on behalf of the proletariat and by placing oneself in its stead, with an honest naivety by the partisans of *Proletkult* and with infamous effrontery by the Stalinists.

Obviously, such an 'assignment of origin' is not simply absurd. But the attitudes of *Proletkult*, fanatical feminists, etc. – or simply a 'genealogy' *à la* Nietzsche, warmed over with a Parisian sauce and served up as a [Foucauldian] 'archaeology' a century later – serve to eliminate the in-eliminable question of *de jure validity*. (That Jefferson owned slaves does not, *ipso facto*, invalidate the Declaration of Independence.) And in their un-fathomable confusion, they simply 'forget' to pose the abyssal question: How can words and works of other times and places still speak to us and, sometimes, make us tremble?

II

Both the term *culture* and that of *democracy* immediately raise a series of interminable questions. Let us take some initial bearings. We shall call *culture* all that, in the public domain of a society, goes beyond that which is simply functional and instrumental in the operation of that society and all that introduces an invisible – or, better, an unperceivable – dimension invested or 'cathected' in a positive way by the individuals of that society. In other words, culture concerns all that, in this society, pertains to the imag-inary *stricto sensu*, to the poietic imaginary, in as much as this imaginary dimension is embodied in works and in patterns of behaviour that go beyond the functional. It goes without saying that the distinction between the functional and the poietic is not itself a material distinction.

The term democracy lends itself to infinitely greater discussion, first because of its very nature and, second, because for a long time it has been the stake in political debates and struggles. In our century, everybody – including the most bloodthirsty tyrants (Nazis and Fascists excepted) – claims to be a democrat. We can attempt to escape from this cacophony of claims by returning to the etymology of this term: democracy is the *kratos* of the *dēmos*, the power of the people. Of course, philology cannot settle political conflicts, but at least it makes us reflect upon the following question: Where in the world today, in what country on this planet, do we see realized the *power of the people?*

Yet at the same time we see this power being affirmed, under the heading of 'sovereignty of the people', in the constitutions of all countries that today call themselves 'democratic'. Leaving aside for a moment the possibility that this affirmation is simply duplicitous, let us accept the letter of the law in order to sift out a meaning for this term that few people would dare to contest: in a democracy, the people are sovereign, that is to say, they make laws and the law. Or else, we may say: Society makes its institutions and its institution; it is autonomous; it self-institutes itself [*s'auto-institue*]. But since every society in fact self-institutes itself, we must add that, at least in part, it self-institutes itself *explicitly* and *reflectively*. I shall return later on to this last term. In any case, a democratic society recognizes in its rules, its norms, its values, and its significations its own creations, whether deliberate or not.

This autonomy, this freedom [of a democratic society] implies and at the same time presupposes the autonomy, the freedom of individuals; the former is impossible without the latter. And yet such individual autonomy, such individual freedom, stated and guaranteed by law, by the constitution, by declarations of the rights of man and of the citizen or by a bill of rights, rests in the last analysis, both *de jure* and *de facto*, on the collective law, which is formal as well as informal. Real, effective individual freedom (I am not speaking of philosophical or psychical freedom) must be decided by a law – even if that law is called a 'Declaration' or 'Bill of Rights' – that no individual could posit or ratify on his own. And within the framework of this law, the individual can in turn define for himself the norms, values, and significations through which this individual will try to order his own life and to give that life a meaning.

This autonomy, or explicit self-institution, which emerges for the first time in the democratic Greek cities and re-emerges, with much greater breadth, in the modern Western world, marks the break that democracy entails *vis-à-vis* all previous social-historical regimes.[1] In the latter systems of rule, which are regimes of *instituted heteronomy*, the source and foundation for the law, as well as for every norm, value, and signification, are posited as being transcendent to society itself: transcendent in the absolute, as in monotheistic societies, and transcendent, in any case, relative to the effective reality of living society (as in the case of archaic societies). Such an assignment of its source and its foundation goes hand in hand with a *closure of signification*; the word of God, or the arrangements bestowed by the ancestors, are taken to lie beyond discussion and to be established once and for all.

What goes for society as a whole also holds for individuals: the meaning of their lives is given, settled in advance, and, for this reason, assured. No discussion is possible concerning institutions – therefore, also, no possible discussion about social beliefs, about what is valid or invalid, about good and evil. In a heteronomous – or simply a traditional – society the closure of signification shuts off in advance not only every political question as well as every philosophical one, but equally every ethical or aesthetic question. In every circumstance, what is to be done is dictated without possible appeal by the law and by collective mores. Nothing in this situation is changed when interminable commentaries or a subtle casuistry is introduced (as with the Talmud, Christian Doctors, or Islamic theologians).

The same thing holds for culture. No doubt, heteronomous societies have created immortal works – or, quite simply, a countless host of beautiful objects. And already, this statement shows – from a democratic perspective, as a matter of fact – the untenability of the historical proscriptions today's new fanatics want to issue concerning cultural matters. Following the logic of certain feminists, for example, I ought to cast out the *Passion According to Saint John* not only because it was composed by a dead and white male but because it gives expression to a religious faith that, in my own view, is alienating.

And yet these immortal works remain forever inscribed within a given social-historical context and horizon. They always also embody imaginary significations as they are each time instituted. This is why the immense majority of works are connected with the sacred in general, or with the politically sacred: they fortify the society's instituted significations through adoration of the divine, hero worship, praise for great kings, or the glorification of warrior bravery, piety, and other virtues consecrated by tradition. Obviously, I am painting a rather rough portrait here, but such is the source upon which the great works bequeathed to us by archaic societies, by the great traditional monarchies, by the true European Middle Ages (that is, from the fifth to the thirteenth century), or by Islam draw their inspiration.

If works and their creators act, so to speak, in the service of instituted significations, what the public in these societies finds in them is the confirmation and illustration of collective and traditional significations and values. And this situation is consonant with the specific mode of 'cultural temporality' of these societies, namely, their extremely slow rhythm, the hidden, subterranean character of the alteration of styles and contents, which is parallel and almost synchronous with changes in language itself. Indeed, it is also consonant with our inability, *ex post facto*, to individuate the creators – an inability that is in no way due to our lack of sufficient information. This is how one paints under the Tang dynasty, one does not paint otherwise; this is the one way to sculpt or build under the twentieth Pharaonic dynasty, and one would have to be a specialist to be able to distinguish such works from those that preceded them or followed them by a few centuries. Thus is there one form, canonically and ecclesiastically regulated down to its tiniest details, for a Byzantine icon of this or that saint or of this or that moment in the life of the Virgin. Anticipating matters somewhat now, let us point out here that, in contrast, it is impossible to confound a fragment composed by Sappho with a fragment from Archilochus, a piece written by Bach with one by Handel, and that, in listening to certain passages from Mozart, one can cry, 'But it's already Beethoven!'

III

The creation of democracy, just like a fragile germ or seed, radically alters this situation. A brief philosophical digression is indispensable here, as it will elucidate, I hope, the question left open above concerning transhistorical validity.[2]

When all is said and done, Being is Chaos, Abyss, Groundlessness. But it is also creation. It is, to employ a Latin expression, a *vis formandi* (a power of formation) which is not predetermined and which superimposes on the Chaos a Cosmos, a World that is organized and ordered somehow or other. In the same way, the human, too, is Abyss, Chaos, Groundlessness – not only in as much as it participates in being in general (for example, *qua* matter and *qua* living matter) but also in as much as we are beings of imagination and of the imaginary. The emergence of these determinations itself manifests the creation and the *vis formandi* that appertain to being as such, but these determinations also concretely realize the mode of being of the creation and *vis formandi* specific to the properly human. Here we can do no more than note the fact that this *vis formandi* is accompanied, in the human sphere, by a *libido formandi*: to the potential for creation found in being in general, the human sphere adds a desire for formation. I call this potential and this desire the 'poietic' element of humanity. Reason itself, in its specifically human form (which is not the same as the rationality intrinsic to animals, for example), is but an offspring thereof.

The 'meaning' with which human beings wish to, and must, always invest the world, their society, their own persons and life is nothing other than this formation, this *Bildung*, this setting into order. Perpetual, and perpetually endangered, this effort is that of a gathering together of all that presents itself, and of all that it itself gives rise to, into an order, an organization, a Cosmos. When man organizes rationally – 'ensidically' [in an ensemblistic-identitary manner] – he does nothing but reproduce, repeat, or prolong already existing forms. But when he organizes poietically, he gives form to the Chaos. This giving-of-form to the Chaos (to the Chaos of what is and that within man himself) – which is, perhaps, the best definition of culture – manifests itself with striking clarity in the case of art.[3] This form is meaning or signification. Signification here is not a simple matter of ideas or representations, for it must gather together – bind in a form – representation, desire, and affect.

This is evidently what religion – all religion – has succeeded so marvellously in doing, so long as it itself has held together. By way of a parenthesis, let us add that we discover here the full meaning of the famous Latin verb *religere*: to bind [*lier*] not only the members of a collectivity but everything, absolutely everything, that presents itself, and to bind the former with the latter.

Religion accomplishes this stupefying *tour de force*, however, only by coupling the significations it creates with a transcendent guarantee – a guarantee for which human beings, quite obviously, have a desperate need. It also couples these significations with a form of closure which seems – but only *seems* – to be consubstantial with the very idea of meaning, but which results, in truth, from this transcendent guarantee itself. Religion establishes this guarantee and this closure by denying to living humanity the possibility of creating meaning: all meaning [*sens*], and all nonsense, has been created once and for all. The *vis formandi* is thus reduced and strictly channelled, and the *libido formandi* is limited to an enjoyment of its past products, without knowing that they are its own doing.

Now, democratic creation abolishes all transcendent sources of signification. They are abolished, in any case, in the public domain, but in fact, if this creation is pushed to its ultimate consequences, they are abolished for the 'private individual', as well, for democratic creation is the creation of unlimited interrogation in all domains: what is the true and the false, what is the just and the unjust, what is the good and what is evil, what is the beautiful and the ugly. It is in this that its *reflectiveness* resides. Democratic creation breaks the closure of signification and thus restores to living society its *vis formandi* and its *libido formandi*. In reality, it does the same thing in private life, since it claims to give to each person the possibility of creating the meaning of her own life. This presupposes that the person has accepted as fact that there is not, as a treasure that has been hidden or that is to be found, any 'signification' in being, the world, history, or our own lives. In other words, it entails acceptance of the fact that we create signification on the basis of the baseless, the groundless, that we too give form to the Chaos through our thought, our action, our labour, our works, and that therefore this signification has no 'guarantee' external to itself.

This means that we are alone in being – alone, but not solipsists. We are alone, already due to the fact that we speak and we speak to ourselves – whereas being itself does not speak, not even to announce the enigma of the Sphinx. But we are not solipsists, since our creation (and already our speech) leans on being, since our creation is constantly relaunched by our confrontation with being and kept in motion by the effort to give form to that which lends itself thereto only partially and fleetingly – whether it be the visible or the audible world, our being in common or our innermost life – and since our creation is thus generally ephemeral, sometimes durable, always risky, and, in the very end, caught within the horizon of destruction – which in being is the flipside of creation.

But then the conditions for cultural creation appear wholly changed. Here we arrive at the heart of our question. Briefly speaking, we may say that in a democratic society the cultural work does not necessarily lie within a field of instituted and collectively accepted significations. It does not find therein its canons of form and content, any more than its author can draw therefrom her subject matter and working methods or the public some support for its show of allegiance. The collectivity itself creates, overtly, its own norms and significations – and the individual is called upon, at least *de jure*, to create, within what in formal terms are quite broad boundaries, the meaning of his life and, for example, truly to judge for himself the cultural works that are presented to him.

Of course, one must be careful not to present this passage in absolutist fashion. There always is a social field of signification, which is far from simply formal in character and from which no one, be she the most original artist ever, can escape: all she can do is contribute to its alteration. We are essentially social and historical beings. Tradition is always present, even if it is not explicitly confining. Both the creation and the acceptance of significations are always social, even when, as in the case of culture proper, they are not formally instituted.

IV

These, we may say, are the basic characteristics of the social field, and it is altered when a democratic society is instaurated. One can see this in the case of ancient Greece, which I shall not discuss here, as well as in the case of modern Europe.

Let us now consider the properly modern phase of the Western world, from the great revolutions at the end of the eighteenth century, which were democratic and in fact de-Christianizing, until around 1950, the approximate date starting from which I believe one can discern the onset of a new situation. What is the field of significations underlying the unprecedented cultural creation that took place over a period of a century and a half? To respond to this question would certainly require an immense social-historical investigation, which there can be no question of undertaking here. I shall limit myself to jotting down a few notes that concern basically the subjective side of the question, that is, the personal translation and expression of these new significations.

On the creator's part, one can no doubt speak of an intense sense of freedom and of a lucid drunkenness accompanying it. There is the drunkenness of exploring new forms, of the freedom of creating them. Thenceforth, these new forms were explicitly sought after for their own sake. They did not arise as a mere outgrowth of the artistic process, as had been the case in previous periods. This freedom, however, remained linked to an object. It entailed a search for and an instauration of a meaning in the form – or better, an explicit search for a form that would be capable of bearing and conveying a new meaning. To be sure, there was also a return to the *kleos* and *kudos* – the glory and renown – of the Ancients. But Proust has already said what is at issue here: the act itself changes us rather profoundly, so that we no longer attach importance to its motives – like the artist 'who set to work for the sake of glory and in the same stroke detached himself from the desire for glory'.[4] Here, the achievement of freedom is freedom in the creation of norms, exemplary creation (as Kant says in the *Critique of Judgment*); and for this reason such creation is destined to endure. This is eminently the case in modern art (in the sense of the period designated above), where there was an exploration and creation of forms in the strong sense. Even if it was not easily accepted by those to whom it was addressed, and even if it did not correspond to 'popular taste', it was thereby democratic – that is to say, liberatory. And it was democratic even when its representatives happened to be politically reactionary, as was the case with Chateaubriand, Balzac, Dostoyevsky, Degas, and so many others.

But above all, it remained linked to an object. If it ceased to be religious, modern art became 'philosophical' – it involved the exploration of ever new strata of the psyche and the social, of the visible and the audible, so that it might, in and through this exploration, and in its own unique way, give form to the Chaos. This does not mean that modern art is philosophy, but it was able to exist only by questioning meaning as it was each time established and by creating other forms for it. It may be recalled at this point that this was the theme of the long meditation that constitutes the last volume of *À la Recherche du temps perdu* (*Remembrance of Things Past*, literally: 'In seach of time lost'), entitled *Le Temps retrouvé* ('time refound'), where Proust finally makes it his object to 'find the essence of things'.

Here again, Kant had seen the thing at hand, although he travestied it when he said that the work of art is 'presentation in the intuition of the Ideas of Reason'. For, what art presents are not the Ideas of Reason, but the Chaos, the Abyss, the Groundlessness to which it gives form. And through this presentation, it is a window on the Chaos; it abolishes our tranquil and stupid assurance about our daily life; it reminds us that we forever live at the edge of the Abyss – which is the main thing an autonomous being knows, although that does not prevent this being from living and creating – like, to cite Proust once again, the 'atheistic artist. . . [who] believes himself obliged to recommence twenty times a piece of work of which the admiration it will arouse will matter little to his worm-eaten body, like the yellow wall section painted with so much knowledge and refinement by a forever unknown artist, barely identified under the name of Vermeer'.[5]

The public, for its part, participates in this freedom 'by proxy', vicariously, using the artist as go-between. Above all, the public is caught up in the new meaning of the work – and it can be so caught up only because, despite inertia, delays, resistances, and reactions, this public itself is creative. The reception of a great new work is never and can never be a matter of mere passive acceptance; it is always also re-creation. And the publics of Western countries, from the eighteenth century down to the middle of the twentieth century, have been authentically creative publics. In other words, the freedom of the creator and her products are, in themselves, socially invested.

V

Are we still living in this situation? A risky question, a dangerous one from which I shall not try, however, to extract myself.

I think that, despite appearances, the rupture of the closure of meaning that was instaurated by the great democratic movements is in danger of being covered back over.[6] On the level of the real functioning of society, the 'power of the people' serves as a screen for the power of money, techno-science, party and State bureaucracies, and the media. On the level of individuals, a new closure is in the process of being established, which takes the form of a generalized conformism.[7] It is my claim that we are living the most conformist phase in modern history. People say each individual is 'free' – but in fact all people passively receive the *sole* meaning the institution and the social field propose to them and in fact impose on them: teleconsumption, which is made up of consumption, television, and consumption simulated via television.

Let me linger briefly over the 'pleasure' of the contemporary tele-consumer. As opposed to the pleasure of the spectator, the auditor, or the reader of a work of art, this sort of pleasure includes only a minimum of sublimation: it involves a vicarious satisfaction of drives through a kind of voyeurism, a bidimensional 'organ pleasure' accompanied by a maximum of passivity. What television presents may in itself be 'beautiful' or 'ugly', but whatever it is it is received passively, in inertia and conformism. If I read a great novel as I would a mediocre crime novel, skipping through the pages to find out 'how it's going to end', at the end of the evening I wind up with a headache. If I read it *as* a great novel, remaining attentive to the time proper to its phrases and narration, I am engaged in a strange and multiple psychical and mental activity that stimulates me without tiring me.

The triumph of democracy has been proclaimed as the triumph of 'individualism'. But this 'individualism' is not and cannot be an empty form wherein individuals 'do what they like' – any more than 'democracy' can be simply procedural in character. 'Democratic procedures' are each time filled by the oligarchical character of the contemporary social structure – as the 'individualistic' form is filled by the dominant social imaginary, the capitalist imaginary of the unlimited expansion of production and consumption.

On the level of cultural creation – where, of course, judgements are most uncertain and most liable to challenge – one cannot underestimate the growth of eclecticism, collage, spineless syncretism, and, above all, the loss of the *object* and the loss of *meaning*, which go hand in hand with an abandonment of the search for form (form always being infinitely more than form since, as Victor Hugo said, it is the bottom that rises to the surface).

The most pessimistic prophecies – from Tocqueville's prophecy of the 'mediocrity' of the 'democratic' individual, passing by way of Nietzsche and his discussion of nihilism ('What does nihilism signify? That higher values are being devalued. It lacks a goal, it is missing the answer to the question "Why?"'),[8] and extending to Spengler and Heidegger and beyond – are now in the process of being fulfilled. They are now even in the process of being theorized in 'postmodernism', whose displays of self-contentment are as arrogant as they are stupid.

If these statements are accurate, be they only partially so, culture in *such a* 'democratic' society runs the greatest of dangers – not, of course, in its erudite, museum-oriented or touristic form, but in its creative essence. Society forms a whole – albeit one that is certainly fragmented, certainly hypercomplex, certainly enigmatic. Thus, just as the current evolution of culture is not wholly unrelated to the inertia and the social and political passivity characteristic of our world today, so a renaissance of its vitality, should it take place, will be indissociable from a great new social-historical movement which will reactivate democracy and will give it at once the form and the contents the project of autonomy requires.

We feel troubled by the fact that it is impossible to imagine in concrete terms the content of such a new creation – whereas in fact that is the very stuff of creation. Cleisthenes and his companions[9] neither could have nor should have 'foreseen' tragedy and the Parthenon, any more than the members of the French Constituent Assembly or the Founding Fathers could have imagined Stendhal, Balzac, Rimbaud, Manet, and Proust or Poe, Melville, Whitman, and Faulkner.

Philosophy shows us that it would be absurd to believe that we might ever exhaust the thinkable, the feasible, the formable, just as it shows that it would be absurd to set limits on the formative potential always stirring within the psychical imagination and within the collective social-historical imaginary. But it does not stop us from noting that humanity has traversed periods of despondency and lethargy that are all the more insidious as they have been accompanied by what some have called 'material well-being'. To the extent, whether frail or firm, that this depends on those who have a direct and active connection with culture, if their work remains faithful to the requirements of freedom and responsibility these persons will be able to contribute to making this phase of lethargy be as short as possible.

Paris, October 1991–April 1994

Notes

1 See, for example, *PoPA* (1988).

2 For what follows, see, for example, *ISR* (1982).

3 See, for example, *DG*, pp. 238–42; also *STCC* (1979).

4 From *La Fugitive*, in *À la Recherche du temps perdu* (Paris: Gallimard [Pléiade edition], 1954), vol. 3, pp. 575–6.

5 For *La Prisonnière*, in ibid., p. 188.

6 I have written abundantly about this topic since 1959. See, for example, *MCR* (1960–1), *CWS* (1982), *DW* (1991).

7 *RA* (1989).

8 *Wille zur Macht*, § 2. See also § 12: 'A goal [*Ziel*] is always a meaning [*Sinn*].'

9 T/E: Cleisthenes was the late sixth-century BCE Athenian reformer generally credited with introducing the political reforms that led to the instauration of democracy at Athens. Castoriadis has contributed a text, 'Athenian Democracy: False and True Questions', for the supplement to a recent translation of Pierre Lévêque and Pierre Vidal-Naquet's classic 1963 study of this 2,500-year-old reform: *Cleisthenes the Athenian. An Essay on the Representation of Space and Time in Greek Political Thought from the End of the Sixth Century to the Death of Plato*, trans. David Ames Curtis (Atlantic Highlands, NJ: Humanities, 1996).

14

Psychoanalysis and Philosophy (1996)*

One of the difficulties inherent in the topic I have chosen, and rather specific to it, is this: Which psychoanalysis, which philosophy? The answer to the second half of this question seems less difficult: to philosophize means, first and foremost, to ask oneself constantly, 'What is it to philosophize and what kind of philosophy does one wish to practise?' Such an interrogation is, at the very most, only implicit in psychoanalysis. Since Freud, one calls psychoanalysis the sort of investigation that concerns what he called psychical reality and, in the main, its unconscious dimension, and at the same time the shared activity of two subjects who aim, via an exploration of this reality, at achieving a certain modification of one of the subjects (this being called, since Freud, 'the end of analysis').

But on the other hand, the question 'Which psychoanalysis?' takes on its full weight when one recalls the multiplicity of psychoanalytic 'schools', their mutual denigration (Leibniz did not say, and never would have said, when reading Spinoza, 'That's not philosophy', whereas 'That's not psychoanalysis' is common currency in polemics among psychoanalysts), the proliferation of interpretations – and, still more, the complexity of Freud's work, his ambiguities, especially the ceaseless unfolding, throughout his life, of his thought, his discovery and his creation of new ideas and ways of seeing.[1] To take but one example, one of Freud's propositions that I consider most important, *Ich bin die Brust* (I am the breast), appears for the first time only in 1939, jotted down on a piece of paper containing only a few lines.[2]

Although it must be stated here, it is therefore tautologous to say that I am speaking on the basis of my own conception of psychoanalysis and of my reworking of the problematic of the psyche, both of which are very different from those that have general currency.

A few words on what psychoanalysis's contribution to philosophy, and more generally to our mode of thinking, is not and cannot be. It is certainly not the idea, as old as philosophy and more than doubtful from the psychoanalytic viewpoint itself, of some sort of determinism of psychical

* Translated from the original unpublished French typescript, 'Psychanalyse et philosophie', which is scheduled to appear in *CL 5*. The translation is forthcoming in a *Festschrift* for Paul Roazen.

phenomena. Nor is it the discovery of the 'splitting of the subject'. Certainly, the 'discovery of the Unconscious' is something basic, and I shall return to it. But, independent of its long and rich philosophical and scientific prehistory,[3] the conscious/unconscious distinction (save for extreme Cartesians, and even then . . .) appertains to something that long ago had attained its philosophical status. The 'splitting of the subject', for example, is envisaged in a much more radical way in Kantian philosophy than it is in the 'subversive' discourses of the past few decades. Indeed, in Kantianism the effectively actual man in his entirety is found to be caught in empirical determinations which act, must (*müssen*, in the sense of the necessity of physical law) act, as 'causes' for his (practical, and certainly also, in strict rigour, cognitive) behaviour in general. Opposed to this effective man is a Transcendental Ego that must (*sollt*, in the sense of the exigencies of law and right) escape these determinations. It changes nothing that in these empirical determinations might be found some motivations generated by egotistical interest (and, for example, a pleasure principle and a reality principle); that these 'interests' might be of a libidinal, economic, or other nature; that they might be conscious or, wholly or in part, nonconscious; that there might even be 'causes' that compulsorily render these motivations unconscious. That would merely serve to underline psychoanalysis's status as a sector of empirical psychology. And the antinomy the Kantian position encounters here – viz., that the effective subject is caught up in effective determinations in which there can be no question of truth or value but simply concatenations of fact, whereas this very assertion stakes a claim to be true – is no different, except for being clearer, than the one a naive psychoanalysis encounters. I shall return to this point below.

Nor is psychoanalysis's contribution to philosophy to be sought on the side of the reinforcement given to the slogan that was fashionable not so long ago, that of the 'death of the subject' (of man, of history, etc.). If psychoanalysis shows anything, it is, rather, the plurality of subjects contained within the same envelope – and the fact that it is very much a question of an agency or instance (*Instanz*) that possesses the essential attributes of a subject. This idea, too, is of venerable antiquity: let us recall the Platonic image of the horses pulling the soul, each in its own direction, and of the rational instance that tends to play the role of auriga (charioteer), an image Freud borrowed almost verbatim. But with the theory of psychical instances, this idea begins to be elaborated in a way that will lead from a simple mention to the intricacies of topographical and dynamic analysis. And far from crying over, or rejoicing over, the death of the subject, it is toward the instauration of the subjective instance *par excellence*, reflective and deliberative subjectivity, that psychoanalysis tends or ought to tend. Psychoanalysis's contribution is to elucidate the structure of every subject, whatever kind it may be – that is, it provides a capital elucidation of the organization of the *for-itself*.

Finally, we may say that, far from teaching us that we should establish the unlimited reign of desire, psychoanalysis makes us understand that such a reign would end, rather, in generalized murder.

Here, in brief, are the principal points whereby, in my opinion, an elucidation of the psyche, one inspired by psychoanalysis but also continuing it, is of capital philosophical importance.

1   *On the level of ontology.* As elucidated by psychoanalysis, the psyche brings into view for us a mode of being that has more or less been ignored by the inherited philosophy. This mode of being is in truth universal, but it appears here with striking clarity.

2   *On the level of philosophical anthropology.* Psychoanalysis obliges us to see that the human being is not a *zoon logon ekhon* [an animal possessing 'reason'] but essentially an imagining being, one endowed with radical, unmotivated, defunctionalized imagination. It also helps us to understand the process of socialization and, thereby, the deep roots of its motivations, and the almost unbreakable solidity of its heteronomy.

3   *On the level of practical philosophy.* As practico-poietic activity, psychoanalysis sheds light on the idea of practice and indicates, in the case of the singular human being, both a path toward the transformation of this being and autonomy as the goal of this transformation.

Ontology

Psychoanalysis obliges us to think, to endeavour to render thinkable, a new mode of being that is embodied in and exemplified by the psyche and that proves, once grasped and elucidated upon the example of this particular being, to be of universal import. I have called this mode of being the magma.[4]

In large part and in its main current, the inherited ontology is founded upon the equation being = being-determined. This latter term does not concern simply the 'determinism' of phenomena (or of 'things', or of 'ideas'), which is but a derivative thereof, but the status of every particular being as well as the 'meaning' (the content, the signified) of the term being as such. This is true even when this determinacy is presented as an inaccessible limit or an ideal. Thus, for example, in Kant the statement '*everything which exists is completely determined*, does not signify only that one of every pair of *given* contradictory predicates, but that one of all *possible* predicates must always belong to a thing'.[5] That Kant considers this requirement unaccomplishable matters little: it is within its horizon – or, to express it better, under its threat – that what it is to exist or to be is defined for him. And this concerns not only the 'effective mode of existence' of things but also the *logical conceivability* of everything that can be an object of thought. It was Parmenides, breaking with the pre-Socratics who preceded him, who first made this decision (in full opposition, for example, to Anaximander and Heraclitus). Limits to this requirement were already laid down, certainly, by Plato (in the *Sophist* and in the *Philebus*) and by Aristotle (this is what the concept of matter, when pushed to the extreme, represents). But these limits (or objections) are, first of all, presented, precisely, as limitations and most often are tied to our human frailties: nothing would be indeterminate for God or for an 'infinitely powerful' mind, both Kant and Laplace went on to say. Second and especially, these limits are never taken into account and elaborated *for their own sake*.

To this ontology corresponds 'ensemblistic-identitary' (for brevity's sake: ensidic) logic. This is the logic of the principle of identity, of contradiction, and of the excluded third, the logic that is at the basis of arithmetic and mathematics in general and that is formally and effectively realized in set theory [*la théorie des ensembles*] and its interminable ramifications. This logic is everywhere present – everywhere 'dense', to use a term from topology – in everything we say and everything we do. It is a logic that must be, and is, each time instituted and sanctioned by society.

Now, in the psyche we are not dealing with a set or an organization or hierarchy of sets. Sets, and determinacy, are present therein, but they far from exhaust the being of the psyche.

This may be seen clearly in the mode of being of that which is the element of psychical life (I mean 'element' here in the sense one speaks of water, earth, and fire as elements): representation, especially unconscious representation, but even already conscious representation. We cannot say how many elements (in the sense, now, of set theory or simply of enumeration) there are 'in' a representation; we cannot even say what makes a representation *one* representation. We cannot apply to representations the basic schema of division [*partition*]. It is impossible to separate my representations into two classes, for example, where the intersection would be empty.

That, far from being limited to the psyche, this mode of being extends at least to the entire human world may be seen immediately when one considers what is basic to language, namely, its significations. Each signification in language, like each psychical representation, *refers* to an indefinite number of other significations, or other representations. This structure of *referral* is here fundamental. It is effectively expressed in the psyche, and in a psychoanalytic setting, through the process of free association. No one can predict, when a patient recounts a dream, where his associations will lead and how they will do so. Despite appearances, Freud knew that very well. Speaking of dream analysis, he wrote:

There is often a passage in even the most thoroughly interpreted dream which has to be left obscure; this is because we become aware during the work of interpretation that at that point there is *a tangle of dream-thoughts which cannot be unravelled* and which moreover adds nothing to our knowledge of the content of the dream. This is the dream's navel, the spot where it reaches down into the unknown. The dream-thoughts to which we are led by interpretation cannot, from the nature of things, have any definite endings; they are bound to branch out in every direction into the intricate network of our world of thought. It is at some point where this meshwork is particularly close that the dream-wish grows up, like a mushroom out of its mycelium.[6]

It is clear, in reading this passage and several others, and contrary to every 'deterministic' exegesis of Freud, that for him (1) not all dreams are inter-pretable and (2) no dream is completely interpretable. And as the passage cited above clearly states, it is not simply resistances on the part of the patient, but the very nature of the psychical world, that is opposed to 'complete' dream interpretation. One could, obviously, say as much about all other phenomena of the unconscious psychism.

In order to illustrate what has been said above concerning the universality of the ensidic element, let me note in passing that, both in psychoanalytic interpretation and in the very being of the dream, ensemblistic-identitary logic is constantly present, it is everywhere dense. Dream interpretation is a strange undertaking, in which one could not take even the first steps without applying this logic and in which one could say nothing essential if one confined oneself to it. This state of affairs results from the very nature of (conscious or unconscious) representation, taken in itself. But it is just as much the manifestation of representation's indistinction (in the classical sense of this term) with respect to the two other vectors of psychical life, from which representation is indissociable: the affect, and intention or desire.

There would certainly be a 'logical' and trivial way of sorting out these three vectors – representation, affect, and desire – and linking them via the mode of determination. For example, one might isolate a representation, which would 'cause' a desire, the satisfaction of which would provoke an affect of pleasure. (And one could, should one wish to do so, change the order of the terms and the direction of causation – which already would, in truth, raise questions profoundly challenging to the very idea of 'causation' in this domain.) Such may be the case in the life of members of the animal kingdom and in certain aspects of conscious human life. But in unconscious life we are truly incapable of performing this separation and this simple linear concatenation. Representation, affect, and desire are mixed together in a *sui generis* fashion, and in general it is impossible, except in trivial cases, to separate them from one another in a clear-cut way and to establish an order for their appearance. In the clinical setting, the processes involved in depression provide an exemplary illustration of this fact. One could also show, in the case of music, that it is meaningless to separate out representation and affect. For lack of space, I cannot insist upon this point here.

Using in particular the example of representation, we can elucidate further what, in the case of the psyche, makes this magmatic state inevitable. First, the ineradicable ambivalence of unconscious affects signifies the coexistence of attitudes of love and hatred toward primordial psychical objects. And this ambivalence, in turn, is the inevitable result of the necessary passage from the initial state of the psychical monad – which is closed upon itself, all-powerful, and all-encompassing within itself – to the socialized state of the singular individual. But obviously, the ambivalence of affects goes hand in hand with the coexistence of opposing – or, in any case, highly different – representations referring to the same 'object'.

Next at issue is the very texture of the representation. What Freud had sifted out as the dream's modes of operation – condensation, displacement, the requirement of 'figurability'[7] – *always* in fact holds for representations and condemns them to polysemy. One need only reflect for a few moments to glimpse that, far from ever being able to be 'clear and distinct', to form a 'mirror of nature', to 'give things in person', etc., representations can only have being by condensing, displacing, and giving figure to that which, in itself, is strictly 'unfigurable' or, in any case, is without any figure previously determined in the psyche. In representation, it may be said that something is *always* there for something else, or for something else as well – or, finally, that, in any case, it can be so. The idea, never thematized as such by Freud (this will have very heavy consequences for his overall views), is nevertheless there under the title – wrongly considered enigmatic – of the *Vorstellungsrepräsentanz des Triebes*, the delegation of the drive (to the psyche and within it) by means of a representation. For humans, there is no representational or 'canonical' object of the drive; contrary to what occurs in animals (though, in certain species, one can glimpse the beginnings of this phenomenon under the form of *imprinting*), its figuration is arbitrary or contingent. This indetermination relative to the representational object of the drive has decisive importance for the process of hominization.

Finally, we must mention the enigma of the relations between body and soul, psyche and soma. Of course, it was not psychoanalysis that discovered this enigma, but psychoanalysis has considerably reinforced its strangeness. I think that the failure of philosophical as well as scientific theories that have aimed at explaining or 'understanding' this relationship comes from the fact that they remain prisoners of ensemblistic-identitary logic: one proceeds, in these theories, as if one were faced with two separate entities, of which sometimes one, sometimes the other would be, according to the personal choices of the theoritst, the 'cause' and the other the 'effect'. But what we notice – already in daily life – is that such a relation does not exist in the present case. The soul depends upon the body (lesions, alcohol, psychotropic substances) and does not depend upon it (one's resistance to or failure to resist pain and torture, the deliberate choice to take one's own life). The body depends upon the soul (voluntary movements, psychosomatic illnesses) and does not depend upon it (at this very moment, fortunately and sometimes un-fortunately, hundreds of billions of cells are functioning within me without my being able to do anything about it).

Despite appearances, therefore, psychoanalysis demolishes the claim of determinism in psychical life. At first sight, to be sure, it 'reinforces' this claim in an infinitely richer and more precise way than had ever been done before when it introduces 'causation' via representation. But this sort of 'causation' is of a strange character. Not only is it not categorical (or even probabilistic), it can never be established except after the fact, which prevents it from having any predictive capacities. But above all, to speak of causation under these circumstances constitutes a monstrous abuse of language: representation cannot be a 'cause' because it is not rigorously determinable and because the incessant flux of representations, affects, and desires is still less so.

This rejection of determinism is not there explicitly in Freud. On the contrary, he certainly considered himself a 'determinist'. It is nevertheless there within his work, between the lines. I have shown it in the case of dreams, and it can also be shown in the famous problem of 'the choice of neurosis', to which Freud returned many times without ever discovering a solution that satisfied him. Starting, notably, in the early 1920s, and in particular in his writings on female sexuality, Freud clearly described several possible 'destinies' for girls and finally admitted that one cannot know what factor determines one personal evolution rather than another. He simply advanced some vague hypotheses concerning the 'quantity' or 'quality' of libido, hypotheses that obviously do not lend themselves to any sort of control. In other contexts during the same period, he spoke of 'temporal modulations' of the libido. (An analogous idea, that of frequency modula-tions in the nervous influxes as carriers of information, was formulated much later by von Neumann.)[8] Often, innate (which does not necessarily mean hereditary) 'constitutional factors' are invoked to account, for example, for the conspicuous phenomenon of early differences among subjects in their levels of tolerance and frustration. Clearly, all this does is recognize, not explain, the singularity of each human subject.

At the basis of indetermination, in the specific case of the human being, we find what radically differentiates this being from any other being, namely the radical imagination. I shall return to this point below.

Philosophical Anthropology

Every living being is a being for itself. This signifies, first and foremost, that it creates its own world – a 'proper world', an _Eigenwelt_. This, in turn, implies that it presents – that it 'has' or that it is (and it is this that makes its being a _living_ form of being) – a soul. Everyday language evinces a clear recognition of this when it opposes animate to inanimate objects, and this is what Aristotle affirms straight out in his text _De Anima_. Although it was clearly discovered by Aristotle in the third book of that treatise under the name _phantasia_, the fundamental determination of the soul – namely, the imagination – has been relegated, by the whole of inherited philosophy, to the status of one 'faculty' or 'function' of the soul among others, a faculty that is treated most of the time as secondary and a function that is generally considered (with the notable exceptions of Kant and Fichte) deceptive.[9]

Imagination is the capacity to make be what is not in the simply physical world and, first and foremost, to represent to oneself and in one's own way – that is, to present for oneself – that which surrounds the living being and matters for it and, undoubtedly also, its own being. In the case of 'external' representation – of perception – this presentation is conditioned, but not caused, by the being-thus of the environment and of the 'objects' it encounters there. At the same time, the living being makes be the equivalent of what we call affect (pleasure/displeasure) and intention (search/avoidance). The living being aims at something, relative to its 'self' and relative to what it creates as its 'environment'. The affect is, to begin with, a decisive 'signal' of its relationship with the environment.

In the case of the simple living being, however, this relationship is in its essence _functional_. The _imagination_ of the living being is, in the main, enslaved to its instrumental functions: conservation and reproduction. (The question, in certain categories of living beings, of the _excess_ of the labour of the imagination over strict functionality is a highly complex one and cannot concern us here. Whatever the conclusions one might reach, they could not affect the principal line of argument being set forth here.) It is easy to see that the living being's creation of a proper world and its self-finality are mutually self-implicating. Its functional enslavement, moreover, goes hand in hand with another of the living being's fundamental traits: closure, the closure of its proper world, which is given once and for all. The products of the generic imagination of each living species are stable and indefinitely repetitive.

Now, the rupture that is expressed in the emergence of the human is tied to an alteration in this imagination – which becomes, henceforth, radical, constantly creative imagination, the uninterrupted surging forth, in the (unconscious as well as conscious) psychical world, of a spontaneous and unmasterable flux of representations, affects, and desires. The key traits may be summarized as follows:

- Human psychical processes become defunctionalized relative to the human being's biological substrate; often they are antifunctional and most of the time they are afunctional. Human sexuality is not functional, nor is war.

- In the human sphere there is a domination of representational pleasure over organ pleasure. This domination is connected to what Freud called the magical omnipotence of thought – which is, in truth, an effective omnipotence within the world of the Unconscious, where to 'think' is to 'do': if a desire arises, the representation that fulfils it also appears immediately.

- The imagination (conceived not only as representational but just as much as affective and desiderative) becomes autonomized. As has already been stated, for the living being creation takes place once and for all and it remains enslaved, in the main, to the functionality of the living being. In the human sphere the spontaneous flux of the specifically human aspects of the imagination is released from the requirements of biological finality. Here we have the condition for the human being's capacity to break the (cognitive, affective, desiderative) closure in which the simple living being remains shut.

These, then, are the attributes of the imagination that, generally speaking, the inherited philosophy has ignored, or in any case has not thematized, by restricting the imagination to the simple reproduction of the already 'perceived' and to the recombination of its elements. Even Kant, who had already raised the idea of a transcendental imagination (which means: the condition for one to have *a priori* knowledge of something), confined this imagination to producing always the same forms (which are enslaved to the functioning of the conscious and knowing Ego; characteristically, he always speaks of the *produktive*, never the *schöpferische Einbildungskraft*). It is this autonomization of the imagination, its disconnection from functionality, that permits human beings to pass from the simple signal to the sign, to the arbitrary *quid pro quo* of language.

It is equally the autonomization of the imagination and the replacement of organ pleasure by the pleasure of representation that is the condition for that decisive determination of the human being without which there would not have been any hominization, viz., sublimation. Sublimation is the capacity to cathect unperceivable, socially instituted 'objects' that have no other kind of existence but a social existence, and to find therein some pleasure (in the psychical sense).

It is not the human being's 'late maturation' that 'explains' socialization and the existence of a society. Nothing would change in a group of chimpanzees if the maturation of the young lasted ten or twelve years instead of one or two. The psychical condition for human beings' 'need' for society is to be sought in the nature of the initial psychical monad, which is closed upon itself, absolutely egocentric, all-powerful, and lives in the felt experience of the original identity that I = pleasure = meaning = every-thing = being. *Ich bin die Brust.* There one finds the prototype of meaning for human beings. This meaning is forever lost due to the very fact that we have exited from the monadic world of psychical self-sufficiency, though we always try to find it again in a mediated way, by means of instituted social imaginary significations, through religion, philosophy, or science. Society always furnishes us with a substitute for it that is nevertheless incapable of measuring up to the initial prototype.

It is through its socialization, its social fabrication *qua* social individual, that the human subject accedes to what we call 'reality' and 'logic'. This socialization is at the same time a *history*, a history of the subject and accession to a collective history – which is something entirely other than a matter of 'apprenticeship' or a 'learning process' (as some would now once again have us believe). It leans on two fundamental psychical modes of operation, projection and introjection, the first of which is always preponderant and the presupposition for the other (whose essential condition is the psychical *cathexis* of that which is internalized). Here we have the role of Eros in *paideia*, which Plato saw in general, though he could not render it comprehensible. Psychoanalysis now permits us to understand it. Through its successive phases, moreover, this history is the origin for the stratification always manifested in the human psyche (absolutely nothing analogous could be said concerning the animal psyche, which has no genuine history), where traces of previous stages coexist with the most recent ones (without their ever being 'harmoniously integrated'), as well as crystallize into psychical 'instances' and persist in a contradictory or incoherent and ever conflictual totality.

I cannot end this part of my presentation without touching upon another point, one that relates, as a matter of fact, to the nature of society. Society is a totality of institutions – but these institutions hold together because they embody, each time, a magma of social imaginary significations. There never has been and there never will be a purely 'functional' society. Social imaginary significations organize the proper world of each society under consideration and furnish a 'meaning' to this world. The proper world of each society must hold together, in and for itself, but it must also furnish meaning to the individuals of that society. This absolute exigency for meaning comes, we may say in concluding this section, from the psyche.

Practical Philosophy

How can psychoanalysis aid in the elucidation of the questions of practical philosophy?

A detour is required before we broach this question. It concerns the antinomy I mentioned at the beginning: psychical reality, with which psychoanalysis is concerned, is pure effective actuality [*effectivité*]. A desire is a desire; it is, as such, neither good nor bad, neither beautiful nor ugly, neither true nor false (it is 'true' only in the sense, simply, that it *is*). How, then, can the psyche maintain any sort of relationship with truth or with value?

In Kantian philosophy, and in nearly all inherited philosophies, this question presents itself as an insoluble antinomy. If everything I say as an effectively actual individual is effectively determined (as it must be, since the psyche exists only as a phenomenon, and therefore is subjected to causality) the term *truth* no longer has any meaning. There are, hypothetically speaking, as many sufficient reasons for saying $2 + 2 = 4$ as for saying the Moon is made of blue cheese. But furthermore, to say that psychical processes are in large part indeterminate does not extricate us from this difficulty: the propositions I state are then, from the standpoint of their truth, simply aleatory. The indeterminacy of psychical processes helps us to elucidate the effective possibility of truth only if this indeterminacy is accompanied, paradoxically, by its contrary: causation via representation. And when we speak of truth, or more generally of value, such causation presupposes sublimation, namely, the cathexis of unperceivable (or, if you prefer, ideal) representations; in psychoanalytic terms it presupposes the conversion of the drive into an intention aimed at a sublimated object. We are capable of truth because we can cathect an activity that offers no libidinal pleasure in the proper sense of the term: the search for what is true. And this possibility refers us back, in turn, to the social-historical: it refers us back to a history wherein the idea of truth has been created and to a society that has found itself capable, somehow or other, of breaking the closure of meaning characteristic of traditional heteronomous societies.

The question of practical philosophy appears in psychoanalysis as the question of the end and the finality of the psychoanalytic treatment, but also that of its 'means' and its 'modes'.

Why are people brought into psychoanalysis? One answer is: because they are suffering. But if it were only a question of easing their suffering, perhaps one might limit oneself to administering them tranquillizers – which, indeed, is what is being done more and more. The finality of the psychoanalytic process is already inscribed in its 'means' and its 'modes': no 'consolation' or 'psychotherapy'; no advice or interventions in reality; the accent is put on the patient's associations and dreams in order that the unconscious psychical flux might come to light; interventions on the part of the psychoanalyst via interpretations ought progressively to give way to reflective self-activity on the part of the patient. Why? Clearly, what is being sought is the patient's gaining access to his Unconscious, namely, his attaining to some lucidity about his own history, his own world, his own desire. Such lucidity can be attained only by means of the patient's self-activity, his own self-questioning, the development of his own reflectiveness. What is sought is certainly also the translation or the expression of this lucidity in the effectively actual life of the patient – and that requires the constitution, the emergence in the patient, of a new psychical instance, a reflective and deliberative subjectivity, one capable of filtering his unconscious pushes and desires, of shattering the coalescence of phantasm and reality, of putting into question not only his thought but also his practices. This emergence of a reflective and deliberative – that is to say, autonomous – subjectivity can be defined as the end of the analytic process ('end' taken here in both senses of the term: the finality or goal and the final ending or termination point).

We can consider this type of subjectivity as the formal norm for human beings. And we can also consider the activity of the genuine analyst – who aims at the emergence of the autonomy of the patient by 'using' for this purpose the potential elements of this same autonomy – as a formal model for all human praxis. Such praxis may be defined as the activity of an autonomy that aims at the autonomy of one or several others – which is what genuine pedagogy and genuine politics also do or should do. Here we find the answer to the question: How is the action of one freedom upon another freedom possible?

Paris, November 1993

Notes

1 See my texts *ETS* (1968) and *PPE* (1977).

2 'Ergebnisse, Ideen, Probleme' (note of 12 July 1938, in London), in *Gesammelte Werke* (hereafter: *GW*), vol. 17, p. 151 = 'Findings, Ideas, Problems' (1941 [1938]), in *Standard Edition* (hereafter: *SE*), trans. James Strachey, rev. edn (London: Hogarth, 1958), vol. 23, p. 299.

3 See, for example, Henri F. Ellenberger, *The Discovery of the Unconscious* (1970; New York: Basic Books, 1979).

4 See, for example, my text *LMQA* (1983), where one will find references to previous texts dealing with this topic.

5 Immanuel Kant, *Critique of Pure Reason*, trans. F. Max Müller (Garden City, New York: Anchor, 1966), p. 388 (emphasis in the original).

6 *GW*, vol. 2, pp. 529–30 (with reference to p. 116, n.) = *SE*, vol. 5, p. 525 (with reference to vol 4, p. 111, n. 1). The emphasis is added.

7 T/E: This is my English translation of the standard French translation of Freud's *Rüchsicht an Darstellbarkeit*. *SE* uses 'conditions of representability'.

8 See J. von Neumann, *The Computer and the Brain* (New Haven, Conn.: Yale University Press, 1958). The texts written by Freud that are alluded to in this paragraph include: 'The Psychogenesis of a Case of Homosexuality in a Woman' (1921), 'Some Psychical Consequences of the Anatomical Distinction Between the Sexes' (1925), 'Female Sexuality' (1931), as well as *Beyond the Pleasure Principle* (1920), *The Ego and the Id* (1923), and 'The Economic Problem of Masochism' (1924).

9 See, for example, my texts *DI* (1978) and *LIR* (1991).

15

Done and To Be Done (1989)*

I can thank the friends who have so kindly contributed to this volume [*Autonomie et autotransformation de la société*] only by sharing with them the emotions I feel at seeing the number and quality of their testimonials. It is with the same emotion that I thank Giovanni Busino, who initiated this volume and brought it to term amid numerous obstacles and personally painful circumstances.

I would have liked to flesh out further these expressions of thanks by responding here to each person in detail, but that would have required a second volume of comparable dimensions and several months of work. That is why – and it will also facilitate the reader's task – I have preferred, rather than to make of this text a series of remarks on the remarks addressed to me, to organize it around a few of the themes that correspond to the main axes of my work and to cover, I hope, a good portion of the criticisms one can read in this volume. Undoubtedly, numerous questions – some that are raised by my friends present here, others that on their own wake me up at night – have not been broached. They remain no less present in my mind and I hope to be able to speak about them elsewhere. In any case, I have endeavoured to underscore, in the most important cases, the tasks that remain and the orientations for the work to come.

Ontology

We do not philosophize – we do not concern ourselves with ontology – in order to save the revolution (Axel Honneth) but in order to save our thought, and our coherency. The idea that an ontology, or a cosmology, might be able to save the revolution belongs to Hegelo-Marxism – that is, to a conception as far removed as possible from my own. An ontological investigation oriented toward the idea of creation leaves room, in the most abstract way, for the possibility of the instauration of an autonomous society as well as for

* 'Fait et à faire', *Revue Européenne des Sciences Sociales*, 86 (December 1989), pp. 457–514. [T/E: This issue is reprinted in book form as *Autonomie et autotransformation de la société. La Philosophie militante de Cornelius Castoriadis*, ed. Giovanni Busino (Geneva: Droz, 1989). It includes thirty discussions of Castoriadis and his work in English, French, German, and Italian.]

the reality of Stalinism and Nazism. At this level, and almost all others, creation has no value content, and politics does not allow itself to be 'deduced' from ontology.

Ontology signifies what is traditionally called metaphysics. I have never thought (Agnes Heller) that I have 'transcended' metaphysics (*MSPI* [1973], in *CL*, pp. 158–9E). As we know, the word is a historical accident. That does not prevent Aristotle, in the book later named by others *Meta ta phusika*, from audaciously affirming: It is a certain kind of science (*epistēmē*) that considers Being/being [*être/étant*] (*on*) *qua* Being/being and appertains to it toward itself (*kath' auto*, in itself). We say: There is a reflection/elucidation, which is concerned with Being/being and which asks itself what appertains to it toward itself and what appertains to it in as much as it is for us – that is, from the fact that we are reflecting upon it. This formulation affirms that it is impossible to separate reflection upon Being from reflection upon beings, as it is impossible and *sinnwidrig* (nonsense) to separate reflection upon being from 'theory of knowledge' (Kant, and his offspring down through our time).

Since total Being/being manifests itself, as well, as concrete and effective organization (order, *kosmos*) – for the moment, we are not deciding whether this organization is total or partial and fragmentary – ontology is also, necessarily, cosmology. It is curious to see the term cosmology used as if it were close to astrology, alchemy, or necromancy. As [Molière's character] Monsieur Jourdain spoke prose without knowing it, Honneth puts the weightiest cosmological postulates into action when he sits down in front of his typewriter or when he goes out into the street: he acts as if he were certain that the former was not going to explode in his hands or that his fellow citizens had not been transformed, overnight, into headhunters. In brief, he is postulating at least a regularity and stability to phenomena, sufficient as to need/usage [as Aristotle would say], which no transcendental consciousness, no *Wesenschau*, no intersubjective communication could produce or draw out of themselves. Perhaps the coherency of experience is only probable (Husserl), but the coherency of certain philosophers appears highly uncertain when they place in doubt or consider in their books as merely probable such facts as their activity shows are taken by them to be categorically assured.

The path of philosophy (ontology, metaphysics) necessarily opens up when one reflects upon mathematics, physics, or biology (*MSPI*). It opens up just as necessarily when one reflects upon the fact, unintelligible from the standpoint of criticism, that there is, in the weightiest sense of the term, a *history* of these sciences (*MSPI, OIHS* [1986]). I was going to write that no one is obliged to take an interest in science, in its results, and in its history, but that would be false. To do philosophy is to take responsibility for the totality of the thinkable, since philosophy is required to reflect upon all our activities. The concrete difficulties this taking of responsibility encounters today pertains to another level of considerations; it does not change anything on the level of principle.

The path of philosophy opens just as necessarily when one reflects upon society, history, or the human psyche. And twice rather than once, for this reflection not only leads to the question, 'What is the mode of being of these beings (society, history, the psyche), "alongside" the mode of being of these other beings that are physical nature and the living being?'; it also confronts us with the question of the being and mode of being of this being *for which* there is a world, nature, or life. The ontology of society, of history, of the psyche is part of philosophy's self-reflection in the strongest sense possible, since it is not only 'under condition' of society, of history, of the psyche that philosophy exists (nature or life is also among its conditions), but also since it appears as a specific creation in and through the domain of being which the social-historical and the psychical make be.

But reflection upon the social-historical and the psychical is philosophically privileged to a third degree, for the fact of being (the effective existence) of the social-historical and its mode of being lead almost directly to weighty conclusions concerning total Being/being as such (toward itself, *kath' auto*). And this, again, twice rather than once: that is, in as much as the social-historical (and the psyche, but I shall concentrate here on the former) manifests a mode of being that, from this very fact, proves to appertain to total Being/being (be it only as one of the latter's strata), since the social-historical could not be excluded from what *is*; and, in as much as the fact of being and the mode of being of the social-historical are not neutral with respect to the mode of being of total Being/being. In other terms: the fact that *there is* the social-historical, and that the latter *is* on the mode of being that is its own, *says something* about the *world* (I shall, for brevity's sake, use this term in the pages that follow).

On this mode of being proper to the social-historical, I have not ceased writing since 1964, and I shall not repeat myself here. It suffices to recall that each society creates a magma of social imaginary significations (henceforth: S.I.S.), irreducible to functionality or 'rationality', embodied in and through its institutions, and constitutive, each time, of its own, or 'proper', world (both 'natural' and 'social').

We remark straight away the immense variety of these proper worlds – of the S.I.S. of different societies and of the institutions that bear/convey [*portent*] them. We then ask ourselves: How is the world *tout court*, since there effectively is this indefinite variety of worlds proper to each society?

The response is: The world lends itself to (is compatible with) all these S.I.S. and privileges none. That means: The world *tout court* is senseless, devoid of signification (save that of lending itself to . . . ; but that is not what we call a signification). The result is that, *at this level*, all 'hermeneutical' discussion, every attempt to see in the creation of S.I.S. 'interpretations' of the world, has no ground to stand on.

We thus remark that all effective institutions of society, and all those we might imagine as effective and viable, necessarily include an ensemblistic-identitary (ensidic) dimension and that the latter has a certain grasp upon the world, sufficient as to need/usage, otherwise these societies could not exist. How is the world *tout court*, then, since the ensidic dimension has, roughly speaking and to a large degree, a grasp upon it?

The response is: The world *tout court* includes *within itself* a dimension that not only *lends itself* to an ensidic organization but *corresponds* to such an organization. The Understanding is socially instituted (*SII* [1975], in *IIS*, pp. 320–39E), but the Understanding would be objectless if the world were *pure* multiplicity of the manifold, of the absolutely diverse (ibid., pp. 340–4E). By an abuse of language, I shall call this the ensidic dimension *of the world*.

The world includes an ensidic dimension; otherwise, for example, the 'unreasonable effectiveness of mathematics' [Wigner] becomes unintelligible. But the world *is not* an ensidic system. First, it is not so since it includes the human imaginary, and the imaginary is not ensidic. Next, the application of the ensidic to the world has a history, which would become unintelligible if the world were wholly ensidic (*MSPI, OIHS*). Finally, even supposing that the world were reducible in an exhaustive way to an ensidic system, this system would be suspended in air since it would still be impossible to account *ensidically* for its ultimate axioms and its universal constants (*MSPI*, in *CL*, pp. 163–4E).

The world indefinitely lends itself to ensidic organizations. The world cannot be exhausted via these organizations. These two statements define a mode of being, which I have called the mode of being of the magma (*MSPI, IIS, LMQA* [1983]) and which we rediscover everywhere (save in mathematical constructions *separated* from their foundations).

We also remark that the diverse creations of S.I.S. are both unmotivated and effective.

S.I.S. are unmotivated for reasons I presented at length in *MRT* (1964–5, in *IIS*, pp. 115–64E). For these reasons it makes no sense to say, for example, that the world of the ancient Egyptians was 'false' (which one would be obliged to say, or at least to discuss, if this world were an 'interpretation' of something with full meaning that would be external to it). We are not saying, moreover, that the world of the Koran, or of the Gospels, is 'false': we are saying (1) that we do not want it beyond the private sphere and (2) that even within this sphere it renders impossible, or meaningless, some objects or activities that we value – for example, genuine philosophy, or theatre (see Borges's Averroes in 'Averroes' Search', *Labyrinths. Selected Stories and Other Writings*, ed. Donald A. Yates and James E. Irby [New York: New Directions, 1962]).

S.I.S. are effective not only for the human beings they socialize but also, in principle, for everyone else, and this not only pragmatically but theoretically: they set *constraints* upon their interpretation. For example, to say that Pharaonic Egypt was capitalist (or feudal) would be false; to say that the signification of Athenian democracy is exhausted in its instauration of the freedom of the community of brothers [Heller] would be inadequate and mutilating.

Let us now examine the question from the other end. Society *is* on the mode of being of the for-itself – and each society is a for-itself. It creates a world of its own, and for it nothing can make sense or simply exist that fails to enter into its proper world in the way this proper world organizes and endows with meaning that which enters therein. The world of the singular psyche is also, to begin with, a world of its own and, in its most deep-seated strata, it remains so until the very end, even if the socialization of the psyche opens it to a larger proper world, the public world of the society that socializes it. This proper world *is* on the mode of *closure* – and its organization is the *a priori* of everything that can present itself – appear, be a phenomenon – to the for-itself under consideration; and this *a priori* is both 'material' (for example, sensoriality) and 'formal' (for example, categoriality).

The existence of proper worlds, the mode of being of the for-itself, its '*a priori*' organization are facts. Curiously, denial of these facts is absurd – by which I mean: if there is a proper world, its organization can only be *a priori*. The idea that electromagnetic waves are coloured in themselves, or that one might be able to discover by induction the categories of the one and the many on the basis of 'observation' (which therefore could not know at the outset whether that which was observed was 'one' or 'many' or both at once) – these ideas are absurd.

But we are obliged to remark that the mode of being of the for-itself, as such, is not specific to the human (whether social or psychical). The living being exists for itself (*MSPI, SST* [1986]). It creates its own world and nothing exists for it (except as catastrophe) that does not enter into this world *according to* the organization of this world.

Let us note in passing that Kant is not interested in this enlargement and that such an enlargement is disturbing for his theoretical philosophy. The admirable paragraphs of the third *Critique*, which *in fact* and despite Kant's precautionary statements establish the ontological autonomy of the level of the living being, do not consider the latter from the *erkenntnistheoretisch* point of view, as organizing a proper world.

For us to halt here would be to accept one of the unacceptable bounds of Kantianism. How does it happen that some for-itself in general, and some living being in particular, exists (and can only exist) by creating a world of its own – and that it is able simply to exist, to subsist in the world *tout court*? It must be remarked that, logically speaking, the problem is the same for the living being *and* for the 'transcendental subject': the effectively actual [*effectif*] world can be effectively organized only if it is organiz*able*, and this is an *attribute of the world*, not of the subject (*SII, LMQA, OIHS*). It is this question that Kant both recognizes and covers over with the famous phrase 'happy accident' [*heureux hasard, glücklicher Zufall*]. Contrary to what Joel Whitebook believes, this nonresponse creates a problem for Kant, not for me. It is Kant who committed himself to sifting out the *a priori* (therefore *necessary*) conditions of experience, who believes he has found them *solely* on the side of the subject, who 'forgets' that there are equally conditions of experience on the side of the 'object', and who places everything under the sign of 'necessity' (after which the 'accident', fortunate [*heureux*] or unlucky [*malheureux*], obviously creates a disagreeable surprise), whereas he is constantly basing himself on raw facts (that *there is* experience, that *there is* 'an art hidden in the depths of the human soul', etc., etc.). As for myself, I certainly shall never claim to be able to bring the ultimate facts (that there is a world, that there is for-itself) under the yoke of any sort of 'necessity' whatsoever or think that one might be able to call 'accident' or 'chance' (*hasard, Zufall*) that which is on the near side or on the far side of the contingent and the necessary, and within which alone contingent and necessary are effectively actual and thinkable.

That does not absolve us from trying to elucidate the various articulations at issue here. That the for-itself as such, and the living being in particular, creates each time a world of its own is only one part of the question. The living being effectively exists. That implies a certain relation between its own world and the world *tout court*. Let us call this relation correspondence in the vaguest sense of this term. It is a fact, a pure fact, a raw fact (and one conditioning an infinity of other facts, for example the existence of philosophers) that this correspondence exists. This fact is neither an accident nor a nonaccident. In a certain regard it is a tautology (the Darwinian tautology: the living being is alive, therefore it is fit for life). In another, much more profound regard, it is in no way at all a matter of a tautology, but of a being-thus of the world – of a given stratum of the world we know. Nothing tells us that some for-itself ought to be able to exist in every possible world.

Freud's 'answer' in *Future of an Illusion* (*SE*, vol. 21, p. 55), invoked by Whitebook, does not surpass the considerations presented above, It is Darwino-Kantian. Kant says: All knowledge (and, more generally, every relation with the world) implies *a priori* structures of the for-itself. He does not say how and why these structures happen to 'correspond' to (have a grasp upon) the world. (One can certainly imagine worlds upon which some of these structures *would not have* a grasp. Moreover, we already positively know some of them: the stratum of microphysics and the psychical stratum, for example. Whence my ever reiterated restriction to the *first natural stratum*.) He says: It's a happy accident. Freud responds to him by invoking a Darwinian genesis of these structures: if the *a priori* structures did not 'correspond' to the world, selection/adaptation would not have allowed the bearers of these structures to exist and to reproduce themselves. The response is, on its own level, correct – but inadequate for the purposes of our discussion. First, it does not draw the ontological implications from the fact that the world in itself is also organizable, that it includes the ensidic. That was not Freud's problem, and it was not for Freud a problem (he never doubted the 'rational' makeup of the physical world). But next and above all, the response on the genetic level – his level – is valid for every effective for-itself, for living being as a whole, and is valid only for the limited quasi-'knowledge' that corresponds, each time, to the category of the living being under consideration. It is valid for bacteria, for sea turtles, for chimpanzees. If these beings exist as living beings – that is to say, as instances of beings-for-themselves – that implies that they have become capable, in one way or another, of creating for themselves proper worlds that happen to have points of contact, sufficient as to need/usage, with the world *tout court*. It is strictly impossible to 'explain' in this way the birth of the theory of *n*-dimensional Hilbertian spaces and the grasp this theory has upon the physical world (or of the birth of psychoanalytic theory itself), unless one postulates an essential homogeneity, without break, stretching from the logic of infraviruses to the logic of Einstein, and also a wholly ensidic organization of everything that is. (It is in this sense that I wrote, irreverently, that 'the *Transcendental Aesthetic* holds good for dogs – and of course for us, too, to the (great) extent that we are related to dogs' (*OIHS*).

One might think that adaptation/selection could 'explain' development of a strictly ensidic and narrowly instrumental kind of human knowledge. In fact, it does not explain even that. It has nothing to say as to what is proper to the human proper worlds (those of various instituted societies) – viz., that the S.I.S. that make them be are not 'adaptive' or 'antiadaptive': they are *elsewhere*. The psyche itself is a massive and monstrous case of *in*adaptation. This inadaptation is, somehow or other, subdued by the social institution and the socialization of the psyche – which certainly has, in this regard, a value, not 'adaptive', but one of survival: if humanity had not created the institution, it would have disappeared as a living species. But this tautology becomes aphonic when faced with the infinite variety of S.I.S.: are the Babylonian gods more, or less, 'adaptive' than the Mayan gods? It also has to occult the decisive dependence of the ensidic dimension of each institution of society – of its *legein* and *teukhein* – with regard to the properly imaginary dimension of its S.I.S. (without Babylonian theology, no Babylonian astronomy). Last and most important, it collapses in the face of the creation of unlimited interrogation, philosophy and science in the true sense of the term. What relation is there between 'adaptation' and the fact that, after hundreds of millennia of instituted (and also more or less 'adapted') existence, certain societies begin to put explicitly into question their institution and their established S.I.S.? What is accomplished thereby is a *shattering of the closure* in and through which the simple living being *is*, an (always imperfect and unfinished) unsettling of one's own world as exclusive, something that *negates head-on* biological 'logic', the creation of a being and of a mode of being that is unprecedented in the history of the world: a being that explicitly puts into question the laws of its own existence and that henceforth *is* in and through this putting into question.

Let me backtrack a moment to explicate the answer to the question I posed in *IIS* by generalizing it: If the for-itself brings everything out of itself, how and why would it ever encounter anything other than its own products? And if it does not do so, this would mean that it 'borrows' or 'copies' its own world from 'without', which is absurd. The *general* answer is: The for-itself can *be* only by creating (only *if* it creates) a world of its own that is sufficiently 'analogous' to traits of the 'external' world; and such a creation is rendered possible by this, that both the proper world of the for-itself and the world *tout court* include an ensidic dimension. The for-itself has to create the ensidic – and there is something ensidic in the world. The for-itself, for example, separates and combines – and there is, in the world, something separ*able* and combin*able*. When it comes to the particular for-itself that is the psyche, this is but a completely inadequate, partial answer (it concerns the debris of animal regulation that subsists within the human being). The essential point here is that, for the psyche, the 'outside world' is the *social* world, that the psyche *is* in and through meaning, and that the social world permits it to create a meaning for it on the basis of social signification. I shall return to this point further on ('Psyche and Society'). As for the proper world of each society, I pose still other problems (see 'Meaning and Validity').

The social-historical is creation: creation once and for all (institution and signification are irreducible to the biological), creation each time of its institution by each society (history is not rational unfolding). The social-historical *is*. *Therefore*, creation *appertains* to Being/being, it has to be counted among the *toutō huparkhonta kath' auto* – to that which appertains to it as such. But this also holds beyond the social-historical: there is living being. The mode of being of a star is not the mode of being of an elephant. (And this is *independent* of the fact that one might eventually show, a possibility Jean-Pierre Dupuy evokes, that under certain conditions the 'inorganic' might be able to 'produce' the 'organic': the living being brings about the appearance of laws and qualities that, as such, have *no meaning* in the physical realm.) It is immediately evident that the emergence of being-for-itself (the living being, psyche, the social-historical) entails an *essential fragmentation* of total Being/being. The extent to which, the manner in which despite and through this fragmentation a *kosmos*, a partially organized and 'coherent' totality, continues to exist is obviously an immense question that remains to be worked out.

The fact of creation also has weighty ontological implications, but I can do no more than allude to them here. It entails the abandonment of the hypercategory of *determinacy* as absolute (and of its avatar, the idea of a complete determinism). But it is a logical error to think – as Honneth and others seem to do – that due to this fact one must replace this hypercategory with the idea of absolute and complete indetermination. My philosophy is not a 'philosophy of indetermination'. Creation means, precisely, the *positing* of *new determinations* – the emergence of new forms, *eidē*, therefore *ipso facto* the emergence of new *laws* – the laws appertaining to these modes of being. At the most general level, the idea of creation *implies* indetermination *uniquely* only in the following sense: the totality of what is is never so totally and exhaustively 'determined' that it might exclude (render impossible) the surging forth of new *determinations*.

The idea of creation is equally foreign to the idea of a full and absolute indetermination from another, equally important point of view. Whatever its specific makeup and whatever the degree of internal indetermination it includes, every form (therefore also every new form) is a *being-this* and a *being-thus*. It would be nothing if it were not an *ecceitas* distinct from the others, a *Dies-heit* and a *Was-heit*, a *tode ti*.

Beyond this point, the discourse has to become specific at each level. The created form can almost exhaust itself in its ensidic determinations (for example, a new mathematical theory) or else reduce these determinations to relatively little (the initial psyche). The mode of being of the indeterminate itself is not purely and simply indeterminate: despite the fact that the indetermination of the Unconscious is, perhaps, the strongest kind we might be given the opportunity to approach, the Unconscious is nevertheless a *this* that is sufficiently distinct for one to be able to state that its indetermination has *no relation* (other than logical and empty) with the eventual indetermination of quantum entities. Society has its own sort of [*propre*] indetermination – and so does *each* particular society.

What is the relation between new and old forms? More generally, what are the forms of relation in general among forms, and among instances (particular exemplars) of each form? What are the relations among strata of Being/being, and among the beings [*étants*] within each stratum? Another immense field, which remains to be worked over. It does not suffice to speak of a 'principle of insufficient reason' (Bernhard Waldenfels): one can say much more than that. A theory of the effective types of connection ought at least to take account of the following modes (indicated here only as examples and without any claim to being systematic or exhaustive):

- the necessary and sufficient condition (as it is encountered in mathematics);

- the simply sufficient condition, what is usually meant by causality (it coincides with the first condition only by adjoining to the latter an indefinite number of necessary conditions picked up under the clause *ceteris paribus*);

- the necessary external condition (the existence of the Milky Way for the composition of *Tristan und Isolde*);

- the necessary internal condition (the previous history of Western music for this same piece);

- the leaning on psychoanalytic meaning;

- the leaning on social-historical meaning;

- the influence of one thought upon another thought (Plato/Aristotle, Hume/Kant, etc.).

These modes are in no way mutually exclusive. In particular, we encounter them in the social-historical field (I have insisted on several occasions, notably in the first part of *IIS* [*MRT*], on the presence and importance of causality in social-historical life). Due to this very fact, it is clear that social-historical creation (as well as, moreover, creation in any other domain), if it is unmotivated – *ex nihilo* – always takes place *under constraints* (it does not occur *in nihilo* or *cum nihilo*). Neither in the social-historical domain nor anywhere else does creation signify that just anything can happen just anywhere, just any time and just anyhow.

Relationship to Inherited Philosophy

Society institutes itself, each time, in the closure of its S.I.S. The historical creation of philosophy is rupture of this closure: explicit putting into question of these S.I.S., of the representations and words of the tribe. Whence its consubstantiality with democracy. The two are possible only in and through an onset of rupture in social heteronomy and the creation of a new type of being: reflective and deliberative subjectivity. The creation of reflection – of thought – goes hand in hand with the creation of a new type of discourse, philosophical discourse, which embodies unlimited interrogation and itself modifies itself throughout its history.

Our relation with the history of philosophy itself creates a philosophical question of the first magnitude (*EP?* [1988]), which is natural since all reflection is also self-reflection, and reflection did not begin today. Among the multiple aspects of this question, one is particularly important here. As rupture of closure, reflection nevertheless tends, in an irresistable manner, to close back upon itself. This is inevitable (even when a philosophy does not take the *form* of a system), since otherwise reflection would limit itself to being an indeterminate and empty question mark. The truth of philosophy is the rupture of closure, the shaking of received self-evident truths, including and especially philosophical ones. It is this movement, but it is a movement that creates the soil upon which it walks. The soil is not and cannot be just anything – it defines, delimits, forms, and constrains. The defining characteristic [*Le propre*] of a great philosophy is what allows it to go beyond its own soil – what incites it, even, to go beyond. As it tends to – and has to – take responsibility for the totality of the thinkable, it tends to close upon itself. If it is great, one will find in it at least some signs that the movement of thought cannot stop there and even some part of the means to continue this movement. Both these signs and these means take the form of aporias, antinomies, frank contradictions, heterogeneous chunks.

This holds, too, on a gigantic scale, for the whole of Greco-Western philosophy – what I have called inherited thought. The soil that limits it, and that constrains us, is the soil of *determinacy* (*peras, Bestimmtheit*). In this regard, there is a closure of ontology and of Greco-Western philosophy. But this closure is not unsurpassable, there is no 'end of philosophy' as is proclaimed amid the sterility and impotence of our age (*EP?*). The closure of inherited thought can and should be broken; not for the mere pleasure of doing so but because such is the exigency with which we are confronted by both things and our own activity of reflection. And – here is the sign of the grandeur of this legacy – a reflection worthy of this name would be able to find in Plato, in Aristotle, in Kant, and even in Hegel the points of departure, and some of the means, for a new movement. I have indicated above some of these points in relation to Kant. I shall do so below apropos of Aristotle.

But such was not my personal itinerary. I was subjugated by philosophy as soon as I knew of it, at the age of thirteen. (A sale of used books at Athens had enabled me to buy with my meagre pocket money a 'History of Philosophy' in two volumes, an honest 'lifting' of Uberweg and Bréhier. Then, at the same time as Marx, came Kant, Plato, Cohen, Natorp, Rickert, Lask, Husserl, Hegel, Max Weber, pretty much in that order.) Since then, I have never ceased to preoccupy myself with it. I came to Paris in 1945 to do a doctoral thesis in philosophy whose theme was that every rational philosophical order culminates, from its own point of view, in aporias and impasses. But as early as 1942 politics proved to be too engrossing and I have always tried to conduct political activity and reflection without directly mixing therein philosophy in the proper sense of the term. It is as political, and not philosophical, ideas that autonomy (*QURSS* [1947], *SB* [1949]), the creativity of the masses, what today I would have called the irruption of the instituting imaginary in and through the activity of an anonymous

collective (*PL* [1951]) made their appearance in my writings; it is starting
from a reflection on the contemporary economy, from an immanent critique
of his economics and his view of society and of history, and not as meta-
physician, that I criticized Marx, then distanced myself from him (*DC*
[1953–4], *CS I–III* [1955–8], *PO* [1959], *MCR* [1960–1]). And it is starting
from a reflection upon history and the diverse forms of society that his system
was finally rejected and the idea of the imaginary institution of society
attained (*MCR, MRT*). Only then – as can be seen in the first part of *IIS* –
was the connection with philosophy proper and its history made, was Marx's
belonging to rational metaphysics described, and were certain of the
premises for the idea of imagination in German Idealism rediscovered. (I
have given a more detailed description of this itinerary in *GI* [1973].) It is
only after the publication of *MRT* (1964–5) and the discontinuation of
Socialisme ou Barbarie that the philosophical work began to absorb the best
part of my free time (I have practically never ceased working professionally
– as an economist until 1970, as a psychoanalyst starting in 1973). But this
work is just as much, if not more, a preoccupation with the presuppositions,
the implications, the philosophical meaning of the sciences, of psychoanalysis, of society and of history as a reflection on the great texts of the past.

Among these texts, none has any 'privilege' – but it is accurate to say that
Aristotle occupies a particular position, for reasons I shall state. It is certainly true, as Heller says, that Aristotle is a philosopher who comes 'after
the Enlightenment' – that therefore, in this sense, his historical situation
offers analogies with our own. But that is only a part of the truth. Aristotle
comes not only after Enlightenment but after the most formidable reaction
against Enlightenment, organized by the greatest philosopher who ever
existed, Plato. (I have never written the absurdity that Heller imputes to
me, viz., that Plato would be a 'theologian'. Plato created, it is true, theological philosophy – which is something else entirely.) But also, Aristotle,
pupil of Plato and inconceivable without him, is in a sense 'before' Plato:
he belongs, to an essential degree, to the fifth century. Certainly, he succeeds in placing at the summit of everything the *bios theōrētikos*. But he is
also, contrary to the interpretational vulgate, a democrat in the Athenian
sense (see *The Constitution of the Athenians*, as well as his ideal *politeia*). If
he posits, by what (also) appears to him as a necessity of thought, a God,
pure thought, pure activity, this God – the sole one worthy of this name –
has no relation with this world; He could not, without toppling over into
ridiculousness, either have created it or have intervened therein. For all
these reasons, the tensions and aporias of Aristotle's thought are particularly fecund.

Aristotle sets the bounds for Greco-Western ontology. On certain
subjects, which in my view are crucial – *phantasia* (*DI* [1978]), *nomos/phusis*
(*VEJP* [1975]) – he straddles this boundary and is on the verge of crossing

it. He does not cross it. He remains within determinacy: pure matter, like pure indetermination, is an abstractive concept, a limit of being and of thought. The idea of creation would have no meaning for him: the theory of *poïēsis* and *technē* is essentially a theory of imitation (T [1973], in *CL*, pp. 231–4E), even if at moments he vacillates. As such, it is obviously inadequate to the thing, and it is no accident that the idea of *mimēsis* returns so often in contemporary authors for whom creation remains an obscene (or divine) term.

Artistotle thinks the fifth century in his *Politics* and in his theory of justice (the fifth book of the *Nicomachean Ethics*). He finds his way back to the fifth century on another point of capital importance – which is connected, moreover, to the preceding one. Not only does he debate constantly with the great Democritus (whose very existence we would have remained ignorant of, had he stuck merely with Plato, the organizer of the first great conspiracy of silence in the history of philosophy), but he positively rediscovers the latter's legacy, as well as that of Herodotus, the Hippocratics, the great Sophistics, in the *phusis/nomos* distinction (obliterated in Plato, where it is replaced with the healthy and the corrupt). No need to recall that Aristotle's thought is essentially a thought of *phusis*. But when he comes to human affairs, he cannot help but find his way back to the question of *nomos*. This explains the chaotic aspects of the *Politics*, and it explains, as well, that in his reflection on the *polis* and justice, when he cannot so easily find his way back to his (or a) *phusis*, he vacillates (*VEJP*). Likewise, in the domain of the psyche he discovers the imagination, but he cannot, despite his efforts in the most aporetic parts of *Peri psuchēs*, articulate it in terms of a functional and rational *phusis* of the soul (*DI*).

Someone who would have reflected solely on the basis of the history of philosophy and of Aristotle's text could, on the basis of these two themes – *nomos* and *phantasia* (which in appearance are strangely, and in truth essentially, connected) – have embarked upon the path of the imaginary institution of society (along which Vico, Montesquieu, Herder, Kant, Fichte, and Hegel would have been at once helpful and treacherous companions). That person could have taken up again the *phusis/nomos* polarity and the aporias to which it gives rise in human affairs, as well as the aporias created by the discovery of the imagination. That person could have accepted these aporias (instead of masking them) and settled them with the decision (which obviously would have engendered new questions): (1) that there is definitely no *phusis* of *nomos*, in any sense of the term; (2) that *nomos* – like *technē* – is created by humans, and that this refers back to a *phantasia* that is not imitative of or complementary to *phusis*; and finally, (3) that there exists at least one type of being, human being, that creates, gives rise to, its own *eidos* in a 'non-natural' fashion, without this *eidos* being found already, *dunamei*, in its determinate potentialities. In taking account of this type of being, not only would the universality of *phusis* be ruptured but every ontology of determinacy, therefore also Aristotelean ontology, would thereby be ruined. *Anthrōpos anthrōpon genna.* And also, by and large, *Athēnaios Athēnaion genna.* But what, then, is the ontological (or physical) place in which being-Athenian is rooted?

Someone could have done it. But why would one have done it? Why, among the innumerable knots of aporias that also constitute the inherited philosophy, would one have chosen those particular two? I have no answer to this hypothetical question, no more than I know why Heller labels 'neo-Artistotelean' an author who began his reflection with a rejection of the central category of Aristotelean ontology. What I do know is that it is not from reading Aristotle or Kant that I got the idea of thinking the imaginary institution of society; rather, my thinking of the latter led me to reread with another regard Aristotle or Kant. Dare I add that these rereadings convinced me of the pertinence of my questions and the inadequacy of their responses?

Let us return to the thing itself. *Phusis* for Aristotle is the end and the norm; but it is also the predominant effective actuality [*effectivité*] (*VEJP*). It has to be both at once. *Phusis* is what is almost always (save for aberrations and monsters) such as it has to be. *Phusis* cannot be a norm external to effective actuality, which would make of Aristotle a strange Platono-Kantian; nor is it a mere raw effective actuality – which, for Aristotle, would deprive it of both unity and intelligibility. Now, these two indissociable components of the idea of *phusis* – without this indissociability Aristotle's ontology would collapse – find themselves irremediably dislocated once one considers the human domain. Aristotle says: *Logos* and *nous* are the end of nature (*to tēs phuseōs telos*) for us humans. How many people effectively realize this *telos*? And how many cities are effectively instituted in order to assure the *eu zein*, the good life, such as the Philosopher would conceive it? And what is the relation, if there is one, between the *eu zein* of the Athenians and that of the Egyptians?

Let us now take all this up again in our own terms. There is, if one wants to call it thus, a *phusis* of man in the sense of universal effective actuality. This *phusis* is, at its core and as *phusis* proper to man, radical imaginary: radical imagination of the psyche, social instituting imaginary at the collective level. But this *phusis* does not coincide with any norm (except in the trivial sense: a human being totally 'without imagination' would be a monster in the Aristotelean sense); nor, as such, does *phusis* permit one to 'deduce' or to 'found' any norms. Certainly, it also appertains to this *phusis* of man to *create* norms, as well as to create (instituting imaginary) significations. But there is *no content* to these norms that allows itself to be sifted out as effectively universal; there is, for humans, no *nomos*, no norm *materialiter spectata* that would be *phusei*, by nature, by human *ousia*. I shall not enter here into the question of social-historical universals, concerning which, as one knows, discussions, revived over the past forty years, have furnished nothing certain. I note simply (1) that one cannot consider as *normative* universals the trivial universals that express the universal constraints under which the social-historical deploys itself (production of 'material' life, sexual reproduction, etc.); (2) that the universals of language, other than phonological ones, can concern only the *ensidic* dimension of language, code and not tongue, the instrumental and not the significant properly speaking (it is here that all 'categorization' of referents brought about by language belongs). In fact, the universals some linguists are trying to sift out all concern language's code: for example, the elementary syntactic structures Chomsky is seeking after simply embody a certain subject/predicate organization and its ramifications; (3) that the sole universals to offer a material normativity are the prohibition of incest and the prohibition of 'free' murder (not murder in general!) *within* the collectivity. But these norms belong to the minimal requisites for the socialization of the psyche (*SII*, in *IIS*, pp. 300–11E; *PoPA* [1988], in *PPA*, pp. 148–9). The institution has to furnish to the psyche diurnal meaning, and to do this it has to force the psyche to exit from its own world, where at the outset desire for the other and hatred of the other know no limit. It is impossible to draw from these two prohibitions any positive, substantive, and universal normative prescription. Obviously, beyond these considerations an immense elaboration remains to be done, an elaboration which, as a matter of fact, is social-historical since both the prohibition of incest and the (limited) prohibition of murder take on some content and have different fields of application in different societies.

The sole 'norm' consubstantial with the *phusis* of man is that man cannot *not* posit norms. Society is human, and not a pseudo-'animal society', in as much as it lays down norms in and through the institution, in as much as these norms embody significations, and in as much as their mode of being and of preservation possesses no specific biological substrate, nor does it answer to any 'functions', 'adaptations', 'learning processes', or 'problems to be resolved'.

Now, starting from *a certain moment* (a very recent one), *certain* (ultrarare) societies raise a hitherto unprecedented question: that of the *de jure validity* of social norms and significations. This, too, is a new social-historical creation, the creation of a new space, of a new mode of being, of new objects, and of new categories – which are consubstantial, obviously, with the creation of philosophy and of politics in the sense I give to this term (PoPA). It is this space that we presuppose, and into which we enter, when we discuss truth or justice. I shall return to this point at length below.

Psyche and Society

The psyche and the social-historical are mutually irreducible. One cannot make society with the psychical (unless one has already surreptitiously introduced the former into the latter, under the form of language, for example). The Unconscious produces phantasms, not institutions. Nor can one produce something of the psyche starting from the social – it is even unclear what this expression might mean – nor reabsorb the psyche totally within the social, not even in an archaic society or in the society of *1984*: people will always dream, they will always desire to transgress the social norm.

This *acknowledgement* seems unacceptable to Whitebook, who on this point happens to be in agreement with Jürgen Habermas: to say that psyche and society are mutually irreducible would, it seems, establish a 'metaphysical opposition' between the two. A curious expression. If what I affirmed above were false, the opposition would not be 'metaphysical', it would be nonexistent. If it is a question of the idea of irreducibility as such, the remark is absurd. If I say that an air chamber and a balloon are (topologically) mutually irreducible, is that 'metaphysical'? One should ask oneself, rather, what metaphysics is hidden behind the idea that every affirmation of irreducibility is 'metaphysical'. The answer is obvious: a unitary and reductionist metaphysics (whether 'materialist' or 'idealist' matters little). That there is nothing that is irreducible signifies: The Essence of the Whole is the Same; phenomenal differences boil down to differences of quantity, combinatory differences, etc. This metaphysics is bad, not because it is 'metaphysical' – but because it is false.

The psyche is not socializable without remainder – nor is the Unconscious translatable, without remainder, into language. The reduction of the Unconscious to language (where Lacan and Habermas curiously meet in agreement) is alien to the thing itself (and obviously also to Freud's thought: 'in the Unconscious there are only representations of things, not representations of words'). *No* dream is fully interpretable, and this is so not in fact but in principle (*ETS* [1968], *SII*). The choice of (figurative, not linguistic) tropes used in the dream is both over- and underdetermined. The requirement of figurability [*Rüchsicht an Darstellbarkeit*] subjects the dream to an essential distortion; starting therefrom, one attempts, in the process of psychoanalytic interpretation, to restitute nonverbal – and, at the limit, nonrepresentable – contents. (It is not because one has *called* something 'drive' that one elicits its essence in language.) The dream-interpretation redoubles this distortion, since the 'dream's navel' is drive-oriented and monadic and since the dream realizes once again the originary indistinction of affect/desire/representation every dreamer is familiar with (except, perhaps, if he is a philosopher). The 'glossification' of the Unconscious not only does not elucidate anything, as Whitebook seems to think, it destroys the essential part of the Freudian discovery by rendering it infinitely flat. In this, it faithfully expresses the 'linguistic turn' (which not only have I *not* 'participated' in but which I have denounced upon several occasions: *MRT, ETS, MSPI, SII*). It also renders incomprehensible the process of socialization, which imposes upon the psyche an each time *singular* tongue. Is one to believe, along with the young pastor in George Bernard Shaw's *Saint Joan*, that the Unconscious speaks English? Are not Yiddish or Viennese German better candidates? A 'linguistic theory' of the Unconscious has to postulate (as Chomsky does) an *a priori*, semantically universal tongue (or the strict isomorphism of every 'empirical' tongue with this *Ur*-tongue).

Can one climb back down and fall back upon a 'potentiality toward language' that would be immanent to the psyche? Whitebook tries to do so. Obviously, everything depends upon the infinitely elastic term *potentiality*. He invokes Ricœur and 'a signifying power that is operative prior to language'. Here again, we must agree on what we are talking about. There is not one 'signifying power' but (at least) two dimensions of the psyche that render it capable of language and, more generally, of socialization (*SII, SST, PoPA*). Both have to do with the radical imagination. From the outset, the psyche is in *meaning*: everything must make sense, on the mode of making sense for the psyche. And almost immediately afterward, the psyche is in the *quid quo pro* (which led Lacan astray); it can see in a thing another thing, this being the subjective correlate of the signitive relation (*SII*). But that does not mean that there is a language of the psyche whose functioning would be disturbed by the 'barrier of repression', or even that there is a 'heterogeneity' between something linguistic that would appertain to the Unconscious and conscious language. There is ontological alterity between (1) a universe that at the outset is monadic, then differentiated, but always tending to close upon itself and in which a representation can be posited as standing [*valant*] for another representation and (2) a diurnal universe of signs, which in good part obeys ensidic logic and bears/conveys *public*, somehow or other shared, significations.

It is said that my conception would render the mediation between individual and society impossible. But it is not a matter of establishing such a 'mediation'. The individual is of the social, it is total fragment of the world as it is each time instituted. It is a matter of elucidating, as far as possible, the fact that the *psyche* is (though never fully) socialized. Whitebook thinks that I 'never . . . adequately theorize' this question, and he believes that the sought-after theorization would be found in an 'immanent potentiality' (dare we say: *Anlage*, disposition?) of the psyche to be socialized. But the postulation of 'immanent potentialities', practised with great success by Molière's doctors, is quite the opposite of theorization: it puts a halt to reflection. That the psyche should be (imperfectly) socializable no more signifies that it possesses an *Anlage* of socialization than the possibility of making a statue from marble signifies that the marble has an *Anlage* of statufication. The 'pre-established harmony' between psyche and society for which Whitebook rightly reproaches Habermas is reintroduced by Whitebook himself if the term 'immanent potentiality' signifies anything else but 'possibility' (*SII*).

Freud said that the Unconscious knows nothing of time and contradiction. Would it be necessary to add, 'But it does not *not* know society, it is very favourably disposed thereto'? This is a question not of orthodoxy but of coherency. If there is a positive social *Anlage* of the initial psyche, then there certainly has to be a positive *Anlage* with regard to all society signifies – the postponement of satisfaction, the renunciation of pleasure, the abandonment of the omnipotence of thought, the abstract rule, the independent other and indefinite others, and so on. None of all that is compatible with what we see daily in the clinical setting or even with a mildly coherent theorization of the psychical world. Society, for the initial psyche, is *Anankē* pure and simple. It does its best to introduce itself to the *infans* under the most benevolent and seductive of guises – those of the mother – but it is still *Anankē*. The profound and almost ineradicable ambivalence toward the mother (reaching, in the adult individual, the point of the most intense hatred I have ever had the chance to observe) has its origin, even beyond the inevitable equation 'absent mother = bad mother', in the mother's decisive role in the breakup of the psychical monad.

We must invert the usual way of looking at things in order to see what within the human being a 'potentiality for socialization' is: it is the beast, the ruins of its animality. Like the majority of mammals, like in any case the higher apes, the 'prehuman' cannot but be endowed with an 'instinctive' quasi-sociality and an essentially ensidic, and nonreflective, 'mental' apparatus, both of them *functional*: social animal, reasonable animal. This is not what is proper to man, any more than what is found in the highly animalistic traits of imitation and learning. What is proper to man is the destruction these two functional apparatuses undergo via the emergence of the psyche in the strict sense. The malignant, as if cancerous, growth of the imagination without regard to functionality shatters these two apparatuses and subjects their debris to nonfunctionality (representational pleasure overtaking organ pleasure). These debris – like, too, for example, the 'perceptual organization' of the world connected to a neurosensorial constitution that is quite obviously quite close, if not identical, to that of higher primates – become, thenceforth, parts or materials with whose aid the institution will construct a human Understanding, a human perception, a genuinely human socialization – all three eminently *variable* across societies and periods.

[No need to discuss the return of confused terms, such as 'animal society' (for example, Maurice Godelier in *La Recherche*, November 1989). The hive or the herd are not societies. There is society where significations are *constitutive* of being-together, as symbolized by and embodied in a network of institutions; or where there is the *explicit nonsensible* borne and conveyed by the 'material-abstract' and participable by an indefinite collectivity. Society is inconceivable without the creation of *ideality*.]

What, then, is there 'in common' between psyche and society, where is the 'mediation' or the 'point of identity'? For both, there is and there has to be *nonfunctional meaning* (meaning in no way signifies *logos*!). But this meaning is, as has already been said, of another nature in each of the two cases. Psyche demands meaning, but society makes it renounce (though never completely) what for the psyche is its proper meaning and forces it to find meaning in the S.I.S. and in institutions. To ask where the 'mediations' are is strange: one could never stop enumerating them (*SII, ISR* [1982], *FISSI* [1985], *SST, PoPA, ISRH* [1988]). 'Abstractly', society furnishes objects to cathect, identificatory models, promises of substitutes (immortality), etc. 'Concretely', socialization can never occur without the total presence and the intervention (be it catastrophic) of at least one already socialized individual, this individual becoming cathected object and way of access to the social world as it is each time instituted.

The mother is society plus three million years of hominization. Anyone who does not see that and asks for 'mediations' shows he does not understand what is at issue. To have shown, in a relatively precise manner (beyond *anthrōpos anthrōpon genna*), the unfolding of this process while taking into account the irreducible specificity of the psyche is the decisive contribution a correctly interpreted psychoanalytic theory can offer to the comprehension not only of the psychical world but also of a central dimension of society. I flatter myself in thinking that, against the sociological lethargy of the psychoanalysts and the psychoanalytic lethargy of the sociologists, I have furnished this correct interpretation in chapter 6 of *IIS*.

All this also goes to show that, if the mode of being of the Unconscious is that of a magma, magma in no way signifies, either here or anywhere else, an 'amorphous clay' – quite the contrary, in fact, since one can 'extract . . . an indefinite number of ensemblist organizations' from a magma (*SII*, in *IIS*, p. 343E) – and it is to this, too, that the 'practically unlimited malleability of the psyche' corresponds. The mode of being of the magma signifies simply that the object under consideration is neither reducible to these ensidic organizations nor exhaustible by them.

To the question of 'how hallucinatory wish fulfilment is ever renounced' by the psyche – which, according to Whitebook, would create insurmountable difficulties both for Freud and for myself – the main response is, obviously, that *the psyche does not renounce it*: the psyche renounces neither dreaming nor the phantasm nor daydreaming. Nor does it renounce any of these in its socialized strata, though there the modalities are different.

Were the delirious crowds standing before Hitler at Nuremburg and the pajdarans ready to die on orders from Khomeini trying to obtain some organ pleasure? But the question is fallacious, it makes sense only upon Cartesian postulates it surreptitiously imputes to its adversary. I have written (*SII*) that the psyche is but the 'form' of the body. If the nursling cannot feel *at the same time* both hallucinatory and 'real' satisfactions, it will die – not from anorexia but from simple starvation. The predominance of representational pleasure over organ pleasure (*SII, SST*) does not signify that organ pleasure is suppressed; if that were so, there would have been no preservation of the individual or sexual reproduction of the species. The body (more exactly, the 'actions/passions' of the body) is source of pleasure, but this pleasure has to be 'doubled' by representation. The nursling's entire fate depends upon the way in which it weaves together, and the way in which its mother leads it to weave together, phantasmatic pleasure and 'real' satisfaction. We are not speaking of a 'Cartesian' psyche, external to the body 'within' which it finds itself imprisoned and with which it has as its sole point of contact the pineal gland. We are speaking of a psyche/soma, of a psyche that is the 'unperceivable' dimension of the body, 'duplicating' it through its entire length. (And obviously, all socialization is also simultaneously socialization of the body, just as the body is, reciprocally, support [*étayage*] for socialization itself.) 'Real' satisfaction is constantly immersed in the imaginary, and it is unclear how, in the human, it could be separated therefrom.

Of the immense work that remains to be done in these domains, here are the directions that to me appear most urgent. First, the elucidation of the specific modes of socialization, as instaurated each time by particular societies. Next, discussion of the nontrivial constants in these modes, beyond the ones I have just mentioned. At the same time, the question of the unity/difference of psyche/soma still also remains obscure, and discussion thereof has to be resumed not only from the 'traditional' ('psychosomatical', etc.) point of view, but also from the point of view of contemporary developments (the neurosciences, the *negative* paradigm of 'artificial intelligence', etc.).

Also to be treated from this angle is the question of the *'concrete' articulation* of society – for example, of intermediate bodies such as family, clan, caste, class, etc., the particular significations attached to them, and the corresponding identifications on the part of individuals. I thank my friends who remind me of the existence of this question – and I permit myself to remind them in turn that it is not because I was unaware of it that I wrote, for thirty years, about classes, informal groups of workers, youths, etc. Would one reproach an algebraist who writes $x + x = 2x$ for ignoring or forgetting that $1 + 1 = 2$?

There is still the prescriptive/normative dimension, namely, the contribution these considerations can bring to a reflection on a form of education oriented toward autonomy.

Finally to be treated more amply than I have done so far (in *SII* and *SST*) is the passage from the psyche and the heteronomous social individual to reflective and deliberative subjectivity (that is, the elucidation of the *two* different modes of sublimation).

Some of these problems are discussed in Hans Furth's text. I am in agreement with the majority of his formulations, including his affirmation that 'action *is* the imaginary product'. But here distinctions are necessary. In *IIS* I consider only the very first phases of psychical life, during which there can be no question of 'action', save in a too abstract and too broad sense – whereas Furth concentrates on the period after two years. But I must also emphasize that, insisting all the while on the fact that the psyche is, indissociably, representational/intentional/affective flux, I had to speak there especially the language of representation for the reason I mentioned above apropos of dreaming: it is this aspect that we can most easily and most directly discuss. And this holds, too, for S.I.S. (*PoPA*). But I would not say, as Furth does, that the child, even at a late stage, 'freely constructs social imaginary significations'. The child's assimilation of S.I.S. is certainly also always self-activity – therefore constructive and even 'creative'. That does not stop it from being essentially *introjection* – which, moreover, begins long before one's seventh year (in fact, as early as one's birth). That introjection presupposes projection (*SII, SST*) is something else. And children's attachment to norms is certain – but late: 'at the outset', such attachment coexists with its opposite, and its roots are to be sought in repetition and the need for regularity and for stable bearings that accompanies the breakup of the psychical monad.

Learning and Progress

A tendency has arisen, for a long time now, to try to make learning play the role of a central category, and even more, of a *deus ex machina* that would miraculously succeed in bridging the gap between the animal world and the human one and, even further, in dissipating by a curious sort of alchemy the question of the new.

But learning – like its cousin, adaptation – as important and ineliminable as it might be, is a *biological* category. I do not need to underscore here what, in strictly biological terms, the notion includes that is both evident and infinitely enigmatic. Whether the biologists know it or not, this notion refers immediately to philosophical questions, those that a philosophy of the living being (and not a 'philosophy of life') ought to elucidate. One could contribute something to the understanding of the human domain if one began to specify what differentiates human 'learning' from animal learning. I do not think that this has yet been done.

One evident fact immediately commands the attention. Whereas animal learning relates to a proper world that is given once and for all and on the basis of 'subjective' apparatuses also given once and for all, learning in the case of the human being concerns only the functions of the human as 'pure animal': gripping, standing erect and walking, etc. – in so far as it might be legitimate to separate them in an abstract manner from the rest. The essential feature of human 'learning' does not concern a proper world given once and for all; it is related to another social-historical world, to other societies. This is manifest not only in the case of one's tongue but also for all of one's behaviour. (One need only have seen Africans and Europeans/Americans dancing side by side to understand that one's relation to one's body is social-historically determined.)

This refers us to two intimately connected points. Without this essential malleability of the human being, which permits it here to learn Bamileke culture and there Florentine culture, there would be no history, no different societies. Now, theories of learning – and, more generally, conceptions of history based upon them – offer nothing capable of elucidating this malleability. At best, it remains for them an indigestible particle. In contrast, an elucidation of the socialization of the psyche on the basis of the imagination and of the imposition on the latter of the each time given institution of society allows us to view the entirety of the phenomena within a framework that renders it, in principle, comprehensible.

Moreover, if human behaviour were only learning, one sees neither why nor how one would ever have exited from the 'first society'. The existence of history and the diversity of societies force one to recognize as essential to the human this capacity for creation that makes it invent new forms of behaviour, as well as to receive, should the case arise, the new (on the cardinal importance of this second aspect, see *SU* [1971], in *CL*, pp. 136–8E). Receiving the new has nothing to do with any sort of learning, since such reception amounts, at minimum, to a massive and sudden modification of the already established 'subjective' mechanisms (in a process where 'trials and errors' play practically no role). Of course, this capacity for receiving the new (always present to a minimum degree, otherwise there would be no alterations of society) itself undergoes an immense transformation with the historical creation of societies that break with the near-absolute closure of traditional societies.

But there is more. One tends, sometimes, to present the whole of the history of humanity as a cumulative 'learning' process across generations and social forms. It is almost fated for this viewpoint to interpret this alleged 'learning' as a more or less successful form of 'problem-solving' and to connect the latter with a 'process of rationalization'. How can one not see in this conception a vulgar, biologistic Hegelo-Marxism that avoids all the questions by means of a dogmatic affirmation and blackmailing of 'rationality'? If man is defined by learning, and if this learning is cumulative, what are we to make of the immense regression and massive losses that characterize Western history from the third to the tenth centuries CE? If this learning is a learning of 'problem-solving', one ought to be able to define what are the problems that are posed in general, everywhere and always, to humanity and in what their solution would consist (*MRT*, in *IIS*, pp. 133–5E). This question is not even envisaged – and if it were, what other response could it receive than false platitudes, of the type: 'satisfaction of needs' or 'better regulation of the metabolism with nature'? Obviously, 'needs' are defined each time by the institution of society (*MRT*), and so are the 'problems'. The 'problems' a *c.*CE 450 member of the Christian faithful has to resolve are in no way the 'problems' a *c.*450 BCE Athenian citizen has to resolve. And I would really like someone to show me, without some fallacious 'dialectic', what 'progress' – or 'cumulation' – there is between one and the other.

The sole 'problem' that the institution of society has to resolve everywhere and always and that, everywhere and always, it *does resolve* in a way that would be practically unassailable, were it not perturbed either from without or by its own imaginary, is the 'problem' of meaning: creating a ('natural' and 'social') world invested with signification (*MRT*, *SII*, *ISR*, *PoPA*). To say that, *in this regard*, there might be 'cumulation' and 'progress' is to subscribe to the incredible, even though banal, idea that there is a 'meaning' of the world and that we are gradually approaching it. (And, subsidiarily, it is to engage in hierarchizing observed societies according to their greater or lesser proximity to this 'true meaning of the world'). It is also to this that the view of the whole of history as 'rationalization' is committed.

It is obvious, and banal, to state that over the whole of human history considered from a bird's-eye view [*en survol*] (though not in its details: see *T*, in *CL*, pp. 241–6E) there is a dimension along which there is 'progress' and 'cumulation': this is the ensidic dimension, *legein* and *teukhein*, the logico-mathematical and the technical (*SII*, in *IIS*, pp. 268–72E). We would be able to draw from this the conclusion that there is 'progress' and 'cumulation' *tout court*, *only if* we reduced the world and human life to ensidic entities – which is clearly absurd. But even in relation to this ensidic dimension we cannot forget that such 'progress' and its maintenance refer back to philosophical questions of capital importance. On the one hand, both are evidently impossible without cosmological conditions (*OIHS*): it is because *there is* an ensidizable dimension of all that is that the Understanding can exercise its 'fantastic potential'. On the other hand, its deployment and unfolding depend on the human imaginary – and so does its *maintenance*, as well as its reception. When I was young, the peasants in Greece (and no doubt in a host of countries) rejected the methods agronomists proposed they adopt, saying, 'That is not what our fathers taught us.' (In this they were not necessarily and always wrong, as the ravages created in Africa by Western 'experts' now show – but that is another story.) This might appear idiotic to a late twentieth-century Western intellectual – idiotic or not, it is, first and foremost, the attitude *princeps* of every human community. And today, the uncritical acceptance by everyone of all that 'modernity' offers is, to begin with, simply a *received* attitude, just as 'idiotic' and, potentially, infinitely more catastrophic. During the supposed destruction by fire of the Library of Alexandria, the Caliph uttered the immortal phrase, 'If these books say what the Koran says, they are useless; if they say something else, they are pernicious' – the story may almost certainly be apocryphal from the point of view of factual truth, but it nevertheless possesses a profound truth from the social-historical point of view. The attitude imputed to the Caliph is the sole one worthy of a true believer; it has been, on a massive scale, that of true Christians over the centuries, when, for example, they covered over Greek philosophical manuscripts in order to write thereon the life and miracles of Saint Paphnutius (learning? problem-solving? progress?). It is also the attitude of the late Pascal.

Ensidic 'progress' wins out in the long run, when it wins out and where it wins out, as a function of the *potential* it confers (this is why the inventions most easily accepted from another culture are inventions having to do with weaponry: from the Arabs to the Indians and to Peter the Great, not to mention Stalin and Brezhnev). This potential assures a sort of quasi-Darwinian 'potential for survival' in the struggle among different societies. But even that is not absolute. The incredible Islamic conquests during the seventh and eighth centuries had nothing to do with some sort of technical superiority; they resulted from traits of the Islamic religion and from its capacity to arouse passion and affects ('fanaticism') and, to a lesser extent, from Islam's social arrangements. But nothing *imposes* philosophy, democracy, the type of society that includes them.

The true questions of historicity are situated beyond 'learning', 'rationalization', 'problem-solving', and 'progress'. The task of elaborating these questions remains for me a priority.

Meaning and Validity

It would seem that I am unaware of the distinction between meaning and validity (*Sinn* and *Geltung*). This criticism, first formulated by Habermas, is now taken up under different forms, notably by Heller and Hugues Poltier. The reproach amounts to saying that I cannot (or will not) distinguish between the statements 'The Eiffel Tower is in London' (a statement that is *sinnvoll*, meaningful, but not valid) and 'The Eiffel Tower is in Paris' (a statement that is both significant and valid). All false statements have a meaning: those that do not have one we call meaningless, absurd, etc. – not false. 'The square root of the Fifth Republic is a jerusalem artichoke' is not a false statement.

Meaning, signification, ideality are created by society; validity, too. The meaning/validity distinction is *constitutive* of the institution of society. It is the presupposition of the distinctions correct/incorrect, licit/forbidden, etc. The attempt to suppress this distinction is the horizon for an unimaginable totalitarianism, brilliantly imagined by Orwell in *1984* as the ultimate objective of Newspeak, when it would finally become not incorrect or illicit but grammatically absurd to say 'Big Brother is ungood.'

This distinction, however, is completely inadequate. Another, much more serious question arises once we recognize, as we are obliged to, that each society creates not only what for it is meaning but also what for it is validity, and valid. One can dispute this only if one totally forgets what history and ethnology have shown us. Paul, who was neither a historian nor an ethnologist, knew it, and he made the same distinction: We preach Jesus crucified, which is for the Jews *skandalon* and for Gentiles *mōria*. For the Jews, the idea that the Messiah was crucified (and not powerful, victorious, etc.) has a meaning, but it is *skandalon* – scandalous, blasphemous, outrageously false. For the Gentiles, the very idea of a Messiah, his crucifixion, and his resurrection is simply *mōria* – childish prattling, meaningless sound. Paul was in the process of instituting a universe full of affirmations (the incarnation of a God who is otherwise transcendent, faith in the Christian sense, etc.) that would not be invalid, or false, but simply absurd (and in fact incomprehensible) for Aristotle. This took place, historically speaking, just yesterday morning. Our philosophers of today have already forgotten it.

The underside, or corollary, of the acknowledgement that each society institutes what is, for it, meaning and validity is that this is not so, in principle, for another one. I say 'in principle' expressly: this affirmation has to be qualified in several ways. There obviously is no 'solipsism' to societies, but there very much is *essential alterity*. If such were not the case, there would be no essential misoxeny (conditioning both racism and wars), or any almost insurmountable difficulties for ethnological and historical knowledge (*GPCD* [1983], in *PPA*, pp. 82–7; *ReRa* [1987]; T/E: *SH* [1991]).

The question presents itself from two angles. First, it must be considered 'in itself' – the way in which each society experiences and *institutes* the other ones. This is a vast domain of research, where one has hardly just begun to break some ground. I shall limit myself to a few general indications.

It is almost an *a priori* proposition that a society could not accept the *validity* of another society's institutions, unless they were 'identical' to its own, or very close to them. Otherwise, it would adopt them (*ReRa*). And it is a fact (the interpretation of which is in no way simple) that this nonacceptance almost never takes the form, 'They are other, they have other institutions', but almost always, 'They are bad, inferior, corrupt, diabolical'. Go reread, then, the foundation of your culture, the Old Testament. You will see what the non-Hebrews were for the Hebrews: not 'barbarians', but sources of defilement. And recall that just yesterday, you burned these same Hebrews and, more generally, those who did not acknowledge the same God as yours, or not in the same way. This becomes truly (though not without difficulty) different only with Greece and modern Europe.

To state this is quite obviously to state that each foreign society makes sense for the society 'Ego' – and that this meaning [*sens*] is affected, as a whole, with a negative (or, at best, deficient) validity. Even if the others are posited as subhuman or nonhuman, they are quite obviously cathected with meaning *in toto* and as such. That is of minor import for the present discussion. On the other hand, what matters is the 'details': to what extent, in what fashion, under what conditions the rules, the acts, the ways of making/doing of society B make sense for society A. This, too, is an immense question that remains to be worked out. But this, at least, is certain: to the extent that A encounters B (trade between tribes, war, etc.), A will have to work out a meaning for the 'acts', etc. of B sufficient as to need/usage. This elaboration will necessarily contain a strong 'projective' element (one need only look at the work of Western ethnologists) – this element already being present, quite obviously, in the postulate that it really is a matter of a society, which has institutions, goals [*finalités*], privileged ways of making/doing 'like ours', even if the 'content' is entirely other. But this elaboration will be almost exclusively *instrumental*: I do not think an Arapesh feels the intense need to 'understand from within' the imaginary significations of the Nugum – any more than Isaiah was trying to understand what might be the religion of the 'idolaters' whom he 'refuted'. What renders possible this elaboration by A of meaning for B is the obligatory ensidic dimension of every social institution. They, like us, know that 100 is greater than 50, that night follows day, that if one wants X one must posit Y, etc. In this ensidic elaboration and the practical syllogisms to which it leads, the 'knowledge' that can exist about the S.I.S. ('irrational beliefs') of the others evidently enters as links in a chain (Cambyses, Egyptians and their cats); no profound understanding is required. One simply acknowledges an 'unanalysed fact'. Here two antinomic considerations intervene. Every society has to institute itself in the ensidic, as well; there is, therefore, something like a nonempty intersection of the institution of all societies (a common part). $2 + 2 = 4$ is instituted (and correct) everywhere. But this dimension (*legein* and *teukhein*) is not absolutely separable from the strictly imaginary dimension of society: Persian cats are not Egyptian cats; in

Christian societies 1 ≠ 3, save when the most important matters are at stake (the three divine persons who are only one while being three). Today's philistine can consider this example merely amusing, forgetting that during several *centuries* countless persons were persecuted, exiled, killed due to subtle variations in the interpretation of the 'equal' sign in 1 = 3; the *Filioque* itself and the great East/West schism are part of it. Today's philosophers of history read too much Kant and not enough history and ethnology, not enough Montaigne, Swift, Montesquieu, and Gibbon. This dependence of the ensidic 'part' of the institution upon its strictly imaginary 'part' illustrates, once again in this case, the magmatic character of S.I.S: the possibility of separating out the ensidic part, the impossibility of doing so without damage.

Meaning and validity are social-historical creations. They constitute the mode of being of the institution, which is without precedent and analogy elsewhere. (I must leave aside here the question of 'meaning' for the living being – as well as meaning for the psyche.) They are expressive of the fundamental fact that each society is a being-for-itself and that it creates a world of its own.

Such is, on the whole, the situation in itself, in effective social-historical life. This does not exhaust the question. For each society, the validity of its institutions is almost always unquestionable and unquestioned. There would have been no combat of the gods in history if, for each society, its gods were not the only 'true' ones and its laws the only valid ones. For us, however, the question cannot stop there. We acknowledge this plurality of incompatible laws, and the domestic validity of each. From then on, two attitudes are possible:

1 We limit ourselves to this acknowledgement, and we proclaim that this difference is indifferent. Did the Aztecs practise human sacrifices? Such is the *nomos* of the Aztecs, such is their 'interpretation' (their hermeneutic) of the world, such is their 'narrative', such is the fashion in which Being was dispensed to them. One can, as one pleases, choose the vocabulary of Critias, Nietzsche, Heidegger, or their Franco-American epigones. The consequence thereof is a compete relativism with respect to both knowledge (philosophy, like differential calculus, is part of the *nomos* or the *epistēmē* of the West, and has validity only in the West) and acting (we do not wish to decide between these different *nomoi* and if, by chance, we might wish to defend our own – it seems that the French Nietzscheo-Heideggerians are now flirting with the 'rights of man', and even with ethics – this is a pure fact: we are like that). It must strongly be emphasized that this relativism, just like all scepticism if it dares be sufficiently radical (which is never the case), is *irrefutable*, both practically and theoretically speaking. Practically, because a consistent sceptic is never lacking in sophisms, changes of definition, eristic arguments, etc. Discussion with him is a combat with the Lernaean hydra. If one

disputes this person with a ten-term statement, he will endeavour to show that each of these terms is ambiguous, contestable, etc. ('You are contradicting yourself.' 'What does "you" mean? I am not me.' Foucault almost literally wrote that.) At the end of n exchanges, there will be 10^n terms in the discussion. The presupposition of every discussion and every refutation is the common aim of truth: what distinguishes the philosopher from the sophist, Aristotle already said, is *proairesis*, the intention. It is also the common acceptance, by the discussants, of a requirement of coherency or of plain noncontradiction – and it is this requirement (this axiom or postulate, if you wish) that the sceptic or the relativist rejects. One cannot force someone to accept the principle of noncontradiction – all the less so as the principle itself has only a restricted or partial validity, as its correct usage requires *phronēsis*, and as its tenor and its reasonable employment wholly change when we pass to higher modes of thought. (Parenthetically, I am completely in agreement with Vincent Descombes on the question of identity. As I already wrote in chapter 5 of *IIS*, identity is never but identity *as to* . . . . See also *LMQA*, in *CR*, p. 294.) There is no answer to the sophist who commands you to say whether capitalist society in 1880 is strictly identical to that of 1890, except to list exhaustively the moments of identity and nonidentity between the two – and who concludes from this, triumphantly, that one cannot speak of capitalist society.

But it is also known, also since Aristotle, that it is not only when faced with the sceptic or the sophist that the principle of identity is unprovable; it is unprovable *in itself*, since every proof of the principle presupposes it. In terms both philosophical and social-historical: identity is inaugural institution; without it, nothing is possible (neither in acting nor in thinking); and it is, moreover, totally insufficient (*SII*, in *IIS*, pp. 205–6E).

2   If we do not want this incoherency, this 'anything goes', we have to introduce an obvious and elementary distinction – but one which opens up a profound, difficult discussion that touches upon the ultimate stakes, at least for our own historical period: the distinction between right and fact. There is not just one form of validity, there are two. (This is what today's incense-bearing altar boys of 'validity' miss without even catching a glimpse of it.) There is social-historically created *de facto* or *positive* validity, which is the validity of each society's institutions for itself (validity, not only prevalence, imposition, etc.; and it is not simply *meaning*: for a traditional society, if there were no meaning/validity distinction, there would be no correct/incorrect distinction). The stoning of adulterers is a valid rule for Judaic society and its validity is unquestionable (it is prescribed by Yahweh). But *we question* this validity. We raise the question of the *de jure* validity of this rule. We ask ourselves: What *ought we* to think of this rule, and what *ought we to make of it*? We acknowledge the indefinite variety of historical *nomoi*, and we pose the question: Do all these *nomoi* have the same *value*, and what *nomos* ought we to want for ourselves? That is equivalent to saying that we introduce (we

accept) the metacategory of *de jure validity*. It is easy to show that this is equivalent to the instauration of *reflection* and *deliberation*, both taken in the radical sense (not halting, for example and especially, before our own institution), or of what is the defensible content of the term *reason* (see the preface to *CL*).

De jure validity gives rise to at least two questions.

First, the question of its social-historical origin. We must exit finally from the (geographical and chronological) provincialism of contemporary philosophers. Humanity, in a meaning congruent with what we today intend by this term (language, institutional social regulation, the antinatural treatment of the dead, etc.), has existed for at least a hundred thousand years. We know very few things about the greatest part of this history and about the majority of types of societies that have existed on Earth, but we can infer much about them, based on the hundreds of savage societies we have been able to observe directly as well as on traditional societies. Not that Australian aborigines 'represent' the universal state of humanity in the year minus 15,000 and the Tupí-Guaraní in the year minus 5000, but it would be somewhat extravagant to suppose that philosophy, for example, abundantly practised by the first Cro-Magnons, subsequently was lost. What is decisive in this regard, and what is of eminent interest to me in this discussion, is what we can presume with great probability about societies that existed between 100000 and 1000 BCE and what we know categorically about almost all societies existing *c.*1900 – and not what happened in Königsberg between 1770 and 1781. Now, the fact, large as the Pyramid of Cheops, is that all these societies are almost totally absorbed within their institution, that is to say, the question of validity is posed in them only as a question of *positive, de facto* validity, in relation to existing institutions (and instituted representations), not as a question of *de jure* validity. This is compatible with the most highly developed intelligence (I have written on several occasions that the intelligence of those who were the first to ascertain, even approximately, the length of the solar year, to invent weaving or pottery, is far superior to, if the expression has any meaning, or at least is infinitely more striking than, that of people today). Expressed in philosophical language: In these societies, all questions can be posed, except the question of principles. Now, reason is not only, but certainly also essentially, the faculty of principles (Kant), or better, the faculty of interrogating oneself about principles. This amounts to saying that reason is unlimited interrogation. This interrogation – and the space of *de jure* validity it constitutes – was created for the first time in ancient Greece, around the end of the seventh century. *De jure* validity, and reason, and truth in the full and strong sense of the term are social-historical creations. This creation undergoes, with true Christianity, a prolonged eclipse. It is reproduced, under the influence of the 'discovery' of the Greeks but also of other historical factors, in Western Europe – and undoubtedly it is not a mere 'repetition', or 'interpretation', of the original creation (as Whitehead thought).

Under these conditions, what does the 'universality' of reason mean? Certainly it means, first of all, the universality of the *object* of interrogation: in principle, no theme is or can be removed from it. It also means something factual: once reason, in the sense indicated, is created, every human being is *amenable* to reason. To call that an *Anlage*, an innate disposition, would be a sophistical tautology. The *Anlage* in question is 'simply' that every human being can, in principle, re*imagine* what another human being has *imagined*. If *Anlage* there be, it is certainly, among all human *Anlagen*, the one whose actualization is the most astronomically difficult. And what does one say of the inverse *Anlage* which led Heidegger to Nazism, Lukács to Stalinism, thousands of intellectuals to a 'sacrifice of conscience', and today still leads some philosophers to religious conversion? What is at stake here is the astonishing potential, and 'universality', of the faculty that is most singular in its texture – the imagination – not the universal innateness of reason. But in order to lead a human being to reason, something else is needed: that his adherence to a heteronomous institution of society, his internalization of the representations in which this institution is embodied, ceases. I willingly would advance the cost if someone would organize a public discussion between two German philosophers and two Iranian mullahs. But I believe that the expense would be in vain: one knows the results in advance. Two years ago, during a colloquium in which Cardinal Lustiger participated, I recalled a phrase from Lessing, viz., that the Enlightenment implies the rejection of all Revelation, of all interventions by Providence in the world, and of any idea of eternal Damnation. The Archbishop of Paris (whose unparalleled intelligence no one will contest) shrugged his shoulders and muttered something like: Why harp on these old-fashioned ideas?

I certainly shall not be insulting Poltier if I say that he is, perhaps, as intelligent as, though certainly not more intelligent than, Saint Augustine. Yet Poltier, despite his eristic sophistics, is right, and Saint Augustine not. For, as Saint Augustine writes in his *Confessions*, no restrictions are acceptable when discussing with our Christian brethren; with them, everything can be put into question. But no discussion is possible with those who would not accept the sacred authority of the Scriptures. For all those for whom a revealed truth exists, whatever their intelligence, their genius, their subtlety, there is a 'principle' before which their mind must halt: the Scriptures. This holds [*vaut*], too, for the immense intellectual effort deployed in the Talmud or on the basis of the Koran. And it also evidently holds, in a pathetically ridiculous mode, for all the 'Marxists', for whom the truth of *Capital* must be saved at any price, via interminable 'interpretations'.

But it is, of course, reason itself that tells us that social-historical origin is not to be confounded with *de jure* validity. Reason is the very establishment of this distinction. And here we come to our second question. Reason cannot be defended *erga omnes*; it can be defended only against those who accept both the distinction between right and fact *and* a certain number of (not simply procedural) rules that render rational discussion possible. That is the *de facto* situation. But there is also a *logical* situation. We are being asked from all sides to furnish a 'rational foundation' for the rational attitude, to justify *de jure* the choice of right, etc. These demands are accompanied by what must very well be called demagogy. For, first of all, those who speak thus would be hard pressed to furnish this 'rational foundation' (we shall soon see why it is excluded *a priori* for them to do so); next, because it is left understood that if one rejects these pretensions, one is fatally 'anti-rationalistic', a cosmologist, a partisan of a 'philosophy of life', and I know not what else.

We pose the question: What is valid *de jure* (as thought, as law, etc.)? We are told: You also have to demonstrate that the question of *de jure* validity is itself valid *de jure*. We are told: You have to prove rationally that reason is valid [*vaut*], you have to furnish a 'rational foundation'. But how can I even raise the question of the *de jure* validity of the question of *de jure* validity without having already raised it and having thus posited both that it makes sense and that it is valid *de jure*? How can I rationally found reason without presupposing it? If a foundation of reason is rational, it presupposes and utilizes what it wants to prove; if it is not (as *is not*, and strikingly so, the idea that 'all men naturally possess reason', assuming that anyone could ever take this as a 'foundation'), it contradicts the result it is aiming at. Not only social-historically, but logically ('transcendentally'), the positing of reason is inaugural, it is *self-positing*. It seems that certain people are entertaining the illusion of a third possibility. But it is impossible to see what it would be. To 'found' reason upon language or communication is absurd under several headings. From the standpoint of the rigorous requirements of what traditionally is called a 'foundation', language, like communication (including the 'intentions of the participants in intersubjective communication'), is a pure fact, which can serve for anything one wants, save for founding anything at all. Language is a necessary condition for reason (for thought), it becomes its living and marvellous body as soon as reason is created, but it does not 'contain' reason. One might say abstractly that the unlimited question is always a possibility immanent to every language – but that would be false; a language can close upon itself in its effective institution and put a halt to interrogation. *Mutatis mutandis*, the same thing is true for communication. The 'foundation' of reason upon reason itself, the rejection of the 'deductive', the announcement of a sort of self-evidence of reason – it is this that really should be called mystical. No great philosopher ever claimed to 'found' reason. Plato postulates the vision of something that is 'beyond essence'; Aristotle postulates a *nous*, concerning which he explicitly states that it is not subject to *logos* (and which is *infallible* as to the *ti ēn einai!*); Kant postulates *at least* the coherency of experience *and* ordinary logic; Hegel postulates nearly everything. From this point of view, I do not feel I am in such bad company.

All this resembles some braggart's tale. No one is holding you back. If you can produce a foundation for reason owing nothing to the usage of reason, why don't you do it? If it is something other than reason that would produce the foundation for the latter, on what, then, would this other thing be founded? *Anankē stēnai*, said a rather well-known simpleton twenty-five centuries ago.

But let us suppose, impossible though it would be, that such a foundation might be exhibited. What then? In what way would that advance us? If reason was capable all alone of producing necessary consequences, starting from this foundation, the ignorant would perhaps have been able to miss them – but what about the philosophers? Why has one been discussing since Thales, and why is one not on the verge of stopping? Has one seen mathematicians disputing for twenty-five centuries about the infinity of prime numbers or the irrationality of $\sqrt{2}$? Would the tribe of philosophers be so corrupt, stupid, and envious that the discovery of a rational *and fecund* founding of reason at Frankfurt, say, remains a local event, confined to a few seminars, instead of provoking a worldwide wave of enthusiasm and unanimous agreement? Why are there oppositions within philosophy, why is there a *history* of philosophy? Were this due to 'empirical' factors (the perverting influence of ruling classes or difficulties in philosophers' digestive systems, whatever), it would still be necessary to admit that in its effective social-historical actuality philosophy is determined much more strongly by nonreason than by reason. But if one cannot find reason in philosophy, where then shall one find it?

I try to reflect and to deliberate. I asked myself (before Habermas or Poltier asked me): And why should I reflect and deliberate? I answer myself (though I would dare not answer this way to Habermas and Poltier): Poor simpleton, in posing this question, you are still in reflection and deliberation, you are posing the question, 'Why should I . . .?', and you are leaving it understood for yourself that you would accept as an answer only 'good reasons' – without yet even knowing, moreover, what defines a 'good reason'. You have already unconditionally given value to unlimited reflection.

Socrates said: *Ho anexetastos bios ou biotos*, The unexamined life, the life without reflection, is not livable, I prefer to die. He was not trying to *demonstrate* to his judges (or to anyone) that one *must* philosophize, nor was he, as he said in other cases, trying to 'force them to admit' (*Symposium* 223d) that. Less naive than the philosophers of the twentieth century, Socrates knew that he could prove it only by philosophizing. But philosophizing and living as he lived, he *showed*, he *realized* the value of philosophy – the *de jure* value of a life devoted to reflection, of someone who refuses to act and to speak without adequate deliberation. And it is on this account that we do not cease looking at him.

Apropos of this – as well as apropos of politics – one speaks of 'voluntarism'. This term of disparagement leaves me cold. Can I reflect without *willing* [*vouloir*] to reflect? Can I deliberate without *willing* to deliberate? Can I try to be free (autonomous) if I do not *will* to be autonomous? But why do you want [*vouloir*] to be free?, Poltier nearly asks me. Are you not a slave to your desire for freedom? According to your ideas, won't an autonomous society be heteronomous in as much as it will be devoted to autonomy? Childish sophisms. When Tocqueville said, in a phrase that no doubt had classical antecedents (and which is certainly inadequate *downstream*): He who wants liberty for something other than liberty is unworthy of it – was he being an 'irrationalist', 'Bergsonian'? There is an inaugural position, a self-positing, which is impossible without the participation of the will: reflecting and deliberating.

What can rightly be called voluntarism is expressed very well in the maxim Waldenfels ironically flings at me: *Wo ein Wille, da ist auch ein Weg* (Where there's a will, there's a way). Its meaning is precise and clear: The will is, by itself alone, the self-sufficient condition for the way, for the solution. Had I ever thought that, I would not have spent the past forty-three years of my life questioning myself without respite about the state and the tendencies of the society in which we live, trying to detect what might herald autonomy in the struggles and the gatherings of French or American workers or the Hungarian and Polish people, in the new movements of students, women, ecologists; nor would I have accorded such heavy weight to the process of privatization in contemporary society (*MCR*) and to its incrustation within a weighty social-historical material situation (*CWS* [1982] and *DE?* [1987]). But Waldenfels, by making a greater effort at reflection, could have found the true maxim, the one that is also my own: *Wo keiner Wille, da ist auch keiner Weg (sondern blosses Geschehen)*, Where there is no will, there is no way, there is only becoming.

A certain intellectualist rationalism has reserved 'will' for 'ethics' or for 'practical reason' – as if there could be a 'subject of pure thought' without will – or as if 'will' were a 'Prussian' or 'Bolshevik' faculty. The will is tension toward . . . reflective and deliberative subjectivity, it is *constitutive* of such subjectivity. It is not a matter of 'psychology' in the derogatory sense of the neo-Kantians and Husserlians. If reflection does not *will* something, it *is* not as reflection. The quest for truth is the will for truth. (This phrase evidently has no meaning if truth is a dispensation of being – which, as one knows, just as well dispenses nontruth, *Verborgenheit* – and if one must '*sein lassen*' both of them.) It is a matter of the ontology of the mode of the for-itself that is reflective and deliberative subjectivity (*SST*). The quest for truth presupposes the will for truth, it also presupposes a cathexis of truth (and not, for example, of saintliness), and both presuppose, already, a certain idea of truth. There is, at this level, no anatomy of subjectivity – or, if one prefers, such an anatomy can only kill subjectivity. The moments of subjectivity – the sublimation of desire into will, of representation into thought, of the pleasure of representation into pleasure in the freedom to do and to think – are indissociable.

To the question 'Why autonomy? Why reflection?' there is no foundational answer, no response 'upstream'. There is a social-historical *condition*: the project of autonomy, reflection, deliberation, and reason have already been created, they are already there, they belong to our tradition. But this *condition* is not a *foundation*. One now offers as an objection to me what I was the first to underscore a long time ago: our tradition does not include only that; it includes the Gulag and Auschwitz as well (*GPCD*). But I have never claimed to have 'founded' the value of autonomy on 'our tradition' (that would be a funny idea). *On the contrary*, the value of our tradition is that it has *also created* the project of autonomy, democracy and philosophy, and also that it has created, and given value to, the possibility of *choice* (impossible, for example, for true Jews, Christians, or Muslims). We value this possibility of choice unconditionally, and we employ it by choosing in favour of autonomy and against the heteronomy present both in our tradition and in our present times, both flabbily and monstrously. No one is preventing Poltier from joining a Nazi or Stalinist party, the order of Jesuits, or the Islamic religion. But this possibility is offered to him only through our social institution, as a realized fragment of the project of autonomy. If someone says he detests this possibility of choice, that he would have infinitely preferred to be born in a society where the very idea of a choice would be by its construction inconceivable, discussion halts, and one can only wish him 'Bon voyage'.

There is, certainly, more. The project of autonomy is not a lightning flash in a clear sky. It *goes with* something else; it conditions, motivates, incites something else: briefly speaking, the best of the creation surrounding us. It can reasonably be defended, at length and substantially, *downstream* from this position and from this choice. It can be so defended, starting from its implications and its consequences. But with regard to whom? With regard to the person who has *already accepted* reasonable discussion, the person who has thereby already situated herself *within* reflectiveness. Would anyone undertake the 'rational refutation' of Pascal or Kierkegaard?

But the most important thing lies elsewhere. The scholarly and scholastic repetition of a pseudo-Kantian arguing gambit occults the great questions that are posed precisely by the fact that we cannot reflect without creating the horizon of *de jure* validity – and that it is *we* who reflect. *We*, this means beings who are also psychical (therefore conditioned by the Unconscious), also social-historical (therefore conditioned by the institution of our society) and always beings for themselves (therefore ones obligatorily placed, even from the most abstract point of view, at a 'point of view', seeing from a 'perspective', creating a meaning and creating it necessarily in a closure). One cannot continue covering up the (second) great black hole of Kantianism: What is the relation of the effective to the transcendental? How can 'we humans' exit from 'empirical' determinations? On this immense question, which governs all the others, I can provide here only two indications (cf. *EP?*).

First, we have to recognize, on the psychical side, the fact of sublimation and the psyche's capacity to sublimate; on the social-historical side, the creation of a space and a time in which the questions of the true and the just can effectively be posed, and are so posed; and, finally, we have to elevate ourselves to another conception of the truth. In brief: if we do not recognize the *philosophical* status of the social-historical, as the site where fact *can* become right and right *can* become fact, we are not being consistent.

The second indication concerns the meaning of this *de jure* validity. Can we qualify it as 'transhistorical' or even 'extrahistorical'? I leave aside the procedural, tautological, and empty answer, viz.: If I could transport myself back two hundred million years, if I were as I am and the rest the same, I would think the same thing for the same reasons. Let us note, first, that the *question* itself has meaning only for a reflective subjectivity and for a society in and through which such a subjectivity has become effectively actual. Things certainly go otherwise for the 'results' of this reflective activity. It seems evident to me not only that the generalized Pythagorean theorem (equality of the square of the measure of the sum of two orthogonal vectors and the sum of the squares of their measure in every pre-Hilbertian space) could be proved to every being capable of following a reasoned argument who would accept certain axioms, *but also* that this very relation between axioms and this conclusion is 'outside time' in the sense that, in the world of 'reinforced' ideality that is that of mathematics, 'time' is as external to the thing as scarlet red or nostalgia. The same goes for the ensidic dimension of all that is (statements bearing on his dimension). Mathematically speaking, the Pythagorean theorem is not only true, in its infinitely thin and infinitely thick truth, 'in every possible universe'; it is (conditionally) true *outside universes*. But the Pythagorean theorem is not and cannot be 'purely mathematical', for it happens that this universe here (and every universe conceivable by us) also includes *in itself* an ineliminable ensidic dimension. To this extent, mathematics is applicable thereto and a mathematical physics results therefrom. The mathematics applicable to our universe includes the Pythagorean theorem (not only, first – which is decisive – in the first natural stratum, but also in the most elaborate conceptions, since in

General Relativity an analogous theorem is locally valid). From this standpoint, the theorem is 'valid' here as well as in a galaxy of the Coma Berenices constellation, now as well as 10^{-40} seconds after the Big Bang. And in the same way (though much more conditionally), the results of mathematical physics are 'valid'. Everything we know and everything we do would collapse into incoherency if we were to suppose that gravitation began only in 1687. Newton certainly did not 'discover', he invented and created, the theory of gravitation; but it happens (and this is why we are still talking about it) that this creation *encounters* in a fruitful way *what is*, in one of its strata. In this case, too, we could show its validity to every being capable of following a reasoned argument who would accept, in addition to the mathematical axioms, certain rules and principles (Ockham's razor, consistency, 'agreement' with observational and experimental facts, etc.; of course, all these terms can and should be discussed in volume after volume).

It is to be noted that such a being, rigorously conceived, would be able to accept the axioms of Newtonian theory but would never be able to *invent* them: it is the theoretical imagination that posits them. No point in entering here into the discussion (the most important of all in this regard) of whether our mathematical physics is also correct for every possible universe – or for every universe that includes a class of effectively actual observers. But one can affirm that, to the extent that it is axiomatized, it is, like the physics of such a universe, also correct *outside universes*.

We create knowledge. In certain cases (mathematics) we also create, thereby, the *outside time*. In other cases (mathematical physics) we create under the constraint of encounter; it is this encounter that validates or invalidates our creations.

In a sense, this also holds for social-historical knowledge. That the Caduveos paint their faces has the same status as every empirical statement bearing upon facts (that there was a supernova in 1987 in the Great Magellanic Cloud, for example). But what about the Caduveos' *significations*? Leaning on certain ensidic elements, we have to try to re-create them – here again, under constraint of the encounter. It is radically false to say that one can 'write history' any way at all. The proof is that the number of stupidities one can say about history (or about societies from other times and places) is unlimited. Why are these stupidities? Because they do not encounter what the society or period considered truly was. Let us leave aside the obvious, but purely negative, criterion of inadequacy or inconsistency (a perfectly coherent paranoidal interpretation of some savage society is not for all that true).

To the extent that we can effectively comprehend something about a foreign society, or say something valid about it, we proceed to a re-creation of significations, which encounter the originary creation. It is again the theoretical imagination (a variant thereof) that, under various constraints, is at

issue here. It is clear, on the one hand, that this task is infinitely more difficult (difficult in another way) than that of theoretical physics, for example;
and on the other hand, that here it does not suffice that a being might be
capable of following a reasoned argument for that being to agree with us. A
being without the re-creative capacity of the imagination will understand
nothing about it. In physics one presents the person with hypotheses, one
assumes that he accepts them, and one draws out the consequences; but the
relation of a society's S.I.S. with its 'observable reality' has nothing to do
with the relation of premises to conclusions, and the S.I.S. cannot be formulated and presented as hypotheses. What could one understand of a
Christian society if one does not understand what faith is? And how can one
present or define faith logically?

If we leave the domain of knowledge, the discussion loses its object. The
question of the transhistorical value of the work of art, for example, plunges
us into aporias I have already discussed (*GPCD*). *The Art of the Fugue* is
central to my Imaginary Museum (and also, I am certain, to Luc Ferry's).
Is there any meaning in saying that it *ought* also to be central to Lady
Murasaki's, or even Aristoxenus', *such as they were*? (That it might *become so
after acculturation* obviously creates a presumption of historicity, and not the
other way around.)

But the same goes for practical values. *Ought* democracy and autonomy
to be valid for the Incas or for the inhabitants of the Kingdom of Dahomey
in the tenth century? This statement is empty, meaningless, pointless. For
something to become an exigency (an 'ought-to-be') it must first *make sense*,
it must *be able* to make sense for the addressee. To say that the people of the
Neolithic age *should have* aimed at individual and social autonomy is to say
quite simply that they should not have been what they were and should have
been what they were not and what no retrospective discourse can make them
become.

Things proceed in quite another direction for those alive today, whatever
their own culture may be, for they can, in principle, accede to this meaning
(to the constellation of significations created in Greco-Western history) –
and they do accede to them in fact (democracy, demanded by the Chinese
last spring [1989], in no way belongs to the Chinese 'tradition'). To 'reasonably convince' people today means to assist them in attaining their own
autonomy. Why do so? Because we want [*voulons*] autonomy for everyone
– because we submit everything, including others' institutions, to the question of right. This is to affirm, Poltier complains, the superiority of Western
culture; it does not respect others' difference. We are not affirming the superiority of Western culture but, rather, one dimension of Western culture,
which we also affirm, as already stated, against another, opposite dimension
of this same culture. If someone does not accept this superiority, it is fitting
that he remain in this culture because chance has put him there, because he

could just as well have become a Buddhist priest or a Sufi, and because, if tomorrow neo-Nazis or neo-Stalinists want to take power in his country, he would find no reasonable reason to combat them – save, possibly, motives of personal convenience.

It is quite obvious that, in defiance of the hardly enticing rose water being amply sprinkled about everywhere today, I do not respect others' difference simply as difference and without regard to what they are and what they do. I do not respect the difference of the sadist, of Eichmann, of Beria – any more than of those who cut off people's heads, or even their hands, even if they are not threatening me directly. Nothing in what I have said or written commits me to 'respect differences' *for the sake of* respecting differences. I do not respect heteronomy; it is something quite else to say that the idea of imposing autonomy by heteronomous means is a pure absurdity, a square circle.

Autonomy: Ethics

It is strange that Heller finds me uninterested in ethics. Certainly, I have never attacked the problem, as decisive as all others: a friend who has entrusted me with something dies; do I or do I not have to return it to his heirs? But one has to be ignorant of all I have written about praxis, and the definition I provide of it (*MRT*, in *IIS*, pp. 75–7E and 101–7E; in *CR*, pp. 150–2 and 177–82), its significance for psychoanalytical, pedagogical, and political activity (ibid., *PPE* [1977], and *EP?*) not to see the basic outlines of an ethics and the content of a maxim that should guide all activity involving human beings (myself as well as others).

This misunderstanding is matched by the strange notion that I have taken up Aristotle's idea of praxis – an idea launched by Habermas. As it is out of the question that neither Habermas nor Heller has not read Aristotle, the only alternative is to assume that they cannot read a contemporary author except as if he had to be copying ancient ones. The same thing goes when I am said to be taking up *legein* and *teukhein* as 'concepts' from Greek philosophy. *Legein* and *teukhein* are not *concepts* of Greek philosophy but Greek *words* I have used to name new concepts I explicated in chapter 5 of *IIS*. One can, strictly speaking, compare *legein* with *some* meanings of *logos* in Aristotle, certainly not all of them, and one would still have to forget that Aristotelean *logos* appertains to the soul, whereas *legein* for me is a protoinstitution of every *society*. Still further removed is the relation of *teukhein* to Aristotelean *technē*, sturdily rooted in *phusis* (*T*). We are sent on an analogous adventure with autonomy in Kant, which is unrelated to the meaning I give to this term. In short: for Habermas and Heller, if someone says 'I think', that person can only be Cartesian.

For Aristotle, praxis is the human activity that has its end in itself, and not in a result that is external to it. Let us note in passing that the Aristotelean *praxis/poiēsis* distinction *depends* on the category of substance, form tied in an ongoing way to matter. What is one to say, then, of Themistocles or of Nijinksy, of the naval battle or the dancer's performance? Do they belong to *praxis* or to *poiēsis*? Let us also note that it is this same distinction, and the category of substance governing it, that 'founds' in Smith, as well as in Marx, the distinction between 'productive' labour (the transforming of material entities according to the Aristotelean categories, including transport, *keisthai*) and 'unproductive' labour (commerce, services, etc.).

For me, praxis is a *modality* of human making/doing (and in no way *identical* to the latter, another misunderstanding that several of my critics have committed). This is the activity that considers the other to be capable of being autonomous and tries to assist him to accede to his autonomy. *Other* is taken here in the broad sense; it includes me as 'object' of my activity. As such, praxis belongs [*est le propre*] not to human beings in general but to reflective and deliberative subjectivity. Therefore, it *does not have* and *cannot have* its end in itself (which is its very *definition* in Aristotle!): it aims at a certain transformation of its (human) 'object'. This 'object' – the other – can be concrete, nominally designated, as in psychoanalysis and pedagogy. It can also be indefinite, as in politics. This is why, taking up the question again (see *ETS*), I ultimately defined psychoanalysis as practico-poietic activity, which holds just as well for pedagogy and for politics (*PsyPo* [1987]).

Does this answer all questions: What am I to do? What can a man encounter in life? Certainly not. But what ethical maxim does? Leaving aside here the *positively immoral* character of an injunction that is impossible to obey and brands as guilty those who fail, does 'Thou shalt love thy neighbour as much as (or more than) thyself' tell me whether I should devote my life to music rather than to philosophy, whether I should join a mass in revolt, go to sleep, or tell them to go home? Do Kant's categorical imperative and maxims tell me whether one should or should not stop, and when, the treatment of someone who is vegetating in an irreversible coma? Does the Christian or Kantian ethic even have the means to respond to the question whether or not it is permissible to kill a brigand or a terrorist in order to save someone else? If human life is an absolute – as it categorically has to be in these two ethics – no arithmetic is allowed. Now, what we have to do is face up to our tragic condition – which is what post-Hellenic ethics, since Plato, have tried to occult: human life ought to be posited as an absolute, but it cannot always be so. People clearly don't like that. They have transferred the Hebraic and Christian Promise onto the requirement for a 'rational foundation' and the Decalogue onto the demand for a book of ethical recipes or for a 'rule' that would give in advance the answer to all cases that might present themselves. Fear of freedom, desperate need for assurance, occultation of our tragic condition.

Human life ought to be posited as an absolute because the injunction of autonomy is categorical, and there is no autonomy without life. But the fact is that there are several lives, they can be opposed to one another, and one might be obliged to choose. I have seen no philosopher pose to himself even for an instant the following question: Is it moral to spend, for a single artificial kidney, in a rich country, the amount that would save hundreds of children from famine in the poor countries? I am certain, even, that he has no moral scruple when he happens to need costly treatment. If we want to exit from the duplicity and hyprocrisy of all ethics, philosophical or instituted, we have to recognize that we are faced with a categorical injunction that we cannot help but relativize.

The Kantian subject, like the Platonic (and Christian) subject, *recognizes conflict only with himself* – and this conflict is not really one: it does not pose any true problem; all problems are, *de jure*, resolved in advance. If this subject suffers, it is that he 'would like' to do what is Good (which he *always* knows or ought to know) but he 'cannot' – or, if he 'can', it is on the basis of 'empirical determinations' and not pure ones. But in truth, no problem is resolved in advance. We have to create the good, under imperfectly known and uncertain conditions. The project of autonomy is end and guide, it does not resolve for us effectively actual situations.

How can one not be struck, and moved, at this place by the unsurpassable depth of the Philosopher? 'Virtue is an acquired deliberative disposition . . . defined by *logos* and as *phronimos* would define it.' *Hexis* is a disposition that is not 'pure', nor is it 'spontaneous': it is, and has to be, acquired (whence the decisive role of *paideia* and of *nomos*). It is *proairetikē*, in two senses. In the sense of its 'object', transitively, it concerns choice; it is a *habitus* bearing on choosing well. But it is also *proairetikē*, deliberative, because it is a *habitus* of deliberation (reflective and deliberative!); it is not mere *habitus*, an automatic mechanical operation; it preserves *proairesis*, intention and choice. It is defined by *logos* – it contains, therefore, a reasonable element open to discussion. But it is neither mechanizable nor simply universalizable: it is such as *phronimos*, the person who possesses *phronimos*, shall define it. Clearly, Aristotle does not know what he is saying: since there is *logos*, what need is there of *phronimos*? And who shall define *phronimos*, and on what basis? He must be forgiven: he did not have the chance to read late-twentieth-century authors.

Phronēsis neither 'founds' autonomy nor allows itself to be 'deduced'. But without *phronēsis* there is no effective autonomy, and no praxis in the sense I give to this term. There is not, moreover, even any *theoretical thought* that truly holds together. Without theoretical *phronēsis*, delirium is close at hand (see Hegel).

Autonomy is not *disinsertion* with regard to effective actuality (as Kantian autonomy is) but, rather, lucid transformation of effective actuality (of oneself and of others), *starting from* this same effective actuality. *Starting from* does not signify that effective actuality furnishes causes, or norms. Here again, we have an original relation, a model of itself, unthinkable within the inherited categories. Autonomy is self-positing of a norm, starting from some content of effective life and in relation to this content.

Norm has no meaning without connection with effective actuality (with the content of life) and a 'transcendental reduction' of this connection is not possible. In the Kantian attempt at reduction, the *pure fact* of the existence of an indefinite multiplicity of subjects (totally heterogeneous to transcendental space) and even of a regularity of the world is implied; otherwise, it would be impossible, short of word games, to give any meaning to the idea of the universality required by the maxim of action (= for anyone under all sufficiently similar circumstances). The effective actuality of the subject's 'empirical' (psychical) 'determination' is implied just as well – otherwise, it is unclear why a norm is needed.

[I note in passing: 'the categorical imperative' wants one 'to regard all human duties as divine commands' (Kant, *Opus Posthumum*, trans. Echart Forster and Michael Rozen [Cambridge, England: Cambridge University Press, 1993]). Kant is far from being a pure *Aufklärer*. The postulates of the existence of God and the immortality of the soul, the rejection of the Revolution, and the above citation show how much, in him, theoretical audacity is wedded with obedience toward the instituted and respect for *Obrigkeit*.]

What remains valid in Kant is the idea of universalization, but in an entirely abstract way. Rid of abstraction, it becomes what I call *reasonability*. The 'maxim' of my act has to be defensible before 'all', and of course before myself, at another moment and in other circumstances. But how far do these 'other circumstances' extend? The entire difficulty lies between the 'maxim' and the 'circumstances'. What is the 'maxim' in the apologue of the thing entrusted without witnesses to someone's care? In truth, it is a *political* maxim, destined to regulate the shared existence of autonomous beings: *pacta sunt servanda*. The trust is a contract. What would happen if some contracts were violated? Kant's pragmatic argument – that there would no longer be any contracts – is naive, for since the beginning of recorded history people have not stopped violating the most important contracts of all, treaties between States, yet this has prevented neither treaties from proliferating nor history from existing. (No need to recall in this connection the congenital blindness of this type of philosophy, and of modern philosophy in general, with regard to the most massive and important facts. All philosophers of the rights of man proclaim the sovereignty of the Nation – but nowhere have I seen any philosophical 'foundation' of this eminent dignity, the Nation. They all also discuss, interminably, the most subtly exquisite ethical cases – but not the ethical character of murder, by tens of millions, during a war. Philosophical Reason, one must conclude, is crushed before *Raison d'État*.) Pragmatic arguments like Kant's can lead only to probabilistic considerations and evaluations.

Kant's pragmatic argument nonetheless masks a profound aporia in his conception: How is one to pass from the abstraction of 'universal law' to the *categorical justification* of the particular 'maxim' that presides over some supposedly ethical act? How is one to justify the maxim's *content*? In fact, in the moral fable of the thing entrusted without witnesses to someone's care the 'maxim', as I said, is *pacta sunt servanda*; its justification is that the respect of mutual commitments is a manifestation of one's responsibility toward oneself and others, which in turn is a *political* exigency that flows from the existence of a collectivity of subjects who aim at autonomy and want to live under the laws they give themselves.

And in fact, Kant's least debatable formulations refer necessarily to some content (*GPCD*, in *PPA*, pp. 90–2E). 'Be a person and respect others as persons' is *empty* without a nonformal idea of the person (who cannot, here, simply be someone who is placed under the 'moral law', for from this standpoint, in Kant's outlook, I could do to him anything you wish, but I could never *reach* him). This content is autonomy such as I define it, and the practical imperative is: Become autonomous, and (not: 'Respect others as autonomous beings', which would once again imply a formal, static, and unreal conception of autonomy, but) Contribute as much as you can to others' becoming autonomous. Respect for others can be required because they are, always, bearers of a virtual autonomy – not because they are 'persons', which they may very well not be (if, once again, *person* has any content at all). It follows immediately that this imperative is not only 'ethical' (concerning the private and private/public spheres, to use terminology I shall explain below) but just as much political (concerning the public/public sphere), since it immediately encounters at once an indefinite number of others – the collectivity – and the conditions for their existence – the institution.

Before arriving there, a final explication concerning the traditional position may be useful.

Waldenfels raises the aporias of 'legislation intimately connected with a factual instance of authority' and evokes the old dilemma: Either the legislative instance acts according to laws, and then it is not autonomous in the radical sense, or else it acts without obeying laws, and then it is not autonomous but anomic. And he adds, making an allusion to a well-known phrase of Heidegger: 'Kant already knew what he was "recoiling" from when he removed practical reason from the competence (from the powers [*attributions*], *Befugnisse*) of a productive imagination.'

But if one conceives autonomy in the 'radical' sense presupposed by Waldenfels, then only the God of Duns Scotus is 'autonomous'. Neither the demiurge of Plato (who is subject to mathematics and to the being-thus of the receptacle) nor the God of Aristotle (who can do only what He does, namely, think Himself) nor a God of Love (tied by His being and loving by necessity) nor, certainly, the practical subject of Kant (to whom, despite the false label of autonomy, the moral law and the categorical imperative are necessarily given as such *and* in their slight content) is autonomous. This 'radical' idea of autonomy is a pseudoidea, that is, an absurdity. It implies a being removed from *all* determination, including that of being itself (it is this absurdity Poltier's eristics is nourishing). I have been denouncing it for a long time (*MRT*, in *IIS*, pp. 103–7E; in *CR*, pp. 179–82). Were one to say that autonomy (Kantian autonomy), lying at an infinite and insuperable distance from all effective actuality, is not affected by these considerations because, as pure requirement, it concerns *nothing* that might ever be determined in any way whatsoever – then it is fitting that this requirement address itself to the *nothing*, not to 'us humans'. But suppose I did respond to this requirement: according to Waldenfels's logic, if I respond to it *motivelessly* (Sartre: nothing can be a motive for an act of freedom), I am simply anomic. If I respond to it because I obey (pure, not empirical) motives, I am conforming to the law (*nomos*) of these motives, I am therefore heteronomous; there are, 'before' autonomy, the *reasons* for which I have to respond to the requirement of autonomy (even if, empirically, this requirement has to remain for ever unfulfilled). More simply: if you can 'found' autonomy 'rationally', then autonomy is *rationally necessary* and it is unclear why you are calling yourself autonomous: you are simply rational (cf., with a different terminology, Spinoza). And why, then, *do I have to* obey rational motives (in the most sublime sense of the term *rational*)? The answer, 'Because man *is* a rational being', infinitely ridiculous in itself, obviously refers back again to a *de facto* being-thus, to a 'nature' of man, and 'flattens the ought-to-be onto being' (which Poltier does while reproaching me for doing it). (Let us note, parenthetically, that behind the scaffolding of his arguments Kant's ultimate position is clear: One ought to want the Good for the sake of the Good. I am still waiting for someone to show me a genuine 'foundation', a *Grundlegung*, for this statement.) But what matters to me is the *effective* autonomy of *effective* men and women, not the fiction of a requirement that itself posits itself straight off as forever unaccomplishable. It is not noticed often enough that the situation is strictly identical to Kant's theoretical philosophy: if the structure of transcendental subjectivity is *effective*, that is to say, *realized* in empirically given exemplars of *wir Menschen*, both the *history* of knowledge, in the weighty sense of this term (*MSPI*, in *CL*, pp. 164–79E; *OIHS*), as well as nontrivial 'errors' become unintelligible. If this structure is simply 'ideal', it is irrelevant. The task of philosophy is not only to raise the question *quid juris*; that is the beginning. Its task is to elucidate how right becomes fact and fact right – which is the condition for its existence, and it is itself one of the first manifestations thereof. *There are* beautiful works; *there are* true thoughts; *there are* (autonomous) ethical acts. A philosophy that begins by positing that, in essence, it is a matter of ever ineffectuable idealities has already smashed to pieces the branch on which it is sitting.

Let us consider now from the *de facto* (*faktisch*) standpoint the instituting imaginary and the radical imagination. Their creation is certainly not 'absolute' (what meaning is one to give to this term, if not again by referring to the God of Duns Scotus?), save in a quite precise sense: the created form is, as such, irreducible to the already-there; it cannot be composed, ensidically, starting from what is already there. (To speak of 'new aspects', as Waldenfels does, only eludes the hard core of the question: When is an 'aspect' new? What is the new?) In this sense, creation is *ex nihilo*. But as I have already written, it is certainly not *in nihilo*, nor is it *cum nihilo* (innumerable passages from *IIS* show this, and I have specified it again recently: *PoPA, ISRH*).

It is thereby also, evidently, limited. But it is really quite unmotivated and lawless. To the question 'Why do certain classes of living beings grasp certain electromagnetic waves *as* colours and *as these* colours?' there is no answer, any more than there is to the question 'Why are the psyche and society always in meaning and signification?' This faculty of making be, of bringing out of itself modes of being, determinations, and laws that will henceforth be that self's laws, determinations, modes of being is what I call radical creation. But what is this 'self' that makes itself be, without 'yet' being a determinate something, but which *is going* to *determine* itself thus and not otherwise? This is what I call the Groundless, the Chaos, the Abyss of the (singular or collective) human being. Here, the term 'nothingness' seems to me mere literary posturing, and a possible source of useless sophisms. But while it is certain that this creation becomes manifest to us in a strong and dense way in the human domain, one cannot remove this domain from total Being/being. If creation appertains to the human, it appertains *due to this fact alone* to total Being/being. Beyond, there are all the elaborations and ontological elucidations that remain to be done.

Let us restrict ourselves to the human domain. Can this self-creation be called autonomy? A gross error. As Dupuy recalls, I radically distinguish self-creation or self-constitution – terms which apply just as well to the emergence of the living being, to paranoidal delusion, and to *every* society that institutes itself in heteronomy – from autonomy. Autonomy, like praxis, is not a 'given' of human nature. It emerges as social-historical creation – more precisely, as creation of a project, which happens to be in part already realized.

Autonomy: Politics

I have defined the object of politics as follows: 'Create the institutions which, by being internalized by individuals, most facilitate their accession to their individual autonomy and their effective participation in all forms of explicit power existing in a society' (*PoPA*, in *PPA*, p. 173). I have added thereto: 'It becomes apparent – this is, in fact, a tautology – that autonomy is, ipso facto, *self-limitation*. . . . This self-limitation can be more than and different from mere exhortation if it is embodied in the creation of free and responsible individuals' (ibid.). As these formulations do no more than condense and prolong what I have written for decades, I find it of no use to discuss the phantasmagorical ideas Heller (that I would be opposed to a Bill of Rights) or Poltier (that I would discredit sites of democratic discussion, or that I might secretly be possessed by the fantasm of indivision) impute to me. It seems to me more useful to discuss the thing itself by extending my reflection and by being more precise about points on which I have until now expressed myself to a lesser extent than other ones.

I shall begin by making an obvious distinction which is there on a factual level, but, without being ignored, remains implicit in all authors (*SRR* [1978]; in *CR*, pp. 218–38; Andrew Arato recalled it in his text). We can distinguish in an abstract way three spheres in which are played out the relations of individuals and the collectivity among themselves and with their political institution: the private sphere (*oikos*); the public/private sphere (*agora*); the public/public sphere, which in the case of a democratic society I shall call for brevity's sake *ekklēsia*. This distinction makes sense, abstractly speaking, for all societies; I mean by this that it permits us to think them all, in a significant way, according to the distinction/articulation they institute among these three spheres.

It is not my fault (I hope Heller will forgive me) if the full deployment of the three spheres and their distinction/articulation in a democratic direction take place for the first time in ancient Greece. It is there that, at the same time the independence of the *oikos* is posited, a free *agora* (the public/private sphere) is created, and the public/public sphere becomes *truly* public. (These latter two aspects have been merged into one in current discussions, in fact since Hannah Arendt, under the heading 'public space'.) The becoming truly public of the public/public sphere is, of course, the core of democracy. As for the rest, here is what Aristotle says about it (*Nicomachean Ethics* 1180a24–9): 'It is only, or almost only, in the *polis* of the Lacedaemonians that the legislator seems to have taken care of education (*sc.* that of citizens) and of occupations, but in the great majority (*pleistais*) of *poleis* these objects have not preoccupied his attention, and each lives as he pleases, legislating Cyclopes-fashion about one's own children and wife.' Aristotle does not express himself here with his usual rigour. In the mythical image of the

Cyclopes (*The Odyssey*), no public or other law prevents the Cyclopes from killing wife and children, which is obviously not the case in any Greek city. But it will be noted that, contrary to the stereotype put into circulation by Benjamin Constant, vulgarized by Fustel de Coulanges, and since then become the meagre stock-in-trade of intellectuals when speaking of the Greek city, the Athenian regime – which left individuals undisturbed to do what they pleased (Pericles in Thucydides 2.37) – is considered, rightly, by Aristotle to be the rule, not the exception. The exception is the *polis* of the Lacedaemonians, where everything is regimented. Why the Spartan mirage, as Pierre Vidal-Naquet has called it, was valued so highly in Modern Times, especially in the eighteenth century and during the French Revolution, is another story.

Totalitarianism is characterized (*SRR*, ibid.) by the attempt to unify by force these three spheres *and* by the full becoming-private of the public/public sphere. The first characteristic is necessary, but not sufficient: the unification of the three spheres is more or less achieved in most archaic societies. This attempt failed to achieve its own goal in the case of Stalinism; its effects were no less terribly real.

I am not trying to do here a general typology of political regimes. I note simply that the emergence of the State and its development (whether it is a matter of 'oriental despotism', absolute Monarchies, or even the modern State) is practically equivalent to the *becoming-private* of the public/public sphere. This is entirely independent of the status of the *oikos* and even of the existence or not of a free *agora*.

The contemporary liberal oligarchies [*liberal* in the Continental sense of a conservative belief in the 'free market'] – the alleged 'democracies' – claim to limit to the maximum or reduce to an unavoidable minimum the public/public sphere. This pretension is clearly deceitful. The most 'liberal' of contemporary regimes (the United States, England, or Switzerland) are profoundly statist societies and committed to remaining so: the rhetoric of Thatcher and of Reagan has changed nothing of importance (the change in formal ownership of a few large enterprises does not essentially alter their relation to the State). The bureaucratic structure of the large firm remains intact, and our political philosophers continue to close their eyes to the question: What is the large modern business enterprise as a *political* structure? Bureaucracy, the interminable and absurd centralized rules and regulations, continues to proliferate. One shamelessly labels 'democracies' societies where not only citizens but even lawyers *do not know the law* and *cannot* know it (for this or that category of case law, you need a lawyer with the corresponding specialization). But there is something more important. The contemporary liberal oligarchies share with totalitarian regimes, Asiatic despotism, and absolute monarchies the following decisive trait: the public/public sphere is in fact, in its greatest part, *private*. It certainly is not so legally speaking; the country is not the domain of the monarch, nor the State the entirety of the servants of its 'house'. But on the factual level the essential features of public affairs are still the private affair of various groups and clans that share effective power, decisions are made behind closed doors, the little that is brought onto the public stage is masked, prefabricated, and belated to the point of irrelevancy.

The first condition for the existence of an autonomous society – of a democratic society – is that the public/public sphere become *effectively* public, become an *ekklēsia* and not an object of private appropriation by particular groups. The implications of this condition are innumerable; they affect the organization of all power existing in society as well as the designation and control of all individuals charged with the exercise of any parcel whatsoever of this power (we can call them *magistrates*), the production and the diffusion of information (a matter that is certainly in no way technical but instead decisively *political*, as I have written since 1957), as well as, at the profoundest level, the *paideia* of individuals (to which I shall return). 'Constitutionally' speaking, the becoming effectively public of the public/public sphere implies that the legislative, judicial, and governmental powers effectively belong to the people and are exercised by the people.

Here we encounter the question of 'representation'. It is saddening to read from Heller's pen that my opposition to the idea of representation comes from the fact that it was not practised at Athens. I have not ceased reiterating that Athenian democracy cannot be for us anything but a *germ*, and in no way a *model*; one would have to be a fool to claim that the political organization of 30,000 citizens might be copied so as to organize 35 or 150 *million* citizens, and someone who has flipped, even casually, through the pages of *CS II* (1957) or *HS* (1976) ought to have glimpsed that this folly is not mine. But there is something graver still. Heller forgets the devastating critique of representation made in Modern Times, at least since Rousseau (I nevertheless recalled it in *GPCD*), as she also forgets – and she is far from alone in this – the equally devastating criticisms of the capitalist 'market' (to which I shall return). She lives in the United States; doesn't she know that a senator, once elected, is practically assured re-election until the end of his days (since all PAC money goes to him)?

More generally, we may ask: Why don't our political philosophers ever mention the *metaphysics* of representation, and why do they disdainfully leave its *effective reality* to 'sociologists'? This is typical of contemporary 'political philosophy' (or theory): the idea of 'representation', which is central, is given *no* philosophical elucidation *and* talk about it has *no relation* to reality. As for myself, as a man who wills to be free, I willingly agree to obey magistrates I have elected so long as they act legally and have not been recalled from office in due and proper form. But the idea that anyone could *represent me* would seem to me unbearably insulting, were it not highly comic.

'Representation' is, inevitably, in the concept as well as in actual fact, *alienation* (in the legal sense of the term: transfer of ownership) of sovereignty, from the 'represented' toward the 'representatives'. In a democratic society, magistrates whose function requires a particular competency are to be elected (not because the Greeks invented elections, which is true, but because elections are the sole reasonable means for choosing in this case: see *GPCD*; in *CR*, pp. 276–7) and subject to recall. Every form of irrevocability, even when 'limited' in time, logically and really tends to 'autonomize' the power of elected officials.

Elections are not the best means of designating magistrates in other cases (where no particular competency is required) for reasons I have explained at length elsewhere (*GPCD*, ibid.) – and that are excellently summarized by Sunil Khilnani: they create a *division of political labour*. Politics has to do with power, and the division of labour in politics does not signify and cannot signify anything other than the division between the governors and governed, dominators and dominated. A democracy will accept, obviously, a division of political *tasks*, not a division of political *labour*, namely, the fixed and stable division of political society between directors and executants, the existence of a category of individuals whose role, whose profession, whose *interest* is to direct others.

It goes without saying that instituted provisions for self-limitation are required in a democratic regime more than in any other. I shall not draft here the Charter of the future society; I am simply recalling that maintaining the gains of democratic revolutions is implicit in everything I have written on the question and that I have emphasized (e.g., in *SAS* [1979], in *PSW* 3, p. 317) that the critique of 'rights' cannot be aimed at their allegedly 'formal' character (as is done by the Marxists) but, rather, at their *partial* character. Rules like those (imperfectly) expressed by the 'rights of man', *nullem crimen nulla poena sine lege*, due process of law, the plea of illegality or unconstitutionality, are an essential minimum.

My friends who felt chagrined by my remarks on constitutions (*GPCD*; in *CR*, pp. 276–7) have misconstrued their meaning. These remarks were directed against the fetishism of constitutionalism, the constitutional illusion; I recalled that the country in which 'human rights' have been perhaps best respected (or least violated) over the past three centuries, Great Britain, has no constitution ('Parliament can do anything, except change a man into a woman' is the English legal saying), whereas perfectly 'democratic' constitutions have served to mask the bloodiest tyrannies and continue to do so. I recalled, too, that a constitution cannot 'guarantee' itself. The question is therefore not 'fundamental'; it is a pragmatic question, one of political symbolics. If I had the opportunity to express myself before an *ekklēsia* on the opportuneness of a constitution, I would certainly be in favour of it, because a condensed text that solemnly affirms certain principles and that could be modified only by means of special procedures and elevated majorities seems to me useful both pragmatically and, above all, pedagogically.

Among these provisions for self-limitation, the 'separation' (though the term is bad) of power seems to me equally basic. It, too, was first broached in ancient democracy: Athenian juries, drawn by lot, did not have to obey the Assembly and could even censure it. This 'separation' has been much developed in theory, though less so in reality, within modern liberal regimes. Here again, the inconsistency of modern 'political theory' leaves one flabbergasted. Under these regimes, legislative power and governmental power are in the hands of the *same* effective instance of authority: the majority party. Where is the 'separation' of powers? Does Mrs Thatcher change her dress when she proposes (imposes) a law and when she makes governmental decisions? And what is the status of the *party* in political philosophy? It would be ridiculous to say that it embodies a pluralism of opinions; it is not their sole conceivable form of expression; in fact, it strangles them, cooks them up, and hardens them. We have been talking for the past forty years about the Party-State in totalitarian countries. Certainly, the situation is tangibly different in liberal regimes. But who reflects on the fact that the *effective site of power*, for the decisions that truly count in liberal regimes, is in parties? Communist constitutions which affirmed 'the leading role of the party' were, on this point, more sincere. And why does political philosophy obliterate the essentially bureaucratic nature of modern political parties, ignoring the fact that power is exercised therein by a self-co-opting hierarchical structure? For my part, I have never proposed the 'prohibition' of parties; the free constitution of groupings of political opinion belongs, obviously, among the imprescriptible liberties of the *agora*. What I said about them, and what Ferenc Fehér seems to me to interpret badly, is that *if* the essential elements of political life continue to unfold within parties, *then* democratic organs of collective power will be emptied of all substance (*CS II*). I mention here, only as a reminder, the judicial power in contemporary societies. Two Republican presidencies in the United States have sufficed to produce a partisan Supreme Court, and the justice system's scandalous dependency upon the Government in France, not only on the factual level but in legal texts, requires no commentary.

I return to the distinction between the three spheres – *oikos, agora, ekklēsia* – and to the question this distinction raises. It is certain that an autonomous society will have to guarantee their greatest possible mutual independence. The freedom of the private sphere, like the freedom of the *agora*, is a *sine qua non* condition for the freedom of the *ekklēsia* and for the becoming public of the public/public sphere. Just this alone makes any idea of 'indivision' – whatever that may mean – absurd.

But no more than any other society, an autonomous society cannot simply 'separate' these three spheres; it must also articulate and join them. Their absolute 'separation' would be an unrealizable absurdity – and it obviously does not take place in the most 'liberal' societies today. The State and law intervene in many ways in the 'private' sphere through the penal and civil code, and especially (to mention only the most important aspect) through the education of children. They also intervene, in innumerable ways, in the *agora*. The incoherency – rather, the shameless trickery – of contemporary 'Liberalism' in this regard defies the imagination. Where and when has one ever seen an economically, politically, and socially neutral budget (on the revenue side as well as the expenditure side)? When, as is the case every-where today, half of the national product goes through the public sector in one way or another (State, local government organizations, Social Security); when between half and two-thirds of the price of goods and services entering into the final national expenditure are in one way or another fixed, regu-lated, controlled, or influenced by state policy, and when one notices that the situation is irreversible (ten years of Thatcher and Reagan made no essential changes therein), neoliberal discourse appears for what it is: a gross farce intended for imbeciles.

An autonomous society will have to guarantee the inviolability of the private sphere, short of criminal laws (I do not think that anyone is proposing that we remain indifferent to spouses murdering each other, or to parents raping their children, penalization of which signifies that the *ekklēsia* inter-venes to limit what can take place in the *oikos*). Short of education, too. It will also have to guarantee the greatest freedom possible for the *agora*, all the while articulating the latter in relation to the *ekklēsia*. This is an immense field, which covers, directly or indirectly, the totality of social life. Let me recall that also belonging here are the question of the ownership of the means of production as well as the prohibition, or not, of 'pornography', the status of theatre or publishing, and the question of the market in general (as one knows, *agora* also signifies 'market'), the utilization of public buildings for public/private meetings as well as the regulation of language (if the Liberals, in their naivety, express astonishment at this last question, I remind them of France's officially sanctioned policy against 'franglais', or, in the United States, the *political* questions raised by the ever stronger challenge to English as the 'national language'). I shall limit myself here to mentioning three points:

1   The relations between the three spheres have nothing 'natural' or self-evident about them; they are always instituted. In the great majority of cases, however, they are instituted in an implicit or tacit way (language, mores, etc.). An autonomous society is a society that self-institutes itself explicitly and lucidly. This explicit and lucid self-institution could never be total and has no need to be (*PoPA*). But nothing, theoretically or 'rationally', allows the limits of this explicit activity – in other terms, what should and what should not be an object of legislation – to be fixed *a priori*, once and for all.

The idea of autonomy, which also takes concrete form in another idea – no autonomous society without autonomous individuals – implies that the *ekklēsia* guarantees and promotes the largest possible sphere of real autonomous activity on the part of individuals and of the groups these individuals form, whatever their nature – therefore, the greatest possible extension of the private sphere and of the private/public sphere. A very strong presumption in favour of *minimal legislation* follows from this. But once again, nothing allows one to settle *in abstracto* this optimal minimum. Whoever would say that legislation ought not – or cannot – intervene in psychical life, or even in the conscious thought of individuals, would show only that she does not know what she is talking about: What else is education (cf. *Nicomachean Ethics* 1179b29ff)? Historically speaking, it never was a question for the Athenians to challenge the status of private property as such, but the Assemblies of the French Revolution on several occasions voted prohibitions against proposing an 'agrarian law' – which shows, precisely, that the question had been posed (and as one knows, it remains so). But these same Athenians never thought of setting by law the permissible modes of sexual relations – whereas only the missionary position is tolerated in the State of Georgia in 1989.

(According to the *International Herald Tribune* of 1 January 1989, p. 3, James D. Moseley, of Decatur, Georgia, served an eighteen-month prison sentence for having had oral sexual relations with his wife. In the State of Georgia 'sodomy', defined to include oral sex, is an offence even among consenting adults. Moseley's wife had accused him of raping and sodomizing her; but, having admitted during the trial that he had engaged in oral sex with his wife, he was sentenced for sodomy without aggravating circumstances. This, too, perhaps is *constitutio libertatis?*)

2   The perversion of Liberalism and, more generally, of what passes now for 'political philosophy' is also the failure to see in the public/public sphere, in the power of the *ekklēsia* (or even of the existing State) *anything but* the question of its relations with the private or public/private sphere – individuals and 'civil society' – and that of their protection. But the public/public sphere has always been, is, and ought in an autonomous society to remain also the domain and the instance where are discussed and decided works [*œuvres*] and undertakings which concern and commit the entire collectivity and which the collectivity cannot, will not, or should not leave to private or private/public initiative: to speak in images here, the erection of the Parthenon, the establishment of the Alexandrian Library, the construction of Campo de Sienna. To say that everything – except, perhaps, prisons (and even then . . .) – has to be left to 'civil society' signifies not only a monstrous misconstruing of the reality of social life (what about urban planning? highways? the environment?) but also, implicitly, a denial of the right and the effective possibility for the collectivity as such to form long-term projects, to

invest its future with a meaning, to see itself and recognize itself in its works. Why? Why would only Messrs Carnegie, Ford, Rockefeller, etc., have the right to establish institutes and foundations, and not the American people?

3 Finally, there is the toughest point, the question of the public/private sphere, of the *agora* – as such in general and as *agora* in the particular sense of the term, that is, as market. Undoubtedly, an autonomous society will not only have to guarantee but actively promote the greatest possible autonomy of the public/private sphere: the sphere where individuals encounter one another and group themselves together without explicit regard to political questions, so as to give themselves over to all activities and all exchanges that may please them. (Here again, I am assuming that no one is proposing to fund or even to tolerate associations of headshrinkers.)

Among these activities and exchanges, there are economic activities and exchanges – production and market, and their organization. On this terrain, too, one observes the same amnesic reversal as on the political terrain. Just as one forgets completely the critiques of the Liberal Republic, just as one does not even bother to discuss the critique of the representational system of government broached at least since Rousseau, continued for two centuries, and corroborated by experience, and just as one limits oneself to the confounding argument, 'Mrs Thatcher or the Gulag', so does the entire critique of capitalism and of the capitalist pseudomarket seem to drop down a memory hole, their reality and their effects are passed over in silence, the sole available choice seems to be between the endless lines in Moscow to obtain a pound of rotten carrots and the Western economy such as it is. While excusable among victims of bureaucratic totalitarianism, who fling themselves upon parliamentarianism and 'the market' as the sole solutions conceivable for themselves (the people of the Eastern-bloc countries have exhibited and continue to exhibit unparalleled courage and tactical genius, but their political imagination, theirs too, is at degree zero – which very well goes to show that this is a universal state), this amnesia is entirely inexcusable when voiced by the 'radical' ex-critics of the Western capitalist system.

Here, ignorance is not an excuse. Where there is capitalism there is no genuine market (*VEJP*, in *CL*, pp. 266–73E), and where there is a market there can be no capitalism. The scaffolding of rationalizations and justifications for the 'economic science' collapsed under the blows struck by the representatives, the best representatives, of this 'science' during the decade from 1930 to 1940 (Straffa, Robinson, Chamberlin, Kahn, Keynes, Kalecki, Schakle, and several others). The quack-remedy salesmen of 'neo-Liberalism' have succeeded, amid the politico-ideological atmosphere of the past fifteen years, in throwing a smoke screen over its ruins, which should be enough to fool hack journalists, not real thinkers. I myself have written at length about these questions and I shall not return to them here. I shall simply recall the most massive points. Political economy does not define and cannot define a concept of capital. It has nothing to say about the distribution of national income. It could never explain, still less justify, wage and income differentials. It has to concede that, under capitalism, there is no spontaneous macroeconomic equilibrium or full employment. I could go on for pages. I shall limit myself here to mentioning the most weighty point (*VEJP*; *RRD* [1974]; *DG*, pp. 128–31): it – like Marx – presupposes that there is a possibility of *imputing* the product in a rigorous way to different 'factors' *and* 'units' of production – whereas this idea is *strictly meaningless*. This destroys any bases for wage differentials other than previously acquired situations and existing relations of force (which, objectively speaking, govern the distribution of income and incomes today).

An autonomous society will instaurate a genuine market, defined by consumer *sovereignty* (not mere freedom) (*CS II*). It will decide democratically the overall allocation of resources (private consumption/public consumption, consumption/investment), aided by a technical device (the 'plan factory') subject to its political control, which will also help to assure general equilibrium. Finally, it is inconceivable that it would institute the self-government of collectivities at all levels of social life and would exclude it in collectivities dealing with production. Self-management of production by the producers is but the realization of democracy in the domain in which individuals spend half of their waking life. (I have already emphasized in *CS II* that there could be no question of 'collectivizing' small producers by force.)

Today

For reasons that will quickly become apparent, I have left aside from this discussion of the project of an autonomous society one point – the equality of wages and incomes – to which I shall return. A few explanations about the status of this project are indispensable before doing so.

The added specifications to the project discussed above, the outline of a 'charter' of an autonomous society, are quite evidently mine. Fehér should not fear that I would want to impose 'a single authentic version of socialism'. A movement that would try to establish an autonomous society could not take place without a discussion and confrontation of proposals coming from various citizens. I am a citizen; I am formulating, therefore, my proposals.

Why must they be formulated in this fashion, which seems to some too precise and to others too imprecise? Apart from flaws on the part of the author, apart, too, from the fact that such an institution can only be the work of collective democratic activity, two considerations have guided me, since 1957 and even earlier, in these efforts. On the one hand, faced with the horrors of 'real socialism', with the discredit into which the idea was falling, with the criticisms of adversaries and with the silence of the 'classics', it seemed to me at the time and it still seems to me now of capital importance to show that the project of autonomy is not just anything, that it can give itself the means for its ends, and that it does not present, as far off as one can see, any internal antinomy, incoherency, or impossibility. On the other hand, it would be both absurd and ridiculous to describe a pseudoconcrete utopia, given that the data change daily, and given, especially, that the alpha and omega of the whole affair is the deployment of social creativity – which, were it unleashed, would once again leave far behind it all we are capable of thinking today.

But on the other hand, let us also recall that, even with the specific formu- lations I have given to it, this project is not 'mine'. Mine is only the labour of elucidation and condensation of a historical experience that began twenty- five centuries ago and that has been particularly dense and rich over the past two centuries. Those who believe that I am inspired exclusively or essen- tially by ancient history simply have not read me completely. My reflection began not with Athenian democracy (only in 1978 did I truly start working on it) but with the contemporary workers' movement. To cite the texts that, since 1946, put this reflection on record would be to cite the tables of contents of the eight volumes of my *Socialisme ou Barbarie* writings [abridged in *PSW 1–3*]; in all these three thousand pages, there is but one allusion to Thucydides and another to Plato. What is constantly discussed, described, analysed, and reflected upon therein is the modern experience: the Russian experience, of course, but also struggles, great and small, of workers in the Western world since 1945, the Hungarian and Polish Revolutions of 1956, the struggles of the 1960s, and so on. *One will not find a single sentence* in *CS II*, for example, that fails to refer to a real historical experience, to a form invented by the workers' movement, to a problem this movement encoun- tered or was inevitably going to encounter had it continued to develop, to a new question posed by changes in the contemporary world. I am saying this, obviously, not in order to 'found' or to 'justify' my ideas (which are based, when all is added up, on a political choice to which they give concrete form), but in order to recall their relevance. If one knows the history of the last two centuries, and quite particularly the twentieth, it is impossible to read me without seeing the guiding thread running throughout my writings: the preoccupation, the obsession with the risk that a collective movement might 'degenerate', that it might give birth to a new bureaucracy (whether totali- tarian or not) – in short, with the question of overcoming the division of political labour, to borrow Khilnani's elegant expression. This 'degenera- tion', this bureaucratization are to be found, and I have found them, in the Russian experience, as well as in strikes of secondary importance, in the student unions, and in tenants' movements.

Khilnani asks to what extent I have remained faithful to my prior formulations. I believe I have already responded to him. I do not see how an autonomous society, a free society, could be established [*s'instituer*] without a genuine becoming-public of the public/public sphere, a reappropriation of power by the collectivity, the abolition of the division of political labour, the unfettered circulation of politically pertinent information, the abolition of bureaucracy, the most extreme decentralization of decision-making, the principle 'No execution of decisions without participation in the making of decisions', consumer sovereignty, the self-government of producers – accompanied by universal participation in decisions that commit the whole and by self-limitation, some of whose most important characteristics I sketched above. On one point *CS II* is 'dated' – and I made the necessary corrections fairly early on, much sooner than others in any case (*RR*, *AR* [1968], and *T*): neither quantitatively nor qualitatively can one attribute any longer to the proletariat, in the proper sense of the term, the privileged role imputed to it by classical Marxism – as had, formally, remained the case in *CS II*.

Has nothing changed, then, since 1957? Oh, yes indeed – and this is what has become the centre of my preoccupations since 1959 (*MCR*, *RR*, *AR*, *GI*, *CWS*). Through a host of factors I do not have to reanalyse here (but which, at bottom, *explain* nothing), the attitudes of labouring people as well as of the population in general have changed profoundly – at least, what is manifest in them. Of the two core imaginary significations whose struggle has defined the modern West – the unlimited expansion of pseudorational pseudomastery, the project of autonomy – the first seems to be triumphing right down the line, the second suffering a prolonged eclipse. The population plunges into *privatization* (*MCR*), abandoning the public domain to bureaucratic, managerial, and financial oligarchies. A new anthropological type of individual emerges, defined by greediness, frustration, *generalized conformism* (which, in the sphere of culture, is pompously labelled post-modernism [T/E: *RA* (1989)]). All this is materialized in structures of massive weight: the mad and potentially lethal race of an autonomized technoscience, consumeristic, televisual, and advertising onanism, the atomization of society, the rapid technical and 'moral' obsolescence of all 'products', 'wealth' that, growing nonstop, melts between one's fingers. Capitalism finally seems to have succeeded in fabricating the type of individual that 'corresponds' to it: perpetually distracted, zapping from one 'pleasure [*jouissance*]' to another, without memory or project, ready to respond to every solicitation of an economic machine that is increasingly destroying the planet's biosphere in order to produce illusions called commodities.

I am obviously talking here about the liberal and wealthy societies (one seventh of the world's population). The image becomes more complicated, but hardly more rosy, when one considers the Third World (which till now has adopted from the West only the worst of what the latter has produced) or even the countries of the East. (The admirable struggles for freedom currently [1989] developing in the latter countries do not succeed in sifting out any new objective – which certainly may be 'explained' historically, but which changes nothing in the diagnosis. That Poland or Hungary might become like Portugal is certainly infinitely preferable to the present-day situation, for the Polish, for the Hungarians, and for everyone. But no one can make me think that Portugal – or even the United States – represents the finally found form of human society.)

Certainly, this situation is deeply menaced by two factors. The first concerns the consequences of the present form of capitalism for the continued self-reproduction of the system. The individuals present-day society fabricates cannot reproduce it in the long run; or, to put it another way, if everything is up for sale capitalism can no longer function. The second deals with the ecological barrier the system will encounter sooner or later. Capitalist 'wealth' has in fact been purchased through the now and henceforth irreversible destruction (continuing at an accelerating pace) of resources of the biosphere accumulated over three billion years.

But this internal antinomy and this external barrier in no way 'guarantee' a 'positive' solution. With the populations of the West such as they are at present, a great ecological catastrophe would probably lead to a new type of fascism rather than anything else.

We thus arrive at the Gordian knot of the political question today. An autonomous society cannot be instaurated except through the autonomous activity of the collectivity. Such an activity presupposes that people strongly cathect *something other* than the possibility of buying a new colour television set. On a deeper level, it presupposes that the passion for democracy and for freedom, for public affairs, will take the place of distraction, cynicism, conformism, and the consumer race. In short, it presupposes, among other things, that the 'economic' cease to be the dominant or exclusive value. This, to respond to Fehér, is the 'price attached' to a transformation of society. Let us put it more clearly still: the price to pay for liberty is the destruction of the economic as central (and, in fact, *unique*) value.

Is this price too high? For me, certainly not: I infinitely prefer a new friend to a new car. A subjective preference, of course. But 'objectively'? I willingly abandon to the political philosophers the task of 'founding' (pseudo)consumption as the supreme value. But there is something more important. If things continue on their present course, this price will have to be paid *anyway*. Who can believe that the destruction of the Earth will be able to continue at its present pace for another century? Who fails to see that it would accelerate further still if the poor countries were to industrialize? And what will the regime do when it no longer is able to exercise a hold over populations by furnishing them constantly with new gadgets?

If the rest of humanity is to escape from its unbearable poverty, and if humanity in its entirety wants to survive on this planet in a steady and sustainable state, it will have to accept a good *pater familias* management of the planet's resources, a radical check on technology and production, a *frugal life*. I have not redone the calculations lately, which in any case would be tainted with immense margins of uncertainty. But, to get a grip on the ideas, one can say: It would already be good if we could assure 'indefinitely' to all the inhabitants of the planet the 'standard of living' of the rich countries in 1929. This can be imposed by a neofascist regime, but this can be done freely by the human collectivity, organized democratically, cathecting other significations, abolishing the monstrous role of the economy as end and putting it back in its rightful place as mere *means* of human life. Independent of a host of other considerations (*HWI* [1974], *SMH* [1974]), it is in this perspective and as a moment of this reversal of values that the equality of wages and incomes appears to be of essential importance (*VEJP*, in *CL*, pp. 329–30E).

Certainly, as I have seen and said before many others, this does not seem to correspond to the aspirations of people today. Even more than that must be said: The world's peoples are in active complicity with the evolution presently under way (*DE?* [1987]). Will they remain so indefinitely? Who can say so? One thing, however, is certain: it is not in running to catch up with 'what is being worn' and 'what is being said', it is not in emasculating what we think and what we want that we will increase the chances for freedom. It is not what is, but what could be and should be, that has need of us.

May–November 1989

Index

Ability, 31, 52, 69, 120, 234, 265; *see also*
Capabilities and capacities
Abolition, abolishing, 44, 45, 47, 50, 57, 60,
83, 87, 91, 101, 103, 106, 128, 134, 169,
185–8, 202, 220, 231, 235, 249, 263–4,
343, 415, 417; *see also* Elimination,
Suppression
Absolute, 11, 108, 109, 141, 146–7, 151,
153–4, 160, 163, 165, 179, 181, 187,
197, 201, 215, 322, 327, 328, 341, 344,
369, 399–400, 404; Idea, 92; Idealism,
296; Knowledge, 146–7, 150–1, 162,
176, 187, 203, 247; Monarchies, 406;
Nonknowledge, 205; and the relative,
160–1, 327; Self, 182; Subject, 154, 188;
Truth, 97
Abstractions, abstracting, abstractive, 96,
107, 111, 173, 181, 219, 229, 236, 240,
373, 379, 402
Abstract, the, 16, 60, 64, 90, 107, 111, 147,
177, 183, 199, 202, 209, 219, 222, 246,
251, 260, 302, 329, 361, 378, 381, 382,
395, 401, 405, 411; *see also* Ideal-abstract
Absurdities, 2, 13, 25, 32, 48, 53, 66, 78,
79, 85, 88, 129, 131, 132, 135, 154, 162,
170, 176, 202, 224–5, 241, 246, 249,
251, 263, 274, 291, 324, 331, 339, 348,
365, 368, 376, 385, 391, 398, 403, 406,
409–10, 414
Abyss, the, 261, 307, 315, 342, 346, 404
Acceptance, 121, 155, 316, 344–6, 365,
384, 394
Accidents, accidental, 58, 129–30, 156, 208,
224, 255, 257, 296; in Aristotle, 213,
217n.21; bad, 228; fortunate, 366; happy,
301, 366; historical, 35–6, 42, 362;
inevitable, 136; non–, 366; unfortunate/
unlucky, 154, 366
Accumulation, 20, 21, 76, 79, 81–2, 110,
123, 164, 174, 220, 254, 264;
bureaucratic, 220; capitalist, 21, 26
Achilles, 284
Acropolis, 277
Actors, 149, 257
Acts, action, acting, activities, 7, 9, 10, 12,
14, 16, 31, 33, 34, 36–8, 48, 49, 51, 52,
53, 60, 61, 72, 84, 85, 86, 91, 106–7,
113, 117, 121, 123–5, 127–30, 134, 136,
145, 147–54, 162, 163, 170, 180–2,
189–90n.1, 191n.12, 198, 199, 209, 221,
223, 230, 235, 236, 240, 241, 243, 246,
250, 251, 263, 268, 272, 274, 275, 278,
281–2, 286, 288, 300, 312–13, 327, 328,
332, 334, 337, 344–5, 347, 359–60,
362–3, 380–1, 386–8, 393, 398, 401,
410; and acting body, 180; autonomous,
3, 48, 50, 59, 136, 152–3, 166, 170, 222,
275, 411–12, 416; collective, 33, 63, 111,
136–7, 272, 313, 337, 413; conscious,
146, 149, 151, 190n.10, 198; economic,
74, 86; effective, 41; ethical, 402, 404;
free/of freedom, 286, 403; human, 123,
144, 148, 150, 189, 262, 281, 284, 399;
instituting, 279, 314; intersubjective, 182;
mass/of the masses, 108–9, 130; political,
3, 90, 128–29, 246, 250–1, 272, 274,
279, 281–2, 286, 371, 398; practico-
poetic/practico-poietic, 190n.6, 351, 399;
pure, 180, 372; rational, 147, 149; real,
107, 152, 163, 173; of reflection/
reflective, 371, 395; reflex, 147, 190n.1;
shared, 349; social, 3, 38, 86, 89, 92,
119, 121, 131, 155, 208–10, 232, 234,
256, 258; technical, 148, 150; trade-
union, 90, 129, 132; workers'/
working-class, 110, 124
Actual, the: and the factual, 322; and the
potential, 332; *see also* Effective
Adaptation and inadaptation, 108, 166,
366–8, 375; and learning, 381
Adherence, adhering, 107, 241, 263, 265,
390; blind, 108; effective, 241
Adikia, 273
Administration, 56–7, 88, 90, 94, 100, 240,
278; of justice, 94; of things, 100
Administrative: bodies, 103; departments,
93; functions, 64–5, mechanisms, 278;
'rights', 93; talent, 256; technique, 59
Adults, 123, 136, 169, 411; and children,
148
Adventurism, 40, 43
Advertising, 158, 281, 321, 415

413; of revolutionaries, 32–3, 135; of workers, 69, 90; *see also* Anonymous collective

Collectivities, 30–2, 56, 83, 116, 133, 134, 157, 160, 163, 276, 281, 288, 308, 313, 325, 343–4, 375, 379, 402, 405, 411, 413, 415–7

Collectivization, 47; of agriculture, 87; of production, 120; *see also* Forced collectivization

Collet, Henri, 104n.18

Colonialism, 106; and the colonized, 135; French, 13

Colour, colours, 323–5, 365, 404

Combat, combativity, 121, 122, 124, 171, 195n.46; of the gods, 387

Combinations, the combinable, 198, 200, 291, 304, 332, 368

Combinatories, combinatorics, 200, 291, 304, 319, 321, 376

Cominform, the, 3

Comitants, 213; essential and accidental, 217n.21

Commentary, 261, 287, 341

Commerce, 56, 64, 88, 335, 399

Commodities, 17–19, 72, 111, 226, 229, 332, 415

Common: affairs, 277–8, 280; good, 288; 'Programme of the Left', 12

Communes, 102, 251; rural, 88–91, 94–5, 99

Communication, 81, 87, 93, 98–9, 159; channels of, 58; intersubjective, 362, 391

Communism, 219, 409; era of, 61; higher phase of, 185–6; in its mythical sense, 185

Communist Parties (CPs), 1–4, 27, 35, 127, 249; French, 2, 43, 245; Yugoslavian, 3; *see also* Bolshevik Party, Communist Party of the Soviet Union, Russian Communist Party

Communist Party of the Soviet Union (CPSU), 219–20; *see also* Bolshevik Party, Russian Communist Party

Communists, 5, 41, 108, 127, 228, 267

Communities, 56, 85, 131, 272, 275, 279–80, 365, 384; political, 277–8; and the State, 277

Compactness, 98

Companies. *See* Enterprises, firms, business enterprises, companies

Compartmentalization, 67; of jobs, 65; of tasks, 64, 115–16; of work, 67; of workers, 313

Compensation: imaginary, 165

Competence, competency, 65, 97 224, 402, 408

Competition, 158, 167; monopolistic, 158

Complete, completion, 160–1, 164–5, 201, 202, 217n.22, 248, 301, 317n.10, 337, 353, 369

Complexity, 25, 39, 75, 97, 116, 117, 119, 140, 150, 165, 178, 205, 211, 215, 236, 241, 290, 294, 347, 349, 356

Components, 207–8; logical, 327

Composers, 324

Composition, composing, 206–7, 212, 297, 326, 404

Computation, 159

Computers, 74, 77, 98, 291

Concealment, 141, 142, 203, 204

Concentration, 45, 231; bureaucratic, 45; of capital, 110, 230–1; economic, 91; of power, 101

Concentration camps, 89, 92, 168, 175

Concepts, 147, 148, 198, 206–7, 305, 322; abstractive, 373; Hegelian, 199

Concrete, concreteness, 34, 37, 56, 102, 107, 117, 123, 129, 130, 144, 150, 152, 160, 161, 181, 204, 209, 221, 232, 241, 278, 347, 362, 379–80, 399, 414

Concretization, 150, 153, 176

Condensation, 354, 414

Conditions, 24, 28, 37, 66, 70, 95, 133, 152, 154, 161, 182, 184, 194n.43, 207, 222, 268, 276, 313, 323, 327, 339, 344, 356–7, 363, 366, 370, 383, 394, 400; for autonomy, 161; efficient, 181; of/for existence, 136, 261, 402–3; of/for heteronomy, 182, 313; 'initial', 24, 75–6, 81, 311–12; necessary, 184, 366, 370, 391; necessary and sufficient, 370; self-sufficient, 393; *sine qua non*, 262, 409; tragic, 399–400; working, 123, 128, 133

Confédération Générale du Travail (CGT), 2, 110

Conflicts, conflictual, 5, 49, 52, 63, 65, 67, 68, 101, 122, 126, 128, 148, 153, 155, 156, 161, 165, 167, 170–2, 174, 178, 191n.19, 203, 207, 220, 223–4, 227, 236, 258, 279, 285, 358, 400; generational, 136; labour, 174; political, 66, 340; social, 66, 170, 241

Conformism, comformists, 124, 166, 168, 259, 347, 416; generalized, 346, 415

Conformity, conformal, 121, 123, 234, 259, 335

Confrontations, 101, 126, 181, 272, 344, 413

Confusions, 36, 39, 43, 54, 55, 57, 86, 90, 134, 152, 156, 160, 162, 181–2, 189, 214, 262, 284, 294, 323–4, 339, 378

Conscious, consciousness, 33, 48, 51, 52, 59, 61, 63, 74, 98, 112, 116, 122, 123, 124, 130, 136, 146, 148, 154, 160, 173, 175, 177, 179, 181–3, 187, 202, 281, 328, 336, 337, 350, 352–3, 411;